Religions of the World

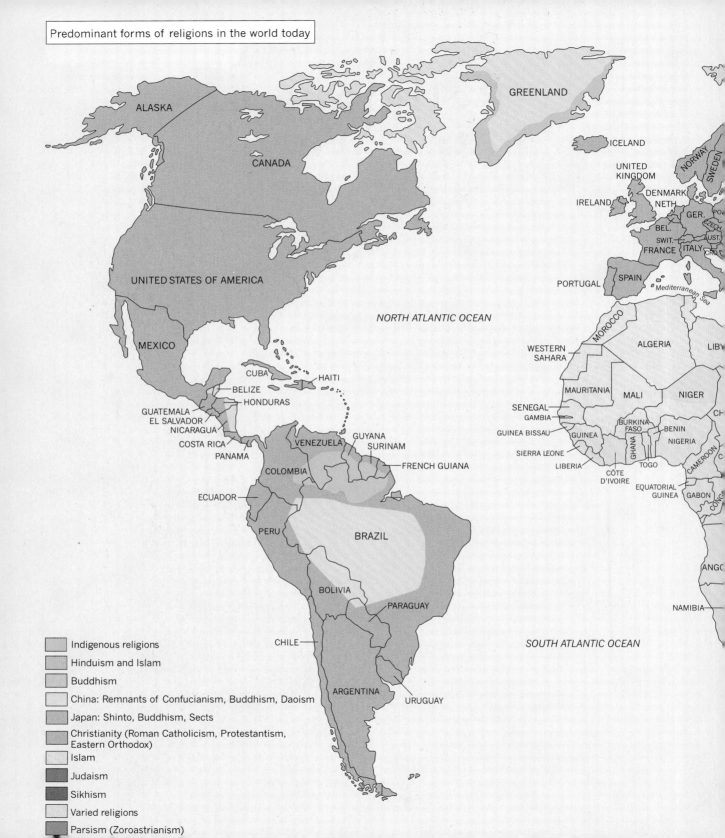

Predominant forms of religions in the world today

Indigenous religions
Hinduism and Islam
Buddhism
China: Remnants of Confucianism, Buddhism, Daoism
Japan: Shinto, Buddhism, Sects
Christianity (Roman Catholicism, Protestantism, Eastern Orthodox)
Islam
Judaism
Sikhism
Varied religions
Parsism (Zoroastrianism)

RUSSIAN FEDERATION

ONIA
LATVIA
LITHUANIA
BELARUS

KRAINE
MOLDOVA

KAZAKHSTAN

MONGOLIA

NORTH
KOREA

SOUTH
KOREA

JAPAN

NORTH PACIFIC OCEAN

GEORGIA

ARMENIA
AZER.

UZBEKISTAN

KYRGYZSTAN

TURKMENISTAN

TAJIKISTAN

TURKEY

SYRIA
LEB.
SRAEL

IRAQ

IRAN

AFGHANISTAN

CHINA

PT

JORDAN

KUWAIT

PAKISTAN

NEPAL

BANGLADESH

TAIWAN

SAUDI
ARABIA

OMAN

INDIA

MYANMAR
(BURMA)

THAILAND

LAOS

VIETNAM

PHILIPPINES

ERITREA

YEMEN

CAMBODIA

DAN

SRI LANKA

MALAYSIA

ETHIOPIA

SOMALIA

SOUTH PACIFIC OCEAN

KENYA

INDONESIA

TANZANIA

PAPUA
NEW
GUINEA

MALAWI

INDIAN OCEAN

ABWE

MADAGASCAR

MOZAMBIQUE

SWAZILAND

AUSTRALIA

LESOTHO

TH
CA

NEW ZEALAND

To Mark R. Woodward for his work on the Eleventh Edition;
and to Savannah Rose, a new generation.
Lavina Hopfe:
Each day we open our eyes to a new world,
new opportunities, and new challenges....(LMH, 1991)
To Savannah Rose, a new generation.

Religions of the World

Eleventh Edition

Lewis M. Hopfe

(Deceased)

revised by

Mark R. Woodward

Department of Religious Studies
Arizona State University

 Read it.
Get it.

New York   San Francisco   Boston   Upper Saddle River
London   Toronto   Sydney   Tokyo   Singapore   Madrid
Mexico City   Munich   Paris   Cape Town   Hong Kong   Montreal

Library of Congress Cataloging-in-Publication Data

Hopfe, Lewis M.
    Religions of the world / Lewis M. Hopfe ; revised by Mark R. Woodward. — 11th ed.
        p. cm.
    Includes bibliographical references and index.
    ISBN 0-13-606177-X
    1. Religions—Textbooks. I. Woodward, Mark R., 1952- II. Title.
    BL80.3.H66 2009
    200—dc22

                                                            2008039861

Senior Acquisitions Editor: Dave Repetto	Image Permission Coordinator: Nancy Seise
Editor in Chief: Dickson Musslewhite	Manager, Cover Visual Research & Permissions:
Editorial Project Manager: Sarah Holle	Karen Sanatar
Editorial Assistant: Pat Walsh	Cover Art: To come
Marketing Assistant: Craig Deming	Senior Media Editor: David Alick
Project Manager: Fran Russello	Full-Service Project Management: Marie Desrosiers
Senior Operations Supervisor: Brian Mackey	Composition: Pre-Press PMG
Operations Specialist: Cathleen Petersen	Printer/Binder: Courier Companies, Inc.
Manager, Visual Research: Beth Brenzel	Cover Printer: Phoenix Color Corp.
Manager, Rights and Permissions: Zina Arabia	VangoBooks Process Coordinator: Xiaohong Zhu

Credits and acknowledgments borrowed from other sources and reproduced, with permission, in
this textbook appear on page 394.

Pearson Education LTD.	Pearson Education Australia PTY, Limited
Pearson Education Singapore, Pte. Ltd	Pearson Education North Asia Ltd
Pearson Education, Canada, Ltd	Pearson Educación de Mexico, S.A. de C.V.
Pearson Education–Japan	Pearson Education Malaysia, Pte. Ltd

10 9 8 7 6 5 4 3 2 1

ISBN 10:   0-13-606177-X
ISBN 13: 978-0-13-606177-9

CONTENTS

CHAPTER 11

Judaism   253

CHAPTER 12

Christianity   292

www.myreligionkit.com*

To the Eleventh Edition

When I first started teaching world religion courses in the mid-1980s, I, and many others, found it necessary to explain to students why it was important to study religion. We usually offered some combination of remarks on the importance of religion in the world's cultures and of the need to promote harmony and understanding among people of different faiths. After September 11, 2001, it was no longer necessary to question the need for the academic study of religion. Policymakers, students, and the public at large came to understand very quickly that religion had replaced economics as the most ideologically potent force in the post–Cold War world. Just as religions include the seeds of peace, they offer the potential for hatred and violence. It is naïve to believe that understanding alone will lead to tolerance and acceptance of the basic humanity of others. Some interpretations of most religions are inherently intolerant and inclined toward violence. Understanding the dark side is, however, essential in the struggle to overcome it. Understanding religions other than our own, even if our own is none, is also necessary if we are to avoid stereotyping all members of a faith because of the violent acts of a few.

In preparing the eleventh edition of Lewis Hopfe's text, I have drawn on my experience teaching the introductory course on world religions to thousands of students over the past decade and living and working in Asian Christian, Buddhist, Confucian, and Muslim societies for extended periods. I have also benefited greatly from seminars and research projects sponsored by the Center for the Study of Religion and Conflict at Arizona State University, and from conversations with faculty and students at the Center for Religious and Cross Cultural Studies at Gaja Mada University in Yogyakarta Indonesia and the S. Rajaratnam School of International Studies at Nanyang Technological University in Singapore—where I have held visiting appointments in recent years.

I have tried to bring the book and the study of world religions into the post–September 11 era and to keep up with the pace of religious change in other traditions and parts of the world. There is expanded coverage of "new religions" and new variants of established traditions. Extremely rapid developments in China and among "overseas" Chinese led to major revisions in Chapter 8, which concerns Chinese religion. Expanded coverage of indigenized or local forms of global religions and of lay forms of Theravada Buddhism are also included. I have unfortunately found it necessary to enhance coverage of religion and violence, including a section in the Introduction on theoretical understandings of this lamentable subject. Discussions of religion and violence have also been included in every chapter. The lists of selected readings have been updated. In this edition, I have included more narrative histories and historical fiction to make the readings more accessible to non-specialist audiences.

This edition of *Religions of the World* is dedicated to people of faith everywhere who draw on concepts of compassion embedded in their religions in the quest for antidotes for the poisons of bigotry and hatred that are all too often spread in the name of most, if not all, of the world's religions. The book is also dedicated to the memory of Dr. Nurcholish Madjid (1939–2005), an Indonesian Muslim scholar who devoted the last decade of his life to an attempt to bring peace and reconciliation to a nation torn by ethnic and religious violence. The last time I spoke with him, Nurcholish said "You know, Mark, I wish I could quit being a politician and go back to writing books." Unfortunately, he never got the chance.

Mark R. Woodward

Why study religion? Students embarking upon a study of the religions of the world, whether for a semester, a year, or a lifetime, must question their reasons. After all, we have been told that religion is a personal matter and that although we should be informed about the nature of our own religion, the religions of others need scarcely concern us. We have heard that religions are of little real consequence, that we might more profitably spend our time studying subjects of immediate practical value in the pursuit of a career, and that religions are becoming passé in a scientifically progressive world. Why, then, should any student take time from an academic career to study the religions of the world?

We might justify the study of religions in the same manner we justify the study of Shakespeare or art history: The subject can be worth studying simply because the student is interested in it. Certainly anyone interested in the history of the world and in the antecedents of his or her own culture will find the study of world religions imperative. An art historian lecturing on the art of sixteenth- and seventeenth-century Europe presented picture after picture of the art of that period, which was filled with religious themes. He said to his class, "Because you may have no religious interest yourself, please do not assume that the people of the past had none." Indeed, we could not understand the art of 90 percent of the world's cultures without knowing the religious themes of those cultures. Likewise, the student of world literature must know religions. We cannot comprehend the *Bhagavad Gita* without knowledge of Hinduism; we cannot truly grasp Hermann Hesse's *Siddhartha* without knowledge of Buddhism; we cannot understand the literature of Herman Melville without a command of Christian themes; even the contemporary literature of a writer such as Philip Roth is misunderstood without knowledge of Judaism.

Religion and Violence

Perhaps the greatest contribution that knowledge of world religions can make to a citizen of the twenty-first century is in the area of world politics. Religion plays an increasingly important role in political conflict at home and abroad. At the time of this writing, as at almost any other time in history, major political conflicts have religious differences at their roots. Religious differences are fundamental to debates concerning civil rights, abortion, and gender relations in the contemporary United States. In other parts of the world, Catholic Christians war against Protestant Christians; Hindus battle Muslims; Buddhists battle Hindus; Muslims are at war against Christians; and Jews struggle with Muslims. Certainly, these conflicts have other dimensions, but the religious differences are imposing. If we are to fully understand these conflicts, we must know that Muslims, Christians, Jews, Hindus, and Buddhists have basic philosophical differences and that religion can be a source of conflict as well as of understanding. In the wake of the tragedies of September 11, 2001, it is clear that we no longer have the luxury of ignorance. It is now essential that government and private sector leaders and the general public be aware of the ways in which religion can exacerbate and ameliorate regional and global conflict.

The world of the twenty-first century pushes us out of our insulated worlds into closer and closer contact with what were formerly considered exotic and distant religions. Television brings instant coverage of events in formerly remote parts of the earth. Industrialization brings us together in urban centers. The most rapidly growing religion in Europe and North America is Islam, due to the influx of Turks, Arabs, Iranians, and Pakistanis, as well as internal conversion. The largest concentration of Hindus outside of India is found in Leicester, England. New York City has a larger Jewish population than the nation of Israel. Hollywood figures proclaim their conversion to Buddhism and pop stars to Islam. Dance clubs play CDs recorded by Sufi devotional singers. Whereas the Hindu, Buddhist, Muslim, or Orthodox Jew may once have seemed a distant and exotic person, known only through books or movies, that person today may well be our neighbor, our co-worker, or a student in our classes. One simply cannot be a well-informed citizen of this era without knowledge of the religions of the world.

If there is to be peace among the nations, cultures, and religions of the world, religious differences must be known and respected. In the early 1960s, a young professor (Lewis Hopfe) and his wife gave a dinner party on a Friday evening. The guest list included Jews, Catholics, and Muslims. The entrée was ham! Jews and Muslims are forbidden by their religion to eat pork, and Roman Catholics of that period abstained from all meat on Fridays. Needless to say, it was not a happy party. Whether the choice of food was made due to ignorance or arrogance does not matter. The guests, because of their religions, were offended. That dinner party was a microcosm of what happens all too frequently because of ignorance of the religions of the world. More sensitive and better-informed hosts would have asked if their guests had any "dietary restrictions," or they would have served a religiously "safe" entrée such as trout. Most of us are familiar with the concept of "kosher" foods that can be eaten by conservative religious Jews. Increasingly one encounters "halal," the Muslim equivalent, in the supermarkets and restaurants of American cities. In August 2002, a street food vendor near the American Museum of Natural History in New York posted a sign stating that his food was kosher and halal—a small sign of hope in a deeply troubled world.

While in North America and Western Europe religion may be a private, personal matter, such is definitely not the case in much of the rest of the world. In Africa, Russia and much of Eastern Europe, the Middle East, and much of Asia, religion plays important roles in public life. In many instances, collective social and political identities are defined on the basis of religious criteria. The end of the Cold War and the collapse of Communist states have vastly increased the importance of religion in world affairs. It is now essential for those who seek to understand regional and global politics, economics, and conflict to be thoroughly grounded in the study of religion.

A Definition of Religion

If we assume an interest in religions and a willingness to study them, what constitutes the subject matter of a course in world religions? Humankind has been on earth a long time. Our cultures, historic and prehistoric, are too numerous to even begin to detail. Which cultures and religions shall we study? Whole texts have been written solely on prehistoric religions, not to mention the great families of religion, such as those found within Hinduism. Therefore, any text or course on religions must be selective about its subject, and a definition of the subject is necessary.

The English word *religion* is derived from the Latin word *religio*, which refers to the fear or awe one feels in the presence of a spirit or god. In Western cultures, we tend to define religion in terms of a set of beliefs having to do with the gods, through which one is taught a moral system. Although this definition contains elements that are found within many of the religions of the world, it cannot do justice to them all. For example, some religions recognize the existence of gods but actually have very little to do with them. Jainism and, to some extent, some forms of Buddhism may be called nontheistic religions because their emphasis is on people's delivering themselves from their plight without the help of gods. Some religions are not naturally tied to moral systems. Most of the religions that have existed on earth have probably been far more concerned with humanity's proper relationship to gods, demons, and spirits, worldly prosperity, and well-being than with ethical relationships among people. One distinctive characteristic of the religion of the early Hebrews was the ethical dimension their God required of them. This emphasis also was found in Zoroastrianism and was in turn passed on to Christianity and Islam. Similar concerns can be found in Buddhism, Hinduism, and other religions that have a broad, universal appeal. Modern adherents to these religions associate the word *religion* with the word *moral*, but among most religions, these terms are not synonymous.

The Christian theologian Paul Tillich defined religion as that which is of "ultimate concern."[1] Taking Tillich's definition one step further, some might say that in its basic form, a person's religion is the concern that is more important than anything else. In this sense, then, the intense patriotism one finds in many nations could be called religion. People have been known to place their families above all other concerns. In terms of this definition, their intense love of family may thus be seen as their religion. However satisfying Tillich's definition may be on philosophical grounds, it is too broad for a world religions course or text.

In *The Varieties of Religious Experience*, William James proposed that because there are so many different definitions of the word *religion*, we should learn that the whole concept is too large for any one definition to fit. Instead, *religion* should be seen as a collective name. James wrote that religion, in the broadest sense, "consists of the belief that there is an unseen order, and that our supreme good lies in harmoniously adjusting ourselves thereto."[2]

The contents of this text have been chosen from the hundreds of world religions on the following six bases: (1) They usually, but not always, deal in some way with people's relationship to the unseen world of spirits, ancestors, gods, and demons; (2) they usually have developed a system of myths about the unseen world and rituals designed for communing with or propitiating it; (3) they usually have developed a system of organized rituals, temples, priests, and scriptures at some point in their history; (4) they usually have some statement about life beyond death, either as survival in some shadowy hades, in some version of heaven and hell, or through reincarnation; (5) they usually have developed a code of conduct or moral order; and (6) they generally have attracted large followings, either currently or at some time in the past.

As there are many religions from which we must choose, so there are many methods by which we might organize them. We might present the religions of the world in terms of their effects on the societies that support them; in terms of their forms or styles of worship; in a comparative manner (in which each religion is compared with the others in terms of its outlook toward its God or gods, the nature of humankind, sin, and so on); or in terms of their histories and impact on the histories of the nations in which they were found. This text combines some of these methods and presents the major religions of the world as simply yet as thoroughly as possible. For each religion, four major points are considered. (1) What culture produced this religion? (2) If there was a founder, and if anything can be known of the founder's life, what factors caused this person to found this religion? (3) If there are scriptures or sacred texts, what do they tell us about this religion? (4) What have been the major historical developments of this religion?

The Universality of Religion

Occasionally, religion is hard to find or pin down, but from the great metropolitan capitals to the least developed areas of the world, there are temples, pyramids, megaliths, and other monuments that societies have raised at tremendous expense as expressions of their religions. Even when we explore the backwaters of time in prehistoric civilizations, we find altars, cave paintings, and special burials that point toward our religious nature. Indeed, no other phenomenon is so pervasive, so consistent from society to society, as is religion.

Theories of the Origin of Religions

From where does religion come? This is a very basic question, as our answer tends to reflect our view of the very nature of religion. Some say human beings developed religion because they were weak and ignorant about the forces of nature that surrounded them; they were at the mercy of these forces and therefore devised a scheme of gods and spirits to whom they could pray for support. According to this view, when human beings come to fully know and understand their universe, they will no longer need the crutch of religion to support them. Others say religion was developed by a few as a means of suppressing the masses. Another school of thought is that religion is based on a combination of psychological fears and needs. Still others say religion developed to give meaning to social institutions and encourage social solidarity. The traditional view held by those who are themselves religious is that a god or other spiritual being revealed religion and religious truths to human beings at some point in their development.

In the nineteenth century, when the social sciences were being developed and anthropologists were first beginning to investigate the remaining "primitive" cultures, certain theories of the origin of religion were proposed. No longer satisfied with mere guessing about the origin of religion or with the orthodox religious views on the subject, early anthropologists based their theories on observations. These nineteenth- and early twentieth-century scholars, enamored of the belief that the biological theories of evolution taught by Charles Darwin could be applied to the social sciences, investigated contemporary "primitive" religions, reread ancient reporters (such as Herodotus), and hypothesized *ad infinitum* about the origin and development of the phenomenon of religion. A few of the more outstanding and enduring of their theories follow.[3]

Animistic Theories

The most outstanding exponent of one animistic theory of the origin of religion was the English ethnologist Edward Burnett Tylor (1832–1917). Although Tylor held no formal degree, he was a leading figure in anthropology for many years. Near the end of his career, he was named Britain's first professor of anthropology (1896–1909). Tylor's greatest contribution to the study of the origin of religions was his book *Primitive Culture* (2 vols., 1871). In the 1850s, Herbert Spencer had theorized that the gods of "primitive" people were based on dreams about the recent dead. According to Spencer, when "primitive" people dreamed of the dead, they came to believe that the former chiefs and heroes were actually alive in another world or another form. Tylor was aware of Spencer's theory, which was called "Manism," but he did not totally accept it.[4] Tylor maintained that "primitive" people developed a sense of other or soul from experiences with death and dreams. According to Tylor, "primitive" people also believed that these souls (Latin, *anima*) were to be found not only in people but in all of nature. There were souls in stones, trees, animals, rivers, springs, volcanoes, and mountains. The entire world, the very air itself, was seen as being alive with spirits of all kinds. These spirits could be helpful or harmful to humans and had personalities that could be offended or flattered. Therefore, it became a part of the life of "primitive" societies to pray to these spirits, offer sacrifices to them, seek to appease them, and avoid offending them.

From the animistic understanding of the world developed the practice of ancestor worship or veneration, in which one attended to the spirits of the dead. An awareness of the existence of spirits in nature led to the worship of various aspects of nature, such as water, trees, stones, and so on. Ultimately, this animistic view of the universe produced the polytheistic religions that worshipped sky, earth, and water deities. Finally, monotheistic religions developed. Tylor's theories were widely accepted and regarded as classic for many years. The term *animism* is still widely used.

Another theory that can be loosely defined as animistic was developed and propounded in 1891 by Bishop R.H. Codrington (1830–1922). During his work as a Christian missionary to Melanesia, Codrington studied the languages and culture of its people. When he returned to Britain, he studied under Tylor at Oxford University. In 1891, Codrington published *The Melanesians*. Although he agreed with much of Tylor's theory, Codrington was more concerned with what native people said about their own religious experience than with the theoretical bases that Tylor and others had built. He took the Melanesian word *mana* to be the basis of religion. *Mana* is defined as a supernatural power that belonged to the region of the unseen. It was experienced emotionally rather than rationally. Codrington theorized that all "primitive" peoples had begun their religions with an awareness of such a force. Investigators studying other "primitive" cultures found a similar phenomenon, although it was called other names.

The Nature-Worship Theory

An alternative theory of the origin of religion was developed by another Oxford professor, Max Müller (1823–1900). Müller's interests were mythology and the religions of India, but he entered the debate over origins with Tylor and others. From his studies, he became convinced that human beings first developed their religions from their observations of the forces of nature. According to this theory, "primitive" people became aware of the regularity of the seasons, the tides, and the phases of the moon. Their response to these forces in nature was to personalize them. Thus they gave a name to the sun, the moon, and so on, and began to describe the activities of these forces with tales that eventually became mythology. An example of this process is found in the Greek myth of Apollo and Daphne. Apollo was in love with Daphne, but she fled from him and was changed into a laurel tree. By searching out the etymology of these names, Müller found that Apollo was the name given the sun and that Daphne was the name given the dawn. Thus, the original myth simply described how the sun chases away the dawn. Müller further believed that all of the stories of the gods and heroes in Indo-European cultures were originally solar myths. Müller became convinced that he had found the key to the origin of all religions: "Primitive" people identified the forces in nature, personified them, created myths to describe their activities, and eventually developed pantheons and religions around them.

The Theory of Original Monotheism

A completely different approach to the origin of religion was presented early in the twentieth century by Wilhelm Schmidt (1868–1954) in *Der Ursprung der Gottesidee.*[5] Schmidt began his career studying the linguistics of New Guinea and then all of Oceania. From his own work, Schmidt came to disagree with the animistic theories of Tylor and others. He noted that all of the hunter-gatherer cultures he had studied (and which were the oldest form of human society to be observed) held a common belief in a distant High God. Although the predominant form of religion for these "primitives" was animism or polytheism, there was always the belief that originally there had been one great god above all others. This god may have been the creator of the world or the parent of the many lesser deities. Usually, the High God is understood to have the qualities of eternity, omniscience, beneficence, morality, and omnipotence. Often, the High God is believed to have been the force that gave society its moral codes. After initially establishing the world, this High God went away and now has little contact with the world. Some of the mythologies go on to say that one day the High God will return and judge the world on the basis of its morality. Usually, the local deities receive the majority of attention and worship, although the distant High God has a small part in mythology. Schmidt inferred from this phenomenon that "primitive" societies were originally monotheistic but that because the worship of one god was difficult, religion was corrupted into polytheism. Later, more advanced religions recovered the true monotheistic religion. Naturally, Schmidt was accused of allowing his Christian prejudices to influence the formulation of this theory.

The Magic Theory

Between 1890 and 1915, Sir James George Frazer (1854–1941), a fellow of Trinity College, Cambridge, produced his encyclopedic work on religion, *The Golden Bough.* Unlike Codrington and Schmidt, Frazer did not personally study contemporary basic religions but constructed his theories by reading the reports of anthropologists, colonial officials, missionaries, and ancient writers. On the basis of his studies, Frazer came to agree with Tylor, that the human mind had developed in a linear fashion in the same way as the process of physical evolution. He taught that humankind had gone through three phases of development regarding the spirit world. First, people had attempted to control the world of nature through magic. When humanity realized nature could not be coerced through magic, it turned to the second stage of development—religion—whose premise seems to be that nature can be implored to cooperate. When religion was also seen to fail, humankind, in a third phase, turned to science, in which a more rational understanding of nature is operative. Therefore, the modern farmer who needs rain turns to neither the magician nor the priest. He turns to the scientist, who will seed the clouds and cause it to rain, although a skeptic might note that there is little proof that seeding the clouds produces rain any more frequently than rain dances or prayers.

Theories of Religion as Projections of Human Needs

One of the most influential thinkers of the nineteenth century was the German philosopher Ludwig Feuerbach (1804–1872). In his influential books *The Essence of Christianity* and *The Essence of Religion*, Feuerbach said religions were essentially projections of the wishes and needs of humanity. He saw religion as a dream or fantasy that expressed the situation of humankind. According to Feuerbach, people tend to see themselves as helpless and dependent when faced with the challenges of life. Therefore, they seek to overcome their problems through imagination; they imagine or project an idealized being of goodness or power who can help them. Humanity is not created in the image of God, but God is created in the image of idealized humanity. Feuerbach believed people seek in heaven what they cannot find on earth. Thus, at its most basic level, religion is a form of wishing. Feuerbach thought that when people become knowledgeable or powerful, religion tends to wither away and be replaced by technology and politics.

A thinker deeply influenced by the theories of Feuerbach was his younger contemporary Karl Marx (1818–1883). Marx added his own distinctive touches to Feuerbach's position on the origin of religion. Marx saw the origin and development of religion in terms of his personal view of history and the economic and social struggle between classes. In words that sound a great deal like those of Feuerbach, Marx said:

Man makes religion, religion does not make man. Religion is the self-consciousness and self-esteem of man who has either not yet found himself or has already lost himself again. . . . Religion is the sigh of the oppressed creature, the heart of a heartless world, just as it is the spirit of spiritless conditions. It is the opium of the people.[6]

Marx also believed that religion was used by the ruling classes to suppress the underclass. The social principles of Christianity preach the necessity of a ruling and an oppressed class, and for the latter all they have to offer is the pious wish that the former may be charitable. The social principles of Christianity declare all the vile acts of oppressors against the oppressed to be either just punishment for original sin and for other sins, or trials which the Lord, in his infinite wisdom, ordains for the redeemed.[7]

Sigmund Freud (1856–1939), the founder of psychoanalysis, gave Feuerbach's ideas a psychological dimension. Freud saw religion as having originated as guilt that men supposedly feel in hating their fathers. Freud saw in the ancient Greek myth of Oedipus a pattern of human experience. Oedipus was a man who, through a long and tragic series of events, killed his father and married his mother. Freud saw that in all males there was a similar tendency to desire their mothers and therefore hate their fathers.[8]

Freud further referred to practices of "primitive" people he believed to be representative of the total human experience. The dominant male/father kept the women of the group for himself and drove the younger males away from his territory. Finally, the younger males joined together in killing the father and eating his flesh. Freud proposed that guilt from this desire for the mother and this great act of patricide lie at the heart of every religion. He believed that totemic religion arose to allay the filial sense of guilt and appease the father through deferred obedience to him and that all later religions are attempts at solving the same problem.[9]

Because of this subconscious hatred and ensuing guilt, Freud believed humans project in the sky a great father image called God. He also thought that religious ideas are "illusions, fulfillments of the oldest, strongest, and most urgent wishes of mankind."[10] The truly healthy and mature person, according to Freud, is content to stand alone and face the problems of life without gods or religions.

Types of Religions

In the long period of human life on earth, there have been thousands of religions. Because recorded history covers only the last 5,000 years of our million-year existence, there are undoubtedly more unknown than known religions. In addition, many religious systems have lived and died within the relatively short span of recorded history. This text does not pretend to address all religions, historical or prehistorical. It deals only with religious systems that are active and viable today. These religions are grouped into four categories.

Basic Religions

The term *basic religion* is generally applied to the religions of contemporary people whose religious ideas are not preserved in written form and to the religions of prehistoric peoples, about whom we know little. This category embraces a great variety of beliefs and practices, including animism, totemism, and polytheism. In the following chapters, we examine Native American and African religions as examples of the basic religions. Probably the most common characteristic of this group is an animistic view of nature. No one knows the number of persons whose religions may be categorized as basic. It is clear that their numbers are rapidly dwindling as conversion of Christianity and Islam proceeds.

Religions Originating in India

Four of the great religions of the world originated in India: Hinduism, Jainism, Buddhism, and Sikhism. India remains the home of Hinduism, Jainism, and Sikhism. Buddhism is now found in other Asian nations, such as China, Japan, Korea, Vietnam, Burma, Cambodia, and Thailand. The basic beliefs of these religions are that there are many gods (Sikhism is the exception, taking its belief in one god from Islam) and that one person may lead many lives through a system of reincarnation. The ultimate concern of these religions is release from the cycle of life, death, and rebirth. Sometimes this goal is achieved through the aid of the gods, but often believers are expected by their actions, or lack thereof, to work out their own release.

Religions Originating in China and Japan

Religions that originated in China and Japan include Taoism, Confucianism, and Shinto. There is some question regarding whether Taoism and Confucianism are truly religions, but because they have at times developed certain religious aspects they usually are listed among the religions of the world. They have in common the belief in many gods and include the worship of nature, the worship or veneration of ancestors, and in the case of Shinto, a reverence for the nation itself.

Religions Originating in the Middle East

Religions originating in the Middle East include Zoroastrianism, Judaism, Christianity, Islam, and Baha'i. All believe in one Supreme Creator God; they believe each person lives only one earthly life; they regard the material universe positively, hold a linear view of time, and believe in divine judgment of the world. Christianity and Islam have been two of the great missionary religions of the world. Today, their adherents are found all over the globe and number in the billions.

Religion and Violence

Religious studies scholars have, until recently, been somewhat reluctant to consider the violent aspects of the religions they study. Many of us avoid the issue entirely and focus on the positive, or at least benign, aspects of religious traditions. Most of us have somewhat of a romantic attachment to the peoples and traditions we study and find it hard to accept that some of these peoples are capable of the worst imaginable atrocities. In the post-9/11 world we now know that this has been a mistake. We now know that religion can be the inspiration—or at least the justification—for horrific acts of violence. Not to address these issues in a book introducing students to the religions of the world is dishonest and irresponsible.

Most people think of their own religion as being peaceful. Jews, Christians, and Muslims all speak of the "Peace of God." Hindus, Jains and Buddhists teach *ahimsa* or nonviolence. There is, unfortunately, a tendency to describe other people's religions as cruel and violent. This is a mistake, and one that helps to promote and perpetuate cycles of violence. People of almost all religions have been victimized because of their beliefs. Most, or almost all have been perpetrators of religious violence. Almost any religion can be used as an excuse or justification for violence. Hindus kill Muslims, Muslims kill Hindus, Jews and Muslims kill each other, Christians kill Hindus and Muslims and Jews. All in the name of religion, adherents of basic religions have engaged in head-hunting and human sacrifice.

In considering "religious violence," it is necessary to distinguish three basic varieties: those intended as punishment for people believed to be evil; acts of violence which are inherently religious; and violent clashes between religious communities. Killings of alleged practitioners of evil magic have occurred throughout history. Large numbers of alleged witches were killed by Christians during the sixteenth century in Europe and North America. Such practices continue throughout Sub-Saharan Africa and parts of Southeast Asia to this day. Human sacrifice among the Moche of ancient Peru and head-hunting among the Naga tribes of Burma and India are examples of the second type of religious violence. In these cultures, killing other people was among the most important ritual acts. The killings were conducted and memorialized with rituals unique to particular religious traditions. Examples have been reported as late as the 1950s.

Far more common today is conflict between communities that define themselves on the basis of religion. Usually the conflicts do not originate in religion, but come to be religious because of the forms that the violence takes. In many, if not most, cases throughout the world these include the facts that collective violence is often used as a tool by political elites, that targets are frequently symbols of collective identity, and that rumors, often grotesque ones, play a major role in fomenting violence. Sexual violence, of which both women and men may be victims, is another common feature. The desecration of corpses in ways that make proper religious funerals impossible is also common. In order to justify these horrible acts it is essential for the perpetrators to define their victims in terms of their own most powerful symbols of evil. Religious violence is particularly pernicious because it strikes at the core symbols of personal and collective identity. Churches, mosques, and temples are among the most frequent targets. Desecrating or destroying them sparks rage and a thirst for revenge. Killing or defiling key religious personnel has similar consequences.[11] The resulting cycles of violence are especially difficult to stop because there is a marked tendency for the victims of violence to become the perpetrators of the same type of violence. [12] For example, when Hindus defile a mosque by killing a pig in it, Muslims are likely to respond by slaughtering a cow in a temple.[13]

Unfortunately, historical and contemporary examples of these patterns are not hard to find. The Crusades of the twelfth and thirteenth centuries, which pitted Christians and Muslims against each other in a struggle over places sacred to both communities, are a clear example of this type of violence conducted on a massive scale. Other recent examples include conflicts pitting Catholic and Orthodox Christians and Muslims against each other in the former Yugoslavia and ongoing Muslim-Hindu and Hindu-Christian violence in India. There are also rare cases where victims and perpetrators share a common faith. Burma is an example. In 1988 and again in 2007, the military government forcefully disrobed, tortured, and executed Theravada Buddhist monks who dared to demonstrate in favor of political and economic reform. The government declared the protesting monks to be "bogus imposters." At the same time, the generals portrayed themselves as the defenders and supporters of Buddhism. [14]

Religion is capable of bringing out the noblest traits of our shared humanity. It can also, unfortunately, motivate or justify the most depraved.

[handwritten margin note: Though mostly women]

STUDY QUESTIONS

1. List several advantages of a knowledge of the differing religious viewpoints of the world.
2. Define *religion*.
3. Name several major theories of the origin of religion.
4. Contrast the Marxist view of religion with the Freudian view.
5. List the four types of religious systems and tell where each may be found. — *final*
6. Define *animism*.
7. Distinguish between three basic types of religious violence.
8. What are some of the factors that perpetuate cycles of religious violence?

PART 1

BASIC RELIGIONS

Basic religions are oral traditions. Their systems of knowledge and behavior are inscribed upon human memory, not in some form of writing. At one time in history, religions may have shared certain characteristics no longer visible in contemporary religions. Through an examination of archaeological and anthropological evidence, the student of religions may be able to gain insight into what the earliest religions may have been. At the same time, by studying the characteristics of these so-called basic religions of the past and present, the student will also learn more about the bases on which such major contemporary religions as Hinduism, Christianity, and Islam rest. We will also come to see that religious concepts and modes of behavior long seen as being central to basic religions can also be found in contemporary formulations of World Religions.

NATIVE AMERICAN RELIGIONS – BASIC TEACHINGS

Native American religions are very diverse.

There are hundreds of Native American religions. It is difficult, if not impossible, to generalize about them. Native American cultures are equally diverse, ranging historically from small bands of hunter-gatherers to large-scale states and empires. Today most Native Americans are Christians, though in many cases they retain elements of traditional beliefs and practices.

Many Native American religions emphasize geographic space and the natural environment.

Plants, animals, and some geographic and geological features are understood as living beings with whom humans can establish relationships. This has often brought native people into conflict with Euro-American communities.

There are many taboos concerning the dead.

In some cases—including the Navajo of Arizona and New Mexico—the dead are greatly feared. Even their clothing and other possessions are avoided. Many Native Americans are greatly concerned by the fact that the skeletal remains of their ancestors have been disinterred and are stored in museums.

Native Americans suffered greatly at the hands of white settlers.

There have been many wars and massacres, some of which rose to the level of genocide. Native peoples were often driven off their lands and forced to relocate in less-productive areas. In many instances, children were taken from their families and placed in boarding schools, where they were forbidden to conduct traditional ceremonies or even to speak native languages.

Today there are religious movements that cross traditional tribal boundaries.

One of the first of these was the Ghost Dance. It began among the Pauite of Nevada and spread rapidly across the Great Plains. It foretold the end of white settlers and the return of the buffalo, which were almost extinct at the time. Some believed that wearing "ghost shirts" would protect them from the U.S. Army's weapons. A more recent movement is the Native American Church, which combines elements of Native American religion with Christianity. It also uses the hallucinogenic peyote cactus in ceremonial ways.

AFRICAN RELIGIONS – BASIC TEACHINGS

Like those of Native Americans, African religions are extremely diverse.

African cultures are also extremely diverse, ranging historically from small bands of hunter-gatherers to states and empires. Today, most Africans are either Christians or Muslims, though in many cases they retain elements of traditional beliefs and practices.

The High God is an important figure in many traditional African religions.

The belief in a High God who created the world but is no longer actively involved in it is very common. In these religions, lesser spirits who were part of his creation are more important in daily life. The earth is often understood to be a goddess and is associated with fertility.

Ancestor veneration is an important element of many traditional African religions.

Ancestors often communicate with the living through dreams. They can be either helpful or harmful, depending on how they are treated. They are offered sacrifices to promote human health, well-being, and prosperity. They are also believed to enforce moral codes by punishing those who violate them.

In some African societies, kings and queens are thought to be divine.

They are the means through which relationships with the spirits and ancestors are maintained. They are the objects of many taboos. In some cases, kings and queens are killed or commit suicide when they become ill or infirm.

In some African religions, it is believed that illness is often caused by witchcraft.

Spiritual healers are employed to counter the effects of witchcraft. A specific person is often identified as the witch. These accusations present difficulties for African governments because people often demand that officials take action against those accused of witchcraft, and modern legal systems make that impossible. There are also cases of revenge killings, especially in countries like South Africa that have witnessed political turmoil.

CHAPTER 1

Basic Religions and World Religions

CHAPTER OBJECTIVES

In this chapter you will:

- Learn some of the features that basic religions share with world religions.

- Become acquainted with theoretical approaches to the academic study of religion.

KEY TERMS

Animism	Taboo	Rites of Passage
Magic	Totemism	Ancestor Veneration
Divination	Myth	

A Timeline of Basic Religions

Unknowable B.C.E.	Origins of religion	17th century–present	Conquest and conversion of indigenous peoples of North America to Christianity
Thousands of years	Oral transmission of myth and ritual		
7,000–3,000 B.C.E.	Neolithic period	19th century–present	Conversion of tribal peoples of Asia and the Pacific to Christianity
1492 C.E.	European discovery of the Americas	19th century–present	Conversion of Africans to Christianity and Islam
16th century–present	Conquest and conversion of indigenous peoples of Central and South America and Mexico to Christianity	20th century–present	Emergence of new forms of Christianity in Africa and Asia

It is impossible to say when people began to be religious. Early theories of culture and religion assumed that there were parallels between cultural and biological evolution. Typically, the religions and total cultures of prehistoric people and the current practices in pretechnological societies were referred to as *primitive*. The word *primitive* carries with it connotations of being backward, simple, even childlike. To the extent that this view persists, the Christian or Muslim or Jew may tend to look down on these religions as being superstitious, uncivilized, or even savage. In studying the religions of the world, we can assume no evolutionary scale that moves from basic religions to Zen Buddhism or any other highly developed religion of the so-called civilized world. An alternative was, and is, to romanticize these religions and to describe them as objects of beauty and simplicity. Both of these views are incorrect. The indigenous religions of Australia, Asia, Africa, and the Americas are as fully intricate in their rituals and **mythologies** and as satisfying to their adherents as those of High Church Episcopalians, Muslims, or Buddhists. There is satisfaction and beauty in all religions; there also is ugliness and violence in all.

Of all of the world's religions, we know least about these basic religions, simply because they spring from prehistory or are practiced in remote places. However, elements of the basic religions are found to some degree in all religions. It is therefore important to study these religions to understand these elements and how they operate. It is also important to study basic religions because they represent the majority of the total religious experience of humankind. With the spread of missionary religions, especially Christianity and Islam, the number of adherents of basic religions has declined dramatically in the last century.

Sources of Information Concerning Basic Religions

Humans have been active on planet Earth for a million or more years, but we know only a tiny fraction of human history. Only within the past 5,000 to 6,000 years has *Homo sapiens* used writing. Although non-written sources (such as cave paintings, burial sites, religious statuary, and archaeological remains) indicate human culture and religious experiences, our strongest source of knowledge is the written record. Of the total period of time during which people have been on Earth, we have written records chronicling perhaps less than one-half of 1 percent. From these records, we know a great deal about different cultures and religious experiences, but there is an enormous amount we do not and cannot know.

There are two primary sources of information about basic religions. The first is contemporary basic religions. The anthropologist visits a contemporary basic culture and studies its religious beliefs and practices. From this study, the anthropologist may infer that many or all basic and prehistoric religions have had similar attitudes and religious practices. Thus, Bishop Codrington studied the Melanesian people during the nineteenth century and reported their awareness of the unseen force called *mana*. Others found a similar phenomenon in different cultures. Therefore, Codrington came to believe that an awareness of such a force as *mana* might have been humankind's original religious impetus.

However interesting the study of contemporary basic religions may be, it obviously leaves much to be desired as a source for knowledge of prehistoric basic religion. The Melanesians of the nineteenth century might have been very different from earlier Melanesians. The Melanesians' religious awareness and practices might have changed within the nineteenth century itself. They might have adopted the belief in *mana* only recently, or they could have been affected by previous visits of missionaries or traders or even by the visit of the anthropologist. All contemporary societies, even the most technologically simple, have long and complex histories. They have developed and evolved over thousands of years in response to ecological and social environments and have built upon the wisdom of many generations. None can be considered really "primitive" or representative of the earliest stages of human development. As anthropological fieldwork has increased our understanding of the diversity of basic religions, it has become more, not less, difficult to use contemporary data to speculate about the origins and earliest forms of religion. The student of religion, like the student of language, must accept the fact that there are some aspects of the origins of the subject that, in all likelihood, we cannot know.

A second source of information is archaeology. Although humans have always been interested in their past and have doubtless always attempted to investigate the physical remains of that past, the scientific examination of those remains is less than two centuries old. In fact, most serious archaeological work has been achieved in the twentieth century. Archaeologists meticulously attempt to uncover the physical remains of past civilizations and to reconstruct the life and history of their cultures. In an archaeological examination of relatively recent cultures, such as the Roman or Mayan, the task is simplified because of the wealth of buildings, burial sites, coinage, and other elaborate artifacts these civilizations left. Archaeologists gain considerable information from scrolls, clay tablets, and inscriptional materials from literate cultures.

In studying prehistoric, or technologically less sophisticated, cultures, the task is more difficult. The main sources of information are likely burial sites, weapons, and tools. Whether the culture is distant or recent, archaeological results depend on the interpretations of the investigator. What one archaeologist calls a temple, another may call a stable; controversy and mistakes within this field are too numerous to list. Therefore, we must be careful to give archaeological investigation its due and no more. Some archaeologists may assure us that Neanderthal people worshipped bears because bear skulls have been found in burial sites. This may or may not have been the case. Perhaps bear skulls were buried with these people as trophies of the hunt. They might also have been the totems of the deceased. With our present limited knowledge about Neanderthals, we cannot be certain about their religion.

Prehistoric Beginnings of Basic Religions
Neanderthal Religion

The earliest hominid for whom much evidence of religion remains is the so-called Neanderthal. It is believed that Neanderthals lived from approximately 125,000 to 30,000 B.C.E. and inhabited Europe, the Middle East, and western and central Asia. Although they were anatomically similar to modern *Homo sapiens*, Neanderthal skeletons reveal that these people were somewhat shorter and more muscular. Their brains were as large as those of

Cave art from Dordogne Valley, Lascaux, France. Typical of prehistoric religious art, this painting may be an example of imitative magic through which a hunter sought to ensure success in a hunt.
(Peter Buckley/Pearson Education/PH College)

contemporary humans. Greater than 100 sites of Neanderthal life have been excavated. These sites reveal that these people were clever workers, using tools made of stone, bone, and wood. They also show that the Neanderthals buried their dead. It is in the circumstances of these burials that one finds clues to Neanderthal religion. In these burials are the remains of animal bones and stone tools, which may indicate that the dead were buried with food, tools, and weapons, perhaps as offerings to gods or as necessary accompaniments into the world of the dead. In addition, archaeologists have found bear skulls, apparently carefully arranged, in Neanderthal burials, which may suggest a worshipful attitude toward the bear.

Cro-Magnon Religion

The Cro-Magnon, the forerunner of modern *Homo sapiens*, replaced the Neanderthal approximately 30,000 years ago. Like the Neanderthals, the Cro-Magnon people left no written records. Again, our only information about their lives comes from the work of archaeologists. Like the Neanderthals, the Cro-Magnons apparently buried tools and weapons with their dead. Graves also have yielded ornaments with which the dead were buried. In addition, some Cro-Magnon graves contain bones painted red. Archaeologists have interpreted these factors as indicative of a concern for life beyond the grave. Sometimes the burials show the corpse was left curled up in a fetal position. To some, this might indicate that the dead were seeking rebirth in the next life.

The most outstanding artifacts associated with the Cro-Magnon are the famous paintings and engravings on the walls and ceilings of caves in France and Spain. These pictures, located in dark recesses far from the entrances, were identified as Cro-Magnon and apparently had been placed in such inaccessible places to keep out the uninitiated. Their location had inadvertently protected them from damage for thousands of years. A few of these paintings depict animals being killed during a hunt. The animals—bison, horses, wild boar, and bears—are shown with arrows and spears entering their bodies at critical points. Although the animals are very lifelike, the humans hunting them are depicted by mere stick figures. The most common understanding of these paintings is that they were placed on the hidden walls of the caves by priests or magicians before the hunt. It is believed that by painting the animals being killed or by retracing the paintings, the priests were hoping to predict the events of a successful hunt. Similar practices are followed by shamans of contemporary basic religions, either in the form of graphic art or a drama in which members of the tribe play the part of animals being killed during a hunt.[1]

In addition to the cave paintings, the Cro-Magnons left figurines carved from stone, ivory, and bone. One of the best known of these is the so-called Venus of Willendorf, a figurine depicting a human female form. Although the figure has no face, its breasts, hips, and abdomen are greatly exaggerated.[2] Similar figurines from historic cultures often indicate worship of a fertility goddess.

Neolithic Religion

Because Neanderthal and Cro-Magnon societies primarily used stone tools and weapons, their cultures are identified archaeologically as the Stone Age. The eras that followed the Cro-Magnon period also featured stone weapons and implements, but they were much advanced in other ways. The Neolithic or late Stone Age ran from approximately 7,000 to 3,000 B.C.E. and was characterized by many new developments in civilization.

One of the advances that greatly influenced the evolution of religion was the development of agriculture as a way of life. When people found they could make their living by planting seeds, harvesting their crops, and storing them against future hunger, their lives changed enormously. For the first time, people did not have to move constantly from place to place in search of game; they could settle and live in one place as long as the soil remained fertile. They now needed more permanent dwellings and could live in larger groups. Agricultural surplus and the ability to store food supplies led to population growth and the development of cities.

In Egypt, agriculture led to land ownership. The sciences of surveying and mathematics were developed to establish ownership of the fields after the annual flood of the Nile Delta. Above all, the development of agriculture gave some people more leisure time than they had ever known. They could, in effect, afford to sit back and allow the soil to provide them with nourishment. For the first time, certain people in the community were free to devote all of their time to the mysteries of religion. In addition, agricultural society first became dependent on the fertility of nature. People grew aware that one year might bring a great harvest, whereas the next might lead to a drought. They became aware of the regularity of the seasons, the tides, the phases of the moon, and the movements of the stars. These factors caused Neolithic people to develop religions based on the fertility of the soil, humans, and animals, as well as mythologies in which deities became personifications of the sun, moon, stars, and seasons.

Archaeological remains from the Neolithic period give some indication of the religious attitudes of the time. Large burials from this era contain the bones of men, women, and animals, along with tools, weapons, and ornaments. This suggests to some that Neolithic people may have buried the chieftain with his wives, servants, and favorite animals, so that they might serve him in the next life.

It also appears that Neolithic societies erected monuments of huge stones called megaliths in many parts of the world. The two best examples of this practice are the great stone monuments raised at Stonehenge in England and the greater than 2,000 megaliths set up in the fields of Brittany in France. Apparently, these massive stones, sometimes weighing as much as 300 tons, were quarried at a distance and transported with great effort to their present sites.[3] Because Neolithic societies left no written records about these stones, no one knows exactly why these people went to such great lengths to set them up or why the practice was so widespread. It is generally assumed that the megaliths had something to do with religion. One of the most common theories is that they were connected to a cult of the dead and to **ancestor veneration.**[4]

Common Features of Basic Religions

The following features appear to be common to many basic religions that still exist or existed in some form in the nineteenth and twentieth centuries, when anthropologists began to study them. These features have also appeared in the historical religions of which we are aware, and many of them are evident in one form or another in the so-called advanced or developed religions. Sacrifice, for example, appears in the earliest form of nearly every extant religion. Finally, some of the features not currently part of religions may be found subliminally in modern cultures. For instance, although few followers of the developed religions would admit that **magic** is part of their theology, belief in the lucky coin, the unlucky day, the avoidance of the number thirteen, spiritual or magical healing, and so on is widely found, even in the most advanced societies of the twenty-first century.

Animism

Sir Edward Tylor theorized that people originally envisioned the world as being alive with souls or spirits and, on the basis of this understanding of nature, developed religions.[5] Indeed, the belief that nature is alive with

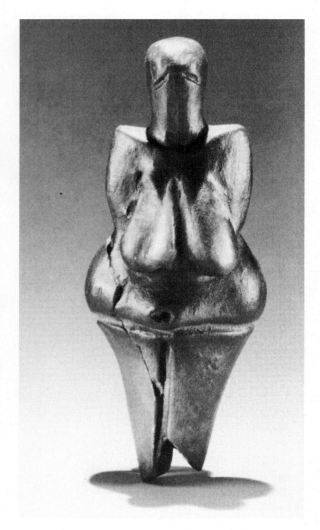

The Venus of Laussel. The exaggerated breasts, hips, and abdomen indicate that this was an image connected with fertility worship.
(Neg. # 329316, courtesy the Library, American Museum of Natural History)

spirits that have feelings and can be communicated with is one of the most common to human religious experience. In many basic religions, people believe that they are not the only spirits—that animals, trees, stones, rivers, mountains, the heavenly bodies, the seas, and the earth itself have *anima* (spirit). It is also believed that these spirits communicate, can be flattered or offended, and can either help or hurt humans. These spirits are therefore believed to be personal. The development of technology and the spread of historical religions have not eliminated these beliefs. Many Christians, Muslims, and Buddhists believe that spirits have the ability to bless or curse human beings.

On the basis of an animistic understanding of life, basic religions and many advanced religions have revered or openly worshipped nearly everything in nature. Almost any animal one can think of has at some time or another been worshipped; stones have been worshipped or have been the sites where gods have spoken to people or received the blood of their sacrifices; mountains have frequently been the objects of worship or the places of revelation; the seas and the creatures in them have been objects of veneration; trees have frequently been the objects of religious cults; the heavenly bodies—the sun, moon, and stars—play a part in nearly every religion; and fire, water, and the earth itself have become objects of worship or important elements in worship. The list of animistic expressions is almost endless.

Modern people place historic stones at the corners of their new buildings; they build expensive, elaborate, useless fireplaces. Christians bring evergreen trees into their homes to celebrate Christmas, even though there is no connection between an evergreen tree and the birth of Jesus; Muslims walk around the sacred black stone and kiss it during their pilgrimage to Mecca; Hindus bathe in the sacred river Ganges; Parsis bring gifts of sandalwood to be burned in the sacred fire temple; Christian and even secular Americans go on pilgrimages to the graves of presidents and rock stars; and on and on. The animistic understanding of life is one of the most pervasive and influential of all of the impulses of mankind—religious and non-religious.

Magic

When modern people speak of magic, they often think in terms of sleight-of-hand tricks or illusions performed by a professional whose job is to deceive and amuse them. In basic religions, the term *magic* takes on a far more serious meaning.

Magicians in basic societies attempt to control nature for either the benefit of their people or the detriment of their enemies. Magicians perceive the world as being controlled by forces that can be manipulated. They know that if they perform their formulas, dances, or incantations correctly, they will in fact be able to control nature; they can make rain, cause crops to be bountiful, create conditions for a successful hunt, or kill their enemies.

According to one theory, the line between religion and magic is drawn by the intent of the practitioner. Magicians believe that by performing rituals they can force nature to act as they desire, whereas the practitioners of religion seek only to implore the gods on their behalf. The magician knows that his or her fiat will be done, but the priest hopes that the gods will act favorably. Actually, the distinction between religion and magic is never absolutely clear, and elements of magic appear in religion, just as

Stonehenge, located on the Salisbury Plain of southern England. It is believed that these massive stones were erected in the second millennium B.C.E. Their exact purpose is open to speculation, but it is believed that the arrangement of the stones was somehow connected to religious ritual.
(British Tourist Authority)

elements of religion appear in magic. Sir James Frazer believed that magic was a phase through which humankind passed on its way to religion and ultimately to science.[6]

Probably the most common form of magic among basic societies is sympathetic or imitative magic. In this form of magic, one attempts to coerce nature into some act by performing that act oneself, but on a smaller scale. An example is the so-called voodoo doll through which the magician seeks to do evil to enemies. The doll is created in the rough image of the enemy and may contain personal elements of the enemy such as bits of hair or nail parings. Practitioners believe that because the doll looks like the victim, whatever is done to the doll will happen to the victim. If the doll is pierced with a needle through the leg, the victim will be injured in the leg; if the doll is pierced through the heart, the victim will be killed or will at least have severe chest pains. In some societies, many of the rain ceremonies and preliminary hunting rituals are based on imitative magic.

Another aspect of magic frequently found in basic religions is the fetish. A fetish is any object used to control nature in a magical fashion. In modern society, such objects are called good-luck charms. For the possessor, the fetish is used to bring good fortune and ward off evil. In basic societies, the fetish may be almost anything: a wooden stick, a stone or a collection of stones, a bone, a feather, even a special weapon. Fetishes may be held singly or collectively, or they may be used as an ornamentation of some kind.

Fetishism is never very far from even the most advanced human society. In any group of people, one is likely to encounter a large collection of lucky coins, rabbits' feet, religious medallions, and so on. The value that most twenty-first-century people place on their fetishes probably varies considerably from that which prehistoric people placed on theirs. Nevertheless, the existence of fetishes and other elements of basic religion in advanced and scientific societies speaks of their enduring appeal to the human race.

In recent decades there has been an animist revival in North America and Western Europe. Many of the so-called "New Age" religions have deep roots in animistic thinking. The Deep Ecology movement, for example, straddles the border between environmentalism and animism. For many supporters of Deep Ecology, the Earth is a spiritual consciousness as well as a planet. The environment is seen as a self-regulating system, all elements of which are to be valued equally. Change or evolution is directed by a spiritual force. Other "New Age" faiths maintain that particular places are vortexes at which a variety of types of spiritual power may be acquired.

Divination

The prediction of the future through **divination** is an important function in basic societies. Usually, this is the work of priests or people who have been specially prepared for the task, and it is accomplished by various means. Frequently, divination is accomplished through the examination of the entrails of a sacrificed animal. Sometimes, it is achieved by observing the flights of birds or by casting sacred dice. In ancient China, a tortoise shell was heated until it cracked, and the pattern of the cracks was interpreted as a prediction of the future. This approach was later refined into the practice of casting yarrow stalks, and these patterns were interpreted in a book called the *I Ching*. Among the ancient Greeks, the future was predicted when a priestess sat on a tripod and breathed in fumes that escaped from the ground at Delphi. What she said after breathing in the fumes was interpreted by a priest as being the message from the gods regarding the future.

Frequently, societies sought knowledge of the future from a member of the group believed to have been possessed by the spirits. Among the peoples of Siberia, this person was called a *shaman*. Although the word *shaman* often connotes an image of a "priest" or "magician," the original meaning related to one who was possessed by the spirits and spoke their messages to the group.

Often, religious societies are served by those who are designated "prophets." In the Hebrew Bible, the prophet revealed the message of God. Sometimes this

Megaliths are still erected in conjunction with mortuary rituals by the Toraja of Indonesia.
(Mark R. Woodward)

message dealt with present events; other times the prophet's words concerned the future. Thus, the word *prophet* in modern English carries the connotation of being a "predictor" or "diviner."

Taboo

In the scheme of life in many basic societies, certain actions must be avoided, lest the spirit world release harmful effects on the person or group; these acts are known by the Polynesian word *tabu* or *tapu*. In basic societies, holy persons, places, and objects are generally considered **taboo** to the ordinary person. Chieftains, priests, sacred places, fetishes, and so on are to be avoided by the unordained, except on special occasions or when there is special preparation. In basic societies, one does not touch the person of the chief, nor does one enter the sacred areas without great fear; great harm can come to someone who violates these tribal taboos. In the Hebrew Bible, we find occasions when people either knowingly or accidentally violate taboos. Second Kings 2:23–25 speaks of an occasion when boys mocked and taunted the prophet Elisha. As a result, the children were mauled by two bears. Second Samuel 6:1–7 tells of a man who merely touched the Ark of the Covenant to prevent its falling off a cart and as a result was struck dead by God. In many other cultures, the person of the king is so sacred that it is considered taboo to come into his presence without special invitation. Until fairly recent times, the Japanese thought it taboo to look upon the face of the emperor, even when he toured the city streets.

Other examples of taboos are numerous. In some basic societies, the birth of twins is considered taboo. Thus, when twins are born they are either killed or exiled, or they are treated as special sacred persons. The dead are often the object of taboos. In many cultures, those who handle the dead for burial are considered ritually unclean, at least for a certain period of time after the handling. One of the most universal taboos regards women during their menses. In some cultures, menstruating women are required to live in houses that are separate from the rest of the group. Some religions prohibit women from prayer during their periods.[7] Many cultures have developed taboos regarding certain foods. Usually, the food set aside for the chieftain is forbidden to the rest of the community. Certain kinds of food, such as pork, beef, or shellfish, are thought of by particular groups as being ritually unclean, and thus taboo. Such beliefs are not restricted to basic societies. Muslims and Jews consider pork unclean. Most Hindus do not eat beef, not because the cow is unclean, but rather because it is viewed as being sacred. Until recently, all forms of meat were taboo for Roman Catholics on Fridays.

Totems

Another practice in some, but by no means all, basic religions is **totemism**. Totemism was first identified by white settlers in the eighteenth century when they discovered the practice among Native Americans. It was later recognized within basic societies in other parts of the world. The word *totem* is a corruption of the Ojibwa word *ototeman*.

Totemism is apparently based on the feeling of kinship that humans have for other creatures or objects in nature. As such, it is an extension and expression of *animism*. Generally, it involves some form of identification between a tribe or clan and an animal, although totems in some parts of the world have been identified as plants or even as the sun, moon, or stars. For example, a clan may believe it is basically related to the bear. The bear may be the ancestor of the clan; the clan may possess the characteristics of the bear (strength, ferocity, or size); or clan members may believe that when they die they will take the form of the bear. If the bear is the totem of the clan, members may not eat or kill this animal except in self-defense or on sacred occasions, when they may eat its flesh in a ceremonial meal that binds the clan closer together. Members of another neighboring clan, whose totem is the deer, may hunt and eat the bear, whereas members of the first clan may hunt and eat the deer.

Highly developed societies, although they do not clearly and religiously adhere to totemism, still retain vestiges of this practice. Nations are symbolized by animals, such as the eagle, bear, or lion, and schools choose mascots to symbolize the spirit of their athletic teams.

Sacrifice

One of the most common practices in all of the religions of the world is sacrifice. Throughout history, people have offered sacrifices of nearly every imaginable material to the gods, spirits, demons, and **ancestor veneration**. Most often, the sacrifices are animals, which are slaughtered and then burned or cooked and eaten before the gods. However, the sacrifice of nearly every other item of value can be found. People have sacrificed grain, wine, milk, water, wood, tools, weapons, and jewelry to the gods. Occasionally, religions call for the sacrifice of a human, but in most religions this is a relatively rare practice. Usually the human who is sacrificed is an enemy taken prisoner in battle; infrequently, it is a beloved child or young person chosen especially for the altar.[8] When human sacrifice is mentioned in religious literature, it usually is considered an extreme but effective method of persuading the gods.[9]

Among the Oche of ancient Peru and the Aztec of pre-Columbian Mexico, human sacrifice was both routine and extremely important. Headhunting, which was thought to ensure the fertility of the land, was practiced by many of the tribal peoples of Southeast Asia well into the twentieth century. There are unconfirmed reports that the practice continues in remote areas.

The act of sacrifice has various meanings. Originally, it probably was considered a means of feeding the residents of the spirit world. How does one feed the spirits? One may pour water, wine, and milk on the ground and believe that as the fluid is soaked up, the spirits are drinking it. One may leave food in a sacred place and assume that when the food has disappeared, the gods have been fed. One may burn meat or grain, and the gods may inhale the smoke of the offerings. Thus, the spirit world is sustained by the human world and acts favorably toward it.

At other times, the sacrifice is understood simply as being a gift of some sort to the spirit world. Gifts of tools, weapons, ornaments, money, incense, or even tobacco may be left in sacred places for the spirits by a person who wishes the favor of the spirits or simply wants to avoid offending them.

Sacrifice in some basic religions also implies the establishment of a communal bond between spirits and human beings. The worshiper brings food to the sacred place, burns a portion of it for the gods, and then eats a portion of it or shares it with the clan. Thus, the spirits and the living share a meal together, and their bond is renewed and strengthened.

Myth

One of the most common characteristics of all religions, basic and advanced, is **mythology**. In modern parlance, the word *myth* connotes a lie or false belief. We speak of the myth of Aryan supremacy or the myth of historical objectivity, and we mean that these concepts are out-and-out fabrications with little or no basis in truth. In the study of religions, the word *myth* is used in another sense. Almost every religion has its stories about the dealings of the gods with humans. We call these stories myths, or poetic ways of telling great truths. Myths are a way of thinking in pictures rather than abstract concepts. Very few people today might believe that the story of Prometheus is a factual account of a great hero of the past; perhaps no one ever did. But the story of Prometheus reveals the truth of the sacrificial love of one divine figure for humanity. In preliterate societies, especially, a religion is sustained and explained by the transmission of its myths from one generation to the next.

Religious myths often are used to explain the whys and hows of the world; they may explain the origin of a people by tracing it back to the beginning of creation. In the Greek myth of Prometheus, for example, there is an explanation for the creation of the world and the origin of fire and civilization. Myths also may explain the power of certain religious functionaries. The Japanese myth of the sun goddess Amaterasu gives background to the belief that the emperor is a divine figure. Often, myths are attached to and explain why the worshipping community keeps certain religious holy days.

Rituals

Every religion has its rituals. These rites or ceremonies may be simple or complex, or so brief that the laity may perform them several times a day, every day. Mealtime prayers

A Mombasa healer in traditional costume in Uganda, East Africa.
(De Cou/Ewing Galloway Inc.)

or libations to African ancestors are examples of these simpler rites. In other cases, community rituals may be so complicated that specific groups of people are set aside as priests to learn, perform, and teach them to others.

Often, religious rituals reenact mythologies. Priests and/or laity take part, wearing the costumes and speaking the lines of the figures from the myth. The historian of religion Mircea Eliade has suggested that the ritual repetition of creation myths is particularly important. Sculptures from the Roman-era religion of Mithraism show members of the order wearing the costumes of lions and ravens, animals that played a part in the cult's myth. They also are shown sitting at a meal of bread and wine in memory of the mythic occasion when Mithras and Sol Invictus ate the flesh of the sacred bull and drank its blood. By acting out the myths, the devotees of the religion identify with the divine characters and their actions.

Rites of Passage

Another universal practice among basic societies is the establishment of certain rituals at key transitional points in the life of the individual. These rituals are called *rites of passage*. The key points of life usually recognized are birth, puberty, marriage, and death. Rituals carried out at these critical periods recall the myths of the culture and symbolize separation from the former status, transition to the new, and incorporation. Often, these rituals involve a dramatic reenactment of a sacred story.

Ceremonies at birth are important. The rites surrounding birth identify the child as a member of the community. In Judaism, male children are circumcised. In many branches of Christianity, there is the ritual of baptism, a ceremony that names the infant and makes him or her a member of the Christian religion.

Basic societies often give their greatest attention to rituals regarding the passage from childhood into adulthood. The rites of passage at puberty are preceded by a period of instruction in the basic knowledge of the society, as well as in such arts as survival, hunting, agriculture, and fire making. At puberty, the child may undergo an ordeal of some kind. Among some Native Americans, children are expected to live apart from their families for a certain period of time, to fast and to seek a vision from the spirits. In other basic societies, children may be painted white or given some other highly visible mark and then sent away to live alone until the paint or the mark disappears. During this time, they are expected to fend entirely for themselves. Some children are not lucky or skillful enough to survive during this period. Those who do survive and return are then initiated into full adulthood. The individual may also be circumcised or given some other mark of identity, such as a facial scar. During these ceremonies, young people are more fully instructed in the religious traditions, secrets, and lore of the society and thereafter may take their place as fully matured members of the group.[10] Modern counterparts to the puberty rites of passage are confirmation for some Christian youths and the Bar Mitzvah or Bat Mitzvah for young Jews.[11]

Other key points at which religious rituals and symbols are important are marriage and death. Marriage is frequently celebrated with fertility rituals and the full attention of religious functionaries. The passage at death is likewise given the attention of religious rituals, both at the time of death and at the burial.

Ancestor Veneration

One final characteristic of basic religions is the veneration or worship of deceased members of the family. Some students of the origin of religion have theorized that because prehistoric people dreamed of their recent dead, they came to believe the dead were not truly gone but lived on in another form or on another planet. According to Spencer, this phenomenon led to ancestor worship and became the first step in the development of religion. Then the ancestors, living in another realm and appearing in dreams, became the gods of early religion. Whether dreams are the means by which ancestors are believed to continue to live is a matter of speculation. From what is known of basic religions, however, these people recognize that the dead live on in some form, at least for a time, and can either help or hurt the living.

Those who believe in the continued life of the ancestors greatly fear the evil the dead might do and frequently take great pains to prevent the dead from returning from their graves to harm the living. Bodies are buried beneath large stones or with stakes implanted in their chests, apparently to prevent them from roaming. Among some basic societies, the names of the dead are dropped from common usage for a time, and the houses in which they died are burned to discourage their return.

At the same time, people of basic societies also seem to feel the dead can benefit the living. Therefore, steps are taken to please the dead. Possessions such as tools, weapons, favorite foods, ornaments, and sometimes even wives and servants are sent to the grave with the dead. Graves and tombs (such as the vast tombs of the Egyptian rulers) are decorated and elaborately tended so the dead might be comfortable. Among the ancient Chinese, grave mounds were rebuilt each year and offerings of food, drink, flowers, and even blankets were left for the comfort of the deceased. Perhaps no people made such a great effort to placate the deceased as the ancient Chinese. Their special concern was to keep alive the memory of their ancestors by memorizing their names and biographies and passing this information on to future generations. Ancestor veneration remains a very important part of traditional Chinese religion, especially among overseas Chinese in places like Taiwan and Singapore where "superstitious" beliefs were not affected by Communist rule. Even some Chinese Christians engage in ancestor veneration to some degree. Saint Andrew's Anglican Cathedral in Singapore, the congregation of which is largely Chinese, holds prayer services in cemeteries on the Saturday before Easter to prepare the ancestors for resurrection.

STUDY QUESTIONS

1. Why do we speak of "basic" rather than "primitive" religions?
2. What are the two primary sources of information about basic religions? How trustworthy are these sources?
3. What do we believe was the purpose of the Cro-Magnon cave paintings?
4. Define *animism*, and give several examples of surviving animism in modern life.
5. Distinguish *magic* from *religion*.
6. Name some taboos in modern life. How are they like those in basic societies? How are they different?
7. In your culture, what are the rites of passage?

8. Name some examples of the ways in which basic religions resemble world religions.
9. What are examples of the basic types of religious violence in the contemporary world?

SUGGESTED READING

Campbell, Joseph. *The Masks of God: Primitive Mythology*. New York: Viking, 1970.

Eliade, Mircea. *The Sacred and the Profane*. Translated by Willard Trask. New York: Harper Torchbooks, 1961.

Evans-Pritchard, E. E. *Theories of Primitive Religion*. New York: Clarendon Press, 1965.

Ferguson, John. *Gods Many and Lords Many: A Study in Primal Religions*. Greenwood, SC: Attic Press, 1982.

Frazer, Sir James. *The New Golden Bough*. Abridged by Theodore H. Gaster. New York: Criterion Books, 1959.

Gill, Sam D. *Beyond "The Primitive": The Religions of Nonliterate People*. Englewood Cliffs, NJ: Prentice Hall, 1982.

Harvey, Graham. *Indigenous Religion, A Companion*. London: Casell, 2000.

Otto, Rudolf. *The Idea of the Holy*. Translated by John W. Harvey. New York: Oxford University Press, 1958.

CHAPTER 2

Native American Religions

CHAPTER OBJECTIVES

In this chapter you will:

- Learn about the great variety of Native American religions.

- Learn about the ways in which Native American religions and cultures have been influenced by contact with Europeans.

KEY TERMS

Mother Earth   Vision Quest   Sun Dance
Great Spirit   Native American Church

A Timeline of Native American Religions

+/– 20,000 B.C.E.	First people arrive in North America Thousands of years of oral tradition	1848	U.S. acquires Southwestern territories at the conclusion of the Mexican War; beginning of large-scale Euro-American settlement and "Indian Wars"
3,500 B.C.E.	Urban centers in Peru created		
1492	European "discovery" of the American begging of Spanish conquest and conversion to Christianity	1862	Homestead Act prompts displacement of many Native American communities
		1863–64	Thousands of Navajo killed by U.S. forces
1540	Spanish arrive in what is now the Southwest United States and establish Roman Catholic missions; beginning of 150 years of conflict	1878–1933	Period of Indian Boarding Schools and involuntary conversion to Christianity
		1890	Battle of Wounded Knee and the end of "Indian Wars"
1607	First successful English settlement in North America; beginning of conflict and missionary activity	1890	Ghost Dance religion
		1918	Incorporation of Native American Church

(Continued)

A Timeline of Native American Religions *(Continued)*

1941–1945	Navajo serve as code talkers during World War II		1978 legalize the use of peyote in religious ceremonies
1968	Dennis Banks founds the Native American Movement to fight for civil rights	2004	Dedication of the National Museum of the American Indian in Washington D.C.
1994	Amendments to the United States American Indian Religious Freedom Act of		

One of the oldest and most enduring forms of religion is that which is practiced by the various Native American peoples. Because of the role played by Native Americans in North American history over the past 400 years, their religious practices have been of interest not only to scholars but also to the general public. In recent years, more and more attention has been focused on the subject. Native Americans have experienced something of a religious revival and have become increasingly concerned with the preservation of their cultural and religious heritage. Many non-native Americans have turned greater attention to the religions of native peoples because of their emphasis on nature and personal religious experience, and the absence of a formal organizational structure.

When speaking of the religion of Native Americans, we must be aware that we are not speaking of a monolithic structure. The people identified as Native Americans arrived on the North American continent 15,000 to 20,000 years ago.[1] Since then, they have lived in nearly every section of America.[2] They have resided in many different climates, with differing lifestyles. Some Native American tribes have been hunting and gathering societies, whereas others lived in settled agricultural communities. Some lived in small nomadic bands, while others built towns, cities, states, and empires. Many now live in towns and cities and are integrated into non-native social and economic systems to a high degree. Many more live on reservations established by treaties with the U.S. government.

Many people tend to identify Native Americans with the nomadic hunting peoples who roamed the western plains of North America in the nineteenth century. The lives of these people centered on the pursuit of the bison. However, many of these tribes were at one time primarily agricultural. All of these hunting societies were influenced by aspects of European culture, particularly the horses and guns that made life on the open plains possible. Because of the long time span involved and the many differing lifestyles, it is impossible to talk about one set "Native American religion."

In studying these religions, one must also be aware of the relative dearth of sources. Although Native American life covers perhaps 20,000 years, literary sources exist from only the last 400 years. Most of the early sources are reports of Christian missionaries and explorers, who may or may not have been sympathetic or objective witnesses. Furthermore, the great bulk of information on Native American religions has been written during the past 100 years—after there had been contact with European civilization, its religions, and its technology. Scholars often debate whether some aspect of these religions truly reflects "pure" Native American religion or whether it developed in response to some aspect of Christianity.[3] While none of the Native American religions have survived unchanged, many have incorporated elements of European culture and religion into native belief systems rather than giving up traditional ways entirely. It is, therefore, still possible to speak of Native American religion in the present tense.

Our primary source of knowledge about Native American religions prior to the arrival of the Europeans is archaeology. Although archaeology can show much about the total culture of a people, it does not tell us much about religion, particularly of those people who did not construct stone monuments or other lasting religious images and structures. Because most pre-Columbian American people were not literate and left few religious artifacts, our knowledge of their religious beliefs is very limited.

To describe Native American religion, we have two major options: We can either describe the specific religion of one tribe at one period in history, or we can make general statements about the entire field of these religions. In this text, we take the second option. Following are some general characteristics of many of the better-known Native American religions.

The Spirit World

To investigate the religions of Native Americans, one might begin by asking whether these religions are basically polytheistic, monotheistic, or monistic. Do they recognize one Supreme God or multiple deities, or do they find the divine present in a variety of forms? Do they follow the theological patterns of Islam and Judaism, or are they more like the polytheistic Graeco-Roman religions with their many gods? Are these religions more like Hinduism, which recognizes a single divine principle that has many outward forms? Unfortunately, there are no easy answers to these questions. In one sense, Native American religions are polytheistic. All nature is alive with spirits. Close at hand are the spirits of animals or plants which appear in visions. There are also the guardian spirits of various animals, and there are the spirits of the dead, who live in the land of the dead. Nature is personified in many spirits. At the heart of nature is **Mother Earth**, who provides the bounty of the earth. Thunder and lightning are believed to be individual beings. Therefore, in the broadest sense of the word, Native American religions are polytheistic. Native Americans believe that many levels of gods and spirits exist in the universe.

However, many forms of Native American religion hold that, in addition to the multiple spirits of nature, there is a single Supreme Being. They believe in the Supreme Being in a manner found in many basic religions. These religions take the position that, above and beyond all the lesser deities, there is a High God. However, this High God is separate from the concerns of Earth. Matters of daily life are the business of the nature spirits and sometimes the ancestors. It is to these spirits that one prays and gives attention. The High God is appealed to rarely, perhaps only in an extreme emergency, and is seldom mentioned in religious conversation. Many of the Native American religions take this attitude toward the Supreme Being.

Amah Kachina Dance, Hopi, Arizona, Southwestern United States.
(Neg. # 928460, courtesy the Library, American Museum of Natural History)

Some Native Americans think of the High God or **Great Spirit** as a personal God. Others understand the High God in a more abstract way. For them, the High God is not a personality, but rather a divine or sacred power that is revealed in humans, nature, and the spirit world. The Dakota (Sioux) belief in Wakan Tanka is an example of this abstract understanding of the High God. Wakan Tanka or the "Great Mysterious" is a creative force found in all beings and spirits. Any object or being that has influence over the course of life is seen as a manifestation of this divine power. Thus, Native American religions have some of the qualities of monotheism, polytheism, and monism.

Animism

Much is made of the contrast between the Native American attitude toward nature and that of the Europeans who came to America. Generally, it is said that Native Americans have a reverent attitude toward the land, trees, rivers, and mountains. On the other hand, the Europeans tended to look upon nature as something to be exploited. Thus, they were willing to sacrifice the beauty and even the life of the land to build a technology that would make life more comfortable and pleasant. Whether this is an accurate characterization of either Native Americans or Europeans is a matter of debate. There are examples of native people who unintentionally abused their environment. In the American Southwest, for example, there are many cases in which overpopulation and the resulting pressure on fragile desert environments led to the decline of large-scale civilizations and long-term environmental change. There are also Europeans who love and respect nature. In general, however, Native Americans have a more reverent attitude toward nature than do most European Americans. This reverence for the land and for nature in general is at least in part the result of the fact that survival within traditional Native American cultures depended on living close to and in balance with nature, rather than on changing the environment to suit human needs.

The term *animism* has been applied to Native American religions by some scholars. In the strictest sense of the word, an animist is one who believes that the trees, rocks, rivers, plants, and animals are spiritually alive. The animist believes that the spirits that exist in nature have the power to help or harm. Therefore, the animist offers some form of worship to these spirits. Native American religions are animistic in a sense. These religions teach that the Supreme Being lives in all creation. If the Supreme Being lives and manifests itself in nature, nature should be respected and cared for. Therefore, nature is not seen as an object to be tamed by humankind. Rather, one must seek to live in harmony with nature.

Hunting was an important part of life in many Native American cultures. Because Native Americans did not keep large domestic animals prior to the arrival of the Europeans, wild game played an essential role in the diets of native people. Animal hides and bones were important raw materials for making clothing, tools, ornaments, and religious objects, and for constructing dwellings. Hunting was also a religious pursuit in which the hunter saw the animal as a fellow creature with a similar spirit. Therefore, a hunter prayed to the spirit of the animal before the hunt. Only those animals that were absolutely needed were killed. After the hunt, one asked the animal for forgiveness. Care was taken to use every part of the slaughtered animal. Nothing was wasted. Sometimes animal bones were buried in such a way that they might be exhumed and used later. These practices were in marked contrast to the actions of Euro-American hunters, who slaughtered great herds of bison for their hides or tongues and left the bulk of the animal to rot. The Euro-American type of hunting led to the destruction of the herds on which many Native Americans depended.

Native Americans who practice agriculture revere the soil, plants, and trees. The soil is often personified as Mother Earth. Planting and harvesting are surrounded with rituals and taboos. Plants, like animals, are thought to have spirits and are treated as persons by many Native Americans. For many Native American people, farming is a religious activity. Many of the Hopi of the Southwest continue to grow corn because of its religious meaning, even when the great bulk of their food comes from "modern" sources. Even the gathering of clay for the production of pottery is done with an understanding of the life in the soil. The Papago women of southern Arizona speak of the clay that they dig for pots: "I take only what I need. It is to cook for my children."[4] Even the cutting of wood has religious overtones. One makes an offering to the tree before cutting it. No wood is wasted because trees are sacred and, like humans, have feelings that must be respected.

The reverent attitude of the Native American toward nature and its contrast to that of many whites is best summarized in the words of a Wintu:

From the Source

The White people never cared for land or deer or bear. When we Indians kill meat, we eat it all up. When we dig roots we make little holes. When we build houses, we make little holes. When we burn grass for grasshoppers, we don't ruin things. We shake down acorns and pine nuts. We don't chop down the trees. We only use dead wood. But the White people plow up the ground, pull down the trees, kill everything. The tree says, "Don't. I am sore. Don't hurt me." But they chop it down and cut it up. The spirit of the land hates them. They blast out trees and stir it up to its depths. They saw up the trees. That hurts them. The Indians never hurt anything, but the White people destroy all. They blast rocks and scatter them on the ground. The rock says, "Don't. You are hurting me." But the White people pay no attention. When the Indians use rocks, they take little round ones for their cooking . . . . How can the spirit of the earth like the White man? . . . Everywhere the White man has touched it, it is sore.[5]

This tale is as much about the coming of the Europeans as it is about the role of nature in Native American religious thought. It is also an example of the way in which many Native Americans understand their relationships with the beings of the natural environment. Rocks, for example, are more than minerals. They are intelligent beings that can communicate with humans. Reverence for nature was part of Native American religion prior to contact with Europeans. Most likely, the encounter with European farmers and ranchers led Native Americans to emphasize this aspect of their religion as they saw environmental change lead to the destruction of their ways of life. Differing understandings of nature and its role in human culture became one of the ways in which Native American peoples distinguished themselves from white settlers. As non-native Americans have become increasingly concerned about the preservation of the natural environment, they have found Native American spirituality increasingly attractive.

Contacts with the Spirit World

Native American people do not tend to see the universe as being under the control of one Supreme God, in the pattern of such religions as Judaism or Islam. They are primarily interested in the day-to-day life among the multiple kinds of beings found in the world. The bulk of their religious attention was directed toward achieving good relations with the spirits of the earth, the forests, the streams, and the animals on which they depended. For Native Americans, the purpose of ritual is not so much to control nature but to communicate and establish good relationships with the spiritual beings that share the world with humans.

Sacrifice

Most of the religions of the world have practiced some form of sacrifice as a way of pleasing the deities.

Religion and Violence

Throughout history, animals, grain, wine, beer, and sometimes humans have been sacrificed to the gods. Such sacrifices are rare in the religions of the native peoples of what are now the United States and Canada, although human sacrifices were an important element of the religions of the Aztec and some other native peoples of Central and South America.[6]

When it occurs, sacrifice is understood as being a gift to the spirits in exchange for assistance to human beings. Some rituals, such as the **Sun Dance** of the native peoples of the Great Plains, require self-torment or sacrifice. This is seen as a way of acquiring the spiritual power necessary for human survival.

Medicine bundles, which are made from animal hides and bones, plants, and minerals, are also sources of spiritual power and are greatly valued both by the people who make them and by those of subsequent generations who treat them as living beings. Many native people are concerned that the medicine bundles found in museums may be in danger of death. While power and gifts are important concepts in native religions, the great blood sacrifices found in many religions are generally not a part of their worship.

Taboos

One of the ways Native Americans protect themselves from possible danger from the spirit world is through taboos. The concept of taboo, as it applies to Native American religions, may be defined in the following manner:

> Taboo are all actions, circumstances, persons, objects, etc., which owing to their dangerousness fall outside the normal everyday categories of existence.[7]

A taboo is a kind of religious action that enables people to avoid doing things that would offend the spirits of nature and the ancestors. A collection of widely held taboos relates to menstruating women. These were particularly strong in societies that depended largely on hunting for survival. In many cultures, women are believed to have special powers for either good or evil, but the menstruating woman is thought to be particularly powerful. During this time, she is obviously set apart by the spirit world as one who can participate in the miracle of child production. Many of the Native American peoples believed in the unusual power of a woman at these times in her life. Therefore, during menstruation, a woman was kept away from ordinary society. In some communities she was required to leave her family and live in a special location because her power could make her especially damaging to the magic necessary for a hunt. It was believed by some that even a glance from a menstruating woman could destroy the hunting ability of a man for the rest of his life. Her gaze could also destroy the magic of hunting weapons, and her presence in the forests might drive away the game forever.

Another widely observed taboo is the avoidance of the dead. No matter how beloved a person may have been in life, the fear is that after death the spirit will continue to stay around its former home and perhaps attempt to take friends and family. At best, the spirits of the dead might haunt their families, causing them bad dreams. This taboo is still widely observed. Among the Navajo and other tribes of Arizona and New Mexico, dead bodies, and even the clothing, belongings, and houses of the dead, are greatly feared, to the extent that many are reluctant to touch the bodies of the victims of automobile and other accidents. Except in extreme emergencies, their care is left to non-native people. Despite this fear of the dead, Navajo have served in the United States Armed Forces in large numbers, many in combat units. Taboos concerning the bodies of the dead may help to explain the high incidence of post traumatic stress disorder and related problems of drug and alcohol abuse among Navajo veterans.

Taboos concerning the dead led Native Americans to be greatly concerned about their final resting places. Often, steps are taken to keep the bodies in the grave and away from contact with the human world. Sometimes, the names of the dead are not spoken for years after their death. In some Native American societies, the dead were buried by special members of the tribe, and not their immediate families. These corpse handlers were considered to be ritually unclean for a period of time after they had touched the body. They were separated from the community for a period of several days and forbidden to eat the regular food of the tribe. Burial grounds and human remains continue to be both sacred and feared and should not be disturbed for any reason. Concern with the dead and their resting places has been the cause of many controversies between Native Americans and the scientific community. Archaeologists and other scientists often study human remains to learn about the diets and health of prehistoric peoples. Native Americans are greatly troubled by what they view as dangerous disrespect for the dead, and they have fought for the return and reburial of the remains discovered and studied by archaeologists.

Ceremonies and Rituals

Along with the observance of taboos, Native Americans often seek to control the forces of the spirit world with ceremonies. As is the case with many other religions, ceremonies are extremely important to the Native Americans. The purpose of their ceremonies, rituals, songs, and dances is not necessarily worship. They are a means of renewing the partnership between humans and the spirit world. Frequently, they involve dancing, singing, fasting, ordeals, bathing, and the observance of certain taboos.

One of the most common elements in Native American religions is the use of dance as a means of contacting the spirit world in preparation for some special event in life. Dance is an event in which the entire community participates. It is used to prepare the tribe for the hunt, for the agricultural season, or for the celebration of tribal gatherings and, previously, the preparation of war. It is also used in the rites of passage. Whatever the occasion, dance is accompanied by song, the beating of drums, the shaking of rattles, and the playing of sacred flutes. The song may be made up of only a few lines repeated over and over again, or it may tell the story of creation or of the great heroes of the past. Some songs speak of the spirits of animals such as deer or bison. The drumbeat might be nothing more than several people beating on a log with sticks, or it might involve complicated rhythms played on animal skin drums, but the hours of song and steady rhythm are hypnotic. Long hours of dancing in this atmosphere prepares the participants for contact with the spirit world.

Among those tribes whose livelihood depended on hunting, rituals prepared the hunters for their work. Hunting, like agriculture, tended to develop highly religious societies because of its capricious nature. During one season, the hunters would go forth and find an abundance of game, their weapons extremely accurate and effective. In the next season, the same hunters could find game scarce or their weapons virtually useless. Therefore, the spirits of the animals and the hunters themselves, along with their weapons, had to be properly prepared to ensure success. The following is a description of a Pueblo ritual before a hunt:

> One of my most dramatic memories is that of standing in the plaza of a Pueblo, in the dark of a January morning, to watch the Mother of Game bring in the deer. It was almost dawn when we heard the hunter's call from the hillside. Then shadowy forms came bounding down through the pinon trees. At first we could barely see the shaking horns and dappled hides. Then the sun's rays picked out men on all fours, with deerskins over their backs and painted staves in their hands to simulate forelegs. They leaped and gamboled before the people while around them pranced little boys who seemed actually to have the spirit of fawns.
>
> In their midst was a beautiful Pueblo woman with long black hair, in all the regalia of white boots and embroidered manta. She was their Owner, the Mother of Game, but she was also Earth Mother, the source of all live things including man. She led the animals where they would be good targets for the hunters, and one by one, they were symbolically killed.[8]

A ritual such as this could be called sympathetic or imitative magic. Those persons imitating the game animals in the ceremony were symbolically called forth and killed in

Oglala Sioux Sun Dance, Pine Ridge Reservation, South Dakota, United States.
(South Dakota Department of Tourism)

the belief that during the actual hunt the real animals would be similarly killed. Because of the identification of a kindred spirit between Native Americans and their game, the ritual of the hunt also included a merciful killing of the animal and festive treatment of its body. For example, there are reports in which hunters apologized to the animal before they killed it. Afterward, the body of the animal was brought back to the tribe and was treated as an honored guest.

The Vision Quest

To gain special power at some point in life, Native Americans often seek visions that put them in contact with the spirit world. Visions are especially sought for young people at the time of puberty. Early in life, children are taught that one day they must go alone into the wilderness and seek a vision of the spirit world. When the time for a **vision quest** arrives, the young person may be sent away from the family and required to live alone until a vision is received. The vision quest is often accompanied by several days of fasting. Usually, the young person on a vision quest lives without food, perhaps without water, and with only the barest of possessions and clothing. This is done to make the individual appear poor and humble before the spirits. Sometimes, the young person's face and body are painted to resemble some special member of the tribe. When the vision comes, the spirits often appear in the guise of animals in a dreamlike or trancelike state. When this happens, the animal becomes the special guardian of the young person, whose name may be changed to include this animal. This practice is known as totemism. The animal that appears in the vision is believed to have a close spiritual bond with the young person throughout life. In some Native American societies, there are also totems for clans or other family groups. The vision may also be of a man or a woman. If the vision does not appear after two or three days of fasting and prayer, the young person may feel compelled to take more extreme measures. One might cut his or her flesh or even chop off a finger as a sign of sincerity. When the vision finally comes, the young person returns to the community as a full member of the group, having moved through this rite of passage.

Visions are sought by Native Americans at other times in life. In the past they were particularly important on the eve of great battles, when extraordinary strength was needed to achieve honors. Visions were also connected with hunting, particularly during the days of the great buffalo hunts in the nineteenth century. Today, they are sought at times of political, economic, or spiritual crisis, and when a person is contemplating a life-changing decision such as marriage, running for a political office, or moving from a rural reservation to an urban area for employment or education.

An example of a communal effort toward achieving visions is the Sun Dance, practiced by the people of the Plains. This dance takes place in summer, often at the solstice, when the heat of the sun is near its peak. Participants in the dance seek a vision and an identification with the divine. They gather in a lodge especially built for this purpose. The center of this lodge is a sacred pole, cut from a tree chosen for the dance. The dance usually lasts three days and nights. During this time, the dancers fast and dance continually. On some occasions and among some tribes, the Sun Dance once involved putting thongs through the flesh of the pectoral muscles of the dancers and hanging them from the center pole of the lodge to attach the dancer to the source of the divine. Because it is dangerous to stay too long in the spirit world, the dancers had to free themselves quickly. At times, the thongs tore through the flesh. As gruesome as this sounds, it apparently inflicted no permanent injury.[9]

Religious Leadership

Native American religions are remarkably free of a priesthood. Although there are those in every tribe who have special connections with the spirit world, basic religious functions are performed by every member of the group. In a sense, Native American religions are very personal in that they encourage individuals to contact the spirit world alone. Prayers, dances, songs, and visions are all performed by every member of the tribe, according to each person's need—not by the specialist in religion. Because there is very limited use of sacrifice, there is little need for the trained professional to perform a ritual on behalf of the untrained layperson—the procedure so common in many other religions. Nevertheless, among Native Americans, several categories of religious specialists are used occasionally in encounters with the spirit world.

The specialist most often connected with Native American religions is the so-called medicine man or woman. The designation "medicine man" was given to the functionary by early white settlers because they recognized this person as one who specialized in healing. To the traditional Native American, sickness is caused by the invasion of the body by a foreign object and healing comes about when the foreign body is removed. It is the job of the healer to remove such objects. The medicine man receives power through visions from the spirit world, which give him power over the forces that cause sickness. The spirits may appear after a period of fasting and prayer, or sometimes without any preparation. They usually take the form of a special animal, such as the bear or badger, because these two animals are connected with healing in Native American mythology. The spirits do not take possession of the healer; they only appear and instruct on a frequent basis, perhaps giving a song or instructing in taboos.

Because of this special contact with the spirit world, medicine men and women are empowered to heal, but they can also curse and bring sickness and even death to those who incur their wrath. This power brings a great responsibility to those who are recognized as healers. If medicine men or women encounter a sickness too serious to be healed, they can claim that it is the work of a more powerful person. But if a number of patients are dying, the healer can be held responsible for the deaths and can even be executed. These beliefs often lead to accusations of sorcery and witchcraft.

The healing process sometimes consists of a sucking ritual. If sickness is caused by the intrusion of a foreign object into the body, it is the healer's job to remove the object. Thus, the healer attempts to literally suck the offensive object or spirit from the body of the sick person. This ritual is often accompanied by songs, dancing, or incantations. At other times, the patient is given various herbs and teas to alleviate pain and induce healing.[10]

Sand paintings are an important element of Navajo healing rituals. *(Neg. # 2A3642 (photo by Boltin), courtesy the Library, American Museum of Natural History)*

Other Means of Contact with the Spirit World

One of the most common elements of Native American religions is the use of tobacco and the sacred pipe in religious ceremonies. Tobacco smoke, a form of incense, is a link with the spirit world. In the past, tobacco was a part of many ceremonies; it was smoked when people gathered to talk of peace, war, or the hunt, and it was smoked by the medicine man during healing ceremonies.

Tobacco was originally grown and used only for religious purposes by Native Americans, although many Native Americans now smoke on a regular basis. One of the reasons tobacco was reserved for special religious occasions was that it was far too strong to be used more frequently. The tobacco used in religious ceremonies is *Nicotiana rustica*, which is far stronger than the tobacco used in cigarettes. The fumes of this tobacco are so strong they can be intoxicating. Smokers who have tried Indian tobacco marvel that anyone is ever able to smoke the six or more puffs required in Native American ceremonies.

The ritual tobacco is occasionally smoked in cigarettes rolled from corn husks, but it is more frequently smoked in pipes. The bowls of these pipes are made from either clay or stone and the stems from reeds. Sometimes, the most ceremonial of the pipes have stems up to four feet long. They are often decorated with paints and feathers and, in the past, were carried into battle or the hunt as tribal talismans.

The use of peyote in Native American religions has received a great deal of attention in recent years. Peyote has been used in religious ceremonies for centuries by the people of Mexico. The practice has spread to North American tribes over the past 100 years.

A Navajo wedding ceremony.
(The Viesti Collection, Inc.)

Peyote is a small, spineless, carrot-shaped cactus growing in the Rio Grande Valley and southward. It contains nine narcotic alkaloids. In pre-Columbian times, the Aztec, Huichol, and other Mexican Indians ate the plant ceremonially, either in the dried or green state. Peyote produced profound sensory and psychic experiences lasting twenty-four hours, a property that led the natives to value and use it religiously.[11] One of the alkaloids found in peyote is mescaline. After a certain quantity of peyote is eaten or ingested in a tea, mescaline produces hallucinations and visions. It is because of these

Religion and Violence

With the military defeats and humiliation Native Americans suffered at the hands of the U.S. government at the end of the nineteenth century, some began to turn to peyote ceremonies. Previously, the vision was sought only occasionally—at the rite of passage at puberty, prior to a great hunt or battle, or by the medicine man at crucial points in his life. However, when so little was left to the Native Americans, and when they had been defeated and crowded into reservations, many felt the need for more frequent visions. Therefore, the peyote cult grew and developed rituals. Today, it plays an important role in the religious lives of many Native Americans, particularly in the Southwestern United States.[12]

A Mission Church in Guadalupe, Arizona, a Yaqui community in the Phoenix metropolitan area.
(Mark R. Woodward)

colorful visions that peyote has been made a part of some religious ceremonies. Peyote and related substances are used by healers and others seeking knowledge and experience of the spirit world in many of the native cultures of South and Central America.

In the early part of the twentieth century, there developed an amalgamation of the peyote cult and a form of Christianity. Many Native Americans had been taught the principles of the Christian religion but also appreciated the values of their own religion and peyote. Some reasoned that Christians used wine and a wafer in celebrating communion and Native Americans used the peyote button and tea in communing with the spirit world. In 1918, the Native American Church, a group that blended Christianity and the peyote cult, was legally organized in Oklahoma. In 1944, the movement became nationwide and was called the Native American Church of the United States. In 1950, it expanded to include Canadian Indians and was called the Native American Church of North America. Currently, it is estimated that this religious movement has about 225,000 members. Members of the Native American Church differ considerably about the importance of Jesus and the Bible. Extreme traditionalists are concerned almost exclusively with traditional beliefs and practices. On the other end of the continuum are church members for whom Christianity is of central importance. The entire range of viewpoints may be found in a single community. There is an unspoken rule that one does not criticize the views of other church members. Many members of the Native American Church refer to peyote as medicine and are convinced that it helps them to cope with and heal from the psychological wounds brought on by war, domestic violence, and alcohol and drug abuse.

The use of peyote in Native American religions has had a running battle with the various courts of the United States. In the early part of the twentieth century, peyote was outlawed by many states because it was considered a narcotic. In 1990, the U.S. Supreme Court upheld state laws that banned the use of peyote in Native American Church rituals. Many Native Americans felt that restrictions on their use of peyote in religious ceremonies violated constitutional guaranties of freedom of religion.[13] An amendment to the Native American Religious Freedom Act passed by Congress in 1994 now permits the use of the substance in Native American ceremonies. The government of Mexico has placed the cactus on an endangered species list and has prohibited its export.

Death and Life after Death

In discussing the beliefs of the Native Americans about death and life after death, we must be reminded again that we are discussing a great variety of people who lived in various climates and had diverse cultural systems. Therefore, attitudes toward death and practices regarding death varied widely. Furthermore, Native Americans have been exposed to Christian eschatology for more than 400 years. It is difficult to distinguish the original Native American view of the dead from the view that evolved in response to Christianity. Therefore, one can no more speak of the Native American concept of life after death than one can speak of the Native American religion; one can only generalize.

As we have noted, Native Americans tend to fear the dead and handle them with great care lest they return and somehow trouble the living. Many of the most serious taboos of Native American life are built around the treatment of the dead.

Young Tlingit dancer standing next to a totem pole, a deeply meaningful object to the coastal peoples of the Pacific Northwest. (Corbis/Bettmann)

Yet despite the fear of the dead, there is apparently little fear of death itself. Missionaries, anthropologists, and other observers have noted again and again the remarkable lack of fear demonstrated by Native American people when facing death.

Generally, traditional Native Americans seem to believe in two souls, neither of which could be considered immortal. One soul is the life, or breath, that accompanies the body. When the body dies, or at least when it decays, this soul also dies. The second soul is what might be called a free soul. This soul wanders about during dreams or leaves the body during sickness. After death, this free soul goes to the land of the dead. Little is said about this land of the dead; sometimes it is considered a happy place, and sometimes it is a place of sadness. Often, the land of the dead seems to be a continuation of this current life but on another plane of existence. Most descriptions of the land of the dead seem to indicate that all go to this land. There is no heaven for those who have been righteous and no hell for those who have been wicked.

Some attempt to aid the deceased in the journey to the land of the dead by burying food and drink with the body. In the past this was sometimes carried further when an important person died. An attempt was made to send along a guide to aid the deceased in finding the land of the dead. Sometimes an animal was killed to act as guide, and on other occasions, an enemy was killed for the same purpose. Among the Natchez people of Mississippi, when a great chieftain died, large numbers of wives, children, friends, and animals were sacrificed to accompany the dead.[14]

When the free soul reaches the land of the dead, it does not necessarily live forever. Perhaps, like the Hebrews' concept of Sheol or the Greeks' idea of Hades, traditional Native Americans believe that the soul exists in the land of the dead only as long as the person is remembered by the living. When the person begins to be forgotten, the free soul begins to fade and eventually disappears.

Occasionally, among Native Americans, references are made to a belief in reincarnation. Sometimes an infant resembles a deceased relative in some fashion, and it is believed that the ancestor might have returned to live again. However, this feature is missing from most Native American religions. There seems to be no widespread belief in reincarnation. Neither is there an emphasis on ancestors in the manner of the Chinese.

Native American Religions Today

With the arrival of European settlers and their religions, Native American cultures have undergone severe stress. In what is now the United States, there were many wars as European settlers moved east from the Atlantic coast and north from Mexico. The last of these, and one of the most tragic, was the consequence of white Americans fear of the Ghost Dance religion. By 1890, when the movement began, almost all of the Native American peoples had been forced onto reservations. The buffalo on which they had formerly depended had nearly vanished. Many faced starvation because the United States government had failed to deliver the supplies it had promised. The Ghost Dance movement began among the Paiute of Nevada and rapidly spread across the Great Plains. The Ghost Dance religion combine elements of Native American religion including visions, song and dance, and Christianity Wovoka, the founder of the movement, believed that he had been visited by Christ, who had taught him songs and dances and foretold the destruction of the white people and the return of the ancestors and the buffalo.

In what is now South Dakota, many of the Lakota people believed that the "ghost shirts" worn by the dancers would protect them from army bullets. On December 29, 1890, units of the U.S. Army 7th Calvary attempted to disarm a band of Lakota at Wounded Knee. A single shot rang out, after which the soldiers used machine guns in a massacre of men, women, and children. As many as 350 Native Americans died. The Massacre at Wounded Knee marked the end of Native American resistance to the United States government. To this day, the Lakota and other Native American peoples have not forgotten what transpired that day.

One of the first acts of the settlers was to seek to convert Native Americans to Christianity. This movement has continued, with varying degrees of success, for more than five centuries. Governments often supported missionaries, thinking that the conversion to Christianity would help to pacify groups opposed to European encroachment on their territory. Some forms of Christianity insist on an all-or-nothing conversion. For native people, this meant that to become Christian they had to turn their backs on their former religion and culture. Other forms of Christianity are more open to native customs and, at least to some extent, religious ideas. The influence of Christianity has been so strong that today most Native Americans are Christians. But Native American Christianity is as complex and variable as the cultures in which it is found. Some Native Americans have almost completely adopted the European style of Christianity. Others have added Christian symbols and myths to native religions. Most Native Americans would probably place themselves between these two extremes.

Many traditional practices and beliefs are continued even by those Native Americans who consider themselves devout Christians. A belief in the power of spirits to cause illness, and of medicine men and women to cure it, is found even in the most urbanized Native American communities. On many reservations, curing combines Native American and biomedical treatment. In hospitals on the Apache reservation in the White Mountains of Arizona, two types of medical practitioners exist. Medical doctors and nurses work by day; by night medicine men and women, many of whom outwardly function as custodians and support staff, perform traditional healing rituals. In many cases, this combination of healing practices is seen as cooperation rather than competition. Increasingly, medical specialists from both traditions have come to respect the healing powers of one another.

Many Native American Christians celebrate Christian holy days in very traditional ways. This is particularly true of Good Friday and Easter, which celebrate the death and resurrection of Jesus Christ. Throughout South and Central America and the Western United States, Holy Week is celebrated with Native American song and dance. Among the Yaqui of Arizona and northern Mexico, Jesus Christ is often associated with the deer because both represent a sacrifice so humans may live and prosper. Many modern Native American songs speak of characters from Bible stories as well as native spirits. Visions of Jesus Christ and his mother, the Virgin Mary, are common in many Native American communities.

Some Native Americans have incorporated elements of Christianity and even missionaries into their own traditions. This practice helps to explain the appeal of the Church of Jesus Christ of Latter Day Saints (Mormons) to Native Americans. Mormons believe that Native Americans are the children of the lost tribes of Israel and that Jesus Christ preached in the Americas during the period between His Crucifixion and Resurrection. This enables some Native Americans to understand Jesus and Christianity as being less foreign. Other Native Americans understand the God of Christianity as being similar to the traditional High God. Christian ritual also can be understood in native terms. In the 1930s, missionaries on the Lakota (Sioux) reservations often observed that hymns were the most effective means of drawing Native Americans to the church. Perhaps it was the Native American belief in the power of song and dance that attracted them to mission churches. Missionaries and their children were often given native names, carrying them into both the community and the spirit world.[15]

In recent decades, traditional Native American religions have experienced both revival and change. Numerous groups have reasserted the values of native culture, including religion. These groups teach that traditional ways are better for Native Americans than those of other cultures. Therefore, there is a resurgence of interest in the study and practice of traditional religion. There are also new developments, including intertribal dances and ceremonies based on aspects of Native American tradition shared by more than a single tribe. These ceremonies reflect and help build a growing sense of Native American cultural identity that transcends tribal boundaries.

There also is a growing interest in Native American arts and religion among non-native peoples, particularly those attracted to "new age" philosophies and religious movements. Native Americans have mixed reactions to this. Many welcome the growing recognition of the universal value of their traditions. Others are concerned that traditional knowledge, objects, and rituals will fall into the hands of non-native people who do not fully understand or appreciate them. This concern has led some Native American artists to make minor changes in traditional music performed or recorded for non-native audiences and to produce works of art that reflect Native American values and symbols that are, from the perspective of Native American religious traditions, secular in nature.[16]

STUDY QUESTIONS

1. Are Native American religions best described as monotheistic, polytheistic, or monistic?
2. Give several examples of animism as it relates to hunting and agriculture.
3. List some of the major taboos of Native American society.
4. What is the purpose of the Sun Dance?
5. In Native American thinking, what is the primary cause of sickness? How should it be cured?
6. Discuss the use of peyote in religious ceremonies. How is peyote involved in the Christian communion ritual in the Native American Church?
7. Distinguish the view of death in Native American religions from that of the traditional Judeo-Christian position.
8. Describe the meaning of music and dance in Native American religions.
9. What is the purpose of the vision quest?
10. How have Christianity and contact with non-native cultures influenced the development of Native American religions?

SUGGESTED READING

Craven, Margaret. *I Heard the Owl Call My Name*. New York: Dell, 1973.

Deloria, Vine. *God Is Red*. New York: Grosset & Dunlap, 1973.

DeMallie, Raymond J., and Douglas R. Parks, eds. *Sioux Indian Religion*. Norman: University of Oklahoma Press, 1987.

Hultkrantz, Ake. *Belief and Worship in Native North America*. Syracuse, NY: Syracuse University Press, 1981.

La Barre, Weston. *The Peyote Cult*. New York: Schocken Books, 1969.

Morrison, Kenneth. *The Solidarity of Kin: Ethnohistory, Religious Studies and the Algonkian-Jesuit Religious Encounter*. Albany: State University of New York Press, 2002.

McLuhan, T. C. *Touch the Earth*. New York: Outerbridge & Dienstfrey, 1971.

Silko, Leslie. *Ceremony*. New York: Penguin, 2006. This is a novel about the struggle of a Native American veteran returning to reservation life.

Underhill, Ruth M. *Red Men's Religion*. Chicago: University of Chicago Press, 1965.

SOURCE MATERIAL

Native American Myths

The following materials demonstrate the perspective on nature held by some Native American religions. The first is the story of a divine visitor to a Sioux tribe and shows the reverence for nature that is an integral part of these religions.[17]

Sioux Legend of the Buffalo Maiden

Braided sweet grass was dipped into a buffalo horn containing rain water and was offered to the Maiden. The chief said, "Sister, we are now ready to hear the good message you have brought." The pipe, which was in the hands of the Maiden, was lowered and placed on the rack. Then the Maiden sipped the water from the sweet grass.

Then, taking up the pipe again, she arose and said: "My relatives, brothers, and sisters: Wakan Tanka has looked down, and smiles upon us this day because we have met as belonging to one family. The best thing in a family is good feeling towards every member of the family. I am proud to become a member of your family—a sister to you all. The sun is your grandfather, and he is the same to me. Your tribe has the distinction of being always very faithful to promises, and of possessing great respect and reverence towards sacred things. It is known also that nothing but good feeling prevails in the tribe, and that whenever any member has been found guilty of committing any wrong, that member has been cast out and not allowed to mingle with the other members of the tribe. For all these good qualities in the tribe you have been chosen as worthy and deserving of all good gifts. I represent the Buffalo tribe, who have sent you this pipe. You are to receive this pipe in the name of all the common people (Indians). Take it, and use it according to my directions. The bowl of the pipe is red stone—a stone not very common and found only at a certain place. This pipe shall be used as a peacemaker. The time will come when you shall cease hostilities against other nations. Whenever peace is agreed upon between two tribes or parties this pipe shall be a binding instrument. By this pipe the medicine men shall be called to administer help to the sick."

Turning to the women, she said:

"My dear sisters, the women: You have a hard life to live in this world, yet without you this life would not be what it is. Wakan Tanka intends that you shall bear much sorrow—comfort others in time of sorrow. By your hands the family moves. You have been given the knowledge of making clothes and feeding the family. Wakan Tanka is with you in your sorrows and joins you in your griefs. He has given you the great gift of kindness towards every living creature on earth. You he has chosen to have a feeling for the dead who are gone. He knows that you remember the dead longer than do the men. He knows that you love your children dearly."

Then turning to the children:

"My little brothers and sisters. Your parents were once little children like you, but in the course of time they became men and women. All living creatures were once small, but if no one took care of them they would never grow up. Your parents love you and have made many sacrifices for your sake in order that Wakan Tanka may listen to them, and that nothing but good may come to you as you grow up. I have brought this pipe for them, and you shall reap some benefit from it. Learn to respect and reverence this pipe, and above all, lead pure lives. Wakan Tanka is your great-grandfather."

Turning to the men:

"Now, my dear brothers: In giving you this pipe you are expected to use it for nothing but good purposes. The tribe as a whole shall depend upon it for their necessary needs. You realize that all your necessities of life come from the earth below, the sky above, and the four winds. Whenever you do anything wrong against these elements they will always take some revenge upon you. You should reverence them. Offer sacrifices through this pipe. When you are in need of buffalo meat, smoke this pipe and ask for what you need and it shall be granted you. On you it depends to be a strong help to the women in the raising of children. Share the women's sorrow. Wakan Tanka smiles on the man who has a kind feeling for a woman because the woman is weak. Take this pipe, and offer it to Wakan Tanka daily. Be good and kind to the little children."

Turning to the chief:

"My older brother: You have been chosen by these people to receive this pipe in the name of the whole Sioux tribe. Wakan Tanka is pleased and glad this day because you have done what is required and expected that every good leader should do. By this pipe the tribe shall live. It is your duty to see that this pipe is respected and reverenced. I am proud to be called a sister. May Wakan Tanka look down on us and take pity on us and provide us with what we need. Now we shall smoke the pipe."

Then she took the buffalo chip which lay on the ground, lighted the pipe, and pointing to the sky with the stem of the pipe, she said, "I offer this to Wakan Tanka for all the good that comes from above." (Pointing to the earth:) "I offer this to the earth, whence come all good gifts." (Pointing to the cardinal points:) "I offer this to the four winds, whence come all good things." Then she took a puff of the pipe, passed it to the chief, and said, "Now my dear brothers and sisters, I have done the work for which I was sent here and now I will go, but I do not wish any escort. I only ask that the way be cleared before me."

Then, rising, she started, leaving the pipe with the chief, who ordered that the people be quiet until their sister was out of sight. She came out of the tent on the left side, walking very slowly; as soon as she was outside the entrance she turned into a white buffalo calf.

Wooing Wohpe

One of the best loved myths of the American Plains people is the story of Wooing Wohpe. Wohpe is the beautiful woman who mediates between the worlds of the human and the divine. The story of her relationship to the Four Winds describes the founding of the four directions.[18]

Before the world, the South Wind, and the North Wind, and the West Wind, and the East Wind, dwelt together in the far north in the land of the ghosts.

They were brothers. The North Wind was the oldest. He was always cold and stern. The West Wind was the next to oldest. He was always strong and noisy. The East Wind was the middle in age and he was always cross and disagreeable. The South Wind was the next to the youngest and he was always pleasant. With them dwelt a little brother, the Whirlwind. He was always full of fun and frolic.

The North Wind was a great hunter and he delighted in killing things. The South Wind delighted in making things. The West Wind was helper of his brother the South Wind and sometimes he helped his brother the North Wind.

The East Wind was lazy and good for nothing.

The little Whirlwind never had to do anything so he played all the time and danced and made sport for his brothers.

After a long time a beautiful being fell from the stars. Her hair was like the light and her dress was red and green and white and blue, and all the colors; and she had decorations and ornaments of all colors.

As she was falling, she met the five brothers and begged them to give her some place to rest.

They took pity on her and invited her into their tipi.

When she came into the tipi, everything was bright and pleasant and all were happy, so all the four brothers wanted her, each for his woman.

So each asked her to be his woman.

She told them that she was pleased with their tipi and would be the woman of the one who did that which pleased her the most.

So the North Wind went hunting and brought to her his game.

But everything he brought turned to ice as soon as he laid it before her.

So that when he laid his presents before her, the tipi was dark and cold and everything was dreary.

Then the West Wind brought his drum and sang and danced before her, but he made so much noise and disturbed things so much that the tipi fell down and she had hard work to put it up again.

Then the East Wind sat down by her and talked to her so much foolishness that she felt like crying.

Then the South Wind made things for her and they were all beautiful so that she was happy and the tipi was warm and bright.

So she said she would be the South Wind's woman.

This made the North Wind very angry, for he claimed that he was the oldest and should have the being by a right.

But the South Wind would not give her up.

So the North and South Winds quarreled all the time about her and finally the South Wind said to his woman that they would go away so that they might live in peace. They started to go away but the North Wind tried to steal her. When she found what the North Wind was trying to do, she took off her dress and spread it out and got under it to hide. So when the North Wind came to the dress, he thought that he had found the beautiful being and he embraced it but everything on it grew hard and cold and icy. He heard the South Wind coming and he fled back to his tipi . . . .

Then the South Wind followed on the trail of the North Wind until he came to the tipi where he found him boasting to the other brothers of what he had done.

The South Wind went in and reproached his brother and they quarreled and finally fought and the North Wind was about to conquer when the West Wind helped the South Wind and they conquered the North Wind. He could not be killed so they bound his feet and hands and left him in the tipi.

The other brothers all sided with the South Wind and determined to live no longer with the North Wind.

So the West Wind went to live where the sun sets and the East Wind went to live where the sun rises and the South Wind went to the opposite of where the North Wind's tipi is, as far as he could go.

The little Whirlwind was too small to have a tipi by himself so he went to live with the South Wind the most of the time, but he was to live with the West Wind sometimes. But the East Wind was so lazy and disagreeable that he would not even visit him . . . .

Thus began the warfare between the brothers which has lasted ever since, to the present time.

CHAPTER 3

African Religions

CHAPTER OBJECTIVES

In this chapter you will:

- Learn about the importance of the High God in African religions.

- Learn about the roles ancestors play in African religions.

- Come to understand the influence of traditional African religions on Afro-American cultures and religions.

- Appreciate the importance of ritual in African religions.

- Understand the importance of witchcraft and accusations of witchcraft in African societies.

KEY TERMS

High God	Yoruba	Ajwaka
Jok	Nuer	Voodoo

A Timeline of African Religions

Tens of thousands of years of oral tradition

1st and 2nd centuries C.E.	Christianity arrives in North Africa	20th century–present	Development of indigenous African Christianities
7th century	Islam comes to North Africa	1960s–1980s	African countries gain independence
1501–1807	Atlantic slave trade brings tradition of African religions to the Americas	1971	Many in Rhodesia believe ancestral spirits aid in independence struggle
1886	Africa divided among European colonial powers	1984	Archbishop Desmond Tutu of South Africa awarded the Nobel Peace Prize
19th century–present	Large-scale conversion to Christianity and Islam in sub-Saharan Africa		

Africa is the second-largest continent. It is home to nearly 3,000 ethnic and linguistic groups totaling over 700 million people. Traditional African societies range from small nomadic bands living deep in the tropical forest and the deserts of North and South Africa to large-scale kingdoms and empires. Because so many Africans were brought to the Americas as slaves and struggled for many centuries to regain freedom and dignity, African religions have had an influence that extends far beyond the continent's borders. In the nineteenth and early twentieth centuries, most of Africa came under European colonial rule. During the last fifty years, colonialism has vanished but its effects remain. The new nations of Africa have become a vocal and active segment of the developing world. Many of them control raw materials vital to the industrialized world. At the same time, poverty and disease are widespread, and many African nations are torn by civil war. Leaders of the industrialized nations must learn to understand and work with Africans on political and business levels if there are to be peace and prosperity in the world. At the same time, African Americans have acquired powerful voices in their own societies and have become increasingly concerned about and interested in their African heritage. It is very significant that the son of an African was a serious candidate for president of the United States in 2008. Understanding African religions is an essential part of developing an atmosphere of trust and cooperation with African leaders and nations, and understanding the problems the continent faces. It is also important for understanding the history and cultures of African Americans. As is the case for most other people, religion is a keystone of African cultures. A basic understanding of African religions will provide knowledge of customs and attitudes toward the family, society at large, the environment, and death and the life beyond.

Perhaps no religions have been more confused in the minds of Western people as those of Africa. Western perceptions and understandings of African religions and cultures have been limited by two quite different stereotypes that have more to do with Western ethnic and racial politics than with the realities of African civilizations. The first presents Africa as a land of savagery and superstition, and has been used all too often to justify white racism and the mistreatment of African and African American people. The other stereotype is more positive but unfortunately no less inaccurate. It values African symbols, literature, and art but treats this vast continent as a unified whole. While this positive stereotype has helped to combat older, negative images of Africa, it contributes very little to the understanding of Africa, its peoples, and its cultures. Both of these images are based on a combination of half-truths and fertile imaginations. To arrive at a genuine understanding of the richness of African civilizations and their contributions to the world, it is necessary to overcome both of these stereotypes.

Native Religions

When discussing African religions, we cannot speak with authority about a single religion, theology, world view, or ritual system. Africa is a huge continent with many varied and ancient cultures. Because most African religions have existed in premodern times, and left few written records, modern students of religion must understand that only the tip of the iceberg can be known. Most of what is known about traditional African religions has been collected by anthropologists and missionaries or remembered from the past by Africans. While in the past the study of African religions was conducted mainly by Europeans and Americans, today African scholars and writers are more and more active in the study and documentation of their own traditions. These African voices help to provide a more balanced and accurate picture of the religious lives of African peoples. As we have come to understand the richness and diversity of African cultures it has become increasingly clear that the religious beliefs and customs of one group of Africans are not necessarily shared by others. Even when we speak of the basic concepts of these religions, we must keep in mind that these ideas are not universally shared or evenly distributed throughout the continent. There is a great variety of beliefs and practices in African tradition.

The Sande mask is worn by the chief dancer of the secret Sande society during a ceremony to initiate young girls into womanhood.
(Kent State University School of Art Gallery)

The High God

The belief that there is a supreme **High God** who created the world and then withdrew from active participation in it is common in polytheistic religions around the world. This belief is shared by many African people. Although most African religions are polytheistic in day-to-day practice, there is a common belief that beyond all of the minor gods, goddesses, spirits, and ancestors there is one High God who created and in some sense still governs the universe.

In many African religions the High God appears as a creator who did his work and retired to a distant place. It is often believed that he has little contact with the world and its daily operation, though he may be appealed to at times of great crisis. The Yoruba story of Olorun is typical of African understandings of this High God. The Yoruba live in the West African nation of Nigeria.[1] In Yoruba mythology, the High God, Olorun, gave the job of creating the world to his eldest son, Obatala. This son failed to complete the task, so Olorun passed it on to the younger son, Odudua—but he too failed. Therefore Olorun had to complete the work of creation himself. He assigned tasks of creation to various *orisha*, who are regarded as lesser deities. After the work of creation was done, Olorun seems to have retired to the heavens with little interest in, or control of, his universe. Although various Yoruba villages have special *orisha* who have saved them or helped them in times of trouble, there is no record that Olorun ever has been of direct assistance. He remains detached from the problems of the world and allows the *orisha* to intervene when necessary.

From the Source

A legend from Mozambique in southeast Africa reveals the retiring nature of the High God even more clearly.

In the beginning Nyambi made all things. He made animals, fishes, birds. At that time he lived on earth with his wife, Nasilele. One of Nyambi's creatures was different from all the others. His name was Kamonu. Kamonu imitated Nyambi in everything Nyambi did. When Nyambi worked in wood, Kamonu worked in wood; when Nyambi forged iron, Kamonu forged iron. After a while Nyambi began to fear Kamonu.

Then one day Kamonu forged a spear and killed a male antelope, and he went on killing. Nyambi grew very angry at this.

"Man, you are acting badly," he said to Kamonu. "These are your brothers. Do not kill them."

Nyambi drove Kamonu out into another land. But after a while Kamonu returned. Nyambi allowed him to stay and gave him a garden to cultivate. It happened that at night buffaloes wandered into Kamonu's garden and he speared them; after that some elands, and he killed one. After some time Kamonu's dog died; then his pot broke; then his child died. When Kamonu went to Nyambi to tell him what had happened he found his dog and his pot and his child at Nyambi's.

Then Kamonu said to Nyambi, "Give me medicine so that I may keep my things." But Nyambi refused to give him medicine. After this, Nyambi met with his two counselors and said, "How shall we live since Kamonu knows too well the road hither?"

Nyambi tried various means to flee Kamonu. He removed himself and his court to an island across the river. But Kamonu made a raft of reeds and crossed over to Nyambi's island. Then Nyambi piled up a huge mountain and went to live on its peak. Still Nyambi could not get away from man. Kamonu found his way to him. In the meantime men were multiplying and spreading all over the earth.

Finally Nyambi sent birds to go look for a place for Litoma, god's town. But the birds failed to find a place. Nyambi sought counsel from a diviner. The diviner said, "Your life depends on Spider." And Spider went and found an abode for Nyambi and his court in the sky. Then Spider spun a thread from earth to the sky and Nyambi climbed up on the thread. Then the diviner advised Nyambi to put out Spider's eyes so that he could never see the way to heaven again and Nyambi did so.

After Nyambi disappeared into the sky Kamonu gathered some men around him and said, "Let's build a high tower and climb up to Nyambi." They cut down trees and put log on log, higher and higher toward the sky. But the weight was too great and the tower collapsed. So that Kamonu never found his way to Nyambi's home.

But every morning when the sun appeared, Kamonu greeted it saying, "Here is our king. He has come." And all the other people greeted him shouting and clapping. At the time of the new moon men call on Nasilele, Nyambi's wife.[2]

The Nuer of the Sudan provide a striking exception to the retiring nature of the High God. The Nuer believe that the High God, known as Kwoth Nhial, or the spirit of the sky, continues to play an active role in the lives of human beings. He is the guardian of moral law, punishing those who do evil and rewarding those who uphold the moral virtues of Nuer society. He is believed to love and care for his creation and is asked for blessings and assistance during troubled times and prior to dangerous undertakings such as battles.

Few African people focus as much attention on the High God as the Nuer do. Most Africans regard the High God as too distant, and too great to pay much attention to the prayers and petitions of human beings. It is the lesser spirits and the ancestors who receive the greatest attention in African religions. Even among the Nuer there is a host of lesser deities known to them as the "children of God."

The Lesser Spirits

When we move beyond tales of the High God that are found in many African religions, we encounter animistic faiths. Like many other peoples, most Africans believe that the universe is populated by spirits as well as humans and animals. The earth, the sky, and the waters are believed to contain spiritual or life forces similar to that of humankind. These forces can be beneficial or harmful. In either case they are subject to prayer, flattery, and sacrifice. Because they have a direct influence on human life, African people try to understand the spirits and seek their favor.

Spirits or life forces are present in the mountains, forest, pools, streams, and many plants and animals. They are also found in storms, thunder, lightning, tides, and other forces of nature. They can be female or male. In some African cultures there are temples and priests dedicated to the worship of storm gods. The earth is also worshipped. As in ancient Europe and many other traditional cultures the earth is often pictured as a goddess and associated with fertility. Among the Ashanti people, for example, there are regular ceremonies for the Earth Mother in which the following prayer is recited:

From the Source

Earth, while I am yet alive,
It is upon you that I put my trust
Earth who receives my body,

We are addressing you,
And you will understand.[3]

Water is often seen as a sacred element. Water is used in religious ritual the world over and is particularly sacred and important in many basic religions, including those of Africa. When the life of a people depends on water in the form of rainfall, rivers, streams, and lakes, it often appears to have a life of its own. When Africans use water for religious rituals such as the washing of the newborn and the dead, the water must come from a source of *sacred, living water*, such as a river or a spring. It must not be heated or boiled, or in modern times treated with chemicals, because that would kill the spirit or power in it. Because snakes are often connected with bodies of water, they too are regarded with awe and are sometimes worshipped as powerful spiritual forces.

Even though nature gods, goddesses, and lesser spirits are not always major elements of African religions, they are recognized and worshipped in most traditional African religions. Their worship varies from elaborate systems of temples, priests, and rituals to less formal worship conducted by individuals and family groups. Perhaps the most common form of worship of these lesser spirits is an offering of food or drink. An African who wishes to acknowledge the spirits or ask them for help will often pour water, wine, beer, or milk on the ground. When more elaborate offerings are required the spirits may be presented with elaborate meals accompanied by singing and dancing. In general they are treated with signs of honor and respect similar to those with which important and powerful people are treated.

The worship of the Yoruba goddess Osun provides an illustration of the ways in which these elements are combined in a major African religion. Osun is one of the most important female *orisha* and is described as a powerful, beautiful, and graceful goddess. She is a strong mother and the guardian of the life force responsible for the fertility of the land and the birth of children. She is worshipped by women and men at an annual ceremony that includes music, dance, and offerings of food and drink. The worshippers celebrate the power of the goddess and her ability to bestow health and fertility on her devotees.[4]

Yoruba Epa mask as worn by a dancing figure. The Yoruba are a tribal people living in West Africa.
(Marsha van der Heyden/Pearson Education/ PH College)

Ancestors

The most commonly recognized spiritual forces in African religions are ancestors. Many Africans believe that departed family members continue to live in the spirit world and that the ancestors, unlike the High God, take an active interest in the well-being of those who live in this world. The ancestors are thought of as being part of a "Cloud of Witnesses." They are believed to watch the spectacle of life and actively participate in the affairs of the living. They can help a person, a family, and even a nation if they wish. Ancestors are often consulted before the birth of a child, at the beginning of the agricultural season, and even prior to battles or political conflicts. In some areas no one may eat the first fruit of the harvest before a portion of it has been offered to the ancestors.

It is the ancestors' ability to harm as well as to help that makes them such a potent force in African religions. Africans' fear of any god is almost unimportant compared with their fear of, as well as respect for, the ancestors. While Chinese and Japanese revere and respect their ancestors, Africans are also often afraid of them. For Africans, ancestors are often capricious and unpredictable. In this way they are much like other powerful people. Despite all of the offerings and respect that they are given, ancestors may turn on a person or even a community. They are often believed to be the causes of famines, droughts, earthquakes, and other natural disasters. They are thought to cause sickness and even death. One of the worst misfortunes that can befall an African couple is childlessness; it is often thought to be caused by the anger of the ancestors. Because respect for and fear of the dead is a basic part of African consciousness, it is the ancestors, rather than the gods, who are believed to enforce social and moral codes.

Because of this great concern for the ancestors, Africans frequently offer gifts and sacrifices to them. It is believed that the ancestors are the actual owners of the land and its products. Therefore, before the living can enjoy the bounty of the land, a portion of it must be offered to the ancestors. At harvest time, rural people make large offerings to them. When new animals are born, some must be slaughtered and offered to the ancestors to ensure continued blessings. Urban Africans continue these traditions, often returning to their native villages to make offerings to their ancestors or finding homes for them in urban places.

Ancestors are believed to communicate with the living in a variety of ways, most often in dreams. At times the message of the dream is clear and direct, but at other times the dreamer must seek the help of a diviner or other religious specialist to understand it. The ancestors might send signs that can be seen in nature or in the organs of sacrificial animals. Diviners who can recognize and explain these signs play important roles in many African religions.

Sometimes, ancestors use more direct means to communicate with the living. Among the Tallensi, there is a story of a young man named Pu-eng-yii who left his own family and settled with a rival group to earn more wealth. By doing this he cut himself off from his ancestors as well as his family, offending them both. In his search for wealth, Pu-eng-yii suffered a serious leg injury in an automobile accident. When he asked a diviner about

Abakweta dancers at an initiation ceremony in the Cape Province of South Africa.
(Homer J. Smith/Pearson Education/PH College)

the cause of the accident he was told that his ancestors were angry. Actually, they had intended to kill him but had failed to follow through with their plan. The diviner told Pueng-yii that he must make restitution to his family and his ancestors and cut his ties with his adopted family. The unfortunate man gave in to these demands, returned to his own family, and offered the proper sacrifices because he feared death.[5]

Diviners who have the ability to contact the ancestors are often asked to inquire about the future. Not only do the ancestors know about what is happening among the living in the present, they also know what the future will bring and are believed to have the power to influence it. Therefore, Africans often consult the ancestors before special events ranging from building a house to fighting a war.

Sacrifice

African religions usually include rituals and sacrifices that seek to appease gods, goddesses, and ancestors, and provide safe and proper transition through the various stages of life. Sacrifice and ritual smooth these transitions and provide a point of communion between humans and the spirit world. Perhaps the most common rituals in African religions are daily offerings to the gods, goddesses, and ancestors. As a display of recognition to the deities and ancestors, those who live in this world pour out a bit of their drink or toss away bits of their food. These simple ritual acts are believed to maintain good relationships with the spirits and ancestors who play such important roles in the daily lives of many African people.

There is animal sacrifice on more serious occasions. The blood of animals such as dogs, birds, sheep, goats, and cattle is poured on the ground to placate deities when they are angry or to ensure their support in some difficult period. Blood sacrifices may be offered when a community is preparing for a battle or, in modern African nations, for an election campaign, when there has been a long drought, or in times of illness. A person engaged in the dangerous business of hunting may wish to offer a sacrifice to one of the deities before the hunt. In modern times, the Yoruba god Ogun, who was for centuries described as the god of iron, has become known as the god of automobiles and trucks. Drivers engaged in the all-too-often deadly business of operating motor vehicles on unsafe roads and streets offer dogs to him and decorate cars and trucks with his symbols. His protection is sought for other iron objects as well, as this sacrificial song illustrates:

From the Source

Ogun, here are Ehun's kola nuts;
He rides a bicycle,
He cultivates with a matchet,
He fells trees with an axe,

Do not let Ehun meet your anger this year,
Take care of him,
He comes this year,
Enable him to come next season.[6]

Often, on the occasion of animal sacrifice, the worshipper shares the flesh of the animal with the deity or ancestor to whom it is offered. After the blood of the animal has been poured on the ground or an altar, the meat is roasted or boiled. A portion is given to the deity by placing it on the altar, and another portion is eaten by the person who brought the sacrifice and his or her family. This establishes a communion between the living and the spirits and is an expression of the almost universal human belief that eating together establishes a social or spiritual bond.

A Peoule wedding in Mali, West Africa.
(*Stock Boston*)

Religion and Violence

Only rarely has human sacrifice been a part of native African religions. The frequency of this practice was grossly exaggerated in movies and in nineteenth-century tales of cannibalism and great stacks of human skulls. Although some African groups did occasionally sacrifice humans to their gods, such sacrifices were rare and occurred only on the most serious occasions. An Akikuyu legend tells of a time when there was a great drought in the land. A diviner determined that it would only rain when a particular girl was sacrificed. The girl was placed in the center of the village, where she gradually sank into the ground. When she had sunk to the depth of her nose, rain began to fall. Her family allowed her to sink completely out of sight as the rain continued. It was only a lover's following her into the earth that spared her life. Eventually, he was able to find her and bring her back to the surface again.[7] This is actually not a tale of human sacrifice, but rather of the salvation of a community through the self-sacrifice of one of its members and her ultimate return to her people. It speaks not of a disregard for human life, but rather of the courage of those who sacrifice themselves for the good of the community.

The most common form of human sacrifice occurred when a great king died and it was believed that he needed servants in the next life. At such times, some people were sacrificed to accompany their leader to the world of the dead. Apparently human sacrifice was practiced only in the most extreme conditions and unlike animal sacrifices was never intended as a regular means of establishing communion with the spirit world. The flesh of the victim was almost never eaten. Cannibalism in any form seems to have been restricted to a very small number of tribal groups.

Rites of Passage

In almost all societies, important points on the pathway of life are marked and celebrated with ritual. These passage points are most often birth, puberty, marriage, and death. In societies where religion is a major force in social life, there is often no clear distinction between the secular and the religious. In Africa, and in many other religious societies, rites of passage are usually regulated by religious practices and functionaries.

Religion and Violence

The birth of a child is a cause for great rejoicing in African cultures. Children are thought of as great blessings from the world of the spirits. A childless couple will go to great lengths to determine the cause of their plight and to alleviate it. Not all childbirths are welcomed, however. Twins, for example, are often thought of as dangerous or evil. Sometimes twins are regarded as a sign that the wife has been unfaithful and that each baby has a different father. Occasionally one or both of the twins is killed. Sometimes, the twins and their mother are forced to live apart from the community. Among other African people, the taboo against twins is reversed and they are considered to be extremely lucky for the community in which they are born.

In many African societies, including the Ashanti, children are not named or given much consideration for the first week of life. Because of the high infant mortality rate, it is considered unwise for a family to become too attached to what might be a ghost child who has come to trick them into loving it. These concerns persist because colonial powers did little to establish adequate health care systems. If the baby lives through the first week or so of life, it is considered to be a real human baby, and attention and joy are lavished on it. At this point, the baby is named. In some cases a lengthy process of divination may be used to choose a proper name for the child. Other African people recite the names of ancestors until the child makes a motion or gesture of recognition. In this manner, the names of the ancestors are kept alive.

The ceremony of naming is often followed by showing the child to the moon. The Gu people of Benin throw their children gently into the air several times, instructing them to look at the moon. The Basuto of South Africa lift their children toward the moon and say, "There is your father's sister."[8] Some African people practice circumcision at birth, but most wait until puberty.

During childhood, young Africans receive instruction in their roles in society as well as training in agriculture, crafts, and increasingly modern education. As they approach puberty, instruction in the norms of social behavior becomes more intensive. Special classes are established separately for boys and girls in which they are taught how to behave as proper young men and women. They are also prepared for the initiation rituals that mark the passage from childhood to adult life. For boys, these rites may involve harsh physical trials including whipping and fasting designed to test their courage and resourcefulness. During these rituals they learn about the religion, myths, and morality of their people. Among some African groups, girls are secluded in special houses and encouraged to eat a great deal and grow plump to make them more attractive as brides. Both boys and girls receive special training in what is considered to be proper sexual behavior and conduct. These puberty rites and initiations may take a few days or several years. In recent years their length and severity have declined because of the opposition of modern governments, the decline in the power of traditional village elders, and the desire of many parents that their children receive as much modern education as possible.

Puberty rites for boys often include ritual circumcision. No one seems to know where or when this practice began, but it is widely practiced in Africa and many other parts of the world. It may be, as Freud suggested, the final domination by the older males of the community over the young. Because circumcision is performed at puberty without any form of anesthetic, it is often regarded as a test of courage. The initiate is expected to endure the operation without crying out, flinching, or showing other signs of pain. Among some African people, the operation is performed by a man wearing a mask who represents the ancestors. This indicates that circumcision may provide a bodily sign of religious and cultural identity as it does for Jews and Muslims throughout the world.

Female circumcision is practiced by some African people, but there is growing opposition to it both among Africans with modern education and the international human rights and feminist communities. As with male circumcision, there seems to be no clear reason for the practice, although it is sometimes described as a means of controlling erotic desire.[9] The severity of both male and female circumcision varies greatly. It ranges from very small cuts that pose no serious health threat to the initiate to extreme forms of genital mutilation that can be life-threatening, particularly when performed in unsanitary conditions.

After puberty rites and initiation, young people are considered to be adults and are expected to assume both the responsibilities and privileges of adult life. One of the first of these adult roles is marriage. There is little of a religious nature about marriage in many traditional African societies. It is often more of a secular contract between the families involved. Virginity is highly prized, particularly among young women. Even after marriage, chastity is considered a virtue by many African peoples and is strongly encouraged by traditional customs and mores. The prevalence of HIV/AIDS shows that values do not always translate into behavior. Polygamy is practiced by the elites of many traditional African societies. Frequently, a husband is forbidden sexual contact with his wife during pregnancy and for as long as she is nursing a child. Because this can often be for as long as two years, it is considered wise for a man who can afford it to have several wives living in separate houses. There are also occasional instances of polyandry, in which one woman is the wife of several brothers.

As in most societies, death is surrounded with a great deal of ritual. The purpose of death rituals is to make the newly dead as comfortable as possible in their new existence so that they will not return to haunt the living. Many steps are taken during and after burial to prevent the dead from returning to their villages, homes, and families. Women fear that their husbands will return as ghosts and cause their wombs to die, making them infertile.

Because of the warm climate of much of Africa, the dead are buried as quickly as possible. On rare occasions, there are attempts to embalm or mummify the bodies of great leaders, such as kings. There are also a few examples of corpses being turned over to hyenas for disposal, but burial is the most common practice. Money, trinkets, tools, and weapons are buried with the body to make life in the next world as comfortable as possible.

In some African societies it is believed that illness, misfortune, and death never "just happen" and are caused by witchcraft or foul play of some kind. In the past, the dead were allowed to identify the person or persons who caused their deaths. Often, corpses would seem to point out the house of the killer or fall from the backs of bearers as they passed the guilty party. Persons accused in this way had to find some means of proving their innocence.

African religions generally do not have a system of eschatology or concepts of judgment and retribution after death. The dead simply move into the world of the spirits and continue to be interested in and effective among the living. Death rituals transform living humans into sacred ancestors. An exception to this is the belief of the LoDagaa people of Ghana. According to their religion, the departed person takes a long journey toward the land of the ancestors. Just before this land is reached, there is a river. A waiting ferryman must be paid to take the deceased across the river. If the deceased has led a good life, the crossing will be easy. If the deceased has been wicked, she or he must swim across the river. This takes three years. People who have debts must wait on the bank until their creditors arrive to be paid. Once the deceased is in the land of the dead, there are further tests and ordeals in which the person's lifetime deeds play a great part. Those who suffer because they are judged to have been evil ask the great god: "Why do you make us suffer?" God replies, "Because you sinned on earth." And they ask: "Who created us?" To which god replies, "I did." And they ask, "If you created us, did we know evil when we came or did you give it to us?" God replies, "I gave it to you." Then the people ask, "Why was it that you knew it was evil and gave it to us?" God replies, "Stop, let me think and find the answer."[10] Here the LoDagaa are asking a very basic religious question shared by all monotheistic faiths: Why should it be that an all-powerful god would allow evil a place in creation?

Religious Leaders

Because a great deal of traditional African religion is based on rituals performed regularly by individuals without the aid of priests, such as offerings of food and drink to the ancestors, the need for religious functionaries is not as great as in religions that rely on complex theology and rituals. Nevertheless, African religions do have leaders and specialists who are essential at critical times or places.

African religions generally do not require a priesthood. In Western Africa, however, some communities maintain temples and altars to the gods. The existence of a temple almost requires a priesthood to maintain and control it. In these areas there are priests and sometimes priestesses who undergo lengthy periods of training in the ritual, mythology, and taboos connected with religion before they are allowed to serve.

One of the most common religious specialists in Africa is the spiritual curer. In almost all premodern societies illness is believed to have religious as well as natural causes. Even in the most advanced industrial societies many people turn to prayer and other religious activities as well as medical science when faced with serious illness. As previously mentioned, many African worldviews do not include the idea of what modern science would call "natural" causes of death and disease. There is generally a spiritual cause for these misfortunes: Someone has cast a spell or placed a curse on the one who has fallen ill, or the sick person has in some way offended one of the lesser spirits or ancestors. It is the spiritual curer's job to find the cause of the illness and prescribe a cure. The curer uses some form of divination to determine the nature of the curse and the one responsible for it. Then the curer, who can be either male or female, uses a combination of spiritual powers, offerings, and herbal remedies to drive away the witchcraft and dispel the curse. Some of these herbal remedies have proven to be effective medicines in the modern sense.

Mami Wata healing ceremony, a priestess sacrifices a chicken to the god Ogun. Cotonou, Nenin, West Africa. *(Peter Arnold, Inc.)*

Religion and Violence

It is also common for African people to call on a spiritual curer to clear a house or other building of witches, spirits, and curses before the owners occupy it. People suspected of sorcery or witchcraft are sometimes killed. Some African communities have been angered when local governments fail to prosecute suspected witches.

Among the Acholi of Uganda, the evil spirits that cause a person to become ill are called *jok*.[11] The healer is called *ajwaka*. When the *ajwaka* enters the presence of the sick person, he attempts to draw the *jok* up into the head of the patient through music and song. When this is accomplished, the *ajwaka* enters into conversation with the *jok*. "Why have you come? What do you want? What is your name?" Finally, the evil spirit is driven out of the sick person by the *ajwaka*, captured in a gourd, and buried in the ground.

The spiritual curer is part religious specialist, part herbalist, and part psychologist. The curer's skills are highly valued and are sometimes imported into modern hospitals and clinics by Africans who don't want to leave anything to chance. For many, modern medicine is understood to be a developed form of herbalism and divination that can treat some, but not all, of the causes of disease and misfortune. Becoming a spiritual curer is a long and involved process. When a young person decides to join or is called to this profession, he or she must apprentice with an established curer for several years to learn the many skills and secrets involved.

In many African communities the role of diviner is closely allied to that of healer. The diviner's task is to use spiritual powers and knowledge to find the causes of present misfortune, past secrets, and things to come. This individual can also ferret out witches and sorcerers. In some African communities, the diviner is primarily one who investigates the causes of trouble. In other communities, the action of prediction is more important.

Among the Ndembu of northwestern Zambia, individuals are chosen as diviners by being inhabited by a spirit. The spirit Kayong'u seeks out those whom he wants to become diviners, and it is believed that he first makes them ill. The deity thus shows people what he wants. A person so selected then goes through an elaborate initiation ritual and a long period of training.

The tools that African diviners use vary widely. Most commonly, they cast the shells of nuts to form a pattern and then read the pattern to find the answer they seek. Among the Yoruba, a diviner shakes 16 palm nuts out into one of 256 possible patterns. Each pattern is associated with several poems, each of which contains a message. Even the beginning diviner is supposed to know from memory a minimum of four poems for each pattern. This means that a person must memorize at least 1,024 poems to be a diviner; an experienced diviner will know many more. When the pattern has been cast and the poems recited, the person who has sought divination selects the poem that he or she

Dogon masked dancers from Mali, West Africa. Most Dogon rituals reenact creation narratives.
(John Elk III)

believes to be the most meaningful.[12] Other methods of divination include casting dice and gazing into a bowl of water. At one time, among many African people, trials by ordeal determined the guilt or innocence of a person accused of a crime. The person being tried was given a poisonous substance to drink. If the person did not die, innocence was proven. In more recent times, a fowl has been substituted. When the fowl dies from the poison, guilt or innocence is determined by the way in which it falls.

Another religious functionary found from time to time in many parts of Africa is the prophet. Like the biblical prophet, this person is seen as one who speaks for the gods.

Usually, African prophetic figures gain their authority by the power of their personalities and their message. They have great influence during their lifetimes, but they seldom leave successors.

Religion and Violence

When there is a political upheaval or religious revival, charismatic leaders appear and proclaim the words of the gods to their people. In the nineteenth century, several prophets led African people in resistance to the slave trade and colonialism. One of these was Ngundeng, who arose among the Nuer of the southern Sudan and who spoke in the name of the sky god, Dengkur.

One of the most enduring of the religious figures in Africa is the chief-king. Although some African societies have no monarchs, those that have kings and queens look upon them with great awe and reverence. These rulers are regarded as the tribal connection to the ancestors and are revered as the living symbol of the tribe. Because of this, they are the objects of many taboos. In some societies, they are considered so sacred that commoners may not look upon their faces. In others, it is regarded as certain death to eat food that has been prepared for the monarch. Some peoples, such as Bantus, actually look upon their rulers as gods incarnate.

Because the rulers represent the community, they must always be in good health. A sick monarch means a sick land.

Religion and Violence

Any infirmity of the ruler must be dealt with quickly. In some societies, rulers are required to take their own lives when ill health or old age begins to weaken them. The queen of the Lovedu of South Africa carries poison with her at all times and is expected to use it to prevent her death by other means. In other areas and at other times, there have been stories indicating that the people felt it necessary to kill an aged or infirm king. In some cases, a substitute king is chosen to rule for a few days and is then ritually killed to spare the true king.

When the monarch dies, the death often is kept secret until a successor can be chosen and enthroned. It is believed that the former king or queen fully becomes a god as he or she enters the land of the ancestors. African monarchies are sometimes hereditary and the child of the monarch automatically comes to the throne. In others the person who is believed to be the wisest or who has been chosen by the gods is selected. Enthroning a monarch often includes very complicated initiation rituals. In many societies the new king or queen is belittled and even physically abused for a period of hours or days to teach lessons in humility before being allowed to assume the position of monarch.

Non-native African Religions

In addition to religions native to Africa, many others have found a home on the continent. Egypt was among the world's first centers of civilization. Later, the urban centers of North Africa were strongly influenced by Greek culture and religion, producing some of the most important scientific and religious innovations of the classical period. Christianity has played an important role in northern Africa since the first century. Judaism has flourished in the region at least since the time of the destruction of the second temple in Jerusalem in 76 C.E. In Ethiopia there is a distinct branch of Judaism among the Falasha people. The Falashas trace their ancestry to the Queen of Sheba in the tenth century B.C.E. and practice a form of Judaism influenced by the Pentateuch, but they are unaware of the Talmud and other later Jewish religious texts. Islam first came to Africa during the lifetime of the Prophet Muhammad, when a party of Muslims fled to Ethiopia to avoid persecution. It became a major force in Africa early in the seventh century and displaced Christianity in many regions. Muslim missionaries have been active in sub-Saharan Africa since at least the seventeenth century. They were followed by Christian missionaries in the early nineteenth century. The greatest growth in Christianity came after the 1950s when the Bible became widely available in African languages. Hinduism, Buddhism, and the Bahá'í faith have come to Africa with immigrants from the Middle East and south Asia in the nineteenth century.

African Religions Today

The past hundred years have been extremely difficult for African religions. The European colonial empires on the continent worked to break up traditional tribal units and to enforce other forms of authority. With the end of colonialism following World War II, Africa was divided into greater than forty nations. The drawing of first colonial and then national boundaries tended to break up tribal life. The pressures of modernization, urbanization, and a rapidly increasing population have further changed African life. If current trends continue, it is likely that conversion to Christianity and Islam will increase. There, are, however, still millions of Africans who practice traditional religions and millions more who combine traditional African beliefs and customs with those of non-native faiths.[13] However, many of the values of these religions will continue; the Christianities and Islams emerging in Africa have distinctive African qualities.

Traditional African religions are closely linked to specific places and to tribal or ethnic groups. Modernization and urbanization have decreased the importance of place and ethnicity in the lives of many Africans. This has encouraged conversion to "world religions," which have a broader, universal message. However, African beliefs concerning the High God have both encouraged conversion and shaped African understandings of these religions. In many places belief in lesser spirits continues in the form of Christian saints and Muslim *jinn* (spirits). Beliefs in divination continue in both Christianity and Islam. Among the Woloff of West Africa, for example, it is believed that there are a large number of non-Muslim spirits who can only be understood and controlled by traditional diviners. In recent years a number of local religious movements that combine African, Christian, and/or Islamic beliefs and rituals have emerged in many parts of the continent.

Similar religious movements can be found among the African American peoples of the Caribbean and South and Central America. So-called **voodoo** cults, which are in reality Christianized versions of African cults focusing on ancestors and spirits, are also found in many urban areas in the United States. At the same time Africans are playing an increasingly important role in more orthodox forms of Christianity and Islam. Struggles for national independence, equality, and human rights have produced strong African and African American voices including such internationally recognized figures as Dr. Martin Luther King, Jr. and Malcolm X in the United States and Archbishop Desmond Tutu in South Africa.

Christianity: Martin Luther King, Jr.

Religion and Violence

Most conflicts in Africa pit rival ethnic groups against one another. However, in countries with large Muslim and Christian populations, including Nigeria and the Sudan, there have been conflicts between the two communities. During a twenty-five-year (1983–2005) civil war in Sudan between the Muslim north and the Christian south, more than two million people died and countless more were driven from their homes. The Lord's Resistance Army, which operates in southern Sudan and northern Uganda, has forced more than half a million people from their homes. It claims to want to establish a government based on the Ten Commandments, and its founder and leader Joseph Kony claims to speak with a host of sprits. The group kills, maims, and rapes seemingly at random. It has abducted thousands of children who have been tortured and forced to become soldiers or sex slaves.

STUDY QUESTIONS

1. Compare and contrast the African idea of a High God with that of Native American religions.
2. Describe the roles of the ancestors in native African religions.
3. What is the most common form of sacrifice in native African religions?
4. Discuss African puberty rites for males and females. How do these rituals prepare them for adult life?
5. What is divination? List several forms of divination in African religions.
6. How have African religions changed in the last century?
7. What are rites of passage? List several forms they take in African religions.

SUGGESTED READING

Badejo, Diedre Osun Seegesi. *The Elegant Deity of Wealth, Power and Femininity.* Trenton, NJ: Africa World Press, 1996.

Courlander, Harold. *Tales of Yoruba Gods and Heroes.* New York: Fawcett Publications, 1973.

Evans-Pritchard, E. E. *Nuer Religion.* New York: Oxford University Press, 1956.

Idowu, E. Bolaji. *African Traditional Religion.* Maryknoll, NY: Orbis Books, 1973.

Magesa, L. *African Religion: The Moral Traditions of Abundant Life.* New York: Orbis Books, 1997.

King, Noel Q. *Religions of Africa.* New York: Harper & Row, 1970.

Parrinder, Geoffrey. *African Traditional Religion*, 3rd ed. New York: Harper & Row, 1976.

Ranger, T. O., and I. N. Kimambo. *The Historical Study of African Religion*. Berkeley: University of California Press, 1972.

Ray, Benjamin C. *African Religions: Symbol, Ritual and Community*. Englewood Cliffs, NJ: Prentice Hall, 1976.

Soyinka, Wole. *You Must Set Forth at Dawn: A Memoir*. New York: Random House, 2007. This is an autobiographical account of life and struggle in post-colonial Africa by the Nobel Prize–winning Nigerian author.

Turner, Victor. *The Forest of Symbols: Aspects of Ndembu Ritual*. Ithaca, NY: Cornell University Press, 1966.

SOURCE MATERIAL

An African Divine King

There are divine kings in many cultures. A careful look into this office and the religious concept that surrounds it often gives the reader an understanding of the supporting culture. The following is a brief description of the life (and death) of the divine king of the people of Malawi.[14]

Mbande is a hill on the plain of north Nyasaland with a commanding view of the surrounding country and well suited to defense. The west side is precipitous and below the scarp edge there used to be a marsh; to the north the hill is protected by a wide reach of the Lukulu River. It is a sacred place and for many generations was the home of the "divine king," the Kyungu. Like the Lwembe he was the living representative of a hero, and was selected by a group of hereditary nobles from one of two related lineages, the office alternating (if suitable candidates were available) between the two. They sought a big man, one who had begotten children and whose sons were already married, not a young man for, the nobles said, "young men always want war, and destroy the country." He must be a man of wisdom (*gwa mahala*) and generous in feeding his people.

The Kyungu's life was governed by taboos even more rigorous than those surrounding the Lwembe. He must not fall ill, or suffer a wound, or even scratch himself and bleed a little, for his ill health, or his blood falling on the earth would bring sickness to the whole country. "Men feared when Kyungu's blood fell on the ground, they said, 'It is his life.'" If he had a headache his wives (if they loved him) told him not to mention it, they hid his illness; but if the nobles entered and found him ill they dug the grave and put him in it, saying, 'He is the ruler (*ntemi*), it's taboo for him to be ill.' Then he thought: 'Perhaps it is so' (with a gesture of resignation)."

Great precautions were taken to preserve his health. He lived in a separate house with his powerful medicines. His food was prepared by boys below the age of puberty lest a menstruating woman, or a youth who had lain with a woman, should touch it and so bring sickness upon him; and his numerous wives were immured in the royal enclosure—a great stockade—and jealously guarded, for any infidelity on their part was thought to make their husband ill, and with him the whole country.

When the Kyungu did fall ill he was smothered by the nobles who lived around him at Mbande, and buried in great secrecy, and with a score or more of living persons—slaves—in the grave beneath him, and one or two wives and the sons of commoners above. And in the midst of all this slaughter the nobles brought a sheep to look into the grave that the dead Kyungu might be gentle (*milolo*) like the sheep!

The living Kyungu was thought to create food and rain, and his breath and the growing parts of his body—his hair and nails and the constantly replaced mucus of his nose—were believed to be magically connected with the fertility of the Ngonde plain. When he was killed his nostrils were stopped so that he was buried "with the breath in his body"; while portions of his hair and nails and of his nasal mucus were taken from him beforehand and buried by the nobles of Ngonde in the black mud near the river. This was "to defend the country against hunger, to close up the land, to keep it rich and heavy and fertile as it was when he himself lived in it."

His death was kept secret—a relatively easy matter since he lived in seclusion—and one of the nobles (*Ngosi*) impersonated him wearing his clothes. After a month or two when the nobles had decided whom to choose as the new Kyungu, the luckless man was summoned to Mbande: "Your father calls you." Then he came with his companions and entered the house to make obeisance; they seized him and put the sacred cloth on him and set him on the stool, *Kisumbe*, saying "Thou Kyungu, thou art he," and he became the Kyungu. Then they struck the drum, *Mwenkelwa*, and everyone knew that the Kyungu had died and another had been installed. Men feared greatly to be seized as the Kyungu, just as they feared to be seized as the Lwembe, because the life of a divine king was short. Ngonde historians quote a number of cases of sons of the Kyungu who fled to escape being set on the stool; once they had sat on it they dared not flee lest they die.

In time of drought the nobles of Ngonde would go to a diviner to inquire who it was who was angry; they would mention all the names of the sacred groves of the Kyungus in turn and he would tell them it was so-and-so. They would inform the living Kyungu and he would give them a bull or a sheep, together with some beer—they would take one of the pots of beer from his own house, brought by his people as tribute. And he would give them some flour and cloths also. Then he would go with them into the grove and build a miniature hut. Next they would kill the beast and hang some of the meat up on a tree—the rest they would eat later outside the grove. Then they would tear up the cloths and fasten some of the pieces on to the hut in the grove—an action they would explain as "giving him cloths." And finally, they would pour out some of the beer and the flour. Nearly always, in time of drought, they would thus build a hut and make an offering in the grove of the Kyungu whom the diviner had mentioned.

But occasionally, if one of the chiefs had recently insulted the Kyungu, they concluded that it was the living Kyungu himself who was angry. They would go to a diviner and mention all the names of the dead Kyungus, but he would refuse to accept any of them: "No . . . no." And at length he would tell them that it was the living Kyungu who was angry because so-and-so had insulted him. Then there would be no sacrifice at the grove at all, but the nobles of Ngonde would go to the one who had insulted the Kyungu and charge him with it, asking him what he meant by thus killing them all, would not the whole land starve? And so the wrongdoer would take a cow to the Kyungu who, thereupon, would address the nobles of Ngonde saying: "If it was my anger which brought the drought then it will rain (for I am no longer angry). But if the rain does not come then it cannot have been my anger, it must have been someone (of the dead Kyungus) whom you forgot to ask about." And if, after that, the rain came soon, then it was not likely that anyone would insult the Kyungu again.

Thus to insult Kyungu was not only treasonable, it was blasphemous, and the whole plain was believed to be cursed with drought or disease in reply. An "insult" might mean any neglect of the obligations of the chiefs and nobles and commoners of the plain to their lord.

The majesty (*ubusisya*) of the Kyungu was cultivated in a variety of ways. He smeared himself with ointment made from lion fat, and his bed was built up with elephant tusks and lion pelts. He was enthroned on the sacred iron stool called Kisumbe, he had a spear, and Mulima, a porous piece of iron "like a mouth organ" used to make rain, all handed down from the first Kyungu. His zebra tails, set with medicines in horn handles, were waved in war and during prayer to the shades, and he also had the famous drum on which the blood of a child was poured.

But the majority of their subjects only worshipped from afar in fear and trembling. At Mbande no ordinary commoner was ever conducted into the sacred enclosure, but only the territorial nobles and the elder chiefs, and they only occasionally; while when the Kyungu traveled through his country all men save the very oldest fled from his approach. Even in speech fearful circumlocutions were used to refer to his journeyings— "The country is on the move"—"the great hill is moving"—"the mystery is coming." It was taboo both for the old men who stayed to see him, and for those who entered the sacred enclosure, ever to greet him in the usual way. Falling down and clapping the hands was the only greeting for the Kyungu.

From the wives of the Kyungu also men fled in terror, fearing lest they be compromised and thrown over the cliff of Mbande, and this both added to the atmosphere of terror that surrounded him and was an expression of it.

An African Creation Story

The following is the creation story of the Boshongo, a Bantu people.[15]

In the beginning, in the dark, there was nothing but water, and Bumba was alone.

One day Bumba was in terrible pain. He retched and strained and vomited up the sun. After that light spread over everything. The heat of the sun dried up the water until the black edges of the world began to show. Black sandbanks and reefs could be seen. But there were no living things.

Bumba vomited up the moon and then the stars, and after that the night had its light also.

Still Bumba was in pain. He strained again and nine living creatures came forth; the leopard named Koy Bumba, and Pongo Bumba the crested eagle, the crocodile, Ganda Bumba, and one little fish named Yo; next, old Kono Bumba, the tortoise, and Tsetse, the lightning, swift, deadly, beautiful like the leopard, then the white heron, Nyanyi Bumba, also one beetle, and the goat named Budi.

Last of all came forth men. There were many men, but only one was white like Bumba. His name was Loko Yima.

The creatures themselves then created all the creatures. The heron created all the birds of the air except the kite. He did not make the kite. The crocodile made serpents and the iguana. The goat produced every beast with horns. Yo, the small fish, brought forth all the fish of all the seas and waters. The beetle created insects.

Then the serpents in their turn made grasshoppers, and the iguana made the creatures without horns.

Then the three sons of Bumba said they would finish the world. The first, Nyonye Ngana, made the white ants; but he was not equal to the task, and died of it. The ants, however, thankful for life and being, went searching for black earth in the depths of the world and covered the barren sands to bury and honor their creator . . . .

When at last the work of creation was finished, Bumba walked through the peaceful villages and said to the people, "Behold these wonders. They belong to you." Thus from Bumba, the Creator, the First Ancestor, came forth all the wonders that we see and hold and use, and all the brotherhood of beasts and man.

PART II

RELIGIONS ORIGINATING IN INDIA

To the modern student of religion, no series of religions is quite as fascinating as those that began in India. The great depth and variety of religious teaching and experience one finds in Hinduism, Jainism, Buddhism, and Sikhism are indeed awesome. Today, the beauty of the great poem of Hinduism (the *Bhagavad Gita*), the complexity of Vedanta philosophy, the mysteries of Zen Buddhism, and the concept of **ahimsa** (non-injury of living beings) taught by the Jains are appreciated by students in Western nations as never before. An understanding of the basic literature, history, and doctrine of these religions is essential for understanding modern Asia and the cultural heritage of Asian peoples living in Europe and the Americas.

HINDUISM – BASIC TEACHINGS
The Vedas are the oldest Hindu religious texts.

Composition of the Vedas probably began between 2,000 and 1,500 B.C.E. The Vedas are a collection of hymns, many of which were recited during sacrifices to the many gods. Indra is the god of thunderbolts, clouds, and rain, and is the ruler of heaven. Agni is the god of fire. He brings offerings to the other gods. Rudra is the god of death and destruction.

In modern Hinduism there are thousands of gods and goddesses.

Some gods and goddesses are worshipped by hundreds of millions; others are only known in particular villages. Hindu divinities come in male and female pairs. Brahma is the creator but is rarely worshipped. His spouse Sarasvati is the goddess of wisdom. Shiva is the god of death, destruction, and dance. His spouse is alternatively Parvati, the female half of the perfect couple, or Kali, who wears a necklace of skulls and is the goddess of smallpox. Vishnu is the preserver of the universe and the god of love. His spouse is Lakshmi, the goddess of wealth and fertility.

Karma is moral action.

The karma one accumulates determines the nature of future existences. Hinduism assumes that there is a constant cycle of birth, life, death, and rebirth. Karma drives this process. One may be reborn as a human or animal and in one of the many heavens or hells. Buddhism and Jainism share this belief with Hinduism.

The Laws of Manu are the "blueprint" for Hindu society.

They provide the outline for the caste system. Castes are hereditary occupational groups. Marriage across caste lines is extremely rare. The four major caste groups are Brahmins (priests), Kshatriyas (rulers and soldiers), Vaishya (artisans, merchants, and farmers), and Shudras (manual workers). There are also Dalits, or Untouchables, who perform the most menial and ritually defiling tasks.

The *Bhagavad Gita* is among the great epic poems of Hinduism.

The *Bhagavad Gita* describes the life and teachings of Krishna, a human incarnation of Vishnu. It was probably composed in the second or third century B.C.E. It is a conversation between Krishna and the young warrior Arjuna as he ponders the folly, human, and karmic consequences of war. Krishna explains that because Arjuna is a Kshatriya, and obligated to fight, he will not suffer the consequences that members of other castes would for joining in the battle.

JAINISM – BASIC TEACHINGS

Jainism was founded in the sixth century B.C.E.

Mahavira, the founder of Jainism, is thought of as a Tirthankara, or "crossing builder," who discovered the path leading out of the cycle of karma and rebirth. He renounced a life of wealth and power and practiced an extreme form of asceticism. He did not wear clothing and sought out the most uncomfortable environments. Some Jain monks starve themselves to death. One of Mahavira's core teachings is that humans must find their own ways to salvation and that gods cannot aid in the process.

The Jain worldview is dualistic.

Jainism teaches that the universe consists of spirit (*jiva*) and matter (*ajiva*). Since both are eternal, there are no Jain creation mythologies. As long as the soul is bound to matter, it is destined to remain caught in the cycle of birth, death, and rebirth.

Non-injury of life (ahimsa) is among the most important teachings of Jainism.

Jainism, Hinduism, and Buddhism all teach that injuring other beings—especially killing them—produces karma that leads to rebirth in abodes of suffering. Jainism places the greatest emphasis on ahimsa. Unlike Hindus and Buddhists, all Jains are vegetarians. They avoid occupations that could lead to the injury of animals. Jain monks sweep the road in front of them as they walk to avoid harming insects. For the most part, Jains have avoided participating in the religious conflicts that have plagued India for much of the last century.

Jain monks follow a strict moral code.

Jain monks vow to always tell the truth and never to take things that are not given to them. Lay Jains also seek to keep these vows. This ethical code has contributed to their reputation as honest and reliable business partners.

There are very few Jains.

Jainism places serious restrictions on one's choice of occupation. It is almost exclusively an urban religion. In India, Jain birthrates are lower than those of Hindus and Muslims, so the proportion of Jains in the total population is declining.

BUDDHISM – BASIC TEACHINGS

Buddhism was founded by Siddhartha Gautama in North India in the sixth century B.C.E.

Like Jainism, Buddhism rejects the authority of the Vedas and the caste system. The only Buddhist society that retains the caste system is Sri Lanka, where there are different monastic orders for different caste groups. Buddhism was the world's first missionary religion. By the third century B.C.E., it had spread throughout much of Asia.

Buddhism is an extremely diverse religion.

The Buddhist schools that have developed over the centuries are very distinct with respect to both their worldview and religious practices. The early Theravada school teaches that there have been many Buddhas, but only one exists at any given time. It also teaches that monks must be celibate and follow a complex set of rules. The later Mahayana schools teach that there are many Buddhas simultaneously. Some allow monks to marry and own property.

Buddhism teaches that the path to salvation is the "Middle Way."

The "Middle Way" lies between worldly life and the extreme forms of asceticism practiced by Jain monks. Most Buddhists believe that to attain salvation it is necessary to renounce the world, but that religious practices that harm the body are counterproductive. Some—but not all—Buddhists are vegetarians. Many maintain that it is the act of killing and not eating meat that has negative karmic consequences.

The most basic Buddhist teachings are those of the Four Noble Truths. These are:

1) Life is suffering, if for no other reason that it will end; 2) Suffering is caused by clinging to and craving worldly pleasures; 3) Nirvana or release from the cycle of rebirth is the alternative to suffering; and 4) The path leading to Nirvana is the path of monasticism—however that is understood.

Bodhisattvas are common to all Buddhist schools, but are understood differently.

Bodhisattvas are future Buddhas. For Theravada Buddhists, they are beings traversing the path to Nirvana. They will come into the world, teach, and die, never to return. For Mahayana Buddhists, Bodhisattvas are almost godlike beings who put off enlightenment until they can guide all beings to it. In Tibet, it is believed that the Dalai Lama and other "reincarnated" Lamas are actually Bodhisattvas who constantly return to the Tibet Buddhist community.

SIKHISM – BASIC TEACHINGS
Sikhism is much younger than other religions that originated in India.

Sikhism emerged in the sixteenth century C.E. While in some respects it resembles both Hinduism and Islam, Sikhs believe their faith to be based on the independent insights of their first teacher, Nanak.

Sikh tradition maintains that when Nanak was approximately thirty years old, God spoke to him and told him that he had been chosen as the Prophet of the True Religion.

After receiving this message, Nanak and his companion wandered across India for many years teaching the unity of Hinduism and Islam. He accepted the teachings of monotheism and that of karma and rebirth.

Nanak was followed by a series of nine teachers or gurus—the last of whom died in 1708 c.e.

Arjan, the sixth guru, was imprisoned and killed by Muslim authorities. Before he died he instructed his son to establish a core of armed guards. This militant tradition has continued because Sikhs have often been the victims of oppression and violence carried out by both Hindus and Muslims.

There are three basic divisions among Sikhs.

The Udasis are an order of holy men whose religious practices resemble those of Buddhist and Jain monks. The Singh represent the warrior tradition. They grow beards, wear turbans, and carry ceremonial daggers. The Sahajdharis are pacifists.

Sikh devotions are very simple.

Nanak rejected the complicated ceremonies of both Hinduism and Islam. Sikh devotions include daily prayers and the singing of hymns. When Sikhs gather for collective meals, there is always a communal prayer or Langer that symbolizes the equality of all humankind.

CHAPTER 4

Hinduism

CHAPTER OBJECTIVES

In this chapter you will:

- Learn about the basic religious teachings and rituals of Hinduism.
- Come to understand the ways in which Hinduism has changed over time.
- Come to understand the caste system.
- Learn about relationships between Hinduism and other religions of India.
- Learn about Hindu/Muslim/Christian conflict in historical and contemporary contexts.

KEY TERMS

Varna	Vedas	Upanishads
Bhakti	Trimurti	Ahimsa
Dharma	Aryan	

A Timeline of Hinduism

2500–1500 B.C.E.	Indus Valley Civilization	788–820	Shankara organizes Vedanta
1750–1200	Aryan migration to South Asia; First Vedas compiled	1510	Portuguese conquest of Goa
400	Vedas completed	1556–1857	Moghul Empire; with few exceptions, characterized by religious tolerance
800–300	Upanishads compiled		
200–200 C.E.	*Bhagavad Gita* compiled	1700	British emerge as major power in India
300–300 C.E.	Laws of Manu compiled; caste system formalized	1774–1833	Life of Ram Mohan Roy
600–1600	Rise of devotional and anti-caste movements	1836–1886	Life of Sri Ramakrishna

(Continued)

A Timeline of Hinduism *(Continued)*

1857	Indian Mutiny; British Christians, Indian Hindus, Muslims, and Sikhs commit atrocities in the name of religion	1947	Independence from Britain; partition of British India into India and Pakistan sparks massive outbreaks of violence among Hindus, Muslims, and Sikhs
1869–1948	Life of Mahatma Gandhi	Late 20th–early 21st century	Growth of Hindu Nationalism leads to increasing Hindu/Muslim/Christian tension and violence
19th and 20th centuries	Emergence of large Hindu communities outside India; large numbers of Dalits (untouchables) convert to Buddhism and Christianity		

Perhaps the oldest and most complex of all the religions of the world is Hinduism. Whereas most of today's active religions seem to have begun sometime around the sixth century B.C.E. or later, Hinduism traces the beginnings of some of its religious themes and forms to the third millennium B.C.E. It is probably the most diverse and varied of all religions. One can find within the Hindu tradition almost any form or style of religion that has been conceived or practiced. Its scope ranges from simple animism to some of the most elaborate philosophical systems ever devised. In this vast diversity, Hinduism allows for literally millions of major and minor gods, their temples, and their priests. Therefore, for the Hindu, the possible religious views are virtually infinite.

Hinduism has also been the source of three other religions. In the sixth century B.C.E., two reform movements, Jainism and Buddhism, arose from within Hinduism and challenged traditional Indian religious concepts. For a time, it appeared that both movements might even replace Hinduism. Within a few centuries, however, their distinctive features were absorbed by Hinduism, which re-emerged as the major religion of India. Today, Jainism is a minority religion in India, and Buddhism, although having great influence in other Asian nations, has only a small following in India. In the fifteenth century C.E., after Muslim invasions of India, Sikhism arose as a religion with features resembling those of both Islam and Hinduism. However, it has never become more than a minority religion and is concentrated in the northwest of what is now modern India. Hinduism faced these challengers by absorbing them and adopting their distinctive features into the mainstream of Hindu thought.

Unlike most of the other major religions of the world, Hinduism has no identifiable founder. Although there have been many great teachers and leaders in its history, there has never been one whose teachings became the wellspring of all later Hindu thought.

The word *Hindu* comes from the Sanskrit name for the river Indus, *Sindhu*. Whereas the designation *Hindu* may refer to a great variety of religious beliefs and practices, it generally applies to the religion of the people of India. Only recently have the people we now know as Hindus begun to use the term to refer to their own religious beliefs and practices. It is believed that the Muslim conquerors of India were the first to use the word *Hindu* to describe religion. They called those Indians who did not convert to Islam "Hindus." The British picked up this usage from the Muslim rulers of India. From English it passed into other European languages. While the vast majority of Hindus live in the modern nation of India, Hinduism flourished in much of Southeast Asia from the seventh to the fifteenth century C.E. and still survives on the Indonesian island of Bali. In the nineteenth and early twentieth centuries, Indian Hindus spread throughout the British Empire. Today, substantial Hindu communities exist in Europe, Africa, the Caribbean, and North America.

The Origins of Hinduism

Pre-Aryan India

The history of Hinduism begins with the migratory waves of Aryan people into India during the second millennium B.C.E. The religion that the Aryans brought with them mingled with the religion of the native people, and the culture that developed between them became classical Hinduism.

Before we can speak of the Aryan religion, however, we must first take note of the pre-Aryan natives of India. Actually, very little is known about these people. Prior to the 1920s, the only source that spoke of the pre-Aryan people was the Vedic literature of early Hinduism. Because this was the religious literature of the Aryans, references to the natives of India and their religions were very negative, and the people were presented as uncivilized and barbaric. Beginning in the 1920s, however, archaeological excavations in northwestern India revealed an entire complex of cities along the Indus River. Contrary to the image presented in the **Vedas**, these excavations showed that as early as 2500 B.C.E. there was an advanced civilization in the Indus valley. The total complex of cities and villages in this area covered nearly one-half million square miles and may represent the largest political entity before the Roman Empire. The cities were laid out in rectangular blocks separated by broad streets with elaborate drainage systems, and they may have supported a population of 40,000 people per city. At the peak of this civilization, houses were made of fired brick, some two stories high, and they contained bathrooms with running water. Cities were supported by advanced agricultural communities. Evidence of complex irrigation systems exists. The cities often contained large granaries for the storage and distribution of food. Archaeologists also found that these pre-Aryan Indians had a written language. Unfortunately, this language has not yet been translated and the great amount of information that it could supply regarding the life and religion of these people remains hidden.

What we know of the religion of the pre-Aryan people is revealed by numerous statues and amulets that archaeologists have found. Many of these bear the image of what have been interpreted as fertility gods and goddesses. Some of the figures sit in the lotus position that was later adopted by Yoga Hinduism and other meditative sects. In addition, archaeologists have found large ceremonial buildings that may have been places of worship. It is therefore assumed that far from being barbarians, the pre-Aryan people were highly civilized city dwellers and that later Hinduism may have taken some of its gods and practices from this early period.[1]

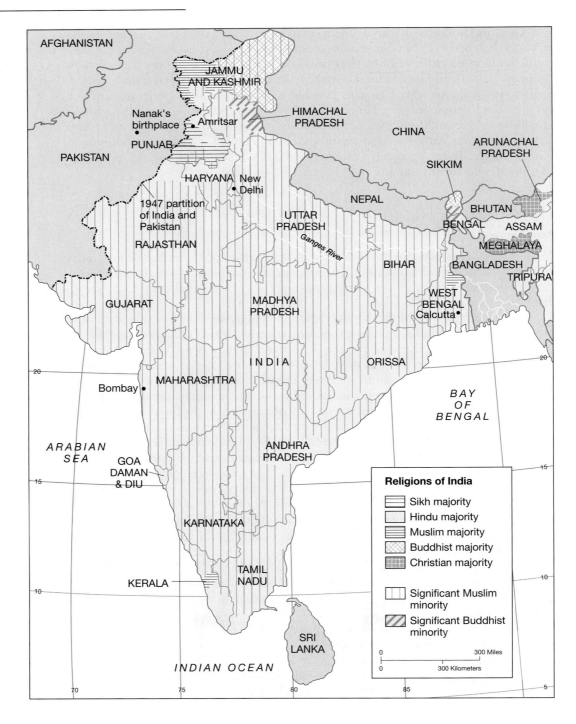

AFGHANISTAN

JAMMU AND KASHMIR

Nanak's birthplace
• Amritsar
PUNJAB

PAKISTAN

HIMACHAL PRADESH

CHINA

ARUNACHAL PRADESH

SIKKIM

HARYANA New Delhi

NEPAL

BHUTAN

1947 partition of India and Pakistan

UTTAR PRADESH

BENGAL

ASSAM

RAJASTHAN

Ganges River

BIHAR

MEGHALAYA

BANGLADESH

TRIPURA

GUJARAT

MADHYA PRADESH

WEST BENGAL
Calcutta •

INDIA

ORISSA

20

Bombay •

MAHARASHTRA

20

BAY OF BENGAL

ARABIAN SEA

ANDHRA PRADESH

GOA DAMAN & DIU

15

15

KARNATAKA

KERALA

TAMIL NADU

10

10

SRI LANKA

INDIAN OCEAN

70   75   80   85   5

Religions of India

Sikh majority
Hindu majority
Muslim majority
Buddhist majority
Christian majority

Significant Muslim minority
Significant Buddhist minority

0   300 Miles
0   300 Kilometers

The Coming of the Aryans

Religion and Violence

To the modern student, the word Aryan usually connotes the various meanings that the twentieth-century Nazi movement gave it. Adolf Hitler, in his attempt to depict his own people as the master race, called the tall, blond, blue-eyed people of the world the "Aryan race." To the Nazis, this superior race had historically given the world its strength and civilization. Other "races," such as the Semitic Jews and Africans, were deemed inferior to the "Aryans." This theory, of course, has no anthropological or historical foundation. The word *Aryan* was first applied to large groups of people in the late nineteenth century, when it was used to designate a family of languages. Later, some attempted to attach the term to a biological or racial unit. However, the word *Aryan* has been used to designate groups as diverse as North Indians, Western Asians, and Europeans. It can scarcely be used as a name for a single racial group.

The term *Aryan* is a Sanskrit word that means "the noble ones"; this word was applied to a group of migrants who moved into the Indus valley in the second millennium B.C.E. from what is now Iran. The Aryans are believed to have been the first to tame horses on a wide scale and use them to pull war chariots.

They spoke an Indo-European language distantly related to English and other languages of Western Europe. Aryans who did not migrate into India became the founders of the ancient Iranian religion Zoroastrianism. There are many similarities between the religion revealed in the Indian Vedic literature and the Gathas of Zoroastrianism. These same people later founded the Persian Empire, which ruled the Middle East from the sixth to the fourth centuries B.C.E. When the modern Persians sought a name for their nation, they called it Iran—that is, the land of the Aryans.

Tanah Laut, an oceanside Hindu temple on the Indonesian island of Bali.
(Mark R. Woodward)

Religion and Violence

During the period between 1750 and 1200 B.C.E., the Aryans came in migratory waves into India. Evidently, the highly civilized city cultures of this region had worn out their environment and were in a state of decline. Some of the excavations demonstrate the evidence of physical conquest, whereas others reveal only the decay of the culture and the abandonment of the site. No one knows whether the Aryans actually invaded and conquered the pre-Aryan cities or simply moved in after their decline.

Of the early Aryans, little is known. Scattered references in the Vedic literature indicate that they were basically nomads following their flocks and herds from place to place. They apparently had no permanent bases or cities. The Aryans of this period were organized along tribal lines and were led by chieftains called *rajas*. It was not until about the sixth century B.C.E. that these people began to settle in cities in the Indus valley and some of the *rajas* began to collect and build minor kingdoms for themselves.

According to early sources, Aryan society began to develop into three basic classes called *varnas*. The highly regarded priests who served the cults of the various Aryan cities were called *Brahmins*. The chieftains and their warriors, also considered to be near the apex of society, were called *Kshatriyas*. The commoners and merchants, regarded as being subservient to the two upper classes, were called *Vaishyas*. A fourth group that may have been made up of those conquered pre-Aryan people were called *Shudras*. *Shudras* were not considered full members of the society and generally held the position of slaves or servants to the Aryans. These divisions were maintained in Indian society for centuries and were later subdivided into the multiple classes that became the basis of the caste system.

Aryan Religion

The best source of knowledge about the religion of the Aryan invaders is the Vedic literature, but this literature was mainly composed after the Aryans had been settled in India for many years and had intermingled with the native people and their religions. What is truly Aryan and what is truly pre-Aryan in the Vedas is therefore difficult to know. Nevertheless, certain basic assumptions about Aryan religion can be made.

It seems clear that the Aryan invaders of India brought with them a polytheistic religion similar to that of other Indo-European peoples. There have been considerable attempts to associate Aryan gods with those of Greece and Rome.[2] The collection of gods that the Aryans worshipped seems to have been personifications of various natural forces, such as the storm, the sun, the moon, and the fertility of the soil. This indicates that the origins of Hinduism are to be found in an even more ancient animistic religion.[3]

The chief manner of worship of the Aryan gods was apparently sacrifice. Because the Aryans were primarily nomadic in the early days of their occupation of India, they built no temples to their gods but rather offered sacrifices to them on altars built in open places. These offerings were frequently animal sacrifices, but they also included the sacrifices of dairy products like butter and libations of milk, which were poured out to the gods. Fire was the basic means through which sacrifices were

"Buffalo from Mohenjo Daro." New Delhi, India.
(© Scala/Art Resource, NY)

offered to the gods. Angi, the god of fire, was the channel through whom offerings were presented to the other gods. Another liquid apparently used as a libation was the juice of the sacred *soma* plant. The exact identification of the *soma* plant is lost to the modern world.[4] The ancient texts describe it as a sacred plant sent to earth by the god Indra. Its juice was described as delicious and invigorating to the worshipper who drank it and shared it with the gods. The plant that modern Indians identify as soma is not delicious and invigorating but produces nausea. Naturally, there are those who suggest that the original soma may have been some form of mushroom or other plant that produced hallucinations.[5]

The Vedas include an extravagant formula for sacrificial offerings. Perhaps the most expensive and elaborate sacrifice ever used in any religion originated among the Aryans—the horse sacrifice. Because of the expense and incredible detail involved, the horse sacrifice was limited to Aryan kings. This sacrifice was believed to have extraordinary effects in atoning and for giving religious power to those who participated in it. The horse sacrifice was also helpful to rulers who wished to expand their territory, and this, of course, was its major attraction to Indian rulers. A young male horse chosen for this sacrifice was set loose to roam the countryside for one year. The attendants of the ruler followed the horse wherever he went. If the horse covered any territory that was not in the domain of the ruler, that *raja* had the right to claim that land as his own. After one year, the horse returned. At that time, as many as 600 other animals, ranging from the bee to the elephant, were sacrificed to the gods. Finally, the sacred horse was strangled and the wives of the *raja* participated in fertility rites with the body of the horse. The carcass was ritually butchered and eaten by the ruler and his family. According to legend, if one man could perform 100 horse sacrifices he would become master over all of the gods and the universe. Unfortunately for those who aspired to this, such an act would have required over 100 years and incredible wealth. Consequently, there is no record of a ruler who could or would perform it 100 times. The horse sacrifice was last performed by an Indian ruler in the eighteenth century C.E.

The Vedic Era
The Vedas

The oldest sacred books of Hinduism are the Vedas. The Vedas are the basic source of the Hindu understanding of the universe. All later texts are seen as mere commentary upon them, even when they include new religious ideas. The Vedas were developed as the Aryans came into India, settled there, and mingled their religion with that of the native peoples. There is dispute over the exact period in which the Vedas were written. Some scholars believe that the earliest of the Vedic hymns may have developed prior to the coming of the Aryans, before 2000 B.C.E., and that they were still developing as late as the sixth century C.E. Others contend that the bulk of the Vedic material came into being between 1500 and 400 B.C.E. As is true of much other ancient religious literature, there is no way of knowing the exact time of the origin and development of these books. Undoubtedly, they were first composed and transmitted orally for many generations before they were committed to writing; thus, centuries may have passed between their origin and completion.

There are four basic Vedic books. The first and most important is the *Rig-Veda* (*Veda* meaning "knowledge" or "sacred lore"), a collection of over 1,000 hymns to the Aryan gods, which contains the basic mythology of these gods.

The second book is the *Yajur-Veda* (knowledge of rites), a collection of materials to be recited during sacrifice to the gods. The third book, the *Sama-Veda* (knowledge of chants), is a collection of verses from the basic hymns recited by priests at sacrifices. The fourth book, second in importance only to the *Rig-Veda*, is the *Atharva-Veda* (knowledge given by the sage Atharva), which contains rituals to be used in the home and popular prayers to the gods, along with spells and incantations to ward off evil.

Brahmins in yellow robes chanting the Ramayana. Varanasi, India.
(Omni-Photo Communications, Inc.)

Each of the Vedic books is made up of four parts;[6] each contains a section of hymns (*mantras*) to the gods. As is the case in many ancient religions, hymns and religious poetry are to be regarded as the most ancient of all religious literature because they reflect the period when statements about and to the gods were memorized, chanted, and passed from one generation to the next without benefit of the written word. Each Vedic book also contains a section of ritual materials (*Brahmanas*) in which the worshippers are given instruction in the proper way to perform their sacrifices, and so on. The Brahmanas are considered to be later than the mantra sections. A third section in each of the Vedas is the so-called Forest Treatises (*Aranyakas*), which are materials for hermits in their religious pursuits. The fourth sections are called *Upanishads* and are made up of philosophical materials. The mantra and Brahmana sections are considered the oldest material in the Vedas, with the Aranyakas and the Upanishads having been added later. The Vedas in their final form are written in a language called *Vedic*, a predecessor of early Sanskrit.

Within the Vedas are basic descriptions and mythology of the various Aryan and pre-Aryan gods. The god who receives the most attention in terms of numbers of hymns is Indra, the god of the thunderbolt, of clouds and rain, and the ruler of heaven. Indra is especially important because he is remembered as the conqueror of Vrtra, the personification of chaos. Contained within the *Rig-Veda* alone are over 250 hymns specifically addressed to him. One of these follows:

From the Source

That highest Indra power of thine is distant: that which is here sages possessed aforetime.

This one is on the earth, in heaven the other, and both unite as flag with flag in battle.

He spread the wide earth out and firmly fixed it, smote with his thunderbolt and loosed the waters.

Maghavan with his puissance struck down Ahi, rent Rauhina to death and slaughtered Vyansa.

Armed with his bolt and trusting in his prowess he wandered shattering the forts of Dasas.

Cast thy dart, knowing, Thunderer, at the Daysu: increase the Arya's might and glory, Indra.

For him who thus hath taught these human races, Maghavan, bearing a fame-worthy title.

Thunderer, drawing nigh to slay the Dasyus, hath given himself the name of Son for glory.

See this abundant wealth that he possesses, and put your trust in Indra's hero vigor.

He found the cattle, and he found the horses, he found the plants, the forests and the waters.

To him the truly strong, whose deeds are many, to him the strong bull let us pour the Soma.

The Hero, watching like a thief in ambush, goes parting the possessions of the godless.

Well didst thou do that hero deed, O Indra, in waking with thy bolt the slumbering Ahi.

In thee, delighted, Dames divine rejoiced them, the flying Maruts and all gods were joyful.

As thou hast smitten Sushna, Pipru, Vrtra and Kuyava, and Samhara's forts, O Indra.

This prayer of ours may Varuna grant, and Mitra, and Aditi, and Sindhu, Earth and Heaven.[7]

Many other Aryan gods are also mentioned in the Vedic literature. Agni, the god of fire, is mentioned in over 200 hymns. He is basically regarded as the god of the priests and the priest of the gods. He leads the gods in proper sacrifice, and as the god of fire, he brings the burnt sacrifices to the other gods. The god Varuna also receives his share of hymns in the Vedic material. He is viewed as the god who presides over the order of the universe and the god who forgives those who have sinned.

From the Source

May we be in thy keeping, O thou Leader, wide-ruling Varuna, Lord of many heroes.

O sons of Aditi, forever faithful, pardon us, Gods, admit us to your friendship.[8]

Vishnu is mentioned briefly in the Vedas; but at the time they were composed, he was not the important deity he was to become in later Hinduism. Another of the gods whose function and name was to change in later Hinduism was Rudra, later known as Shiva, the god of death and destruction. In later times, Shiva and Vishnu become two of the most popular gods in Hinduism. The god of the dead who receives attention in the Vedas is Yama, who was supposed to have been the first man to die.

From the Source

Honor the King with thine oblations, Yama, Vivasvan's Son, who gathers men together,
    Who travelled to the lofty heights above us, who searches out and shows the path to many.

Yama first found for us a place to dwell in: this pasture never can be taken from us.
    Men born on earth tread their own paths that lead them whither our ancient Fathers have departed.[9]

In addition to hymns to the many gods of the Aryan pantheon, the Vedas also contain legendary and mythological material from early Indian life. One of the most interesting of these is the story of Manu, which speaks of the origin of women and the subsequent growth of the human race. As in other Vedic texts, sacrifice plays an important role in the story.

From the Source

They brought water to Manu for washing, as it is now usual to bring it for washing hands. When he was washing, a fish came into his hands.
    It said to him in words, "Bring me up, I shall save you." "From what will you save me?" "A flood will carry away all the creatures. I shall save you from that flood." "How can I bring you up?"
    "Fish swallow fish. So long as we remain small, destruction awaits us. Keep me first in a jar. When I outgrow it, dig a pond and keep me in it. When I outgrow that also, take me to the sea. Then I shall be beyond danger."
    It quickly became a Jhasa, which become the largest. Then it said, "The flood will come in such and such a year. Take my advice then, and build a ship.

Enter it when the flood rises, and I shall save you from the flood."
    After rearing the fish thus, Manu took it to the sea. In the year indicated to him by the fish, he acted according to the advice of the fish and built a ship. When the flood rose, he entered it. The fish then swam to him. He tied the rope of the ship to the horn of the fish and thus reached swiftly the Northern Mountain there.
    The fish then said, "I have saved you. Tie the ship to a tree and do not let the water leave you stranded when you are on the mountain. Descend as the water subsides." Thus gradually he descended, hence that slope of the Northern Mountain is called "Manu's Descent." The flood carried off all the creatures, Manu alone survived.

> Wishing for a progeny, he began to worship and do penance. Then he performed a sacrifice of cooked meal. In the waters he offered melted butter, buttermilk, whey, and curd as oblations. In a year, a woman was created out of them. She rose dripping, melted butter collected at her footprints.

> Wishing for progeny, he continued to worship and perform penance along with her. Through her this race was generated by him. This is the race of Manu. Whatever blessings he desired through her were all conferred on him.[10]

In modern Hinduism, the Vedic literature is held in high regard, but its texts are known by only a few scholars. Some of the gods mentioned in the Vedas are no longer worshipped. This ancient sacred literature serves mainly as background for other developments in Hinduism in much the same way that the Hebrew Bible serves as background for the development of Christianity and Islam.

The Upanishads

As noted earlier, the fourth section of each of the Vedas is the Upanishads.[11] Within these materials, one finds the early philosophical statements that became the basis for later Hindu philosophy. Although there originally may have been more of these treatises, there are currently about 200 Upanishads, varying in length from one to over fifty pages. Of these, fourteen are called the principal Upanishads. Scholarly research indicates that the earliest Upanishads probably originated in the ninth century B.C.E.

Some scholars contend that the Upanishads are an integral part of the Vedas and that they are a natural commentary on the early hymns and ritual texts. These scholars tend to see the Upanishads as the philosophical expression of what one finds in the rest of the Vedas. Others disagree and point out the basic disharmony between the two. Whereas the hymns, chants, legends, and rituals in the rest of the Vedic material are clearly polytheistic, giving instruction on the proper worship of myriad gods, the Upanishads operate from a monistic presupposition. The gods of the earlier Vedic literature are not very important. The Upanishads assume that there is only one reality, the impersonal god-being called Brahman. All other beings are but an expression of Brahman. All that is not Brahman is not real. Humans have a false knowledge (*maya*) when they believe that this life and our separation from Brahman are real. Not only is there this basic distinction between the Upanishads and the rest of the Vedic material, but the Upanishads also seem to have been written as a reaction to the priestly form of worship prescribed by the other Vedic books. Whereas most of the Vedas seem to teach that the proper way to worship is by

The Buddha and lay devotees. Borobudur, ninth-century Buddhist Stupa near Yogyakarta, Indonesia. (*Mark R. Woodward*)

sacrifice to the various Aryan gods, the Upanishads emphasize meditation as a means of worship. They teach that people's real problem is ignorance (*avidya*) of their plight and that only when people realize this ignorance and come to true knowledge will they find release. Those scholars who point to these essential differences between the Upanishads and other portions of the Vedas believe that the Upanishads may have had a different origin and became attached to the Vedic literature at a later time. It probably is fair to say that although the Upanishads have been tremendously influential as the basis for later Hindu philosophy, they have never been extremely popular, except among intellectuals. They are complicated and difficult discussions, and they require the acceptance of a worldview that is not easily understood.

As we have indicated, the fundamental assumption of the Upanishads is that there is but one true reality in the universe—Brahman. Brahman is eternal, infinite, unknowable, sexless, without a past, present, or future, and totally impersonal.[12]

From the Source

Verily, in the beginning this world was Brahman, the limitless One—limitless to the east, limitless to the north, . . . limitless in every direction . . . .

Incomprehensible is that supreme Soul, unlimited, unborn not to be reasoned about, unthinkable—He whose soul is space![13]

The living beings that inhabit our world are really only expressions of the Brahman. They are souls (*atman*) that are a part of the great ocean of souls that make up the Brahman. Therefore, all phenomenal existence is illusion (*maya*) arising from ignorance of the true nature of reality. A person's individuality apart from the Brahman—the world in which one lives, that which one sees, hears, touches, and feels—is all an illusion, a dream.

From the Source

This whole world the illusion-maker projects out of this [Brahman].
And in it by illusion the other is confined.

Now, one should know that Nature is illusion,
And that the Mighty Lord is the illusion-maker.[14]

The plight of human beings is that they are bound up in this world of illusion and ignorance, thinking that it is real, unaware of their true identification with Brahman. "Those who worship ignorance (*avidya*) enter blinding darkness."[15] This ignorance is often illustrated by the parable of the tiger who was orphaned as a cub and reared by goats. All of his life, he believed that he too was a goat; he ate grass and bleated like a goat. One day he met another tiger who took him to a pool where the first tiger saw his true image. The second tiger then forced him to eat meat for the first time, and he slowly came to realize his tiger nature. In a similar manner, humans are deceived about their true nature. It is the task of religion to reveal the divine within us and to show us how to live on the new plane.

In discussing the nature of life, the Upanishads introduce the concept of karma. What makes one person different from another? Why is one person kind, intelligent, talented, or wise, and a brother or sister the opposite? Modern answers to these questions often center around a debate over the effects of heredity or environment. Ancient Indian thinkers preferred to attribute virtue or evil to choices made by the individual. They introduced the concept of karma into religious language. The Sanskrit word *karma* comes from a root that means "to do or act." In the classical period, Indians came to believe that every action and every thought had its consequence, marking the individual internally, an effect felt either in this life or in a succeeding one. Therefore, the person who seems to have positive innate qualities is merely a demonstration of positive actions in the past. Likewise, the person who is criminal is acting out the consequences of choices made in the past.

Along with the idea of *karma*, Indian thinkers introduced the concept of *samsara*, literally "to wander across." Indian religions believe that the life force of an individual does not die with the death of the body, but instead "wanders across." The life force moves on to another time and body, where it continues to live. Many Western thinkers have proposed this idea as "reincarnation" or the "transmigration of souls." Some see this process as a blessing; but in Indian thought, *samsara* may be thought of as a curse. One is bound to life in ignorance and pain, living over and over again through countless generations. Indeed, the goal of most Indian religions is to break the cycle of *karma* and *samsara* and be free from the burden of life. This breaking free from life is called *moksha*.

In the Upanishads, release from life comes when there is true knowledge of the illusion of life. "By knowing God man is freed from all bonds."[16] When true knowledge of the illusion of life is realized, one can be freed from the bondage of life and achieve unity with the Brahman. This is difficult. It comes only after much study, and requires many lifetimes. "Arise, awake, go to the sages and learn. The wise say that the path is sharp like the edge of a razor, hard to walk on, and difficult to obtain."[17]

Within the Upanishads, one finds a collection of materials similar to that found in the Jewish Talmud. Various legends and tales are used to illustrate the philosophical material of these books. They are frequently cast in the form of a student's discussion with a guru and apparently have been collected over centuries of use. The Chandogya-Upanishad records a conversation between a son and his father. The father instructs his son in the following manner:

From the Source

"Put this piece of salt in the water and come to me tomorrow morning." [Svetaketu] did as he was told. [Then his father] said to him: "[Do you remember] that piece of salt you put in the water yesterday evening? Would you be good enough to bring it here?"

He groped for it but could not find it. It had completely dissolved.

"Would you please sip it at this end? What is it like?" he said.

"Salt."

"Sip it in the middle. What is it like?"

"Salt."

"Sip it at the far end. What is it like?"

"Salt."

"Throw it away and then come to me."

He did as he was told but [that did not stop the salt from] remaining ever the same.

[His father] said to him: "My dear child, it is true that you cannot perceive Being here, but it is equally true that it is here.

"This finest essence, the whole universe has, as its Self; That is the Real: That is the Self: That you are, Svetaketu!"

"Good sir, will you kindly instruct me further?"

"I will, my dear child," said he.[18]

The Law of Manu

Another piece of traditional Indian literature produced during the classical era is the ethical *Law of Manu*. This law, which was probably written at some point between 300 B.C.E. and 300 C.E., is of value not only because of its religious teachings but also because of what it reveals about Indian life during the period. Within this book, the student finds the ethical and social standards that were held as ideals during the classical era of Indian history and the effects that the religious and philosophical teachings of the Vedas had on Indian society. Furthermore, one finds here the roots of many of the social and religious traditions that characterize modern Hinduism.

One of the basic assumptions of the *Law of Manu* is the varna system, which had apparently developed from the early Aryan divisions of society. The description of the varna system included in this text is based on an earlier account in the *Rig-Veda* that describes the gods' sacrifice of the cosmic man Purusa as the origin of Hindu society.

From the Source

When they divided Purusa, into how many parts did they separate him?

What did his mouth become? What his two arms? What are declared to be his two thighs, his two feet?

The Brahman [priest] was his mouth. His two arms became the Raja [ruler]; his two thighs are the Vaishya [artisans, merchants and farmers], from his two feet the Sudra [servant] was produced.[19]

The *Law of Manu* is more explicit concerning the duties of the four varna. It specifies particular occupations for each of the four social groups, which are seen as being divinely ordained.

For the growth of the worlds, (Brahman) created Brahmanas (Brahmins), Kshatriyas (warriors), Vaishyas (traders) and Shudras (manual workers) from his face, arms, thighs, and feet respectively.[20]

The first three are called "twice born" and the fourth, the Shudras, the "once born." Members of each group have specific duties (*dharma*) and opportunities and must obey them only.[21]

From the Source

For the Brahmanas (Brahmins), he created teaching, studying, sacrifice, officiating at sacrifice, giving gifts, and accepting gifts.

For the Kshatriya, he created in short the protection of people, giving gifts, performing sacrifices, studying, and nonattachment to sense pleasures.

For the Vaishya, he created the protection of cattle, charity, performance of sacrifices, studying, trading, lending on interest, and agriculture.

The Lord created only one profession for the Shudra: service without envy of the above three castes.[22]

At this time, Brahmins were expected to lead a religious life and to devote themselves to the study of the Vedas and the practice of their teachings. Members of the other varna were expected to perform their duties faithfully and to move gradually through the system, incarnation by incarnation. Even at this early stage, Indian society was stratified into fixed classes. Mobility through the system could only be achieved through reincarnation.

The *Law of Manu* also demonstrates the state of the understanding of reincarnation at this period.

From the Source

Man obtains the life of motionlessness (of plants, and so on) as a result of the evil committed by the body, the life of birds and beasts because of the evil committed by speech, and the life of the lowest born because of the evil committed by mind.

If a man performs only good actions, he will be born a god; if he performs mixed actions, he will be born a man; and if he performs only evil actions, he will be born a bird or an animal. The result of evil speech is the destruction of knowledge, that of evil mind is the loss of the supreme destiny; and that of the evil body is the loss of the worlds. So let one protect the three in every way. The punishment prescribed for evil speech is silence; that for evil mind is fasting; and that for evil action is breath control.[23]

Mountaintop Hindu Temple dedicated to Vishnu and Lakshmi found in Central Bali, Indonesia. *(Mark R. Woodward)*

Another central teaching of the *Law of Manu* is the various stages of life through which upper-caste men were expected to pass. In the first stage of life, the typical upper-caste Indian male is supposed to be a student, studying the Vedas and giving careful attention to a teacher. In the second stage, he is to become a householder and marry within his caste. In the ideal marriage described in the *Law of Manu*, the man is to be considerably older than his wife. The role of householder and provider is one of the most important, for the householder is seen as one of the cornerstones of society. This is also the time when a man enjoys whatever wealth and pleasure may come into life. When his duties as a householder are finished (typically when the grandchildren are grown), a Hindu man may retreat to the forest and live there for some years as a hermit, meditating and offering sacrifices. During this time, he learns nonattachment to the things of the world. Finally, when the hermit life is completed, Hindus may become wandering beggars (*sannyasi*). These four stages are only the ideals of the twice-born males (the three higher castes); the role of the Shudra is to serve the higher castes.

Sadhu, Hindu holy man in Bombay India. This man has entered the final stage of life and has given himself totally to meditation and acts of devotion.
(*Eugene Gordon*)

The four stages of life are only for men. Women are supposed to stay in the home under the control and protection of the chief male of the household. Even at home nothing should be done independently by a woman, whether she is a young girl, a youthful maiden, or an old lady. When young, she should be in the control of her father and in her youth of her husband. When the husband dies, she should be in the protection of her sons. She should not love independence. She should never desire separation from her father, husband, or children. Separated from them, she brings bad name to both the families.[24] Women are meant for children. They are for the good and light of home. They are to be worshipped. In a home there is no difference between a woman on the one side and wealth, beauty, and splendor on the other.[25]

The *Law of Manu* is mainly a statement of the moral and ethical ideals of the period. It contains the prohibitions that one would expect against murder, theft, and sexual immorality. The moral aims of the era are summed up in the following ten characteristics: pleasantness, patience, control of mind, non-stealing, purity, control of the senses, intelligence, knowledge, truthfulness, and non-irritability.[26]

It is notable that even at this early date, Indian society placed a premium on the life of cattle and imposed penalties on those who slaughtered them.

The Vaishya, having gone through the sacraments, and having accepted a wife, should engage himself in trade and in the protection of cattle.[27]

Among the greatest of sins is listed the killing of cows.[28] For those who have committed great sins, the remedy is to live with cows for a year controlling his mind, studying sacred texts.[29]

The *Law of Manu* is also helpful in providing an understanding of the Indian conception of divine time, which is virtually endless.

Eighteen movements of the eyelid are called Kashta, Kala is thirty Kashtas, thirty Kalas constitute a Muhurta, and thirty Muhurtas make a day and night.

The night and day are divided by the sun for men and gods. The night is meant for the sleep of beings and the day for their work.

The night and day of ancestors is one month of men. Its black fortnight is meant for their action and the white for their sleep.

The night and day of gods is the year of men. Its division again is into the summer solstice as the day and the winter solstice as the night.

Now, understand the night and day of Brahman and their duration, and also each of the aeons in succession.

The Krita aeon consists of 4,000 years. Four hundred years before and four hundred after are the intervening times for this aeon. In the case of the other three aeons with their prior and posterior twilights, the number of thousands and hundreds is to be less and less by one. The aeon of the gods is said to be 12,000 times the four aeons counted previously. One thousand times the aeon of the gods is the day of Brahman. His night also is as long.

The knowers of day and night call the day of Brahman, which is 1,000 aeons long, the auspicious day. His night also is such.[30]

In general, ancient Indian philosophy saw time as moving endlessly through various cycles. At the beginning of a cycle, the world is created by Brahman. At first there is peace, abundance, and morality. Then the world begins to decay. Vishnu intervenes on behalf of humanity; but in the long run, the world continues to decay. Famines, wars, and general immorality become the rule. Finally, the world is destroyed by Shiva. When one cycle of time is completed, the world dissolves and all souls depart into suspended being. After a period of repose, the world begins again and the souls take up new bodies.

Jainism and Buddhism

In the sixth century B.C.E., two new religions arose in India and offered alternative paths within the Indian worldview. They are discussed in detail in later chapters, but it is worth noting at this point in our discussion of classical Hinduism that they did arise as serious challenges to the mother religion.

Both Jainism and Buddhism rejected the sacrifice system taught in the Vedas. Both taught that one achieved release from life not by offering sacrifices to the gods or by any form of worship but through accomplishments in one's own life. Both rejected the Vedas as sacred scripture, and both taught that anyone of any caste who lived properly might find release.

Jainism taught that one found release from life through asceticism. The more one denied pleasures and satisfactions to the body, the more likely that person was to achieve freedom from the endless cycle of birth and rebirth. In addition, the founders of Jainism expanded on the traditional Indian concern for cattle and taught that all forms of life were sacred and were to be loved and preserved whenever possible (*ahimsa*). Although Jainism had its moments of popularity, it demanded too much of the average person for it to become a mass movement. In the centuries following Jainism's origin, Hinduism absorbed its concern for asceticism and *ahimsa*. Today, Jainism has only about two million followers in India out of a population of greater than a billion.

Krishna dancing the Dance of Life (Rasa Lila) with Radha and the cowherd women. Krishna is worshipped by Hindus as the eighth avatar (incarnation) of the Hindu god Vishnu. As a youth, Krishna was a cowherd who made a reputation for himself as a lover, and when he played the flute, the gopis (wives and daughters of the cowherds) came to dance with him.
(Rajput; Rajasthan, Nathadwara. "Rasa Lila: Krishna Dances with Radha and with each of the Village Gopis", early 20th century. Opaque watercolor on cotton. Height 110 in., width 103 in. Williams College Museum of Art, Gift of Karl Mann, 92.12.3.)

Buddhism grew out of many of the same longings and beliefs that formed the basis for Jainism. However, it taught that although one could find release from life without priests and a sacrifice system, the extremes of asceticism were not necessary. For a time, Buddhism, with its more moderate ways, appeared to have become the religion of India. It became a missionary religion, sending its preachers to other Asian nations. However, Hinduism eventually reasserted itself and absorbed the distinctive features of Buddhism. Gautama Buddha, founder of Buddhism, was made a member of the Hindu pantheon, and some of his teachings became a part of Hinduism. He is said to have been an incarnation of the god Vishnu. By the fifteenth century C.E., few Buddhists were left in India. Buddhism did, however, become the dominant religion of many other Asian nations and survives in them today. The rise and popularity of Jainism and Buddhism in the sixth century C.E. demonstrates that not all Indians found satisfaction in the teachings of classical Hinduism.

Bhagavad Gita

Perhaps the concluding statement on classical Hinduism is the great epic poem of Indian culture and religion, the *Bhagavad Gita*. This poem is to Hinduism what the Homeric epic poems are to Greek and Hellenistic culture. Like the Homeric poems, the *Gita* is about a great battle; it relates the stories of the struggles of notable heroes and gods and contains much of the basic philosophy of the culture.

The *Bhagavad Gita* is found within the text of a longer epic called the *Mahabharata*.[31] The *Mahabharata* is the story of the struggles between the two leading families from the beginning of Indian history. Finally, these two families come together in the battle of Kurukshetra, which historians roughly place between 850 and 650 B.C.E. Just prior to this battle, one of the warriors, Arjuna, contemplates his fate and the struggle before him. His charioteer, Krishna, enters into the dialogue with him. Their conversation, found between chapters 25 and 42 of the *Mahabharata*, makes up the *Bhagavad Gita*.

Although the *Mahabharata* is believed to have been composed over a very long period, beginning perhaps as early as the ninth or eighth century B.C.E., the *Gita* is believed to have been composed at some point between the second century B.C.E. and the third century C.E. The eighteen chapters that comprise the Gita are divided into three sections of six chapters each. In the first section, Arjuna (the young warrior) looks out on the battlefield and contemplates the coming war and his part in it.

Religion and Violence

There as they stood the son of Pritha saw fathers, grandsires, teachers, uncles, brothers, sons, grandsons, and comrades, fathers-in-law and friends in both armies, and seeing them, all his kinsmen, [thus] arrayed, the son of Kunti was filled with deep compassion and, desponding, spoke these [words]:

"Krishna, when I see these mine own folk standing [before me], spoiling for the fight, my limbs give way, my mouth dries up, trembling seizes my body, and my [body's] hairs stand up in dread. [My bow,] Gandiva, slips from my hand, my very skin is all ablaze; I cannot stand and my mind seems to wander. Krishna, adverse omens too I see, nor can I discern aught good in striking down in battle mine own folk. Krishna, I do not long for victory nor for the kingdom nor yet for things of pleasure. What should I do with a kingdom? What with enjoyments or [even] with life?[32]

"O let the sons of Dhritarashtra, arms in hand, slay me in battle though I, unarmed myself, will offer no defense; therein were greater happiness for me."[33]

(Continued)

Religion and Violence (*Continued*)

Thus, like other warriors in all ages, Arjuna ponders the folly of war, particularly interfamily war, and contemplates going into battle unarmed and thus committing suicide. Arjuna's contemplation is answered by his charioteer, Krishna. The remainder of the poem is the conversation between Arjuna and Krishna about the nature of life and one's duties in life. In the second section of the poem, Krishna reveals that he is the incarnation of the god Vishnu. As such, he has come to earth to help mortals who are struggling with their problems. In the third section, Krishna and Arjuna continue to discuss the problems of life that confront mortals.

Much of the advice and teaching that Krishna gives Arjuna is a reflection of the philosophy of the Upanishads, that most of what mortals see as life and its problems is merely illusion. The most direct teaching that Krishna gives to Arjuna is that he should not dread going into battle because he is a member of the Kshatriya class and as such it is his duty (*dharma*) to be a warrior and to kill. If Arjuna were a member of another class, such as the Brahmin, he might have reason to reject the battlefield. However, battle is the dharma of the Kshatriya, and Arjuna has an obligation to obey that duty.

From the Source

Not by leaving works undone does a man win freedom from the [bond of] works, nor by renunciation alone can he win perfection's prize. For not for a moment can a man stand still and do no work, for every man is powerless and made to work by the constituents born of Nature.[34]

The basic teachings and religious implications of the *Bhagavad Gita* are many. The obvious teaching is that individuals should perform the duty of their caste and thus avoid *karma*, the force that binds people to the endless cycle of birth, death, and rebirth.[35] The obligations that are placed upon each caste are raised to the level of religious duties.

A second feature of Indian religion apparent in the *Gita* is its openness to a variety of means of religious expression. People can achieve release from life (*moksha*) through asceticism, meditation, devotions to and worship of the gods, or obedience to the rules of caste. It is for this reason that Hinduism is often described as the most tolerant of all the world religions.

Perhaps the most lasting teaching of the *Gita* is its picture of Vishnu as a god who loves and is concerned about human beings. His concern is such that he takes various forms and comes to earth at certain times to aid mortals in their struggles. As Krishna says;

From the Source

For whenever the law of righteousness withers away and lawlessness arises, then do I generate myself [on earth].[36]

In postclassical Hinduism, Vishnu became one of the most popular gods. The *Bhagavad Gita* makes clear that one of the legitimate aspects of Hinduism is devotion (***bhakti***) to gods like Vishnu.

Arjuna, be sure of this: none who worships Me with loyalty and love is lost to Me.

From the Source

For whosoever makes Me his haven, base-born though he may be, yes, women too, and artisans, even serfs, theirs it is to tread the highest way. How much more, then, Brahmans pure and good, and royal seers who know devoted love. Since your lot has fallen in this world, impermanent and joyless, commune with Me in love. On Me your mind, on Me your loving service, for Me your sacrifice, to Me be your prostrations: now that you have thus integrated self, your striving bent on Me, to Me you will [surely] come.[37]

Postclassical Hinduism

With the completion of the *Bhagavad Gita*, the classical era in Indian religion came to a close. This period began with the coming of the Aryans to India. It included the development of the Vedas and other religious literature, such as the *Law of Manu*, the Upanishads, and the Bhagavad Gita. This material, its philosophy, and the pantheon of gods that it presented became the basis for later Hinduism.

Some scholars distinguish between the religion of the classical era and that of the postclassical period by referring to the earlier religion as Brahminism and the later as Hinduism. Within Brahminism, the religion of the Indian people was much like that of the Graeco-Roman world. Gods were worshipped with sacrifices offered on altars built in the open. Priests who were experts in rituals and methods of sacrifice were very important.

After the close of the classical period, subtle changes gradually were introduced into the religion of India. Although the existence of many gods was still acknowledged, interest tended to center on the worship of a few major deities, who were, however, worshipped in many forms. Worship came to be love and devotion to those gods. Temples were built to honor them, and hymns were composed about their outstanding qualities. Whereas the literature of the classical period tended to deal with the great epics of Indian history, the literature of the postclassical era tended to center on gods and goddesses. The major gods were seen as taking various forms and becoming involved in the affairs of humans. The wives and consorts of the gods were particularly important in postclassical Hinduism. Some of these goddesses became as popular as their mates; many of the people of India became devotees of these goddesses, developed cults about them, and built temples for their worship. Particularly in south India, major temple festivals celebrate the marriages of gods and goddesses. Hindu gods and goddesses have many human qualities, but on a grand scale. They can be kind and loving or cruel and violent; they can be erotic and life-affirming or practice severe austerities. Some of the tales of the gods and goddesses are romances that tell of love and desire; others concern battles between gods and demons.

Some scholars also point to the change that occurred in the basic attitude toward life in India between the classical and postclassical eras. When the Aryans came to India, they were an aggressive, optimistic people. Pessimistic and passive peoples do not migrate thousands of miles from their homes, conquer a land, and establish themselves as its rulers. By the beginning of modern Hinduism, however, one sees certain negative and life-denying forces emerging in Hindu philosophy. If the basic worldview of Hinduism is that life is an endless cycle of birth, life, death, and rebirth, and that the goal of religion is to cease living, then this is essentially a negative and world-denying religion. The ascetic who refuses the pleasures and comforts of this life (and not the warrior) becomes the religious and cultural hero.

None of these changes occurred overnight or even over one century. Their roots appear even in the Vedas. By the beginning of the Common Era, however, certain changes in the basic religious structure did appear.

Devotion to Three Major Gods

Hinduism offers its devotees many paths. Individuals may find release from life by devotion to one or more of the Indian gods. They may give full religious attention to each of these gods or goddesses by worshipping at their temples, offering sacrifices, praying, supporting the priests of the temple, and so on. In this manner, the gods or goddesses may look with favor upon the devotees, support the believers in life, and help in the struggles of life. This path is called *bhakti-marga* ("the way of devotion").

Brahman, who is ultimate reality, is at the core of Hindu thought. He is one and undivided. Yet postclassical Hinduism sees him in terms of three forms or functions. These three (called the *Trimurti*) are creation, destruction, and preservation. Each of these three functions of Brahman is expressed by a god from the classical literature: Brahma, the creator; Shiva, the destroyer; and Vishnu, the preserver. Devotees of any of these three gods tend to see all of the functions of Brahman in their chosen deity. Devi, the great goddess, represents the feminine principle in Hindu thought. She is the creative power worshipped in female form and is believed to be the all-pervasive energy (*Sakti*) of the gods as well as the slayer of demons. Other goddesses are thought to be manifestations of Devi in much the same sense that the gods can be seen as manifestations of the supreme god Brahman.

BRAHMA. Of the three leading deities of the Hindu pantheon, Brahma receives the least attention.[38] Although Brahma is widely respected and recognized as being the creator of the world, only two temples are specifically dedicated to him in all of India, and he has no cult of devotees. When Brahma is depicted in Indian art, he is shown as red, with four bearded faces and four arms. His chief wife, Sarasvati, is the goddess of knowledge, speech, poetry, and wisdom. In Hindu Bali she is also regarded as the primary patron of the performing arts. Although Brahma is not mentioned in the Vedas, considerable mythology has accumulated during the post-Vedic era about him and his work of creation.

SHIVA. Among the most popular gods in postclassical Hinduism is Shiva, known as "the destroyer." Shiva is the god of death, destruction, and disease. Like Brahma, Shiva does not appear in Vedic literature, but he is believed to have been developed from the Aryan god Rudra.

The functions of Shiva are many. Not only is he the god of death, disease, and destruction, he is also the god of the dance. In the mythology connected with Shiva, there is frequently some statement about his dancing. He is a special god to Hindu ascetics, probably because in the process of tormenting and destroying their flesh, this terrible deity is the one who is closest to reality for them. One of the most common symbols of Shiva is the trident. Frequently, ascetics are seen carrying a trident or have the form of a trident painted on their faces.

Perhaps the most important reason for Shiva's popularity is that he is also the god of vegetable, animal, and human reproduction. In Indian thought, death is but the prelude to rebirth. Therefore, it follows that the god of death will also be a god of reproduction and sexuality. In the mythology of Shiva, he is described as having a constantly erect penis and as being sexually alert at all times. Other symbols that depict Shiva are the *lingam* and the *yoni*, the male and female sexual organs, respectively. Thus Shiva becomes the special deity of those who seek fertility or who use sex as a basis for religion.

A Hindu goddess in a temple in Kuala Lumpur, Malaysia. Hindus are a substantial minority in the predominantly Muslim country in Southeast Asia.
(Mark R. Woodward)

Devotees of Shiva are known as Shivaites (or Shaivites). Several sects of Shivaism (Shaivism) exist in Hinduism today. All regard the Vedas and special Shivaite texts as scriptures. Their philosophical stance is that Shiva is ultimate reality; he is creator, preserver, and destroyer. Humans are thought to be separated from Shiva because of ignorance, karma, and illusion. To achieve union with Shiva, people must follow a prescribed path and worship and attend Shiva in his temples. They must also meditate and study under the direction of a guru. Some Shivaites require the repetition of a special mantra. All of these acts culminate in a union between Shiva and the worshipper and ultimately result in *moksha* (release from the death-rebirth cycle).

Fully as popular as Shiva are his various consorts. Numerous goddesses are associated with him; but the most important and most popular are Kali or, as she is sometimes called, Durga, and Paravati. Kali is, if anything, more terrible than Shiva. She is frequently depicted as wearing a necklace of human skulls, tearing away the flesh of sacrificed victims, and drinking blood. Mythology connects her with the founding of the modern city of Calcutta.

From the Source

When Kali died, Shiva was both grief-stricken and angry. He placed her corpse on his shoulders and went stamping round the world in a dervish dance of mourning which became more furious the longer it lasted. The other gods realized that unless Shiva was stopped the whole world would be destroyed by his rage, which was unlikely to end as long as he had his wife's body on his shoulders. So Vishnu took up a knife and flung it at the corpse, dismembering it into fifty-two pieces which were scattered across the face of the earth. By the side of a great river in Bengal the little toe of the right foot landed, and a temple was built there, with an attendant village, and the people called this place Kalikata.[39]

Paravati is very nearly the opposite of Kali. She is the daughter of the Himalayas and the female element of the perfect loving couple when paired with the gentler aspect of Shiva. Paravati is often depicted as the perfect wife and mother. Because of her desire to marry Shiva, she undertakes the practice of asceticism. It is her responsibility to persuade Shiva to stop his meditation and use his powers for the benefit of the world. She is also a fertility goddess. Like that of Shiva, the mythology of Paravati emphasizes the aesetic as well as the erotic aspects of her personality. In her destructive mode, she is often depicted riding a lion.[40]

VISHNU. The third god of the postclassical Hindu triad is Vishnu, the preserver. In contrast to Shiva, Vishnu is known as a god of love, benevolence, and forgiveness. One of his chief characteristics is his love of play. He plays and joins humanity in play. He enjoys tricks and pranks. The chief feature of Vishnu is his concern for humanity, which he expresses by appearing on earth a number of times in various forms (*avatars*). According to mythology, Vishnu has appeared on earth in nine forms. In some incarnations, he has come as a man. According to the *Bhagavad Gita*, he has appeared as Krishna. As Hinduism absorbed the distinctive features of Buddhism, it was taught that Vishnu had appeared as Gautama, the Buddha. He has purportedly also come to earth as various animals and creatures involved in helping people. For example, it is believed that Vishnu appeared as Matsya, the fish who saved Manu from the great flood. In every case, he has come to aid humankind because he is the preserver and the restorer. The tenth *avatar* of Vishnu will occur at the end of the age, when he will appear as Kalkin on a white horse. He will bring time to an end, punish the wicked, and reward the virtuous.

Ganesha is one of the most popular Hindu gods. He is the son of Shiva and Paravati. He is known as the patron of scribes and accountants and as "the remover of obstacles." Every Hindu divinity is associated with an animal. Ganesha's is the rat pictured here.
(Mark R. Woodward)

Devotees of Vishnu are known as Vaishnavites. In India, they are noted for their deep love of God and for the poems and songs they write in his praise. Kabir and Nanak, the founders of Sikhism, were poets in this tradition. Like the Shivaites, the worshippers of Vishnu regard their god as ultimate reality. Generally, they emphasize the love and grace of Vishnu rather than the actions of devotees.

Lakshmi is the wife of Vishnu. She is believed to have risen from the ocean to ensure the fertility and welfare of the world. She is the goddess of fertility and wealth and also of victory. On the Indonesian islands of Java and Bali, where she is known as Sri, she is worshipped as the goddess of rice. She is often seen as a mediator between humans and Vishnu, who is sometimes too remote for humans to approach directly. Lakshmi is also known for her complete devotion to her husband, despite his frequent extramarital affairs. The love of Vishnu and Lakshmi is the central theme in the second of the great Indian epic poems, the *Ramayana*. In this tale, Vishnu and Lakshmi are born in the world as Rama and Sita. The story focuses on Rama's quest to find and rescue his beloved Sita when she is kidnapped by Rawana, the king of the demons.

An extreme example of devotion to one god has become familiar in many major American cities in the past few decades—the so-called *Hare Krishna* movement. This group of devotees of the god Krishna traces its origin to the appearance of Krishna in human form, as recorded in the *Bhagavad Gita*. From that time onward, a group of people in India has devoted themselves totally to the worship and adoration of Krishna.

Devotion to Knowledge

In postclassical Hinduism, people could choose one or more of the gods and devote themselves to those gods and their temples. This was probably the most acceptable and convenient path for most people. An equally acceptable way for those who could follow it was the so-called way of knowledge (*jnana-marga*). For the wealthy or the intellectual who had the time to spend studying the various philosophical implications of sacred writings, the way of knowledge had merit.

Generally, when one speaks of the way of knowledge in Hinduism, one refers to the various systems of philosophy (*darshan*). These systems are Sankhya, Yoga, Mimansa, Vaisheshika, Nyaya, and Vedanta. All claim to be based on the Vedas, all aim at release, and all believe in rebirth and pre-existence. Although the number of philosophical systems usually is limited to these six, many other lesser systems and variations exist within the six.

THE SANKHYA SYSTEM. The Sankhya system of philosophy is said to have been founded by the sage Kapila, who lived during the sixth century B.C.E. The Sankhya system arose during the era of the founding of Jainism and Buddhism; it apparently influenced both of these religions and was in turn influenced by them. Like Jainism and early Buddhism, the Sankhya system recognizes no personal gods and may be viewed as an atheistic approach to life. As does Jainism, it sees the universe as a dualism of the forces of spirit (*purusha*) and matter (*prakriti*). All that exists are these two forces, and from them springs all that we know in the world.

THE YOGA SYSTEM. Of all the Hindu philosophies, Yoga is the best known to Westerners, although they tend to think only of physical (*Hatha*) Yoga, or of the various extremes of asceticism that the Yogin may achieve. The word Yoga is derived from the root *yuj*, "to yoke" or "to join." Yoga basically follows the philosophical views of the Sankhya system, viewing the world as a dualism and teaching that one should attempt to yoke or join the individual spirit to god, the atman, to Brahman.

Statues and seals depicting persons in various yogic positions have been found in the remains of the pre-Aryan cities dating back to the third millennium B.C.E. However, the philosophy of Yoga as it is known today was developed by the sage Patanjal, who lived in the second century B.C.E. and codified the teachings of Yoga in his *Yoga Sutra*.

Lakshmi Puja, worship of the Goddess of Prosperity and Fertility in Central India.
(Doranne Jacobson/International Images)

The main feature of all Yoga is meditation. Meditation is necessary even for the gods if they are to find release from the cycle of birth, death, and rebirth. There are several forms of Yoga, each having several features and each emphasizing a different one. Raja Yoga stresses mental and spiritual development. In this form of yogic discipline, one works through various stages to free the mind from anger, lust, hatred, greed, and so on. According to the *Yoga Sutra*, there are eight steps one must take to achieve trance or the superconscious level in Raja Yoga.

1. Before one can progress, one must take certain vows of restraint (*yama*). These are vows against harming living creatures and against unchastity.
2. At this stage, one attempts to achieve internal control, calmness, and equanimity (*niyama*).
3. In the third stage, one learns and practices certain bodily postures (*asana*) designed to help one achieve the aims of Yoga.[41]

4. Once the postures have been mastered, one works on breath control (*pranayama*).
5. The fifth stage is control of the senses (*pratyahara*), in which one seeks to shut out the outside world.
6. The sixth stage is extreme concentration on a single object (*dharana*).
7. Then, one seeks to achieve meditation (*dhyana*).
8. Finally, the Yogin seeks a trance (*samadhi*), in which the Yogin becomes one with the Brahman.

Those who work through these steps achieve great physical powers and remarkable abilities of concentration. The ascetics who master Yoga are those who perform the outstanding feats of asceticism that have come to be identified with Yoga in the Western mind.

THE MIMANSA SYSTEM. Purva Mimansa, the full name of the Mimansa system of philosophy, means "early examination" of the Vedas. The primary scriptures for the advocates of this system are the Vedas and the *Mimansa Sutra*, which was written about 200 B.C.E. The leading advocates of the Mimansa philosophy were Kumarila and Prabhakara, who lived in the eighth century C.E.

Vishnu, the preserver, one of the three most important gods of Hinduism, is depicted with Garuda, a mythological bird, at a Balinese temple, ca. 1600 C.E. *(Mark R. Woodward)*

The primary concern of Mimansa is the avoidance of rebirth. This is accomplished by obeying the laws laid down in the Vedas and by performing the rites established in them. Early advocates rejected the existence of gods, but by the eighth century B.C.E. some philosophers of this system were known to offer prayers to Shiva.

THE VAISHESHIKA SYSTEM. The root meaning of Vaisheshika is "particularity." The Vaisheshika system of philosophy probably arose in the sixth century B.C.E. at the time of the founding of Buddhism and Jainism. The founder of Vaisheshika was Kanada, who wrote the primary document, the *Vaisheshika Sutra*. In contrast to the philosophies that teach that there is no reality except Brahman, the Vaisheshika teaches that the universe is composed of nine distinct elements: earth, water, air, fire, soul, mind, ether, time, and space. Because these elements are eternal and uncreated, no gods are needed in the universe. Later philosophers of this system adopted the idea of a Supreme Being who guides the universe.

THE NYAYA SYSTEM. The Nyaya philosophical system has adopted the metaphysical scheme of the Vaisheshika system and is often paired with it by those who classify Indian philosophies. Nyaya was founded by a man named Gautama who lived in the third century B.C.E. and wrote the *Nyaya Sutra*. Gautama has been called "the Aristotle of India" by some students of philosophy. Like the advocates of Vaisheshika, he was essentially atheistic and believed in the reality of the world. He therefore reasoned that individuals can have a real knowledge of the world. Thus, the Nyaya system is primarily concerned with logical analysis as a means of arriving at a truth about the world.

THE VEDANTA SYSTEM. The term Vedanta is usually translated "the end of the Vedas," thus indicating that the major materials in these systems are taken from the Upanishads, which are placed at the end of the Vedic literature. The term is also translated as "the acme of the Vedas," indicating that the Vedanta philosophy is the very peak of the religious teaching found in the Vedas. Regardless of the interpretation, Vedanta philosophy is based on the Upanishadic writings and their outlook on life. It is believed that the Vedanta philosophy was first formulated by a sage named Badarayana, who may have lived during the first century B.C.E. and may have written the *Vedanta Sutra*.

In contrast to the Sankhya system, the Vedanta is monistic and assumes only one true essence in the universe. This essence may be called God, or Brahman. Nothing else exists but Brahman. The world of humankind, its bodies, souls, and material substances, does not really exist. The world as we perceive it is based on false knowledge (*maya*), which conceals the reality of Brahman. Humans do not recognize Brahman but instead try to cling to the objects of life, which are like mirages—they keep slipping from our grasp. In truth, only Brahman is real. Therefore, humankind's basic problem is not wickedness but ignorance. People are ignorant about the true nature of reality and believe that they are separated from Brahman. This ignorance thus binds them endlessly to the cycle of birth and rebirth until they can achieve liberation through knowledge.

One branch of Vedanta that developed in the ninth century C.E. is called Advaita, which means "non-dual" and indicates its monistic viewpoint. Its founder was Shankara (788–820 C.E.), who was perhaps the most outstanding scholar of medieval Hinduism. Although he was a famous ascetic and teacher in his time, he is best known for his philosophical approach in interpreting the Upanishads. His abilities and reputation as a philosopher have prompted some Western readers to refer to Shankara as the "Aquinas of Hinduism." His most outstanding literary contribution is a commentary on the *Vedanta Sutra*. This commentary has become such a classic in Hindu literature that it has been the object of several commentaries. In his commentary, Shankara asserted the absolute oneness of Brahman in the classic manner of the Upanishads. Brahman is all there is. All else in the universe is an illusion, and people are bound up in endless reincarnations until they rip aside the veil of this illusion. Shankara himself was a devotee of Shiva, because he believed that Shiva was the best representation of the true nature of Brahman.

Shankara is also remembered for his fierce opposition to Buddhism. It is thought that his leadership against Buddhism was a major factor in destroying this religion in India and restoring Hinduism to its dominant position.

According to one story, Shankara did not die; he simply disappeared. Consequently, some Shivaites believe that the great scholar was actually an avatar of Shiva.

Prambanan, a tenth-century Hindu temple dedicated to the three major gods, Brahma, Vishnu, and Shiva, near Yogyakarta, Indonesia.
(Mark R. Woodward)

A second philosopher of the medieval period in Hinduism, who represents a side in the debate over the true meaning of the Vedas, was Ramanuja (ca. 1056–1137 C.E.). Ramanuja believed that devotion to the gods was extremely important. He was himself devoted to the worship of Vishnu. He reasoned that if Shankara were correct and if each person were merely a part of the god Brahman, then devotion to god would not be possible, for how can one be devoted to oneself? Although he could not move away from the traditional Vedanta position of the oneness of god, Ramanuja taught a qualified dualism in which he asserted that the human soul and the divine soul were united and yet somehow separate. The analogy that he used was the human body and spirit—one cannot exist without the other, but they are separate entities.

The third point of view in this debate was presented by the philosopher Madhva (1199–1278 C.E.). Like Ramanuja, Madhva was devoted to the god Vishnu and believed strongly in devotion to the gods as the only proper religious expression. He was willing to go further than Ramanuja, however. He took the side of dualism even though he remained in the general school of Vedanta. He abandoned completely the notion that god was all and that all else was illusion. To him, the world and individual souls were completely separate from Brahman and separate from one another. Thus, each individual and separate soul is able to worship properly the separate nature of god.

Muslim Influences in India

In the seventh century C.E., a new and vital religion sprang from the deserts of Arabia. Within a few decades, the religion of Islam had spread, through conquest and conversion, across the entire Middle Eastern world. By the eighth century, it was on the verge of moving into Europe. Muslims also moved eastward and by the eighth century had conquered Persia and Afghanistan and made occasional raids into India.

Portions of northwest India were conquered by Muslim leaders as early as 712 C.E. In the eleventh century, the Turkish general Mahmud of Ghazni invaded India seventeen times and brought a vast treasure to his headquarters in Afghanistan. By the thirteenth century, Islam was so well entrenched in India that there was a Sultanate of Delhi. In the sixteenth century, a dynasty of Turkish rulers, known as the Moghuls, established an empire and ruled most of the subcontinent of India. Most of the Moghul emperors sought to accommodate their Hindu subjects. By the eighteenth century, however, this empire had run its course and had decayed into many small warring states that became easy prey for the invading British armies. Despite its political and economic decline, the Moghul Empire retained its symbolic importance until its final destruction in 1857.

Religion and Violence

In 1857, Hindu and Muslim *sepoys* (soldiers) of the British East India Company joined together in a rebellion against the British when they began to use a combination of beef suet and lard to grease rifles. The beef suet was considered to be defiling by Hindus and the lard equally so by Muslims. This led to one of the deadliest outbreaks of religious violence in history. Hindus and Muslims massacred Christians and were in turn massacred by them with the aid of Sikhs. Strangely, the British spared the last of the Moghul emperors, Bahadur Shah Zafar II. He was sent to Rangoon, Burma, in exile, where he died in 1862. He was buried in an unmarked grave. The location was not discovered until 1991. It has since become an important pilgrimage site for Indian Muslims, particularly politicians.

Today, there are more Muslims on the Indian subcontinent than there are anywhere else in the world. India has the world's second-largest Muslim population. Only Indonesia's is larger. Relations between Hindus and Muslims have always been touchy. Indeed, it would be difficult to find two religions more different than Hinduism and Islam. Whereas Muslims are staunchly monotheistic, Hindus tend to be limitlessly polytheistic; whereas Muslims disdain the representation of Allah in any form, Hindus have richly decorated temples, their homes, and in modern times their cars and trucks with images portraying their many gods; whereas Muslims sacrifice cattle and other animals in commemoration of the Biblical and Quranic account of Abraham's willingness to sacrifice his son at God's command, Hindus regard the cow as a sacred animal and seek to protect it from any harm; and whereas Muslims regard every person as equal before Allah, Hindus have traditionally followed a caste system that divides society into classes, with the upper classes having more religious privileges than the lower.

Early Muslim visitors to India were amazed at the openness of Hindu theology. Al-Biruni, a Muslim writer from the eleventh century, described the Hindus in the following terms:

From the Source

They totally differ from us in religion, as we believe in nothing in which they believe, and vice versa. On the whole there is very little disputing about theological topics among themselves; at the utmost, they fight with words, but they will never stake their soul or body or their property on religious controversy.[42]

Despite these vast differences, Hindus and Muslims have managed to live side by side for more than 1,000 years. Hinduism has not altered its basic theology in light of its contacts with Islam, but Indian society has adopted many of the elements of the Muslim culture. Particularly during the years of the Moghul Empire, Indian society was influenced by the art, architecture, sciences, and even the dress styles of the Muslim world. Over the centuries, Hinduism and Islam have also converged in important ways. Many Muslims have adopted caste as a mode of social organization. There are also shrines and saints that both members of both communities venerate.

In the fifteenth century, there arose the most notable attempt at reconciliation between Islam and Hinduism: the religion of Sikhism. Sikhism is discussed in detail in Chapter 7; however, it must be said at this point that Sikhism managed to attain a harmony between the uncompromising monotheism of Islam and the doctrines of illusion and reincarnation of Hinduism. It must also be said that, whereas Hindus and Muslims have somehow managed to live together in India, the religious and political differences between the two peoples are one of the major problems facing India today.

Modern Hinduism

Hinduism, like all major religions, has had to face the rigors of the modern age, with its nationalistic movements, its social reforms, its encounters between religions, and its scientific revolutions. Of the factors of the modern era that have affected Hinduism, one of the most important has been its encounter with Christianity and its European and American representatives. According to tradition, Christianity was brought to India by the disciple Thomas in the first century C.E. Christian communities existed in southern India many centuries before the arrival of the Europeans. However, Christianity had little effect on the vast majority of Indian people until more recent times. In premodern times, Christians were treated as simply another caste, in much the same way Muslims were in large parts of India. However, when Christianity was encountered in conjunction with the political power of the British Empire and modern scientific knowledge, it had to be taken as a more serious challenge.

The first significant encounter between India and the modern European nations came in 1510, when the Portuguese conquered Goa. In the seventeenth century, the British invaded India and established the British East India Company. This began three centuries of British rule in India. Though the British were present in India as merchants and soldiers, it was not until the nineteenth century that they allowed missionaries to

Images of Gods and Goddesses in a Hindu shop in Singapore.
(Mark R. Woodward)

enter the country to try to convert the Indians. One of the reasons for this late entry was that many Protestant denominations did not actively seek to send missionaries earlier.

One of the British missionaries to enter India was the Baptist William Carey (1761–1834). Like many other missionaries of the nineteenth century, Carey was concerned not only with preaching the gospel of his faith but also with raising the living and educational standards of the people to whom he ministered. He was the first to begin modern printing in India, and he also initiated many new educational programs for the Indian people. Carey, along with other missionaries, was alarmed at several practices he felt were inhuman and harmful within Indian social life. One of these was the *suttee*, in which an Indian widow was expected to be placed on the funeral pyre of her dead husband and be destroyed with his remains. *Suttee* was more social than religious in origin. Indeed, passages in Hindu sacred literature speak against the practice. *Suttee* had also been rejected by many Hindu reformers, such as Ram Mohan Roy. At the insistence of Christians and reform-minded Hindus, the British government outlawed the practice in 1829. Another practice that was abhorrent to the European missionary was child marriages. It had become common in India for parents to betroth their young children to ensure a suitable marriage.[43] One of the primary concerns of parents in arranging marriages was that their children should marry within their caste. Frequently, this meant the betrothal of very young children and the marriage of nine- and ten-year-olds, which was particularly harsh for girls, who might have been promised by their parents to men twenty or thirty years their senior. This practice tended to ensure that when a husband died he left behind a fairly young widow who was not allowed to remarry and in some cases was expected to destroy herself. Eventually, child marriage also was officially outlawed in India.

The late nineteenth and twentieth centuries saw several reform movements in Hinduism. One of the earliest reformers was Ram Mohan Roy (1774–1833), who was called "the Father of Modern India." As noted above, Roy opposed *suttee* and pressured the British government to outlaw the practice. He saw in Christianity many elements he appreciated, although he did not accept the divinity of Jesus. Ram Mohan Roy tended to be a monotheist and sought to suppress what he perceived to be the polytheism and idolatry of Hinduism. To continue his work after his death, Roy organized the Brahmo Samaj (The Society of God), which became a major force in the renewal of India in the nineteenth and twentieth centuries.

Perhaps the greatest religious reformer of the nineteenth century was Sri Ramakrishna (1836–1886). Once a priest of Kali in Calcutta, Ramakrishna was philosophically a follower of non-dualistic Vedanta. He later became convinced that behind all religions was a single reality that might be called God. His religious experience with Christians and Muslims, as well as Hindus, convinced him that truth was essentially one. The teachings of Ramakrishna might have died with him in India had it not been for one of his disciples, Narendranath Dutt (1863–1902), who was later known as Vivekananda. Vivekananda became a member of the Brahmo Samaj early in life. Later, he met Ramakrishna and became his apostle. After a period of several years of retreat in the Himalayas, he set forth to be the first Hindu missionary to the modern world. Vivekananda traveled widely, lecturing about the virtues of Vedanta Hinduism, which he described as "the mother of all other religions." He made his greatest impression at the Parliament of Religions in Chicago in 1893 as the representative of Hinduism. Wherever he went, this spokesman for the oneness of God captivated audiences and produced converts. Vivekananda was followed by Paramahansa Ananda (1893–1952), who came to the United States in 1920 and founded the Self Realization Fellowship, which teaches a form of Vedanta philosophy that draws its inspiration from the Christian gospels as well as the sacred texts of Hinduism. The Fellowship is particularly active in California, and also has branches in India, Europe, and most of the major cities of the United States.

The best known Indian reformer of the twentieth century was Mohandas K. Gandhi (1869–1948). Gandhi is chiefly remembered for his work in bringing political and social benefits to the Indian people near the end of British rule, through a combination of religious idealism and civil disobedience. In his childhood, Gandhi was deeply influenced by Hinduism, its literature and ideals. He also encountered Jains, Muslims, and Parsis. Gandhi was originally trained as a lawyer in England, where he came into contact with many of the social and political ideas of the nineteenth century. He also was introduced to Christianity, especially to Jesus' Sermon on the Mount. These factors, along with the ideals of his Hindu heritage, molded Gandhi. As the leader of the Indian people in their struggle for freedom from British rule, he personally led many fasts and strikes against various British policies and usually was victorious. In addition to espousing civil disobedience and non-violence, Gandhi also was influenced by the Jain teaching of non-injury of life (*ahimsa*). Thus, he was a vegetarian and stoutly defended the Indian practice of cow protection. Gandhi also read the works of the American Henry David Thoreau

(1817–1862), who advocated passive resistance to civil authority. In turn, Gandhi became one of the models for the political thinking of Martin Luther King, Jr., who led the Civil Rights movement in the United States during the 1960s. Gandhi, who advocated non-violence, was assassinated by an extremist Hindu Nationalist 1948, just a few months after his people won their independence.

An object of special concern for internal and external reformers is the caste system. Although the ancient Hindu literature spoke of society's being divided into four *varnas* (colors), the full-blown caste system is a relatively modern development. In early Hinduism, there is evidence of social intercourse among classes. At some point after 700 C.E., the modern caste system began to develop. The four basic social groups proceeded to divide into literally thousands of castes. Most frequently, these castes are based on vocations. There are castes of metal workers, weavers, warriors, priests and many other professions. Other castes developed along ethnic or religious lines. Tribal communities, as well as Muslims, Christians, and Jews, were incorporated into Hindu society as distinct caste groups. Ultimately, more than 3,000 separate castes emerged in Indian society. When the Portuguese came to India in the sixteenth century, they gave their word *casta* (breed, race) to these divisions.[44]

The caste system dominates every aspect of life in traditional Hindu society. One enters a caste by being born to parents of that caste. One's caste dictates diet, vocation, place of residence, and choice of mate. Complex rules regulate social intercourse among members of different castes. Caste hierarchy is based on concepts of purity and pollution. The greater one's contact with the sources of pollution—blood, death, and dirt—the lower one's position in the system. Many Brahmins, who are the highest caste, refrain from any contact with pollution and consequently are strict vegetarians. One can accept cooked food only from people of equal or higher rank. Consequently many restaurants are run by Brahmins.

Dalits, the lowest caste, who are sometimes referred to as untouchables, perform such tasks as sweeping streets, cleaning latrines, handling the dead, tanning leather, and washing clothes, which bring them into constant contact with sources of pollution. With these vocations come the lowest wages, the worst living conditions, and little hope of improvement. Generally speaking, members of higher castes have few, if any, social contacts with members of these groups. They will give gifts to or accept gifts from them. Traditionally, they were forced to live in segregated compounds on the east sides of villages for fear that the prevailing westerly winds might exposes other castes to airborne pollution. It is, however, important to note that despite the fact that the untouchables are thought of as defiled, Hindu society cannot function without them because their work enables members of the higher castes to live without coming into contact with polluting substances.[45]

Traditional Hinduism seems to justify the status of the outcasts. Because the untouchables are in this situation in life, it must be because their karma from a previous life dictates it. If the outcasts accept the *dharma* (duty) of this life and do not rebel against it, they may hope for a better caste in the next life. As a result of the efforts of reformers like Gandhi, discrimination against the outcasts was officially forbidden in the 1948 *Constitution of the Republic of India*. Gandhi referred to the untouchables as *harijan* (children of God) and taught that because of their long and quiet suffering they had earned the respect and affection of both the gods and humans. Many lower-caste Hindus converted to Islam or Christianity. Conversion is not a fully effective remedy for the inequalities of caste because upper-caste Hindus continue to treat the converts as they always have. The long-standing, firmly entrenched rules of caste die slowly in modern India.

Hindu Holy Days

Because Hindus worship a variety of gods and goddesses, there are a tremendous variety of festivals, fasts, feasts, and pilgrimages in Hinduism. Millions of Hindus make pilgrimages to the holy Ganges River each year to bathe in its waters and to fulfill their vows. In addition to the holy days dedicated to the various deities and holy places, festivals are held in relation to the seasons. It would be impossible to describe all of these holy days in one brief chapter; however, several general festivals that are celebrated throughout India will be discussed.

Holi

Holi is the most popular festival. It is celebrated each year during February/March to welcome spring. Holi is dedicated to the god Krishna, and it was once a fertility ceremony. This festival also celebrates the destruction of demons. During the days of Holi, many of the caste and taboo restrictions are set aside and pleasure is emphasized.

Divali

In November, Hindus welcome the new year, which is also a festival of lights. The goddesses Kali (the consort of Shiva) and Lakshmi (good fortune) are connected to Divali.

Hindu pilgrims bathing in the Ganges, the most sacred river in India.
(Air India Library)

Devotees may choose to make pilgrimages to the holy sites connected to the story of Kali at this season. Lakshmi visits every house that is lit with a lamp and brings to it prosperity and good fortune.

Dasehra

Nine days in October are reserved for this celebration in honor of Durga, a consort of Shiva. Dasehra celebrates Durga's victory over the Buffalo demon. Presents are exchanged, and dances and processions are held to honor the goddess.

Hinduism Today

Like all religions, Hinduism today must struggle with the issue of modernity. Its primary home, India, is the world's largest democracy; therefore, the demands of its people must be heard. Perhaps for the first time in its history, Hinduism must deal with such issues as birth control and the problems raised by urbanization. In the past, people were taught to accept their lots in life and not complain, in that the next life might be better. If problems became so severe that one could not endure them, there was always the alternative of life as an ascetic.

Religion and Violence

Conflicts between religious communities are still an important issue. There is a long history of what is called "communal violence" in India. The partition of British India into India and Pakistan in 1947 led to horrific acts of violence in both countries. The rise of Hindu fundamentalism and the demand for the establishment of India as a Hindu theocracy in the 1990s has heightened the tension between the Hindus and Muslims. The inability of India and Pakistan to resolve their differences concerning the Muslim majority state of Kashmir is a continuing source of tension and intermittent violence. In 2002, as many as 2,000 people were killed—many of them burned alive—in riots sparked by a dispute over a shrine in the city of Ayodhya that Muslims consider to be the oldest mosque in India and that militant Hindus believe to be the birthplace of the Hindu god Rama. The violence has led to increasing segregation along religious lines. In many cities in Northwest India traveling to a Muslim area is now referred to as "going to Pakistan." The continuing demands of militant Sikhs to create an independent state have led to even further complications. The conversion of Dalits to Christianity has led Hindu extremists to attack churches and violently disrupt worship services. In areas of Northeast India, where the vast majority of the population are Baptists, there have been insurgencies since the earliest days of independence. Hindu extremists refer to the insurgents as "Christian terrorists." The insurgents call themselves "Baptist Nationalists." The bloodshed between religious groups is likely to continue into the future.

In other parts of the world, Hinduism faces different challenges. The Balinese Hindus are a small minority in the overwhelmingly Muslim nation of Indonesia. Their minority status, coupled with the increasing role of Islam in public life, sometimes makes it difficult for the Balinese to fully participate in national affairs. Hindus in Western countries are faced with the difficulties of maintaining a religious identity in societies in which they are very small minorities and have limited access to sacred texts, temples, and religious specialists.

Hinduism is an ancient religion and has withstood many challenges over the centuries. New religions have been established and absorbed by Hinduism. Social changes have come and gone, and Hinduism remains a viable force in the lives of millions of people. Its temples, gods, and festivals continue to fulfill a need in the lives of Indians and Hindus throughout the world.

STUDY QUESTIONS

1. Outline the early history of Hinduism. How did the gods and rituals brought by the Aryans blend with native religions to produce classical Hinduism?
2. Define the *Rig-Veda*, the *Upanishads*, and the *Law of Manu*. Show how these three bodies of literature demonstrate basic Hindu religious concepts.
3. Discuss Jainism and Buddhism as heresies of Hinduism. What was the fate of these two religions in India? Elsewhere in Asia?
4. What central lesson must Arjuna learn from his conversation with Krishna in the *Bhagavad Gita*?
5. List the three major gods of modern Hinduism and give a brief description of each.
6. Discuss the role of goddesses in Hinduism.
7. Describe the central features of the caste system.
8. Contrast Hinduism with Islam.

SUGGESTED READING

Chaudhuri, Nirad C. *Hinduism*. New York: Oxford University Press, 1979.

Dalrymple, William. The Last Mughal: The Fall of a Dynasty: Delhi 1857. London: Knopf, 2006. This is a history of Delhi during the Indian Mutiny of 1857.

Dirks, Nicholas B. *Castes of Mind: Colonialism and the Making of Modern India*. Princeton: Princeton University Press, 2001

Eck, Diana. *Darsan: Seeing the Divine Image in India*. Chambersburg: Anima Books, 1985.

Dimmitt, Cornelia, and J. A. B. van Buitenen. *Classical Hindu Mythology. A Reader in the Sanskrit Puranas*. Philadelphia: Temple University Press, 1978.

Feldhaus, Anne. *Water and Womanhood. Religious Meaning of Rivers in Maharashtra*. New York: Oxford University Press, 1995.

Hopkins, Thomas J. *The Hindu Religious Tradition*. Encino, CA: Dickenson, 1971.

Hume, Robert Ernest. *The Thirteen Principal Upanishads*. New York: Oxford University Press, 1971.

Koller, John M. *The Indian Way*. New York: Macmillan, 1982.

Zaehner, R. C., trans. *The Bhagavad-Gita*. New York: Oxford University Press, 1969.

SOURCE MATERIAL

Selections from the *Rig-Veda*

The basis of all later Hindu scripture is the *Rig-Veda*, the ancient collection of hymns to the Aryan gods. The following are representative selections from this book.

Varuna and Indra
Rig-Veda, IV. 42, 1–7, 10

1. I am the royal Ruler, mine is empire, as mine who sway all life are all the Immortals. Varuna's will the Gods obey and follow. I am the king of men's lofty cover.
2. I am King Varuna. To me was given these first existing high celestial powers. Varuna's will the Gods obey and follow. I am the King of Men's most lofty cover.
3. I Varuna am Indra; in their greatness, these the two wide deep fairly fashioned regions. These the two world-halves have I, even as Tvashtar knowing all beings, joined and held together.
4. I made to flow the moisture shedding waters, and set the heaven firm in the seat of Order. By Law, the son of Aditi, Law-Observer, hath spread abroad the world in threefold measure.
5. Heroes with noble horses, fain for battle, selected warriors, call on men in combat. I Indra Maghavan, excite the conflict; I stir the dust, Lord of surpassing vigour.
6. All this I did. The god's own conquering power never impedeth me to whom none opposeth. When lauds and Soma juice have made me joyful, both the unbounded regions are affrighted.
7. All beings know these deeds of thine; thou tellest this unto Varuna, thou great Disposer! Thou art renowned as having slain the Vritras. Thou madest flow the floods that were obstructed . . . .
10. May we, possessing much, delight in riches, Gods in oblations and the kine in pasture; And that Milch-cow who shrinks not from the milking, O Indra-Varuna, give to us daily.[46]

"What God Shall We Adore with Our Oblation?"
Rig-Veda, X. 121, 1–10

1. In the beginning rose Hiranyagarbha, born Only Lord of all created beings. He fixed and holdeth up this earth and heaven. What God shall we adore with our oblation?
2. Giver of vital breath, of power and vigour, he whose commandments all the gods acknowledge; The Lord of death, whose shade is life immortal. What God shall we adore with our oblation?
3. Who by his grandeur hath become Sole Ruler of all the moving world that breathes and slumbers; He who is Lord of men and Lord of cattle. What God shall we adore with our oblations?
4. His, through his might, are these snow-covered mountains, and men call sea and Rasa his possession; His arms are these, his are these heavenly regions. What God shall we adore with our oblation?
5. By him the heavens are strong and earth is steadfast, by him light's realm and sky-vault are supported; By him the regions in mid-air were measured. What God shall we adore with our oblation?
6. To him, supported by his help, two armies embattled look while trembling in their spirit. When over them the risen Sun is shining. What God shall we adore with our oblation?

7. What time the mighty waters came, containing the universal germ, producing Agni, Then sprang the Gods' one spirit into being. What God shall we adore with our oblation?

8. He in his might surveyed the floods containing productive force and generating Worship. He is the God of gods, and none beside him. What God shall we adore with our oblation?

9. Ne'er may he harm us who is earth's Begetter, nor he whose laws are sure, the heaven's creator, he who brought forth the great and lucid waters. What God shall we adore with our oblation?

10. Prajapati! thou only comprehendest all these created things, and none beside thee. Grant us our heart's desire when we invoke thee; may we have store in riches in possession 47

Selections from Upanishads

Upanishads are philosophical writings from the classical teachers of Hinduism. The following is a description of the moment of death.[48]

When this self gets to weakness, gets to confusedness, as it were, then the breaths gather round him. He takes to himself those particles of light and descends into the heart. When the person in the eye turns away, then he becomes non-knowing of forms.

(When his body grows weak and he becomes apparently unconscious, the dying man gathers his senses about him, completely withdraws their powers, and descends into the heart. *Radhakrishnan.*)

He is becoming one, he does not see, they say; he is becoming one, he does not smell, they say; he is becoming one, he does not taste, they say; he is becoming one, he does not speak, they say; he is becoming one, he does not hear, they say; he is becoming one, he does not think, they say; he is becoming one, he does not touch, they say; he is becoming one, he does not know, they say. The point of his heart becomes lighted up and by the light the self departs either through the eye or through the head or through other apertures of the body. And when he thus departs, life departs after him. And when life thus departs, all the vital breaths depart after him. He becomes one with intelligence. What has intelligence departs with him. His knowledge and his work take hold of him as also his past experience. (*Brihad-aranyaka Upanishad,* IV. 4, 1, 2.)

Verily, when a person departs from this world, he goes to the air. It opens out there for him like the hole of a chariot wheel. Through that he goes upwards. He goes to the sun. It opens out there for him like the hole of a lambara. Through that he goes upwards. He reaches the moon. It opens out there for him like the hole of a drum. Through that he goes upwards. He goes to the world free from grief, free from snow. There he dwells eternal years. (Ibid, V. 11, 1.)

Selections from the *Law of Manu*

Asceticism has been associated with forms of Hinduism from its beginning. The following is a description of the life of an ascetic:

Law of Manu, VI. 33–36, 41–43, 45–49, 60–65.[49]

33. But having thus passed the third part of (a man's natural term of) life in the forest, he may live as an ascetic during the fourth part of his existence, after abandoning all attachments to worldly objects.

34. He who after passing from order to order, after offering sacrifices and subduing his senses, becomes, tired with (giving) alms and offerings of food, an ascetic, gains bliss after death.

35. When he has paid the three debts, let him apply his mind to (the attainment of) final liberation; he who seeks it without having paid (his debts) sinks downwards.

36. Having studied the Vedas in accordance with the rule, having begat sons according to the sacred law, and having offered sacrifices according to his ability, he may direct his mind to (the attainment of) final liberation.

41. Departing from his house fully provided with the means of purification (Pavitra), let him wander about absolutely silent, and caring nothing for enjoyments that may be offered (to him).

42. Let him always wander alone, without any companion, in order to attain (final liberation), fully understanding that the solitary (man, who) neither forsakes nor is forsaken, gains his end.

43. He shall neither possess a fire, nor a dwelling, he may go to a village for his food, (he shall be) indifferent to everything, firm of purpose, meditating (and) concentrating his mind on Brahman.

45. Let him not desire to die, let him not desire to live; let him wait for (his appointed) time, as a servant (waits) for the payment of his wages.

46. Let him put down his foot purified by his sight, let him drink water purified by (straining with) a cloth, let him utter speech purified by truth, let him keep his heart pure.

47. Let him patiently bear hard words, let him not insult anybody, and let him not become anybody's enemy for the sake of this (perishable) body.

48. Against an angry man let him not in return show anger, let him bless when he is cursed, and let him not utter speech, devoid of truth, scattered at the seven gates.

49. Delighting in what refers to the Soul, sitting (in the postures prescribed by the Yoga), independent (of external help), entirely abstaining from sensual enjoyments, with himself for his only companion, he shall live in this world, desiring the bliss (of final liberation).

60. By the restraint of his senses, by the destruction of love and hatred, and by the abstention from injuring the creatures, he becomes fit for immortality.

61. Let him reflect on the transmigrations of men, caused by their sinful deeds, on their falling into hell, and on the torments in the world of Yama,

62. On the separation from their dear ones, on their union with hated men, on their being overpowered by age and being tormented with diseases,

63. On the departure of the individual soul from this body and its new birth in (another) womb, and on its wanderings through ten thousand millions of existences,

64. On the infliction of pain on embodied (spirits), which is caused by demerit, and the gain of eternal bliss, which is caused by the attainment of their highest aim, (gained through) spiritual merit.

65. By deep meditations, let him recognize the subtle nature of the supreme Soul, and its presence in all organisms, both the highest and the lowest.

Selections from the *Bhagavad Gita*

The *Bhagavad Gita,* "The Song of the Blessed Lord," is the classic poem of India. In this massive poem about a great battle, the gods take human forms and talk with mortals. In the following sections, the god Krishna speaks with the poem's hero, Arjuna, about the nature of life, death, and the gods.[50]

II. 16–27

Of what is not there is no becoming; of what there is there is no ceasing to be; for the boundary line between these two is seen by men who see things as they really are. Yes, indestructible [alone] is That—know this—by which this whole universe was spun: no one can bring destruction on That which does not pass away. Finite, they say, are these [our] bodies [indwelt] by an eternal embodied [self],—[for this self is] indestructible, incommensurable. Fight then, scion of Bharata. Who thinks this [self] can be a slayer, who thinks that it can be slain, both these have no [right] knowledge: it does not slay nor is it slain. Never is it born nor dies; never did it come to be nor will it ever come to be again: unborn, eternal, everlasting is this [self],—primeval. It is not slain when the body is slain. If a man knows it as indestructible, eternal, unborn, never to pass away, how and whom can he cause to be slain or slay? As a man casts off his worn-out clothes and takes on other new ones, so does the embodied [self] cast off its worn-out bodies and enters other new ones. Weapons do not cut it nor does fire burn it, the waters do not wet it nor does the wind dry it. Uncuttable, unburnable, unwettable, undryable it is—eternal, roving everywhere, firm-set, unmoved, primeval. Unmanifest, unthinkable, immutable is it called: then realize it thus and do not grieve [about it]. And even if you think that it is constantly [re-]born and constantly [re-]dies, even so you grieve for it in vain. For sure is the death of all that is born, sure is the birth of all that dies: so in a matter that no one can prevent you have no cause to grieve.

XI. 15–21, 24, 25, 31–34

Arjuna said: O God, the gods in your body I behold and all the hosts of every kind of being; Brahma, the lord, [I see] throned on the lotus-seat, celestial serpents and all the [ancient] seers. Arms, bellies, mouths and eyes all manifold—so do I see You wherever I may look—infinite your form! End, middle, or again beginning I cannot see in You, O Monarch Universal, [manifest] in every form! Yours the crown, the mace, the discus—a mass of glory shining on all sides—so do I see You—yet how hard are You to see,—for on every side there is brilliant light of fire and sun. Oh, who should comprehend it? You are the Imperishable, [You] wisdom's highest goal; You, of this universe the last prop—and resting place, You the changeless, [you] the guardian of eternal law, You the primeval Person; [at last] I understand. Beginning, middle, or end You do not know,—how infinite your strength! How numberless your arms,—your eyes the sun and moon! So do I see You,—your mouth a flaming fire, burning up this whole universe with your blazing glory. By You alone is this space between heaven and earth pervaded,—all points of the compass too; gazing on this, your marvellous, frightening form, the three worlds shudder, [All-] Highest Self!

Lo! These hosts of gods are entering into You; some terror-struck, extol You, hands together pressed; great seers and men perfected in serried ranks cry out, 'All hail,' and praise You with copious hymns of praise.

Ablaze with many-coloured [flames] You touch the sky, your mouths wide open, [gaping,] your eyes distended, blazing: so do I see You and my inmost self is shaken: I cannot bear it, I find no peace, O Vishnu!

I see your mouths with jagged, ghastly tusks reminding [me] of Time's [devouring] fire: I cannot find my bearings, I cannot find a refuge; have mercy, God of gods, home of the universe.

Tell me, who are You, your form so cruel? Homage to You, You best of gods, have mercy! Fain would I know You as You are in the beginning, for what You are set on doing I do not understand.

The Blessed Lord said: Time am I, wreaker of the world's destruction, matured,— [grimly] resolved here to swallow up the worlds. Do what you will, all these war-riors shall cease to be, drawn up [there] in their opposing ranks. And so stand up, win glory, conquer your enemies and win a prosperous kingdom! Long since have these men in truth been slain by Me: yours it is to be the mere occasion. Drona, Bhishma, Jayadratha, Karna, and all the other men of war are [as good as] slain by Me. Slay them then,—why falter? Fight! [for] you will conquer your rivals in the battle.

Shankara on the Nature of the Brahman

Shankara, an Indian philosopher of the ninth century C.E., was one of the founders of the non-dualistic schools of Hindu thought. His understanding of the nature of the world and of God is based on the Upanishads.[51]

But, it may be asked, is Brahman known or not known (previously to the enquiry into its nature)? If it is known we need not enter on an enquiry concerning it; if it is not known we cannot enter on such an enquiry.

We reply that Brahman is known. Brahman, which is all-knowing and endowed with all powers, whose essential nature is eternal purity, intelligence, and freedom, exists. For if we consider the derivation of the word "Brahman," from the root brih, "to the great," we at once understand that eternal purity, and so on, belong to Brahman. Moreover the existence of, Brahman is known on the ground of its being the Self of every one. For every one is conscious of the existence of (his) Self, never thinks "I am not." If the existence of the Self were not known, every one would think "I am not." And this Self (of whose existence all are conscious) is Brahman. But if Brahman is gen-erally known as the Self, there is no room for an enquiry into it! Not so, we reply; for there is a conflict of opinions as to its special nature. Unlearned people and the Lokay-atikas are of opinion that the mere body endowed with the quality of intelligence is the Self; others that the organs endowed with intelligence are the Self; others maintain that the internal organ is the Self; others, again, that the Self is a mere momentary idea; others, again, that it is the Void. Others, again (to proceed to the opinion of such as acknowledge the authority of the Veda), maintain that there is a transmigrating being different from the body, and so on, which is both agent and enjoyer (of the fruits of action); others teach that being is enjoying only, not acting; others believe that in addition to the individual souls, there is an all-knowing, all-powerful Lord. Others, finally (i.e., the Vedantins), maintain that the Lord is the Self of the enjoyer (i.e., of the individual soul whose individual existence is apparent only, the product of Nescience).

Thus there are many various opinions, basing part of them on sound arguments and scriptural texts, part of them on fallacious arguments and scriptural texts, part of them on fallacious arguments and scriptural texts misunderstood. If therefore a man would embrace some one of these opinions without previous consideration, he would bar himself from the highest beatitude and incur grievous loss.

That same highest Brahman constitutes—as we know from passages such as "that art thou"—the real nature of the individual soul (i.e., *atman*), while its second nature, i.e., that aspect of it which depends on fictitious limiting conditions, is not its real nature. For as long as the individual soul does not free itself from Nescience in the form of duality—which Nescience may be compared to the mistake of him who in the twilight mistakes a post for a man—and who does not rise to the knowledge of the Self, whose nature is unchangeable, eternal Cognition—which expresses itself in the form "I am Brahman"—so long it remains the individual soul. But when, discarding the aggregate of body, sense-organs and mind, it arrives, by means of Scripture, at the knowledge that it is not itself that aggregate, that it does not form part of transmigratory existence, but it is the True, the Real, the Self, whose nature is pure intelligence; then knowing itself to be of the nature of unchangeable, eternal Cognition, it lifts itself above the vain conceit of being one with this body, and itself becomes the Self, whose nature is unchanging, eternal Cognition. As is declared in such scriptural passages "He who knows the highest Brahman becomes even Brahman" (*Mundaka Upanishad*, III. 2, 9). And this is the real nature of the individual soul by means of which it arises from the body and appears in its own form.

There is only one highest Lord ever unchanging, whose substance is cognition (i.e., of whom cognition is not a mere attribute), and who by means of Nescience, manifests himself in various ways, just as a thaumaturg appears in different shapes by means of his magical power . . . . To the highest Self which is eternally pure, intelligent and free, which is never changing, one only, not in contact with anything, devoid of form, the opposite characteristics of the individual soul are erroneously ascribed; just as ignorant men ascribe blue color to the colorless ether.

A man may, in the dark, mistake a piece of rope lying on the ground for a snake and run away from it, frightened and trembling; thereon another man may tell him, "Do not be afraid, it is only a rope, not a snake"; and he may then dismiss the fear caused by the imagined snake, and stop running. But all the while the presence and subsequent absence of his erroneous notion, as to the rope being a snake, make no difference whatever in the rope itself. Exactly analogous is the case of the individual soul which is in reality one with the highest soul, although Nescience makes it appear different.

As therefore the individual soul and the highest Self differ in name only, it being a settled matter that perfect knowledge has for its object the absolute oneness of the two; it is senseless to insist (as some do) on a plurality of Selfs, and to maintain that the individual soul is different from the highest Self, and the highest Self from the individual soul. For the Self is indeed called by many different names, but it is one only. Nor does the passage, "He knows Brahman which is real, knowledge, infinite, as hidden in the cave" (*Taittiriya Upanishad,* II. 1), refer to some one cave (different from the abode of the individual soul). And that nobody else but Brahman is hidden in the cave we know from a subsequent passage, viz., "Having sent forth he entered into it" (*Taittiriya Upanishad,* II. 6) according to which the creator only entered into the created beings.—Those who insist on the distinction of the individual and the highest Self oppose themselves to the true sense of the Vedanta-texts, stand thereby in the way of perfect knowledge, which is the door to perfect beatitude, and groundlessly assume release to be something effected, and therefore non-eternal. (And if they attempt to show that *moksha,* although effected, is eternal) they involve themselves in a conflict with sound logic.

That Brahman is at the same time the operative cause of the world, we have to conclude from the circumstance that there is no other guiding being. Ordinarily material causes, indeed, such as lumps of clay and pieces of gold, are dependent, in order to shape themselves into vessels and ornaments, on extraneous operative causes such as potters and goldsmiths; but outside Brahman as material cause there is no other operative cause to which the material cause could look; for Scripture says that previously to creation Brahman was one without a second. The absence of a guiding principle other than the material cause can moreover be established by means of the argument made use of in the Sutra, viz., accordance with the promissory statements and the illustrative examples. If there were admitted a guiding principle different from the material cause, it would follow that everything cannot be known through one thing, and thereby the promissory statements as well as the illustrative instances would be stultified. The Self is thus the operative cause, because there is no other ruling principle, and the material cause because there is no other substance from which the world could originate.

The entire complex of phenomenal existence is considered as true as long as the knowledge of Brahman being the Self of all has not arisen; just as the phantoms of a dream are considered to be true until the sleeper wakes. For as long as a person has not reached the true knowledge of the unity of the Self, so long as it does not enter his mind that the world of effects with its means and objects of right knowledge and its results of actions is untrue; he rather, in consequence of his ignorance, looks on mere effects (such as body, offspring, wealth, etc.) as forming part of and belonging to his Self, forgetful of Brahman being in reality the Self of all. Hence, as long as true knowledge does not present itself, there is no reason why the ordinary course of secular and religious activity should not hold on undisturbed. The case is analogous to that of a dreaming man who in his dream sees manifold things, and, up to the moment of waking, is convinced that his ideas are produced by real perception without suspecting the perception to be merely an apparent one.

CHAPTER 5

Jainism

CHAPTER OBJECTIVES

In this chapter you will:

- Learn about the Jain concept of *ahimsa,* or non-violence.

- Learn about the life of Mahavira, the founder of Jainism.

- Explore Jain religious teachings and sects.

- Examine the position of the Jain community in contemporary India.

KEY TERMS

Tirthankara
Moksha

Jiva
Ajiva

Svetambara
Digambara

A Timeline of Jainism

599–527 B.C.E	Life of Mahavira		Muslims, and Sikhs commit atrocities in the name of religion; some Jains killed in the fighting
1st century B.C.E	Distinction between Svetambara and Digambara sects emerges		
9th–11th century C.E	Digambara Jains supported by South Indian kings	19th–21st century	Jains are among India's best educated and most prosperous communities
1473	Emergence of Sthanakavasi sect		
1700	British emerge as major power in India	20th century	Emergence of Jain communities worldwide, especially in former British colonies
1857	Indian Mutiny; British Christians, Indian Hindus,		

In the sixth century B.C.E., two protests arose in India against Hinduism. These were Jainism and Buddhism, and each offered an alternative to that presented in the Vedic literature and taught by the Brahmins. Both Jainism and Buddhism denied the validity of the Vedas as inspired scripture, and both rejected the religious implications of the Indian caste system. Of these two new religions, Jainism was probably the first.

The Life of Mahavira

It is difficult to determine precisely the origin of Jainism, although Nataputta Vardhamana, who became known to his followers as Mahavira ("great hero"), has traditionally been identified as its founder. The story of Mahavira's life, however, obviously has been covered with legend. Actually, in orthodox Jainism, Mahavira was only the last in a long line of founders. It is believed that over enormously long periods of time the truth is discovered, fades and is lost, and is found again. Theravada Buddhists and Jains share this understanding of time and religion. Twenty-three figures preceded Mahavira in the establishment of Jainism. These people, together with Mahavira, are called *Tirthankaras*, or "crossing builders." They are believed to be those ideal persons who forged a bridge between this life and Nirvana. A total of twenty-four *Tirthankaras* receive the veneration of Jains in their temples.

Most sources suggest that Mahavira lived between 599 and 527 B.C.E., although some authorities place his death as late as 467 B.C.E. This means that he was contemporary with Siddhartha Gautama, Confucius, Lao-tzu, and the great Hebrew prophets of the sixth century B.C.E. (Jeremiah, Ezekiel, and the anonymous author or authors of Isaiah 40–66).

The reported details of the life of Mahavira are similar in many respects to those of the life of the Buddha, and some suggest that these details are taken from Buddhism. Others suggest that Buddhists borrowed them from Jains. Like the Buddha, Mahavira was born in the sixth century B.C.E. to parents of the Kshatriya caste; his father was a minor ruler. Mahavira was the second of two sons. According to legend, the family possessed great wealth and lived in luxury. They resided in Vaisali, the capital city of the region of Magadah in north India. At the proper age, Mahavira married and had a daughter. Despite his position and wealth, he was not happy and sought a religious answer to this unhappiness. When a group of wandering ascetics came to dwell in his village, Mahavira became interested in them and longed to join their order. Being a dutiful son, however, he waited until his parents died and the business affairs of the family had been taken over successfully by his older brother.[1] Then he bade farewell to his family, turned his back on his wealth and luxury, tore out his hair and beard by the handfuls, and went off to join the ascetics.

Mahavira did not find what he had sought among this group of ascetics. He came to believe instead that one must practice a more severe asceticism than they practiced to find release of the soul from this life. In addition to his concern for extreme asceticism, Mahavira eventually felt that one must also practice *ahimsa* (non-injury to life) to find release. Therefore, he went forth on his own path.

The legends concerning this period of Mahavira's life emphasize the extreme measures of asceticism that he imposed on himself. Because he did not wish to become attached to people or things, he never stayed more than one night in any place when he traveled. During the rainy season, he stayed off the roads to avoid walking where he might inadvertently step on an insect. During the dry season, he swept the road before him as he walked to avoid crushing insects. He strained all the water he drank to prevent swallowing any creature it might contain. Like any true ascetic, he begged for his food; but he refused to eat raw food and preferred to eat only that which had been left over from the meal of some other person, so that he might not be the cause of death. To better torment his body, he sought out the coldest spots in the winter months and the hottest climates in the summer, and he always went about naked. Whenever angry or vile persons sent their dogs after him, Mahavira allowed himself to be bitten rather than resist them. Legend also tells of a time when Mahavira was meditating and some people built a fire beneath him to see if he would resist; he did not. After twelve years of the harshest forms of asceticism, he achieved release (*moksha*) from the bonds that tie one's soul to the endless cycle of birth, death, and rebirth. Thus, he became known to his followers as a *Jina* (conqueror) because he had heroically conquered the forces of life. Although he had achieved moksha, Mahavira lived for another thirty years and died at the age of seventy-two.

The Teachings of Jainism

Like other Indian religions, Jainism views life in terms of endless reincarnation. People are born, live out their lives, die, and are born again. This is the problem around which Indian religions revolve. How does a person get off the wheel of lives and cease to live? Hinduism offers a variety of answers, as do Buddhism and Sikhism. Jainism views people as bound to life because of the karma they acquire.

From the Source

All living beings owe their present form of existence to their own Karma; timid, wicked, suffering latent misery, they err about (in the Circle of Births), subject to birth, old age and death.[2]

Mahavira taught that *karma* was built up in an individual as the result of activity of any sort. Thus, the ideal life for a Jain might simply be to do as little as possible and thereby escape karma and be freed from life.

From the Source

Liberation is absolute from the totality of actions through the absence of the causes of bondage and exhaustion (of past karmas).[3]

The philosophical worldview of Jainism is dualistic. According to Jainism, the world is comprised of essentially two substances—soul (*jiva*) and matter (*ajiva*). Soul is life; it is eternal and valuable. Matter is lifeless, material, and evil. The entire universe can be identified as either soul or matter. All persons are seen as soul encased in matter. Matter clings to the soul because of past actions (*karma*). As long as soul is enmeshed in matter, it can never be free and is bound to remain in the end-less cycle of lives. Thus, it is the goal of Jainism to liberate the soul from matter. This philosophical basis views the flesh as being evil, because it traps the spirit. If the flesh is evil, then the ascetic answer is to release the soul by tormenting the flesh in some manner. This answer to the human plight is found in some form in Hinduism, Buddhism, Christianity, Islam, and nearly every other major religion in the world. Whereas these religions also have other solutions to the problem of humankind's plight, Jainism is consistent. It views the world as a dualism. Its answer to the dualistic nature of the world is severe asceticism. Since not all Jains can be free from the responsibilities of life and dedicate themselves to the ascetic life, it is believed that the Jains who do are closest to release from the cycle of birth, life, and death. Mahavira set the pattern by turning his back on the wealth and pleasures of his home and submitting his body to the rigors of asceticism; thus, he found release.

Jainism maintains that release from the cycle of life, death, and rebirth must be accomplished by the individual. The soul can be freed from matter only by the actions of the person involved, and that person cannot receive help from outside. Therefore, the gods are of little consequence in Jainism. Jains have no need for a creator god because they believe that matter is eternal. Thus there never was a creation of the world. It has been here forever and will continue to exist forever. If Jainism has any awareness of gods, it is that they are simply creatures living on a different plane from that of humankind. These gods cannot help humans in their search for release. Therefore, prayer and worship are worthless. Although Jainism may acknowledge the existence of gods, it does not rely on them.

A Jain pilgrim wears a mask to prevent swallowing of insects as he walks and sweeps the road before him with a broom to prevent crushing of life. Thus he adheres to the principles of *ahimsa* (non-injury of life). *(Ann and Bury Peerless Picture Library)*

In the practice of their religion, Jains tend to divide themselves into two distinct groups: the majority, who cannot afford to leave their homes and accept the rigors of the ascetic life, and the minority, who can and do become monks. The latter group represents the ideal life of a Jain. Jain monks take five vows to guide their lives.

From the Source

1. *They vow non-injury of life (ahimsa).* According to Jain tradition, Mahavira taught:

He who injures these (animals) does not comprehend and renounce the sinful acts; he who does not injure these, comprehends and renounces the sinful acts.

Knowing them, a wise man should not act sinfully toward animals, nor cause others to act so, nor allow others to act so. He who knows these causes of sin relating to animals, is called a reward-knowing sage. Thus I say.[4]

This vow has become the most dominant characteristic of all Jains and the mark by which they are known to the world. A Jain will go to great lengths to avoid harming any living creature, as they are vegetarians and avoid leather products, which necessitate killing. Some Jains are so concerned with avoiding meat products that they will not eat food that has been cooked in pans previously used to cook meat. Jain monks, following Mahavira's example, sweep the path before them when they walk to avoid treading on insects, and they strain the water they drink to protect whatever life may have been in it. In certain extreme cases, Jains have been known to extend this care to rats.[5] Most Jains avoid occupations, including agriculture, that involve even the possibility of harming a person or other living creature. For this reason, Jainism is almost exclusively an urban religion. The Jain principle of not injuring life has had widespread influence among non-Jains, such as Mohandas Gandhi and Albert Schweitzer. There have, however, been Jain kings who have waged war. Jainism does not require complete pacifism. Some Jains hold the view that it is permissible to use weapons but only in self-defense, although monks are not permitted to use them under any circumstances.

2. *Jain monks vow to always speak the truth.*
   Because of this vow, they are widely respected for their truthfulness. In its search for truth, however, Jainism has tended to view truth as relative rather than absolute.[6]

3. *Jain monks vow to refrain from taking anything that is not given to them.*
   This too has added to the Jains' reputation for honesty.

4. *They renounce sexual pleasures.*
   In keeping with traditional asceticism, which views the pleasures of the flesh as evil, because sex is one of the greatest pleasures of the flesh, it must be forsaken. (Mahavira went even further, by not only renouncing sexual pleasures but by also renouncing women in general. He is said to have declared that "women are the greatest temptation in the world.")

5. *They renounce all attachments.*
   Attachments to and love for other persons or things is one of the elements that keep humans bound to life. (It was for this reason that Mahavira renounced his family and possessions and refused to stay in any place longer than one day, lest he form new attachments.)[7]

Generally, all Jains seek to follow the first three vows as much as possible; those who enter the monastic life keep all five. Thus, a Jain layperson may marry and have a family and possessions—with the understanding that he or she is not leading the ideal life and may not expect release in this life.

The scriptures of the Jains are called *Agamas*, or "precepts," or *Siddhantas*, or "treatises." Orthodox Jains believe these Agamas are the actual sermons or teachings Mahavira gave to his disciples. The various Jain sects differ regarding the number of Agamas they consider genuine and authoritative. Many of the lesser-known Agamas have not yet been translated into English.

Jain Sects

By 80 B.C.E., the Jains were severely divided over what was to be the true meaning of Jainism, and they split into two sects that exist today. The sect that interprets Jain teachings more liberally is the *Svetambara* (literally, "the white-clad"). This group is now

The Badri Das at the Parasnath Jain Temple which is covered with mother-of-pearl and is the centre of the Jain system in Calcutta. *(Omnia/Getty Images Inc.—Hulton Archive Photos)*

located mainly in the northern part of India. They are liberal in their interpretation of Mahavira's teachings regarding the wearing of clothing and are called "white-clad" because they reject the necessity of nudity and allow their monks to wear a white garment. They are also liberal in that they allow women into the religion and into their monasteries and even accept the possibility that a woman may find release. Of the two sects, the Svetambara is the more popular.

The second sect, the *Digambara* (literally, "the sky-clad"), is the more conservative of the two, and its members live mainly in southern India. The Digambaras adhere to the old ideals and require their monks to go about nearly nude; total nudity is reserved only for those of greatest holiness. In addition, they believe women have no chance of achieving release and are to be regarded as the greatest of all temptations to a man. Therefore, women are prohibited from entering the monasteries and temples. The Digambaras even refuse to believe that Mahavira was ever married.

In 1473, a third sect arose as a splinter group from Svetambara. This group, known as the *Sthanakavasi*, is distinguished by its opposition to temples and idols. It also differs from other Jain sects by accepting only thirty-three Agamas as authoritative, whereas others accept as many as eighty-four.

The Shatrunjaya Hill in Palitana is an important pilgrimage for the followers of Jainism. This site contains over 863 temples of worship. Palitana, Gujarat, India. *(Getty Images/Digital Vision)*

Jain Festivals

Although Jains do not place heavy emphasis on corporate worship and rituals, they do celebrate certain major annual festivals. These festivals are connected with the five major events in the life of each of the *Tirthankaras*. They coincide with *Tirthankaras'* entering into the womb, birth, renunciation, attainment of great knowledge, and final release from this life. Mahavira's birthday is celebrated in early April.

Paijusana

This celebration comes at the end of the Jain year, usually in the month of August or September, and it is the most popular festival. During this eight-day period, each Jain fasts and attends special worship. All Jain laity are encouraged to live as monks for at least one twenty-four hour period. During this time, the layperson is to live in a monastery, fast, and meditate. At the conclusion of this period, Jains perform acts of penance and seek forgiveness to begin the new year with a clean slate. The festival ends with a procession of adherents carrying the image of a *Tirthankara* through the village and of giving alms to the poor.

Divali

Jains have appropriated the Hindu holiday of Divali, which is celebrated in November. Instead of worshiping the Hindu goddess, Kali, Jains use this period to remember the liberation of Mahavira by the lighting of lamps. In addition to these festivals, Jains fast at each full moon and make pilgrimages to various holy sites.

A Statue of Mahavira. In this portrayal, the founder of
the Jain path of purification and release exhibits the
serenity of Jain who has "conquered" *samsara*.
(Robert Radin)

Jainism Today

Hinduism was affected by Jain teaching and was moved to accept its emphasis on asceticism and *ahimsa*. Although Jainism and its ascetic movement may have been very popular in India at one time, today it is a minority religion.

Religion and Violence

At times Jains have been subject to persecution by Hindus. One of the most famous incidents was the execution of approximately 8,000 Jains in Karnataka in Southwest India in the eleventh century because they refused to convert to Hinduism.

Worldwide, there are an estimated four million Jains, most of whom live in urban areas in Western India. There are fewer than 6,000 Jain monks.[8] Because of their overwhelming concern for the sacredness of life, Jains are forbidden from entering certain occupations.

Religion and Violence

No Jain can belong to any profession that takes a life or profits from slaughter. For example, they cannot be soldiers, butchers, leather workers, exterminators, or even farmers, since farmers regularly plow the soil and might kill worms and insects that live in it. In the past, however, there have been Jains who were soldiers and emperors. These prohibitions have forced Jains to enter the commercial professions. This fact, along with their reputation for honesty and morality, has made them excellent businessmen. It is paradoxical that a sect that began with the intention of asceticism and poverty has become, by virtue of its respect for life, one of the wealthiest classes in India. Jains have not actively participated in the religious and ethnic violence that is all too common in modern India, though some have been caught in the crossfire.

They are very strict vegetarians. Some Jains refuse to eat in restaurants that are not entirely vegetarian for fear that the subtle essence of meat will slip into the vegetarian food. A Jain professor in the United States explains that, for similar reasons, he would not consider ordering a half-cheese, half-pepperoni pizza when eating out with friends.

Although Jains have no need for gods, they do venerate the twenty-four *Tirthankaras* and have erected over 40,000 temples in India to worship these figures. Many of these temples are renowned for their beauty; the temple on Mount Abu is considered one of the seven wonders of India. Apart from adoring the *Tirthankaras* in temples, Jain worship includes many rituals in the home. This may include reciting the names of the *Jinas* (saints from the past), bathing idols, and offering flowers and perfumes to them. Worship also may include meditation and the observance of vows during their worship.

STUDY QUESTIONS

1. Describe the movement begun by Mahavira as a reaction to classical Hinduism.
2. According to Jainism, how is one able to free oneself from the cycle of endless lives?
3. Define *ahimsa* and give examples of this teaching in the life of Mahavira.
4. What is the greatest contribution of Jainism to world religions?
5. How does the teaching of *ahimsa* influence the daily lives of lay Jains?

SUGGESTED READING

Frost, S. E., ed. *The Sacred Writings of the World's Great Religions.* New York: McGraw-Hill, 1972.

Jaini, Jagmanderlal. *Outlines of Jainism.* Cambridge: Cambridge University Press, 1940.

Jaini, Padmanabh. *The Jaina Path of Purification.* Berkeley: University of California Press, 1979.

Mahapragya, Nathamal. *Jain Ethics and Morality.* London: Amol, 2000.

Rankin, Adian. *The Jain Path: Ancient Wisdom for the West.* Winchester UK: O Books, 2006.

Shah, Bharat. *An Introduction to Jainism.* Charlestown, South Carolina: BookSurge, 2003. (Available from Amazon.com.)

SOURCE MATERIAL

A Jain Parable: The Man in the Well

Jainism, along with many other Indian religions, has historically taught that there are few yes or no answers to the problems of life. This has never been better illustrated than in the Jain parable of the man in the well. The story also is found in many other cultures and literatures.[9]

Haribhadra, 'Samara-dityakatha,' II. *55–88*

A certain man, much oppressed by the woes of poverty,

> Left his own home, and set out for another country.

> He passed through the land, with its villages, cities, and harbors,

> And after a few days he lost his way.
> And he came to a forest, thick with trees . . . and full of wild beasts. There, while he was stumbling over the rugged paths, . . . a prey to thirst and hunger, he saw a mad elephant, fiercely trumpeting, charging him with upraised trunk. At the same time there appeared before him a most evil demoness, holding a sharp sword, dreadful in face and form, and laughing with loud and shrill laughter. Seeing them he trembled in all his limbs with deathly fear, and looked in all directions. There, to the east of him, he saw a great banyan tree. . . .

> And he ran quickly, and reached the mighty tree.

> But his spirits fell, for it was so high that even the birds could not fly over it,
> And he could not climb its high unscalable trunk. . . .
> All his limbs trembled with terrible fear,
> Until, looking round, he saw nearby an old well covered with grass.
> Afraid of death, craving to live if only a moment longer,
> He flung himself into the well at the foot of the banyan tree.
> A clump of reeds grew from its deep wall, and to this he clung,
> While below him he saw terrible snakes, enraged at the sound of his falling;
> And at the very bottom, known from the hiss of its breath, was a black and mighty python
> With mouth agape, its body thick as the trunk of a heavenly elephant, with terrible red eyes.
> He thought, "My life will only last as long as these reeds hold fast,"
> And he raised his head; and there, on the clump of reeds, he saw two large mice,
> One white, one black, their sharp teeth ever gnawing at the roots of the reed clump.
> Then up came the wild elephant, and, enraged the more at not catching him,
> Charged time and again at the trunk of the banyan tree.
> At the shock of his charge a honeycomb on a large branch
> Which hung over the old well, shook loose and fell.
> The man's whole body was stung by a swarm of angry bees,
> But, just by chance, a drop of honey fell on his head,
> Rolled down his brow, and somehow reached his lips,
> And gave him a moment's sweetness. He longed for other drops,
> And he thought nothing of the python, the snakes, the elephant, the mice, the well, or the bees,
> In his excited craving for yet more drops of honey.
> This parable is powerful to clear the minds of those on the way to freedom,

Now hear its sure interpretation.
The man is the soul, his wandering in the forest the four types of existence.
The wild elephant is death, the demoness old age.
The banyan tree is salvation, where there is no fear of death, the elephant,
But which no sensual man can climb.
The well is human life, the snakes are passions,
Which so overcome a man that he does not know what he should do.
The tuft of reed is man's allotted span, during which the soul exists embodied;
The mice which steadily gnaw it are the dark and bright fortnights.
The stinging bees are manifold diseases,
Which torment a man until he has not a moment's joy.
The awful python is hell, seizing the man bemused by sensual pleasure,
Fallen in which the soul suffers pains by the thousand.
The drops of honey are trivial pleasures, terrible at the last.
Now can a wise man want them, in the midst of such peril and hardship?

Jain Respect for Life

Ahimsa (the vow of non-injury to life) is one of the primary doctrines of Jainism and may be its chief contribution to other religions. The selection from the *Akaranga-Sutra* details Jain respect for all life.[10]

Akaranga-Sutra, *I. 1*

Earth is afflicted and wretched, it is hard to teach, it has no discrimination. Unenlightened men, who suffer from the effect of past deeds, cause great pain in a world full of pain already, for in earth souls are individually embodied. If, thinking to gain praise, honour, or respect . . . or to achieve a good rebirth . . . or to win salvation, or to escape pain, a man sins against earth or causes or permits others to do so, . . . he will not gain joy or wisdom. . . . Injury to the earth is like striking, cutting, maiming, or killing a blind man. . . . Knowing this, man should not sin against earth or cause or permit others to do so. He who understands the nature of sin against earth is called a true sage who understands karma.

And there are many souls embodied in water. Truly water . . . is alive. He who injures the lives in water does not understand the nature of sin or renounce it. . . . Knowing this, a man should not sin against water, or cause or permit others to do so. He who understands the nature of sin against water is called a true sage who understands karma.

By wicked or careless acts one may destroy fire-beings, and moreover, harm other beings by means of fire. . . . For there are creatures living in earth, grass, leaves, wood, cowdung, or dustheaps, and jumping creatures which . . . fall into a fire if they come near it. If touched by fire, they shrivel up . . . lose their senses and die. . . . He who understands the nature of sin in respect of fire is called a true sage who understands karma.

And just as it is the nature of a man to be born and grow old, so is it the nature of a plant to be born and grow old. . . . One is endowed with reason, and so is the other; one is sick, if injured, and so is the other; one grows large, and so does the other; one changes with time, and so does the other. . . . He who understands the nature of sin against plants is called a true sage who understands karma.

All beings with two, three, four, or five senses, . . . in fact all creation, know individually pleasure and displeasure, pain, terror, and sorrow. All are full of fears which come from all directions. And yet there exist people who would cause greater pain to them. . . . Some kill animals for sacrifice, some for their skin, flesh, blood, . . . feathers, teeth, or tusks; . . . some kill them intentionally and some unintentionally; some kill because they have been previously injured by them, . . . and some because they expect to be injured. He who harms animals has not understood or renounced deeds of sin. . . . He who understands the nature of sin against animals is called a true sage who understands karma.

A man who is averse from harming even the wind knows the sorrow of all things living. . . . He who knows what is bad for himself knows what is bad for others, and he who knows what is bad for others knows what is bad for himself. This reciprocity should always be borne in mind. Those whose minds are at peace and who are free from passions do not desire to live (at the expense of others). . . . He who understands the nature of sin against wind is called a true sage who understands karma.

In short, he who understands the nature of sin in respect of all the six types of living beings is called a true sage who understands karma.

CHAPTER 6

Buddhism

CHAPTER OBJECTIVES

In this chapter you will:

- Learn about the life of the Buddha.

- Come to understand basic Buddhist teachings.

- Understand the differences between Theravada and Mahayana Buddhism.

- Become familiar with the outlines of the history of Buddhism outside of India.

- See how Buddhism can be a religion of peace but that Buddhists are not necessarily peaceful.

KEY TERMS

Buddha	Nirvana	Anatman
Sangha	Theravada	Arhat
Dharma	Mahayana	Bodhisattva

A Timeline of Buddhism

480–405 B.C.E.	Life and teaching of the Buddha	1st century C.E.	Transmission of Buddhism to Southeast Asia and China
405	First Buddhist Council		
350	Second Buddhist Council	4th century	Transmission of Buddhism to Korea
200–200 C.E.	Development of Theravada Buddhism	550	Transmission of Buddhism to Japan
297	Spread of Buddhism in India encouraged by Emperor Asoka	700	Transmission of Buddhism to Tibet
		845	Persecution of Buddhists in China
247	Transmission of Buddhism to Sri Lanka	1200	Growth of Zen in Japan
250	Third Buddhist Council distinction between Theravada and Mahayana schools emerges	1250	Decline of Buddhism in India
		1617–1682	Life of the fifth Dalai Lama; beginning of monastic rule in Tibet

(Continued)

A Timeline of Buddhism   (*Continued*)

19th century	Initial transmission of Buddhism to Europe and North America	1959–present	Dalai Lama in exile; spreads message of Tibetan Buddhism throughout the world
1949–1976	Communist persecution of Buddhism in China	1963–present	Buddhism used to justify military rule and human rights abuses in Burma
1950	Tenzin Gyatso becomes Dalai Lama; China invades Tibet and begins persecution of Buddhists	1950–present	Rapid growth of Buddhism in Europe and North America
1975–1979	Severe persecution of Buddhists by the Communist Khmer Rouge in Cambodia	1980s–present	Emergence of Socially Engaged Buddhism
1976–present	Buddhist revival in China	2008	Hundreds killed in pro-independence demonstrations in Tibet

Buddhism began in India in the sixth century B.C.E. as another interpretation of the Hindu religious system. In many respects, it resembled Jainism because it rejected the authority of the Vedas and offered a vision of salvation based on individual effort. It differed from Jainism in that the Buddha taught a "middle way" between worldliness and the extreme asceticism of Mahavira. As such, it held great appeal in India for several centuries. By the third century B.C.E., Buddhism developed something unusual for any version of Hinduism: a missionary imperative. The rulers of India, who were enamored of this new religion, sent Buddhist missionaries into neighboring Asian countries. At the same time, Buddhism was developing new philosophies that became more and more attractive to the Asian peoples. This combination of missionary thrust and new philosophies made it a sweeping success in China, Japan, Korea, and Southeast Asia. Yet while Buddhism was becoming a success in foreign missions, it was slowly being pushed aside in India by a resurgent Hinduism. The Muslim conquest of India led to the further decline of Buddhism there. While new converts have emerged in the twentieth and twenty-first centuries, particularly among lower-caste Hindus, and many Tibetan refugees who now live in India, today the vast majority of Buddhists are found in East and Southeast Asia.

The Life of Gautama

The founder of Buddhism was a man named Siddhartha, who was a member of the Gautama clan. The dates usually given for his life are 560–480 B.C.E.; however, the life of Gautama, as he has come to be known, is surrounded by legend and the exact dates of his life are subject to question.[1] Nevertheless, he probably lived during the sixth century B.C.E. and was a contemporary of Mahavira.

Gautama was the son of a Kshatriya *raja* (king) called Suddhodana and his wife, Maya. The legends say that the birth of the child was surrounded by extraordinary events and portents. According to one story, a soothsayer predicted that the child would

Buddha statue, Thailand.
(Getty Images, Inc.—Photodisc)

either become a great king, who would rule the entire world, or a great Buddha (Enlightened One). Gautama's mother died soon after his birth, and he was reared by his maternal aunt, who became his father's second wife.

When Gautama was born, it was predicted that he could become a great king, but that if he ever saw the sights of human misery or the tranquility of a monk, he would grow up to be a religious teacher. Because his father did not wish this, he sought to protect him from the ugliness and distress of humanity. The *raja* specifically sought to keep the young prince from seeing four sights: a dead body, an aged person, a diseased person, and an ascetic monk. Thus, Gautama grew up surrounded by youth, beauty, and health. He received a normal education for a prince of that era. He studied the arts and warfare and received some training in philosophy. When he was nineteen, he married his cousin and they shared a happy home. They had one child, a son, Rahula.[2]

As Gautama neared his thirtieth birthday, he gradually became aware of the ugliness of the real world. According to some of the legends, the gods, wishing to awaken the future Buddha from the wasteful life he was leading, conspired to break through the walls of youth and beauty that had been erected around him. One by one, he began to see the things his father had forbidden. He saw a wrinkled and bent elderly person, a man with a loathsome disease, a rotting corpse, and finally a peaceful monk, who had renounced the world in search of a release from his suffering. Gautama, reaching his mature years, became aware that life always involves suffering and pain. It is said that he once entered his harem room where there were some of the most beautiful young women in the kingdom. There he received a vision that these women would soon become wrinkled, gray, and stooped. These revelations made it impossible for the young prince to continue to live in his palace surrounded by ease and plenty; one night, he decided to leave his home. He crept into his wife's bedroom and said farewell to her and their infant son. Then he took his best horse and rode off into the night. After riding a certain distance, he clipped off his hair and beard and sent his horse back. He changed clothes with a beggar and began a period of searching for answers to life's miseries.

At first, Gautama thought the answers to the questions that troubled him were to be found in the various schools of philosophy. Therefore, he attached himself to a guru and studied with him for some time; but he received no satisfaction in his studies. A second avenue Gautama tried was asceticism. As a solution to the problems of life, asceticism was an acceptable pursuit in the sixth century B.C.E., as can be seen from the life of Mahavira and his followers. Gautama joined five other monks and with them began a life of severe asceticism that lasted six years. The ascetic measures Gautama took were as severe as any recorded in the history of religion. According to legend, he became something of a champion ascetic. Gautama sought out anything that was unpleasant, painful, or disagreeable as a means by which he might find release. He is supposed to have practiced fasting until he reached the point of living on a single grain of rice per day.

Many Westerners tend to think of Buddha as a fat, jolly person because they have been influenced by Chinese statuary depicting plump figures as "Buddhas" often found in Chinese restaurants and grocery stores. These images, however, are not attempts to depict the historical Buddha.[3] At this time in his life, Gautama reportedly became so thin that when he grasped his stomach he touched his backbone. He wore irritating garments and sat in awkward and painful positions for hours. He sat on thorns and for a time slept in a cremation ground among rotting corpses. In the tradition of many ascetics, Gautama allowed filth and vermin to accumulate on his body. But despite these heroic efforts at asceticism, he did not find the enlightenment he was seeking.

Apparently, the turning point in Gautama's quest came one day when he was walking near a stream. Because he had been terribly weakened by his ordeals, he fainted and fell into the stream. The cold water revived him; when he was able to contemplate his situation, he realized that although he had done everything that could be expected of an ascetic, he still had not found satisfaction. He therefore arose, walked to a nearby food stand, and ate a meal. Another tradition states that he received his first meal from a village woman named Sujata.[4] His five friends happened to pass by; when they saw him eating and drinking and enjoying himself, they spurned him as a traitor. When Gautama had finished his meal, he went to the banks of a river and sat down under the shade of a fig tree and began to meditate.[5] He decided to meditate until he received enlightenment. At last, after a period of meditation, Gautama was enlightened; from then on, he was known as the Buddha (Enlightened One). In his meditation, the Buddha had a vision of the endless cycle of birth and death that is the lot of humankind. It was revealed to him that people were bound to this cycle because of *tanha* (desire, thirst, craving). It is desire that causes *karma* and thus fetters people. The Buddha had desired enlightenment and had sought it through asceticism and knowledge, but it had eluded him. When he had ceased to desire it, he found enlightenment.

The first step the Buddha took after his enlightenment was to travel to the holy city of Banaras and locate the five ascetic friends who had spurned him. He found them in Deer Park; though at first they had contempt for him, they listened as he preached. In his first sermon, the Buddha taught that neither the extreme of indulgence nor the extreme of asceticism was acceptable as a way of life and that one should avoid extremes and seek to live in the middle way. The five ascetics noted the change that had come over the Buddha, and they accepted his teachings. These five formed the first *Sangha* (Buddhist monastic order).

The Buddha became enlightened when he was about thirty-five years old. He spent the remaining years of this life teaching his growing band of disciples. Unlike orthodox Hindus, he taught that any person of any caste or sex could find the same enlightenment he knew.[6] Therefore, his followers included a wide variety of persons. When women asked to join his group, the Buddha was at first reluctant, but he eventually relented and allowed them to form an order of nuns. According to legend, the Buddha's stepmother and former wife were among the first women to seek admission to this group. Unlike orthodox Hinduism and Jainism, early Buddhism taught that women as well as men could achieve enlightenment. People who seriously joined the Buddha as monks shaved their

A statue of the Buddha carved in Java, which was located in the Southeast Asian island nation of Indonesia during the ninth century. While today Java is overwhelmingly Muslim, it was, at that time, home to Buddhist and Hindu civilizations.
(Mark R. Woodward)

heads and wore coarse yellow robes. Their only possession was a bowl they carried when they begged for food. Their creed is said to have been, "I take refuge in the Buddha; I take refuge in the **Dharma** (law); and I take refuge in the *Sangha.*" Lay Buddhists supported the *Sangha* with gifts of food, clothing, and other necessities of life.

Lay Buddhists also were expected to observe five basic rules of moral conduct: abstain from killing, stealing, lying, engaging in improper sexual conduct, and partaking of intoxicants. The monks sought to observe the following rules of conduct, as described in the Pali Sermons.

From the Source

And How, O king, is a monk accomplished in morality?

Herein a monk abandons the killing of living things and refrains from killing; laying aside the use of a stick or a knife he dwells modest, full of kindliness, and compassionate for the welfare of all living things. This is his behavior in morality.

Abandoning the taking of what is not given he refrains from taking what is not given, he takes and expects only what is given, he dwells purely and without stealing.

Abandoning incontinence he practices continence and lives apart, avoiding the village practice of sex intercourse. Abandoning falsehood he refrains from falsehood, he speaks truth, he is truthful, trustworthy, and reliable, not deceiving people.

Abandoning slanderous speech he refrains from slanderous speech; what he has heard from one place he does not tell in another to cause dissension. He is even a healer of dissensions and a producer of union, delighting and rejoicing in concord, eager for concord, and an utterer of speech that produces concord.

Abandoning harsh speech he refrains from harsh speech; the speech that is harmless, pleasant to the ear, kind, reaching the heart, urbane, amiable, and attractive to the multitude, that kind of speech does he utter.

Abandoning frivolous speech he refrains from frivolous speech; he speaks of the good, the real, the profitable, of the doctrine and the discipline; he is an utterer of speech worth hoarding, with timely reasons and purpose and meaning.

He refrains from injuring seeds and plants.

He eats only within one meal time, abstaining from food at night and avoiding untimely food.

He refrains from seeing dancing, singing, music, and shows.

He refrains from the use of garlands, scents, unguents, and objects of adornment; from a high or large bed; from accepting gold and silver; from accepting raw grain and raw meat.

He refrains from accepting women, girls, male and female slaves, goats and rams, fowls and pigs, elephants, oxen, horses, mares and farm-lands.

He refrains from going on messages and errands; from buying and selling; from cheating in weighing, false metal, and measuring; from practices of cheating, trickery, deception, and fraud; from cutting, killing, binding, robbery, pillage, and violence.[7]

The Buddha reportedly died at the age of eighty after eating spoiled pork curry.[8] According to tradition, his final words were, "Subject to decay are all component things. Strive earnestly to work out your own salvation."

The Teachings of the Buddha

There is nothing in the life and teachings of the Buddha to indicate that he intended to found a new religion. He understood life in Hindu religious categories and taught his followers using those categories and vocabulary. The Buddha was opposed to many of the various existing forms of religious worship; he certainly was opposed to the Brahmin system of animal sacrifice. In addition, he rejected the authority of the Vedas. The

Buddha accepted many Hindu teachings concerning the gods but considered them mortal beings, subject to the laws of *karma* and rebirth. While Buddhism teaches that gods have great powers, the Buddha was much more concerned that people find their own enlightenment than appeal to the gods for help and support.

Among the unique teachings of the Buddha was that the soul did not exist. According to Buddha, people live in a state of **anatman** (the absence of enduring souls). What is called a soul is actually a combination of five mental or physical aggregates: the physical body, feelings, understanding, will, and consciousness. This combination, which makes up the human personality, is bound up in the endless cycle of birth, death, and rebirth that is typical in Indian religions. The Buddha's understanding of humankind's plight is presented in the classic Buddhist statement of the Four Noble Truths:

From the Source

And what, monks, is the Middle Path, of which the Tathagata has gained enlightenment, which produces insight and knowledge, and tends to calm, to higher knowledge, enlightenment, Nirvana?[9] This is the noble Eightfold Way, namely right view, right intention, right speech, right action, right livelihood, right effort, right mindfulness, right concentration. This, monks, is the Middle Path, of which the Tathagata has gained enlightenment, which produces insight and knowledge, and tends to calm, to higher knowledge, enlightenment, Nirvana.

Now this, monks, is the noble truth of pain: birth is painful, old age is painful, sickness is painful, death is painful, sorrow, lamentation, dejection, and despair are painful. Contact with unpleasant things is painful, not getting what one wishes is painful. In short the five groups of grasping are painful.

Now this, monks, is the noble truth of the cause of pain: the craving, which tends to rebirth, combined with pleasure and lust, finding pleasure here and there, namely the craving for passion, the craving for existence, the craving for non-existence.

Now this, monks, is the noble truth of the cessation of pain, the cessation without a remainder of craving, the abandonment, forsaking, release, non-attachment.

Now this, monks, is the noble truth of the way that leads to the cessation of pain: this is the noble Eightfold Way, namely, right views, right intention, right speech, right action, right livelihood, right effort, right mindfulness, right concentration.[10]

The person who follows the Eightfold Path will break the bonds that tie one to life and will achieve release from the cycle. The word used to describe this release is **Nirvana**, which basically means "extinguished" or "put out like a candle." Thus the goal of basic Buddhist practice is not the achievement of a state of bliss in some heaven but the extinguishing of *tanha* (desire, thirst, craving). When *tanha* is extinguished, one is released from the cycle of life that includes birth, suffering, death, and rebirth. One who has followed the Eightfold Path and has arrived at the point of achieving *Nirvana* is called **arhat**, or "saint."

The teachings of the Buddha became the basis for an organization that took on many of the components of a religion. His followers organized themselves into a monastic order (*Sangha*). His teachings became codified in the laws of that order and in various forms of scripture. The Buddha himself came to be regarded as the greatest of beings. The rules under which early Buddhist monks were expected to live are noteworthy because they demonstrate the practical outworking of the Buddha's teachings.

The Development of Buddhism

The teachings of the Buddha differed radically from those of the Indian religions of his day. He denied the relevance of the gods and the necessity of worship or sacrifice. Although the Buddha shared the Indian idea that the goal of life was release from existence, he taught that release depends totally on the works of the individual. Persons attracted to the teachings of the Buddha during his life must have been a special group of very intelligent people who were dissatisfied with life and had the capacity to discipline themselves. Had Buddhism remained as it was in the beginning, it is doubtful that more than a handful of people would have been interested in it. In the twenty-first century, however, Buddhism is one of the major religions of the world. Its devotees are found in nearly every Asian nation and in many other parts of the world. The path by which Buddhism was transformed into one of the largest religions is fascinating indeed.

As in the case of almost every other founder of a religion, before the Buddha had been dead very long his followers were debating the meaning of his teachings. According to one tradition, a schism occurred between the disciples the day after his death. Within a year of his death, his followers called a council to try to determine the true meaning of his teachings. This council failed to bring unity; within a short period, there were four major Buddhist factions. During the next ten years, the number increased to more than sixteen.

In 390 B.C.E., a second council was called and a conservative minority declared the majority of Buddhists to be heretics. From this point onward, Buddhism has been divided into these two major camps, which have in turn subdivided into numerous sects. The smaller and more conservative wing of Buddhism is known as Hinayana (the exclusive way). At one time, there may have been as many as eighteen schools within the Hinayana movement. Today, the only remaining Hinayana school is **Theravada** (the tradition of the elders).[11] The larger and more liberal segment is known as **Mahayana** (the expansive way). The basic differences between these two sects are discussed later in this chapter.

Buddhism received its greatest impetus when the emperor of India, Asoka, converted to the new religion. It is said that Asoka was to Buddhism what Constantine I was to Christianity. In both cases, these rulers of large empires were converted to what had previously been small, struggling religions. Both emperors then threw the power of their thrones behind their new faiths; from that point onward, these religions grew rapidly. Asoka, who ruled from 268 to 232 B.C.E., had been converted to Buddhism in 297 B.C.E. He became convinced that, unlike other religions of India, Buddhism was potentially the religion for all the peoples of the world. Thus, he was the first Buddhist to send out missionaries to carry the teachings of Gautama and urge non-Indians to accept them. Asoka sent his son Mahinda to Ceylon (present-day Sri Lanka), where the king and his court were converted. Today, Sri Lanka boasts the longest history of Buddhism of any Asian nation outside of India. Other emissaries carried the Buddhist message to Burma. The thirteenth rock edict of Asoka claims that the missionaries went as far west as Syria and Greece.[12] Asoka's decision to spread his religion proved to be the salvation of Buddhism, because Buddhism virtually ceased to exist in India centuries later. Asoka also called the third council of Buddhism in 247 B.C.E. to determine the authoritative list of Buddhist scriptures.

Despite the enormous unifying work of Asoka and others, by the first century C.E. many major and minor sects existed within Buddhism. The most distinct split was along the lines of the differences between Theravada and Mahayana.

Theravada Buddhism

Theravada Buddhism is the more conservative of the two major divisions within this religion. As such, it believes itself to be closer to the original teachings of the Buddha. The major locations of Theravada Buddhism today are Sri Lanka and the Southeast Asian nations of Burma, Thailand, Cambodia, and Laos. There are also large and growing communities of Theravada Buddhists in Europe, Australia, and North America.

According to Theravada Buddhism, people must achieve enlightenment for themselves without reliance on the gods or on any force beyond themselves.[13] For this reason, the monk is the ideal figure. It is he who shaves his head, puts on the yellow or orange robe, takes up a begging bowl, and seeks release from life through meditation and self-denial. His home is the *Sangha*, as it was in the days of the Buddha. When a monk achieves the goal he is seeking, he becomes an *arhat* and when he dies is released from the cycle of birth, death, and rebirth—the common lot of humankind.

From the Source

There is no suffering for him who has finished his journey, and abandoned grief, who has freed himself on all sides, and thrown off all fetters.

They exert themselves with their thoughts well-collected, they do not tarry in their abode, like swans who have left their lake, they leave their house and home.

Men who have no riches, who live on recognized food, who have perceived void and unconditioned freedom [Nirvana], their path is difficult to understand, like that of the birds of the air.

He whose appetites are stilled, who is not absorbed in enjoyment. . . .

The gods even envy him whose senses, like horses well broken in by the driver, have been subdued, who is free from pride, and free from appetites;

In a hamlet or in a forest, on sea or on dry land, wherever venerable persons [Arananta] dwell, that place is delightful.[14]

If a Theravada Buddhist cannot or will not join the *Sangha* and become a monk, then that person must be content to lead the life of a layperson, supporting the needs of the monks and hoping to be in a better position in another life to become a saint. One need not make a lifelong commitment to the monastic life. Most Theravada men become monks as a rite of passage from youth to adulthood. Many Theravada Buddhists temporarily "put on the robes," as ordination is called, for a period of weeks or months to mark critical stages in the course of life or when life's pressures become too much to bear. Monks are free to leave the *Sangha* at any time. Sponsoring the ordination of a monk or novice is thought to be a potent source of good *karma,* or merit, as it is commonly known. Because they cannot be ordained themselves, many women encourage their sons, grandsons, and even husbands to join the *Sangha* and sponsor their ordinations.

Theravada Buddhism, like that of the Buddhism of Gautama, teaches that the goals of religion are reached through the efforts, meditation, and achievements of the individual.

The gods, sacrifice, and prayer are of minor consequence. However, certain traditional religious elements have evolved. For example, relics of the life of the Buddha have become important to Theravadins. His bones and possessions have become objects of veneration at many of the important sites of Theravada life. Paying homage to these relics is considered to be as meritorious as paying homage to a living Buddha. Control and veneration of relics also plays an important role in the legitimation of Theravada Buddhist politics. This is as true in modern states as it was in traditional kingdoms, and plays a role in international affairs as well as in domestic politics. China, for example, periodically sends a tooth relic on tours of other Buddhist countries, allowing local Buddhists to make large stores of merit and presumably incurring the gratitude and support of their governments. The cult of relics is as important in Mahayana as it is in Theravada Buddhism. Chinese relics have even toured Taiwan, China's archrival. Indeed, relic veneration is a complex ritual that binds Buddhists together despite enormous doctrinal, philosophical, and cultural differences. Nowhere is this more clear than in the southeast Asian city-state of Singapore, which is predominantly Chinese. There the charismatic Chinese Mahayana monk Shi Fa Zhao recently sponsored the construction of a Buddha Tooth Relic Temple supported by public donations and the national government. The relic was obtained from a Theravada monk in Burma.

There are many ways for lay Theravada Buddhists to make merit. One of the early Buddhist missionaries reportedly took a branch from the sacred *bo* tree under which the Buddha found enlightenment and planted it in Sri Lanka. The resultant tree is thought to be the world's oldest living tree. Cuttings from this tree have been planted in many Buddhist countries. One often encounters offerings of candles and incense at their roots.

Offering food to monks is among the most important ways of making merit for Theravada Buddhists. Despite the fact that refraining from killing is a core Buddhist doctrine, few Theravada Buddhists, including monks, are vegetarians. Indeed, rich, fatty, pork curry is among the foods that Burmese Theravada Buddhists consider to be especially appropriate for offering to monks. This is also true among Mahayana Buddhists. While some are vegetarians, the Chinese are famous for their love of pork and duck, as the Japanese are fond of fish. The eating of meat is often justified by the teaching that eating the flesh of an animal does not generate negative *karma* or demerit because the animal was not intentionally killed for one's use. Nonetheless, Theravada Buddhists avoid occupations that involve killing. In Mandalay, an old royal city in Burma, for example, cattle and goats are slaughtered by Muslims and hogs by the Chinese. Chickens and ducks are processed by members of both communities. Burmese fisherman often justify their occupation by stating that they do not kill fish but only take them out of the water. This is also true in Mahayana Buddhism. At the same time, releasing animals, birds, and fish destined for slaughter is considered to be a meritorious act. In Thailand, Burma, and other Theravada Buddhist countries, there are temples dedicated to the release of such practices.

As Jains believe that there were many Tirthankaras in the past, Theravada and other Buddhists believe that there have been many Buddhas in the past and that there will be more in the future. A Buddha, after all, is only a human being who has discovered the path to *Nirvana* through his own efforts. There are also many stories concerning the former lives of the Buddha Gautama known as *Jatakas*. The *Jatakas* are among the most common themes in Buddhist art and are the subject of sermons and popular religious texts in all Theravada societies.[15]

The characteristic physical structure of Theravada Buddhism is a complex of buildings which in Thai is called a *wat*.[16] The most important building in the *wat* is the *bot* or *vihara*, a hall used for teaching, preaching, and meditation. Usually, this hall contains a statue of the Buddha, with attending altars, candles, and incense. Another portion of the hall may have raised seats for lecturing teachers and preachers. Other buildings include the living quarters for the monks and a number of graceful towers known as *stupas* or *pagodas*. Some speculate that the *pagodas* may have begun as relic mounds, but today they serve as worship or festival centers for the Buddhist community. Some of these *pagodas* are believed to contain relics of the Buddha or *arahats*. Others contain manuscript copies of Buddhist texts or large images of the Buddha. Lay people often visit and make offerings at these shrines. Their purpose, however, is not to worship the Buddha or the enlightened saints, but to pay respect to the ideas of Buddhahood and *Nirvana* and dedicate themselves to the quest for liberation. These devotional acts are also said to produce merit.

The wealthy also make merit by constructing or repairing pagodas and monasteries. In the past, Buddhist kings and nobles engaged in massive Buddhist building programs, erecting hundreds of shrines and dedicating tax revenues for their maintenance. Today, politicians and wealthy businesspeople continue this practice, though on a lesser scale. Even the poor can engage in this type of merit making by dropping a few coins in the collection boxes found in most *pagodas*.

Monks should not be concerned with making merit. Monastic life is structured in ways that block the acquisition of either merit or demerit—both of which lead to rebirth and impede progress toward enlightenment. Instead, through meditation and the study of Buddhist scriptures, they cultivate the types of mental states and knowledge that lead toward enlightenment. *Pagodas* are used as places of meditation by both monks and lay Buddhists. Today there are meditation centers that are used as retreats for those who want to devote themselves fully to the practice for a period of time. There are two types of Theravada meditation. *Sammatta* meditation involves intense concentration, the purpose of which is the attainment of the spiritual states that open the path to enlightenment. *Vipassana* is insight meditation; its purpose is the sudden, intuitive realization of Buddhist truths, and it is modeled on the experience of the Gautama under the *bo* tree.

Mahayana Buddhism
The Principles of Mahayana

In the third century B.C.E., while King Asoka was spreading the teachings of Buddhism through his missionary efforts, certain subtle changes began to occur in the religion. One of the basic assumptions underlying these new developments was that, in addition to what the Buddha had openly taught his disciples, there were many other principles he had secretly taught, but only to a select group who could properly understand them. A favorite story of the Mahayanists is that, as the Buddha was teaching, he took a handful of leaves from the forest floor and explained to his disciples that as the leaves in his hand were less than the total leaves of the forest, so were the teachings that he had given them openly less than the total amount of truth that could be imparted in secret. Mahayana

Buddhism simply picked up a few more leaves. Once this assumption was accepted, it was possible to accept fresh and expansive interpretations of basic Buddhist concepts as part of the Buddha's original teachings.

A second principle that began to develop in Mahayana Buddhism between the third century B.C.E. and the first century C.E. was that Gautama was really more than a man. In contrast to the teachings of early Buddhism and those of the Theravada school, the Mahayanists began to teach that the Buddha was really a compassionate, eternal, and almost divine being who came to earth in the form of a man because he loved humankind and wished to be of assistance.

The third principle the Mahayanists put forth was that Gautama was not the only Buddha to whom people could appeal. If Gautama was an eternal being who had come to earth to help people, the Mahayanists maintained that there must be many others. The Mahayana teaching is that there are many Buddhas located in different parts of the cosmos, all of whom are capable of helping people on the path to enlightenment.[17] This new idea did more than anything else to broaden the appeal of Buddhism: If there were many such eternal beings who were compassionate and had come to earth to help suffering people, then these beings were worthy of veneration and respect. Whereas Gautama had been unconcerned about the gods and worship had meant little in his scheme of things, Mahayanists could now focus their religious attention on these many eternal Buddhas. They could study their lives and build temples for them. Clergy could be trained in worshipping them; and cultic systems of ritual, sacrifice, hymns, and the like could be established on their behalf. It also meant that people could appeal to them for assistance. This remains an important part of Mahayana devotionalism.

This development also was essential to the Buddhist missionary movement. When Buddhist missionaries entered a new country, they did not have to ask the natives to give up their old gods; these gods were seen as various incarnations of the Buddha, and their cults could continue. In the same way that Hinduism absorbed Buddhism by saying that Gautama was really an *avatar* of Vishnu, Buddhism absorbed many other religions by saying that their gods were really incarnations of one of the Buddhas.

Mahayanists also developed a class of beings called **Bodhisattvas**, who could provide help for humans struggling with the problems of life. It was taught that certain beings had taken vows to become *Bodhisattvas* (future Buddhas) at some point during their lifetimes. Then, by living exemplary lives, they could acquire merit. Following death, these *Bodhisattvas* postponed their achievement of *Nirvana* until such time as all living beings could attain it and shared their merit with humankind. Some of the *Bodhisattvas* were thought to reside in heaven, while others continued to be incarnated as human beings. They were all believed to respond to the prayers of those who needed their help. The Mahayana concept of the *Bodhisattva* is based on the older early Buddhist and Theravada *Jataka* tradition, in which the future Buddha is referred to as the *Bodhisattva*. Mahayana differs from the older, more conservative, Buddhist tradition in that *Bodhisattvas* came to be seen as saviors and as one of the primary objects of popular devotion.

The Spread of Mahayana Buddhism

The teachings of the Buddha were carried into China soon after they became popular in India. There is some evidence that Hinayana Buddhism had achieved a foothold in

China by the first century C.E. However, it was not until the third century, when Mahayana was introduced, that Buddhism really began to take hold there. From that era onward, Buddhism became one of the three major religions of China, alongside the native Confucianism and Taoism.

From China, Mahayana Buddhism spread to other East Asian nations. Because of its close ties to China, Korea was brought under the influence of Buddhism as early as the fourth century C.E. The spread to the East continued in the sixth century, when Buddhism entered Japan. The Japanese at first refused to accept this new religion; but after a short time, they embraced it to the point that it came to share religious leadership with the native Shinto. Mahayana Buddhism also spread to the Indonesian islands of Java, Sumatra, and Bali. Chinese pilgrims en route to India often stopped for a period of months or even years in island Southeast Asia to improve their knowledge of Sanskrit and Buddhist doctrine. Other Asian nations, such as Mongolia and Tibet, also accepted versions of Mahayana Buddhism. Because of the remote location of these countries, their versions of the religion developed along slightly different lines than it did in other places, and today they remain unique.

Quan Yin, the Chinese Bodhisattva of Compassion. Quan Yin is an important female figure in Chinese Buddhism.
(CMCD/Getty Images, Inc.)

While Buddhism was becoming a great success as a missionary religion in the East and Southeast Asia, it was gradually dying in India. Buddhism suffered from absorption by Hinduism. Because Hinduism was able to absorb the distinctive qualities of the major challenging religions of Jainism and Buddhism. By the seventh century, it had absorbed many Buddhist features—simply by stating that Gautama was an *avatar* of Vishnu. Therefore, anything new, important, or distinctive about Buddhism came to be understood as an expression of Vishnu within the Hindu scheme of things. In predominately Buddhist countries, images of the Buddha can be found in Hindu temples often with inscriptions describing him as an avatar of Lord Vishnu. Waves of invasions, particularly the Islamic invasions in the eleventh through thirteenth centuries, destroyed many Indian centers of Buddhist learning. In those times, many Buddhists converted to Islam. With the destruction of Buddhist kingdoms, monasteries and temples found it difficult to survive. Although Hinduism somehow had the resiliency to survive the transition to Muslim rule, Buddhism—in India—did not.

Mahayanist Sects

Mahayana Buddhism began as a religion open to innovation and change. As it spread and developed in various Asian nations, it acquired many new concepts from these peoples. Therefore, we do not speak of Buddhism today as a single religion but as a family of religions; within this family, many forms of religious expression may be found.

The Pure Land Sect (Ching-t'u, Jodo). One of the most popular and widespread branches of Mahayana Buddhism is the so-called Pure Land sect. The goal of its adherents after death is a paradise called "the Land of Bliss." Mahayanists believe there have been many Buddhas and *Bodhisattvas*. Among these are the Dhyani Buddhas, who preside over heavenlike Buddha-lands, in which it is possible to cultivate Buddhist virtues and in which evil does not exist. One of the most popular of these cosmic Buddhas is Amitabha.[18] Amitabha presides over a Western paradise called "the Pure Land." His followers believe that living a virtuous life and reciting Amitabha's name will lead to rebirth in his world.

From the Source

This world Sukhavati,[19] Ananda, which is the world system of the Lord Amitabha, is rich and prosperous, comfortable, fertile, delightful and crowded with many Gods and men. And in this world system, Ananda, there are no hells, no animals, no ghosts, no Asuras and none of the inauspicious places of rebirth. And in this our world no jewels make their appearance like those which exist in the world system Sukhavati.

And that world system Sukhavati, Ananda, emits many fragrant odors, it is rich in a great variety of flowers and fruits, adorned with jewel trees, which are frequented by flocks of various birds with sweet voices, which the Tathagata's miraculous power has conjured up. And these jewel trees, Ananda, have various colors, many colors, many hundreds of thousands of colors. They are variously composed of the seven precious things, in varying combinations, i.e., of gold, silver, beryl, crystal, coral, red pearls or emerald. Such jewel trees, and clusters of banana trees and rows of palm trees, all made of precious things, grow everywhere in the Buddha field.[20]

To the Pure Land Buddhist, the emphasis is on faith in Amitabha. Some members of this sect believe that simply uttering the name Amitabha many times during the day will aid in one's achieving the Land of Bliss. With faith in Amitabha as its central premise and eternity in the Pure Land as its goal, this version of Buddhism is quite different from that originally taught by the Buddha. It is possible for the Pure Land monk to marry, have children, and live in the world in a manner very similar to that of the laity. Worship for the Pure Land devotee often occurs in what may be best described as "churches"; in fact, some Pure Land congregations in Western nations use that title. Pure Land Buddhists may have "Sunday schools" for the religious instruction of their children, may meet for worship in congregations, may hear sermons from their clergymen, and may offer prayers to Amitabha.

The Intuitive Sects (Ch'an, Zen). There has always existed a group within Buddhism that has emphasized that the truths of religion do not come through rational thought processes, study of scripture, or faith, but rather through a sudden flash of insight. These groups usually trace their origin to the experience of the Buddha under the *bo* tree. Recall that here the Buddha realized he had not found the truth he sought through study with the Brahmin *gurus*, or after five years of extreme asceticism. He therefore resolved to meditate. He sat under the *bo* tree for several weeks and the truth came to him in a flash of inspiration. Advocates of this position maintain that the intuition or inspiration that comes after a period of meditation is the key to Buddhist truth. These groups have been known throughout the Buddhist world as being meditative or Intuitive Buddhists. In India, the word for meditation is *dhyana*; in Theravada countries, it is associated with vipassana meditation schools; in China, it is ch'an; and in Japan, it is Zen.

Although these Buddhists believe that the Buddha himself received his knowledge intuitively and taught his disciples in this manner, the actual founding of the Intuitive

Young Theravada Buddhist monks and novices at the Shwedagon Pagoda in Rangoon, Burna.
(Corbis)

sects did not take place until sometime in the fifth century C.E., with the work of a monk named Bodhidharma. A great deal about the life of Bodhidharma is legendary; however, it seems clear that in the late fifth or early sixth century, the concepts of Intuitive Buddhism entered China from India. From China, they were carried to Korea and Japan, where this version of Buddhism is known as Zen. According to legend, at the invitation of the Chinese emperor, Bodhidharma went as a missionary from southern

India to Canton in 470 C.E. There, he taught the emperor that his scripture, monasteries, and philanthropy availed him nothing; the truth of Buddhism, he taught, is to be found only through meditation and sudden insight. Again, according to legend, when he had finished teaching the emperor, Bodhidharma retired to a cave in the mountains where he spent ten years meditating while facing a wall; during this time, his lower limbs withered and he was no longer able to walk.

A purely apocryphal story says that Bodhidharma wished to stay awake for many hours and meditate, but he kept falling asleep. In a fit of anger at his own inability to stay awake, the monk took a knife and cut off his eyelids. The eyelids fell to the ground and sprang up as the tea plant. Therefore, depictions of Bodhidharma show him with harsh, staring eyes and no eyelids. Legend also has it that Bodhidharma brought tea from India to China. It is true that at about this time tea was introduced from India to China and later to Japan, and that the Intuitive monks began to heavily use caffeinated tea as a means of staying awake to meditate longer.

The basic principle behind all of the Intuitive sects of Buddhism is that enlightenment is an individual matter and therefore one cannot receive much help from other persons or institutions. Individuals find enlightenment through meditation and the realization that the Buddha nature is within themselves. While the externals of religion, including the study of texts, monastic discipline, temples, and images, are important in Zen Buddhism, only direct insight can yield enlightenment. Zen teaches that all people must learn the real truth about religion and life for themselves, through their own experience. One can become enlightened while sitting under a tree or sweeping a floor.[21]

According to the Intuitive sects, reason is to be distrusted because it cannot possibly lead people to real truth. In fact, people must deliberately confuse reason before they can find the truth. Therefore, Zen Buddhism uses riddles that are carefully constructed to go beyond reason or confuse reason in order to lead the initiates into enlightenment. Such riddles of Zen are called *koans* (case studies). Entire books have been filled with these riddles, tales, and short statements used by Zen masters to aid their pupils. Perhaps best-known to Westerners is the simple statement, "You have heard the sound of the clapping of two hands, but what is the sound of one hand clapping?" This question makes no sense, but it is designed to induce the initiate to go beyond sense or reason and to ponder. Another *koan* frequently given to students is, "What was your face before your parents were born?" Still another is, "From where you are stop the distant boat from moving across the water."

The pupil of Zen first meditates. When the pupil's mind is cleared of day-to-day matters and is ready to be released from reason, the master gives the student a riddle. It is hoped that while the novice meditates on one of these nonsense statements a flash of enlightenment (*satori*) will lead the initiate to the truth beyond reason.

In addition to the riddles, Zen masters use other devices to bring a student to insight. Generally, any device that confuses the reasoning processes of the pupil will be used.

Religion and Violence

A Zen master might suddenly shout at or even slap or kick the student to do this. Tales from Zen monasteries tell of masters striking their pupils with sticks or even cutting off one of their fingers in an attempt to cause the intuitive flash. The occasions of brutality are the exception rather than the rule, however.

It is in Japan that Intuitive Buddhism has had its most profound effect on society. The Zen principles of beauty, simplicity, and profundity have deeply touched many areas of Japanese life. Because tea was introduced along with Intuitive Buddhism, tea drinking and the rituals that surround it have been affected by Zen principles. The architecture of the teahouse, the pottery used in the tea ceremony, the music played during the tea ceremony, the poetry that is recited, and the floral arrangements that decorate the teahouse all reflect the principles of Zen. In Japanese art, what is most highly valued is "the controlled accident"; that is, art that is not purely planned or contrived is valued above that which is planned. A teapot that is accidentally broken and glued back together with gold-colored cement is more valued because of the beautiful "accidental" lines of the breakage than a teapot with a contrived design painted on it. A drawing on very porous paper with pen and ink that cannot be erased and corrected is considered more beautiful than one that has been planned, worked out carefully, and corrected by an artist. Thus, the concepts of beauty in Japanese life are heavily influenced by the nonrational approach of Zen.

THE RATIONALIST SECT (T'IEN-T'AI, TENDAI). Whereas the Intuitive sects, Ch'an and Zen, tended to distrust the rational process and felt they had little need for scripture in their search for enlightenment, another group that arose in China in the sixth century taught that in addition to meditation one should use reason and study the scriptures to discover the truth about Buddhism. This sect, which was called T'ien-t'ai, was founded by a monk named Chih-I. According to Chih-I, the Buddha had used various methods during his lifetime to teach his truths. At one point, he taught the Theravada doctrines; at another time, he felt he could communicate better by teaching the Mahayana doctrines; and at still another point, he taught in a manner similar to that used by the Intuitive sects. In reality, there is only one true Buddhist teaching; individuals must study the scriptures of Buddhism to know this truth. Therefore, although meditation may be helpful at certain times, it is not the only path, and rational thought and study should not be disregarded. In the ninth century, the teachings of Chih-I were introduced into Japan, where this sect became known as Tendai.

THE SOCIOPOLITICAL SECT (NICHIREN). From time to time, the various sects of Buddhism have come to have great effect on the social and political life of various nations. One such sect is the so-called Nichiren (sun lotus) Buddhist group, which is a purely Japanese phenomenon. The founder of Nichiren lived in Japan in the thirteenth century. The son of humble parents, at age fifteen he entered a Tendai Buddhist monastery. During his ten years there, he came to believe that all of the current sects of Buddhism were a perversion of the true teachings of the Buddha. He also came to believe that the *Lotus Sutra* was the only scripture a person needed to study to become a correct Buddhist. While meditating on this *sutra*, he underwent a conversion. He changed his name to Nichiren, took a vow to faithfully follow and teach the *Lotus Sutra*, and set forth on a career of preaching and polemics with a fervor reminiscent of many of the Jewish prophets. He preached that he alone understood the truth of pure Buddhism and that the other Japanese sects—Zen, Pure Land, and so on—were preaching falsehoods and leading people to hell. Because most Japanese people followed these "false" sects, the nation was suffering from internal and external woes. Naturally, this kind of preaching aroused powerful enemies; Nichiren was twice deported and twice condemned to death by the Japanese authorities.

Throughout its history, Nichiren Buddhism has expressed hostility toward the rituals and teachings of other Buddhist sects. Consequently, it has always been a small, persecuted minority. The Nichiren sect has also stressed a simpler form of Buddhism and uncompromising patriotism and loyalty to Japan. It teaches that when Buddhism becomes purified in Japan, it will reach out to the rest of the world. Although Nichiren has only slightly over two million followers today, it was the source of another Buddhist sect, Soka Gakkai, which is much larger.

Tibetan Buddhism

Another aspect of Mahayana Buddhism is represented by sects that emphasize the use of magical words or formulas as a means of achieving various goals. In Buddhism, as in nearly every other religion, there are those who believe that the recitation of certain phrases, names, or "magical" words achieves certain ends. The largest and best known of these sects is the religion that once was a dominant force in Tibet.

Native Tibetan religion emphasized incantations and spells to protect people from the demons and spirits that lurked in the shadows and dark places of that harsh land. When Buddhism entered Tibet, it apparently took this concern for magic and protection from demons as a major emphasis. Today, this variant of Tibetan Buddhism is known as Bon, a form of folk Buddhism that is more concerned with life in the world than with the attainment of enlightenment.

Buddhism was officially introduced into Tibet in the seventh century, when King Srong-brtsan-sgam-po, who was interested in bringing the benefits of Indian and Chinese culture to his people, came to the throne. One of his wives was Chinese, and another was Indian; both were Buddhist, therefore, he sent them back to their respective homelands and asked them to return with Buddhist books and teachers. In the eighth century, the spread of Buddhism was interrupted when local shamans convinced the Tibetans that a certain epidemic was the result of the native deities' anger. This interruption did not last long, however; soon the Buddhists were allowed to return to continue their missionary activities.

The philosophy of Tibetan Buddhism is much like that found throughout the Mahayana world; but because of the isolation of this nation, many unique features have been developed and maintained. The most important practical feature of Tibetan Buddhism is its concern for magic as a means of coping with the problems of life. Tibetan Buddhism is frequently referred to as Tantric Buddhism because of its heavy reliance on manuals (*tantras*) that teach the various magical words and spells that help one deal with the unknown and are believed to guide the quest for positive rebirth and eventually enlightenment. Tantric religion is found in several sects of both Hinduism and Buddhism. In original Indian thought, it was

Chinese Mahayana Buddhist layman paying homage to the Buddha. Buddah Tooth Relic Temple (Singapore).
(Mark R. Woodward)

believed that within each deity there were two elements: the male and the female. Sometimes these elements were separated in the minds of the devotee into a god and his consort, or wife, as in the case of Shiva and Kali. The awareness of these two divine elements led certain Hindus and, later, Buddhists to seek a mystical union with them through sexual practices. It was also believed that people could conquer passion with an excess of that passion. Therefore, in addition to bringing about a union between the devotee and the god/goddess, Tantric religion sought enlightenment and conquest over the flesh by carrying passion to excessive lengths. It also was believed that people could conquer their desire for meat, wine, or other forbidden items by overindulging in them. This form of religion became popular in early medieval Tibet. Reform came under the direction of a monk named Atisa (982–1054 C.E.), and Tibetan Tantric Buddhism was purged of much of its eroticism and given a more spiritual foundation.

Another feature of Tibetan Buddhism is its use of the phrase *Om mani padme hum*, which means, "Om, the jewel in the lotus, hum." This expression is used to invoke the *Bodhisattva* Avalokiteshvara. While Avalokiteshvara is known in many schools of Mahayana Buddhism, he is particularly important in Tibet. He is revered as the patron of the Tibetan people and is worshipped because of his great compassion and ability to rescue his disciples from the perils of the world, as well as to guide them on the path to enlightenment.

Tibetan Buddhist prayer wheel. The cylinder contains a prayer text. Spinning it is thought to yield as much positive karma as reciting the text.
(Mark R. Woodward)

Another feature of Tibetan Buddhism that seems to be unique is the prayer wheel. No one knows the origin of this device, but it has been used primarily among Tibetans. One form of the prayer wheel is a cylinder that contains various prayers and ritual incantations; within this cylinder is an agitator. It is believed that by turning the agitator and stirring the prayers, they are somehow prayed. The most common form of the prayer wheel is a small model that can be carried on one's person and activated regularly. Other larger models are found in monasteries. Inventive Tibetan Buddhists have even been known to set up prayer wheels near streams, where they are turned by water power.

Still another distinctive feature of Tibetan Buddhism is its clergy, the *lamas*. The word *lama* basically means "superior one." From the earliest days, men who have spurned the normal pursuits of life to enter monasteries have been unusually powerful. As early as the ninth century, the kings of Tibet gave the *lamas* certain land for their monasteries and with these lands the power to gather funds from the people. By the fourteenth century, the leaders of the monasteries had become more powerful than the kings. The kings disappeared; for all practical purposes, the country was ruled by the Buddhist priests. Although the *lamas* had originally taken vows of celibacy, by the fourteenth century they had rejected it and lived in lordly splendor with their wives and children. During that same century, however, reforms were introduced and celibacy was restored.

The *lamas* of Tibetan Buddhism basically have been divided into two orders: The larger of the two is identified by Western scholars as the Yellow Hat school; the other is identified as the Red Hat school. One of the most interesting contributions of the Red Hat school is their scriptural book, *Bardo Thodol* (The Book of the Dead). It is believed that this book came to written form sometime in the eighth century C.E., although it may contain materials that are centuries older. Of course, it contains some teachings that are pre-Buddhist in nature. It teaches essentially that after death the human soul abides for forty-nine days in a dreamlike state called the *Bardo*. During this period, the ultimate destiny of the soul is determined. Individuals who have lived virtuous lives will achieve *Nirvana* from the *Bardo*; if, on the other hand, a karmic pull has built up during an individual's life, then that person will be drawn again to rebirth.[22] It also is believed that the immediate predeath hours can influence the soul in its stay in the *Bardo*. Therefore, Tibetan Buddhist monks are trained to help the dying through this experience. Western witnesses have sometimes observed the elaborate rituals and efforts of monks as they seek to help the dying.

The leader of the Yellow Hat group has been known for centuries as the Dalai Lama and by virtue of his position essentially has been the ruler of Tibet.[23] When one Dalai Lama dies, an extensive search is made for his successor. A group of monks scours Tibet for a child who seems to have the qualities and characteristics of the dead Dalai Lama, because it is believed that following his death he will reincarnate himself in the body of his successor. When the group has found such a child and agrees that this is the new Dalai Lama, the boy begins a long period of preparation for leadership of the nation.

By the twentieth century, Tibet had become a nation in which the clergy once again ruled the land. The Dalai Lama served as both spiritual and temporal leader, and the position of *lama* became so popular and so important that it was estimated in 1950 that almost 20 percent of the male population lived in monasteries.

Religion and Violence

This came to an abrupt end in 1950, when China invaded Tibet. For centuries, Tibet was claimed by China, but because the claim was rarely pressed, Tibet enjoyed a virtually independent existence. In 1950, China occupied Tibet and set up a puppet government. In 1959, under the leadership of the young Dalai Lama, the Tibetans attempted to overthrow Chinese rule, but their revolution was crushed. The Dalai Lama and many of his followers escaped to India. In exile, the Tibetan Buddhists have maintained their identity and carried on missionary work in India, Europe, and North America. The Dalai Lama has become an international spokesman for peace and human rights and has received the Nobel Prize. He is particularly adept at translating the message of Buddhism into terms that Western people can understand easily. Recent changes in Chinese policy provide some hope that Buddhism in Tibet may be revived, but no hope that the Dalai Lama will be allowed to return to his homeland.

Buddhist Festivals and Holy Days

Because Buddhism is divided in many ways according to philosophy and geography, there is great variety in its holy days. Some Theravada Buddhist monks have as many as forty holy days each year, but they are not celebrated by all Buddhists. The major festivals recognized by most Buddhists follow.

New Year

In Theravada Buddhist countries, the new year is celebrated in April. This holiday often lasts three days and has a certain carnival-type atmosphere. During the first two days, there is a time of washing, cleaning, and preparing for the new year. In Burma, water is thrown on passersby. On the third day, there is a rededication to the Buddhist way of life; worshippers visit the temples and make offerings in preparation for the new year.[24]

Buddha's Birthday

The birth of Gautama is celebrated on April 8 in China and Japan and on the last full moon in May in Southeast Asia. Japanese Buddhist temples have a flower festival during this holiday. Other Buddhist communities celebrate by washing the statue of the infant Buddha in a basin of fragrant water filled with flower petals to honor the gods who bathed the Buddha immediately after his birth. Sometimes, there is a procession of Buddha images through the streets, accompanied by cheers and firecrackers. Buddhist children dress up as the little Buddha on this holiday.

The Festival of Souls (Ullambana)

During July (in Japan) or August (in China), Buddhists believe that purgatory is opened and the souls of the dead are allowed to wander about the world. Out of compassion,

This Singapore Buddha Tooth Relic Temple. The veneration of relics plays an important role in Buddhist piety that crosses sectarian divides. In this case the Temple was built by a Chinese Mahayana monk who obtained the relic from a Burmese Theravada monk. In Buddhist countries, relics play a significant role in public diplomacy as they are periodically sent on tour to foster goodwill among Buddhists abroad. China, India, Singapore, and Sri Lanka have all sponsored relic tours.
(Mark R. Woodward)

families leave gifts of food for these wandering spirits. During the middle of the month, elaborate rituals are performed by priests to provide comfort and release from purgatory to the souls of the dead.

The Robe Offering

In November, at the end of the rainy season, Theravada Buddhists celebrate the sending forth of the first Buddhist missionaries in the days of Asoka. The laity present new yellow robes to the monks of their region, as well as other gifts. A public feast and display of the robes on a "wishing tree" make up the ceremony. The season ends with the making and presentation of the *mahakathina* (great robe). This robe is one that has been made in a single day or night—from spinning the thread to stitching the cloth. The robe commemorates the act of the Buddha's mother, who upon hearing that the Buddha was to renounce his worldly life, wove his first mendicant robe in one night.

Buddhism Today

After the great missionary movements in the first fifteen centuries of its existence, and after such Asian nations as Sri Lanka, Burma, Thailand, China, Japan, and Korea had been converted, Buddhism slipped into a state of quiescence. For centuries, there were no great movements or changes. Within the twentieth century, however, Buddhism began to revive and grow again. There are several reasons for this revival.

Strangely enough, one of the factors in renewed interest in Buddhism has been the work of Christian missionaries and other Western Orientalists. As Europeans entered Asian nations in the nineteenth and twentieth centuries, they felt the need to know more about Buddhism. They therefore initiated translations of ancient Buddhist texts. Some actually converted to Buddhism.[25] This marked the beginning of Western fascination with Buddhism, which has continued until the present day.

A second factor that has contributed to the revival of Buddhism, particularly Theravada Buddhism, has been the rise of Asian nationalisms. With the collapse of the colonial empires after World War II, many new Asian nations began to take pride in being Buddhist. In the past, it was in vogue to be Western, to speak a European language, and to study Christianity. After World War II, Theravada Buddhism attracted renewed attention in such nations as Burma and Thailand. Some modernist interpretations of Buddhism and Hinduism, claim that with their theories of endless ages, they are much more in tune with science than the Judeo-Christian story of creation. Furthermore, Buddhism's message of peace and tolerance seemed to fit the needs of the nuclear age. Therefore, some Buddhists have come to see their religion as being the religious option for the modern world. These concerns have led to a renewed emphasis on missionary efforts, as well as to an ecumenical Buddhist movement known as Socially Engaged Buddhism, which minimizes sectarian differences and emphasizes such universal Buddhist teachings as nonviolence and compassion for all living beings. While it is true that Buddhism can be understood as a religion of nonviolence, Buddhists can be as violent as any other people. Throughout their histories, Burma and Thailand have fought many wars. While contemporary Tibetan Buddhists stress a nonviolent, psychologically oriented interpretation of their faith, in the eighteenth and early nineteenth centuries they enjoyed a well-deserved reputation as ferocious warriors. Indeed, some of the world's most brutal governments have been led by Buddhists. Today, Burma provides the clearest example. Even monks have been victims of this brutal, totalitarian regime. In Sri Lanka, Buddhist nationalism is used to promote discrimination against ethnic and religious minorities and to justify brutal counterinsurgency operations.

Historically, the chief locations for Mahayana Buddhism have been China, Japan, Vietnam, and Korea. Following World War II, Buddhism suffered severe losses in China. With the establishment of the People's Republic of China in 1949, Buddhism was suppressed. It suffered more serious losses with the Chinese Cultural Revolution, beginning in 1966. Today, however, there seems to be renewed Buddhist activity in China. At the conclusion of the Vietnam War, great numbers of Vietnamese, Lao, and Thai Buddhists migrated to the United States. Zen, Nichiren, and Tibetan Buddhism have also attracted many converts in America and Europe over the past few decades. Today it is not unusual to find large communities of Buddhists of many sects and varieties in major American urban centers. American Buddhism is beginning to acquire its own unique characteristics. Popular Buddhist magazines like *Tricycle* include articles about many different forms of Buddhism, emphasizing the study and practice of meditation and social and ecological responsibility. They place relatively less emphasis on monastic life, which few Americans find appealing. These trends are contemporary examples of the ways in which Buddhists have tried to apply the teachings of the Buddha in widely different cultural, social, and historical contexts.

In Japan and Korea, Mahayana Buddhism remains a vital force in people's lives. In recent decades, Japanese forms of Buddhism (such as Zen, Nichiren, and Pure Land) have attracted much attention in Western nations. Today, Buddhist temples and shrines are found in many of these countries, and Buddhist literature is widely read. Buddhism, it would seem, is in the process of another great missionary outreach. Its world population is currently estimated at approximately 324 million.[26]

STUDY QUESTIONS

1. Compare the life of Gautama to that of Mahavira. Why are the details of their lives similar?
2. List the four passing sights that Gautama saw. Why did these sights cause him to begin a search for religious answers?
3. What are the Four Noble Truths that Gautama taught in his Deer Park Sermon at Banaras?
4. What is there in the teachings of Gautama that caused Buddhism to be called "the middle way"?
5. According to the Buddha, what is the central problem of humanity that keeps it bound to the endless cycle of life?
6. What is the significance of King Asoka in the development of Buddhism into a world religion?
7. List four basic differences between Mahayana and Theravada Buddhism.
8. Distinguish between the Pure Land and the Intuitive sects of Mahayana Buddhism.

SUGGESTED READING

de Bary, William Theodore, ed. *The Buddhist Tradition.* New York: Vintage, 1972.
Beyer, Stephen. *The Buddhist Experience.* Encino, CA: Dickenson, 1974.

Conze, Edward. *Buddhist Scriptures.* New York: Penguin, 1959.

Fields, Rick. *How the Swans Came to the Lake. A Narrative History of Buddhism in America.* Boston: Shambala Publications, 1992.

Gyatso, Tenzin. *The Buddhism of Tibet and the Key to the Middle Way.* London: George Allen and Unwin, 1975.

Kuah, Pearce. *State Society and Religious Engineering: Towards a Reformist Buddhism in Singapore.* Singapore: Eastern Universities Press, 2003.

Küng, Hans, et al. *Christianity and the World Religions: Paths of Dialogue with Islam, Hinduism, and Buddhism.* Translated by Peter Heinegg. New York: Doubleday, 1986.

Robinson, Richard H., and Willard L. Johnson. *The Buddhist Religion.* Belmont, CA: Wadsworth, 1997.

Spiro, Melford. *Buddhism and Society. A Great Tradition and Its Burmese Vicissitudes.* Berkeley: University of California Press, 1982.

Strong, John. *The Experience of Buddhism. Sources and Interpretations.* Belmont, CA: Wadsworth, 1995.

Suzuki, Daisetz T. *Zen and Japanese Buddhism.* Boston: Charles E. Tuttle, 1958.

SOURCE MATERIAL

Gautama Speaks of His Ascetic Practices

Before Gautama achieved enlightenment under the *bo* tree, he had struggled for many years. One of his paths led him to practice extreme asceticism. In the following passage, Gautama relates his experiences to one of his disciples.[27]

Majjhima-Nikaya. *XII*

Aye, Sariputta, I have lived the fourfold higher life;—I have been an ascetic of ascetics; loathly have I been, foremost in loathness, scrupulous have I been, foremost in scrupulosity; solitary have I been, foremost in solitude.

(i) To such a pitch of asceticism have I gone that naked was I, flouting life's decencies, licking my hands after meals, never heeding when folk called to me to come or to stop, never accepting food brought to me before my rounds or cooked expressly for me, never accepting an invitation, never receiving food direct from pot or pan or within the threshold or among the faggots or pestles, never from (one only of) two people messing together, never from a pregnant woman or a nursing mother or a woman in coitu, never from gleanings (in time of famine) nor from where a dog is ready at hand or where (hungry) flies congregate, never touching flesh or spirits or strong drink or brews of grain. I have visited only one house a day and there take only one morsel; or I visited but two or (up to not more than) seven houses a day and taken at each only two or (up to not more than) seven morsels; I have lived on a single saucer of food a day, or on two, or (up to) seven saucers; I have had but one meal a day, or one every two days, or (so on, up to) every seven days, or only once a fortnight, on a rigid scale of rationing. My sole diet has been herbs gathered green, or the grain of wild millets and paddy, or snippets of hide, or water plants, or the red powder round rice-grains within the husk, or the discarded scum of rice on the boil, or the flour of oil-seeds, or grass, or cow-dung. I have lived on wild roots and fruit, or on windfalls only. My raiment has been of hemp or of hempen mixture, of cerements, of rags from the dust-heap, of bark, of the black antelope's pelt either whole or split down the middle, or grass, of strips of bark or wood, of hair of men or animals woven into a blanket or of owl's wings. In fulfillment of my vows, I have plucked out the hair of my head and the hair of my beard, have never quitted the upright for the sitting posture, have squatted and never risen up, moving only a-squat, have couched on thorns, have gone down to the water punctually thrice before nightfall to wash (away the evil within). After this wise, in divers fashions, have I lived to torment and to torture my body—to such a length in asceticism have I gone.

(ii) To such a length have I gone in loathness that on my body I have accumulated the dirt and filth of years till it dropped off of itself—even as the rank growths of years fall away from the stump of a tinduka-tree. But never once came the thought to me to clean it off with my own hands or to get others to clean it off for me;—to such a length in loathness have I gone.

(iii) To such a length in scrupulosity have I gone that my footsteps out and in were always attended by a mindfulness so vigilant as to awake compassion within me over even a drop of water lest I might harm tiny creatures in crevices;—to such a length have I gone in scrupulosity.

(iv) To such a length have I gone as a solitary that when my abode was in the depths of the forest, the mere glimpse of a cowherd or neatherd or grass cutter, or of a man gathering firewood or edible roots in the forest, was enough to make me dart from wood to wood, from thicket to thicket, from dale to dale, and from hill to hill,—in order that they might not see me or I them. As a deer at the sight of man darts away over hill and dale, even so did I dart away at the mere glimpse of cowherd, neatherd, or whatnot, in order that they might not see me or I them;—to such a length have I gone as a solitary.

When the cowherds had driven their herds forth from the byres, up I came on all fours to find a subsistence on the drippings of the young milch-cows. So long as my own dung and urine held out, on that I have subsisted. So foul a filth-eater was I.

I took up my abode in the awesome depths of the forest, depths so awesome that it was reputed that none but the passionless could venture in without his hair standing on end. When the cold season brought chill wintry nights, then it was that, in the dark half of the months when snow was falling, I dwelt by night in the open air and in the dank thicket by day. But when there came the last broiling month of summer before the rains, I made my dwelling under the baking sun by day and in the stifling thicket by night. Then there flashed on me these verses, never till then uttered by any:

Now scorched, now froze, in forest dread, alone.

naked and fireless, set upon his quest.
the hermit battles purity to win.

In a charnel ground I lay me down with charred bones for pillow. When the cowherds' boys came along, they spat and staled upon me, pelted me with dirt and stuck bits of wood into my ears. Yet I declare that never did I let an evil mood against them arise within me.—So poised in equanimity was I.

(80) Some recluses and Brahmins there are who say and hold that purity cometh by way of food, and accordingly proclaim that they live exclusively on jujube-fruits, which, in one form or other, constitute their sole meat and drink. Now I can claim to have lived on a single jujube-fruit a day. If this leads you to think that this fruit was large, in those days, you would err; for, it was precisely the same size then that it is today. When I was living on a single fruit a day, my body grew emaciated in the extreme; because I ate so little, my members, great and small, grew like the knotted joints of withered creepers; like a buffalo's hoof were my shrunken buttocks; like the twists in a rope were my spinal vertebrae; like the crazy rafters of a tumble-down roof, that start askew and aslant, were my gaunt ribs; like the starry gleams on water deep down and afar in the depths of a well, shone my gleaming eyes deep down and afar in the depths of their sockets; and as the rind of a cut gourd shrinks and shrivels in the heat, so shrank and shriveled the scalp of my head,—and all because I ate so little. If I sought to feel my belly, it was my backbone which I found in my grasp; if I sought to feel my backbone, I found myself grasping my belly, so closely did my belly cleave to my back-bone;—and all because I ate so little. If for ease of body I chafed my limbs, the hairs of my body fell away under my hand, rotted at their roots;—and all because I ate so little.

> Other recluses and Brahmins there are who, saying and holding that purity cometh by way of food, proclaim that they live exclusively on beans—or seasamum—or rice—as their sole meat and drink.

(81) Now I can claim to have lived on a single bean a day—on a single seasamum seed a day—or on a single grain of rice a day; and (the result was still the same). Never did this practice or these courses or these dire austerities bring me to the ennobling gifts of super-human knowledge and insight. And why?—Because none of them lead to that noble understanding which, when won, leads on to Deliverance and guides him who lives up to it onward to the utter extinction of all ill.

The Buddha Explains the Eightfold Path

At the heart of Buddha's teaching about the nature of life and death and the proper way to live is the Eightfold Path. The following selection contains the Buddha's explanation of this path.[28]

Samyutta-nikaya V, 8,

"The Noble Eightfold Way, monks, I will expound and analyze to you. Listen to it, reflect on it well, I will speak." "Even so, Lord," the monks replied to the Lord.

The Lord said, "What, monks, is the Noble Eightfold Way? It is namely right view, right intention, right speech, right action, right livelihood, right effort, right mindfulness, right concentration."

"And what, monks, is the right view? The knowledge of pain, knowledge of the cause of pain, knowledge of the cessation of pain, and knowledge of the way that leads to the cessation of pain: that, monks, is called right view."

"And what is right intention? The intention to renounce, the intention not to hurt, the intention not to injure: that, monks, is called right intention."

"And what is right speech? Refraining from falsehood, from malicious speech, from harsh speech, from frivolous speech: that, monks, is called right speech."

"And what is right action? Refraining from taking life, from taking what is not given, for sexual intercourse: that, monks, is called right action."

"And what is right livelihood? Here a noble disciple abandoning a false mode of livelihood gets his living by right livelihood: that, monks, is called right livelihood."

"And what is right effort? Here a monk with the non-producing of bad and evil thoughts that have not yet arisen exercises will, puts forth effort, begins to make exertion, applies and exerts his mind; with the dispelling of bad and evil thoughts that had arisen he exercises will, puts forth effort, begins to make exertion, applies and exerts his mind; with the producing of good thoughts that had not arisen he exercises will, puts forth effort, begins to make exertion, applies and exerts his mind; with the fixing, freeing from confusion, increasing, enlarging, developing and filling up of good thoughts that had arisen he exercises will, puts forth effort, begins to make exertion, applies and exerts his mind: that, monks, is called right effort."

"And what is right mindfulness? Here (1) on the body: a monk abides contemplating the body, ardent, thoughtful, and mindful, dispelling his longing and dejection toward the world; (2) on feelings: he abides contemplating the feelings, ardent, thoughtful, and mindful, dispelling his longing and dejection toward the world; (3) on thoughts: he abides contemplating thoughts, ardent, thoughtful, and mindful, dispelling his longing and dejection toward the world. That, monks, is called right mindfulness."

"And what is right concentration? Here (1) a monk free from passions and evil thoughts attains and abides in the first trance of joy and pleasure, which is accompanied by reasoning and investigation and arises from seclusion. (2) With the ceasing of reasoning and investigation, in a state of internal serenity, with his mind fixed on one point, he attains and abides in the second trance of joy and pleasure arising from concentration, and free from reasoning and investigation. (3) With equanimity and indifference toward joy he abides mindful and self-possessed, and with his body experiences pleasure that the noble ones call 'Dwelling with equanimity, mindful and happy,' and attains and abides in the third trance. (4) Dispelling pleasure and pain, and even before the disappearance of elation and depression, he attains and abides in the fourth trance, which is without pleasure and pain, and with the purity of mindfulness and equanimity: that, monks, is called right concentration."

The Infinite Compassion of the *Bodhisattva*

One of the important figures in Mahayana Buddhism is the *Bodhisattva*. They may have lived as humans and have delayed their achievements of *Nirvana* because of their compassion for humankind. In this passage from *Shikshasamuccaya* (pp. 280–82) is a statement about the compassion of the *Bodhisattva*.[29]

A Bodhisattva resolves: I take upon myself the burden of suffering. I am resolved to do so, I will endure it. I do not turn or run away, do not tremble, am not terrified, nor afraid, do not turn back or despond.

And why? At all costs I must bear the burdens of all beings. In that I do not follow my own inclinations. I have made the vow to save all beings. All beings I must set free.

The whole world of living beings I must rescue, from the terrors of birth, of old age, of sickness, of death and rebirth, of all kinds of moral offense, of all states of woe, of the whole cycle of birth-and-death, of the jungle of false views, of the loss of wholesome dharmas, of the concomitants of ignorance,—from all these terrors I must rescue all beings. I walk so that the kingdom of unsurpassed cognition is built up for all beings. My endeavors do not merely aim at my own deliverance. For with the help of the boat of the thought of all-knowledge, I must rescue all these beings from the stream of Samsara, which is so difficult to cross, I must pull them back from the great precipice. I must free them from all calamities, I must ferry them across the stream of Samsara. I myself must grapple with the whole mass of suffering of all beings. To the limit of my endurance I will experience in all the states of woe, found in any world system, all the abodes of suffering. And I must not cheat all beings out of my store of merit, I am resolved to abide in each single state of woe for numberless aeons; and so I will help all beings to freedom, in all the states of woe that may be found in any world system whatsoever.

And why? Because it is surely better that I alone should be in pain than that all these beings should fall into the states of woe. There I must give myself away as a pawn through which the whole world is redeemed from the terrors of the hells, of animal birth, of the world of Yama, and with this my own body I must experience, for the sake of all beings, the whole mass of all painful feelings. And on behalf of all beings I give surety for all beings, and in doing so I speak truthfully, am trustworthy, and do not go back on my word. I must not abandon all beings.

And why? There has arisen in me the will to win all-knowledge, with all beings for its object, that is to say, for the purpose of setting free the entire world of beings. And I have not set out for the supreme enlightenment from a desire for delights, not because I help to experience the delights of the five-sense qualities, or because I wish to indulge in the pleasures of the senses. And I do not pursue the course of a Bodhisattva in order to achieve the array of delights that can be found in the various worlds of sense-desire.

And why? Truly no delights are all these delights of the world. All this indulging in the pleasure of the senses belongs to the sphere of Mara.

The Importance of Sitting

In that branch of Mahayana Buddhism known in Japan as Zen, meditation is the key to enlightenment. The following text from Shobogenzo Zuimonki speaks of the importance of meditation in Zen.[30]

When I stayed at the Zen lodge in T'ien-t'ung (China), the venerable Ching used to stay up sitting until the small hours of the morning and then after only a little rest should rise early to start sitting again. In the meditation hall we went on sitting with the other elders, without letting up for even a single night. Meanwhile many of the monks went off to sleep. The elder would go around among them and hit the sleepers with his fist or a slipper, yelling at them to wake up. If their sleepiness persisted, he would go out to the hallway and ring the bell to summon the monks to a room apart, where he would lecture to them by the light of a candle.

"What use is there in your assembling together in the hall only to go to sleep? Is this all that you left the world and joined holy orders for? Even among laymen, whether they be emperors, princes, or officials, are there any who live a life of ease? The ruler must fulfill the duties of the sovereign, his ministers must serve with loyalty and devotion, and commoners must work to reclaim land and till the soil—no one lives a life of ease. To escape from such burdens and idly while away the time in a monastery—what does this accomplish? Great is the problem of life and death; fleeting indeed is our transitory existence. Upon these truths both the scriptural and meditation schools agree. What sort of illness awaits us tonight, what sort of death tomorrow? While we have life, not to practice Buddha's Law, but to spend the time in sleep is the height of foolishness. Because of such foolishness Buddhism today is in a state of decline. When it was at its zenith monks devoted themselves to the practice of sitting in meditation (zazen), but nowadays sitting is not generally insisted upon and consequently Buddhism is losing ground."

Upon another occasion his attendants said to him, "The monks are getting over-tired or falling ill, and some are thinking of leaving the monastery, all because they are required to sit too long in meditation. Shouldn't the length of the sitting period be shortened?" The master became highly indignant. "That would be quite wrong. A monk who is not really devoted to the religious life may very well fall asleep in a half hour or an hour. But one truly devoted to it who has resolved to persevere in his religious discipline will eventually come to enjoy the practice of sitting, no matter how long it lasts. When I was young I used to visit the heads of various monasteries, and one of them explained to me, "Formerly I used to hit sleeping monks so hard that my fist just about broke. Now I am old and weak, so I can't hit them hard enough. Therefore it is difficult to produce good monks. In many monasteries today the superiors do not emphasize sitting strongly enough, and so Buddhism is declining. The more you hit them the better," he advised me.

CHAPTER 7

Sikhism

CHAPTER OBJECTIVES

In this chapter you will:

- Study the lives of Nanak and the other Sikh *gurus*.

- Come to understand how Sikhism stands between Islam and Hinduism on many issues.

- Understand the tension between pacificism and militancy in Sikh tradition and history.

KEY TERMS

Granth

Singhs

Udasis

Sahajdharis

A Timeline of Sikhism			
1491–1539 C.E.	Life of Guru Nanak		British occupy the Punjab; end of Sikh independence
1658–1707	Persecution of Sikhs during reign of Emperor Arungzeb	1857	Sikh forces aid in suppression of Indian Mutiny; British Christians, Indian Hindus, Muslims, and Sikhs commit atrocities in the name of religion
1699	Militarization of the Sikh community		
1700	British emerge as major power in India	19th and 20th centuries	Sikh immigration to Britain, Africa, North America, and other English-speaking colonies/countries
1780–1839	Ranjit Singh rules Sikh kingdom in the Punjab; encourages religious tolerance;		

(Continued)

A Timeline of Sikhism (*Continued*)			
1947	Independence from Britain; Sikh demands for independent state ignored; Partition of British India into India and Pakistan sparks massive outbreaks of violence among Hindus, Muslims, and Sikhs		Indian army storms Golden temple; thousands die in outbreaks of Hindu rioting
		1984	Assassination of Indian Prime Minister Indira Gandhi triggers Hindu violence in which thousands of Sikhs are killed
1983	Sikh militants occupy Golden Temple	2004	Monmohan Singh, a Sikh, becomes first non-Hindu Prime Minister of India

Sikhism originated in the sixteenth century C.E. in the Punjab in northwestern India. Sikhs believe their faith to be a new and independent religion based on the insights of their first teacher, Nanak. Scholars have long held that Sikhism developed in the context of a religious conversation between devotional Hinduism and Islamic mysticism. Like Buddhism and Jainism, Sikhism takes much of its worldview from and seeks to reform certain elements of Hinduism. Unlike other reform movements in Hinduism, however, Sikhism endeavors to accommodate elements from another major world religion, Islam. Many Sikh spiritual leaders have also been warriors.

Sikhism has always been a minority religion in India. Today, Sikhs number only about 19.1 million worldwide.[1] Sikhs are still found mainly in the Punjab, although substantial communities also are found in other regions of India, Europe, North America, and Southeast Asia.

The Life of Nanak

From the tenth century onward, various Muslim groups invaded India from their bases to the west. These invasions eventually resulted in the domination of India by the Moghul rulers. Although all of India faced Muslim conquest at one time or another, the northwest section was invaded most frequently. Here, Islam made its greatest number of converts and established its strongest bases. Because Islam and Hinduism were basically so different in so many areas, the encounters between Muslims and Hindus often were hostile and violent.

From the earliest days, however, there were teachers who did not believe the two religions had to be antagonistic and thought a synthesis could be reached. The reformer best remembered for attempting to bring Hinduism and Islam together was Kabir (1440–1518 C.E.). By this time, Hinduism and Islam had grown closer than they had been at the time of the initial Muslim conquest. Hindus and Muslims revered many of the same holy men and sometimes shared shrines and other places of religious devotion. This was possible because Hinduism teaches that gods appear in many forms, while Sufism, the mystical branch of Islam, believes in saints whose tombs become objects of veneration. There were some, Hindu and Muslim alike, who took these similarities as a sign that the two religions pointed to a common sacred reality.

Kabir was born a Muslim, but he found it possible to worship with his Hindu neighbors. While worshipping the Hindu deities, he was also teaching that the true God was one. The oneness of God is the most basic Muslim teaching. Kabir was later accepted as a holy man or saint by Hindus and Muslims and made a profound impression on the Sikhs and their literature.

The founder of Sikhism was a man named Nanak (1469–1538 C.E.), a later contemporary of Kabir. Nanak was born into a Hindu home in the Punjab about forty miles from the city of Lahore. Because of the mixed nature of the region, Nanak's schoolmaster was a Muslim and surely influenced him.

Nanak is pictured as a dreamer who had little grasp of the day-to-day world of business or practicality. His interests and talents leaned more toward poetry and religion. His father tried to place him in a variety of occupations, but Nanak failed at all of them. He was betrothed to a young woman when he was twelve, and their marriage was consummated when he was nineteen. Two sons were born of this marriage. Nanak eventually left his wife and sons and went to the city of Sultanpur to earn his living. Here he was a bit more successful in his business pursuits.

During his stay in Sultanpur, when he was about thirty years old, Nanak received a vision from God that was to change his life. According to some stories, God spoke to him while he was meditating in the forest. The message of the vision was that Nanak had been singled out as a prophet of the true religion. His message was to be, "There is no Muslim and there is no Hindu." Thus, he was to become an evangelist, preaching a gospel of unity between these two religions. Along with his constant companion, Mardana, Nanak became a wandering preacher of this new message. The two traveled widely in India over the next decades, preaching the essential unity of Islam and Hinduism. To emphasize his message, Nanak wore a mixed costume, made up of the clothing of both Hindus and Muslims. Wherever he went, he sought to organize communities of people who accepted his teachings. Each of his followers became known as a Sikh, a Punjabi word for "disciple." In his travels, Nanak even made the pilgrimage to Mecca, although he antagonized the people there because of his unwillingness to display the proper respect for Muslim shrines.

After many years of wandering, Nanak returned home to northwest India, where he continued to teach and form communities of Sikhs. According to a charming Sikh legend, as Nanak was about to die, his followers were still divided over their basic religious loyalties. Those who originally had been Hindus planned to cremate his remains, whereas those who originally had been Muslims wished to bury him. Nanak, aware of this dispute over his body, requested that each group place flowers beside him, and the group whose flowers were still fresh on the following day could have his body. When the two factions agreed and placed their flowers beside him, Nanak covered himself with a sheet and died. When the sheet was removed the next morning, the Sikhs found that both sets of flowers were still fresh but that Nanak's body had disappeared. Thus, according to this legend, the peaceful and loving Nanak, even in death, sought to bring harmony between Muslims and Hindus.[2]

The Teachings of Nanak

Nanak, like Kabir and others, endeavored to synthesize elements of Islam and Hinduism. He took from each religion what be believed to be of most importance. From Islam he took the teaching that there is but one God. Although Hindus may see this God at work in many ways and in various disguises, still God is basically one. Sikhs refer to this God as The True Name.

Nanak also taught that The True Name is the creator of the entire universe and that human beings are God's supreme creation. Thus Nanak rejected the teaching of *ahimsa*, which is so important to many Indian religions. Because people are the primary creation, they are free to kill and eat animals. Sikhs are among the few Indians who may legitimately eat meat.

Nanak did adopt several elements of Hinduism. He accepted the principle of reincarnation, which is basic to many Indian religions. Sikhs came to believe that the spirit of Nanak was reincarnated in the bodies of those *gurus* who succeeded him as the leaders of Sikhism. Nanak also taught the Indian principle of *karma* and believed that people continue to acquire *karma* and live again and again until they are freed from this cycle by The True Name.

Nanak rejected the ceremonialism and rituals of both Hinduism and Islam. He taught a very plain and simple form of religion that distrusted and rejected ritual.

From the Source

The Musalamans praise the Sharia, read it, and reflect on it:

But God's servants are they who employ themselves in His service in order to behold him.

The Hindus praise the Praised One whose appearance and form are incomparable;

They bathe in holy streams, perform idol-worship and adoration, use copious incense of sandal.

The Jogis meditate on God the Creator, whom they call the Unseen,

Whose form is minute, whose name is the Bright One, and who is the image of their bodies.[3]

According to one story, Nanak was once ejected from Muslim worship because he laughed aloud during the sermon of the imam. When asked why he was so disrespectful to Muslim worship, he replied that he had perceived that the imam was not really thinking about God while he was preaching but was in fact thinking about his horse and worrying lest the horse fall into a well. This perception struck Nanak as being so ludicrous that he burst into laughter.

Religion and Violence

Another element in the religion of Nanak was his pacifism. In all of his travels and with all of the rejection he received, Nanak maintained the stance of a pacifist. He never struck out at his enemies and apparently taught his disciples to follow this pattern. In contrast to the teachings of Nanak, Sikhs, in their later history, became known as the most militant of warriors. Many Sikh spiritual leaders have also been warriors.

A Sikh preacher addresses an audience in the Golden Temple in Amritsar, India. The Golden Temple houses the Holy Granth and is the most sacred of all Sikh shrines.
(UN/DPI PHOTO)

The Historical Development of Sikhism

Upon the death of Nanak, the leadership of the new movement was taken over by Angad, who ruled until 1552. Nanak and Angad were the first two in a series of ten *gurus* who led Sikhism until the eighteenth century. Usually, the word *guru* in Indian religions carries the connotation of "teacher"; but to the Sikhs, it means "leader." The first four of the ten *gurus* of Sikhism tended to follow the teachings of Nanak and be rather pacific toward their enemies. Angad is remembered because he devised a new script and began to compile the Sikh scriptures. Other *gurus* followed similar paths.

With the ascension of the fifth *guru*, Arjan Dev (1581–1606), both the office and the religion underwent significant changes. Arjan is remembered for beginning the compilation of the official scriptures of Sikhism, the *Adi Granth*. The *Granth* has become increasingly important in Sikhism since the days of the *gurus*. Basically, it is a collection of hymns, a large portion of which came from Nanak. The remainder of the hymns that make up the *Granth* came from Kabir and other *gurus*. The *Granth* contains 3,384 hymns and is roughly three times the size of the *Rig-Veda*.

Religion and Violence

In addition to his contribution as the compiler of the *Granth*, Arjan is recognized for giving Sikhism its militant aspect, in direct contrast to the pacifism of Nanak and the earlier *gurus*. Between the time of Nanak and Arjan, the Sikh movement had grown and was beginning to be recognized as a threat by the Muslim authorities. The Muslim emperor ordered Arjan to remove from the *Granth* any doctrine that was contrary to the teachings of the *Qur'an*. When Arjan refused, he was jailed and tortured to death. Before his death, however, he instructed his son Har Gobind, who was to become the sixth *guru* (1606–1645), to arm and surround himself with bodyguards. The advice of Arjan was accepted, and henceforth the Sikhs were more militant and aggressive in their attitude toward their enemies.

The last of the Sikh *gurus* was Gobind Singh (1675–1708). He assumed the leadership of the Sikhs when he was only a boy because his father, the ninth *guru*, had been imprisoned and executed by the Muslims. It was Gobind Singh, more than any other *guru*, who organized and prepared the Sikhs for self-defense and war. He introduced into Sikhism the worship of the terrible Hindu goddess of death, Durga. He also established the *Granth* as the final word for Sikhs. Because Sikhs were to be governed by the *Granth*, *gurus* did not exist after Gobind Singh's death. Because of his love of weapons, he is said to have introduced the baptism of the sword as a religious ritual. To strengthen his people further and prepare them for war, he developed an elite class of Sikhs who made unusually fine warriors. This corps was known as *Singhs* (Lions)

and was distinguished in the following ways: They wore the *kes* or long hair on their heads and faces and adorned their hair with the *kangha* (comb); they wore *kachk* (short trousers); they wore a *kara* (steel bracelet); and they were equipped with a *kirpan* (steel dagger). The members of this corps were not allowed to use wine, tobacco, or any other form of stimulant. They were encouraged to eat meat. The order of the Singhs was open to men of all castes. These factors, combined with the theology of reincarnation, made the Singhs incredible warriors.

Gobind Singh, the last of the *gurus*, was assassinated in 1708. From that time until the present, the Sikhs have been governed by their scripture, the *Granth*, and their history has been full of strife. At certain times, the Sikhs have been the victims of violence; at other times, they have been the aggressors. By the early nineteenth century, they controlled most of the Punjab region. When the British sought to enter that area, the Sikhs fought bloody wars against them but were finally subdued. Because of the Sikhs' valor as warriors, the British came to admire and use the Sikhs as soldiers and policemen throughout India. Even today Sikhs are employed as bank security guards as far away from the Punjab as northern Burma and southwest China. With the departure of the British in the 1940s and with the partition of India into Hindu and Muslim states by the United Nations in 1947, the Sikhs were located in the Indian state of Punjab. There, their numbers were only slightly larger than those of the Hindus.

Divisions within Sikhism

Modern Sikhs are found mainly in India, although Sikh communities are found in many other parts of the world. Within the main body of modern Sikhism are three divisions. Each division accepts the central teachings of Nanak, each accepts the *Granth* as sacred scripture, and each accepts the ten *gurus* as inspired leaders of the faith.

The first sect, known as the *Udasis*, is basically an order of holy men. These Sikhs follow many of the same principles and rules that govern the ascetics of Hinduism,

Buddhism, and Jainism. They are celibate and wear coarse yellow garments like the Buddhist monks, or they go naked like Jain monks. Their only possession is a begging bowl. Unlike other Sikhs, the Udasis frequently shave their heads and beards. Often, they are active missionaries, seeking to convince nonbelievers of the merit of their religion.

The second sect of Sikhs is known as the *Sahajdharis* (conservative, slow-going). Their development as Sikhs seems to have stopped at some point before Gobind Singh. They reject the militant characteristic of much of Sikhism today and prefer to be clean-shaven. The third sect, the Singhs, have already been described.

Sikh Religious Life

The religious life of the modern Sikh tends to be simple, probably because of the distrust of elaborate ceremonies that moved the early founders of this religion. One joins the Sikhs not by being born into a Sikh family but by undergoing a ritual of baptism when one is mature enough to accept it. In this ritual, a bowl of sweetened water is stirred by a dagger; the water is then sprinkled on the initiate as the initiate is instructed in the truths

Communal meal at a Sikh Gurdwara (temple) in New York City. After the religious service, everybody partakes in the traditional Sikh communal meal called Langer. This communal meal symbolizes that all are equal.
(Eugene Gordon/Pearson Education/PH College)

Sikh man on his way to prayer.
(Mark R. Woodward)

and prohibitions of the faith. Just as the initiatory ceremony of Sikhism is simple, so are the ceremonies surrounding marriage and death.

Daily rituals for a Sikh include an early-morning bath, followed by the reading of certain hymns and the recitation of prayers. At night, there is another ritual involving hymns and prayers. When Sikhs gather for congregational worship, they meet in temples called *gurdwaras*. In these temples, the central object of worship is a copy of the sacred *Adi Granth*. Congregational worship involves prayers to the *Granth*, various hymns, a sermon, and a communion meal. There are no Sikh priests, and the group services may be led by any member of the community. In addition, there are no caste or sexual differentiations in worship.

An object of special attention to Sikhs all over the world is the *Takht* (throne) of Sikhism at Amritsar. Although there are three other such thrones throughout the Sikh world, the one at Amritsar, within the golden temple, is central. It is here that the authorities of the Sikh world make decisions regarding the worship and practice of their people. Although Nanak specifically prohibited pilgrimages as being worthless for true religion, most Sikhs like to go to Amritsar and plan to visit there at least once in their lives.

Sikh Holy Days

Because of the extreme simplicity and personal nature of Sikhism, this religion does not have an elaborate calendar or set of festivals. As residents of northern India, the Sikhs celebrate Holi and Divali with their Hindu neighbors.[4] In June, the Sikhs celebrate the martyrdom of Guru Arjan, the compiler of the *Adi Granth* and the builder of the Golden Temple at Amritsar. The Sikhs also celebrate annually the birthdays of Nanak in November and Guru Arjan in December or January. These celebrations include communal processions and sacred meals.

A Sikh Gurdwara in Singapore.
(Mark R. Woodward)

Sikhism Today

Religion and Violence

The life of the Sikhs has become increasingly precarious in modern India. In the Punjab region, the growth of Hindus and other religious groups has once again made the Sikhs a minority group. Because they are neither Hindu nor Muslim, Sikhs lack the political strength of the major religions of India. Therefore, radical factions in Sikhism have begun to demand that the Punjab be declared an independent Sikh nation.

When combined with the Sikh warrior tradition, political radicalism has a strong potential for violence. This combination of factors has sometimes led to armed conflict with the government of India. In 1984, when Indian Prime Minister Indira Gandhi was assassinated by her Sikh bodyguards, there were anti-Sikh riots in Delhi in which large numbers of innocent people were killed.

In recent years, Europeans and Americans have been attracted to Sikhism primarily because of its simplicity and tolerance, and its emphasis on the religious equality of men and women. For the most part, these converts follow the pacifist tradition associated with Kabir and Nanak. Because many Indian Sikhs living in the West follow a worldlier path, tension sometimes exists between the two communities.

STUDY QUESTIONS

1. Discuss Sikhism as a syncretism between Hinduism and Islam. Which features has it taken from each religion?
2. What factors worked to turn the pacific movement of Nanak into the warrior caste of later Sikhism?
3. List the three major sects of Sikhism. What are the major characteristics of each?

SUGGESTED READING

Archer, John Clark. *The Sikhs*. Princeton, NJ: Princeton University Press, 1946.
Banerjee, Anil Chandra. *Guru Nanak and His Times*. Columbia, MO: South Asia Books, 1971.
Fenton, John Y. et al. *Religions of Asia*. New York: St. Martin's Press, 1983. (See the section on Sikhism.)
Singh, Harbans. *The Heritage of the Sikhs*. New York: Asia Publishing House, 1964.

SOURCE MATERIAL

The Japji

The following material, which is called the Japji, is extremely important to Sikhs. It is to be memorized and recited each day and is believed to be essential to understanding all scripture. According to tradition, the Japji was written by Nanak, the founder of Sikhism.[5]

A Book of Psalms of Guru Nanak Nirankari

> Unity, Active Om, True Name!
> Actor, Pervader, Fearless, devoid of Enmity,
> Whom Time and the Ages do not cumber,
> Self-existent, perceptible Guru—
> Praise!
> Pre-eminent Truth, primordial Truth,
> Truth that is, saith Nanak, and will abide forever.

1. Thinking comprehendeth him not, although there be thoughts by the thousands,
   Silence discovers him not, though it be continuous silence;
   Man is persistently hungry, though he eats of tasty abundance;
   Not one of a hundred thousand artful devices avails him!
   How may the truth be attained, the bonds of falsehood be broken?
   By obeying the will of God as surely recorded, saith Nanak.

2. Forms have come of his order, but his order goes still undetected;
   Life has come by his will, through which comes life's exaltation.

High and low are his will, and joy and sorrow his pleasure;
In his will alone is he blessed who runs the round of his nature.
All are subject to him, not one beyond his jurisdiction.
If any perceives his will, he humbles himself, saith Nanak.

3. Some sing his power who themselves are feeble,
Some sing his gifts—such as they may know;
Some sing his attributes, his glory and his precepts,
Some sing the substance of his vital wisdom;
Some sing his altering of bodies into ashes,
Some sing his gift of vitality to matter,
Some proclaim him manifest, albeit at a distance,
Some sing him present and immediately beholding;
There is no end of the multitude of sayings—
Sayings, sayings by the million millions;
He bestows and men grow weary getting,
And go on eating, eating through the ages;
He goes on ever willing his good pleasure,
Making progress undismayed, saith Nanak.

4. The Lord is true, plainly known, his loving kindness infinite:
To those who crave and seek he gives, gives with full abandon.
What indeed must he be offered to throw his court wide open?
What words must lips be uttering to make his love responsive?
At deathless dawn give Sat Nam thought and glory,
Put on the garb of deeds—and salvation's way is open!
Be sure that he himself is fully true, saith Nanak.

5. He is not fabrication, nor subject to man's making.
Intrinsically devoid is he of passion;
Who does him homage meets in turn with honor.
Whoever sings and listens, heart-felt praise retaining,
His sorrows fade and he will dwell in blessing.
The Guru has a voice, speaks wisdom, teaches patience,
Whether he be Shiva, Vishnu, Brama, Parbati—
If indeed I knew him, would I not describe him?
Words are vain, but teach me the mystery, O Guru,
Of him who giveth life—such wisdom may I cherish!

6. At the place of pilgrimage no bath avails without his favor,
The whole creation that I see, it came of his exertion,
Counsel glows like priceless gems, if one harkens to the Guru.
Teach me the mystery, O Guru,
Of the life thou givest—such wisdom may I cherish!

7. To live four ages or even ten times longer,
Winning ninefold fame with every man's devotion,
Winning a good name through the whole earth published—
Lacking God's good grace, none will care about him.
A worm is but a worm, and sin rests on the sinner,

But he forgives, saith Nanak, adds virtue unto virtue—
No man exists who needs not added virtue.

8. Responding to the Name come lords, gods, saints and masters,
   The white bull earth and sky are made by harkening,
   Worlds, nether regions, islands came by harkening,
   Death itself is overcome by harkening.
   Devotion leads to happiness, saith Nanak,
   Sins and sorrow are destroyed by harkening.

9. Brahma, Shiva and Indra came by harkening,
   Which prompts their lips the Gayatri to utter,
   Yoga skill and mystery come by harkening,
   By harkening come Vedic praise and wisdom.
   Devotion leads to happiness, saith Nanak,
   Sins and sorrow are destroyed by harkening.

10. Truth, knowledge and contentment come by harkening
    By harkening comes the bathing places' merit,
    Honor and the art of reading come by harkening,
    And by it the last stage of meditation.
    Devotion leads to happiness, saith Nanak,
    Sins and sorrow are destroyed by harkening.

11. By harkening one knows the avataras,
    The role of prelates, saints and rulers come by harkening,
    The blind find their own paths by harkening,
    By harkening streams impassable are forded.
    Devotion leads to happiness, saith Nanak,
    Sins and sorrow are destroyed by harkening.

12. His state is indescribable who keeps the Name in mind,
    He repents it afterwards who undertakes description,
    No use of pen or paper is availing,—
    Let them think it in the prose of meditation.
    The Name is such to him devoid of passion,
    He knows him in his heart on due reflection.

13. Wisdom comes and understanding by reflection,
    By reflection comes the knowledge of creation,
    Slights and slaps are nothing by reflection,
    Death's ties are cut asunder by reflection.
    The Name is such to him devoid of passion,
    Who knows him in his heart by due reflection.

14. One's path is rid of hindrance through reflection,
    Through reflection one appears at last with honor,
    By reflection one may journey quite unshaken
    And find companionship at last with Dharma.
    The Name is such to him devoid of passion,
    Who knows him in his heart by due reflection.

15. Salvation's doors are opened by obedience,
    And one may save his family by obedience,
    Obedience to the Guru gets salvation,
    Who obeys, saith Nanak, is ne'er a lifelong beggar.
    The Name is such to him devoid of passion,
    Who knows him in his heart by due reflection.

16. Some saints are genuine and some impostors,
    Some receive their honor at the threshold,
    Some saints shine at the gateway of the ruler,
    And some think sincerely of the Guru.
    Though thought and speech be far extended,
    This measures not the works of the creator,
    Not by the bull but by the law of mercy
    Joy becomes man's guardian and guidance.
    Who comprehendeth this hath truth discovered,
    Nor rests his burden faithless on the bull,
    There are so many earths, another and another,
    A burden far beyond his power to uphold it.
    Creatures, castes, of many shades of color,
    Have ever been described in varied phrase,
    Many who have known the art of writing
    Have written many essays on such themes.
    Impressive are the varied forms of beauty,
    Who knows the generous bounty of the whole?
    How many issues out of one source flowing—
    A hundred thousand rivers from one spring.
    What mighty power for man to fix his thought on!
    No self-denial comprehends it all,
    To please thee is a man's best aspiration,
    O thou who art eternal, ever dwelling in repose.

17. Countless repetitions, countless salutations,
    Countless genuflections and numberless tabus,
    Countless recitations of the Vedic writings,
    Yogis beyond number all indifferent to the world;
    Countless devotees with minds intent on virtue,
    Countless the generous and those who are sincere,
    Countless warriors with their steel unflinching,—
    Incomparable the minds in their silent, fixed attention.
    What mighty power for one to fix his mind on!
    No self-denial comprehends it all,
    To please thee is man's best aspiration

PART III

RELIGIONS ORIGINATING IN CHINA AND JAPAN

Until fairly recent times, the religions of China and Japan were relatively unknown to the Western world. Unlike religions originating in the Middle East or South Asia, East Asian religions have never had a strong missionary spirit. Thus, their influence was limited to the East Asian nations of China, Japan, Korea, Mongolia, and Vietnam. However, in the last century, increased political, cultural, and commercial contacts with East Asia and the Christian missionary movement have brought us the texts and traditions of Taoism, Confucianism, and Shinto, along with East Asian forms of Buddhism, and within these a deep and modern love for the beauty of nature and the family. Today there are substantial populations of people of East Asia heritage throughout Europe, the Americas, and Southeast Asia.

CHINESE RELIGION – BASIC TEACHINGS

Chinese Religions are syncretic.

Most Chinese people see no conflict between Taoism, Confucianism, Buddhism, and the practices of divination and ancestor veneration.

Each set of practices and beliefs is part of a total religious and social system and serves its own purposes.

Yin and *Yang* are basic philosophical concepts.

Yin is dark, cool, and female. *Yang* is light, warm, and male. The two forces must be in balance for life to flow smoothly.

Ancestor veneration and filial piety are important social and religious concepts.

The Chinese believe that children have an obligation to take care of their parents in their old age and even after they are dead. There are small shrines dedicated to the ancestors in most Chinese homes. Offerings are made to them in Buddhist and Taoist temples. These may include food, incense, and even reproductions of paper money, credit cards, cars, and houses.

Taoism emerged from the teachings of Lao-tzu, who is believed to have lived in the sixth century B.C.E.

The most basic Taoist teaching is that the course of life is governed by a mysterious force know as the Tao. Ideally, people should strive to flow with the Tao, and not to struggle against it. Accordingly, life itself is the greatest of all possessions. Life should be lived simply—ideally in small communities. Wealth and social position are to be rejected. Many believe that those who truly master the Tao will become immortal.

Confucianism provided the moral basis for most historical and some contemporary Chinese societies.

Confucius lived in the sixth century B.C.E. He was as much a social and political thinker as he was a religious thinker. His teachings emphasize order, propriety, and respect for authority. Over time, he came to be regarded as a religious figure and temples were dedicated to him. Confucianism and all other forms of religious thought were severely repressed after the Communist Revolution. There has been a religious revival in China since the end of the Cultural Revolution in 1976. All forms of Chinese religion have continued to flourish in Hong Kong, Singapore, and Taiwan.

SHINTO – BASIC TEACHINGS

Shinto is the indigenous religion of Japan.

For centuries, some variants of Shinto have been closely associated with the Japanese Imperial House. Japanese mythology maintains that the Emperor of Japan is a descendant of the Sun Goddess Amaterasu. Shinto also includes elements of ancestor veneration and animism. Some Shinto rituals are conducted in the numerous shrines found throughout the country and others in private homes

While the term is hard to define—even for the Japanese—kami play a central role in Shinto religious beliefs and practices.

Kami can be viewed as spiritual beings, but they are more than that. The term also refers to the spiritual beings and forces that give life to the natural world. They have the power to inflict pain and suffering as well as to come to the aid of humans.

Some variants of Shinto have been militaristic.

Bushido, or the "way of the fighting knight," was important during the Tokugawa period. It emphasized loyalty, bravery, respect for authority, and benevolence. State Shinto was instituted in 1899. The newly modernizing state took over 110,000 shrines and used state Shinto to encourage patriotism and support for Japanese military adventurism. It was abolished after World War II.

Sectarian Shinto is the public dimension of Japanese popular religion.

There are at least thirteen sects emphasizing mountain and other forms of nature worship, shamanism, divination, and Japanese mythology.

Domestic Shinto is the household religion of many Japanese.

Almost every Japanese home has a kami-dana, or household altar. It usually contains plaques inscribed with the names of ancestors, objects bought at national shrines, and images of divinities who have helped the family in the past. Offerings include food, drink, and flowers.

CHAPTER 8

Chinese Religions

CHAPTER OBJECTIVES

In this chapter you will:

- Learn how Chinese religion combines elements of animism, Doais, Confucianism, and Buddhism, and about the basic teachings of each of these traditions.

- Explore the historical development of the syncretic traditions.

- Discover some of the ways in which Chinese governments have tried to regulate religion.

- Learn about Chinese minority religions, including Christianity, Islam, and New Religious Movements.

KEY TERMS

Ancestor Veneration	Yang	Tao
Filial Piety	Li	Falun Dafa
Yin	Shang Ti	

A Timeline of Chinese Religion

11th century B.C.E.	Development of belief in Shang Ti	1503	Ritual veneration of Confucius suppressed
6th century	Life of Lao-tzu	1851–64	Tai Ping Rebellion
4th century	Composition of *Tao Te Ching*	19th century	Large-scale Christian missionary activity
551–479	Life of Confucius		
468–390	Life of Mo-tzu	1949	Communist revolution founding of People's Republic of China
3rd century	Buddhism enters China		
298–238	Life of Mencius	1966	Cultural Revolution; severe repression of religions
195	Ritual veneration of Confucius begins	1977	Death of Chairman Mao; relaxation of restrictions on religions

Western students often find the syncretic nature of Chinese religion puzzling. The average European or American finds it difficult to advocate more than one religion at a time. The Christian may be tolerant of the views of a Jewish or Muslim neighbor but could never say, "I am a Christian, and I am a Jew," or "I am a Christian, and I am a Muslim." The very nature of these religions makes it almost impossible to adhere to more than one at a time. This is not the case with Chinese religions. It is perfectly acceptable for the traditional Chinese to be a Buddhist, Taoist, and Confucian. This is illustrated in the story of the emperor who asked a Buddhist scholar if he were a Buddhist. The scholar pointed to his Taoist cap. "Are you then a Taoist?" the emperor asked, and the scholar pointed to his Confucian shoes. "Are you then a Confucian?" the emperor asked, and the scholar pointed to his Buddhist scarf. It is not at all unusual for a Buddhist priest to attend a Taoist temple and to memorize the teachings of Confucius. Many Chinese temples are shared by adherents of all of these religions. An additional element that makes the study of Chinese religions difficult for the modern student is that for the past fifty years the government of China has been at best neutral and sometimes hostile to any form of religion. All missionaries have been excluded, and the teachings of Lao-tzu and Confucius were suppressed as hostile to modern China. In recent years, the government of China has softened its attitude toward religion, which has led to a resurgence of religion and tradition similar to that in Eastern Europe and the former Soviet Union. Even during the period when the Chinese government was most hostile toward religion, millions of Chinese living outside of their ancestral homeland continued to practice traditional Chinese religions.

The history of religion in China falls into several broad categories. From the earliest recorded history until the end of the Shang dynasty in the eleventh century B.C.E., the Chinese people apparently followed a basically polytheistic religion intermingled with ancestor worship. From the development of the Chou dynasty in the eleventh century B.C.E. until the beginning of the Common Era, a portion of the Chinese literati concluded that there was one Supreme God above all other gods and spirits. The second period also was characterized by an emphasis on morality, particularly the morality of the rulers. This was the era that produced Lao-tzu (the legendary founder of Taoism) and Confucius. From the beginning of the Common Era until the eleventh century C.E., Buddhism and religious Taoism developed in China; for the first time, fully developed religious cults were found. The fourth general period of religious development extends from the eleventh century to the present. In this period, we find an eclectic movement, bringing about a synthesis among Buddhism, Taoism, and Confucianism for most of the Chinese people.

Basic Chinese Religious Concepts

From earliest times, the Chinese have held certain religious concepts and practices that later played a part in the development of the philosophies of Taoism and Confucianism.

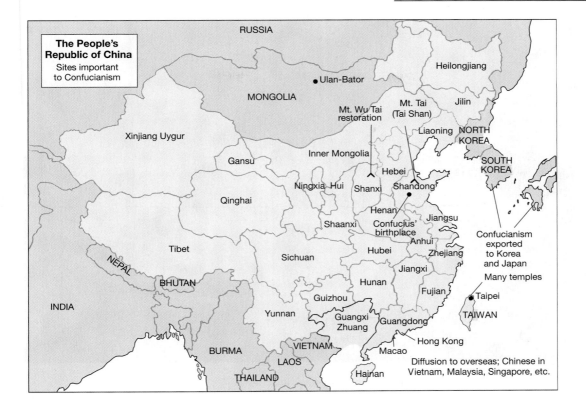

The People's
Republic of China
Sites important
to Confucianism

RUSSIA

Ulan-Bator

MONGOLIA

Heilongjiang

Jilin

Mt. Wu Tai
restoration

Mt. Tai
(Tai Shan)

Liaoning

NORTH
KOREA

Xinjiang Uygur

Inner Mongolia

SOUTH
KOREA

Gansu

Hebei

Ningxia Hui   Shanxi   Shandong

Qinghai

Henan

Shaanxi   Confucius'
birthplace

Jiangsu

Confucianism
exported
to Korea
and Japan

Tibet

Anhui

Sichuan

Hubei

Zhejiang

Many temples

NEPAL

Jiangxi

BHUTAN

Hunan

Fujian

INDIA

Guizhou

Taipei

Yunnan

Guangxi
Zhuang   Guangdong

TAIWAN

BURMA

VIETNAM   Macao

Hong Kong

LAOS

Diffusion to overseas; Chinese in
Vietnam, Malaysia, Singapore, etc.

THAILAND

Hainan

Although the ancient records are sketchy in their description of these concepts, we must examine them first to better understand Chinese religions.

Recognition of Multiple Gods and Spirits

As already stated, the earliest religion of the Chinese people seems to have been based on the recognition of many gods and spirits that controlled the universe. As was the case of many other basic religious groups, the ancient Chinese were apparently polytheistic and animistic in their understanding of the cosmos. The gods of the heavens and the earth received particular attention and sacrifice. In the spring and fall, the emperors of ancient China performed elaborate and expensive sacrifices to the gods of the heavens and the earth. Many of these rituals were intended to ensure the fertility of the soil and bountiful harvests. Lesser rulers and the common people also performed sacrifices to these spirits.

In addition to the major deities of the heavens and the earth, the Chinese also recognized several kinds of local deities and spirits. In general, the beneficial spirits were known as *Shen*. They were to be found in the bright and lighted places of the earth and were associated with the sun and the spring. The evil spirits were known as *Kuei* and were associated with dark and gloomy places. Generally, the common people performed sacrifices and rituals to put themselves on good terms with the *Shen* and protect themselves from the *Kuei*. Usually, animals or grain were sacrificed, but occasional records

Central altar of a Chinese temple, Semarang, Java, Indonesia.
(Mark R. Woodward)

exist of human sacrifice being the supreme offering to the deities. Archaeological investigations have revealed wealthy men's tombs that contained the bodies of hundreds of servants and wives who were presumably buried alive with their masters. One record speaks of an emperor who was buried along with all of his wives who had failed to bear him children. One wonders if this was a matter of religious sacrifice or simple revenge. By the end of the Chou dynasty, before the Common Era, this practice had ceased. Apparently, the practice of burying straw figures or paper likenesses of the wives was instituted as a substitute. Today it is common for the Chinese to offer stylized paper money and even "heaven visa" cards to the ancestors.

Yin and *Yang*

In searching for a principle to explain the true nature of the universe, the ancient Chinese philosophers developed the concept of the *yin* and the *yang*. What made the universe operate the way it did was understood to be a balance between these two forces. The *yin* was the negative force in nature. It was seen in darkness, coolness, femaleness, dampness, the earth itself, the moon, and the shadows. The *yang* was the positive force in nature. It was seen in lightness, brightness, warmth, maleness, dryness, and the sun.

The interaction between *yin* and *yang* was understood as one of the factors in the operation of the universe. Except for a few objects, such as the sun or the earth, which were clearly *yin* or *yang*, all the rest of nature, humankind, and even events were a combination of both forces. When these two forces were at work in harmony, life was what it should be.

Filial Piety and Ancestor Worship

A characteristic of the Chinese people throughout history has been their respect for and even veneration of aged members of the family. Perhaps the most difficult aspect of Chinese life for modern Western students to understand is this veneration of old age. The legendary founder of Taoism was Li-poh-yang, but his disciples called him *Lao-tzu*, which means "Old Master" or "Old Boy."

To the Chinese, the terms *old* or *aged* are not the signs of disrespect that they often are in many Western countries; rather, they are the ultimate terms of respect. To the Chinese, life may truly be said to begin at sixty, when a person reaches the age when he or she is respected. Historically, it is the aged father, mother, grandfather, or grandmother who dominates the Chinese home. It is the obligation of the children to support the elderly, to obey them, and to give them proper burial after death. Even after the parents' death, the child is obligated to maintain their grave site, to remember them and their deeds, and to offer sacrifices to them.

Western students of Chinese life have often referred to this attitude as "ancestor worship." Indeed, there is a religious aspect to these practices: Individuals revere their parents while they are alive and after they are dead. While they are alive, the aged represent the wisdom of the family; after their deaths, they may be in a position to help the family further because of their contact with the spirit world. Therefore, support of the dead ancestors with remembrance and sacrifices is essential. The Chinese who forget their ancestors are disgraced and will one day become homeless ghosts. It is also commonly believed that those lacking filial piety will be afflicted by dangerous spirits. Historically, the Chinese home has tended to have a small shrine or altar at which the names and deeds of many previous generations of the family are remembered and where small sacrifices of rice and wine may be offered. Imitation paper money, often inscribed as being issued by the "Bank of Hell," is another common offering. Ancestral tablets are also often placed in Chinese temples and family meeting centers.

Divination

Like many other basic religious groups, the early Chinese believed that the unity of the universe allowed future events to be predicted by some means. Whereas certain ancient religions sought out the future in the patterns of the flight of birds, in the entrails of sacrificed animals, or in the sayings of various oracles, the ancient Chinese sought the future in the patterns of the shell of the tortoise or in stalks of grain. The shell of the tortoise was thought to be especially in tune with the rhythms of the universe because of the long life of its inhabitant. Frequently, the shell was heated and the future was divined by the cracks that appeared in it. Divination among the ancient Chinese probably reached its peak in the development of a book called the *I Ching* (The Book of Changes), which was edited by Confucius and is still used today. With the casting of coins or stalks of a plant, certain patterns emerge. By identifying these patterns among some sixty-four hexagrams presented in the *I Ching*, a statement or prediction is evoked.

Development of Belief in the Shang Ti

Chinese religion is basically polytheistic, as previously described. However, in the eleventh century B.C.E., certain political events affected the religious thinking of the Chinese, perhaps for all time. In that century, the Chou clans rebelled against the ruling Shang dynasty. By the end of the century, the Chou warriors had effectively completed the rebellion and had begun a new dynasty that was to rule China for several centuries. The Chou rulers began to assert that the right to rule had to be based on morality and religion. They further asserted that one Supreme God controlled the destinies of all humankind. This God was Shang Ti, who had previously been regarded as the patron ancestor of the Shang dynasty. The Chou rulers asserted that Shang Ti was more than an ancestor; he was the Supreme God, and he had been responsible for the fall of the Shang dynasty because of their immorality. Shang Ti was seen as the rewarder of good morality and the punisher of immorality, particularly among rulers. Therefore, government had to be founded upon virtue. Although Shang Ti might delight in elaborate sacrifice and ritual, he still loved morality more; all the sacrifices in the world could not cover up evil. We read of his concern for morality in the ancient *Shu Ching* (Book of Documents).

From the Source

The capital of Shang was full of crime. [The king] was not distressed that the kingdom of Yin was mined. Nor did he care that the fragrance of virtue should rise up from the sacrifices to plead with T'ien (Shang Ti). Instead the complaints of the people and the rank odour of drunken orgies were felt on high. Therefore T'ien determined to destroy Yin. It loved Yin no more, because of Yin's excesses. It is not T'ien that is cruel. It is people who bring evil on themselves.[1]

His [King Wen's] fame reached up to Shang Ti who blessed him. T'ien therefore bestowed its great command on King Wen to extirpate the dynasty of Yin, to receive the mandate, and take over its territories and people, that they might be well governed.[2]

Some scholars have suggested that the Chinese during this period were very close to developing an ethical monotheism similar to that enunciated by the Hebrew prophets in the eighth century B.C.E. However, the emphasis on morality as a means of satisfying the High God remained in the hands of the rulers, and prophets never arose in this period of Chinese history. Nevertheless, the emperors of China held their thrones with one eye on the heavens and a concern for personal morality and good government.

Decline of the Feudal System

During the Chou dynasty, China had been organized and governed by a feudal system similar to that of medieval Europe. The empire was divided into vassal states whose princes were subject to the emperor. The states in turn were subdivided into districts ruled by governors who were vassals to the princes. Each substate supported its lord financially, while the lord in turn provided protection for the state. Society was then stratified into ranks. Members of the society knew their ranks and duties. They also knew who was above and below them.

In the five centuries between the eighth and third centuries B.C.E., the feudal system in China began to break down. Lords were no longer able to protect their vassals from invading armies. This led to the development of warlords who could provide protection and command respect. Serfs sometimes became landowners in these upsetting times. Merchant classes began to appear in the cities, and their economic power began to be felt. Old aristocratic families began to find themselves without either wealth or power. In general, the feudal world turned upside down. Into this era came the great Chinese schools, each with its own distinctive answer to the problems facing the nation. The Confucians dreamed of a restored idealized form of feudalism as the best government; the Legalists wanted nothing to do with feudalism but wished for a strong centralized government; the Taoists wanted no government at all, or at least as little government as possible. It was out of this confused milieu that the great Chinese philosophy-religions were born.

Confucius depicted wearing the robes of a scholar of a later age. *(Collection of the National Palace Museum, Taiwan, Republic of China)*

Taoism

Taoism is extremely difficult to define. It can be described in terms of its history and its effects on the Chinese people, but it cannot be clearly delineated as a religion with a certain body of doctrines and rituals as can Islam or Christianity. Its origins are lost in the mists of Chinese antiquity. Little is known of its founder; indeed, there are those who even deny his existence. Its sacred book is more a brief poetical statement of philosophy than a scripture. The name Taoism is taken from the title of this book, *Tao Tê Ching*, and it is probably best translated as "the way" or "the way of nature." In spite of this seemingly religious title, the earliest teachers of Taoism were only vaguely theistic in their beliefs. By the early centuries of the Common Era, however, Taoism had been converted into a religion complete with gods, priests, temples, and sacrifices. In modern China, Taoism is mainly associated with charms, exorcisms, and magical attempts to prolong life. A philosophy of nature, a religion, a system of magical practices—Taoism is all of these.

The Life of Lao-tzu

Traditionally, the founder of Taoism is thought to be Lao-tzu, who lived in the sixth century B.C.E., although the basic philosophy of Taoism is probably much older. Little is known about Lao-tzu, and some scholars doubt that he was a historical figure. Legends about him state that he was born approximately fifty years before Confucius; according to Confucian sources, there was a meeting between the two. His original name was Li-poh-yang, but he was given the title *Lao-tzu (Old Master or Old Boy)* by his disciples as a title of respect. It is said that he was the keeper of royal archives in the court of the Chou dynasty during the tumultuous period when order was breaking down. He tired of the artificial life in court and retired from his post. Journeying westward, he reached a pass in the mountains at the northwest boundaries of China, where he sought to leave the country. The guard of the pass recognized the wise man and refused to allow him to leave until he had committed to writing the sum of his wisdom. Thereupon, Lao-tzu sat down and wrote the *Tao Tê Ching*. When this was completed, he was allowed to leave the country and was never seen again. The truth of this story has never been verified. Certainly, we know less about the founder of Taoism than we know about any of the other founders of world religions.

The *Tao Tê Ching*

The book that Lao-tzu was supposed to have written in the sixth century B.C.E., the *Tao Tê Ching*, has become the most influential book in Chinese literature, except for the *Analects of Confucius*. The title literally means "The Classic of the Way and Its Power or Virtue." It is a small book, made up of slightly more than 5,000 words contained in eighty-one chapters, and it is usually translated in poetical form. It has been the object of at least a thousand commentaries and has been translated into English more than forty times. In fact, it has been translated more times than any other book in the world except the Bible and thus is probably the best known of all Chinese books.[3]

Whether the *Tao Tê Ching* was written by Lao-tzu in the sixth century B.C.E. as he waited to be allowed to leave China has been the subject of much scholarly debate for some time. It is generally agreed that the book was developed over many centuries and evolved into its present form around the fourth century B.C.E. Arthur Waley suggests that the book was written in the third century B.C.E. as a polemic against the Confucians and Legalists who wished for either an idealized form of feudalism or some strong central government.[4] The theme of the *Tao Tê Ching* is that all human achievements are folly, especially elaborate government.

Teachings of the Early Taoist Philosophers

The beliefs of the early Taoists are difficult to ascertain. Our two major sources for Taoism before the Common Era are the *Tao Tê Ching* and the work of a fourth-century B.C.E. disciple of Lao-tzu, Chuang-tzu. Chuang-tzu covered the field of Taoism as it was practiced by the early devotees. He collected this material into a book and with it tried to convince the Chinese to accept Lao-tzu instead of Confucius as their main teacher. The teachings of early Taoism center on the following themes:

1. *The basic unity behind the universe is a mysterious and indefinable force called the Tao.* Usually the word *Tao* is defined as "the way," and it may be best understood in terms of "the way of the universe" or perhaps "nature's way." Yet the true *Tao* is impossible to define. The *Tao Tê Ching* begins with the following admonition:

From the Source

The Way (*Tao*) that can be told of is not an Unvarying Way (*Tao*). The names that can be named are not unvarying names.[5]

Nameless and undefinable though it may be, the Tao is the source of the universe.

It was from the Nameless that Heaven and Earth sprang;

The named is but the mother that rears the ten thousand creatures, each after its kind.[6]

Even the gods, along with all the rest of the universe, seem to have evolved from the flow of the *Tao*.

Though the *Tao* is defined as "the way," it is most often compared to a stream or a moving body of water as it progresses endlessly and inexorably. As water wears away the hardest stone or metal and carries off buildings in its path, it is useless to struggle against the *Tao*. Therefore, the ancient Taoist philosophers believed that all humankind's accomplishments and monuments will sooner or later be destroyed by the *Tao*. The greatest buildings will fall into decay, hard-won knowledge will be superseded, wealth will fail, and even the sharpest sword will become dull. For this reason, it behooved people not to struggle against the *Tao* but to seek to blend with it and be guided by it. True Taoists live quiet and simple lives. They avoid any achievement except that of seeking to understand the *Tao*.

2. *Life is the greatest of all possessions.* Because of their belief in the *Tao* as the source of all life and their belief in the folly of achievement, the early Taoist philosophers taught that life itself was the greatest of possessions; all others were doomed to decay. Fame, wealth, power, and education were mere flitting, transient illusions. If people were not interested in the acquisition of goods, power, or education, then they could give their full attention to the enrichment of their own lives. This led the Taoists to search for a way to lengthen life; eventually, they employed various magical practices in an attempt to prolong and enrich life.

3. *Life is to be lived simply.* Believing that all life originated from the *Tao*, which would ultimately destroy people's achievements, the early Taoists turned their backs on civilization with all of its ills and benefits and sought to live life as simply as possible. The Taoist philosophers may have carried this dream to its greatest extreme. They considered education, wealth, power, and family ties worthless, in fact, impediments to living.

From the Source

Banish wisdom, discard knowledge,
  And the people will be benefited a hundredfold.
Banish human kindness, discard morality,
  And the people will be dutiful and compassionate.
Banish skill, discard profit,
  And thieves and robbers will disappear.

If when these three things are done they find life too plain and unadorned,
  Then let them have accessories;
  Give them Simplicity to look at, the Uncarved Block to hold,
  Give them selflessness and fewness of desires.[7]

Ideally, individuals should turn their backs on the advancements of civilization and live as simply and as quietly as possible. The word *innocence* characterizes the ideal state. Like the plants and creatures of the earth, innocent human beings are content with what the *Tao* has ordained for them. According to early Taoist philosophers, there should be little government in the ideal state. In fact, it was an axiom of Taoists that the least government is the best government. Lao-tzu is remembered for saying, "Govern a great nation as you would cook a small fish"—do not overdo it.[8] The small village is the ideal unit of society. The best ruler is the one who rules least and is virtually anonymous. If all this were realized, all striving, quarrels, and wars would cease. Taoism is pacific, not out of any moral commitment to pacifism but because warring is useless and wasteful. If a larger, stronger state wished the territory of the quiet Taoist village, the village should simply submit to the larger state. In the long run, there would be no grief due to this decision and the village ultimately would conquer the large state with its humility.

The early Taoists looked upon the innocence of the child as an ideal toward which all human beings should strive. The infant knows no craft and has no ambitions but to live; yet the child is cared for, fed, and clothed. The weakness and softness of the infant are the ideals of Taoism.

4. *Pomp and glory are to be despised.* Because the Taoists were concerned with living according to the path of nature (i.e., as simply as possible), they despised the fame, pomp, and glory that most people seek. They saw such things as the cause of strife and discord in society. If each person were only content to live as the *Tao* intended, without seeking to rise above other people, then life would be as it was intended. This attitude also contained a condemnation of pride. It was a Chinese belief, perhaps older than Taoism, that pride invited destruction, that the tree that stood taller than its neighbors would be the first felled by the woodsman. Therefore, better to be humble, small, or imperfect than to stand out from all the rest.

From the Source

To remain whole, be twisted!
  To become straight, let yourself be bent.
  To become full, be hollow.
  Be tattered, that you may be renewed.
  Those that have little, may get more,
  Those that have much, are but perplexed.
  Therefore the Sage
  Clasps the Primal Unity,
  Testing by it everything under heaven.
  He does not show himself; therefore he is seen everywhere.

He does not define himself, therefore he is distinct.
  He does not boast of what he will do, therefore he succeeds.
  He is not proud of his work, and therefore it endures.
  He does not contend,
  And for that very reason no one under heaven can contend with him.
  So then we see that the ancient saying "To remain whole, be twisted!" was no idle word; for true wholeness can only be achieved by return.[9]

Perhaps the best example of the Taoists' contempt for pomp, glory, rank, and wealth is the story of Chuang-tzu, the fourth-century B.C.E. Taoist philosopher. Chuang-tzu was widely regarded for his wisdom and was offered the position of prime minister by Prince Wei of Ch'u. When the messengers of the prince brought this offer, Chuang is said to have replied in the following manner:

From the Source

You offer me great wealth and a proud position indeed; but have you never seen the sacrificial ox? When after being fattened up for several years, it is decked with embroidered trappings and led to the altar, would it not willingly then change places with some uncaring pigling? . . . Begone! Defile me not! I would rather disport myself to my own enjoyment in the mire than be a slave to a mire of a state. I will never take office. Thus I shall remain free to follow my own inclinations.[10]

History does not record the response of the prince whose offer was spurned with such contempt.

There is little theism in early Taoism. The *Tao* itself is an impersonal, vague force behind the universe and is more of a First Cause than a god in any traditional sense of the word. In one translation of the *Tao Tê Ching*, the word "god" is used only once; in many translations, it does not appear at all.[11] Only rarely does the term "heaven" appear. The *Tao* is not conceived of as a force to whom one can pray or sacrifice, and the early Taoists seem to have had no rituals for worship. In fact, they may have been rejecting religion and all of its accoutrements as part of their rejection of the Confucians, who placed a very high value on rituals.

The early Taoists also seem to have had little concern for life after death. One of the most frequently remembered tales of Chuang-tzu concerns an occasion following his wife's death. His disciples sought to comfort him in his time of mourning but found him singing and beating time on a wooden bowl.

From the Source

"To live with your wife," exclaimed Hui-tzu, "and see your eldest son grow up to be a man, and then not to shed a tear over her corpse—this would be bad enough. But to drum on a bowl and sing; surely this is going too far!" "Not at all," replied Chuang-tzu. "When she died I could not help being affected by her death. Soon, however, I remembered that she had already existed in a previous state before her birth, without form or even substance; that while in that unconditioned condition, substance was added to spirit; that this substance then assumed form and that the next state was birth. And now, by virtue of a further change she is dead, passing from one phase to another like the sequence of spring, summer, autumn and winter. And while she is thus lying asleep in eternity for me to go about weeping and wailing would be to proclaim myself ignorant of these natural laws. Therefore I refrain."[12]

In general, the early Taoists were concerned about the quality of life as it is lived on a day-to-day basis, without much interest in the heavens, the gods, rituals, or life after death.

Schools that Rivaled the Early Taoists

The fourth and third centuries B.C.E. were eras of chaos in China. The old governmental structure of feudalism was breaking down, invaders regularly made inroads into the country, the social order was in a state of flux, and the ancient systems of values were seriously being questioned. The Taoist philosophers and their challenge to existing values and structures were, of course, a part of that era. Other philosophers, politicians, and teachers held other views of life and government and toured the nation. According to Arthur Waley,

Every court in China was infested by "journeying philosophers" each in turn pressing upon a bewildered ruler the claims of Activism, of Quietism, of morality, of nonmorality, of force, of non-resistance, of individualism, of State supremacy. In one thing only were they united; each claimed to possess the secret "art of ruling" whereby the Ancestors had grown mighty in the past.[13]

In addition to the Taoists, three major schools of thought were dominant in those days: the Confucians, the Legalists, and the Mohists.

THE CONFUCIANS. More will be said about the school of Confucius in a later section. However, it must be noted here that its members were rivals of the Taoists in the fourth and third centuries B.C.E. in advising the rulers of China on government. Whereas the Taoists believed that the least government was the best government, the disciples of Confucius believed that an idealized feudal system was the best form of government. Whereas the Taoists had little use for formal religion, the Confucians at least believed that the rites and rituals of religion served the function of uniting the people. Whereas the Taoists believed that the best society was one with little structure, the Confucians taught that society needed an elaborate structure, reinforced by etiquette, to be effective.

THE LEGALISTS. A second group that vied for the attention of the rulers of China during this period was a large one that followed no specific teacher; its members were known as Legalists or Realists. They believed that human nature and the condition of China at the time demanded strong leadership. To them, human nature tended to be wicked and lazy. People followed the path of least resistance. Left to their own devices, people made decisions that were bad for society as a whole. Therefore, government should be run under what Westerners might call Machiavellian principles. Government should not be affected by morality or pity. People did not need love or pity; they needed food and houses. Thus, leaders of government should determine what would be best for the majority of society and take the difficult steps necessary to achieve these ends. Any resulting hardship for the minority should not affect decisions. Legalists had no room for religion. Money and time spent on sacrifices to the gods were better spent on good government. Naturally, these teachers had little in common with the passive Taoist sages.

THE MOHISTS. The third group that sought to influence government during the fourth and third centuries B.C.E. was the Mohists. These teachers were disciples of Mo-tzu, who lived in the fifth century B.C.E. (ca. 468–390 B.C.E.). Mo-tzu began his career as a Confucian but later broke away to form his own distinctive philosophy. He and his disciples believed that the best government operated under the direction of the traditional Chinese religions. Under these religions, people were taught to love one another; thus, the government would operate from a position of love. The Mohists were pacifists, yet they recognized the necessity of self-defense and allowed the building of fortifications.

Though there were probably many representatives of each of these distinct philosophies, it is doubtful that any of them had serious influence on the governors of China, except perhaps the Legalists. Nevertheless, the teachings of the Taoists, the Confucians, and the Mohists have been held as ideals for the Chinese people—in a strange eclecticism—for thousands of years.

Later Development of Taoism

Basically, Taoism as it is seen in the *Tao Tê Ching* and in the essays of Chuang-tzu was concerned with living life in harmony with the basic force behind nature, the *Tao*. As a pure philosophy, this appealed to a small group of persons, malcontent with the intricacies of society and government, but it probably never had wide appeal for the populace.

After the period of the early philosophers, however, Taoism did develop wide appeal for the masses and is frequently listed among the major religions of the world. This development from a philosophy for the few to a religion for the many is a fascinating story.

Following the period of the early Taoist philosophers, two kinds of Taoists developed. One group followed the philosophical writings of Lao-tzu and Chuang-tzu. The second group was searching for immortality, not in the sense of life after death, as taught by many other religions, but in an endless extension of the present life through various devices. The philosophers had taught that life was the greatest of all possessions and that the person whose life was properly attuned to the Tao might have a long life. This appealed to the Chinese, who look forward to old age and the relative ease and honor that it has traditionally brought in Chinese culture. Taking up this aspect of Taoism, scholars, priests, and magicians began to seek the means whereby life could be extended indefinitely. They sought every possible means, including special dietary regulations. Some came to believe that all foods, particularly solid foods, were poisonous; thus, they tried to train their bodies to live on very little liquid food. Some claimed that eventually they were able to live on only saliva and air. Others practiced fasting and breath control, in a manner similar to that of the Indian Yogin.

Still another popular means of extending life was alchemy. Some believed that because dead meat could be preserved from decay by salt, living flesh might be preserved by some other mineral, such as gold. One can only guess at the outcomes of some of these experiments in longevity. Nevertheless, the hope that immortality might be achieved did not die out among the Chinese. Regarding one of the leaders of these movements, it was said by a contemporary:

From the Source

He abstained from cereals, escaped old age, knew the method to avoid dying, and transmuted cinnabar. When he died, it was said that he had been transformed and, on opening the tomb several years later, they found no corpse there but only his cap and clothing.[14]

The Taoist alchemist seeking to work his magic soon became concerned with gods that might be involved in the process. Because the alchemists worked at the stove, they began to offer sacrifices to the god of the stove, Tsao Chün. Thus it is said that Tsao Chün, by the third century C.E., became the first god of Taoism. The process of apotheosis continued until there were many Taoist gods. And so a philosophy that began by essentially denying personal gods developed its own gods.

By the second century C.E., the *Tao Tê Ching* had been officially recognized as a Chinese classic and was soon on its way to becoming the Taoist scripture. Those seeking immortality came to believe that the only way they could achieve it was through the practice of morality and virtuous deeds toward their fellow human beings.

Also in the second century C.E., the Han dynasty, which had ruled China for several centuries, began to break down. During this time of chaos, certain charismatic Taoist leaders appeared. Several of them not only led the search for immortality but also gathered great armies of followers and participated in wars in a most un-Taoist fashion. With the organization that these people brought, the concern for faith healing, the search for immortality, and the other accoutrements of gods, morality, temples, priests, rituals, and so on, Taoism became one of the religions, if not the religion, of the masses of the Chinese people by the beginning of the third century C.E.

Because there were contacts between India and China from very early times, and because Buddhism under the influence of Asoka had become a missionary religion, no doubt there were Buddhist missionaries and traders in China as early as the third century B.C.E. However, early Chinese contacts with Buddhism were with the Theravada branch. It is likely that this version of Buddhism, with its emphasis on the monastic life, was far too Indian for the Chinese; therefore, it made little headway in China. In later years came the development of Mahayana Buddhism, with its elaborate rituals and many gods. Extraordinary missionaries also came, such as the legendary Bodhidharma, who brought the *dhyana* version of Mahayana Buddhism from India to China in the fifth century C.E. In China, as in most other Asian nations, this version of the teachings of the Buddha appealed tremendously to the masses.

By the fourth century C.E., Mahayana Buddhism was a force to be reckoned with by the Taoists. At first, there seems to have been no rivalry between the two religions. The Taoists helped the Buddhists translate their texts into Chinese, and the Buddhists used Taoist terms to explain Buddhist concepts. As Buddhism became more popular among the Chinese, however, the Taoists began to recognize it as a threat. Fierce struggles arose between the two groups to determine who would have influence with the various rulers and thus control the provinces. In a most uncharacteristic fashion, each religion became hostile to the other and persecution developed. In the ninth century C.E., Emperor Wu Tsung, who was greatly influenced by Taoist priests, persecuted the Buddhists on a vast scale, destroying numerous temples. At other times, Buddhists influenced the rulers to discriminate against the Taoists.

The struggle between the Buddhists and Taoists was settled more by syncretism than by persecution. Each religion borrowed from the other until both became associated, along with the teachings of Confucius, as the common religion of the people. Taoism borrowed widely from the Mahayana teachings of an afterlife, with heavens and hells and judgment. The Buddhists followed their traditional pattern of accepting the native gods and heroes of the land as Buddhist *Bodhisattvas*, and the Taoists sought to turn the tables by asserting that Lao-tzu and others were created before the foundations of the earth and thus were superior to the Buddha. All in all, the Taoists seem to have copied the most. By the sixth century C.E., the Taoists had taken up the Buddhist pattern of monasticism. Their priests could now live in monasteries and in some cases were commanded to be celibate. Nunneries were established for Taoist women who desired celibacy. By the tenth century, the shape of Taoism was established; it changed little during the next ten centuries.

Taoism, with its religious side fully developed and its traditional emphasis on a magical means of extending life, continued to have a hold on the common people into the twenty-first century. The Chinese upper classes and intellectuals continued to read the *Tao Tê Ching* and other classics of philosophical Taoism, but they tended to regard the religion itself as being fit only for the ignorant masses.

Confucianism

Because Confucianism is generally considered one of the major religions of the world, it might be appropriate to discuss it in a separate chapter rather than to include it as part of a general chapter on the religions of China. However, in its origins and development, Confucianism, like Taoism, is inextricably interwoven into the total philosophy of the Chinese people. Therefore, to discuss Confucianism in a chapter separate from Taoism and Chinese religious thinking would be to present it in an unreal setting.

Some contend that the teachings of Confucius and his disciples were never intended to be a religion, that Confucius was probably an atheist who discouraged prayer to the gods as worthless and that his main concern was the nature of human society. If Confucianism is a religion, it is a very different kind of religion. It has no priesthood; its sacred writings, although important, have never been considered a divine revelation like the Vedas or the *Qur'an*; it has frowned upon asceticism and monasticism; and it has no doctrine of an afterlife. In spite of all of these "non-religious" aspects, there have been some cultic developments in the history of Confucianism, and its philosophy has deeply affected the Chinese character. Therefore, Confucianism deserves to be examined at least as a possible world religion.

The Life of Confucius

The man whom the West knows as Confucius was really named Kung. When he became a famous teacher, his disciples referred to him as *K'ung Fu-tzu* (Kung, the master). As his teachings became known to Western missionaries and scholars, the name was Latinized to "Confucius."

Although Confucius was born in the sixth century B.C.E., the biographical material about him is extensive and fairly reliable because of the influence that he and his disciples had on the Chinese people. This is in marked contrast to the life of Lao-tzu, who also lived in the sixth century B.C.E. but about whom we know almost nothing. The earliest and most authentic material about Confucius is contained in the *Analects of Confucius*, a collection of his teachings compiled about seventy years after his death. In addition to the biographical material in Confucian literature, Confucius is mentioned in the writings of contemporary Taoists and Mohists. No one seriously doubts the historicity of Confucius.

Confucius was born in 551 B.C.E. in the state of Lu (now in modern Shantung). He was the child of an aristocratic family that had lost its wealth and position in the decline of the feudal states of China during that chaotic period. His father was said to have been a famous warrior of gigantic size and strength who was seventy years old when Confucius was conceived. The father died shortly before the birth of the child, and Confucius was reared in poverty by his widowed mother. Although his mother had to struggle for survival, she was determined to provide her son with an education. Therefore, Confucius was allowed to study with the village tutor. The biographies say he studied subjects that were the traditional fare of Chinese students of his time: poetry, Chinese history, music, hunting, fishing, and archery. Even as a youth, he seems to have been extremely interested in the interworkings of society, particularly in what constituted good government. This was to be his main theme for the rest of his life.

In his late teens, he accepted a minor position in government, where he closely observed the ruling process. He married and fathered one son, but the marriage ended in divorce. We know little about the wife or family of Confucius beyond these scanty facts. However, there are still Chinese today who claim to be the physical descendants of

Confucius. While Confucius was in his mid-twenties, his mother died; being a devoted son, Confucius mourned her for three years.

During his twenties, Confucius began his true career, that of teacher. His reputation as a man of learning allowed him to establish himself as a teacher of young people. In the following years, his reputation spread widely, and he attracted many students. They lived in his home and followed him on his journeys. He taught them history, the principles of good government, and divination.[15]

Legend has it that at the age of fifty, Confucius was finally able to put into practice some of his principles of good government when he was asked to join the government of the Duke of Lu as its prime minister. According to these Confucian legends, Confucius' government was ideal. During his leadership, the state was so well-governed that the crime rate dropped to almost nothing. People stopped locking their doors, and a wallet that was dropped on the street was left untouched for days. However, the enemies of

Chinese civil service examination. For many years, a knowledge of the writings of Confucius was required for entry into Chinese civil service.
(From "The Horizon History of China," by the editors of Horizon Magazine, *American Heritage Publishing Co., Inc., NY © 1969. Bibliotheque Nationale de France)*

Confucius became jealous of his success and conspired against him. Consequently, he was forced to retire from government at the age of fifty-five.

During the next twelve years of his life, Confucius held no position. He wandered from place to place with a few of his faithful disciples. Sometimes he was accepted by the populace and treated hospitably. At other times he and his friends were jeered and even jailed. Finally, when he was sixty-seven years of age, a position was found for him as an adviser to the Duke of Ai. Although this was not as important as the position he had formerly held, it at least gave Confucius a home for himself and his disciples. During the next years, he taught and compiled some of the classical Chinese texts. The master died in the year 479 B.C.E. and was widely mourned by his disciples. According to one tradition, his most faithful disciple built a hut beside the grave and stayed to mourn Confucius for three years.

The Teachings of Confucius

Confucius' attitude toward religion has been a point of great debate; on the one hand, some regard him as the founder of one of the world's great religions; on the other hand, some believe he was an agnostic, if not an atheist. The truth about Confucius' teachings on religion probably lies somewhere between the two extremes. Relative to his contemporaries, he was somewhere in the middle of the spectrum, with Lao-tzu on the left, denying the validity of religions, and Mo-tzu on the right, advocating a return to the ancient religions of China.

Confucius seems to have believed that, although the gods existed and worship and rituals were of value in bringing people together, these things were of secondary importance to an equitable social order. Praying to the spirits should not interfere with one's proper social duties. His attitude seems to have been that, ideally, one should respect the spirits but keep them at a distance.[16] Even though Confucius was not an atheist or antireligious, no evidence suggests that he was interested in starting a religion. Rather, he developed a system of ethics, a theory of government, and a set of personal and social goals that deeply influenced the Chinese for almost twenty-five centuries.

The teachings of Confucius are based on certain central themes. One of these themes is represented by the word *li*, variously translated as "propriety," "rites," "ceremonies," or "courtesy." Originally, it may have meant the grain found in wood or the pattern in jade. Basically, *li* seems to mean "the course of life as it is intended to go"; of course, it has religious and social connotations. When society lives by *li*, it moves smoothly: men and women respect their elders and superiors; the proper rituals and ceremonies are performed; everything and everyone is in its proper place.

Naturally, the principle of *li* was most closely followed when an idealized form of feudalistic government existed. In such a state, all people know their superiors and inferiors and are able to act in the genteel manner that Confucius believed was necessary for a smoothly functioning society. Furthermore, Confucius believed that China in his day was in a state of chaos because the people were no longer living according to the principles of *li*.

One of the Confucian classics, the *Li Chi*, whose primary subject is *li*, records the following conversation:

From the Source

Duke Ai asked Confucius, "What is the great li? Why is it that you talk about li as though it were such an important thing?"

Confucius replied, "Your humble servant is really not worthy to understand li."

"But you do constantly speak about it," said Duke Ai.

Confucius: "What I have learned is this, that of all the things that people live by, li is the greatest.

Without li we do not know how to conduct a proper worship of the spirits of the universe; or how to establish the proper status of the king and the ministers, the ruler and the ruled, and the elders and the juniors; or how to establish the moral relationships between the sexes; between parents and children and between brothers; or how to distinguish the different degrees of relationships in the family. That is why a gentleman holds li in such high regard.[17]

According to Confucius, there are five basic relationships in life. If *li* were present in these relationships throughout society, the social order would be ideal. These five relationships are as follows:

1. *Father to son.* There should be kindness in the father and filial piety in the son.
2. *Elder brother to younger brother.* There should be gentility in the elder brother and humility in the younger.
3. *Husband to wife.* There should be righteous behavior in the husband and obedience in the wife.
4. *Elder to junior.* There should be consideration among the elders and deference among the juniors.
5. *Ruler to subject.* There should be benevolence among the rulers and loyalty among the subjects.

In Confucian ideals, the principle of *li* is the outward expression of the superior individual toward others in his society. The inward expression of Confucian ideals is called *jen. Jen* is frequently translated as "love," "goodness," or "human-heartedness." According to Confucius, only the great sages of antiquity truly possessed *Jen* but it is a quality that all should seek to develop. The pursuit of this quality is mentioned many times in the *Analects of Confucius.*

From the Source

Jen is of more importance to people than fire and water. I have seen men die through walking through water or fire, but I have never seen a man die through walking in Jen.[18]

Jen is self-denial and a return to propriety (li). For by self-denial and a return to propriety the whole world would return to Jen.[19]

Thus, Confucius taught that people should love one another and practice respect and courtesy toward each other in their daily lives. He did not go so far as Jesus did and command that people should exchange good for evil, nor did he command, "So whatever you wish that men would do to you do so to them . . . ."[20] Rather, Confucius taught that society was best served when people acted with reciprocity (*shu*) toward each other.

From the Source

Tzu Kung asked: "Is there any one word that can serve as a principle for the conduct of life?"	Confucius said: "Perhaps the word, 'reciprocity': Do not do to others what you would not want others to do to you."[21]

If the principles of *li* and *jen* were present and operative in a person, the end product would be the Confucian goal, the superior human being.

Apparently, Confucius believed in the natural goodness, or at least in the natural perfectibility, of humankind, although it is not as clear in his teachings as it is in the work of his disciple Mencius. This teaching places the Confucians in direct contrast to those philosophies like Christianity, which maintain that humanity's natural state is evil and that it needs divine intervention for salvation. Confucius apparently believed that under the proper circumstances it was possible for individuals to achieve goodness and eventually to achieve the status of the superior human being.

One requirement for people to achieve goodness is good government. Confucius believed that poor government with bad laws caused people to do evil, and that a generation of good rulership could cure most of the moral ills of people. A good example set by the ruling classes will bring out the true morality of people. Because of the natural morality of humanity, Confucius believed that it was unnecessary to offer people rewards or punishments to induce them to good conduct. Good conduct is its own reward. Therefore, whatever Confucius might have believed about the gods, he never spoke of an afterlife in heaven or hell to reward good deeds or punish evil. Under the proper conditions, people simply grow and develop into what Confucius called the "Superior Man."

The Development of Confucianism

When Confucius died in 479 B.C.E., his teachings were remembered and followed by only a small group of disciples. He had not had the success as a ruler that he had hoped for, and his teachings had not received widespread support—nor did the rulers of China open their doors to his immediate disciples. During the following 500 years, however, the disciples of Confucius began to take a major part in training and advising the rulers of China, to such an extent that his teachings became an integral part of Chinese culture.

After the death of Confucius, approximately seventy of his disciples scattered across the empire. Some sought positions as adviser to rulers and others tried to establish their own schools. They were not spectacularly successful in either of these attempts for at least two reasons. First, they faced the opposition of rival schools—Taoists, Legalists, and later Mohists—who all claimed to have the key to good government for the official who would listen. Second, the disciples of Confucius taught that the best form of government was an idealized feudalism—and they were teaching this in a time when the feudal society was breaking down all over China; they were out of step with their time. Nevertheless, the disciples did manage to reach a few receptive ears with their teaching and advising; Confucius' teaching was thereby perpetuated. In the fourth and third centuries B.C.E. arose two of the most outstanding Confucians of all times, Mencius and Hsün Tzǔ, who did much to popularize and spread the teachings of Confucius.

In Chinese thought, the Chinese sage second only to Confucius is his latter-day disciple, Mencius.[22] Mencius was born approximately 100 years after the death of Confucius and lived from 372 to 289 B.C.E. We are not certain about a great many details in his life; but as is true of many of the ancients, there is an abundance of legend about him. Much of this legendary material apparently is intended to draw parallels between him and Confucius. We are told that, like Confucius, Mencius was the only child of a poor widow who struggled to support her son and provide him with an education. As did Confucius, Mencius became a teacher and sought a position as a political adviser. Also as was true for his master, his advice was not wanted; he too wandered about teaching his disciples. More substantial tradition says that Mencius studied under the disciples of Tzu Ssu, the grandson of Confucius, and was in fact an ineffective adviser to some of the Chinese rulers of his day.

The teachings of Mencius have been maintained in the *Book of Mencius*. From this text and others, his contribution as a Confucian scholar can be learned. Like Confucius, Mencius was not terribly interested in religion. Little is said about the gods in his writings, and no attempt is made to influence people to return to the worship of the traditional Chinese gods. Mencius' major ethical position was a reinforcement of Confucius' teaching of the natural goodness of human beings. Whereas this teaching had not been terribly clear in the writings of Confucius, it became crystal clear in those of Mencius. The latter strongly asserted that human nature was basically good. He observed that not all people act virtuously, but that this is because of their environment. Given the proper environment, he taught, it is possible for all people to be virtuous. Naturally, the best environment for a Confucian scholar features a government based on paternalistic feudalism operated for the benefit of the people. Thus, Mencius distinguished between the feudal tyrant and the sage-king.

From the Source

He is a tyrant who uses force while making a show of benevolence. To be a tyrant, one must have a large kingdom at one's command. He is a true king who practices benevolence in a virtuous spirit. To be a true king, one need not wait for a large kingdom. T'ang ruled over seventy square li, and King Wen over a hundred. When men are subdued by force, it is not their hearts that are won but their strength that gives out. When men are won by goodness, their hearts are glad within them and their submission is sincere.[23]

Because war destroyed the possibility of the kind of just and honorable conditions under which human goodness could develop, Mencius opposed war. On the other hand, because people were the most important element in any state, Mencius believed that people had the right to revolt against an oppressive government. In many ways, Mencius sharpened the focus of Confucius' teachings; in other ways, he added his own distinctive ideas to the Confucian canon.

The second most famous Confucian interpreter was Hsün tzǔ, who lived in the generation after Mencius (298–238 B.C.E.). Whereas Mencius has come to be regarded as the orthodox interpreter of Confucius, Hsün tzǔ is regarded as the heterodox interpreter; however, Hsün tzǔ had a greater impact in his time. Some authorities even give him credit for the development of Confucianism during the Han dynasty (206 B.C.E. to 220 C.E.).[24] He was a native of Chao and a widely respected and revered scholar. In his later years, he served as a magistrate of the city of Lan-Ling. Beyond these bare facts, we know little about him.

Hsün tzǔ is remembered for two major contributions to Confucian thought. First, even more than Confucius himself, he believed in the worth of rites (*li*) as devices to bring people together and educate them.

From the Source

What is the origin of rites? I say: Man is born with desires. If he does not get what he desires, he can but seek for it. If there are no degrees or limits to his seeking, he can but contend with others. Contention leads to disorder and disorder leads to exhaustion. As ancient kings hated such disorder, they established rites and moral principles to bring about the proper shares in order to nourish men's desires and meet their demands. They made it possible that men's desires did not exhaust the material supplies and the material supplies did not suppress the desires. Both desires and material supplies support each other and thus grew. This is how rites originated.[25]

The second contribution of Hsün tzǔ, and the one for which he is more famous, is his denial of the basic goodness of humankind. In direct contradiction of the teachings of Mencius, Hsün tzǔ contended that people were basically evil in nature. He believed that goodness comes only through proper training. Therefore, training, laws, and restraint are necessary so that society might survive. This made rites even more important, because it is through rites that people are trained in proper living. Added to this teaching was Hsün tzǔ's belief that the spirits of the heavens were basically impersonal forces. For this reason, Hsün tzǔ appears as the most non-religious of all of the early Confucian scholars.

The rise of the Han dynasty marked a new era in Chinese history. The period preceding it had been one of political upheaval. When the Han rulers came to power, they needed great numbers of new administrators and advisers. This new market for political theorists attracted many scholars who had been trained by the disciples of Confucius. The Confucians' position was further strengthened when in 136 B.C.E. they were placed in charge of the education of Chinese youth, particularly those youths who would eventually govern. The civil service examinations were based on the teachings of Confucius. From that date until 1905 C.E., Chinese education included a study of the teachings of Confucius. Master Kung himself could not have devised a system in which his philosophy would have had more influence over the future of China.

In addition to the development of Confucianism as the leading educational theory of China, a cult of Confucius himself developed during the years of the Han dynasty. The ruler of the state of Lu is said to have mourned Confucius after his death and built a shrine to him. With the coming of the Han rulers and the ascendancy of the Confucian scholars, however, reverence for him increased dramatically. In 195 B.C.E., the first of the Han emperors visited the grave of Confucius and offered a pig, a sheep, and an ox as sacrifices. Fifty years later, a temple was built to honor Confucius in his native town. By 8 B.C.E., titles and land were given to his descendants. The practice of awarding posthumous titles to Confucius himself began, and he was given the title of Duke. Gradually, the temples and ceremonies increased all over China. By the sixth century C.E., every prefecture in China had a temple to Confucius and some people came to look upon him as a god. However, no popular religion developed about Confucius. He was generally regarded as the patron saint or ancestor of the Chinese scholar, and he was remembered and revered as one would remember any ancestor.

The growth of the Confucian cult was set back in 1503, when the government ordered the removal of the images of Confucius from the temples and replaced them with wooden tables on which his teachings were inscribed. In addition, all of the titles that had been given were removed, and he was known simply as "Master Kung, the perfect teacher of antiquity." In 1906, an attempt was made to restore the Confucian cult to some of its original glory; but with the birth of the People's Republic of China, the sacrifices to Confucius, along with the other "great sacrifices," were abandoned.

Traditional Chinese Holidays

Holidays in Chinese communities are based on various religious and secular foundations. Ancient holidays associated with the various agricultural seasons and other holidays are connected to Taoism, Confucianism, and Buddhism. Some holidays celebrate the births of the various gods and the founders of Chinese religions. A list of some of the traditional festivals celebrated in Chinese communities follows. The Chinese year is based on a lunar calendar, and festival dates vary from year to year in relation to a solar calendar.

Chinese New Year

The New Year is celebrated at the end of January or the beginning of February. Each year is associated with a particular animal. The New Year celebrations' emphasis is on cleansing and renewal to prepare for the new year and the coming planting in the spring. Often, businesses are closed for several days. Houses are cleansed in preparation for feasts and guests. On the eve of the New Year, families gather to worship various gods and to venerate ancestors. The acts of worship are followed by a feast of many courses. This is also a time of new clothes and presents for children. Firecrackers and parades are a part of this holiday. Chinese New Year celebrations continue until the full moon of the first month.

Pure and Bright Festival

In early April, Chinese people celebrate another festival that involves the ancestors. This celebration includes ritual baths and the building of new fires that symbolize the newness of the spring season and the renewal of the *yang* forces in nature. Families also use this season as an occasion to clean and redecorate the graves of ancestors.

Food is offered to the departed family members at the graves, and the living family enjoys a picnic.

The Dragon Boat Festival

In June, the Chinese people celebrate the beginning of summer with the Dragon Boat Festival. This season is celebrated with dragon boat races and the eating of rice cakes. The beginning of summer is believed to be the high point of *yang* power in the earth (the longest day of the year) and the beginning of *yin* power. Taoist rituals exorcise pestilent spirits during this season.

All Souls' Day

The festival of All Souls' Day occurs in late August. It is the Chinese version of the Buddhist Ullambana. The Buddhist idea of purgatory is combined with traditional Chinese concern for the welfare of the ancestors. It is believed that souls are released from purgatory in a kind of amnesty. Money and other offerings are made to the spirits of the ancestors. Food and flower offerings are left outside for wandering spirits. Some people light fires in the streets to drive spirits and ghosts away. On this day, families join together for another feast.

Autumn Harvest Festival

The Chinese celebrate the autumn harvest during the full moon of the eighth lunar month (September). This holiday includes the enjoyment of the full moon and the eating of fresh fruits and sweet pastries, called moon cakes. The festival also features the reading of poetry and a general spirit of thanksgiving for the autumn harvest.

Winter Holidays

The winter season includes the Taoist holiday of the renewal of the universe (*Chiao*) at the time of the winter solstice. During the late autumn and early winter days, there are also celebrations of the birthdays of various heroes, gods and goddesses, and patron saints.

Religion in China Today

Throughout the centuries, Chinese governments have attempted to manage or control religion, in part because in traditional China religion and politics were so closely intertwined. While religion provided the basis for political authority, it also contained the seeds of rebellion. The nineteenth and twentieth centuries were difficult times for religion in China. During the mid-nineteenth century, natural disasters and political and military intervention by European powers yielded social and economic chaos in much of the country. There were many religious responses that offered hope of a return to peace and prosperity.

Religion and Violence

The most disastrous of these was the Taiping Rebellion, which raged between 1851 and 1864. Its leader, Hung Hsiu-chuan, combined elements of traditional Chinese religion and Protestant Christianity in a revolutionary ideology. Hsiu-chuan believed that he was the younger brother of Jesus Christ and that he had been sent by God to destroy demons and those who worshipped them. These included Buddhists, Daoists, and Confucians. Hsiu-chuan was also dedicated to the destruction of the ruling Qing Dynasty. He declared a new "Kingdom of Heavenly Peace," of which he would be the "Heavenly King." In his teachings, he combined Christian notions of Christ as the king of heaven, with Chinese concepts of the authority of heaven. The rebellion attracted an enormous following and spread rapidly over much of southeastern China. By the time it ended in 1864, nearly thirty million people had died.

In 1949, China underwent a revolution and became the People's Republic of China, under the direction of a Marxist government. The official attitude of this government toward religion was that it was a vestige of the feudal past and would gradually fade away from a modern society. Theoretically, at least, the government allowed freedom of religious belief. However, Taoism and Confucianism were regarded with great suspicion because Confucianism seemed so clearly tied to the feudalism of the past and Taoism was seen as superstition. Buddhism was viewed as an imported religion and was therefore suspect. Large numbers of Buddhist monks fled the country, contributing to the development of intellectually stronger, more sophisticated communities in Taiwan, Hong Kong, Singapore, and the West. Christianity was associated with the imperialistic Western nations. Therefore, Christian missionaries were expelled from China by 1952. Islam was a more delicate matter for the new government. Most Muslims in China live in the western part of the nation and are members of various minority ethnic groups related to the Turkic peoples of central and western Asia. Even though Islam had been brought in from outside China, the government of the People's Republic did not suppress it; however, Islamic education was severely restricted. Despite the official government position, many temples, mosques, and churches closed or were converted to other uses in the years following 1949. Christians were required to join together in the so-called Three-Self Movement[26] to protect themselves against foreign intervention or control. Those who refused and formed independent Christian communities (often called "house churches" in English) suffered persecution. The Chinese government refused to recognize the authority of the Pope to appoint bishops. Generally, post-1949 China was not a healthy place for organized religions, although some adherents of all five faiths maintained their practices.

Religion and Violence

During the period of the Cultural Revolution, which began in August 1966, all religions in China were severely repressed. For three years, the leaders of the Cultural Revolution moved actively against anything that represented the four "olds": old ideas, old culture, old customs, and old habits. The remnants of religion were inviting targets. Temples and churches that had managed to survive until 1966 were closed. Buddhist temples were especially singled out to be plastered and painted with slogans. Their statues were smashed and dragged through the streets. Confucius was called "the number-one criminal of feudal thinking." His birthplace was raided, and the temple there was destroyed. People who dared to celebrate Taoist festivals were arrested and accused of wrong thinking. Many Taoist shrines, tablets, altars, and relics were destroyed in the purge.

In 1977, after the death of Mao and with the thawing of relationships between China and Western nations, the government became more open to religions. In 1982, the Chinese Communist Party declared its respect for religion—until the time comes it disappears. Churches and temples were allowed to reopen and hold services. The University of Nanking established a Center for Religious Studies in 1979. Chinese students are now enrolled in religious studies departments at several American universities. The Chinese government is paying the costs for a translation and publication of the Bible, and subsidizing the studies of Chinese Muslim students in Egypt. Despite these liberalizing trends, the position of religion in Chinese society remains precarious. The government tolerates only those religious organizations willing to accept strict regulation. Religions must be free from foreign influence. To be officially recognized, religious organizations must accept government censorship of religious writings and guidance in the selection of clergy, and limit religious activities to approved locations. Only five religions are officially recognized: Taoism, Buddhism, Roman Catholicism, Protestant Christianity, and Islam. The government does not recognize individual Protestant denominations.

Religion and Violence

Unrecognized religious organizations and those the government declares to be "cults" are subject to severe repression. Roman Catholics who remain loyal to the Pope, Protestant "house churches," and conservative Muslims who refuse government regulation continue to suffer. Falun Dafa, a mystical group that seeks to establish inner peace and physical health through a combination of meditation and exercise, has been singled out for especially harsh repression. The government considers Falun Dafa practice to be a dangerous, superstitious cult. Members of the organization have been jailed, sent to re-education camps, and harshly treated by security forces. It is likely that the cause of this wave of repression is the fact that Falun Dafa is a new religious development that has attracted millions of followers and that the government and the party are unable to control it. Demonstrations by Tibetans calling for impendence and the return of their spiritual leader, the Dalai Lama, from exile are violently suppressed. The latest of these took place in March of 2008. According to the Tibetan government in exile, approximately 130 people were killed by security forces. Officials are also concerned about the possible development of political Islamic movements, especially in Muslim majority regions in the western part of the country. This concern motivated the government to limit "Year of the Pig" celebrations in 2007 to avoid offending Muslims who consider pigs to be defiled. What the future holds for religion in China is unclear. What is clear is that Marxist attempts to build a non-religious society failed in China in much the same way they did in the former Soviet Union and Eastern Europe.

It is also clear from the examples of Hong Kong, Singapore, and Taiwan—where modernity and religion thrive together—that the party's depiction of religion as a source of backwardness is incorrect.[27]

STUDY QUESTIONS

1. Are Taoism and Confucianism truly religions? Argue both sides.
2. Describe the Chinese concept of the *yin* and *yang* as a unifying explanation for the universe.
3. How could the hexagrams of the *I Ching* be viewed as a means of divination? How could they be seen as having personality and wisdom of their own? Note the editorial work of Confucius.

4. Why did the decline of the feudal system in ancient China set the stage for both Taoism and Confucianism?

5. Contrast the view of the best government as it is revealed in the *Tao Tê Ching* and in the teachings of Confucius.

6. By what process did Taoism become magic?

7. How would the current leaders of China regard Taoism? How would they evaluate the teachings of Confucius?

8. What political difficulties do religions face in China today?

SUGGESTED READING

Bush, Richard C. *Religion in Communist China*. Nashville, TN: Abingdon Press, 1970.

Giles, Herbert A. *Religions of Ancient China*. Salem, NH: Books for Libraries Press, 1969.

Hung Lou Meng. *The Dream of the Red Chamber*. West Stockbridge, MA: Publisher, 2003. This is one of the classics of Chinese literature. It is the very long and complex tale of a pair of male and female spirits who are reincarnated into a noble human family.

Kohn, Livia. *Daoism and Chinese Culture*. Cambridge, MA: Three Pines Press, 2001.

Overmyer, Daniel C. *Religion in China Today*. Cambridge, Cambridge University Press, 2003.

Reilly, Thomas H. *The Taiping Heavenly Kingdom: Rebellion and the Blasphemy of Empire*. Seattle: University of Washington Press, 2004.

Smith, D. Howard. *Chinese Religions*. New York: Holt, Rinehart and Winston, 1968.

Thompson, Laurence G. *The Chinese Religion: An Introduction*, 3rd ed. Belmont, CA: Wadsworth, 1979.

Waley, Arthur, trans. *The Analects of Confucius*. New York: Vintage, 1938.

———, trans. *The Way and Its Power*. London: George Allen & Unwin, 1956.

SOURCE MATERIAL

Selections from Sacred Chinese Literature

The source book for Taoism is the *Tao Tê Ching*. According to tradition, it was written by Lao-tzu as he sought an exit from China in the sixth century B.C.E. Modern scholars believe that these poems were really compiled over a long period by many Taoist sages. One can gather a sense of the message of the *Tao Tê Ching* in the segment called "The Tao of Heaven."

Tao Tê Ching[28]

CHAPTER I

The Way that can be told of is not an Unvarying Way;

The names that can be named are not unvarying names.

It was from the Nameless that Heaven and Earth sprang;

The named is but the mother that rears the ten thousand creatures, each after its kind.

Truly, "Only he that rids himself forever of desire can see the Secret Essences";

He that has never rid himself of desire can see only the Outcomes.

These two things issued from the same mold, but nevertheless are different in name.

This "same mold" we can but call the Mystery,

Or rather the "Darker than any Mystery,"

The Doorway whence issued all Secret Essences.

CHAPTER II

It is because every one under Heaven recognizes beauty as beauty, that the idea of ugliness exists.

And equally if every one recognized virtue as virtue, this would merely create fresh conceptions of wickedness.

For truly Being and Not-being grow out of one another;

Difficult and easy complete one another.

Long and easy complete one another.

Long and short test one another;

High and low determine one another.

Pitch and mode give harmony to one another.

Front and back give sequence to one another.

Therefore the Sage relies on actionless activity,

Carries on wordless teaching,

But the myriad creatures are worked upon by him; he does not disown them.

He rears them, but does not lay claim to them,

Controls them, but does not lean upon them,

Achieves his aim, but does not call attention to what he does;

And for the very reason that he does not call attention to what he does,

He is not ejected from fruition of what he has done.

CHAPTER XIV

Because the eye gazes but can catch no glimpse of it,

It is called elusive.

Because the ear listens but cannot hear it,

It is called the rarefied.

Because the hand feels for it but cannot find it,

It is called the infinitesimal.

These three, because they cannot be further scrutinized,

Blend into one.

Its rising brings no light;

Its sinking, no darkness.

Endless the series of things without name

On the way back to where there is nothing.
They are called shapeless shapes;
Forms without form;
Are called vague semblances.
Go toward them, and you can see no front;
Go after them, and you see no rear.
Yet by seizing on the Way that was
You can ride the things that are now.
For to know what once there was in the Beginning,
This is called the essence of the Way.

CHAPTER XXVII

Perfect activity leaves no track behind it;
Perfect speech is like a jade-worker whose tool leaves no mark.
The perfect reckoner needs no counting-slips,
The perfect door has neither bolt nor bar,
Yet cannot be opened.
The perfect knot needs neither rope nor twine,
Yet cannot be untied.
Therefore the Sage
Is all the time in the most perfect way helping men,
He certainly does not turn his back on men;
Is all the time in the most perfect way helping creatures,
He certainly does not turn his back on creatures;
This is called resorting to the Light.
Truly, "the perfect man is the teacher of the imperfect;
But the imperfect is the stock-in-trade of the perfect man."
He who does not respect his teacher,
He who does not take care of his stock-in-trade,
Much learning though he may possess, is far astray.
This is the essential secret.

CHAPTER LVII

"Kingdoms can only be governed if rules are kept;
Battles can only be won if rules are broken."
But the adherence of all under heaven can only be won by letting-alone.
How do I know that it is so?
By this.

The more prohibitions there are, the more ritual avoidances,

The poorer the people will be.

The more "sharp weapons" there are,

The more benighted will the whole land grow.

The more cunning craftsmen there are,

The more pernicious contrivances will be invented.

The more laws are promulgated,

The more thieves and bandits there will be.

Therefore a sage has said:

So long as I "do nothing" the people will of themselves be transformed.

So long as I love quietude, the people will of themselves go straight.

So long as I act only by inactivity the people will of themselves become prosperous.

So long as I have no wants the people will of themselves return to the "state of the Uncarved Block."

CHAPTER LXXVIII

Nothing under heaven is softer or more yielding than water; but when it attacks things hard and resistant there is not one of them that can prevail. For they can find no way of altering it. That the yielding conquers the resistant and the soft conquers the hard is a fact known by all men, yet utilized by none. Yet it is in reference to this that the Sage said "Only he who has accepted the dirt of the country can be lord of its soil-shrines; only he who takes upon himself the evils of the country can become a king among those that dwell under heaven." Straight words seem crooked.

The *Analects of Confucius*

The *Analects* are a collection of the sayings of Confucius and his disciples, dating from the fifth century B.C.E. The following selections are representative of its concern for a well-ordered society.[29]

BOOK III

1. Master K'ung said of the head of the Chi family when he had eight teams of dancers performing in his courtyard, "If this man can be endured, who cannot be endured!"
2. The Three Families used the *Yung Song* during the removal of the sacrificial vessels. The master said,

   "By rulers and lords attended,
   The Son of Heaven, mysterious————"
   What possible application can such words have in the hall of the Three Families?

3. The Master said, "A man who is not Good, what can he have to do with ritual? A man who is not Good, what can he have to do with music?"
4. Lin Fang asked for some main principles in connection with ritual. The Master said, "A very big question. In ritual at large it is a safe rule always to be too sparing

rather than too lavish; and in the particular case of mourning-rites, they should be dictated by grief rather than fear."

5. The Master said, "The barbarians of the East and North have retained their princes. They are not in such a state of decay as we in China."

6. The head of the Chi family was going to make the offerings on Mount T'ai. The Master said to Jan Ch'iu, "Cannot you save him from this?" Jan Ch'iu replied, "I cannot." The Master said, "Alas, we can hardly suppose Mount T'ai to be ignorant of matters that even Lin Fang inquires into!"

7. The Master said, "Gentlemen never compete. You will say that in archery they do so. But even then they bow and make way for one another when they are going up to the archery-ground, when they are coming down and at the subsequent drinking-bout. Thus even when competing, they still remain gentlemen."

8. Tzu-hsia asked saying, "What is the meaning of

Oh the sweet smile dimpling,
The lovely eyes so black and white!
Plain silk that you would take for colored stuff."

The Master said, "The painting comes after the plain groundwork." Tzu-hsia said, "Then ritual comes afterwards?" The Master said, "Shang it is who bears me up. At last I have someone with whom I can discuss the Songs!"

9. Someone asked for an explanation of the Ancestral Sacrifice. The Master said, "I do not know. Anyone who knew the explanation could deal with all things under Heaven as easily as I lay this here"; and he laid his finger upon the palm of his hand.

10. Of the saying, "The word 'sacrifice' is like the word 'present': one should sacrifice to a spirit as though that spirit was present," the Master said, "If I am not present at the sacrifice, it is as though there were no sacrifice."

11. Wang-sun Chia asked about the meaning of the saying,

"Better pay court to the stove
Than pay court to the Shrine."
The Master said, "It is not true. He who has put himself in the wrong with Heaven has no means of expiation left."

12. The Master said, "Chou could survey the two preceding dynasties. How great a wealth of culture! And we follow upon Chou."

13. When the Master entered the Grand Temple he asked questions about everything there. Someone said, "Do not tell me that this son of a villager from Tsou is expert in matters of ritual. When he went to the Grand Temple, he had to ask about everything." The Master hearing of this said, "Just so! such is the ritual."

14. The Master said, "The saying

In archery it is not the hide that counts,
For some men have more strength than others, is the way of the Ancients."

15. Tzu-kung wanted to do away with the presentation of a sacrificial sheep at the announcement of each new moon. The Master said, "Ssu! You grudge sheep, but I grudge ritual."

16. The Master said, "Were anyone to-day to serve his prince according to the full pre-scriptions of ritual, he would be thought a sycophant."

17. When talking to the Grand Master of Lu about music, the Master said, "Their music in so far as one can find out about it began with a strict unison. Soon the musicians were given more liberty; but the tone remained harmonious, brilliant, consistent, right on till the close."

18. The Master spoke of the Succession Dance as being perfect beauty and at the same time perfect goodness; but of the War Dance as being perfect beauty, but not perfect goodness.

19. The Master said, "High office filled by men of narrow views, ritual performed without reverence, the forms of mourning observed without grief—these things I cannot bear to see!"

Book IV

1. The Master said, "It is Goodness that gives to a neighborhood its beauty. One who is free to choose, yet does not prefer to dwell among the Good—how can he be accorded the name of wise?"

2. The Master said, "Without Goodness a man

   Cannot for long endure adversity,
   Cannot for long enjoy prosperity."
   The Good Man rests content with Goodness; he that is merely wise pursues Goodness in the belief that it pays to do so.

3,4. Of the adage "Only a Good Man knows how to like people, knows how to dislike them," the Master said, "He whose heart is in the smallest degree set upon Goodness will dislike no one."

5. "Wealth and rank are what every man desires, but if they can only be retained to the detriment of the Way he professes, he must relinquish them. Poverty and obscurity are what every man detests, but if they can only be avoided to the detriment of the Way he professes, he must accept them. The gentleman who ever parts company with Goodness does not fulfill that name. Never for a moment does a gentleman quit the way of Goodness. He is never so harried but that he cleaves to this, never so tottering but that he cleaves to this."

6. The Master said, "I for my part have never yet seen one who really cared for Goodness, nor one who really abhorred wickedness. One who really cared for Goodness would never let any other consideration come first. One who abhorred wickedness would be so constantly doing Good that wickedness would never have a chance to get at him. Has anyone ever managed to do Good with his whole might even as long as the space of a single day? I think not. Yet I for my part have never seen anyone give up such an attempt because he had not the strength to go on. It may well have happened, but I for my part have never seen it."

7. The Master said, "Every man's faults belong to a set. If one looks out for faults, it is only as a means of recognizing Goodness."

8. The Master said, "In the morning, hear the Way; in the evening, die content!"

9. The Master said, "A Knight whose heart is set upon the Way, but who is ashamed of wearing shabby clothes and eating coarse food, is not worth calling into counsel."

10. The Master said, "A gentleman in his dealings with the world has neither enmities nor affections; but wherever he sees Right he ranges himself beside it."

11. The Master said, "Where gentlemen set their hearts upon moral force (*tê*), the commoners set theirs upon the soil. Where gentlemen think only of punishments, the commoners think only of exemptions."

12. The Master said, "Those whose measure are dictated by mere expediency will arouse continual discontent."

13. The Master said, "If it is really possible to govern countries by ritual and yielding, there is no more to be said. But if it is not really possible, of what use is ritual?"

14. The Master said, "He does not mind not being in office; all he minds about is whether he has qualities that entitle him to office. He does not mind failing to get recognition; he is too busy doing the things that entitle him to recognition."

15. The Master said, "Shên! My Way has one (thread) that runs right through it." Master Tsêng said, "Yes." When the Master had gone out, the disciples asked, saying "What did he mean?" Master Tsêng said, "Our Master's Way is simply this: Loyalty, consideration."

16. The Master said, "A gentleman takes as much trouble to discover what is right as lesser men take to discover what will pay."

17. The Master said, "In the presence of a good man, think all the time how you may learn to equal him. In the presence of a bad man, turn your gaze within!"

18. The Master said, "In serving his father and mother a man may gently remonstrate with them. But if he sees that he has failed to change their opinion, he should resume an attitude of deference and not thwart them; may feel discouraged, but not resentful."

19. The Master said, "While father and mother are alive, a good son does not wander far afield; or if he does so, goes only where he has said he was going."

20. The Master said, "If for the whole three years of mourning a son manages to carry on the household exactly as in his father's day, then he is a good son indeed."

21. The Master said, "It is always better for a man to know the age of his parents. In the one case such knowledge will be a comfort to him; in the other, it will fill him with a salutary dread."

22. The Master said, "In old days a man kept a hold on his words, fearing the disgrace that would ensue should he himself fail to keep pace with them."

23. The Master said, "Those who err on the side of strictness are few indeed!"

24. The Master said, "A gentleman covets the reputation of being slow in word but prompt in deed."

25. The Master said, "Moral force (*tê*) never dwells in solitude; it will always bring neighbors."

26. Yzu-yu said, "In the service of one's prince repeated scolding can only lead to loss of favor; in friendship, it can only lead to estrangement."

The Meaning and Value of Rituals

One of the greatest interpreters of Confucius was Hsün tzǔ. In the following section, Hsün tzǔ states the Confucian view of the value rituals have for a society.[30]

Rites (*li*) rest on three bases: Heaven and earth, which are the source of all life; the ancestors, who are the source of the human race; sovereigns and teachers, who are the source of government. If there were no Heaven and earth, where would life come from? If there were no ancestors, where would the offspring come from? If there were no sovereigns and teachers, where would government come from? Should any of the three be missing, either there would be no men or men would be without peace. Hence rites are to serve Heaven on high and earth below, and to honour the ancestors and elevate the sovereigns and teachers. Herein lies the threefold basis for rites.

In general rites begin with primitive practices, attain cultured forms, and finally achieve beauty and felicity. When rites are at their best, men's emotions and sense of beauty are both fully expressed. When they are at the next level, either the emotion or the sense of beauty oversteps the others. When they are at still the next level, emotion reverts to the state of primitivity.

It is through rites that Heaven and earth are harmonious and sun and moon are bright, that the four seasons are ordered and the stars are on their courses, that rivers flow and that things prosper, that love and hatred are tempered and joy and anger are in keeping. They cause the lowly to be obedient and those on high to be illustrious. He who holds to the rites is never confused in the midst of multifarious change; he who deviates therefrom is lost. Rites—are they not the culmination of culture?

Rites require us to treat both life and death with attentiveness. Life is the beginning of man, death is his end. When a man is well off both at the end and the beginning, the way of man is fulfilled. Hence the gentleman respects the beginning and is carefully attentive to the end. To pay equal attention to the end as well as to the beginning is the way of the gentleman and the beauty of rites and righteousness.

Rites serve to shorten that which is too long and lengthen that which is too short, reduce that which is too much and augment that which is too little, express the beauty of love and reverence and cultivate the elegance of righteous conduct. Therefore, beautiful adornment and coarse sackcloth, music and weeping, rejoicing and sorrow, though pairs of opposites, are in the rites equally utilized and alternately brought into play. Beautiful adornment, music, and rejoicing are appropriate on occasions of felicity; coarse sackcloth, weeping, and sorrow are appropriate on occasions of ill-fortune. Rites make room for beautiful adornment but not to the point of being fascinating, for coarse sackcloth but not to the point of deprivation or self-injury, for music and rejoicing but not to the point of being lewd and indolent, for weeping and sorrow but not to the point of being depressing and injurious. Such is the middle path of rites.

Funeral rites are those by which the living adorn the dead. The dead are accorded a send-off as though they were living. In this way the dead are served like the living, the absent like the present. Equal attention is thus paid to the end as well as to the beginning of life.

Now the rites used on the occasion of birth are to embellish joy, those used on the occasion of death are to embellish sorrow, those used at sacrifice are to embellish reverence, those used on military occasions are to embellish dignity. In this respect the rites of all kings are alike, antiquity and the present age agree, and no one knows whence they came.

Sacrifice is to express a person's feeling of remembrance and longing, for grief and affliction cannot be kept out of one's consciousness all the time. When men are enjoying the pleasure of good company, a loyal minister of a filial son may feel grief and affliction. Once such feelings arise, he is greatly excited and moved. If such feelings are not given proper expression, then his emotions and memories are disappointed and not satisfied, and the appropriate rite is lacking. Thereupon the ancient kings instituted rites, and henceforth the principle of expressing honour to the honoured and love to the beloved is fully realized. Hence I say: Sacrifice is to express a person's feeling of remembrance and longing. As to the fullness of the sense of loyalty and affection, the richness of ritual and beauty—these none but the sage can understand. Sacrifice is something that the sage clearly understands, the scholar-gentleman contentedly performs, the officials consider a duty, and the common people regard as established custom. Among gentlemen it is considered the way of man; among the common people it is considered as having to do with the spirits.

CHAPTER 9

Shinto

CHAPTER OBJECTIVES

In this chapter you will:

- Learn about the various forms of Shinto.
- Discover how Shinto interacts with Buddhism and Confucianism.
- Learn about the role of Shinto in politics in pre-modern and early modern Japan.

KEY TERMS

Kami

Samurai

Bushido

Amaterasu

Tenrikyo

A Timeline of Shinto			
522	The term "Shinto" is used to distinguish Buddhism from local religion	1868	Meji state religion
		1887	Buddhism is allowed
8th century	Composition of Shinto classics	1889	Religious freedom
800–1700	Shinto is combined with other religions	1946	State Shinto is abolished
1700	Revival of the ancient tradition		

Shinto, a loosely organized native Japanese religion, embraces a wide variety of beliefs and practices. The variety is so wide that it is difficult to define Shinto precisely. Therefore, we can only list some of the areas it covers. In one sense, Shinto is a religious form of Japanese nationalism. Its mythology describes the formation of Japan as a land superior to all other lands; its shrines commemorate the great heroes and events in the history of Japan.

Historically, it has taught the Japanese people that their emperors were descendants of the sun goddess. Western commentators have frequently compared Japanese Shinto to the feeling that Americans have when visiting Gettysburg or the Washington Monument. Perhaps the closest comparison would be what takes place in some American towns on Memorial Day, when people recall great events in national history, visit the graves of war dead, and ask God to bless the nation on a beautiful late spring day.[1]

Shinto is more than religious nationalism, however. It also involves the Japanese in a worshipful attitude toward the beauties of their land, particularly its mountains and forests.[2] It includes aspects of *animism* and ancestor worship. Large-scale, public Shinto rituals take place in shrines throughout Japan. Private family rituals are carried out in small shrines in Japanese homes. Highly organized and active religious sects also have developed from basic Shinto. Thus, the term *Shinto* may refer to a multitude of varying Japanese religious and cultural practices.

The word *Shinto* itself was not officially coined until the sixth century C.E. It was developed then to distinguish native Japanese religion from the newer religions—Buddhism, Taoism, and Confucianism—being imported from China and Korea during the period. The word *Shinto* actually comes from the Chinese words *shen* and *tao*, which may be roughly translated in this context as "the way of the gods." The preferred Japanese term that describes this native religion is *kami-no-michi*, which also may be defined as "the way of the gods."

Japanese Mythology

To understand Japanese religion before the sixth century C.E., we must look at some of the traditional myths surrounding the origin of Japan, its native gods, and its early history. In the beginning, there were the **kami**, usually defined as "gods," which is inexact. Some scholars have chosen to define *kami* as *mana*. "Kami, in its original meaning, is practically identical with mana, the name adopted by science from the language of the Melanesians to indicate the occult force that preliterate man found emanating from objects and experiences that aroused in him emotions of wonder and awe."[3]

Others have identified the *kami* with the Greek term *daimon*. However, this too is inadequate. Even eighteenth-century Japanese Shinto scholar Motoori Norinaga confessed, "I do not yet understand the meaning of the term kami."[4] *Kami* certainly refers to the deities of heaven and earth worshipped by the Japanese people, but it can also refer to the spirit that is in human beings, animals, trees, plants, seas, and mountains. Any thing, person, or force that possessed superior power or was awesome in any way was described by the ancient Japanese as *kami*. Although *kami* may be defined in these broad terms, in mythology it generally refers to gods or to humans with godlike powers.

The major source for our knowledge of Japanese mythology is the *Kojiki*, "Chronicles of Ancient Events." These chronicles were collected in the seventh and eighth centuries C.E. as a response to the entrance of Chinese culture and religions. In these centuries, the Japanese, although willing to accept the advanced culture of the Chinese, sought their own heritage. The results of this search yielded the chronicles, which contain a section called "The Age of the Gods." In this material, one finds the mythological background of Japanese culture. The *Kojiki* includes stories that describe the special creation of the Japanese islands by two *kami*, Izanagi and his consort, Izanami. These two become the divine parents of the other *kami* in Japanese mythology. The chief of these spirits is **Amaterasu**, the sun goddess. All of the Japanese emperors are believed to have descended from the line of Amaterasu.

The History of Shinto
Shinto Prior to 300 C.E.

According to mythological tradition, the first Japanese emperor was enthroned in the seventh century B.C.E., but most modern scholars agree that the actual history of Japan does not begin until the third century C.E. At that point, the Japanese became known to other nations and began to keep historical records. Therefore, Japan's is among the youngest cultures of all of the Asian nations.

It is difficult to say what the exact worship of the Japanese was prior to this period. The coming of Buddhism in the sixth century C.E. caused the Japanese to collect their various myths and rituals under the title of *kami-no-michi* to distinguish native religion from those religions brought in by the Chinese and Koreans. Prior to this, Japanese worship probably consisted of a loosely organized, widely varying collection of practices. The myths allowed for a limitless number of gods, goddesses, and spirits; ancestor worship; and various forms of *animism*. Shrines were established throughout the Japanese islands for the worship of the various **kami**, and shrines were built in individual homes for ancestor and **kami** worship. Amaterasu and Susa-No-O were probably the most popular gods and received more than their share of attention at the shrines built for them and in private homes. Beyond these very general statements, it is difficult to say anything about Japanese worship in its prehistoric period.

Chinese Influence on Shinto

Early in its history, Japan became an object of interest to Chinese and Korean merchants and missionaries. These persons brought with them much of the older culture of China, including its arts, language, and system of writing and, of course, its various religions and ethical systems. After the fourth century C.E., the Japanese came under the influence of Buddhism, Taoism, and Confucianism. All of these had a lasting effect on Japanese civilization. The *Kojiki* records the entrance of Chinese culture into Japan.

In the years that followed, intercourse between China and Japan greatly increased. Before this period, the Japanese had no written language. They subsequently adopted the Chinese script and many other elements of Chinese culture. Confucian ethics were welcomed because Japan was governed by a feudal system, and Confucianism provided an ethical foundation for the Japanese political system. Ancestor worship had always been practiced in Japan; thus, the Confucian and Taoist elements that emphasized filial piety were readily accepted. The Chinese arts, particularly those connected to Buddhist ritual, were also adopted. Altogether, the period between the fourth and eighth centuries C.E. was one of dramatic change for Japan.

The introduction of Chinese and Korean Buddhism was extremely important in the development of Japanese religion. According to the Japanese chronicles, the emperor was presented with an image of the Buddha and several volumes of Buddhist scripture in

522 C.E. The emperor was delighted, but his advisers warned him that the introduction of a foreign god might arouse the anger of the native *kami*. Shortly after the introduction of the Buddha, a plague broke out in Japan. The emperor was afraid that the plague was the work of vengeful *kami*. He had the Buddha image thrown into a canal and the temple built to house it burned. The chronicles explain that the emperor's rejection of the foreign religion brought the plague to an end.

Buddhism could not so easily be turned away from Japan, however. In succeeding generations, other statues of the Buddha were introduced, as well as prayers and rituals. By the end of the sixth century C.E., Mahayana Buddhism had taken a firm foothold in Japan.

Japanese reaction to Buddhism was fourfold. First was the introduction of the name *Shinto* or *kami-no-michi* to distinguish the native Japanese religion from the new foreign religion. This was probably the time at which the Japanese actually began to think of their native worship as a distinct religion.

The second reaction was for the Japanese advocates of Shinto to recognize the many Buddhas and *Bodhisattvas* of Buddhism, but to think of them as the revelation of the *kami* to the Indian and Chinese people. Naturally, the Buddhists tended to reverse this line of thinking and to identify the *kami* as Japanese revelations of the Buddhas and *Bodhisattvas*.

The third reaction was Ryobu (Two Aspect Shinto), a syncretism between Shinto and Buddhism that developed in Japan between the sixth and ninth centuries C.E. An identification gradually developed between the various Shinto kami and the Buddhist deities. Little by little, the boundaries between the two religions disappeared. Buddhist priests began to officiate at Shinto shrines. The rituals performed in these sanctuaries made little distinction between the two religions. Buddhist architectural elements were added to Shinto temples. Generally, Japanese life began to be divided into two spheres. The concerns of day-to-day life became the domain of the Shinto side of the religion, and concerns for the afterlife were served by the Buddhists. Thus, a traditional citizen of Japan might be said to have been born a Shintoist but to have died a Buddhist. For ten centuries, Shinto and Buddhism lived side by side in Japan, each serving a special need of the people.

The fourth reaction of the Japanese to Buddhism was the development of some distinctively Japanese forms of Buddhism. Mahayana Buddhism is an extremely elastic religion, allowing for variations to such a degree that it may be considered a family of religions rather than a single branch of Buddhism. Within a few centuries of the time that Buddhism came to Japan, new variations on the Buddhist theme began to develop. Buddhism had emphasized meditation (*dhyana*) as a means of insight into religious truth. The Chinese Buddhists had picked up this emphasis through the missionary work of Bodhidharma and called it their branch of Buddhism Ch'an. The Japanese developed meditative Mahayana Buddhism even further under the name Zen. The Japanese also originated or developed other forms of Buddhism, such as Pure Land and Nichiren.[5] These and other forms of Buddhism became so popular in Japan that even though Shinto was intermingled with them, it was almost forgotten as a viable religion for the Japanese people.

The Revival of Shinto

From the eighth century C.E. onward, Shinto and Buddhism merged into a syncretistic form of religion, to the point that Shinto almost disappeared as an independent religion.

Kiso Province, Japan. Shinto priest with a mother and child for ceremony after the birth of a baby.
(Ms. Michal Heron Photography)

Nevertheless, many reformers wished to revise and revitalize the native religion of Japan. As early as the fourteenth century, various scholars tried to point out the strengths of Shinto and restore it to a place of prominence. However, it was not until the seventeenth century and the rise of the Tokugawa regime (1600–1867) that Shinto received official support. In this era, the Japanese were unified by tough-minded military leaders who sought to isolate the nation from outside influences.

Religion and Violence

Because Buddhism and Christianity were foreign-born, they were pushed aside; since Shinto was native to Japan, it was given new strength and support by the national government. Large numbers of Christians were executed when they refused to renounce their faith. A Japanese version of Confucianism was the only foreign system that was allowed support during this period, because Confucian ethics were supportive of the militaristic Tokugawa regime.

One of the most colorful aspects of Japanese life during the Tokugawa era was the feudal knight, called **samurai**. Throughout the history of Japan, individual warriors hired themselves out as bodyguards or mercenary soldiers to lords; but in the Tokugawa era, the samurai was idealized and a code of conduct was established for him. In the seventeenth century, the government set up the Chu Hsi (*Shushi*) School of Confucianism as the orthodox model for the conduct of the upper classes. A leader of this school, Yamaga Soko (1622–1685) led in combining Shinto and Confucianism to develop the warrior code called **Bushido**, "the way of the fighting knight." The standard of conduct established for the Japanese feudal knight was similar in many respects to that of the idealized Christian knight of medieval Europe, except for the absence of romantic love. Generally, Bushido may be summarized under the following categories:

1. *The* samurai *is bound to be loyal to his master in the hierarchy of the feudal system.*

(Continued)

Continued

The extremes to which this loyalty was carried are best illustrated by one of the most famous stories in Japanese literature, the tale of the forty-seven *ronin*. In 1702, a certain lord was insulted by a government official. He drew his sword and wounded the official. For this act, the lord was required to commit suicide and his property was confiscated by the government. He had in his employ forty-seven *samurai* who, because their lord was dead, were officially known as *ronin* (men without a master). These knights took a vow of vengeance for the injustice brought against their master. To avoid suspicion, they disbanded and acted publicly as if they had no concern for their master. When their enemies ceased to be watchful, they gathered together, attacked the castle of the one who had humiliated their master, and killed him. Then they quietly waited for the government to order them to commit suicide. Thus, the forty-seven *ronin* became the ideal examples of the loyalty that *samurai* are to have toward their masters.

2. *The* samurai *must have great courage in life, in battle, and in his willingness to lay down his life for his master.*

3. *Above all, the* samurai *is to be a man of honor.* He prefers death to dishonor and is expected to take his own life rather than face a situation in which he is dishonored.

4. *Like a true Confucian, the* samurai *is expected to be polite to his master and to people in a position of authority.* However, this politeness and gentility did not extend to everyone in society. There are stories of *samurai* who felt quite justified in trying out the edge of their swords on peasants if there was no battle at hand. The age-old story of the man who struck a peasant with his sword seven times and had no apparent effect until the peasant fell into eight pieces probably originated in *samurai* lore.

5. *Despite his attitude toward peasants, the* samurai *is expected to be a gentleman in every sense of the word.* He is supposed to be benevolent, to right wrongs, and to bring justice to the victims of injustice. A popular Japanese movie, "The Seven Samurai," is a good example of this sense of justice.

The willingness of the proper *samurai* to commit suicide rather than face dishonor and the attitude of the Japanese people toward suicide as a whole have long amazed Westerners. Many European religious traditions forbid suicide. In Japan, however, suicide has often been encouraged as a means of avoiding dishonor, as a means of escaping a bad situation, as a means of protest, and in World War II as a very effective means of destroying enemy warships. Perhaps no other culture in the history of the world has had this attitude toward suicide.

In Bushido, the warrior is expected to kill himself in a slow, painful manner called *seppuku*. (Westerners prefer the term *hara-kiri*,[6] which means "belly slitting.") This is suicide by disembowelment. At the proper time, the warrior is expected to slit open his abdomen so his intestines fall out. In recent times, it has become common for a friend to chop off the head right after the necessary slitting has taken place. This form of death was reserved for warriors and nobility. Women and peasants are forbidden to commit *seppuku* and were expected to kill themselves in a quicker manner by stabbing themselves in the throat. A. B. Mitford, a secretary to the British consulate in Japan in the nineteenth century, was allowed to witness a ritual suicide; he recorded the incident in the following manner:

The condemned man was Taki Zenzaburo, an officer of the Prince of Bizen, who gave the order to fire upon the foreign settlement at Hiogo in the month of February, 1868.

The ceremony, which was ordered by the Mikado himself, took place at 10:30 at night in the temple

(Continued)

Religion and Violence (*Continued*)

of Seifukukji, the headquarters of the Satsuma troops at Hiogo. A witness was sent from each of the foreign legations. We were seven foreigners in all.

After an interval of a few minutes of anxious suspense, Taki Zenzaburo, a stalwart man, thirty-two years of age, with a noble air, walked into the hall attired in his dress of ceremony, with the peculiar hempen-cloth wings which are worn on great occasions. He was accompanied by a kaishaku and three officers, who wore the jimbaori or war surcoat with gold-tissue facings. The word *kaishaku*, it should be observed, is one to which our word "executioner" is no equivalent term. The office is that of a gentleman: in many cases it is performed by a kinsman or friend of the condemned and the relation between them is rather that of principal and second than that of a victim and executioner. In this instance the kaishaku was a pupil of Taki Zenzaburo, and was selected by the friends of the latter from among their number for his skill in swordsmanship. With the kaishaku on his left hand, Taki Zenzaburo advanced slowly towards the Japanese witnesses, and the two bowed before them, then drawing near to the foreigners they saluted us in the same way, perhaps even with more deference: in each case the salutation was ceremoniously returned. Slowly, and with great dignity, the condemned man mounted to the raised floor, prostrated himself before the high altar twice, and seated himself on the left carpet with his back to the high altar, the kaishaku crouching on his left-hand side. One of the three attendant officers then came forward, bearing a stand of the kind used in temples for offerings, on which, wrapped in paper, lay the wakizashi, the short sword or dirk of the Japanese, nine inches and a half in length, with a point and an edge as sharp as a razor's. This he handed, prostrating himself, to the condemned man, who received it reverently, raising it to his head with both hands, and placed it in front of himself.

After another profound obeisance, Taki Zenzaburo, in a voice which betrayed so much emotion and hesitation as might be expected from a man who is making a painful confession, but with no sign of either in his face or manner, spoke as follows: "I, and I alone, unwarrantably gave the order to fire on the foreigners at Kobe, and again as they tried to escape. For this crime I disembowel myself, and I beg you who are present to do me the honor of witnessing the act."

Bowing once more, the speaker allowed his upper garments to slip down to his girdle, and remained naked to the waist. Carefully, according to custom, he tucked his sleeves under his knees to prevent himself from falling forwards. Deliberately, with a steady hand, he took the dirk that lay before him; he looked at it wistfully, almost affectionately, for a moment seemed to collect his thoughts for the last time, and then, stabbing himself deeply below the waist on the left-hand side, he drew the dirk slowly across to the right side, and, turning it in the wound, gave a slight cut upwards. During this sickeningly painful operation, he never moved a muscle of his face. When he drew out the dirk, he leaned forward and stretched out his neck; an expression of pain for the first time crossed his face, but he uttered no sound. At that moment the kaishaku, who, still crouching by his side, had been keenly watching his every movement, sprang to his feet, poised his sword for a second in the air; there was a flash, a heavy, ugly thud, a crashing fall; with one blow the head had been severed from the body.

A dead silence followed, broken only by the hideous noise of the blood throbbing out of the inert heap before us, which but a moment before had been a brave and chivalrous man. It was horrible.[7]

The willingness of warriors to die in such a manner for personal honor or for the good of the Japanese nation may seem out of place to the Westerner trained in the sacredness of life and the evils of suicide, but in the coming together of the Shintoist's love of and worship for the nation and its heroic figures and the Confucian's high sense of honor, *seppuku* is considered very religious.

The Modern Era

During the Tokugawa era, Japan did its best to avoid foreign influence in any form. It closed itself off from foreign trade, diplomatic missions, and foreign religions. During this period, it attempted to draw only from its native resources. In the meantime, the rest of the world, particularly the West, moved toward industrialization. In 1853, Japan was brought to a sudden confrontation with the modern world when Commodore Perry of the U.S. Navy appeared in Tokyo Bay and asked that the Japanese ports be opened and trade relations established between the United States and Japan. In 1854, Perry appeared again with more ships, troops, and cannons; the Japanese rulers were forced to open their nation to foreigners.

After a period of some confusion over what role religion was to play in the new Japan, it was decided, in the Constitution of 1889, that the nation would follow the pattern of many Western nations in that there would be a state-supported religion but that all other religions would be allowed to exist and propagate. There would be state-supported Shinto that would essentially consist of patriotic rituals at certain shrines. In addition, those who wished could develop Shinto sects, which would be supported by their adherents. Further, Shinto could be carried on in every home around simple domestic shrines. Beyond these forms of Shinto, any other religion—Buddhism, Christianity, and so on—was free to exist in Japan. However, only the patriotic rituals at the state shrines would receive financial support from the government of Japan.

Torii gate at Hiroshima-Miyajima. The symbol of Shinto is the torii.
(Dallas and John Heaton/Stock, Boston)

Three Forms of Shinto

State Shinto

Following the Constitution of 1889, the state took over the support of some 110,000 Shinto shrines and approximately 16,000 priests who tended these shrines throughout the nation. This version of Shinto (sectarian) became known as *Jinja* (shrine) to distinguish it from the more religious *Skuha* versions.

Each shrine supported by the state was dedicated to some local deity, hero, or event; the grand imperial shrine at Ise was dedicated to the mother goddess of Japan, Amaterasu. The visitor approaches the shrine through a distinctive Japanese archway, called a *torii*, which is so inseparably connected to Shinto that it has become known worldwide as its symbol.

The typical major shrine consists of two buildings, an inner and an outer shrine. Both are built of unpainted wood and must be torn down and rebuilt once every twenty years. Anyone may visit the outer shrine, but the inner one is reserved for priests and government officials. The inner shrine contains objects of importance to the deity or event it commemorates. For example, at the grand imperial shrine, the sacred objects are a mirror, sword, and string of beads, all of which are important to the myth of Amaterasu. On certain occasions or holidays, these relics are publicly displayed.

The visitor who enters the outer shrine meditates on the importance of the deity or the event celebrated there and offers a modest offering and perhaps a brief prayer. No one is obligated to visit the shrine, but it is an unwritten assumption that every loyal Japanese will try to visit the shrine at Ise at least once during his or her lifetime.

Religion and Violence

State Shinto was established to engender patriotism and loyalty toward the nation of Japan. It established a religious foundation for the Japanese nation but had no other religious functions. After the 1889 Constitution, the Japanese government forbade the priests who tended the state shrines and were supported by the state from performing any religious act, such as conducting funerals. The Constitution of 1889 began with these words: "The Empire of Japan shall be reigned over and governed by a line of Emperors unbroken for ages eternal. . . . The Emperor is sacred and inviolable."[8] This constitution also made the military leaders responsible to the emperor rather than to the parliament. State Shinto therefore became an instrument of support for the military in the wars in which Japan participated during the last part of the

nineteenth century and the first part of the twentieth. It was particularly supportive of the Japanese war effort during World War II. Shinto had become such an inseparable part of Japanese militarism that the American occupation forces felt it necessary to abolish state support for Shinto in December 1945. In January 1946, the occupation forces directed the emperor to issue a statement declaring that he was not divine.[9]

Since 1945, the shrines once supported by the Japanese government have continued to exist but are now sustained by the financial support of private citizens. Immediately following World War II, attendance at these shrines dropped off and many fell into disuse. In the ensuing years, however, interest in them revived.

Sectarian Shinto

With the developments of the Meiji era (1868–1912), specifically when the government treated Shinto as a nationistic and militaristic institution, the religious side of Shinto was forced to identify itself separately and find its own support, as were all other religions in Japan. (The adherents of these religions are thought to number over eighteen million; however, statistics regarding any religion are always suspect, and this is especially true in Japan, where a person may in good conscience be a Buddhist, a Confucian, and a member of a Shinto sect all at the same time.)

The thirteen major sects of Shinto may be divided into three categories. First are the sects whose primary emphasis is on mountain worship. The beautiful, graceful mountains of Japan have always been objects of reverence to its people. At some point in time, it became popular for people to climb the mountains during seasonal pilgrimages, in a combination of nature worship and asceticism. Some made exhausting climbs from the valleys to the peaks, while others took up temporary dwellings in the mountains for ascetic purposes. Mountains Ontake and Fuji were the special favorites for these purposes. During the Meiji era, three groups dedicated to nature worship and asceticism became established Shinto sects.

A second category developed from the basic practices of shamanism and divination of the Japanese peasants. The basic appeal of these sects in modern Japan is their promise of faith healing. Representative of such sects is **Tenrikyo** (Teaching of Heavenly Reason). Tenrikyo was founded in the nineteenth century by a peasant named Nakayama Miki (1798–1887). When she was forty-one years old, she felt she was possessed by the *kami* of Divine Reason. She believed she had been miraculously healed from a serious illness and began to teach others as a result of this experience. Her religion emphasized various elements that had always been a part of the basic religion of the Japanese peasant, such as shamanism, ecstatic dance, and faith healing. Today, this sect emphasizes volunteer labor for public charity and, of course, faith healing.

A third type of sectarian Shinto includes sects classified as more or less pure Shinto. When the rulers of Japan took over the shrines of Shinto in the Meiji era and used them for political purposes, this left behind a basic residue of the religious tradition of Shinto, its mythology, and its rituals. Three major sects developed to emphasize these religious elements and revived the myths of the origin of Japan from the ancient chronicles. They believed that there were religious, ethical, and political aspects to Shinto. They emphasized purification of the body through fasting, breath control, bathing in cold water, chanting, and many other devices similar to those of the Yoga cults of Hinduism. Today, these sects seem to be losing ground among the people of Japan, while groups like Tenrikyo are growing.

Domestic Shinto

In addition to the organized forms of state and sectarian Shinto is another, more basic form. This is the very simple and common form of Shinto that takes place in many Japanese homes. The basic unit or symbol of domestic Shinto is the *kami-dana* (god shelf), which is found in many Japanese homes. The *kami-dana*, whether it is elaborate or simple, contains the symbols of whatever may be of religious significance to the family. It usually contains the names of the ancestors of the family, because a part of the religion of the household is filial piety. The *kami-dana* might contain statues of the gods that have been beneficial to the family or are highly regarded. In the homes and shops of many Japanese artisans are the images of the various patron deities. The literature of Japan contains many stories of skilled workers creating masterpieces under the direction of an unseen patron god.

The traditional *kami-dana* contains objects that have been bought at the great shrines, such as the one at Ise. Any object the family considers sacred is fit for veneration at the god shelf. There is a story that the *kami-dana* in one household contained the cast-off shoes of a man who had been a benefactor of the household when it was in trouble. The shoes were believed to be symbolic of the friend's goodness or to contain the *mana* or *kami* that prompted the good deeds. At any rate, they became objects of veneration.[10]

Worship at the *kami-dana* in the Japanese home is a simple affair. Offerings of flowers, lanterns, incense, food, and drink may be placed before this altar each day. A simple daily service in which the worshippers wash their hands, make an offering, clap their hands as a symbol of communication with the spirits, and offer a brief prayer

Fortune prayers are tied to a fence at this Shinto temple in Kyoto.
(Paul Fusco Magnum Photos, Inc.)

may also be held here. On such special occasions as holidays, weddings, or anniversaries, more elaborate ceremonies may be held at the *kami-dana*. However, if the occasion is decidedly religious—a funeral, for example—the Japanese family turns not to the Shinto deities or priest but to the Buddhist priest. In the special religious syncretism of Japan, Shinto is for this life but Buddhism is for the life beyond. Therefore, in addition to their *kami-dana*, many Japanese homes have a *butsu-dan*, a Buddhist household altar, where worship of the Buddhist deities is also held.

As we have seen, Shinto, the native religion of Japan, is many things to many people. To some Japanese, it is a set of myths and rituals that remind them of the special origin of their nation. They are occasionally reminded of these myths and rituals on national holidays or during visits to a national shrine. Religion in terms of more regular worship and a concern for the future life is likely to be Buddhism. To those who are members of specific Shinto religious sects, Shinto may be related to faith healing, ascetic practices, or purification of the body. To many rural families of Japan, Shinto includes the daily worship that is carried on in the home at the *kami-dana* and contains elements of ancestor worship and *animism*.

Japanese Festivals

Traditional Japanese holidays are a combination of secular, agricultural, Buddhist, and Shinto celebrations. At times, one tradition or religion dominates; at others, all sources blend together. Various festivals are held at local Shinto shrines throughout the year.

New Year (Shogatsu)

The most widely celebrated holiday is the Japanese New Year. In the past, when a lunar calendar was used, this holiday was kept in February; but today, it is celebrated January 1 through January 6. During this period, businesses close and people gather with their families. Each family purifies and cleans the house in preparation for the new year. On New Year's Eve, special food is eaten and offerings are made to the ancestors. At Buddhist temples at midnight, gongs are struck 108 times for 108 kinds of passions to be purged in the new year. On New Year's Day, families visit places of worship. Some go to Buddhist temples, but most go to Shinto shrines. At the end of the season, the New Year's decorations are burned in bonfires.

Buddha's Birthday

In Japan, Buddha's birthday is celebrated on April 8. At Buddhist temples, the priests pour flowers and sweet tea over the statues of the Buddha as a remembrance that on the day of his birth flowers and sweet tea came down from heaven. December 8 is celebrated as the traditional day of the Buddha's enlightenment. Zen Buddhists participate in an all-night meditation to welcome this day.

All Souls' Day (Ullambana)

Among Japanese Buddhists, Ullambana (the festival for dead ancestors) is celebrated in mid-July. As in other Buddhist nations, this holiday is an occasion to welcome the spirits of the dead into homes. In this season, the graves are swept and decorated. It also is a time of parades, dancing, and bonfires.

Autumn Festival (Niiname-sai)

A combination agricultural and Shinto holiday is Niiname-sai, celebrated on November 23 and 24. At this time, the emperor offers the first fruits of the autumn harvest to Amaterasu and the other *kami* at Ise. Although this is the national festival of the harvest, various local thanksgiving ceremonies are held throughout Japan during October and November.

Shinto Today

Following the defeat of Japan at the end of World War II, several events occurred that made the future of Shinto uncertain. The most direct threat to this religion was the removal of official government support for state Shinto. The second threat came from Japan's rapid industrialization. Within a few decades, Japanese industry and science caught up to most Western nations and, in many cases, surpassed it. In this environment of quick movement into the twentieth, and now the twenty-first, centuries, it would seem that an ancient religion like Shinto would have little chance of survival. In addition to a struggle with the modern world, Shinto faced its old rival, Buddhism. Most Japanese think of themselves as being primarily Buddhist. Shinto is viewed as a secondary practice. Therefore, one might think that Shinto, with its ancient myths, rituals, and shrines, would quickly fade away.

But Shinto has not faded at all. It is as strong as ever in Japan today. It has survived the withdrawal of support by the state and continues to exist on private donations. New Shinto sects, which emphasize faith healing, positive thinking, and chanting, have been accepted by millions of Japanese. In some cases, adherents of these new forms of Shinto have entered politics and taken up the causes of certain labor unions. The new forms of Shinto have also provided an outlet for the religious aspirations of urban people, helping them cope with the day-to-day stress of modern life. Therefore, Shinto, in its many forms, still remains an important force in Japanese culture.[11]

STUDY QUESTIONS

1. Discuss Shinto as a reverential form of Japanese patriotism and as a religion. Can the two be clearly distinguished?
2. Review Japanese mythology and connect the imperial family to the *kami*.
3. What effect did the entrance of the Chinese and of Buddhism into Japan have on Shinto?
4. What is the connection between Shinto and the *samurai* class?
5. List the three forms of Shinto in modern Japan.

SUGGESTED READING

Anesaki, Masaharu. *Religious Life of the Japanese People*. Tokyo: The Society for International Cultural Relations, 1961.

de Bary, William I., ed. *Sources of Japanese Tradition*. New York: Columbia University Press, 1958.

Davis, Winston. *Dojo Magic and Exorcism in Modern Japan*. Stanford: Stanford University Press, 1980.

Earhart, H. Byron, ed. *Religion in the Japanese Experience: Sources and Interpretations*. Encino, CA: Dickenson, 1974.

————, ed. *Japanese Religion: Unity and Diversity*, 2nd ed. Encino, CA: Dickenson, 1974.

Kitagawa, Joseph M. *Religion in Japanese History*. New York: Columbia University Press, 1966.

Nelson, John. *A Year in the Life of a Shinto Shrine*. Seattle: University of Washington Press, 1996.

Ross, Floyd Hiatt. *Shinto, the Way of Japan*. Boston: Beacon Press, 1965.

Yamamoto, Yukitaka. *Way of the Kami*. Stockton, CA: Tsubaki American Publications, 1987.

SOURCE MATERIAL

Shinto Myths

The *Kojiki* (The Chronicles of Ancient Events) contain the myths of ancient Japan. These chronicles were compiled in the seventh and eighth centuries C.E. at a time when Japan was being deeply influenced by Chinese Buddhism. At that time, the Japanese felt a need to remember their own heritage.[12]

Myths Regarding the Plain of High Heaven

Birth of Kami

At the beginning of heaven and earth, there came into existence in the plain of High Heaven the Heavenly Center Lord Kami, next, the Kami of High Generative Force, and then the Kami of Divine Generative Force. Next, when the earth was young, not yet solid, there developed something like reedshoots from which the Male Kami of Excellent Reed Shoots and then Heavenly Eternal Standing Kami emerged.

The above five kami are the heavenly kami of special standing.

Then, there came into existence Earth Eternal Standing Kami, Kami of Abundant Clouds Field, male and female Kami of Clay, male and female Kami of Post, male and female Kami of Great Door, Kami of Complete Surface and his spouse, Kami of Awesomeness, Izanagi (kami-who-invites) and his spouse, Izanami (kami-who-is-invited).

Solidification of the Land and the Divine Marriage

The heavenly kami at this time gave the heavenly jeweled spear to Izanagi and Izanami and instructed them to complete and solidify the land. Thus, the two kami, standing on the floating bridge in Heaven, lowered the spear and stirred around, and as they lifted up the spear, the brine dripping from the tip of the spear piled up and formed an island. This was the island of Onogoro.

Descending from heaven to this island, Izanagi asked his spouse Izanami as to how her body was formed. She replied, "My body is formed in such a way that one spot is not filled." Then Izanagi said, "My body is formed in such a way that there is one spot which is filled in excess. How would it be if I insert the portion of my body which is formed to excess into that portion of your body which is not filled and give birth to the land?" Izanami replied, "That would be excellent." Then Izanagi said, "Let us then walk around the heavenly pillar and meet and have conjugal intercourse."

Birth of Other Kami

After giving birth to the land, they proceeded to bear kami [such as the kami of the wind, of the tree, of the mountain, and of the plains]. But Izanami died after giving birth to the kami of fire.

Izanagi, hoping to meet again with his spouse, went after her to the land of hades. When Izanami came out to greet him, Izanagi said, "Oh my beloved, the land which you and I have been making has not yet been completed. Therefore, you must return with me." To which Izanami replied, "I greatly regret that you did not come here sooner, for I have already partaken of the hearth of the land of hades. But let me discuss with the kami of hades about my desire to return. You must, however, not look at me." As she was gone so long, Izanagi, being impatient, entered the hall to look for her and found maggots squirming around the body of Izanami.

Izanagi, seeing this, was afraid and ran away, saying, "Since I have been to an extremely horrible and unclean land, I must purify myself." Thus, arriving at [a river], he purified and exorcised himself. When he washed his left eye, there came into existence the Sun goddess, or Heavenly illuminating Great Kami (Amaterasu), and when he washed his right eye, there emerged the Moon Kami (Tsukiyomi). Finally, as he washed his nose there came into existence Valiant Male Kami (Susanoo).

Greatly rejoiced over this, Izanagi removed his necklace, and giving it to the Sun Goddess, he gave her the mission to rule the Plain of High Heaven. Next he entrusted to the Moon Kami the rule of the realms of the night. Finally, he gave Valiant Male Kami the mission to rule the ocean.

The Conflict between Amaterasu and the Storm God Susa-No-O

The following selection from the Nihongi, I, 40NN45 relates the tale of a struggle between Amaterasu and her kinsman, Susa-No-O. It explains some of the features of the cult of Amaterasu.[13]

After this, Susa-No-O Mikoto's behavior was exceedingly rude. In what way? Amaterasu (the Heaven-shining Deity) had made august rice fields of Heavenly narrow rice fields and Heavenly long rice fields. Then Susa-No-O, when the seed was sown in spring, broke down the divisions between the plots of rice, and in autumn let loose the Heavenly piebald colts, and made them lie down in the midst of the rice fields. Again, when he saw that Amaterasu was about to celebrate the feast of first-fruits, he secretly voided excrement in the New palace. Moreover, when he saw that Amaterasu was in her sacred weaving hall, engaged in weaving garments of the Gods, he flayed a piebald colt of Heaven, and breaking a hole in the roof tiles of the hall, flung it in. Then Amaterasu started with alarm, and wounded herself with the shuttle. Indignant of this, she straightway entered the Rock cave of Heaven, and having fastened the Rock-door, dwelt there in seclusion. Therefore constant darkness prevailed on all sides, and the alternation of night and day was unknown.

Then the eighty myriads of gods met on the bank of the tranquil River of Heaven, and considered in what manner they should supplicate her. Accordingly Omoio-kane no Kami, with profound device and far-reaching thought, at length gathered long-singing birds of the Eternal Land and made them utter their prolonged cry to one another. Moreover he made ta-ji-kara-o to stand beside the Rock door. The Ame no Koyane no Mikoto, ancestor of the Nakatomi Deity Chieftains, and Futo-dama no Mikoto, ancestor of the Imibe Chieftains, dug up a five-hundred branched True Sakaki tree of the Heavenly Mount Kagu. On its upper branches they hung an august five-hundred string of Yasaka jewels. On the middle branches they hung an eight-hand mirror.

On its lower branches they hung blue soft offerings and white soft offerings. Then they recited their liturgy together.

Moreover Ama no Uzume no Mikoto, ancestress of the Sarume Chieftain, took in her hand a spear wreathed with Eulalia grass, and standing before the door of the Rock-cave of Heaven, skillfully performed a mimic dance. She took, moreover, the true Sakaki tree of the Heavenly Mount Kagu, and made of it a head-dress, she took club moss and made of it braces, she kindled fires, she placed a tub bottom upwards, and gave forth a divinely-inspired utterance.

Now Amaterasu heard this, and said: "Since I have shut myself up in the Rock-cave, there ought surely to be continual night in the Central Land of fertile reed-plains. How then can Ama no Uzume no Mikoto be so jolly?" So with her august hand, she opened for a narrow space the Rock-door and peeped out. Then Ta-jikara-o no Kami forthwith took Amaterasu by the hand and led her out. Upon this the Gods Nakatomi no Kami and Imibe no Kami at once drew a limit by means of a bottom-tied rope (also called a left-handed rope) and begged her not to return again (into the cave).

After this, all the gods put the blame on Susa-No-O, and imposed on him a fine of one thousand tables, and so at length chastised him. They also had his hair plucked out, and made him therewith expiate his guilt.

PART IV

RELIGIONS ORIGINATING IN THE MIDDLE EAST

At the dawn of the twenty-first century, Christianity and Islam have more adherents than any other religions, sharing almost half of the world's population between them. Their influence on the values and aspirations of humanity is therefore enormous, and a basic knowledge of them is essential. These two giant missionary religions arose from the milieu of the ancient Middle East, which first produced Zoroastrianism and Judaism. It was from these two religions that Christianity and Islam drew much of their worldview, ethics, and especially their concept of world history, beginning with a creation and ending with a divine judgment. Baha'í grew out of Islam in the nineteenth century. Study of these religions is essential for the student to be truly aware of the past and future of many of the people of planet Earth.

Zoroastrianism—Basic Teachings
Zoroastrianism is one of the world's oldest living religions.

Textual sources indicated that it was founded by Zarathustra between 1400 and 1000 B.C.E. It was the religion of the ancient Persian Empire that once ruled most of the Middle East. It influenced the development of later religions, including Christianity and Islam.

Zoroastrianism is monotheistic.

Ahura Mazda is the one god who created the earth. Ahura Mazda has both masculine and feminine characteristics. There are also angels who can come to the aid of humans.

Zoroastrianism is dualistic.

Two spirits emanate from Ahura Mazda, one good and the other evil. They have existed since the beginning of time and are interrelated. Just as there are angels who can come to people's aid, there are demons who torment them.

It is believed that after death the soul remains in the body for four days, after which it goes to the place of judgment.

The souls of people who have done more good than evil go to a garden like heaven, while the souls of the wicked are tormented in hell. Bodies are exposed to the elements in a structure called a *dakhma,* where they are consumed by vultures.

Most Zoroastrians have fled Iran because of persecution.

There are small communities in Western nations and approximately 100,000 in Bombay in India. There they are known as Parsis (Persians) and are very prosperous. There is some concern that the religion may vanish entirely because birthrates are low, and Zoroastrianism does not allow conversion from other faiths.

Judaism—Basic Teachings

Judaism is based on the assumption that there is a covenant between God and the Jewish people.

Over the centuries, interpretations of this teaching have taken many forms. The Hebrew Bible mentions God appearing to or talking with Abraham and other patriarchs. It also describes the ways in which he destroys the enemies of the Jewish people and punishes them when they are disobedient. The covenant is also interpreted politically because the Hebrew Bible describes the territory on the east shore of the Mediterranean Sea as the "Promised Land."

Prophets were the moral voice of ancient Israel.

Prophets often denounced the wicked ways of all classes of people, including kings, and called on them to comply with the term of the covenant. They also offered hope in troubled times, including the period of the Babylonian Exile.

Contemporary Judaism has a complex set of taboos.

Many of these concern the Sabbath and dietary laws. Jews are forbidden to work on the Sabbath (Saturday). For some, this means that even simple acts such as turning on lights is prohibited. Dietary laws regulate the ways in which animals are slaughtered and what foods can be eaten. Pork and shellfish are prohibited, as is mixing milk and meat. Foods that are allowable are known as kosher.

Jews have suffered from oppression—primarily by Christians—for centuries.

In Europe during the Middle Ages, there were restrictions on where Jews could live and what work they could do. They were expelled from several European countries. Many moved to Muslim lands to avoid persecution. Zionism, a movement seeking a Jewish homeland, developed as a result of continued persecution in the nineteenth and twentieth centuries. The worst case was the Holocaust, in which the Nazis murdered more than three million Jews.

Contemporary Judaism is extremely diverse.

Orthodox Judaism is the largest variant. It stresses dietary laws and the Sabbath. It requires that men and women be separated in the synagogue. Reform Judaism is the most liberal variant. Few reform Jews are concerned with dietary laws. They do not require separation of the sexes in worship services. Conservative Judaism is located between these extremes. Most Conservative Jews "keep kosher." Their Sabbath restrictions are milder than those of the Orthodox, and they make more extensive use of vernacular languages in worship services. There are also large numbers of secular Jews, for whom Judaism is a cultural rather than religious identity.

Christianity—Basic Teachings

Christianity is based on a belief in the unique character of Jesus of Nazareth, and that by his death and resurrection he provided for the redemption of humanity.

Jesus' life story and teachings are the subject of the four Gospels. They place him in the context of the first century C.E. Judaism. His ministry is described as a combination of preaching, healing, and ministry. It is not clear that Jesus saw himself as the founder of a new religion. Many Christian rituals, including baptism and the Lord's supper, are based on episodes in his biography.

Paul was among the most important of the early Christian missionaries.

Paul was at first strongly anti-Christian and joined in early persecutions. He was converted when he was struck down by a light from Heaven. He did much to establish Christianity as a distinct religion and carried its message to non-Jews.

There have been many theological interpretations of the nature of relationships between Jesus and the other two persons of the Trinity: God the Father and the Holy Spirit.

These debates were particularly important in the early centuries of the tradition. Gnostics taught that Jesus was purely spirit and only appeared to be human. In the second century C.E., Marcion taught that the God of the Old Testament was not the same as that of the Gospels, who was the father of Jesus. During the same period, Montanus taught that the Holy Spirit continues to speak to humanity and that religious truth can be found outside the Gospels. The position that emerged as "orthodox" maintains that Jesus was both fully human and fully God.

In 313 C.E., Christianity was legalized by the Roman Emperor Constantine.

It rapidly became the official religion of the Roman Empire. As the empire collapsed in western Europe, the bishop of Rome, or the Pope came to be increasingly important. His authority was not accepted by the churches of the eastern part of the empire. This and ritual differences led to the division of the church into Eastern Orthodox and Roman Catholic branches in 1054 C.E.

The Protestant Reformation initiated by Martin Luther in 1517 split the Western Church, and led ultimately to the formation of thousands of Protestant denominations.

Martin Luther sought to purify the church, which in his day was notoriously corrupt. He taught that the Scripture and reason were the only sources of religious authority, and that all Christians should read and interpret the Bible. He also taught that faith was the only source of salvation and that rituals were useless. He rejected the veneration of saints, an important part of the Roman Catholic and Orthodox faiths. A second great reformer was John Calvin, who broke with the Roman Catholic Church in 1534. His teachings emphasized the doctrine of predetermination—that souls were selected for Heaven or Hell at the time of creation.

Islam—Basic Teachings
Islam is based on the life and teachings of the Prophet Muhammad.

Islam means "Submission to God." *Allah* is the Arabic word for God. This is the same God worshipped by Jews and Christians. The Prophet Muhammad was born about 570 C.E. Tradition holds that he received his first revelation from God in 610, a process that continued until his death in 632 C.E. Together, these revelations are the Qur'an, which Muslims believe to be the speech of God.

Muhammad was the political leader of the Muslim community as well as a Prophet.

Following years of persecution, he led the Muslim community from Mecca to Medina in what is now Saudi Arabia in 622 C.E. For the next eight years, there was intense and often violent conflict with the people of Mecca, who sought to destroy the new religion. Mecca was taken in 630 C.E. and Islam rapidly became the religion of almost all Arabs.

Following the death of the Prophet Muhammad, Islam entered a period of expansion that continues today.

While it originated in Arabia, today only a small minority of Muslims are Arabs. Iranians are not Arabs. Most are found in south and southeast Asian countries. The most populous Muslim country is Indonesia. Today, Islam is expanding in Africa, Europe, and North America.

There are many Islamic taboos.

Muslims are prohibited from eating pork, birds of prey, dogs, donkeys, and mules, and from drinking alcohol and gambling. They must also abstain from eating, drinking, and engaging in sexual acts between dawn and sunset during the month of Ramadan.

The most basic sectarian dispute is that between Sunnis and Shi'ites.

This division is based on an early dispute concerning leadership of the Muslim community. The Sunni maintain that decisions about leadership were the prerogative of the Muslim community; the Shi'ites believe that it should be in the hands of Imams, who were descendants of the Prophet Muhammad. Since the death of Husayn, the grandson of the Prophet Muhammad, in the Battle of Karbala in 680 C.E., the division between them has been bitter, often sparking sectarian violence. Approximately 85 percent of Muslims are Sunni; 15 percent are Shi'ite. The Shi'ite are concentrated in Iran and Iraq.

The most basic aspects of Muslim ritual are the five pillars.

The first is accepting the confession of faith: There is no God but God and Muhammad is the messenger of God. The others are the five daily prayers, fasting during the month of Ramadan, charity, and pilgrimage to Mecca (for those who can afford it).

Baha'i—Basic Teachings
Baha'i began as a sect of Shi'ite Islam.

It was founded in 1863 C.E. in Persia (Iran) by Husayn Ali. The Baha'i have been persecuted in Iran throughout their history. In part because of flight from persecution, and in part from missionary ventures, the faith has spread throughout the world.

The Baha'i quickly began to think of themselves as a distinct, universal religion.

The most basic Baha'i teaching is that all religions come from the same source. It teaches the revelation is a continuous process. It maintains that there have been numerous revelations in the past, including those of the Buddha, Jesus, and Muhammad, and that there will be more in the future.

Baha'i emphasizes modernity and social reform. All forms of religious persecution are condemned. Gender equality, the harmony of religion and science, modern education, social and economic justice, and the establishment of world peace are emphasized.

Baha'i ritual practices are similar to those of Islam.

There are three required daily prayers. In another sense, the totality of life should be understood as prayer. There is an annual fasting period of nineteen days, during which eating and drinking are prohibited between dawn and sunset. Marriage requires the consent of both sets of parents.

CHAPTER 10

Zoroastrianism

CHAPTER OBJECTIVES

In this chapter you will:

- Learn about the history of one of the world's oldest religion.

- Explore relationships between Zoroastrianism and Vedic religious traditions.

- Understand the role of human choice in Zoroastrianism.

- Learn about the roles of Zoroastrians (Parsis) in modern India.

KEY TERMS

Gathas
Ahura Mazda

Saoshyants
Spenta Mainyu

Angra Mainyu

A Timeline of Zoroastrianism

1600 B.C.E.	Birth of Zarathustra (date contested—alternative is 1400 and 628 B.C.E.); revelation of basic texts during his lifetime	1640–1720	Continued persecution and forced conversions in Iran and Afghanistan
600 B.C.E.	Zoroastrianism expands in Iran; first written Zoroastrian scriptures	1878	First fire temple in the United States
		1890–1979	Liberalization and lessening of persecution of Zoroastrians in Iran
220–650 C.E.	Zoroastrian Sasanid Empire in Iran	1979	The Iranian Revolution leads to increased persecution and migration to India, Europe, Australia, New Zealand, and the United States
651 C.E.	Defeat of Sasanids by Arab Muslims, beginning of persecution		
900 C.E.	Beginning of migration to India		
1381 C.E.	Thousands of Zoroastrians killed by Mongol invaders in Iran	2000	Possibility that Zoroastrianism will survive only among the Parsis

Zoroastrianism is one of the oldest living religions. It may be as many as 3,000 years old. Unlike its kindred religions, Christianity and Islam, Zoroastrianism today is small, with only about 250,000 adherents. Nevertheless, it cannot be overlooked in any study of the religions of the world because of its great contributions to Judaism, Christianity, and Islam. It should also be studied by the student of world history because it was the religion of the ancient Persian Empire, which once controlled the entire Middle East and attempted to conquer the Greek city-states in the fifth century B.C.E. Students of philosophy may be interested in the founder of this religion, Zarathustra,[1] who was chosen as the key figure in Friedrich Nietzsche's *Also Sprach Zarathustra* (Thus Spoke Zarathustra.)

Pre-Zoroastrian Persian Religion

The origins of Zoroastrian religion are shrouded in mystery. Existing literary sources are contradictory regarding dates and events. Naturally, our knowledge of the pre-Zoroastrian Persians and their religion is also incomplete. The major literary sources that deal with this period are the **Gathas**, or hymns, of early Zoroastrianism.[2] The Gathas are to the people of this religion what the *Torah* is to the Jews. These hymns are considered the very words of the prophet Zoroaster, and all remaining scriptural books are based on them. Naturally, these books disparage the earlier religious practices of the Persian people; for this reason, the truth about these practices is difficult to ascertain.

The ancient inhabitants of the land that later became the Persian Empire were a group of people generally known as *Aryans* (noble ones).[3] A portion of the Aryan population migrated into the Indus valley and laid the foundations for the Indian peoples and their religion. Other Aryans continued to live in the region east of Mesopotamia and became the basis of the Medo-Persian Empire. Originally, both the Aryans who migrated to India and those who remained probably worshipped the same deities.

The Gathas indicate that the Aryans were nature worshippers who venerated a series of deities. Many of these gods are also mentioned in the Indian Vedic literature. They were generally known as *daevas* and were associated with the sun, moon, earth, fire, and water. Above this series of *daevas* were higher gods, such as Intar, the god of war; Asha, the god of truth and justice; and Uruwana, a sky god. The most popular and most important of all of these gods was Mithra, known as the giver and benefactor of cattle, a god of light, and the representative of loyalty and obedience. Although Zoroaster attempted to discount all gods but one, Mithra could not be displaced in the minds of the Aryan people. He reappears as a judge in the Zoroastrian Judgment Day; he is seen as Mitra in the Indian Vedic literature; and in the times of the Roman Empire, a religion based on the myth of Mithra became popular among Roman soldiers and merchants and rivaled Christianity in some parts of the Empire.

Above and beyond the local nature gods, one Supreme Lord was recognized as the one reality, called **Ahura Mazda** (The Wise Lord). As was the case in many other basic religions, one Supreme Deity was recognized but the actual day-to-day worship seemed to revolve around less important localized gods. Because the predecessors of Zoroaster were nomadic, it is likely that they worshipped the nature gods on altars, with blood sacrifices. They also favored the sacramental use of the juice of the sacred *haoma* plant. The reason for this is not clear, but some suggest that the juice may have been drunk by the worshipper for its psychedelic qualities.[4] The worship of fire and water may also have been part of the religion of the ancient Aryans.

The pre-Zoroastrian Aryans also believed that whenever religious practices strayed from the truth, prophets or reformers called **Saoshyants** (those who benefit the community) would restore the purity of the religion. They believed that before Zoroaster there had been a series of *Saoshyants* who had restored pure religion, and some saw Zoroaster himself as one of the last and greatest of these reformers.

The Life of Zoroaster

Several diverse sources provide information about the life of the prophet Zoroaster. There are, of course, the Gathas, which reveal many of the events of his life. In addition, there are the writings of many ancient Greek and Roman authorities, who showed a great interest in Zoroaster's life. Such writers as Plato, Pliny, and Plutarch made many references to Zoroaster. It is said that Plato attempted to travel to Persia to study with the magi, the Zoroastrian priests, but was forbidden because of the outbreak of war between Greece and Persia. Some of the material in these sources is obviously legendary, but some bears the mark of authenticity.

Zoroaster's birth date is uncertain. Many of the ancient Greek writers placed it at various points between 1000 and 600 B.C.E. Others place it approximately 300 years before the time of Alexander the Great. Modern investigation into the Gathas seems to indicate a date between 1400 and 1000 B.C.E.[5]

Because biographical materials are scanty and many are heavily laced with legend, it is difficult to know more about Zoroaster than the broad outline of his life. His name, Zarathustra Spitama, indicates that he was born into a warrior clan connected to the royal family of ancient Persia. The name Zarathustra may mean "possessor of camels" and is taken by some to indicate that he came from a nomadic family. Little is known about his early life. Legendary material states that demons attempted to kill the infant Zoroaster several times because they recognized him as a potential enemy.

Zoroastrian priest with the sacred fire dedicated to Ahura Mazda.
(Magnum Photos, Inc.)

They rush away shouting, the wicked, evil-doing Daevas; they run away shouting, the wicked, evil-doing Daevas; "Let us gather together at the head of Aresura! For he is just born, the holy Zoroaster, in the house of Porushaspa. How can we procure his death? He is the weapon that fells the friends; he is a Druj to the Druj!" Vanished are the Daeva-worshipers, the Nasu made by the Daevas, the false speaking lie.[6]

Each attempt on the infant's life was thwarted by the powers that watched over him. We have no information about Zoroaster's childhood beyond the fact that at age fifteen he put on the *kusti*, the sacred string belt symbolic of his passage into manhood as a member of his religion. Later, Zoroaster became a priest in his religion. He was therefore the only founder of a world religion to be trained as a priest. The literature on his life informs us that Zoroaster had three wives and was the father of six children.

At this most critical time in his life, he was wandering about seeking answers to religious questions that troubled him. By the banks of a river, he had a vision of the angel Vohu Mana, who appeared nine times the size of a man. In this meeting, the angel told Zoroaster that there was only one true God, Ahura Mazda, and that Zoroaster was to become his prophet. During the next ten years, Zoroaster had other visions in which each of the archangels of Ahura Mazda appeared and revealed further truth to him. He began to preach his new revelation at once but with absolutely no success. For ten years, no one converted to the message of this new prophet. He was condemned by his people as a heretic and sorcerer and was tempted by evil spirits to cease his preaching. Finally, he converted his cousin Maidhyomah.

The turning point in the career of Zoroaster came when he and his cousin journeyed to Bactria to the court of the monarch Vishtaspa. Zoroaster sought an audience with Vishtaspa in an attempt to convert him, but neither the audience nor the conversion was easy to attain. Although the stories of these events are mixed, it seems clear that Zoroaster stayed at the court of Vishtaspa for several years. During that time, rival priests conspired against him and had him thrown into prison. Finally, however, he converted the prince to his new religion. Some of the legends say that the conversion was achieved when Zoroaster healed the favorite horse of Vishtaspa. At any rate, Vishtaspa and his entire court and kingdom became followers of the prophet.

In the ensuing years, Zoroastrianism spread rapidly in the lands of the Aryan people. Sometimes the conversion rates were speeded up by holy wars. During a war with the Turanians, the city in which Zoroaster lived was invaded. An enemy soldier found the seventy-seven-year-old prophet tending the sacred flame in the fire temple and killed him.

The Teachings of Zoroaster

The Nature of God

As it was with the life of Zoroaster, so it is with his original teachings: The sources are distant and confused. The problem is compounded by the fact that over the years other teachings and legends have been added to the original message of the prophet. However, the central teaching of Zoroaster seems clear: There is only one true God in all the world and his name is Ahura Mazda. It is He who created the world.

From the Source

This I ask Thee, tell it to me truly, Lord! Who set firmly earth below and kept the sky Sure from falling? Who the streams and trees did make? Who their swiftness to the winds and clouds hath yoked? Who, O Mazda, was the Founder of Good Thought?

This I ask Thee, tell it to me truly, Lord! Who, benignant, made the darkness and the light? Who, benignant, sleep and waking did create? Who the morning, noon and evening did decree As reminder, to the wise, of duty's call.[7]

With this point, Zoroaster began. All the many gods of nature (*daevas*) that his people worshiped and the gods to whom they offered sacrificial animals were declared false gods. For its time, Zoroaster's monotheism must have been revolutionary. Before him were few who believed that there was only one God. Moses, who probably lived in the thirteenth century B.C.E., is said to have taught the Israelites that they were to have no other gods before YHWH (discussed in the next chapter, Judaism), but he never denied the existence of other gods. It is no wonder that Zoroaster's assertion that there was only one God was so controversial.

The one true God in Zoroaster's religion, Ahura Mazda, was the same God who had been worshiped by the Aryans for centuries as the distant High God. Zoroaster simply declared that he was the only God. The name Ahura, "lord," indicates one who created and governs the universe. The name Mazda means "all wisdom." Thus, Ahura Mazda is usually translated "Wise Lord." Zoroastrian scripture attributes another twenty names to this God, such as He of Whom Questions Are Asked, Giver of Herds, Strong One, Perfect Holiness, Understanding, Blessing, the Unconquerable, Healing, the Creator, and so on.[8] Ahura Mazda is understood to be the invisible and intangible creator and ruler of the universe.

In Zoroaster's understanding, Ahura Mazda revealed himself to humankind through the agency of six modes, the *Amesha-Spenta* (usually translated "Holy Immortals"). Western scholars have tended to equate these six modes with the archangels in Christian theology or with some form of secondary deity. The analogy is not exact, however. The six figures are really six outstanding attributes of Ahura Mazda. Because people cannot properly comprehend the nature of God, Ahura Mazda comes to them as one of these aspects of his total nature. Three of the immortals bear masculine names and carry masculine qualities, and the other three bear feminine names and represent feminine qualities. Thus, the total nature of Ahura Mazda is an equal balance of the male and female. The three masculine or father types of these immortals are Asha (knowledge of the law of God and the law itself), Vohu-Mana (love), and Kshathra (loving service). The three feminine immortals are Armaiti (piety), Haurvatat (wholeness or perfection), and Ameretat (immortality). Faithful Zoroastrians pray that these six immortals may come into their homes and bless them.

In addition to these expressions of the total nature of Ahura Mazda, other beings who serve him may be helpful to human beings. If the six immortals are the archangels of Zoroastrianism, the multiple Yazata (Adorable Ones) are the hosts of angels surrounding the throne of God. They are limitless in number, but only about forty are mentioned in the Zoroastrian texts and only three receive any regular mention. These angels are Sraosha, the guardian of humanity who shows obedience to the law of God; his sister and feminine counterpart, Ashi Vanguhi, the rewarder of good deeds; and the ever-popular Mithra, the strongest of these beings and the ideal of soldiers.

The God of Evil

Perhaps Zoroaster's greatest contribution to the religions of the world was in the area of the problem of evil. The world is full of both good and evil. It is easy enough to ascribe the good in the world to the good God who has created the world, but who is responsible for the evil? If the creator God is responsible for the evil of the world, then where is his goodness and justice? Many religions have their powers of darkness, their demons; but it remained for Zoroaster to systematize and delineate the forces behind the world's evil.

Zoroastrianism is often referred to as dualistic—that is, as a religion that sees two supreme forces contending with each other for control of the universe. The usual interpretation of Zoroastrianism is that it recognizes a good God and his angels, who are in charge of the good that happens in the world, and it recognizes an evil god and his demons, who are responsible for all the world's evil. But if this were Zoroaster's understanding of the universe, then he would not be teaching a monotheism but a dualism. In the same vein, one might say that because Christianity recognizes a Satan figure, it too is not monotheistic. This is not the case in the teachings of Zoroaster. According to him, two spirits emanate from Ahura Mazda; one is **Spenta Mainyu**, the Beneficent Spirit; the other is **Angra Mainyu**, the Evil Spirit. These two have co-existed since the beginning of time.

From the Source

Now the two primal Spirits, who revealed themselves in vision as Twins, are the Better and the Bad in thought and word and action. And between these two the wise once chose aright, and the foolish not so.

And when these twain spirits came together in the beginning, they established Life and Not-Life, and that at the last the Worst Existence shall be to the followers of the lie, but the Best Thought to him that follows Right . . . .[9]

These two spirits do not exist independently but relate to each other and meet in the unity of Ahura Mazda. In this sense they are much like the *yin* and *yang* of Taoism. Neither is free from the influence of the other, and each is bound by the other. In the truest sense, Zoroastrianism remains a monotheism, with the forces of both good and evil under the control of Ahura Mazda.

Angra Mainyu is also known by other names. He is sometimes known as Ahriman and at other times Shaitin or Satan. He is surrounded and abetted by a host of demons who do his bidding, tempting and tormenting human beings. Zoroastrianism may have been the first religion to develop a full scheme of demonology. All the *daevas* of pre-Zoroastrian Aryan religion came to be identified as demons in the corps of Angra Mainyu. One of the most frequently mentioned of these demons is Aeshma, the demon of wrath.[10] Aeshma is second-in-command to Angra Mainyu and stalks the earth, polluting it and spreading disease and death.

The Nature of Humankind

Zoroaster saw the forces of good struggling with the forces of evil in the world, and he taught that human beings played a part in this struggle by cooperating with either of the forces. To Zoroaster, men and women were born in a pure, sinless state and could choose to serve either good or evil. Their lives and ultimate destiny depended on the exercise of their free will. If they wished, individuals could serve the forces of evil—they could cooperate in lies, hate, corruption, and every other sort of evil—but they could also choose to be a part of good acts that would improve the world. The choice of conduct was entirely up to the individual. In this respect, Zoroastrianism is markedly different from the various deterministic views of human conduct. Some religions see a deity controlling the choices people make; others see human conduct determined by economic or social factors. Unlike these philosophies of human nature, Zoroastrianism taught that men and women were genuinely free to decide if they would do good or evil, and thus were to be held accountable for those choices.

From the Source

Hear with your ears the Highest Truths I preach,   Deciding man by man, each one for each;—
And with illumined minds weigh them with care,   Before the great New Age is ushered in
Before you choose which of Two Paths to tread,—   Wake, up, alert to spread Ahura's Word.[11]

By exercising the reason with which they were endowed, it is possible for human beings to choose the path of righteousness and in fact achieve perfection in this life. Therefore, a scheme of multiple lives, such as that of Hinduism, is not necessary for Zoroastrianism.

From the Source

Within the span of this life of Earth   Ardent in zeal, sincere in their toil.[12]
Perfection can be reached by fervent souls,

Thus we see that in Zoroastrianism, perhaps more than in any other religion, ethical conduct is urged. Ethical conduct is possible because people have free choice, and ethical conduct is important because it determines people's ultimate destiny.

The Destiny of Humankind

Because people have freedom of choice, they must stand responsible for their choices. Each deed, either good or evil, will bear its own fruits. Therefore, Zoroastrianism sees a law of retribution at work in this life. That which is called *karma* in Hinduism, and that which is stated by St. Paul as "whatsoever a man soweth, that shall he also reap,"[13] is also taught in Zoroastrianism. "Evil to Evil, Good to Good."[14]

From the Source

Falsehood brings on age-long punishment,   And Truth leads on to fuller, higher life.[15]

Another of Zoroaster's gifts to the world of Western religions was his organized scheme of eschatology (belief concerning the end of the world). In religions prior to Zoroastrianism, elaborate preparations were sometimes made for life beyond the grave, as with the ancient Egyptians. In most religions, however, it was simply assumed that with death, life essentially came to an end. The ancient Hebrews of the pre-exilic period (before 586 B.C.E.), for example, believed that the dead lived in a realm called *Sheol* for a time and then gradually faded into nothingness. Perhaps the Aryan kinsmen of Zoroaster living in India had begun to think in terms of reincarnation by this time, but that is not clear. Zoroaster and his followers developed a complete eschatology that was the consistent outworking of his theology of free choice and complete responsibility.

According to Zoroastrianism, the soul stays with the body for three days after the individual's death and meditates on the deeds that were done in life. On the fourth day, the soul journeys to the place of judgment. There, Mithra judges the soul according to the deeds performed during life. These deeds are balanced on a scale. If the preponderance of a person's life has been given over to evil, that person's soul will be sentenced to hell; but if the scale tips even slightly toward good, that person's soul will go to paradise. The soul on its way to paradise crosses the Chinvat Bridge, which is a wide, easy path. The soul is greeted by beautiful maidens who escort it into heaven. Zoroastrian paradise is a place of beauty, light, pleasant scents, and noble souls who have lived life according to Zoroastrian ethics.

For the person whose balance is weighted down by evil deeds and thoughts, the Chinvat Bridge becomes an entirely different experience. Once condemned, the soul is forced out on this bridge, which turns up on its edge and becomes as hard to walk on as the edge of a sword. Moreover, the soul is tormented by an old hag and eventually falls off the bridge into hell. Zoroastrian hell is one of the most terrible hells of all. It is vividly described in a work called the *Vision of Arda Viraf*, which was written sometime between 226 and 641 C.E. In this work, the hero is allowed to travel to both heaven and hell and sees the delights and miseries of their inhabitants.

From the Source

I saw the greedy jaws of hell: the most frightful pit, descending, in a very narrow, fearful crevice and in darkness so murky that I was forced to feel my way, amid such a stench that all whose nose inhaled that air, struggled, staggered, and fell, and in such confinement that existence seemed impossible. Each one thought, "I am alone"; and when a mere three days had elapsed supposed that the end of the nine thousand years of time had come, when time would cease and the resurrection of the body occur. "The nine thousand years are run," he would think, "yet, I am not released." In that place even the lesser noxious creatures are as high as mountains, and these so tear, seize, and worry the souls of the wicked as would be unworthy of a dog. But I passed easily thereby in the guidance of Obedience and Thought.

I saw the soul of man through whose fundament a snake went in, like a beam, and came forth out of the mouth; and many other snakes ever seized his limbs. "What sin," I inquired, "was committed by this body whose soul suffers so severe a punishment?" "This," I was told, "is the soul of a man who, in the world, committed sodomy."

A woman's soul I saw, to whom they gave to drink one cupful after another of the impurity and filth of men. I asked, "What sin was committed by the body whose soul thus suffers?" "Having failed to abstain," they replied, "this wicked woman approached water and fire during menstruation." I saw also, the soul of a man, the skin of whose head was being flayed . . . who, in the world, had slain a pious man. I saw the soul of a man into whose mouth they poured continually the menstrual discharge of women, while he cooked and ate his own child . . . "While in the world," I was told, "that wicked man had intercourse with a menstruating woman."[16]

The scene continues with all sorts of horrors. It seems that the Zoroastrian hell is filled with men and women who have broken the laws of clean and unclean, and who are being punished accordingly. There also is a large category of men and women who have violated the sexual taboos of Zoroastrianism and are being punished in a particularly horrible manner.

In the Zoroastrian scheme, the souls of the dead abide in their heaven and hell until that point when time ends. The cycle of time will run out at a specified point in the future, and the world will come to its final consummation—as established by Ahura Mazda when he created the world. He will wipe out every trace of the evil work of Angra Mainyu. The souls from hell will be brought up and purified and will join the resurrected souls of the righteous. Then the world will enter a new cycle without the evil and misery of the past. The Saoshyant will restore the world; and in this restored world, no one will ever grow old or decay. Angra Mainyu and his demons will be destroyed forever, and the will of Ahura Mazda will reign supreme.

Zoroastrian Ethics

Because the essence of Zoroastrian theology is that people are free to choose between good and evil in this life and will be held responsible for their choices in an afterlife, one would expect Zoroastrians to have a lengthy and involved code of ethics. This is in fact the case, and Zoroastrians as a people have long been noted in both the ancient and modern world for their high ethical standards.[17]

The basis for much of Zoroastrian ethics and worship is the understanding of the sacredness of the elements of earth, fire, water, and air. Whatever violates or pollutes these sacred elements is wicked. Thus, in the Zoroastrian hell, those who have polluted the earth or water with their excrement are subject to unusually harsh punishments. The concern for the elements is seen again and again in Zoroastrian life.

Zoroastrianism also teaches a concern for *Humata, Hukhta,* and *Hvarshta*: good thought, good word, and good deed. A prayer is

From the Source

Henceforth let me stand firm for good thoughts, good words, and good deeds, which must be well thought, must be well spoken, and must be well done.[18]

Based on these rather general concerns are the specific demands of Zoroastrianism for righteousness as expressed in truthfulness, chastity, justice, compassion, care of the soil and cattle, charity, education, and service. The ancient Persians were known to the Greek historians for these virtues, particularly for the virtue of truthfulness. In modern India, where most contemporary Zoroastrians live, they are known for their purity of life, for their honesty as businesspeople, and for their concern over the education of their children.

Zoroastrian Worship

Pre-Zoroastrian Aryan worship depended heavily on blood sacrifices to the various deities, but Zoroaster drastically changed these patterns. Zoroastrian worship consists mainly of prayers offered to Ahura Mazda requesting assistance in living a righteous life and in avoiding temptations. The only form of sacrifice that currently exists is the offering of sandalwood to sacred flames that burn eternally in Zoroastrian fire temples. These fires are tended by priests who have been specially trained for their tasks and who wear surgical masks over their faces lest their breath contaminate the sacred flames. On special occasions during the year, Zoroastrians visit the fire temple, offer bundles of sandalwood, and receive the ashes of the sacred flames.

In addition to these forms of worship, Zoroastrian rituals exist for each of the points in life normally associated with rites of passage, such as ceremonies that attend the birth of a child. Zoroastrian scripture lays out explicit regulations regarding the state of purification of the household and mother at the time of the birth of a child.

At a certain age (seven years in India and ten years in Iran), young Zoroastrian boys and girls are received into their religion with the investiture of a sacred shirt (*sadre*) and sacred thread (*kusti*). Except when bathing, they must wear these two items for the rest of their lives. The *kusti* is to be tied and untied on at least five occasions during each day, as a form of prayer. This sacred belt is made up of seventy-two threads that represent the seventy-two chapters of the Zoroastrian scripture, the *Yasna*.

Zoroastrians are traditionally placed in a *dakhma* (tower of silence) at death. Because Zoroastrians consider corpses to be polluting and soil, water, and fire to be holy, this is an acceptable manner to dispose of the dead.
(Robert Harding World Imagery)

Of course, Zoroastrian ceremonies also occur at other important points in life, such as marriage, periods of purification, and initiation into the priesthood for those who choose it. The most distinctive ritual of all, however, occurs at death. If one believes that earth, fire, water, and air are the most sacred elements in life, and if one believes that the corpse is the most contaminating element of all, how is one to dispose of the dead? The body cannot be buried lest it contaminate the soil; it cannot be cremated lest it contaminate the sacred fire; and it cannot be buried at sea lest the water be polluted. The Zoroastrian solution to this problem has attracted widespread attention.

When a Zoroastrian dies, the corpse is washed, a clean suit of clothes is placed on it, and the *kusti* of the deceased is wrapped around the body. After certain purification ceremonies, the body is carried out of the house by corpse bearers. The corpse bearers, along with the mourners, take the body to an enclosure called a *dakhma*, or tower of silence. This enclosure looks something like a small version of an American football stadium. It is a round structure, open to the sky. Inside the *dakhma* are open compartments and, in the center, a dry well. The body is placed in one of the compartments and its clothing is either removed or torn open. The mourners leave the site and within a few moments vultures descend on the body and begin to strip it of its flesh. In an area where there are fairly frequent deaths, a large number of vultures usually stay near the *dakhmas*; within thirty minutes, they can strip the body clean. After a time, when the bones are dried out by the sun, they are washed down into the central well of the *dakhma*. Thus, the body of the Zoroastrian is disposed of without risking contamination of soil, fire, or water.

The principle of exposing the dead to birds and beasts of prey seems to have been a part of Zoroastrian life from earliest times. The *Zend-Avesta* commands the following procedure:

From the Source

And two men, strong and agile, having changed their garments, shall lift the body from the clay or the stones, or out of the plastered house, and they shall lay it down at a place where they know that there are always corpse-eating dogs and corpse-eating birds.[19]

Zoroastrian disposal of the dead occasionally runs into problems when the community is small and deaths are so infrequent that there are not large numbers of vultures about the *dakhmas*. On some occasions, non-Zoroastrian majorities protest against this procedure. In such situations, it is permissible to bury the body in a stone casket lined with lead to prevent contamination of the soil. Modern Zoroastrians sometimes live in cities where the practice of exposing the dead may be frowned upon. This has caused them to think of alternatives, such as cremation by means of electrical heat. In this manner, the flame may not be contaminated. Another alternative is to bury a body in a completely sealed casket so there is no chance of contaminating the earth.

Historical Development of Zoroastrianism

Apparently, Zoroastrianism was well-established as the religion of the Persian people by the sixth century B.C.E. It was therefore the religion of Cyrus the Great when he founded the Medo-Persian Empire and ruled from 558 to 530 B.C.E. Cyrus is mentioned in the Hebrew Bible as the liberator of the Jews from Babylonian captivity in 538 B.C.E. However, Zoroastrian sources do not mention Cyrus or his contemporaries. The earliest sources of information on the religion of the Persian Empire are inscriptions from the time of Darius the Great (521–486 B.C.E.). Although they indicate that the people of that era worshipped Ahura Mazda, they do not mention Zoroaster.

From the Source

A great god is Ahuramazda, who created this excellent work which is seen, who created happiness for man, who bestowed wisdom and activity upon Darius the king.

Says Darius the king: By the favor of Ahuramazda I am of such a sort that I am a friend to the right, I am not a friend to wrong; it is not my desire that the weak man should have wrong done to him by the mighty; nor is that my desire, that the mighty man should have wrong done him by the weak.

What is right, that is my desire. I am not a friend to the man who is a Lie-follower. I am not hot-tempered. What things develop in my anger, I hold firmly under control by my willpower. I am firmly ruling over my own [impulses].[20]

Zoroastrian influence of people and religions other than the Persians is also a matter of some speculation. Many ancient Greek and Roman writers were apparently enamored of Zoroaster and his thoughts, and he is featured in many of their writings. However, the Persian emperors of the fifth century B.C.E. failed in several attempts to conquer Greece. Consequently, Persian influence was never strong there. Persia did conquer and hold the Middle East for two centuries, and its influence was very strong on the peoples of that area. The Jews came under Persian control in 538 B.C.E. when Cyrus conquered Babylon, where many Jews lived in captivity. According to the Hebrew Bible, Cyrus allowed the captive Jews to return to Jerusalem.[21] Apparently, a minority of the Jews returned, but most stayed in Mesopotamia and became a part of the culture there. If the book of Esther is correct, a Jewish woman even became the wife of the king of Persia.

How much influence did Zoroastrianism have on Judaism during this period? We cannot be sure. However, there are certain changes in the theology of Judaism between the pre-exilic days of 586 B.C.E. and the post-exilic period beginning in 538 B.C.E. Biblical books that reflect the period prior to 586 B.C.E. have no Satan figure. However, the literature that was written after the exile speaks of a Satan figure four times.[22] In the intertestamental literature, Satan and his demons are mentioned frequently; in the New Testament literature, they are accepted as a regular part of life.[23] Jesus is confronted by Satan as he begins his public ministry, and a large part of that ministry is devoted to exorcising demons. Pre-exilic biblical books have no mention of a resurrection of the body, little concern for life after death in either a heaven or hell, no reference to God's plan for bringing the earth to an end, only an occasional mention of angels, and no word about a day of judgment. Each of these themes, which were part of the teachings of Zoroastrianism, developed in Judaism after the exile, and each had become a vital part of the religion by the time of Jesus.

The early Christians incorporated these items into their religion. In later years, it was the eschatology of Judaism and Christianity that most deeply influenced the prophet Muhammad; judgment day, resurrection, heaven, hell, Satan, demons, and angels all became vital parts of Islam. It may be that all of these major religions drew their eschatology from Zoroastrianism.

The Persian Empire was conquered by Alexander the Great in the fourth century B.C.E. In the years that followed, Zoroastrianism suffered a decline. The entire Persian culture was invaded by the pervasive Hellenistic culture. During the era of the Roman Empire, Zoroastrianism also was quiescent. All that seems to have been active in this period was the cult of Mithra. The Roman Empire became acquainted with Mithra in the first century C.E. Mithra, the god of light and obedience, appealed especially to the Roman soldier; thus, Mithraic cults were established throughout the entire Mediterranean world. The worship of Mithra became so popular that some suggest it was a major rival to early Christianity. When Christianity was declared the official religion of the Roman Empire, however, Mithraism was suppressed.

A revival of Zoroastrianism occurred in the third century C.E. under the Sassanid rulers of Persia. These rulers established official support for Zoroastrianism and had the ancient scriptures translated into contemporary language.

Religion and Violence

The religion continued to flourish until the seventh century C.E. At this time, Islam was arising out of the desert regions to the south of Persia. By 642 C.E., Muslim warriors, with three major battles, had caused the collapse of the Sassanid Empire. At first, the Muslims tolerated the Zoroastrians. The latter were, after all, a people with a book (scripture) and worshipped only one God. By the ninth century C.E., however, Muslim persecution of the Zoroastrians had grown to such a point that most Zoroastrians were forced to either convert to Islam or flee the country. Those who chose to flee followed the path of their ancient Aryan relatives to India.

In India, Zoroastrians found tolerance by the Hindu majority and were known as the Parsis (those who came from Persia). They remained an insignificant minority in India until the nineteenth century, when the British arrived. Because the Parsis were not encumbered by a caste system or intricate food taboos, and because they valued education, they quickly became favorites of the British. As a result of this favored position in British India, the modern Parsi community leads in such fields as education, business, and finance to a far greater measure than its minority status would indicate.

Zoroastrian Holy Days

In the history of Zoroastrianism, there have been several sacred calendars. The current calendar contains twelve thirty-day months, which begin in February or March. An additional five days are included each year to match the solar calendar.

The Jasans

In each month of the Zoroastrian year, regular *jasans*, or feasts, take place. Each *jasan* falls on the day that bears the name of that particular month. The feast is in honor of the *Amesha-Spenta* or the *Yazad* to whom the month belongs. The most popular of these feast days is Farvardin jasan, held on Farvardin, the nineteenth day of the first month. Farvardin is honored on the grounds of the towers of silence because it is believed that he presides over the spirits of departed ancestors. During this ten-day period, it is thought that departed spirits visit their descendants.

New Year's Day (NôRûz)

New Year's Day is celebrated on the first day of the first month of the year—Farvardin. Zoroastrians believe this day to be one of good fortune. It is celebrated with a joyous feast that sees the renewal of creation as the earth moves into the spring season.

Also in the month of Farvardin is the celebration of the birth of Zarathustra on the sixth of the month. The death of Zarathustra is commemorated on the eleventh day of the tenth month.

Seasonal Feasts (Gahambars)

In addition to the aforementioned festivals, Zoroastrians keep six seasonal feasts called *Gahambars*, which are scattered throughout the year. Each of these feasts lasts five days and is connected to an aspect of creation. The Gahambars are respectively dedicated to the creation of heaven, water, earth, trees, animals, and humans.

All Souls' Day (Muktad)

All Souls' Day is similar to Farvardin in that it also honors departed ancestors. During the period of Muktad, the dead are believed to return to their homes, where they are welcomed. In every home a platform is erected, on which is placed water, fruit, and flowers for the ancestors. Special lamps and sandalwood sticks are burned to welcome the guests. Other food is cooked and placed near the platform for the returning spirits to enjoy.

Zoroastrianism Today

Religion and Violence

Zoroastrianism is one of the smallest religions in the modern world. Approximately 11,000 Zoroastrians remain in Iran. They have always been regarded with suspicion by Shi'ite Muslims, who are the majority in Iran. The Zoroastrians who remained were called *Gabars* (infidels) by the Muslims. Their situation became much more difficult after the Islamic Republic was established in Iran in 1979. At that time, the shah of Iran was overthrown and the country came under the strict Islamic rule of Ayatollah Ruhollah Khomeini. Since then, non-Muslims, including Zoroastrians and Baha'is, have suffered much persecution.

The Parsi community in India is small but prosperous. It numbers perhaps 100,000 people, most of whom live in Mumbai (Bombay). Its members tend to be leaders in many fields and are highly valued. However, the Parsi birthrate lags behind that of the rest of India and, because it does not allow conversion, Zoroastrianism is not a growing religion. Parsis are found in many other parts of the world, including North America. The total world population of Zoroastrians is estimated at 250,000.

The small and diminishing size of the community is a matter of great concern to many Zoroastrians. The dispersion of much of the Iranian population has led many to fear that the religion may soon vanish. Zoroastrian leaders very strongly condemn intermarriage with members of other faiths, which is increasingly common, especially in the small communities in Europe and North America. They regard it as the road to extinction. In this respect Zoroastrian view are similar to those of many Orthodox Jews. It is likely that within a few decades the Bombay Parsis will be the only remaining viable Zoroastrian population.

STUDY QUESTIONS

1. Zoroastrianism is called a dualism. What does this mean? Contrast the dualism of Zoroastrianism with the monotheism of Judaism or Islam.
2. One of the great contributions of Zoroastrianism to Western religions is its eschatology. Show how Zoroastrian eschatology influenced Judaism, Christianity, and Islam.
3. How does the Zoroastrian scheme of the afterlife affect the ethical teachings of this religion?
4. Discuss why Zoroastrians refuse to bury or burn the bodies of the dead.
5. Compare the position of Zoroastrians in Iran and India.

SUGGESTED READING

Boyce, Mary. *A History of Zoroastrianism*, 2 vols. Leiden: E. J. Brill, 1975, 1982.

Karaka, Dosabhai. *History of the Parsis: Including Their Manners, Customs, Religion, and Present Position.* 2 vols. Mumbai: Adamant Media Corporation, 2000.

Duchesne-Guillemin, Jacques. *Symbols and Values in Zoroastrianism.* New York: Harper & Row, 1966.

Masani, Sir Rustom. *Zoroastrianism: The Religion of the Good Life.* New York: Macmillan, 1968.

Vermaseren, M. J. *Mithras, The Secret God.* Translated by Therese and Vincent Megaw. New York: Barnes & Noble, 1963.

Zaehner, R. C. *The Dawn and Twilight of Zoroastrianism.* New York: Putnam, 1961.

SOURCE MATERIAL

Zoroastrian Eschatology

One of the major contributions of Zoroastrianism to the religions of the world is its eschatology. The Zoroastrian understanding of the judgment of the soul after death, life after death either in Paradise or Hell, and the end of the world was paralleled in the eschatology of Judaism, Christianity, and Islam. The following materials, taken from Zoroastrian sources, illustrate some of these concepts.[24]

Roads to the Netherworld

Put not your trust in life, for at the last death must overtake you; and dog and bird will rend your corpse and your bones will be tumbled on the earth. For three days and nights the soul sits beside the pillow of the body. And on the fourth day at dawn (the soul) accompanied by the blessed Srosh, the good Vay, and the mighty Vahram, and opposed by Astvihat (the demon of death), the evil Vay, the demon Frehzisht and the demon Vizisht, and pursued by the active ill-will of Wrath, the evil-doer who bears a bloody spear, (will reach) the lofty and awful Bridge of the Requiter to which every man whose soul is saved and every man whose soul is damned must come. Here does many an enemy lie in wait. Here (the soul will suffer) from the will of Wrath who wields a bloody spear and from Astvihat who swallows all creation yet knows no sating, and it will (benefit by) the medication of Hihr, Srosh, and Rashn, and will (needs submit) to the weighing (of his deeds) by the righteous Rashn who lets the scales of the spiritual gods incline to neither side, neither for the saved nor yet for the damned, nor yet for kings and princes; not so much as a hair's breadth does he allow (the scales) to tip, and he is no respecter (of persons), for he deals out impartial justice both to kings and princes and to the humblest of men.

And when the soul of the saved passes over that bridge, the breadth of the bridge appears to be one parasang broad. And the soul of the saved passes on accompanied by the blessed Srosh. And his own good deeds come to meet him in the form of a young girl, more beautiful and fair than any girl on earth. And the soul of the saved says, "Who art thou, for I have never seen a young girl on earth more beautiful or fair than thee." In answer the form of the young girl replies, "I am not girl but thy own good deeds, O young man whose thoughts and words, deeds and religion were good: for when on earth thou didst see one who offered sacrifice to the demons, then didst thou sit (apart) and offer sacrifice to the gods. And when thou didst see a man do violence and rapine, afflict good men and treat them with contumely, and hoard up goods wrongfully obtained, then didst thou refrain from visiting creatures with violence and repine of thine own; (nay rather,) thou wast considerate to good men, didst entertain them and offer them hospitality, and give alms both to the man who came from near and to him who came from afar; and thou didst amass thy wealth in righteousness. And when thou didst see one who passed a false judgment or took bribes or bore false witness, thou didst sit thee down and speak witness right and true. I am thy good thoughts, good words, and good deeds which thou didst think and say and do . . . ."

And when the soul departs from thence, then is a fragrant breeze wafted toward him,—(a breeze) more fragrant than any perfume. Then does the soul of the saved ask Srosh saying, "What breeze is this, the like of which in fragrance I never smelt on earth?" Then does the blessed Srosh make answer to the soul of the saved, saying, "This is a wind (wafted) from Heaven; hence is it so fragrant."

Then with his first step he bestrides (the heaven of) good thoughts, with his second (the heaven of) good words, and with his third (the heaven of) good deeds; and with his fourth step he reaches the Endless Light where is all bliss. And all the gods and Amahraspands come to greet him and ask him how he has fared, saying, "How was thy passage from those transient, fearful worlds where there is much evil to these worlds which do not pass away and in which there is no adversary, O young man whose thoughts and words, deeds and religion are good?"

Then Ohrmazd, the Lord, speaks, saying, "Do not ask him how he has fared, for he has been separated from his beloved body and has traveled on a fearsome road." And they served him with the sweetest of all foods even with the butter of early spring so that his soul may take its ease after the three nights' terror of the Bridge inflicted on him by Astvihat and the other demons, and he is sat upon a throne everywhere bejeweled. And for ever and ever he dwells with the spiritual gods in all bliss for evermore.

But when the man who is damned dies, for three days and nights does his soul hover near his head and weeps, saying, "Whither shall I go and in whom shall I now take refuge?" And during those three days and nights he sees with his eyes all the sins and wickedness that he committed on earth. On the fourth day the demon Vizarsh comes and binds the soul of the damned in most shameful wise, and despite the opposition of the blessed Srosh drags it off to the Bridge of the Requiter. Then the righteous Rashn makes clear to the soul of the damned that it is damned (indeed).

Then the demon Vizarsh seizes upon the soul of the damned, smites it and ill-treats it without pity, urged on by Wrath. And the soul of the damned cries out with a loud voice, makes moan, and in supplication makes many a piteous plea; much does he struggle though his life-breath endures no more. When all his struggling and his lamentations have proved of no avail, no help is proffered him by any of the gods nor yet by any of the demons, but the demon Vizarsh drags him off against his will into nethermost Hell.

Then a young girl who yet has no semblance of a young girl, comes to meet him. And the soul of the damned says to that ill-favored wench, "Who art thou? for I have never seen an ill-favored wench on earth more ill-favored and hideous than thee." And in reply that ill-favored wench says to him, "I am no wench, but I am thy deeds,— hideous deeds,—evil thoughts, evil words, evil deeds, and an evil religion. For when on earth thou didst see one who offered sacrifice to the gods, then didst thou sit (apart) and offer sacrifice to the demons. And when thou didst see one who entertained good men and offered them hospitality, and gave alms both to those who came from near and to those who came from afar, then didst thou treat good men with contumely and show them dishonour, thou gavest them no alms and didst shut thy door (upon them). And when thou didst see one who passed a just judgment or took no bribes or bore true witness or spoke up in righteousness, then didst thou sit down and pass false judgment, bear false witness, and speak unrighteously.

Then with his first step he goes to (the hell of) evil thoughts, with his second to (the hell of) evil words, and with his third to (the hell of) evil deeds. And with his fourth step he lurches into the presence of the accursed Destructive Spirit and the other demons. And the demons mock at him and hold him up to scorn, saying, "What grieved thee in Ohrmazd, the Lord, and the Amahraspands and in fragrant and delightful Heaven, and what grudge or complaint hadst thou of them that thou shouldst come to see Ahriman and the demons and murky Hell? for we will torment thee nor shall we have any mercy on thee, and for a long time shalt thou suffer torment."

And the Destructive Spirit cries out to the demons, saying, "Ask not concerning him, for he has been separated from his beloved body, and has come through that most evil passage-way; but serve him (rather) with the filthiest and most foul food that Hell can produce."

Then they bring him poison and venom, snakes and scorpions and other noxious reptiles (that flourish) in Hell, and they serve him with these to eat. And until the Resurrection and the Final Body he must remain in Hell, suffering much torment and many kinds of chastisement. And the food that he must for the most part eat there is all, as it were, putrid and like unto blood.

Zoroastrian Dualism

One of the unique contributions of Zoroastrianism was its dualistic understanding of the world. Zoroaster saw the forces of good and evil struggling for control of the universe.[25]

GREATER BUNDAHISHN *I.* 18–22

18. Ohrmazd, before the act of creation, was not Lord; after the act of creation he became Lord, eager for increase, wise, free from adversity, manifest, ever ordering aright, bounteous, all-perceiving.

19. (First he created the essence of the gods, fair movement, that genius by which he made his own body better) for he had conceived of the act of creation; from this act of creation was his lordship.

20. And by his clear vision Ohrmazd saw that the Destructive Spirit would never cease from aggression and that his aggression could only be made fruitless by the act of creation, and that creation could not move on except through Time and that when Time was fashioned, the creation of Ahriman too would begin to move.

21. And that he might reduce the Aggressor to a state of powerlessness, having no alternative he fashioned forth Time. And the reason was this, that the Destructive Spirit could not be made powerless unless he were brought to battle.

22. Then from Infinite Time he fashioned and made Time of the long Dominion: some call it finite Time. From Time of the long Dominion he brought forth permanence that the works of Ohrmazd might not pass away. From permanence discomfort was made manifest that comfort might not touch the demons. From discomfort the course of fate, the idea of changelessness, was made manifest, that those things which Ohrmazd created at the original creation might not change. From the idea of changelessness a perfect will (to create) material creation was made manifest, the concord of the righteous creation.

CHAPTER 11

Judaism

CHAPTER OBJECTIVES

In this chapter you will:

- Learn the history of the growth of the Hebrew Bible.

- Explore the history of the Jewish people.

- Come to understand Jewish taboos, including Kosher food laws.

- Know about the varieties of Judaism in the modern world.

- Understand the Holocaust.

KEY TERMS

Torah	Kosher	Anti-Semitism
Talmud	Exodus	
Mishnah	Holocaust	

A Timeline of Judaism

3760 B.C.E.	Traditional date for creation of Adam and Eve[1]	825	Construction of First Temple completed
1812	Traditional date for the birth of Abraham	586	Destruction of First Temple; beginning of Babylonian exile
1312	Traditional date of the Exodus from Egypt	537	Persians allow return from exile
		352	Construction of Second Temple
1000–586	Approximate dates of the biblical Israelite kingdoms	63 C.E.	Roman Conquest of Israel
1200–400	Period in which the Torah was compiled	70	Romans destroy Second Temple; Jewish population dispersed the Roman Empire

[1]Dates for biblical events cannot be independently verified

(Continued)

A Timeline of Judaism   (*Continued*)

219	Completion of the Mishnah	1933	Hitler comes to power in Germany
499	Completion of the Talmud	1938	Beginning of the Holocaust
1135–1204	Life of Maimonides	1948	Establishment of the modern state of Israel. Many Palestinian Muslims flee or are forced into exile.
1215	Fourth Lateran Council promotes persecution of Jews in Christian Europe		
1492	Jews expelled from Spain; many find refuge in Muslim lands	1948–present	Political conflict between religious and secular Jews in Israel
1791–1917	Emancipation of Jews from legal discrimination in most of Europe	1967	Israel occupies East Jerusalem and the West Bank territories
1810	Construction of the first Reform synagogue in Seesen, Germany	1972	First woman rabbis ordained
1881	Large-scale Jewish immigration to North America begins	1990–present	Alternating Israeli-Palestinian conflicts and peace talks
1897	First Zionist Conference	2003	Israel begins construction of security fence

One of the most perplexing problems that arises in any discussion of Judaism is its definition. If we were to define Judaism as we define any other religion, we might say that a Jew is anyone who adheres to a certain set of Jewish religious beliefs or practices. Indeed, in many cases this may be a very effective definition. Unfortunately, the issue has been clouded, so it is not always so simple. Alan W. Miller, in his introduction to *The God of Daniel S.: In Search of the American Jew*, lists eight different types of persons who are called Jews in American society. These range all the way from the extremely orthodox Hasidic Jew to the person whose parents or grandparents happened to be born Jewish. In the modern nation of Israel, a continuing and perplexing problem is "Who is a Jew?"

Judaism cannot be defined primarily in terms of religious beliefs, because some people are called Jews but consider themselves atheists. Adolf Hitler found it expedient to define Judaism in terms of race, but Jewish people display the physical characteristics of nearly every race. There are European Jews, African Jews, and Asian Jews. Nor can Judaism be defined in linguistic or ethnic terms. Jewish people have spoken and written many languages and have acquired much of the cultures of the lands in which they have dwelt.

If we cannot define Judaism in terms of all people who might be called Jews, we can speak of those people who identify themselves with the religion of Judaism. Though religious practices differ widely among Jews, generally the unifying feature among all Jews is a belief in the oneness of a God who works in and through historical events and who has in some manner chosen the Jewish people as agents. Numerous forms of Judaism are built around this basic principle.

Biblical Patriarchs

Because Judaism is concerned with God's activity in history, it is necessary to describe Jewish beliefs and practices historically. According to the Bible, God found it necessary to call out one man and his family from all the people on earth. This calling of Abraham is recorded in Genesis 12. It came after a series of disastrous dealings with all humankind (Adam and Eve, Cain and Abel, the Flood, the Tower of Babel, and so on). Because of these disasters, God chose to communicate with only one nation, the descendants of Abraham.

According to the Book of Genesis, Abraham was promised that he would become the father of a great nation, possess a land, and become a blessing to all people if he were faithful to his part of a covenant with God. Abraham is succeeded in this covenant by his son Isaac, his grandson Jacob (or Israel), and Jacob's twelve sons. These figures are called the patriarchs of the Jewish people because they are the physical forbearers of the nation. Their stories are found in Genesis 12–50; these tales were probably authored generations after the times of the patriarchs. Though some scholars doubt the historicity of these figures, their names and their ways of life fit into the history of the Fertile Crescent at the beginning of the second millennium B.C.E.[1]

If people like Abraham and Isaac were the ancestors of the Jews, what was the nature of their lives and their religion? The biblical narratives present the patriarchs as nomads, following their flocks from place to place. Abraham is described as a citizen of the city of Ur of the Chaldees (Genesis 11:31) who left his home to follow the voice of God to the land of Canaan, on the western side of the Fertile Crescent. Historically, he could have been one of the waves of Amorites who flooded the Fertile Crescent between 2000 and 1750 B.C.E. The Mari letters from Mesopotamia in this era reveal the use of such names as *Benjamin* and *Jacob,* thus indicating the historical plausibility of the biblical narrative.

The Bible does not give the reader a systematic presentation of the religious beliefs and practices of the patriarchs, but it does reveal a great deal about their theology. They worshipped one God who guided their destinies. The generic name for God among ancient Semitic peoples was El. This name is frequently used in various combinations in the patriarchal literature to refer to their God. The God is called El Shaddai (God of the mountains); El Elyon (God Most High); El Olam (God Everlasting), and most frequently, Elohim (Gods).[2]

This God was worshipped by burning animal sacrifices on altars built in the open. The Israelites apparently did not worship their God in a building or temple until the time of Solomon (961–922 B.C.E.). There also are indications of basic animistic practices in the worship of the patriarchs. Abraham made a covenant with Abimelech in Beersheba and called upon the name of God. To seal the covenant, Abraham planted a grove in Beersheba (Genesis 21:32, 33). God appeared to Isaac and reaffirmed the covenant while

Menorah in front of the Knesset, Israel's parliament. The seven-branched candelabrum is one of the oldest symbols of Judaism.
(Consulate General of Israel in New York)

Isaac was digging wells near Beersheba (Genesis 26:17–25). Jacob slept on certain stones; in Jacob's dreams, God spoke to him and renewed the covenant (Genesis 28:11–16). The connection between the appearance of God, the reaffirmation of the covenant, and the typical animistic symbols of trees, wells, and stones may be significant.

From very early on in the worship of the patriarchs, circumcision of the male was practiced. Genesis traces the ritual back to a commandment of God to Abraham (Genesis 17:10, 11). However, circumcision is a very ancient and widespread religious custom, which probably did not originate with Abraham. In addition, the practice of keeping a Sabbath may have been a part of the worship of the patriarchs. Genesis attaches the custom to the days of creation, when God rested on the seventh day after laboring for six days (Genesis 2:2). In the patriarchal stories, it is not clear what the Sabbath practices of these figures were.

Exodus

Whatever their religious practices may have been, and whatever gods they may have worshipped, the stories of the patriarchs exist in Genesis to provide the reader with a reason for the most important event in Judaism—the **Exodus**. God promised Abraham that a great nation would arise from his seed, that this nation would have a homeland (Canaan), and that the entire world would be blessed by this nation. The Book of Genesis closes with a great nation springing up from the descendants of Abraham, but they were not in Canaan. They were in Egypt, where they were bound in slavery. Therefore, the Exodus from Egypt and their slavery, the journey back to Canaan, and the conquest of the land had to be accomplished before God's promise to Abraham could be fulfilled. The events and characters of the Exodus became the heart and soul of the Jewish religion. God acted to save his chosen people, the Israelites, miraculously delivered them from slavery (from the most powerful nation in the world at that time), revealed to the leaders the divine name and laws, and finally brought the former slaves, as a conquering army, into Canaan. These events are remembered annually in the various major holidays of Judaism. The legal material, which is attributed to the Sinai experience, became the most important material in the Hebrew *Bible*.

The Book of Exodus opens with the descendants of Abraham, the Israelites, crying out for deliverance from their enslavement by the Egyptians.[3] The key figure in this drama of salvation is Moses. Like many great figures in religion, Moses was endangered as an infant by the forces of evil and was miraculously delivered. He was rescued and reared by the daughter of the pharaoh of Egypt. Because the name *Moses* is Egyptian, there may be a factual basis for the story.

After recognizing his Israelite heritage and killing an Egyptian in defense of a slave, Moses was exiled to the Sinai Desert, where he lived for forty years as a shepherd. In the desert, the God of Abraham was revealed to Moses and spoke through a bush that

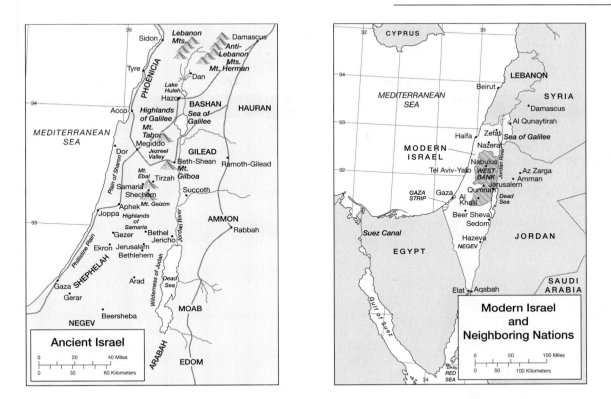

burned but was not consumed. The God declared that his name was YHWH and commanded Moses to lead the Israelites from their slavery.[4] Moses returned to Egypt and, after a series of ten miraculous plagues upon the Egyptians, was able to gain the release of the Israelites. The final plague was death to the firstborn of every house in Egypt. Israelites who ate a sacred meal of roasted lamb, bitter herbs, and unleavened bread and who smeared lamb's blood on their doorposts were passed over by the angel of death.

When the Israelites fled Egypt, they were pursued by the pharaoh, who had changed his mind about their release. The waters of the Sea of Reeds were parted by YHWH, and the Israelites crossed through on dry land.[5] When the Egyptians attempted to follow them, the waters returned and the Egyptians were trapped and drowned. This event, along with the Passover, became a part of Jewish history—an act in which God intervened to deliver his chosen people.

Sinai and the Law

The next significant event was the giving of the law on Mt. Sinai. After crossing the Sea of Reeds, the Israelites came to Mt. Sinai on their journey to Canaan. From this mountain, YHWH communicated the law to the Israelites through Moses. Ten absolute laws that are basic to Jewish life are found in Exodus 20:1–17 and in Deuteronomy 5:6–21. They may be summarized as follows:

From the Source

1. I am the Lord your God, who has brought you out of the land of Egypt, out of the house of bondage. You shall have no other gods before me.
2. You shall not make any graven image.
3. You shall not take the name of the Lord your God in vain.
4. Remember the Sabbath day, to keep it holy.
5. Honor your father and your mother.
6. You shall not kill.
7. You shall not commit adultery.
8. You shall not steal.
9. You shall not bear false witness against your neighbor.
10. You shall not covet your neighbor's property.[6]

An Israeli family prays at the start of their Seder dinner celebrating the traditional week-long festival of Passover, which commemorates the Israelite exodus from Egypt. *(Max Nash/AP/Wide World Photos)*

Basically, these commandments stress obedience and loyalty to YHWH and decent behavior toward members of the community. The Books of Exodus and Leviticus and portions of Numbers and Deuteronomy elaborate codes of law that regulate every area of life. These laws are purported to have been given by God through Moses during the wilderness experience, but many of them reflect a community that has been established in agricultural life for centuries.

Whenever they may have been codified, the legal material in the Pentateuch (the first five books of the Bible) became the single most important part of the Bible for Judaism. It is to this material that Jews have turned for centuries, looking for inspiration and guidance. This material became the basis for the later Mishnah and **Talmud**, which in turn became central for Judaism. It is at this point that Judaism is defined as a religion of the law and Jews as a people primarily concerned with obedience to the laws of God.

Post-Sinai Religious Institutions

In addition to the laws of God, the years in the Sinai wilderness gave the Israelites two other religious institutions, the Ark of the Covenant and the Tent of Meeting. The Ark of the Covenant was a coffinlike box that contained the sacred relics of the Exodus and may have been the portable throne of YHWH. This box was the most treasured sacred possession of the Israelites and was eventually placed in Solomon's temple, in the Holy of Holies, in the tenth century B.C.E. It presumably remained there until the temple was destroyed by the Babylonians in 586 B.C.E. The Tent of Meeting was not so popular or long-lived as the Ark. It was literally a tent that could be moved from place to place with the nomadic Israelites. It provided a place to worship YHWH. After the Israelites entered Canaan, it is mentioned only once in connection with the cult at Shiloh.

After their period of wandering in the wilderness, the Bible records that the Israelites conquered the territories on the East Bank of the Jordan River. Then, under the leadership of Joshua, Moses' successor, they crossed the Jordan and conquered the cities of Canaan. Two conflicting accounts are given. According to the Book of Joshua, the Israelites swept across the country and destroyed the Canaanites. The Book of Judges tells another story, however. Here we have a picture of the worshippers of YHWH living side by side with the native dwellers of Canaan, and sometimes even being subject to them. Later events seem to support the second story.

When the Israelites settled in Canaan, they renewed their covenant with YHWH. The cult of YHWH, its ark, its priests, and its sacrifices were centered in Shiloh. Worship at this time seems to have been a rather informal matter. The cultic priests attended to those who came on special days to the sanctuary for special needs. They were in turn supported by the gifts of those who came to worship and perhaps by the donations of the various tribal groups who surrounded the cult center.

Religion in the Time of the Hebrew Monarchy

The religion of Israel took a more formal turn when David became the first truly effective king of the Israelites. David, who was from the southern portion of the country, needed a central capital and a cult to unify his nation. He captured Jerusalem in the central hill country and made it his capital. Jerusalem had little to recommend it except its location, its easily defended hills, and perhaps a history as a sacred site. David, as well as later historical events, parlayed these features and made Jerusalem one of the most important, most disputed cities in the world. David's abilities as a military leader and administrator helped Israel develop into a fairly powerful and wealthy small nation of the ancient Middle East. Hebrew scripture indicates that David wished to build a magnificent temple in Jerusalem but was forbidden by YHWH.

The Temple

It remained for Solomon, David's son and successor, to build the temple. With all the wealth his father had amassed, Solomon built a palace for himself and a temple for his God. Strangely enough, the temple was designed by Tyrian builders who were worshippers of the Baalim, the gods of the Canaanites and Phoenicians, and who were condemned in the Bible. The temple naturally took the form of other Canaanite temples built for the Baalim. The Ark of the Covenant was placed in the temple, and a class of priests was attached to the temple. Worship of YHWH thus took on a more formal status. The main form of worship remained the animal sacrifice, with its flesh burned in the courtyard. In the temple, prayers were offered to YHWH, and if the example of David is typical, there may also have been sacred dancing before the Ark (II Samuel 6:14).

The Prophetic Movement

With the development of the temple cult, another aspect was introduced into the worship of Israel. Other ancient religions, including that of the worship of the Baalim, had developed bodies of religious leaders called prophets. In their earlier forms, the prophetic figures were persons involved in the ecstatic aspects of worship. Unlike the priests, whose duties involved the proper offerings of sacrifices, the prophets of ancient religions danced, sang, breathed incense, and worked themselves into an ecstatic state to hear the voices of their gods. The prophets of Israel may have begun in this fashion.[7] They healed the sick, cursed, blessed, and produced food for their followers, and worked other miracles.[8]

Eventually a portion of the Israelite prophetic movement became attached to the royal household. The first of these prophets to be involved with the palace was Nathan, who was part of the court of David. It was Nathan who accused the king after David had murdered his faithful servant, Uriah; but it also was Nathan who was instrumental in placing Solomon on the throne at the death of David. Others who were more or less attached to the royal houses, or at least had the ear of the kings, were Elijah, Isaiah, and Jeremiah. Still other prophets were commoners who preached fiery denunciations against wickedness among peasants and royalty alike. Outstanding in this group were Amos and Micah. These prophets must have been but a few of many who preached in troubled times. Their messages were remembered and preserved by their disciples and eventually written into the Bible.

In contemporary English, the word *prophet* has the connotation of prediction; but to label all of the works of the prophets of Israel as predictions is to do them injustice. In the social and political upheavals of the eighth century B.C.E., the prophetic movement produced four classic figures—Amos, Hosea, Isaiah, and Micah—who are remembered not so much for their predictions as for the boldness with which they denounced the social injustices of their times and for the beautiful, poetic language with which they bade the Israelites to return to their God.

From the Source

Thus says the Lord:
"For three transgressions of Israel,
and for four, I will not revoke the punishment;
because they sell the righteous for silver,
and the needy for a pair of shoes—
they that trample the head of the poor into the dust of the earth,
and turn aside the way of the afflicted."[9]

Seek good, and not evil,
that you may live;
and so the Lord, the God of hosts, will be with you,
as you have said.
Hate evil, and love good,
and establish justice in the gate;
it may be that the Lord, the God of hosts,
will be gracious to the remnant of Joseph.[10]

These are not the words of seers predicting the future but of people who were busy speaking the word of God to their people. The prophetic movement of ancient Israel stands out as one of the major moral and literary contributions to any religion of the world.

Exile and Return

In 922 B.C.E., after the reign of Solomon, a rebellion split the nation of Israel into two nations. The northern nation, called Israel, was the larger and more productive of the two. It was destroyed by the Assyrians in 721 B.C.E., and its people disappeared from history. Its population was either killed or deported and enslaved. Whatever their fate, they were never to be a distinctive people of Israel again; they are known as the ten lost tribes.

Religion and Violence

The southern nation, called Judah, was made up of the remainder of David's kingdom. Judah survived the Assyrian years but was eventually destroyed by the Neo-Babylonian Empire in 586 B.C.E. With the Babylonian conquest, the city of Jerusalem was destroyed, Solomon's temple was torn down, and the citizens of Judah were either killed or deported. Whereas the northern nation had simply ceased to exist after its destruction, the people of Judah held on to their identity, customs, and religion while in captivity. They were led by a man who was both a prophet and a priest, Ezekiel. Ezekiel and others so forged the identity of the Jews in captivity that when the Persians captured Babylon in 538 B.C.E., many Jews were freed and returned to Jerusalem to re-establish their lives and their temple there.

During the Babylonian captivity, certain theological changes were forced upon the Jews. Previously, they had thought of YHWH as their local deity, perhaps residing in the temple at Jerusalem. Now the temple was destroyed and the people were scattered in a strange land. An unknown poet of that period wrote of their sadness:

From the Source

By the waters of Babylon,
there we sat down and wept,
when we remembered Zion,
On the willows there
we hung our lyres.

For there our captors required of us songs,
and our tormentors, mirth, saying,
"Sing us one of the songs of Zion!"
How shall we sing the Lord's song
in a foreign land?[11]

Ezekiel answered that YHWH was mobile and was available to his people in Babylon as easily as in Jerusalem.[12] Another prophet, Isaiah, stated that YHWH was no longer just the God of the Israelites but was in fact the one true God for all the people of all the world.[13] Even the Zoroastrian Cyrus, king of Persia, was but an instrument of YHWH.

From the Source

Who says of Cyrus, "He is my shepherd,
and he shall fulfill all my purpose";

saying of Jerusalem, "She shall be built,"
and of the temple, "Your foundations shall be laid."[14]

Indeed, the mission of the Jews as YHWH's chosen people is to present his message to all the nations of the world.

Among the most influential Jews to return from Babylon to Jerusalem was Ezra (ca. 428 B.C.E.). Ezra was a priest who brought with him a copy of Scripture that he read to the citizens of the rebuilt Jerusalem. The nature and exact content of this book are unknown, but it had a profound effect on the people. They reformed their lives according to the laws in this book. For all times, Jews became identified not only as a people of God's laws but as a people centered around a book. Ezra probably began the process of canonizing books as the word of God. From this time onward, it was believed that God no longer spoke through the prophets but through his book. It remained only for the followers of YHWH to read this book and interpret it for their lives.

In addition to the growth of a scriptural canon, the religion of the period of the second temples (520 B.C.E. to 70 C.E.) included sacrifices at the rebuilt temple, with a cult of priests, singers, and attendants. At first, the temple (which was rebuilt in the sixth century B.C.E.) was a rather simple structure. In the time of Herod the Great (37–4 B.C.E.), and later, it was restored and decorated to a magnificent state, far beyond the glory of Solomon's temple. Just a few years after the second temple was finally finished, it was destroyed by the Romans in 70 C.E.

Diaspora

The years following the Assyrian destruction of Israel (721 B.C.E.) saw the beginning of the Diaspora, the scattering of the Jewish people all over the world. Sometimes it was forced on them, as in 586 B.C.E. by the Babylonians. In other cases, Jews moved by choice to other nations or stayed by choice in such nations as Babylon and Persia. By the year 250 B.C.E., there was such a large Jewish community in Alexandria, Egypt, that it was necessary to translate the Hebrew Bible to Greek.[16] Jews in Babylon apparently lived well under Persian rule. According to the Book of Esther, a young woman from the Jewish community actually became queen of Persia in the fifth century B.C.E. In later years, Jews were found in such prominent cities as Toledo, Lyons, Cologne, Bonn, and most major cities throughout the Roman Empire.[17]

The Synagogue

Judaism away from the land of Israel was forced to accept a new concept of God and new institutions of worship. The notion of YHWH as the only God of all the peoples of the world, as enunciated by Isaiah, was accepted; various books were accepted as Scripture. Because they were separated by great distances from the temple in Jerusalem, the

Jews of the Diaspora developed the institution of the synagogue as a local center for prayer and study.

The English word *synagogue* is derived from the Greek word *synagoge*, or "assembly." The synagogue is literally an assembly. A synagogue can exist wherever there is a copy of the Scripture (**Torah**) and ten adult (over thirteen years of age) Jewish males. Ten adult males constitute a quorum, or a *minyan*. Whenever this combination exists, there can be prayer and instruction. Synagogue may be held in many kinds of places. It can be under a tree, in the back room of a home, or in an elaborate building set aside for the purpose. No one knows exactly when the institution of the synagogue developed; whatever the specific date, it arose during the Diaspora, when Jews could no longer worship at the temple in Jerusalem, and it serves Judaism to this day.

A Rabbi and other men read from an open Torah at Temple Beth Or, Everett, Washington, United States.
(Bill Aron/Photo Edit)

Along with the synagogue arose the figure of the rabbi. The rabbi is not a priest or a minister in the traditional sense. The word *rabbi* literally means "my master." With the establishment of the Torah as the voice of God, there also arose the need for someone to spend time studying the Scripture and teaching the community. Those persons who had the time, interest, and intelligence to study gradually began to be singled out and sought after by inquiring members of the Jewish community. They eventually became known as rabbis.

As rabbis sought to interpret Scripture to Jews living lives very different from those of Abraham, Moses, or David, many problems arose. How does one apply laws intended for nomadic or agricultural peoples of the Iron Age to persons living in imperial Rome in the time of Augustus Caesar? Rabbis struggled with these problems, sought hermeneutical (interpretive) principles, and interpreted God's laws to their people. Outstanding rabbis arose; their fame as wise men and interpreters spread; students came to study with them; great rabbis disagreed and entered into debate with one another. Gradually, an accepted corpus of rabbinic opinion developed.

In addition to the synagogue and the rabbis, the Diaspora communities maintained other distinctive features that set them apart from the gentiles who surrounded them, and Jews maintained their separateness. Jews separated themselves from gentiles by refusing to work on the Sabbath. In the worlds of the Greeks and the Romans, where only religious holidays were days of rest from labor, the Jews were regarded as lazy because of their refusal to work one day out of seven. In addition, Jews refused to eat certain foods that gentiles ate. Kosher (clean, fit) food laws in the early Diaspora were not as broad or complex as they later became, but Jews of the Diaspora doubtless had to refuse many foods their neighbors ate. The story of Daniel, in which a Jewish captive in Babylon refuses to eat the king's food, must have been representative of the plight of many. Jews also practiced circumcision. This ritual was looked upon with disgust, at least by the Greeks, who believed in the beauty of the unmarred human body.

Sources as diverse as the Jewish historian Flavius Josephus, the **Mishnah**, the New Testament, and Roman historians speak of theological diversity in Diaspora Judaism. Such parties as the Pharisees, the Sadducees, and the Essenes are often mentioned in these works. They differed over such issues as the belief in the resurrection of the dead, the authority of the temple and its priests, and the way in which Jews should live their religion. Another party, the Zealots, argued for a rebellion against the Roman government based on theological and political grounds.

Literary sources that describe Diaspora Judaism also speak of the hopes that God would send a messiah to defeat the enemies of the Jews and re-establish the ancient kingdom of David. The various parties in Judaism had differing views of the messiah. For some, the messiah was undoubtedly a spiritual concept. For others, there seems to have been the expectation that God would literally send a military leader to defeat the Roman forces and sit upon David's throne in Jerusalem.

Religion and Violence

In 66 C.E., the cup of bitterness between Jews and Romans in Judea overflowed into violent revolution. At first, the Jews were successful, but by 68 C.E., the tide had turned. The Romans, under Titus, gradually subdued the land and finally besieged Jerusalem. By the summer of 70 C.E. the city was defeated. Jewish revolutionaries were slaughtered or enslaved by the thousands. Worst of all, the magnificent temple was looted and burned, never to be rebuilt. This was surely the most severe blow of all to the Jews.

From the ashes of destruction arose a new Judaism. The phoenix was modest indeed. A rabbi living in Jerusalem during the siege, Yohanan Ben Zakkai, escaped in a coffin borne by his disciples to the tent of Titus. The rabbi asked permission to establish an academy on the Mediterranean coast of Israel at the town of Yabneh to discuss the future of Judaism. Titus granted permission, and Ben Zakkai gathered about him the rabbis of Israel to discuss and debate the future of Judaism. Among the issues debated was the authority and inspiration of books that belonged in the sacred Torah. The books of the law (Genesis through Deuteronomy) were widely accepted, as were most of the books of the prophets.[18] The books that were the object of the greatest debate were called "the writings," and included the Psalms, Job, Esther, Ruth, Tobit, Judith, and I and II Maccabees.

The Mishnah

After the years at Yabneh, the leadership of Judaism moved to the region of Galilee. Here, the debates over the meaning of the law continued for years. The greatest leader of Jews during the second century C.E. was Judah ha-Nasi (Judah the Prince). Judah's great contribution to Judaism was to bring together all the legal commentary that had been collected since the days of Ezra. The commentary, along with the disputes, was collected into a series of tractates arranged in six divisions. This collection by Judah was called the Mishnah (repetition), and it became one of the great literary milestones in Jewish history.

Within the pages of the Mishnah, the reader finds the attempt of second-century Jews to live by the law of God. At this time, there was no Jewish nation; after 135 C.E., there was no hope of rebuilding the temple or re-establishing a priesthood. All that was left was the law. How does one keep the law? By building a structure of additional, complementary laws as an adjunct to the primary law, so that in keeping the second law the first will not be violated. For example, the Ten Commandments say, "Remember the Sabbath day, to keep it holy." People must not work on the Sabbath, but what does that mean? The only form of work specifically forbidden in the Bible is lighting a fire. Some literalists would have had the observant Jew simply sitting in cold and darkened rooms all during the Sabbath.

The rabbis who produced the Mishnah tried to interpret what the Torah really meant by keeping the Sabbath. They tried to develop interpretations and secondary laws that would make the Sabbath a day of worship and joy. One entire section of the Mishnah is set aside for opinions relating to the Sabbath to make the house more cheerful. Gentiles could be employed to light or extinguish cooking fires on the seventh day.

From the Source

If a gentile lighted a lamp an Israelite may make use of the light, but if he lighted it for the sake of the Israelite it is forbidden. If he filled (a trough) with water to give his cattle to drink, an Israelite may give his own cattle to drink after him, but if the gentile did it for the Israelite, it is forbidden. If he made a gangway by which to come down (from a ship) an Israelite may come down after him, but if he did it for the Israelite, it is forbidden. Rabban Gamaliel and the elders were once traveling in a ship, and a gentile made a gangway by which to come down, and Rabban Gamaliel and the elders came down by it.[19]

According to the Mishnah, the Sabbath was to be a happy day. The best food the family could afford was to be served, the best clothes were to be worn, and emergencies that might arise were to be taken care of by the rabbis. Every step was taken to preserve the sanctity of the law, on the one hand, and to make life under the law as comfortable and agreeable as possible, on the other hand.

The Talmud

Following the compilation of the Mishnah, the center of Jewish life and learning gradually moved from Galilee to Babylon, where Jews had lived since 586 B.C.E. Although there was occasional persecution of the Jews by the Zoroastrians of that area, life for the Jews in Babylon was easier and more prosperous than it had become in Galilee.

In 323 C.E., Constantine I became the sole emperor of what was left of the Roman Empire. Because of his wife and mother, Constantine was favorably inclined toward Christianity and took steps toward making it the official religion of the Empire; this was finally accomplished near the end of the fourth century. The rise of Christianity brought about pressure and hostility against the Jews in Galilee and throughout the rest of the Empire.

Christianity had begun as a sect of Judaism, with Jesus and all of his immediate disciples as practicing Jews. Christianity drew its scripture, its forms of worship, and its eschatology directly from Judaism. In fact, the early church first met in synagogues throughout the Roman Empire.

The New Testament records the first split between Judaism and Christianity. In the middle of the first century, Peter and Paul invited non-Jews into Christianity. Not only were non-Jews brought in, but they came without benefit of circumcision or **kosher** food laws. These laws prohibit Jews from eating pork and shellfish. They did not have to convert to Judaism or keep its laws. Whether it was Judaism drawing away from Christianity or the reverse is not clear, but the schism occurred and intensified. After 70 C.E., Jesus' messiahship was one of the issues of separation, without a doubt, but it was not the only issue. Jews were willing enough to accept potential messiahs, such as Simon Bar Kochba in the second century and Shabbatai Zevi in the seventeenth century. The greatest issue must have been the Christian acceptance of gentiles who were not required to keep the laws of Judaism.

Christian hostility toward Judaism centered on Jewish refusal to accept Jesus as the Messiah and the supposed guilt of all Jews for the death of Jesus. Jewish minorities living in Christian-dominated lands began to feel the hostility from the majority. Byzantine Christianity soon made life for Jews in Palestine less pleasant than it had been under pagan Roman domination, and life in Zoroastrian Babylon became more appealing and acceptable.

In the Jewish community of Babylon, the discussion over the laws of God continued. Additional interpretative, illustrative, and sermonic material was brought together under the title of Gemara. Gemara was more than additional commentary on the Mishnah and Torah; this body of literature dealt with every area of Jewish life. Gemara developed in both the Palestinian and Babylonian communities. When Gemara was added to the Mishnah, the result was called the Talmud.

The Palestinian Talmud was completed about 425 C.E. The body of this Talmud is about one-third the size of its Babylonian counterpart. Both Talmuds are written mainly in Aramaic, with some Hebrew mixed in, whereas the Mishnah texts are entirely in Hebrew. The Babylonian Talmud is the larger (it runs to 2.5 million words) and more influential of the two; it was completed about 500 C.E. Both Talmuds are made up of two kinds of material: Halachah (the proper way), which consists of legal material, discussions, and decisions; and Haggadah (tale, narrative), which has sections concerning history, folklore, and sermons. About 30 percent of the Babylonian Talmud is Haggadah. The following tale is an example of Haggadic material found in the Talmud.

From the Source

Another time the Emperor said to R. Joshua B. Hananiah, "I wish to see your God." He replied, "You cannot see him." "Indeed," said the Emperor, "I will see him." He went and placed the Emperor facing the sun during the summer solstice and said to him, "Look up at it."

He replied, "I cannot." Said R. Joshua, "If at the sun which is but one of the ministers that attend the Holy One, blessed be He, you cannot look, how then can you presume to look upon the divine presence?"[20]

As the repository of the oral law, the Talmuds became the most important non-Biblical material in Judaism. Since their completion, they have been the object of many commentaries and endless study by all generations of Jews.

With the completion of the Talmuds in Babylon at the beginning of the sixth century C.E., a portion of the life of Judaism came to an end. Scholars who had compiled the Talmud were followed by scholars who founded and ran academies for its study. The presidents of these academies were called *Gaon* (excellency), and the period 600–1000 C.E. was known as the Gaonic period. These *Geonim* lived mainly in Babylon and were the leading religious authorities in Judaism during that period. The last of the great *Geonim* was Saadiah ben Joseph (882–942), who became *Gaon* of the academy at Sura in Babylon. Saadiah was best known as the leading spokesperson of Talmudic Judaism against the Karaites, a group within Judaism that denied the authority of the Talmuds and desired to live exclusively by the legal material within the Hebrew Bible. With the passing of Saadiah, the great Jewish academies of Babylon faded.

Medieval Judaism
Judaism and Islam

In the seventh century C.E., a new religion and a new culture sprang from the Arabian desert; the religion was Islam. Muhammad (570–632), the founder and prophet of Islam, had contact with Judaism through the Jewish tribes in Arabia. He learned stories from the Jewish Bible and knew of Judaism's worship of one eternal God and its condemnation of idolatry.

In the years following the death of Muhammad, the religion of Islam exploded out of Arabia into the entire Fertile Crescent and across North Africa. By the end of the seventh century and beginning of the eighth century, Jews living in Babylon, Palestine, Egypt, Turkey, North Africa, and Spain came under the control of Muslim rulers. Muslims treated Jews and Christians better than other non-Muslims under their control. Muslims considered Judaism and Christianity to be God-given faiths. Jews and Christians were not polytheists and had sacred books (Scripture), which Muslims accepted as revelations from God. However, the Muslim toleration of the Jews was sometimes uneven.

Religion and Violence

The Umayyad Caliphs, who were the first Muslim dynasty (640–750), sporadically persecuted then tolerated the Jews.

The Abbasid dynasty, which followed the Umayyads, was known for religious tolerance. Its capital at Baghdad became the center of science, philosophy, and medicine in the Middle Eastern world. Jews became part of a golden society. Arabic became their language, and the Bible was translated into it. Jewish and Muslim scholars worked side by side to translate into Arabic the works of Greek and Latin philosophers. Thus, these writings were saved from the neglect and destruction of classical materials that occurred in much of Europe during this period. Later, European scholars would rediscover Aristotle and other classical philosophers when their works were translated back from Arabic. It was in this tolerant Islamic world that the Jewish academies flourished, and Baghdad became the center of Jewish religious authority during this period.

The golden age did not last long, however. In 847 C.E. heavier taxes were levied against non-Muslims, and some Jewish synagogues were converted into mosques. The Jewish world also was torn internally. One group of Jewish leaders, the *exilarchs*, struggled against the academic heads, *Geonim*. The Karaite heresy challenged Talmudic authority and drained the energies of the community. With the exception of Saadiah, no outstanding minds arose to lead the academies. Gradually, the academies declined and closed down. The leadership of Jewish life and thinking passed across the Mediterranean to Spain.

Judaism in Spain

Jews were in Spain as early as the first century C.E., and St. Paul mentions his hopes of visiting the Jewish community there.[21] When the Roman Empire converted to Christianity in the late fourth century, Jews in Spain were given the choice of conversion or expulsion. Apparently, however, this was not evenly enforced; Jews continued to survive in Spain as Jews. Judaism probably welcomed the conquest of Spain by the Muslims in 711. With the Muslim conquest began a golden age of freedom and tolerance for Jews. They freely entered the fields of government, science, medicine, philosophy, and literature. With the decline of the Babylonian community, Spanish Jews became the leaders of worldwide Judaism.

There were many outstanding Jews in Spain in the early Middle Ages. Samuel Ibn Nagdela was the grand vizier of Granada and wrote an introduction to the Talmud. Judah ha-Levi was a physician and a Hebrew poet. Moses Ibn Gikatella was a Biblical scholar who advanced the theories of Biblical criticism not espoused by Christian scholars for almost 1,000 years. Moses ben Nachman (Nachmanides, 1195–1270) was a Talmudic authority who was challenged to debate Judaism against Christian monks before the king of Aragon in 1263. He debated so rationally and refuted the Christian claims so clearly that he was rewarded by the king. Even so, he was banished in 1267 and spent his last years in Jerusalem.

By far the greatest figure from Spanish Judaism spent most of his life out of Spain. He was Moses ben Maimon (Maimonides, 1135–1204). Like others of his time, Maimonides was an expert in several fields. He was an outstanding philosopher, a Talmudist, and a physician. He and his family fled from religious persecution in Spain when he was thirteen. After traveling many lands, they eventually settled in Egypt, where Maimonides became the personal physician of Saladin, the Sultan of Egypt. Maimonides' two most famous works are his *Mishneh Torah* and *Guide to the Perplexed*. The *Mishneh Torah* contains fourteen volumes and is a summary of the laws of the Talmud. *Guide to the Perplexed*, completed in 1190, is an attempt to harmonize Judaism with the philosophy of Aristotle. This book caused a storm of controversy among the Jews of the time.

Religion and Violence

Muslim Spain began to decline at the beginning of the thirteenth century. The subsequent rise of Christian rulership meant hardship for the Jewish people. Persecutions and forced conversions increased. Thousands of Jews were massacred in 1391. Many accepted conversion rather than endure persecution, while others converted openly but secretly continued to practice Judaism. These persons were called *los conversos* (the converts). The pressure continued until 1492, when King Ferdinand and his queen, Isabella, not only sent Columbus on his historic mission but also expelled the Jews and Muslims from Spain. Thousands of Jews fled to Italy, Morocco, the Balkans, and Turkey from yet another area that had once been their home.

Judaism in Other European Nations

Although Jews resided in most of the European regions from the time of the Roman Empire onward, Babylon and Spain were the favored sites for Jewish life in the early medieval period. With the decline of these areas, Jews began to move throughout Europe in greater numbers. They were found in Italy, Germany, Portugal, and England. There were small but influential Jewish communities in India and China. In some cases, Jews were well-treated and actually prospered.[22] On the whole, however, the condition of Jews in Muslim lands was far better than it was in Christian Europe.

The Crusades

Religion and Violence

The Christian Crusades set off widespread attacks on Jews in Europe. The Crusades were instituted by Pope Urban II in 1095. He urged Christian rulers to attack the Muslims and win back the holy places in Palestine. Christian princes and their knights took up the challenge for a variety of religious, economic, and political reasons. However, it was easier to attack defenseless Jews who lived in Europe than it was to vanquish Muslim armies in Palestine. Jewish communities all over Europe, particularly those in the Rhineland, were ravaged by the Crusaders. Many were killed, others were forced to convert to Christianity, and still others committed suicide. A few were hidden by sympathetic Christian bishops. The wave of persecution set off by the Crusades was so severe by 1286 that many Jews fled to Poland or to Islamic countries, where authorities were more tolerant.

The Kabbalah

Jewish mysticism is as old as Judaism. Elements of the occult in Judaism have been found in the Bible, the Talmud, and in the writings of many of their leading figures. The concern for angels, demons, magical incantations, charms, witches, ghouls, interpretation of dreams, the date of the coming of the Messiah, numerology, and the name of

God have been lumped together under the term *Kabbalah* (tradition). The codification of these elements in Judaism probably began in Babylon between approximately 500 and 900 C.E., when books containing speculations in these areas began to appear. The outstanding book from this period was the *Sefer Yetzirch* (the book of creation), which came from the Babylonian Jewish community. After this period, the Kabbalahlistic movement shifted to Spain, Italy, Germany, and Poland.

By far the most outstanding compilation of Kabbalahlistic material was the *Sefer Hazohar* (the book of splendor), more simply known as the *Zohar*. The book is attributed to Tanna Simeon Ben Yohai, a Jewish leader of the second century C.E. Internal evidence has caused modern scholars to attribute the *Zohar* to Moses de Leon, a thirteenth-century Spanish mystic from Cordova. De Leon probably attempted to attribute the book to a figure 1,000 years earlier to give it more authority. Whoever its author may have been, the Zohar soon became the most widely read book of Judaism, replacing even the Talmud for a time.

The *Zohar* is concerned with such themes as the nature of God, the theory of the emanations from God, cosmogony, the creation of humankind and of angels, the existence of evil, and the work of angels in the world. Like some of the Gnostics, the Kabbalahists asked how an essentially good and spiritual God could have created this sensual world. The answer that most satisfied them was that the nature of God is truly incomprehensible to humanity. Therefore, God reveals himself to the world through ten emanations, named for the various attributes of God, such as "wisdom," "strength," and "beauty." It was through the work of these ten forces that the sensual world was created. Humans are the highest of all creation and are endowed with three souls. These souls are pre-existent and immortal. The Kabbalahists also taught that evil is non-existent. That which is called evil is but the negative side of good. By such teaching, Kabbalahism differed markedly from Orthodox Judaism.

To achieve its unorthodox teachings, the followers of Kabbalah used unique and far-fetched systems of interpretation. For example, in reading the story of Abraham and the angels who visited him at Mamre (Genesis 18:2a), the Kabbalahists found the following phrase: "Behold, three men stood in front of him." Nowhere in the text are the angels named, but the Kabbalahists ascertained that they must have been Michael, Gabriel, and Raphael. They achieved this knowledge by totaling the numbers of the letters in the phrase. Hebrew, like Latin and Greek, uses the letters of its alphabet for numerals. Therefore, by adding the numerical values of the letters used in the Hebrew phrase, "Behold, three men stood in front of him," the interpreter totals 701. The numerical value of the names Michael, Gabriel, and Raphael is also 701. Therefore, the Kabbalahists reason, these three must have been the angels who visited Abraham.

One of the outstanding Kabbalahistic groups was founded in upper Galilee in the village of Safed by Jews fleeing from Spain in the sixteenth century. They were led by Isaac Luria (1534–1572). Luria and his friends established a whole system of amulets, words, and numbers to overcome evil. Luria himself is said to have believed that he was Elijah, the forerunner of the Messiah. Wherever Jews were found during these troubled times, they studied the Kabbalahistic literature and dreamed of the Messiah.

The Kabbalahistic literature became popular with Jews during a very difficult time for them. At the close of the Middle Ages, Jews had been officially expelled from most European nations. The Babylonian Jewish community had collapsed. World Judaism had entered a period of persecution, exile, poverty, and depression. The Talmud is intended for reasonable people who live under rather normal circumstances. The Kabbalahistic literature is for the oppressed and despised who have little hope. Jews fleeing from Spain and from ghetto to ghetto in Europe needed a messiah to deliver them more than ever. Therefore, they searched the *Zohar* for magical clues that would lead them to the Messiah and to salvation.

Judaism and the Modern World

Religion and Violence

By the end of the fifteenth century, Jews had been officially expelled or made to feel unwelcome in nearly every European nation. Most devastating was the expulsion of the Jews from Spain in 1492. Other nations had officially taken this step earlier: Edward I of England expelled them in 1290; Philip the Fair of France moved to drive all Jews from his country in 1306; they were driven from Germany in the fourteenth century. Portugal followed Spain's example: After 1498, there were no overt Jews in that country. Many fled the persecution of Christian governments and found homes in the Muslim states of the Ottoman empire. In the Ottoman world, Jewish refugees from Spain and Portugal became known as Sephardim and developed their own *lingua franca*, which was mainly Spanish with some Hebrew loan words. The Sephardim also developed their own liturgy and a distinctive pronunciation of Hebrew.

Other refugees turned to Eastern Europe. Poland particularly attracted persecuted Jews because authorities allowed Jews to enter many vocations that were closed to them in other nations. Many became landlords and tax collectors for the absentee Polish nobility. By the end of the sixteenth century, it is estimated that there were more than a half million Jews in Poland, the largest concentration of Jews in the world. Jews in Eastern Europe became known as Ashkenazim. Their language was Yiddish, a combination of Middle High German and Hebrew, written in the Hebrew alphabet.

In the sixteenth century, Christianity was seized by a revolution that became known as the Protestant Reformation. The leader of this movement in Germany was Martin Luther. Luther was a biblical scholar who knew Hebrew and emphasized the study of both the Old and New Testaments as a true basis for faith. In his early writings, he denounced the Catholic Church for its treatment of Jews. However, when it became apparent that Jews were no more interested in converting to his brand of Christianity than they had been in converting to the Catholic faith, Luther turned against them and made fierce anti-Jewish statements in his later writings. The Counter-Reformation of the Catholic Church against the Protestant movement in the sixteenth century reinstituted the Inquisition, and the Jews again became its victims.

Another feature of the Counter-Reformation in Rome was the formation of the Ghetto. Jews of that city were forced to move into a special section, known as the Ghetto, where they were confined. Later, ghettos were found wherever Jews lived throughout Europe. At first, they probably entered these ghettos voluntarily for their own protection and because it was a place where they could maintain their culture; but later, they had no choice. The ghettos became crowded, sunless places in the very worst parts of the cities. They were walled, and their gates were locked after a certain hour each day, thus enforcing a curfew upon the inhabitants. To ensure that Jews could be distinguished from gentiles, the fourth Lateran Council in 1215 decreed that Jews should wear a yellow badge. In addition, many European communities demanded that Jews wear distinctive hats or caps.

In the seventeenth century, Jews living in Poland saw the end of their sheltered existence. In 1648, the Cossacks and the Ukrainian peasants rose in revolt against the Polish nobility. The Jews who had served the nobility became the objects of pogroms: outbreaks of cruel abuse, robbery, rape, and slaughter. Between 1648 and 1656, an estimated 300,000 to 500,000 Jews were slaughtered. Many of those who survived fled into Western Europe.

Responses to Modernity
Shabbatai Zevi

Because of the misery of the Jews in the ghettos, there arose a strong messianic hope. The object of this hope in the seventeenth century was a charismatic figure named Shabbatai Zevi, who was born in Smyrna (now Izmir) in 1626. As a young man, he studied the mysticism of the Kabbalah and eventually gathered around him a band of disciples. Shabbatai Zevi and his followers wandered from place to place in the Middle East. In Egypt, he married a young woman named Sarah, who claimed that she was destined to be the bride of the Messiah; Shabbatai Zevi was eventually declared the Messiah by his disciples. These claims raised Jewish hopes all over the world. Jews danced for joy in the streets of many European cities; bets were taken in Lloyd's of London as to the exact day when Shabbatai Zevi would enter Jerusalem. In 1665, the Messiah and his party entered Constantinople with the purpose of dethroning the sultan of Turkey. The Turkish rulers imprisoned him and gave him the choice of conversion to Islam or death. Shabbatai Zevi converted and thus bitterly crushed the hopes of Jews everywhere.

Mendelssohn

Where Shabbatai Zevi had failed (after conversion to Islam), another figure arose in Germany; his life and influence would do much to deliver the Jews from their misery. In 1743, a frail, hunchbacked boy appeared at the only gate through which a Jew could enter Berlin. When asked his purpose in the city, he replied that he had come to learn. This was Moses, the son of Mendel of Dessau. He had been born in 1729, and learning was indeed his passion. The long hours spent studying under poor conditions had ruined his health and stooped his shoulders. After his arrival in Berlin, he spent his time learning and soon began to write essays in German that caused him to be widely accepted by the poets and philosophers of eighteenth-century Germany and the court of Frederick the Great. Moses germanized his name to Mendelssohn.

That a Jew could write in German prose and be accepted by the learned of that nation was phenomenal. Mendelssohn became the friend of German critic and dramatist Gotthold Ephraim Lessing and is believed to be the hero of his play *Nathan the Wise*. Mendelssohn encouraged the Jews to leave the ghettos and enter the modern world, to write and speak German rather than Yiddish.

Baal Shem Tov

At the same time, another movement that would influence modern Judaism was developing in Poland. About 1750, in Podolia, a simple, uneducated man named Israel ben Eliezer (1699–1760) began to preach to his Jewish brethren that God was not to be found in scholarly research in the Bible or the Talmud but in simple, heartfelt faith. Israel became known to his followers as Baal Shem Tov (master of the good name), and his followers became known as the Hasidim. The following is an example of the teaching of the Baal Shem Tov.

From the Source

Frequently we observe a Zaddik lamenting unto the Lord because of his poverty, yet failing to gain any improvement of his position. This should not be construed to mean that the Lord does not concern himself for the Zaddik. Nay, it is rather a sign of God's great love for him. A parable will illustrate this: A prince of tender age built himself a little house of toy boards. A careless servant inadvertently struck it with his foot, and the fragile structure fell to pieces. The weeping child complained to the king and besought him to punish the servant. The king, however, had secretly intended to surprise his beloved son by building for him a miniature palace of solid and beautiful materials. Therefore, knowing of the rare gift in store for the prince, he did not act upon the lad's complaint.

It is the same with Zaddik, God's cherished son. The Lord has made ready for him a splendid abode in Paradise. He therefore gives slight attention to the Zaddik's complaints of temporary discomforts in this insignificant world below.[23]

The Hasidic movement was widely accepted by the Jews of Eastern Europe, despite the strong disapproval of the Orthodox rabbis. One could not find more distant opposites than the two stellar figures of Judaism in the eighteenth century, Moses Mendelssohn and the Baal Shem Tov.

The end of the eighteenth century brought new winds of thought to Europe and North America, and these were to have an effect on Judaism. In North America, there was a revolution and a subsequent constitution, which stated that all people are to be treated equally under the law. For the first time in modern history, a gentile nation declared that Jews were to be granted the same rights as others. In France, the revolution of 1789 was followed by the Declaration of the Rights of Man, including the Jews. Wherever the armies of France went in the following years, ghettos were torn down and Jews were given civil rights. In that same year, Jews were first admitted to European universities. On the one hand, Mendelssohn encouraged the Jews of Western Europe to come out of the ghettos and join Christian societies in the adventure of modernity. On the other hand, the Baal Shem Tov and his followers in the Hasidic movement encouraged the Jews of Eastern Europe to search within their own traditions and find the resources to maintain Judaism as an independent entity in the midst of Christian societies.

Reform Judaism

With Jews following the lead of Mendelssohn and entering European society on all levels, the demand for reforms in Judaism became apparent. If Jews were to be a part of Western civilization, many felt, some of the historical practices of Judaism were out of place. In 1843, a group of German Jewish leaders met and made the following declarations:

From the Source

1. There is a continuation in the development of Judaism.
2. The Talmud has no authority for the modern Jew.
3. We seek no Messiah, and we know no homeland but the land of our birth.

This declaration became the basis for Reform Judaism. Reform Jews began to use more vernacular and less Hebrew in their worship; their synagogues were called temples; kosher food laws were relaxed; choirs and organs were introduced. Indeed, reform worship in the nineteenth century was in many respects like Protestant Christian worship. Many of the Jewish immigrants to the United States in the early nineteenth century were Reform.

Religion and Violence

While Jews were enjoying new freedoms and rights in Western Europe in the nineteenth century, the lot of their kinspeople in Eastern Europe had scarcely changed in 200 years. Czarist Russia allowed fierce pogroms against its Jewish population. Harassment and second-class citizenship were their lot. In Russia, Jews were squeezed into certain areas called the Pale of Settlement and were forbidden to travel even into other parts of the empire. In 1881, after the assassination of Alexander II, the worst series of pogroms against the Jews broke out. As a result, a great exodus from Eastern Europe took place. Thousands of Jews fled to any country that would have them; the greatest number took refuge in the United States.

Religion and Violence

Zionism

In Western Europe, Jewish people may have believed that they had been accepted into the modern world as equals. Indeed, civil rights had been granted and Jews were making great contributions in every profession. But the anti-Jewish feeling of Christian Europe still lay beneath the surface. These feelings were brought into the open by the Dreyfus case. In 1894, Captain Alfred Dreyfus was accused of betraying French military secrets during the Franco-Prussian War. On the basis of flimsy evidence, Dreyfus was convicted and condemned to life imprisonment on Devil's Island. During the trial, the hostility of the French toward the Jewish Dreyfus and all other Jewish people erupted. Captain Dreyfus was granted amnesty in 1899; seven years later, his court-martial was declared "erroneous."

The Dreyfus case was to have long-range effects on modern Judaism because of a young Austrian journalist named Theodor Herzl, who covered the trial for his newspaper. Herzl and others came to believe that regardless of the liberal facade of European countries, Jewish people would never be treated fairly until they had a land of their own. In a movement known as Zionism, Herzl and others pleaded the case for a Jewish state. Attempts were made to find land anywhere in the world where Jews might develop their own state; but in Jewish hearts, all locations took second place to the land they had left hundreds of years before, the land that had been called Palestine since the second century C.E.

In the early 1900s, Jews began buying land and developing settlements in Palestine. Herzl's work did not produce immediate results, but the seeds had been sown for what would eventually become the nation of Israel. In 1909, the Jewish city of Tel Aviv was founded; by 1920, approximately 50,000 Jews had migrated to Palestine. Many American Jews were suspicious of the Zionist program because they felt that it raised questions about their loyalty to their homeland.

(Continued)

Religion and Violence   (*Continued*)

With the end of World War I, the defeat of the Turks, and the breakup of the Ottoman empire, Palestine became governed by mandate by the British. In 1917, Chaim Weizmann, a Zionist who had rendered service to the British as a chemist, persuaded British Foreign Secretary Lord Balfour to issue a declaration that said: "His Majesty's government views with favour the establishment in Palestine of a national home for the Jewish people." With the issuance of this document by a sympathetic government that ruled Palestine, it would seem that it should have been clear sailing for Zionists. Their objective, however, was not to be easily achieved.

The native populations of Palestine, which included both Arab Christians and Muslims, reacted strongly against the great number of Jewish immigrants and put pressure on the British to restrict immigration. By 1928, there were 100,000 Jews in Palestine; by 1931, 175,000; by 1933, 220,000. The Arabs, fearing a new form of European colonialism and the loss of their land, reacted with riots and strikes. In 1939, the British government issued a white paper that set a quota, limiting Jewish immigration to 15,000 per year for the next five years. This quota came at a time when the Jews of Europe were desperately seeking refuge from the Nazis.

Anti-Semitism and the Holocaust

In 1933, Adolf Hitler became chancellor of Germany. Very quickly thereafter, that nation was changed into an anti-Semitic, Nazi dictatorship. Little by little, the rights of the Jews in Germany were taken away. The Nuremberg Laws of 1935 reduced Jews to second-class citizens who could not vote, hold office, work in most professions, or marry non-Jews. Jews who could see the handwriting on the wall fled to whatever refuge they could find. Immigration laws in the United States prevented large numbers of Jews from entering. Palestine was virtually closed as a result of the British white paper of 1939.

When Hitler's armies began to move across Europe in 1939 and throughout the rest of World War II, millions of Jews fell into their hands. In many cases, the non-Jewish citizens of these countries were only too happy to cooperate with the Nazis on the "Jewish question." The yellow badges and ghettos of the Middle

Children behind a barbed wire fence at the Nazi concentration camp at Auschwitz, southwest Poland. (*Getty Images Inc.—Hulton Archive, Photos.*)

Ages were restored for the Jews. How was the extermination of European Jews to be accomplished? Millions of Jews were trapped in Europe, and their numbers made a "solution" to the "Jewish problem" difficult. The first "solution" was the deportation of all Jews in Nazi-occupied countries to concentration camps in the East. Hundreds of thousands were jammed into cattle cars and sent to Eastern Europe, mainly Poland, where they were forced to work until they died.

By 1941, a "final solution" was reached by the Nazis: The Jews were to be annihilated in extermination camps set up for that purpose. Many extermination methods were attempted, but the one that was eventually accepted as the cheapest and most efficient was death by Zyklon B gas. Methodically, Jews in the death camps were driven into gas chambers and asphyxiated. Their bodies were shorn of all valuables, including hair and gold fillings. Skin, bones, and even body fat were put to use by the thorough Nazis. Bodies that were no longer of any use were then cremated in special ovens.

(Continued)

Religion and Violence (*Continued*)

There are various estimates regarding the number of Jews killed during the Nazi years. The usual number given is six million. In Poland alone, the Jewish population was 3,500,000 prior to World War II. In 1945, only 500,000 Jews remained. Few Jews remain in Western Europe.

One might ask how such a thing could happen in the twentieth century, in one of the most civilized nations in the history of the world. Germany had given the world great musicians, philosophers, theologians, scientists, and leaders in nearly every profession, art, and craft. How could such a nation produce such evil? A number of explanations for the Nazi **Holocaust** have been suggested:

1. *German ethnocentricim and racism.* Adolf Hitler appealed to a very basic emotion in his people when he asserted that the so-called Aryans were the master race and that others, especially the Jews, were inferior. He also condemned, and subsequently executed, Roma (Gypsies) and mentally and physically handicapped people.
2. *German troubles following World War I.* Germany had been defeated in World War I and humiliated by the peace treaty that followed. German pride demanded that some reason be found for the defeat. The most common excuse was that Germany had been "stabbed in the back," and the traitor was supposedly the Jews. Germany also suffered from an economically disastrous inflation following the war, and this too was blamed on the Jews. The fraudulent *Protocols of the Elders of Zion,* written by officers of the Russian Secret Service, was believed to be the plan for an international Jewish conspiracy to destroy the economies of Christian nations. Many Americans, including Henry Ford, agreed with these views. Many Germans also believed that the Jews were behind an international Communist conspiracy. Therefore, Jews were accused of being the international bankers and financiers who would wreak havoc in the world economy—at the same time that they were accused of being

the Marxist enemy of capitalist economies! Nothing could have been more absurd.
3. *Nazi madness.* It would seem that in some cases the destruction of the Jews was more important to the Nazis than anything else. There were occasions when trains that were needed to take German troops and supplies to the front were diverted to take Jews to extermination camps instead.
4. *Modern efficiency.* The very number of Jews murdered could not have been achieved at any other time in history. Neither the Romans nor the Cossacks could have killed so many persons in such a short period of time. Only modern technology made such a mass killing possible.
5. *The silence of the rest of the world.* At a time when Jews most needed a refuge, doors were shut to them all over the world. Many Christian leaders did very little to rescue the victims, and little protest was raised. No attempt was made by Allied bombers to wreck the machinery of the Holocaust. It was as though the rest of the world was willing to allow Hitler to have his way with the unfortunate Jews in his trap.

The Holocaust reduced the world population of Jews by as much as one-third. When the enormity of the crime was made public in the Nuremberg trials of 1946 and the Eichmann trial of 1960, it had a profound effect on Jewish thinking. It was one of the primary causes of the development of the nation of Israel in the years after World War II. The Holocaust may have had a lasting effect on Jewish theology also. At least one Jewish thinker, Richard Rubenstein, said in his book, *After Auschwitz,* that God died in the Holocaust for Judaism. Before the Nazi years, whenever there was a serious threat to the Jews, no matter how severe it was, God somehow answered the cries of his people. At Auschwitz and other death camps, there seemed to be no answer to their prayers as Jews were led to the gas chambers. The full story of the Holocaust and its effects on Judaism has not yet been told. **Anti-Semitism** has not vanished. It remains in Europe,

(Continued)

Religion and Violence (*Continued*)

Latin America, and the United States. In the 1960s, many Jews fled the American South in fear of the violent and anti-Semitic Ku Klux Klan. Neo-Nazis have also demonstrated in largely Jewish suburbs of Chicago.

The State of Israel

The birth of the state of Israel came quickly after World War II. By 1947, it was obvious that Britain could no longer control Palestine and its two warring factions. Zionists were determined to build a home for

Shrine of the Dead Sea Scrolls. The Isaish Scroll is pictured here. ISRAEL
(Israel/Ancient Art and Architecture/Danita Delimont.com)

the thousands of displaced Jews, and the Palestinian Arabs were just as determined that it would not be established in Palestine, fearing that they might become the next group of displaced persons. In 1947, the United Nations voted to partition Palestine into a Jewish and an Arab state. The British left Palestine in May 1948, and Israel immediately proclaimed its statehood. Ironically, the United States and the Soviet Union vied to see who would be the first to recognize the new nation. Immediately, Israel was attacked by five neighboring Arab states. It survived these attacks and others and has answered, at least in part, the Zionists' dreams of a homeland for the Jews.

Unfortunately, with the development of the state of Israel, thousands of Palestinian Arabs were forced from or simply fled their homes in what became the new nation. Since 1948, many of them have eked out miserable existences in various refugee camps. During the Arab-Israeli war of 1967, more Arab territories were occupied by the Israelis, including the city of Old Jerusalem and one of the most sacred shrines of all to the Jews, the Wailing Wall, that portion of the temple remaining after the war of 70 C.E. The governance of the city of Jerusalem and the West Bank of the Jordan and an equitable solution to the displacement of the Palestinian refugees remain serious problems. The peace treaty between Israel and Jordan and the establishment of the Palestinian Authority on the West Bank of the Jordan River and the Gaza Strip were first steps toward resolving these problems, but much remains to be done before true peace is established in the region. The fact that Muslims as well as Jews regard Jerusalem as sacred territory makes the resolution of these problems even more difficult and even more important for the future of all of the people of the area.

Current Variations in Judaism

Recent statistics estimate that there are 14,117,000 Jews in the world.[24] More than 1.8 million live in New York City, making it the largest concentration of Jews anywhere in the world. As already stated, the term *Jew* covers a multitude of religious practices and beliefs. The Jews of the world are widely divided in terms of these beliefs and practices.

Orthodox Jews are the largest group within Judaism. Orthodox Judaism strives to preserve traditional Jewish culture and religion and resist the secularizing elements of modernity. Orthodox Jews attempt to stay as close as possible to the nature of Biblical and Talmudic Judaism. Kosher food laws are stressed, along with strict observance of the Sabbath. In worship, men and women are separated in the synagogue and both must cover their heads. Hebrew is the language of Orthodox worship.

Reform Judaism is popular mainly in the United States and Europe. The Reformist tradition emphasizes the universality of traditional Jewish values, interfaith dialogue, and social activism. It attempts to be as modern as possible in its beliefs and practices. Its worship is usually on Friday evenings, and its synagogues are called temples. Men and women sit together with uncovered heads. The vernacular is used throughout most of the service, with Hebrew interspersed only occasionally. Organ music and choirs are common. Few members of Reform temples attempt to keep all of the kosher food laws or the Talmudic restrictions on the Sabbath. One of the most important developments in Reform Judaism is the ordination of women as rabbis.

Between the Orthodox and the Reform is the Conservative movement, which arose in the nineteenth century, led by Sabata Morais, as a reaction against the perceived extremes of the Reform movement. Shocked at the excesses of the Reform leaders at the Pittsburgh Conference of American Rabbis in 1885, Sabata Morais and others organized the Jewish Theological Seminary of America in New York City. This seminary has been the voice of Conservative Judaism in the United States ever since. Conservative Judaism is firmly rooted in the rabbinical tradition but is somewhat more relaxed in matters of religious practice than is the Orthodox movement.

Jewish men at the Wailing Wall in Jerusalem.
(Pawel Kumelowski/Omni-Photo Communications, Inc.)

Conservative Judaism is distinguished from Orthodox Judaism by its greater concern with the scientific study of the Bible and rabbinical material. In its worship, the vernacular is used more than Hebrew. Unlike Reform Jews, Conservatives tend to worship on Saturday morning. Men are required to cover their heads with the traditional skullcap (*yarmulke*) during worship. Many Conservatives attempt to abide by the Biblical and Talmudic laws regulating food and Sabbath observance.

Growing out of the Conservative movement is Reconstructionist Judaism. Mordecai M. Kaplan, a professor of homiletics at the Jewish Theological Seminary in the 1930s, is regarded as the founder of Reconstructionism. He understood Judaism to be not only a religion but a culture, with its own history, laws, and arts. Therefore, it is not enough to practice Judaism as a religion only; the entire Jewish culture must be studied and experienced. The numerous Jewish community centers in American cities today are an organizational attempt to deal with Kaplan's ideals. Naturally, the Reconstructionists provide complete support to the state of Israel as the home of Jewish culture.

In both the United States and Israel there are now fundamentalist Jewish sects that demand complete acceptance of traditional Jewish law and are overtly hostile to non-Jews and to those Jews who do not accept their extreme views. Some of these groups have gone so far as to plan the destruction of Muslim shrines in Jerusalem and the reconstruction of the Temple of Solomon. Many of them are active in the settlement movement that establishes Jewish enclaves in Muslim areas on the West Bank of the Jordan River. Unlike most other Jewish communities, many of these groups have missionary agendas, directed almost exclusively at less observant Jews.

Jewish prayer book for morning services; ink, watercolor, gouache, and gold paint on parchment. Ashkenazi Europe, 1725.
(*The Jewish Museum, NY/Art Resources, NY*)

There also are large numbers of secular, or non-observant, Jews. Many value their Jewish culture and heritage but do not share the religious beliefs or practices of Jewish communities. Many celebrate traditional Jewish holy days in much the same way secular people of Christian heritage celebrate Christmas and Easter. They are celebrations of family, community, and tradition, but no longer of faith.

Throughout the world there are numerous smaller Jewish sects that because of geographical isolation or differing religious practice are out of the mainstream. The Beta Israel of Ethiopia, a group of black Ethiopians numbering between 15,000 and 25,000, practices a form of Judaism that retains Jewish beliefs and practices from the first century C.E. Other small variant Jewish groups exist in India and China.

Jewish Festivals and Holy Days

Judaism has always been defined and understood by its adherents in terms of the actions of God. Therefore, commemorations of these acts of God tend to be extremely important. The holidays on which these great events are remembered are a unifying factor, bringing together Jews of all degrees of belief and practice. Judaism also depends on the community for its very existence. Therefore, although many portions of its annual festivals may be carried out in the Jewish home, most depend heavily on the community meeting in the synagogue. Because of this reliance upon the group, the events of Bar Mitzvah and Bat Mitzvah (when the young are officially recognized as adult members of the Jewish community) also comprise a significant festival.

Sabbath (Shabbat)

The most important and distinctive of all Jewish holidays is the Sabbath. Judaism gave the world the six-day work week, with the seventh day reserved for worship and rest. The Sabbath begins on Friday at sundown and continues until sundown on Saturday. On Friday night, the Sabbath is ushered in with the Kiddush, the benediction over wine or bread, and the lighting and blessing of Sabbath candles by the woman of the house. Traditionally, the best food of the week is served at the Friday evening meal. Conservative and Orthodox Jews attend synagogue on Saturday morning and also read the week's section of the Torah. Orthodox observance of the Sabbath forbids lighting or extinguishing fires or lights, riding in automobiles, smoking, carrying money, or performing any type of labor.

Passover (Pesach)

Another important festival in Judaism is the celebration of Passover. This holiday begins on the fifteenth of the Hebrew month of Nisan (March–April) and lasts for eight days.[25] It commemorates the deliverance of the Israelites from slavery in Egypt. On the first two nights of Passover, the Jewish family gathers for a ritual meal called Seder. The foods associated with the Exodus (lamb, unleavened bread, bitter herbs, and so on) are eaten as the family engages in rituals that recall the Exodus.

The Feast of Weeks (Shavuot)

Fifty days after Pesach—i.e., on the sixth and seventh days of Sivan (May–June)—the Celebration of Weeks, or Shavuot, occurs. This holiday is called the Pentecost in the New Testament. Shavuot was originally a festival celebrating the first grain harvest, but later it was related to the Exodus event—when Moses received the Ten Commandments on Mt. Sinai. Jewish homes and synagogues are decorated with plants and flowers during the celebration of this holiday.

Jewish men praying at the Western Wall of the Temple in Jerusalem.
(Corbis)

New Year (Rosh Hashanah)

The Jewish New Year is celebrated on the first and second days of the month of Tishre (September–October). Tradition says that the days of Rosh Hashanah were also the first days of creation. The season begins a period of penitence that culminates in the next holiday, the Day of Atonement (Yom Kippur). The New Year is celebrated by special prayers and by eating sweets in the hope of a good year to come.

The Day of Atonement (Yom Kippur)

The holiest of all Jewish holidays is the Day of Atonement. It is celebrated on the tenth of Tishre and at the end of the period of penitence begun at Rosh Hashanah. The day is traditionally observed by abstinence from work, food, and drink. The day is to be spent in the synagogue, where prayers are offered for forgiveness of sins and reconciliation. It is also an occasion for charity.

The Feast of Tabernacles (Sukkot)

Five days after Yom Kippur, on the fifteenth of Tishre, the Feast of Tabernacles is celebrated. Originally, this was a celebration of the autumn harvest. As did many of the other holidays, Sukkot became attached to the Exodus experience and is now kept as a remembrance of the times when the Israelites wandered in the Sinai wilderness and lived in makeshift tabernacles (*sukkot*). For either reason, the festival is a joyous one.

The Feast of Dedication (Chanukah)

On the twenty-fifth of the month of Kislev (November–December), Jews celebrate one of the few holidays not associated with the Exodus. In 165 B.C.E., Judas Maccabaeus retook the Temple from the Syrian Greeks and rededicated it. Only one small container of oil was available to light the temple. It should have lasted only one day. Miraculously, however, the oil lasted eight days. In remembrance of that event, Jews light a candle each day for eight days. It is thus a festival of lights as well as a festival of dedication. Chanukah had been a minor holiday in Judaism until fairly recent times. It has become increasingly important for Jews in the United States because of its proximity to Christmas.

Purim celebration, Brooklyn, New York. Purim is a festive Jewish holiday, with prizes. noisemakers, costumes and treats. This holiday commemorates a major victory over oppression and is recounted in the scroll of the story of Esther.
(Getty Images, Inc.)

The Feast of Lots (Purim)

Another festival not associated with the Exodus is Purim, celebrated on the fourteenth of Adar (February–March) as a remembrance of Jewish victory over gentile foes. The Book of Esther says that Esther, who had become the Queen of Persia, learned of a plot to destroy her people. By boldly approaching the king and revealing this plot to him, Esther saved her people from a massacre and saw her enemies hanged upon the gibbet they had prepared for the Jews. Because lots were cast to determine the day when the Jews were to be destroyed, the festival is known as Purim (lots). On this day, the scroll of Esther is read, gifts are exchanged, and a special meal is eaten. Generally, it is a day of great joy and merrymaking.

The Son of the Commandment (Bar Mitzvah)

Though the Bar Mitzvah is not an annual festival in the Jewish calendar, it is an important occasion in the life of the community. According to Judaism, a boy is technically a man when he reaches his thirteenth birthday. He can be one of the ten adults necessary for a minyan. Usually, the boy is prepared for the occasion by several years of instruction in his religion and in Hebrew. On the Sabbath after his thirteenth birthday, he reads from the scripture at synagogue and may deliver a speech. This is a festive occasion for the boy and his parents, and the young man may receive many presents from his friends. The Bar Mitzvah may have been introduced as late as the fourteenth century, as a counter to Christian confirmation, although the age of thirteen has always been the age of majority in Judaism. A modern innovation is the Bat Mitzvah (daughter of the commandment), a similar ceremony for girls. The Bat Mitzvah is practiced mainly by Reform congregations.

When a Jewish child reaches the age or maturity (12 for girls, 13 for boys), that child becomes responsible for him/herself under Jewish law. The event is commemorated with a Bat Mitzvah/Bar Mitzvah. (Lawrence Migdale/PIX)

Judaism Today

At the beginning of the twenty-first century, one of the primary tasks of Judaism continues to be interpreting the Holocaust. Throughout its history, Judaism has always sought to understand God through history. The biblical material seeks to understand the Exodus experience. The postexilic books try to make sense of the Babylonian exile. The Mishnah and Talmud seek to reinterpret Jewish life after the destruction of the temple. Kabbalahistic literature is the Jewish response to the expulsion from Europe in the fifteenth century. The single greatest tragedy for Judaism in the modern world was the murder of six million Jews by the Nazis. Does this event mean that God is dead for the Jews, or that he has turned his back on them, or that they were being punished for some sin? Does it mean that all Christians are hostile and murderous toward Jews? These and many other questions continue to be asked by the Jewish thinkers of today.

Religion and Violence

As we have noted, one major response to the Holocaust was the founding of the state of Israel. Although the rest of the world may look upon Israel as just another nation, it is far more to Jews. Israel is seen as a refuge for Jews who need to flee from oppressive governments around the world. Israel is seen as the culmination of all of Judaism's dreams for a homeland after 2,000 years of wandering. It is seen by many Jews as almost filling the role of God's Messiah. Therefore, the peace, safety, and well-being of Israel are central concerns to modern Judaism. Anyone of another religion who does not understand this one fact does not understand modern Judaism.

Israel's survival after the battles that occurred in 1948, 1956, 1967, and 1973 is seen in a theological light. The 1978 peace treaty with Egypt is seen by many as a harbinger of peace that is to come with all of its neighbors in the future. The peace treaty with Jordan and the establishment of the Palestinian Authority with limited autonomy in the West Bank territories and the Gaza Strip was an extension of this process. Others look on these developments as a serious threat to Israel's national security and to that of Judaism as a religious community. Sharp disagreements occur over these issues in Israel and among Jews in the United States and Europe. The assassination of the Israeli Prime Minister Yitzhak Rabin in 1995 by a Jewish extremist in an attempt to stop the peace process indicates the depth of these divisions. The Palestinian uprising that began in 2001 and the harsh Israeli response have further deepened these divisions. The rise of the militant group Hammas has only made the situation more difficult. Further difficulties have arisen from the spread of European style anti-Semitism in the Muslim world. Translations of books such as the *Protocols of the Elders of Zion* now circulate widely even in countries where there are no Jews, such as Indonesia and Malaysia.

As has been the case many times in the past, Judaism today struggles with the issue of its place in a predominantly gentile society. There is a long-standing debate about whether Jews should compromise with the values of society at large, or whether they should find their values only in historical Judaism. One greatly feared compromise is intermarriage with gentiles and the consequent loss of Jewish offspring. This concern has created a revival of interest in forms of Orthodox Judaism such as Hasidism. Many of these movements are of great interest to modern young Jewish people.

STUDY QUESTIONS

1. Is Judaism a religion, a culture, a race, or something else? Defend your answer.
2. Using material from the Bible, explain how Judaism provided the moral foundation for much of Western culture.
3. Define *prophet* in the biblical sense of the word.
4. How did the Babylonian exile of 586 B.C.E. change the Jewish understanding of God?
5. Explain the value of the synagogue to a dispersed Judaism. Why are some modern synagogues called *temples*?
6. What were the factors in the development of the Talmud? List the various parts that went into it.
7. Why was Kabbalahistic literature important to the Jews of the sixteenth century?
8. List four major divisions within modern Judaism. Explain how they differ from one another.
9. Explain the importance of the Nazi Holocaust to Jewish thinking. Discuss the state of Israel as a response to the Holocaust.

SUGGESTED READING

Baron, Salo W. *A Social and Religious History of the Jews*, 3 vols. New York: Columbia University Press, 1952.

Bokser, Ben Zion. *The Jewish Mystical Tradition*. Long Island City, NY: Pilgrim Press, 1981.

Buber, Martin. *Tales of the Hasidim*, 2 vols. New York: Schocken Books, 1948.

Chabon, Michael. *The Yiddish Policemen's Union: A Novel*. San Francisco: Harper Collins, 2007.

Cohen, A., ed. *Everybody's Talmud*. New York: Schocken Books, 1975.

Hertzberg, Arthur, ed. *Judaism*. New York: George Braziller, 1961.

Küng, Hans. *Judaism: Between Yesterday and Tomorrow*. Translated by John Bowden. New York: Crossroads, 1992.

Lachs, Samuel T., and Saul P. Wachs. *Judaism*. Niles, IL: Argus Communications, 1979.

Neusner, Jacob. *The Way of the Torah. An Introduction to Judaism*. Belmont, CA: Wadsworth, 1988.

Plaskow, Judith. *Standing Again at Sinai. Judaism From a Feminist Perspective*. San Francisco: HarperCollins, 1990.

Trepp, Leo. *Judaism: Development and Life*. Encino, CA: Dickenson, 1966.

SOURCE MATERIAL

Selections from Hebrew Scriptures

Jewish Scripture and commentary is so widely available and abundant that it is difficult to select a truly representative collection. However, the following materials tend to be illustrative of at least early Jewish thought. The Book of Deuteronomy, from the Old Testament, though it claims to be the words of Moses, is believed by many scholars to be the work of the disciples of the eighth century B.C.E. prophets. It also is believed to have been the book found in the rubble of the Temple in the sixth century B.C.E.(see II Kings 22). Deuteronomy 5 contains one version of the Ten Commandments; verses 4 and 5 of chapter 6 contain the Shema (the creedal assertion of Judaism that God is one). The

Psalms make up a large part of the poetical material of early Israel. Psalm 1, with its praise for the person who "delights in the law of the Lord," shows the growing concern for Scripture in Israel. Micah is representative of the prophetic movement in Israel, particularly with his strong emphasis on social justice.[26]

Deuteronomy

5 [1]And Moses summoned all Israel, and said to them, "Hear, O Israel, the statutes and the ordinances which I speak in your hearing this day, and you shall learn them and be careful to do them. [2]The Lord our God made a covenant with us in Horeb. [3]Not with our fathers did the Lord make this covenant, but with us, who are all of us here alive this day. [4]The Lord spoke with you face to face at the mountain, out of the midst of the fire, [5]while I stood between the Lord and you at the time, to declare to you the word of the Lord; for you were afraid because of the fire, and you did not go up into the mountain. He said:

[6]"I am the Lord your God, who brought you out of the land of Egypt, out of the house of bondage.

[7]"You shall have no other gods before me.

[8]"You shall not make for yourself a graven image or any likeness of anything that is in heaven above, or that is on the earth beneath, or that is in the water under the earth; [9]you shall not bow down to them or serve them; for I the Lord your God am a jealous God, visiting the iniquity of the fathers upon the children to the third and fourth generation of those who hate me, [10]but showing steadfast love to thousands of those who love me and keep my commandments.

[11]"You shall not take the name of the Lord your God in vain: for the Lord will not hold him guiltless who take his name in vain.

[12]"Observe the Sabbath day, to keep it holy, as the Lord your God commanded you. [13]"Six days you shall labor, and do all your work; [14] "but the seventh day is a Sabbath to the Lord your God; in it you shall not do any work, you or your son, or your daughter, or your manservant, or your maidservant, or your ox, or your ass, or any of your cattle, or the sojourner who is within your gates, that your manservant and your maidservant may rest as well as you. [15]You shall remember that you were a servant in the land of Egypt, and the Lord your God brought you out thence with a mighty hand and an outstretched arm; therefore the Lord your God commanded you to keep the Sabbath day.

[16]"Honor your father and your mother as the Lord your God commanded you; that your days may be prolonged, and that it may go well with you, in the land which the Lord your God gives you.

[17]"You shall not kill.

[18]"Neither shall you commit adultery.

[19]"Neither shall you steal.

[20]"Neither shall you bear false witness against your neighbor.

[21]"Neither shall you covet your neighbor's wife; and you shall not desire your neighbor's house, his field, or his manservant, or his maidservant, his ox, or his ass, or anything that is your neighbor's.'

[22]"These words the Lord spoke to all your assembly at the mountain out of the midst of the fire, the cloud, and the thick darkness, with a loud voice; and he added no more. And he wrote them upon two tables of stones, gave them to me . . . .

6 [1]"Now this is the commandment, the statutes and the ordinance which the Lord your God commanded me to teach you, and you may do them in the land to which you are going over, to possess it; [2]that you may fear the Lord your God, you and your son and your son's son, by keeping all his statutes and his commandments, which I command you, all the days of your life; and that your days may be prolonged. [3]Hear therefore, O Israel, and be careful to do them; that it may go well with you, and that you may multiply greatly, as the Lord, the God of your fathers, has promised you, in a land flowing with milk and honey.

[4]"'Hear O Israel: The Lord our God is one Lord; [5]and you shall love the Lord your God with all your heart, and with all your soul, and with all your might. [6]And these words which I command you this day shall be upon your heart; [7]and you shall teach them diligently to your children, and shall talk to them when you sit in your house, and when you walk by the way, and when you lie down, and when you rise. [8]'And you shall bind them as a sign upon your hand, and they shall be as frontlets between your eyes. [9]And you shall write them on the doorposts of your house and on your gates.

[10]"And when the Lord your God brings you into the land which he swore to your fathers, to Abraham, to Isaac, and to Jacob, to give you, with great and goodly cities, which you did not build, [11]and houses full of all good things, which you did not fill, and cisterns hewn out, which you did not hew, and vineyards and olive trees, which you did not plant, and when you eat and are full, [12]then take heed lest you forget the Lord, who brought you out of the land of Egypt, out of the house of bondage. [13]You shall fear the Lord your God; you shall serve him, and swear by his name. [14]You shall not go after other gods, of the gods of the people who are round about you; [15]for the Lord your God in the midst of you is a jealous God; lest the anger of the Lord your God be kindled against you, and he destroy you from off the face of the earth.

[16]"You shall not put the Lord your God to the test as you tested him at Massah. [17]You shall diligently keep the commandments of the Lord your God, and his testimonies, and his statutes, which he has commanded you.

[18]And you shall do what is right and good in the sight of the Lord, that it may go well with you, and that you may go in and take possession of the good land which the Lord swore to give to your fathers [19]by thrusting out all your enemies from before you, as the Lord has promised.

[20]"When your son asks you in time to come 'What is the meaning of the testimonies and the statutes and the ordinances which the Lord our God has commanded you?' [21]then you shall say to your son, 'We were Pharaoh's slaves in Egypt; and the Lord brought us out of Egypt with a mighty hand; [22]and the Lord showed signs and wonders, great and grievous, against Egypt and against Pharaoh and all his household, before our eyes; [23]and he brought us out from there, that he might bring us in and give us the land which he swore to give to our fathers. [24]And the Lord commanded us to do all these statutes, to fear the Lord our God, for our good always, that he might preserve us alive, as at this day.

[25]And it will be righteousness for us, if we are careful to do all this commandment before the Lord our God, as he has commanded us.'"

The Psalms, Book I

Blessed is the man
who walks not in the counsel of the wicked,
or stands in the way of sinners,
nor sits in the seat of scoffers;
but his delight is in the law of the Lord,
and on his law he meditates day and night.
He is like a tree
planted by streams of water,
that yields its fruit in its season,
and its leaf does not wither.
In all that he does, he prospers.
The wicked are not so,
but are like chaff which the wind drives away.
Therefore the wicked will not stand in the judgment,
nor sinners in the congregation of the righteous;
for the Lord knows the way of the righteous,
but the way of the wicked will perish.

Micah

6 Hear what the Lord says:
Arise, plead your case before the mountains,
and let the hills hear your voice.
[2]Hear, you mountains, the controversy of the Lord,
and you enduring foundations of the earth;
for the Lord has a controversy with his people,
and he will contend with Israel.
[3]"O my people, what have I done to you?
In what have I wearied you? Answer me!
[4]For I brought you up from the land of Egypt,
and redeemed you from the house of bondage;
and I sent before you Moses,
Aaron, and Miriam.
[5]O my people, remember what Balak king of Moab devised,
and what Balaam the son of Be'or answered him,
and what happened from Shittim to Gilgal,

that you may know the saving acts of the Lord."

6"With what shall I come before the Lord.

and bow myself before God on high?

Shall I come before him with burnt offerings,

with calves a year old?

7Will the Lord be pleased with thousands of rams,

with ten thousands of rivers of oil?

Shall I give my first-born for my transgression,

the fruit of my body for the sin of my soul?"

8He has showed you, O man, what is good;

and what does the Lord require of you

but to do justice, and to love kindness,

and to walk humbly with your God?

9The voice of the Lord cries to the city—

and it is sound wisdom to fear thy name;

"Hear, O tribe and assembly of the city!

10Can I forget the treasures of the wickedness in the house of the wicked,

and the scant measure that is accursed?

11Shall I acquit the man with wicked scales

and with a bag of deceitful weights?

12Your rich men are full of violence; your inhabitants speak lies,

and their tongue is deceitful in their mouth.

13Therefore I have begun to smite you,

making you desolate because of your sins.

14You shall eat, but not be satisfied,

and there shall be hunger in your inward parts;

you shall put away, but not save,

and what you save I will give to the sword.

15You shall sow, but not reap;

you shall tread olives, but not anoint yourselves with oil;

you shall tread grapes, but not drink wine.

16For you have kept the statutes of Omri,

and all the works of the house of Ahab;

and you have walked in their counsels;

that I may make you a desolation, and your inhabitants a hissing;

so you shall bear the scorn of the peoples."

The Mishnah: Pesahim (The Feast of Passover)

The Mishnah is representative of rabbinic Literature, which became so important to later Judaism. It is a collection of rabbinic opinions about how to keep the laws of God. It is believed that the Mishnah was collected and codified in the second century C.E. The following selection is taken from the section that deals with keeping the feast of Passover. Exodus 12:19 forbade the presence of any form of leaven or yeast in a Jewish household during the seven days of the feast of Passover. But what is yeast (*hametz*)? Where is it found? And to what lengths should one go to get rid of it? This section of the Mishnah attempts to answer these questions.[27]

1. These must be removed at Passover: Babylonian porridge, Median beer, Edomite vinegar, and Egyptian barley-beer; also dyers' pulp, cooks' starch-flour, and writers' paste. R. Eliezer says: Also women's cosmetics. This is the general rule: whatsoever is made from any kind of grain must be removed at Passover. These are included in the prohibition, yet punishment by Extirpation is not thereby incurred.

2. If dough remained in the cracks of a kneading-trough and there was an olive's bulk in any one place, it must be removed. If there was less than this it is negligible in its scantness. So, too, in a matter of uncleanness: he that is scrupulous about it must make a partition; if he wished it to remain it can be reckoned as (one with) the kneading-trough. Dough that is still "dumb" is forbidden if other dough like it has already fermented.

3. How is the dough-offering set apart of a Festival-day if the dough is unclean? R. Eliezer says: She should not designate it (Dough-offering) until it is baked. R. Judah b. Bathyra says: She should throw it into cold water. R. Joshua said: Such hametz is not included in the prohibitions Let it not be seen, and Let it not be found; but rather, she should set it apart and leave it until evening, and if it become hametz it becomes hametz.

4. Rabban Gamaliel says: Three women may knead dough at the same time and bake it in the same oven one after the other. But the Sages say: Three women may occupy themselves (at the same time) with the dough, one kneading, one rolling it out, and one baking. R. Akiba says: All women and all kinds of wood and all ovens are not equal. This is the general rule: if the dough swells let her slap it with cold water.

5. Dough beginning to ferment (si'ur) must be burnt; but he that eats it is not culpable. Dough wholly fermented (sidduk) must be burnt and he that eats it is liable to punishment by Extirpation. What is si'ur? (Dough) on which the cracks are all entangled together. So R. Judah. But the Sages say: If a man ate either (of these) he is liable to punishment by Extirpation. But what is si'ur? (Dough) whose surface turns pallid like a man's face when his hair stands on end.

6. If the 14th falls on a Sabbath all hametz must be removed before the Sabbath. So R. Meir. But the Sages say: (Not until) its appointed time. R. Eliezer b. R. Zadok says: Heave-offering (must be removed) before the Sabbath, but common food (not until) its appointed time.

7. If a man was on the way to slaughter the Passover-offering or to circumcise his son or to eat the betrothal meal at his father-in-law's house and he remembered that he had left hametz in his house, if he has yet time to go back and remove it and return to fulfill his religious duty, let him go back and remove it: but if not, he may annul it

in his heart. (If he was on the way) to render help against ravaging soldiery or a flood or a fire or a falling building, he may annul the hametz in his heart; but if it was but to keep the Feast at a place of his own choice he must return at once.

8. So, too, if a man had gone forth from Jerusalem and remembered that he still had with him flesh that was hallowed, if he had already passed Zofim he may burn it there and then; but if not, he must return and burn it before the Birah with wood for the Altar-hearth. By reason of how much (flesh or hametz) must they return? R. Meir says: In either case an egg's bulk. R. Judah says: In either case an olive's bulk. But the Sages say: An olive's bulk of hallowed flesh or an egg's bulk of hametz.

CHAPTER 12

Christianity

CHAPTER OBJECTIVES

In this chapter you will:

- Learn about the life of Jesus.
- Come to understand why Christianity became fragmented into many denominations.
- Come to understand the relationship between Judaism and Christianity.
- Learn how Christian teachings have developed and changed over the centuries.

KEY TERMS

Gospel
Epistles
Evangelical

Apostle
Missionary
Ecumenical

Sacraments
Indulgences

A Timeline of Christianity

B.C.E./C.E. 0	Birth of Jesus	379—395	Reign of Emperor Theodosius, who proclaims Christianity the official religion of the Roman Empire
29–33	Crucifixion of Jesus		
50–60	Missionary travel of Saint Paul		
150	Completion of New Testament writings	1054	Split between Eastern Orthodox and Roman Catholic churches
313	Edict of Toleration issued by Emperor Constantine legalizes Christianity following periodic persecution	1095–1300	The Crusades
		1232	Start of the Inquisition
		1517	Martin Luther begins Protestant Reformation
325	Council of Nicaea issues credo affirming the divinity of Christ	1520–present	Proliferation of Protestant denominations

(Continued)

A Timeline of Christianity *(Continued)*

1562–1648	European Wars of Religion pits Protestants against Catholics	1895	Origin of Protestant Fundamentalism at Princeton University
1562–1649	The Peace of Westphalia brings the Wars of Religion to an end and establishes the basis for the modern political order of nation states	1917	Communist Revolution in Russia sparks persecution of Christians
1611	King James translation of the Bible produced	1945–present	The end of colonialism leads to the development of new local Christianities in Africa and Asia
1820s–present	Expansion of Protestant missionary activities	1945–present	Rapid growth of secularism in Europe and North America
1830	Joseph Smith presents the Book of Mormon and founds the Church of Jesus Christ of Latter Day Saints (Mormons)	1962–1965	Second Vatican Council
1830–1847	Violent persecution of Mormons in the United States	1965–present	Controversies concerning the roles of women, gays, lesbians, and transgendered persons in most Christian denominations
1834	Spanish Inquisition ends	1991–present	The collapse of Communism in the Soviet Union and Eastern Europe leads to the end of persecution and sparks major religious revivals in many formerly Communist countries
1869	First Vatican Council		
1870	Roman Catholic Church adopts doctrine of Papal infallibility		

Christianity is the largest religion in the world. Today there are more than two billion Christians.[1] This means that approximately one out of every three persons on earth is identified in some way with Christianity. Naturally, a religion that encompasses so many people contains a great variety of beliefs and practices. In general, Christians share a common belief in the uniqueness of Jesus of Nazareth, that he in some way provided for the redemption of humankind by his death and was himself resurrected from the dead. Christians generally also believe in baptism as an initiation into the religion, and in the communion meal. They hold to the idea that believers have one life in which to determine their destiny for life after death. This destiny is usually thought to be either an eternity of bliss in heaven or an eternity of torment in hell. Around these basic themes are many variations within the body of Christianity.

The World of the First Century C.E.

Christianity began as a sect of Judaism in the first century C.E., when the Roman Empire was at its peak and Augustus Caesar (63 B.C.E. to 14 C.E.) ruled. Some knowledge of the condition of both Judaism and the Roman Empire of those days will help us understand the forces that created Christianity.

In the first century C.E., much of Europe, North Africa, and the Middle East were under Roman rule. The Mediterranean Sea was a "Roman lake." The various peoples of the Empire shared a common language and a common intellectual culture that combined elements of Greek and Roman philosophy and religion. Under the rule of Augustus Caesar and his successors, the Roman legions had conquered almost everything that could be conquered. Wherever they went, they took with them Roman civilization, efficient administrators, and thorough engineers. They built cities and roads to link them. They swept the Mediterranean of pirates and made sea travel safe. Communication and travel across the vast area had never been safer or more sure. When Christian missionaries, such as the Apostle Paul, began to spread the **gospel** of Christianity, the Roman Empire provided the path.

In addition to material benefits, as mentioned above, the Roman Empire gave the world one language. Each captive nation continued to speak its own native tongue, of course, but wherever one went in the Roman world, the leaders of government and business would, in addition, be able to speak *Koine* Greek.[2] Although the language of the common people of Rome was Latin, many of the leaders had been educated by Greek slaves and tutors; they found Greek a more beautiful and expressive language. Furthermore, Alexander the Great had conquered much of the world that later became the Roman Empire, and he had sowed the seeds of Hellenistic culture and its Greek language wherever his armies had gone. Because ancient Greece had been the home of philosophy, the beautiful and accurate language of Greece is considered by many to be one of the best vehicles for expressing philosophical and theological thought. A Christian **missionary** (e.g., Paul) could go anywhere in the Roman Empire and be sure that he could converse with the populace in *Koine* Greek. He could also write letters or **epistles** to Christian communities in Greek and know that they would be read and understood.

The world of the first-century Roman Empire was one of political stability. The Romans governed with great cruelty, but they produced a world of relative peace. Augustus and his successors imposed their *pax romana* (the peace of Rome); though it was harsh, it was peace nonetheless. To be sure, there were local revolts against Roman government, such as the Jewish revolt of 66–70 C.E.; but there were no major international wars during this period. Christianity developed in a time of stable government and international calm.

The Roman world of the first century had no major religious commitment. The Greeks and Romans had their pantheons, but belief in them had largely ceased, at least among the ruling elite. Sacrifices to the Roman gods were still carried on officially, but there was little popular support for them. The nations within the Empire had their own national religions, and many of these were alive and well. In Judaism, the rabbis were developing material that would eventually become the Mishnah and the Talmud. Indeed, Judaism was finding many converts from other religions. However, the Empire itself had no vital official religion during this era, and many people were seeking a new religion to take the place of the dead or dying faiths.

Many sought out astrology as a solution to the problems of life. Others turned to new religious cults that developed from various Eastern religions. Mithraism, which was a development from Persian thought, entered Roman life during the reign of Nero and quickly became a popular cult among Roman soldiers. The cult of Osiris spread from Egyptian religions into the Empire. In Greece, the worship of Dionysus was popular.

These and other so-called mystery religions gained large followings among the citizens of the Roman Empire. Each offered the believer life after death in one form or another. Many had secret rituals to which only the initiated were invited. Many had sacred communion meals and baptisms that aided the participant in the search for eternal life. Most of the mystery religions accepted people into their groups without regard to race or social status. In the homogenized life of the Roman Empire, where a large portion of the population was made up of slaves, this was an important feature.

Another aspect of the first-century world (in Judaism and possibly other religions) that is becoming increasingly clear today is that there was an anticipation among some that the world was nearing its end or at least nearing a climactic moment. Among the political groups of Palestine was the hope that a messiah would emerge and lead the people in the overthrow of the Roman monster. This was therefore a time in which many would identify themselves, or at least would allow themselves to be identified, as Messiah. Among the people living at Wadi Qumran by the Dead Sea, who produced those documents popularly called the Dead Sea Scrolls, there was an anticipation of a swiftly approaching end of time. These people were so certain that the end was near that they had left their normal lives and come to this lonely wilderness to await the coming of the Lord. Into this forlorn and hopeful world came Jesus of Nazareth.

The Life and Teachings of Jesus

Jesus of Nazareth was not mentioned in non-Christian literature until the end of the first century C.E. Even then, references to him were vague and not very helpful in constructing the events in his life. Non-Christians sometimes assert that Jesus was not a historical figure, because up until the end of the first century there were only Christian stories about his life.[3] Whether or not this is true cannot be proved, but it is fact that there is limited first-century, non-Christian material about his life. The only truly objective facts we have about the life of Jesus are that a group of people called Christians began to be recognized in the Roman Empire around 60–65 C.E. and that they aroused hostility and persecution in an empire that was normally tolerant of religious variations. Christianity became the object of many official and unofficial persecutions, but it continued to grow until the fourth century, when it became the official religion of what remained of the Roman Empire. Although modern students of Christianity may not know exactly what the early church taught, the existence of this group cannot be questioned.

Religion and Violence

Central to the existence of early Christians was the idea that Jesus of Nazareth had been crucified in Jerusalem during the reign of Pontius Pilate and had been resurrected from the dead. Christianity is among the few religions in which accounts of violent acts are of central significance. Christians commemorate the death and resurrection of Jesus every year during Holy Week.

About forty years after his death, members of this group began to write biographical statements about Jesus, centered on his death and resurrection. These books, or Gospels, are not biographies in the true sense of the word but give most of their attention to the last few months in the life of Jesus. Only rarely are Jesus' childhood or early adult years mentioned, and none of the Gospels contains a physical description of Jesus. Even the exact details of Jesus' last few months differ among the four Gospels. If the earliest Gospel was written forty years after the death of Jesus, and if all of the Gospels were written by confessed Christians who had a biased point of view, then admittedly they may not be the most reliable sources of objective material. With all of their imperfections, however, the Gospels still provide the best information we have about the life of Jesus.

Shrine of the Virgin Mary. National Cathedral, Jakarta, Indonesia.
(Mark R. Woodward)

Two Gospels, Mark and John, begin with the ministry of a mature Jesus. Only Matthew and Luke speak of his birth, and only Luke contains materials relating to Jesus' childhood. The reader must assume that for the early church, the years before Jesus' actual ministry were not terribly important. In those Gospels that do tell of his birth, there are problems in harmonizing details. They do agree, however, that Jesus was born in the ancestral home of David: Bethlehem. Matthew places the time of Jesus' birth in the years prior to the death of Herod the Great (4 B.C.E.).[4] Both Matthew and Luke assert that Jesus' birth was unique in that he was born of Mary, who was a virgin. They tie this event to the words of the eighth-century B.C.E. Hebrew prophet Isaiah: "Behold, a young woman [virgin][5] shall conceive and bear a son, and shall call his name Immanuel."[6]

All of the Gospels agree that Jesus was a resident of the village of Nazareth in the province of Galilee. About his childhood and young maturity, we are told only of the event recorded in Luke, in which the twelve-year-old Jesus went to Jerusalem for a festival with his parents and became so involved in a discussion with the teachers of the law that he failed to find his way to the party returning to Nazareth. Except for this lone incident, the life of Jesus prior to his thirtieth year is not mentioned. Naturally, this blank has led to all sorts of speculation by Christians and non-Christians.

The Gospels all place Jesus within the background of first-century Judaism. He quotes the Hebrew Scriptures in his teaching. Each Gospel writer sees Jesus as a fulfillment of the promises of the Hebrew Bible. Jesus and his **Apostles** used the Jewish synagogue as the starting point of their ministry. The New Testament shows them celebrating the Jewish holidays and being concerned with the correct interpretation of Jewish laws. Jesus is often presented in variance with some forms of first-century Judaism, but the similarities are much more common.

The Gospel of Luke tells its readers that Jesus was about thirty years of age when he began his ministry, and all of the Gospels agree that his first public act was his baptism by John the Baptist in the Jordan River. The figure of John also is not clear in the Gospel accounts. Luke says that he was Jesus' second cousin. Whatever his relationship may have been, John was a powerful and charismatic figure in Judea. When he preached his message of repentance, large crowds came down to the Jordan River to hear him. A body of disciples followed him. Years later, the Apostle Paul encountered Jews in Ephesus who had heard of John but not of Jesus.[7]

After his baptism, Jesus went into the nearby Judean wilderness where he fasted for forty days and pondered the nature of his ministry. According to the **Gospels**, Jesus was tempted by Satan to accept a wide variety of easy paths to glory during this time. After the period of temptations, Jesus returned to Galilee, where he began to preach. From the Galilean villages, he chose a band of followers who would be his disciples for the next few years. Some of them had originally been disciples of John the Baptist. The Gospels list twelve disciples, but this number must have varied. There were times in Jesus' ministry when only three or four disciples of this group were close to him. At other times, he seems to have been followed by thousands of disciples.

The exact length of Jesus' public ministry is not known. The events of this ministry given in the synoptic Gospels (Matthew, Mark, and Luke) could fit into one year, beginning and ending at Passover. However, the Gospel of John presents Jesus' ministry over several seasons that seem to fit into a three-year period. Traditionally, Christians accept John's outline and talk of a three-year ministry. The location of Jesus' ministry is also a matter of some dispute. The synoptic Gospels present Jesus working mainly in Galilee and appearing in Jerusalem only for special occasions. John's account has Jesus spending more time in the province of Judea, around Jerusalem.

Hispanic man witnesses African-American woman being baptized by African-American Roman Catholic priest. *(Michael Newman/Photo Edit)*

All of the Gospels agree that during his public ministry Jesus spent his time teaching and healing; whether to a small group of disciples or a large crowd in a public place, he was a teacher. In the truest sense of the word, he was called *rabbi* by his disciples. Both the form and content of Jesus' teachings are recognized and respected as being outstanding among those of the world's great religious teachers.[8] Occasionally, Jesus conveyed his message in direct, simple statements, such as the Beatitudes from the Sermon on the Mount:

From the Source

Blessed are the poor in spirit, for theirs is the kingdom of heaven.

Blessed are those who mourn, for they shall be comforted.

Blessed are the meek, for they shall inherit the earth.

Blessed are those who hunger and thirst for righteousness, for they shall be satisfied.

Blessed are the merciful, for they shall obtain mercy.

Blessed are the pure in heart, for they shall see God.

Blessed are the peacemakers, for they shall be called sons of God.

Blessed are those who are persecuted for righteousness's sake, for theirs is the kingdom of heaven.

Blessed are you when men revile you and persecute you and utter all kinds of evil against you falsely on my account.

Rejoice and be glad, for your reward is great in heaven, for so men persecuted the prophets who were before you.[9]

Jesus is most often remembered, however, for his use of a teaching device called the parable. The parable is a short, easily recognized story about very human characters and events. Because of the brevity and beauty of these stories, the parables of Jesus are among the best remembered and most quoted teachings of all of the religions of the world. The Gospel of Luke is particularly well stocked with Jesus' parables. Here the reader finds the stories of the prodigal son, the lost sheep, and (perhaps the best known of all) the parable of the Good Samaritan.

From the Source

A man was going down from Jerusalem to Jericho, and he fell among robbers, who stripped him and beat him, and departed, leaving him half dead. Now by chance a priest was going down the road; and when he saw him he passed by on the other side. So likewise a Levite, when he came to the place and saw him, passed by on the other side. But a Samaritan, as he journeyed, came to where he was; and when he saw him, he had compassion, and went to him and bound up his wounds, pouring on oil and wine; then he set him on his own beast and brought him to an inn, and took care of him. And the next day he took out two denarii and gave them to the innkeeper, saying, "Take care of him; and whatever more you spend, I will repay you when I come back."[10]

It is difficult to find one central theme in all of the teachings of Jesus. Different groups within Christianity tend to isolate those statements that seem to support their position and claim that this was indeed the main message of Christ.

Many of Jesus' teachings seem pacifistic. For example:

From the Source

You have heard that it was said, "An eye for an eye and a tooth for a tooth." But I say to you, Do not resist one who is evil. But if any one strikes you on the right cheek, turn to him the other also; and if any one would sue you and take your coat, let him have your cloak, as well; and if any one forces you to go one mile, go with him two miles.[11]

Yet it would be a mistake to say that pacifism was Jesus' total answer to the problems of his times. At one point, he urged his disciples to be armed (Luke 22:36); and at another, he stated that he had not come to bring peace but a sword (Matthew 10:34).

Other groups within Christianity contend that the central message of Jesus was people's superiority over the Jewish law. Indeed, many of Jesus' actions and teachings seem to suggest an attitude of indifference toward the laws of Judaism. He healed on the Sabbath, and he allowed his disciples to pluck grain on the Sabbath while they walked through the fields. He also stated,

From the Source

"Not what goes into the mouth defiles a man, but what comes out of the mouth, this defiles a man."[12]

This statement seems to put Jesus in conflict with the kosher food laws. However, at times, Jesus had a very reverent attitude toward the laws of Judaism:

From the Source

Think not that I have come to abolish the law and the prophets; I have come not to abolish them but to fulfill them. For truly I say to you, till heaven and earth pass away, not an iota, not a dot, will pass from the law until all is accomplished. Whoever then relaxes one of the least of these commandments and teaches men so, shall be called least in the kingdom of heaven; but he who does them and teaches them shall be called great in the kingdom of heaven.[13]

Indeed, many of the teachings of Jesus are similar or parallel to those of the great rabbis of that era, whose words are remembered in the Mishnah.

Still others have chosen to see the central message of Jesus in terms of an overwhelming concern on his part for the coming end of the age. Albert Schweitzer, in his classic *The Quest of the Historical Jesus*, has pointed out the heavy emphasis on eschatology found in the words of Jesus.[14] Those who agree with Schweitzer see Jesus as a leader who believed that the world was very near the end of an old age and the beginning of a new one.

Many associate this new age with the return of Jesus, the resurrection, and the judgment of the dead.

There are many aspects of the teachings of Jesus as found in the Gospels. Like all great teachers, Jesus was concerned with human values, warning people about the perils of riches and preaching compassion among humans. Yet he also was a man of his times, aware of the hateful oppression of his people by the Romans but similarly aware of the disastrous possibilities of revolution against the Romans. He had been schooled in the laws of his religion and saw in them the great potential for human good if properly applied, as well as the potential for oppression if improperly applied. Jesus also was a man of his times in that he, like the monks of the Essene community who lived at Wadi Qumran near the Dead Sea, was acutely aware that the age was drawing to a climax. Therefore, Jesus cannot easily be forced into one dogmatic mold.

All of the Gospels record that Jesus was a worker of miracles. Regardless of either the attitude that modern readers may have toward the nature of miracles or the embarrassment that miracles may cause some modern Christians as they try to find a rational explanation for them, the Gospels and the sermons of the early Christians are quite clear: Jesus worked miracles. He healed the sick, the blind, and the lame; he fed the hungry; he raised the dead; he cast out demons; he walked on the waters and stilled the storms. Miracles were a very real part of the world of Jesus, and he performed them regularly, without great fanfare.

After a time of public ministry, the opposition against Jesus began to grow. It became necessary for him to go away from the crowds of both friends and enemies and rest periodically. On one such occasion, he went to the north to Caesarea Philippi to be alone with his closest disciples. Here he asked his disciples:

From the Source

"Who do men say that I am?" And they told him, "John the Baptist; and others say, Elijah; and others one of the prophets." And he asked them, "But who do you say that I am?" Peter answered him, "You are the Christ."[15]

This is the clearest statement of Jesus' identification as a messianic figure by his disciples and by himself. He followed this statement with the warning that he would soon go to Jerusalem and be put to death.

After these events, Jesus and his followers began their journey southward to Jerusalem. They arrived at the time of celebration of the Passover, when the city was crowded with pilgrims from the Diaspora communities all over the world. It was a season of great expectation because it commemorated YHWH's greatest intervention in history on behalf of his people. On the Sunday before his death, Jesus entered the city and was widely accepted and acclaimed by the citizens. On this day and those that followed, Jesus spent much time in the temple teaching and engaging in debates with his opponents. Each afternoon, he left the city and went a few miles to the village of Bethany, where he stayed at the home of his friends Mary, Martha, and Lazarus.

On Thursday evening, Jesus entered Jerusalem and partook of a final meal with his disciples. It is not clear in all of the Gospels whether this was the Passover Seder or simply a common meal. He shared bread and wine with his disciples. The Gospel of Luke describes this final meal as follows:

From the Source

"Then he took a cup, and after giving thanks he said: 'Take this and divide it among your selves; for I tell you that from now on I will not drink of the fruit of the vine until the kingdom of God comes.'

Then he took a loaf of bread, and when he had given thanks, he broke it and gave it to them saying:

'This is my body, which is given for you. Do this in remembrance of me.'

And he did the same with the cup after supper, saying:

'This cup that is poured out for you is the new covenant in my blood,'"[16]

For Christians these verses are among the most important in the entire Bible. They have inspired the most common and universal of Christian rituals—the Lord's Supper—but are also the source of great controversy. Some Christians, particularly Roman Catholics, have maintained that Jesus' statements support the doctrine that in the ritual bread and wine are transformed into the body and blood of Christ. Most Protestants believe that the bread and wine are symbolic of Christ and are a reminder of his sacrifice, but that they are not literally transformed into his body and blood. It is unlikely that this controversy will ever be resolved.

The Last Supper, Hubert Ruland (1854–1906).
(*SuperStock, Inc.*)

Following the meal, Jesus and his party went out of the city to the Garden of Gethsemane, where Jesus prayed for a few hours. Here he was betrayed by Judas, one of his closest disciples, and arrested by the temple guards. He was tried by the Jewish high court, the *Sanhedrin*, early the next morning. This trial was followed by a hearing before Pontius Pilate, the Roman procurator of Judea, and a beating by his troops. Jesus was also interviewed by Herod Antipas, the governor of Galilee.

Finally, at about nine o'clock in the morning, he was sent out of the city and crucified with two felons. The Gospels record that a series of cataclysmic events occurred as Jesus was dying. By three o'clock in the afternoon, he was dead. He was taken from the cross and buried in a nearby borrowed tomb.

The Gospels state that the opposition to Jesus and the responsibility for his death came mainly from within the body of Jewish leadership, especially from the party of the Pharisees. The Pharisees were a group within Judaism made up mostly of the common people. They were fairly liberal and progressive in their theological outlook. They believed in the resurrection of the dead and accepted as canon books in the Bible beyond the first five books of Moses. The New Testament lists several of Jesus' disciples as Pharisees, including Paul, the great **missionary** of the early church. In truth, there were more similarities between Jesus and the Pharisees than there were differences. Some have suggested that Jesus himself was a Pharisee.

Other opposition came to Jesus from the Sadducees, an aristocratic group who controlled the temple in Jerusalem. Theologically, they were very conservative, accepting only the first five books of the Bible as the word of God. The Gospels present the Sadducean leaders as the ones who tried Jesus in Jerusalem and were ultimately responsible for his death.

Undoubtedly, Jesus was opposed by another party within Judaism, the Zealots. The Zealots, who had arisen in Galilee soon after the birth of Jesus, were fanatical anti-Roman patriots who stirred up revolution at every opportunity. Even though one of Jesus' closest disciples is listed as a Zealot, this party could not have been pleased with Jesus because he refused to be the leader of a political revolution against Rome.[17]

Religion and Violence

Although the Gospels fix the major share of the opposition to Jesus on these groups within Judaism, the ultimate and fatal opposition must surely have come from the Roman government. Because of the Zealots and other dissident groups, Roman rule of Judea was never easy. From the time of Pompey's entry into Jerusalem in 63 B.C.E., through the reign of Herod the Great in the first century B.C.E., and into the period of 130–135 C.E., Judea was not quiet for the Romans.

The Gospels say that Jesus began the last week of his life by entering the city of Jerusalem during Passover week, riding a donkey and being received by the crowds as though he were a conquering hero. Because Jesus was from Galilee, the home of the Zealots, and because some of his close followers were known to be armed, it was only natural for the Roman authorities to assume that this was a potentially dangerous man.

(Continued)

Religion and Violence   (*Continued*)

The Gospel accounts place the responsibility for Jesus' death upon the Jewish leaders and the crowds in Jerusalem who were there for the Passover. These accounts lay the foundation for much of the anti-Jewish feeling and persecution that followed for more than 2,000 years.[18] Jesus surely would not have been executed had it not been the wish of the Roman authorities. He was crucified Roman-fashion, by a group of Roman soldiers, by order of the Roman procurator of Judea, Pontius Pilate. Moreover, the Gospels make it clear that Jesus died to save all humans from sin, which can only mean that all share equally in the responsibility for his death.

Jesus was crucified on Friday and was placed in the tomb by Friday evening. When women came to tend to his body the following Sunday morning, they found the tomb empty. The four Gospels tell different tales about the events that followed: Mark records that the women found the tomb empty and conversed with a young man there who told them that Jesus had risen and gone into Galilee. The other Gospels present more elaborate statements. In them, Jesus appeared to different groups of disciples in Jerusalem and Galilee at various times over the next forty days. Eventually, he gathered his friends together at the Mount of Olives outside of Jerusalem and ascended into heaven. All of the Gospels agree, however, that the tomb was empty and that Jesus had conquered death. Most agree that he was seen after his resurrection by a number of reputable witnesses. Luke mentions that some of the Apostles doubted the rise of Jesus, and that he ate a piece of broiled fish to prove to them that he was not a ghost or spirit but a living man.[19] The Resurrection event became central to the early Christian church and almost all subsequent Christian groups and denominations.

Early Christianity
The Jerusalem Church

After Jesus' resurrection and ascension, his followers met in Jerusalem. They probably banded together out of fear that they might share Jesus' fate. At the festival of Shavuot[20] (fifty days after Passover), however, the Christians were feeling more courageous because of the coming of the Holy Spirit and went out into the streets of Jerusalem to preach about their faith. Miraculously, they were able to preach in languages that they had not known before and as a result persuaded many people to join them.

It is important to note that this original group of Christians in Jerusalem and those groups that later sprang up throughout the world were considered by themselves and others to be another sect of Judaism. The members of this group were Jewish by background; their Bible was the Hebrew Bible; and they continued to worship at the Temple in Jerusalem. The only thing that distinguished them from other Jews was their belief that Jesus of Nazareth was somehow unique. The exact faith of these early Christians is difficult to define precisely. The systemization of Christian theology was not to come for several centuries, and after long years of debate.

Our knowledge of the Jerusalem church is drawn from the accounts of the New Testament book, Acts of the Apostles. The leadership of the group seems to have resided in two men. The first was Simon Peter, who had been among the inner circle of Jesus' disciples. Though the organization was loose in the early days, Simon Peter was certainly a major spokesperson for the church. Others of Jesus' disciples are mentioned in Acts, but none seems to have had Simon Peter's authority. A second leader who came to have more and more influence in Jerusalem was James, the half-brother of Jesus. Tradition says that James was not a follower of Jesus during his ministry but came to believe in him after the Resurrection. James assumed leadership of the Jerusalem church when Simon Peter moved out to other communities. Beyond these two, there seems to have been no official leadership.

The Acts record that seven men were chosen to serve the Christians of Jerusalem in the distribution of charity. One of these was Stephen, who not only acted as a servant of the church but also preached in the streets. His preaching so enraged the authorities in Jerusalem that he was officially denounced and stoned to death. Thus Stephen became the first martyr of the Christian faith. His death was but one event in a series of persecutions against the Christians in Jerusalem as hostility against them increased. These persecutions caused many Christians to leave Jerusalem and carry their faith elsewhere in Judea and into other centers of the Roman Empire.

The Life of Paul

Because almost half of the Book of Acts is devoted to the missionary activities of Paul, and because he is traditionally considered the author of fourteen books of the New Testament, Paul is the best known early Christian. Undoubtedly, other missionary figures in the early church went as far and did as much as Paul, but they escaped the attention of the New Testament. Not only was Paul important as a missionary of the early faith, but he also made a great contribution as a theologian. He was among the first to attempt to state systematically the beliefs of Christianity. Indeed, Paul is sometimes called the "Second Founder of Christianity."

According to the biographical material presented in Acts and that which may be gathered from his epistles, Paul was reared in the Diaspora Jewish community of Tarsus in Asia Minor. He was educated in both Judaism and Hellenistic traditions. He studied with the great Rabbi Gamaliel and was a member of the Pharisee party.

Religion and Violence

Paul was originally strongly anti-Christian, and when opposition to the Christian sect in Jerusalem became active persecution, Paul became a leader and observed the stoning of Stephen. On a mission to persecute the Christians in Damascus, he was struck down by a light from heaven and became converted from an enemy of the Christians to a spokesperson for them.

After a time of study, he began to preach on behalf of Christianity. With various companions, he traveled across the Roman Empire, preaching first in the Jewish synagogues and then to gentile audiences. It was Paul, perhaps more than anyone else, who led the movement to allow gentiles to become Christians without first becoming Jews and following the laws of Judaism. This became both the strength and the weakness of Christianity. Its strength lay in the fact that converts could come very easily into the church from almost any background, without a lengthy and arduous preparation for

Judaism. This made it possible for Christianity to become an independent universal religion rather than a sect of Judaism. Its weakness was that it set the wedge between church and synagogue, a wedge that has never been removed.

Religion and Violence

Paul and his companions carried out three missionary journeys, which are discussed in Acts. These journeys took them to many of the cities of Asia Minor and Greece. Upon completion of his travels, Paul returned to Jerusalem, where he was arrested by the Roman authorities. He was imprisoned in Caesarea for several years and eventually sent to Rome, where he was to be tried by Caesar. Acts concludes with Paul's entering Rome somewhere around 60 C.E., and there is no biblical material about the remainder of his life. Tradition says he was imprisoned in Rome during the period of the Neronic persecution of the church (64 C.E.) and executed.

Tradition also states that Simon Peter, who had become bishop of the church at Rome, was executed there at approximately the same time. *The Annals* of Tacitus, a Roman historian who wrote approximately fifty years after Nero's persecution, claims that Nero set out to persecute the Christians to shift the blame from himself for having set a great fire in Rome. This was the first of the official persecutions of the Christians by the Roman government.

The Worship of the Early Church

Clearly the church modeled its worship after the forms used in the Jewish synagogue. The Jerusalem church, which continued to exist and exert authority until its destruction along with the city in 70 C.E., still used the Temple as a place of worship. It may even have continued to practice the animal sacrifice that was a part of Temple worship at that time. Wherever Paul went, he first sought out and preached at the local Jewish synagogue. Undoubtedly, the prayers, the Scripture reading, the hymns, and the simple sermons that were so much a part of synagogue worship were also a part of early Christian worship.

In addition to these modes of worship, Christians added others. Baptism was apparently a part of Christian worship from the earliest times. Baptism as an initiation into a new faith was practiced by the Pharisees when they took converts into Judaism. John the Baptist baptized people in the Jordan River as a symbol of repentance. Jesus' disciples baptized converts even during his ministry, and Paul baptized converts wherever he went.

Both the mode and the meaning of Christian baptism have been objects of debate throughout the history of the church. The word *baptize* comes from the Greek word *baptizein*, "to immerse." Presumably, John immersed his converts in the Jordan River. As Christians grew in number, the inconvenience of finding a body of water large enough to immerse the candidate may have ushered in a more moderate form of baptism. Pouring or sprinkling water on the head became accepted as the proper mode of baptism.[21] Some Christian communities continue the practice of baptism by immersion.

It is not clear why Jesus' disciples baptized, nor does the New Testament tell the reader clearly why the early church continued the practice. It appears originally to have been an outward sign of the change in status from the pagan life to the Christian life. In later years, it took on deeper meanings. Eventually, baptism was understood to be the washing away of original sin. In the New Testament accounts, the converts who were baptized were adults, but baptism became more and more important to salvation; eventually infants were baptized to wash away the stain of original sin as quickly as possible.[22] This is easy to understand when we recall that at the time the practice was initiated, infant mortality rates were extremely high. Whatever the original manner and meaning of baptism may have been, before long it was administered by a sprinkling of water on the infant children of Christian parents and became a **sacrament** of the church.

The second addition of the early Christians was the Eucharist, or communion meal. This was probably modeled on the Seder meal of Judaism, in which the community recalls divine history as they partake of sacred foods. Specifically, it was adopted by Christians from the model of Jesus' last supper with his disciples on the evening before his death. In the early years of the church, it became customary for Christians to gather together and eat a meal recalling the death of Jesus. Perhaps it was simply a meal of bread and wine, or it may have included other foods.[23] Again, both the manner and meaning of the communion meal have been debated within the church. Eventually, the Eucharist became a sacred meal in which the bread and wine actually became the flesh and blood of Jesus; individuals who received these elements were actually eating and drinking the body of Jesus and thus their souls were sanctified and aided in their journey toward eventual salvation.

Leadership in the Early Church

The early church was not a highly organized structure. It was small and not quite sure of itself. Both Acts and the Epistles of Paul indicate that many Christians were expecting Jesus to return to earth at almost any time, and therefore the church had no need for a highly organized structure. As the years passed and it became apparent that Jesus was not returning immediately, as the number of Christians grew, and as the various interpretations of Christianity increased, it became necessary for the church to organize more fully. There had always been outstanding leaders, such as Simon Peter, Paul, and James; apparently, they held no titles and drew whatever authority they had from their relationship to Jesus and the force of their personalities. The Roman Catholic Church claims that Simon Peter was intended by Jesus to be the cornerstone of the Church. This claim is based on the following biblical passage:

From the Source

Simon Peter replied, "You are the Christ, the Son of the living God." And Jesus answered him, "Blessed are you, Simon Bar-Jona! For flesh and blood has not revealed this to you, but my Father who is in heaven. And I tell you, you are Peter [Greek Petros], and on this rock [Greek petra] I will build my church, and the powers of death shall not prevail against it. I will give you the keys of the kingdom of heaven, and whatever you bind on earth shall be bound in heaven, and whatever you loose on earth shall be loosed in heaven."[24]

Although it is not mentioned in the New Testament, a strong tradition says that Simon Peter went to Rome and became the leader of the church in that city. The bishops who were his successors became the Popes of the Roman church.

The New Testament mentions several kinds of leaders in the early church, but their roles are never clearly delineated. One such leader was the bishop. The Greek word for *bishop*, *episkopos*, literally means "shepherd." Qualifications for this office were laid out by Paul in the epistles to Timothy and to Titus, and the bishop seems to have managed the church in a certain geographical area. Another officer was the deacon. The first seven servants chosen by the church of Jerusalem are frequently referred to as deacons, although the New Testament never calls them this. The office of deacon was, as the word *diakonos* (servant) implies, one of service.[25] The qualifications for deacon were as stringent as those for bishop.

Elders (*presbyteroi*) are also mentioned as leaders of the church. Acts makes a clear connection between the elders of Judaism and those of the church. Apparently, the latter were older persons who had been given authority to make decisions on religious matters by virtue of their age and wisdom. Paul's letters indicate that the elders also taught and preached. In addition to these offices, the New Testament mentions evangelists, prophets, apostles, pastors, and teachers. Never, however, is the reader given a complete list of the functions of these leaders.

The Christian church of the New Testament period (ca. 30–150 C.E.) seems to have been amorphous both in belief and structure. No strong organization imposed a creed on the Christian groups; therefore, they varied greatly in what they believed and practiced. Paul was constantly having to correct what he considered false doctrine among Christians in various parts of the Roman world. He disagreed with many of the Jerusalem leaders about the admittance of gentiles into the church. The churches of the various cities within the Roman Empire seem to have been loosely organized, meeting in the synagogues when they were welcome and in private homes when no other arrangements could be made. They soon changed their day of worship from the Jewish Sabbath of Saturday to Sunday, the day when Jesus rose from the dead. Their clergy apparently had little official status and usually were not paid for their preaching. Occasionally, offerings were taken for Christian preachers, but for the most part they lived by whatever trade or skills they had.

The Production of the New Testament

The Bible of the early church was the Hebrew Bible. Christians read the prophets Isaiah, Micah, and Zechariah and saw in them predictions of the life of Jesus. As the years passed, specific Christian literature began to develop. Probably the earliest Christian writings were the letters (epistles) that Paul wrote to the Christian congregations he had established. These letters began in the '50s and '60s of the first century C.E. Fourteen of the current twenty-seven books of the New Testament are letters attributed to Paul, although modern scholars doubt that all fourteen came from his pen.[26] These letters are an anthology of Pauline thought. They contain advice to the early church on doctrine, leadership, and worship. Additionally, they contain some biographical material about Paul and other early church leaders not found elsewhere. In his letters to the Romans and Galatians particularly, Paul sets forth the first systematic understanding of the importance of the life, death, and Resurrection of Jesus.

In the years following Jesus' death, Christians undoubtedly wrote their remembrances of the events of his life as well as his sayings. We may speculate that collections of his teachings were compiled for use in the instruction of converts. However, Christians may not have made a careful attempt to write the story of Jesus because they were expecting his imminent return. As the years passed and as the people who personally knew of Jesus began to die (either from old age or persecution), fewer and fewer Christians were able to recount the events in Jesus' life with any certainty.

Religion and Violence

In 70 C.E., the Roman armies closed in on Jerusalem to finish off the Jewish revolution that had begun four years earlier. By the end of the summer, Jerusalem and its temple were destroyed, along with the Jerusalem church and many witnesses to the life of Jesus. It may have been this event that caused a Christian to collect a brief statement of the events in the last few months of Jesus' life and to publish it as the Gospel of Mark. In the next decade, two more elaborate Gospels, Matthew and Luke, were written using Mark's as a base.

The Gospel that differs most from the others in terms of content, chronology, and message is the Gospel of John. This work supposedly was written between 90 and 100 C.E., although its date is by no means certain. The account of the early church in Jerusalem, Acts of the Apostles, was probably written by the author of Luke as a sequel to that Gospel.[27]

Other epistles by anonymous authors were probably written between 90 and 150 C.E. and make up eight books in the current New Testament. In addition to these books, there were many other epistles, Gospels, and histories written in these early centuries that were circulated and read by Christians; but they were not popular or authoritative enough to have been maintained. The exact list and number of the books of the New Testament probably remained in flux for the first centuries of the life of the church. By the fourth century, Athanasius of Alexandria placed his authority behind the twenty-seven books that make up the New Testament. Despite official endorsement of the canon, questions remained about such books as Hebrews, James, and the Revelation as late as the sixteenth century.

Early Theological Controversies

As we have noted, because early Christianity was not a highly organized body with an established creed, and because it encompassed a wide variety of members, many different beliefs were held by early Christians. In subsequent years, the church established creeds and supported an orthodox theology. Later Christians, looking back on the early believers who did not conform to the content of these creeds, referred to their predecessors as heretics.

The most famous controversy within the early church centered around the widespread and diverse group called Gnostics.[28] The term *Gnostic* has come to encompass so many beliefs and practices among early Christians that it is difficult to define it accurately. However, most authorities seem to agree that the Gnostics had in common a belief in a divine spark within all humans. This spark is immortal and came from an unknown god. Gnostics also believed that the universe as we know it is controlled by evil forces. Therefore, it was necessary for a redeemer figure to come to earth from the unknown god and provide knowledge, whereby the divine spark in humanity might be able to rejoin its maker. Some Gnostics seem to have believed that spirit was good and flesh was evil. Therefore, the Supreme God, who was pure spirit, could not have created this fleshly world; it must have been created by some secondary deity.

The major thrust of Gnosticism against orthodox Christianity was that it denied that the godly Christ could have been fully identified with the human Jesus. Many of the Gnostics said that Jesus only appeared to be human but was actually pure spirit; therefore, his life, teachings, and death and resurrection were of little consequence.[29] Gnosticism also was a syncretistic movement, taking its doctrines from late Judaism; Christianity; Greek, Persian, and Egyptian religions; Greek philosophy; and the mystery religions. Though the Gnostics were branded as heretics and their teachings condemned by the early church councils, their belief that flesh is evil and spirit divine had its long-range effects on Christianity. The church has historically placed more emphasis on the divinity of Jesus than on his humanity, and Christians have been encouraged to deny the flesh to glorify the spirit.

A representative collection of early Christian Gnostic literature was discovered at Nag Hammadi in Egypt in 1945. After many years of study, editing, and translation, the corpus of these Gnostic books is available for study in English.[30] For the first time, students of Gnosticism can rely on first-hand Gnostic materials in the pursuit of an understanding of this fascinating heresy.

Another early controversy concerned Marcionism. Marcion, son of the Bishop of Pontus, came to Rome in 140 C.E. seeking an office in the church. It is not clear that Marcion was a true Gnostic, but he shared many of their doctrines. Apparently, he believed in a dualism. He taught that there were two gods: a world god of justice, who created the world, and a god of goodness, who was the father of Jesus Christ. He taught that all humankind are by nature the children of the god of justice. Jesus came into the world to save us from that god. Marcion believed that the creator god was the deity taught in the Old Testament. Therefore, Christians should not have the Old Testament in their Bible. Because Marcion and his followers had no use for the created order, they were ascetic and refused to marry.

Although this theology attracted many followers, Marcion was excommunicated in 144 C.E. He died in 160 C.E., but his teachings continued to be popular in some circles. Even today, one still hears Christians saying that the God of the Old Testament is a God of wrath and judgment, while the God of the New Testament is a God of love.

Another controversy that sprang up in early Christianity concerned Montanism. In the middle of the second century, Montanus taught that the Holy Spirit, the third member of the Trinity (Father, Son, and Holy Spirit), was not to be stifled by dogma but was to be free to move among Christians, causing them to speak in tongues and prophesy. He also taught that the end of the world was coming soon, along with the return of Christ. Although Montanus had a zealous band of disciples, his movement had almost died out by the fourth century. Still, there have been occasional charismatic movements similar to Montanism throughout the history of the Christian church.

To counter these and other "heretical" groups, it became necessary for orthodox Christians to develop a statement of faith. The statement had to be simple enough to be memorized and used regularly; at the same time, it had to be thorough enough to combat the heresies effectively. The result was the so-called Apostles' Creed. The critical mind cannot believe that this creed was developed by Simon Peter, James, and John, although it does have the ring of early authority. The following statement of this creed comes from about 340 C.E.:

From the Source

I believe in God almighty

And in Christ Jesus, his only son, our Lord

Who was born of the Holy Spirit and the Virgin Mary

Who was crucified under Pontius Pilate and was buried

And the third day rose from the dead

Who ascended into heaven

And sitteth on the right hand of the Father

Whence he cometh to judge the living and the dead.

And in the Holy Ghost

The holy church

The remission of sins

The resurrection of the flesh

The life everlasting.[31]

Growth of the Church of Rome

In the early years of Christianity, Jerusalem exercised leadership over the church. After 70 C.E., other cities, such as Alexandria and Antioch, took over this leadership. These cities produced many of the outstanding thinkers, known as the church fathers, whose writings have influenced Christianity for all time. Each of the great cities of the Roman Empire had a bishop; the larger and more influential the city, the greater the authority of its bishop. The bishops of Alexandria, Antioch, Caesarea, and Rome were all considered to be leaders in the early church. Eventually, the bishop of the Church of Rome came to be recognized as the most important bishop of all and finally was designated Pope. There were several reasons for this ascendancy.

First, Simon Peter, whom Jesus had singled out as the rock upon which he would build his church, had become the first bishop of the Roman church and had passed on his authority to the bishops who succeeded him. Thus, the Roman church had a very strong tradition.

Second, Constantine, the first Roman emperor to support Christianity, moved his political capital from Rome to Byzantium in 330 C.E., which left the city of Rome without a strong political leader. A series of strong bishops of the Roman church filled this void and were looked on by Western rulers as being extremely important.

Third, the churches of the East were split apart by various doctrinal controversies, and no one bishop could speak for all Eastern Christians. The West, however, was relatively free from these controversies; the bishop of Rome was the spokesperson for a widely accepted orthodoxy.

Thus, through a combination of fortuitous events and able leadership, the Church of Rome came to be the dominant church in Christendom, and its bishops became the Christian Popes.

Emergence of Christianity as the Religion of the Roman Empire

Religion and Violence

During the period between 64 and 330 C.E., Christianity went through several periods of persecution and acceptance by the Roman Empire. Officially, the Empire was tolerant of all religions. However, the Christians occasionally found themselves in trouble because of their refusal to accept the official Roman gods and to worship them on state occasions. Jews also were in turmoil over this issue. In addition, the Christian sect was accused by the Romans of a variety of evils. Because Christians were often from the slave classes and often met in secret, they were accused of performing evil secret rituals that included eating human flesh and drinking human blood. They also were accused of sexual immorality.

As the number of Christians grew, as they refused to give first allegiance to the emperor, and as they occasionally refused to be members of the Roman army, opposition to them grew. Frequently, persecution was the result. Nero's persecution of Christians was local and brief. Emperor Domitian (who ruled from 81 to 96 C.E.) insisted that citizens of the Empire worship his person, and he instituted the first widespread persecution of Christians who refused to worship him. This persecution may have formed the background from which the Revelation of John was written. Early persecutions of Christians also led to the development of traditions concerning the sanctity of martyrdom that persist to this day.

In the second century C.E., quiet periods were again followed by severe persecutions. The legal status of Christians in the Empire was never secure; at any time, local officials could begin to persecute them. Widespread persecution broke out under Hadrian (emperor from 117 to 138 C.E.) and Marcus Aurelius (emperor from 161 to 180 C.E.). In this era, the old Roman Empire was falling apart from internal and external forces and the emperors frequently looked on the Christians as a threat to the unity and strength of the old Roman ways. Therefore, they persecuted Christians in hopes of restoring Rome to what it had been in the days before Christianity.

The on-again, off-again persecution of Christians reached its peak in 303 C.E. under Diocletian (emperor from 284 to 305 C.E.) in an empire-wide movement that lasted for more than ten years. This period was followed by the reign of Constantine. Constantine was not Christian but was strongly influenced by his wife and mother, who were. In 313 C.E., Constantine issued the Edict of Milan, which gave Christianity the same privileges as other religions. The official persecution of Christians was over. In 325 C.E., Constantine called the Church Council of Nicaea to stop the warring within Christian factions over the nature of Christ. Twelve years later, when he was dying, Constantine finally accepted baptism and officially became a Christian.

Several emperors who followed Constantine tried to reverse the tide and return to the old Roman religions. But with the reign of Theodosius (emperor from 379 to 395 C.E.), Christianity officially became the religion of the Roman Empire and all other religions were suppressed.

Augustine

Perhaps no other Christian after Paul and Constantine so deeply influenced the life and direction of Christianity as did Augustine (354–430 C.E.). Like many of the other leaders of the early church, he was born in North Africa. His mother was a devout Christian, but his father was pagan. Although he received Christian instruction as a child, he did not accept the faith until later in life. As a young man, he took a concubine and had a

Christmas Mass at Saint Peter's Basilica in Vatican City.
(Corbis)

child by her. For a time, he was interested in Manichaeism, a religion that was a syncretism of Christian and Zoroastrian ideas. After a few years with Manichaeism, Augustine followed the teachings of Neoplatonism, but he was not completely satisfied with this either.

In Milan, Italy, Augustine came under the influence of the Christian bishop Ambrose. In a very dramatic conversion experience, Augustine became a Christian. He returned to North Africa, where he became a writer and eventually the bishop of Hippo. Two of his writings have become classics in Christian literature: his autobiographical *Confessions* and his *City of God*, an interpretation of history written in response to those who blamed the Christians for the fall of the city of Rome to the Goths.

Augustine is also widely known for his formulations of the doctrine of original sin, the fall of man, and predestination. Taking his support from Paul's Letter to the Romans, he believed that the original man and woman had willfully chosen to sin against God and thus had passed to all future generations a sinful nature. For this reason, all humankind was incurably sinful and fallen. To Augustine, God in his infinite mercy had sent his son to die for the sins of a handful of sinners who had been predestined for salvation. All the rest of humankind was doomed to eternal damnation. Augustine was challenged in these views by the monk Pelagius, who believed that humankind was free to act as it would.

Therefore, to Pelagius and his followers, salvation was something initiated and mainly carried through by human will. Only a little help from God was needed.

Although the Pelagians were denounced by orthodox Christianity, the teachings of Augustine on predestination never really became orthodox either. It was not until the time of John Calvin, in the Protestant Reformation of the sixteenth century, that Augustine's doctrines received wider attention.

The Monastic Movement

Introduced by the early medieval church, the monastic movement became a major part of Christianity. Of all the major religions of the Western world, Christianity is the only one to encourage monastic orders. Neither Judaism nor Islam has encouraged its members to live alone apart from the evils of normal life, although there have been minor movements in both religions in that direction.

The monastic movement in Christianity did not really begin to develop until the third century C.E. To be sure, there were statements in the New Testament from both Jesus and Paul that supported some forms of celibacy, fasting, and sharing of possessions with the needy. Nevertheless, the first two and a half centuries of Christianity saw no widespread application of these teachings in the form of monasticism. The tradition of celibacy for the bishops, priests, and deacons was established in the Western churches by the end of the fourth century. The Eastern churches commanded celibacy for the bishops, but priests and deacons were allowed to marry before they were ordained.

The movement toward asceticism and monastic community life apparently began in Egypt in the middle of the third century C.E. Christians in Egypt may have been influenced by the asceticism of native Egyptian religions, or they may have been influenced by the basic distrust of the flesh taught by the Manichaeans, the Gnostics, and the Neoplatonists. Egypt itself, with its deserts and wild places, offered the ideal setting for men and women who wanted to leave the problems of normal life behind them and seek solitude in the wilderness. Some began to sell their possessions and go out into the desert regions to live simple lives dedicated to God. A number of them were widely known for their feats of asceticism. Simeon Stylites (d. 459 C.E.), for example, is said to have lived atop a pillar in the desert of Syria for thirty-six years. Others fasted for long periods, went without sleep, ate only the simplest of food, gave up bathing, and wore garments that were irritating to the skin. Still others gathered together and formed monastic communities.

The first Christian monastery is attributed to Pachomius, who was born in Egypt in the last decade of the third century. For a variety of reasons, the monastic movement soon became popular throughout Christendom.

Basically, monasteries were secluded places where people dedicated themselves to a simple life of hard manual labor, prayer, fasting, and sometimes study. What little learning and scholarship existed in the medieval period was kept alive in monasteries. Historically, some of the best minds of the church were produced by these communities. Jerome (345?–420 C.E.), who translated the Hebrew and Greek biblical material into the Latin Vulgate—the standard Bible for the Roman Catholic Church for over 1,500 years—was a product of the monastic movement. Some have suggested that the vitality and strength of the monasteries at any given time was an accurate gauge of the vitality of the entire church.

Medieval Christianity

The period between the fall of the Roman Empire and the rise of the modern European nations is usually called the medieval period or the Middle Ages. During this period, the Christian church was a major force in the total culture of Eastern and Western Europe.

Division between Eastern and Western Christianity

From the time of the establishment of the city of Constantinople as the new capital of the Roman Empire (330 C.E.), there developed a gradually widening division between the Christians of the East and those of Western Europe. This basic division was political and geographic as well as theological. When Constantine set up his capital in the East, he took an active role in the development and direction of the church and called the Council of Nicaea to settle theological differences. His successors followed his example and usually took an active part in directing religion. In the West, Rome had been left without an effective political leadership. Into this vacuum stepped the able bishops of the Roman church, who even took some of the titles of the ancient caesars. When the barbarians massed at the walls of Rome, it was the Popes who negotiated with them for the city.

The theological differences between East and West were basic. Most of the great thinkers and leaders of the early church were from North Africa and Asia Minor. Most of the early councils that established Christian doctrine were held in the East. Eastern Christians tended to be more interested in theological formulations and became bitterly divided over certain issues. Western Christians tended to be more practical and were concerned with survival in a hostile, decaying world. Eastern theologians tended to emphasize the divine nature of Christ, whereas those of the West emphasized his humanity.

Greek Orthodox priests celebrating Christmas in Bethlehem.
(Micha Bar Am/Magnum Photos, Inc.)

The largest issue dividing Eastern and Western Christians was the papacy. The great cities of the East had outstanding bishops who became known as patriarchs. Although Constantinople was the capital, its patriarch could never gain authority over the patriarchs of the other major cities. In the West, there was only Rome; and the bishop of that city clearly led the Western church. Gradually, the bishop of Rome claimed to be the leader of all Christendom, but the Eastern patriarchs refused to accept his authority.

Numerous minor differences also developed between these churches, which came to be known as Eastern Orthodox and Roman Catholic. The Eastern church used icons—two-dimensional pictures of Jesus, Mary, and the disciples—in their worship, whereas the Western church allowed statues. The East baptized infants by immersion, whereas the West allowed sprinkling. The East gave the people both bread and wine in the communion meal, whereas after the tenth century, the West gave them only bread. The East allowed its clergy the possibility of marriage before ordination, whereas the West came to insist on celibacy. The East used Greek as its language of worship, whereas the West used Latin until the mid-twentieth century.

The rift between the two branches of Christendom continued to grow during its first thousand years. Western Christians were busy repelling various barbarian invasions and building what has become Western Europe, while the East saw almost all of its empire fall into the hands of Muslim invaders in the seventh and eighth centuries. Antagonism reached a climax in 1054, when Leo IX sent delegates to Constantinople to excommunicate the Patriarch Cerularius. Even this breach might have been healed, but Christian Crusaders from European nations stopped at Constantinople in 1204 on their way to the Holy Land and sacked the city. Even today, the modern **ecumenical** movement within Christendom is still seeking a reunion between these two branches of the church.

Eastern Orthodox Christian Easter celebration in Karpathos, Greece.
(The Viesti Collection, Inc.)

The Medieval Papacy

Because of its great missionary activities and basic attractiveness, Christianity had become virtually the only religion of Western Europe by the medieval period. The thrust of the Muslim movement into Western Europe was stopped by Charles Martel at the Battle of Tours in 732. Although Spain was Muslim for another seven centuries, the rest of Western Europe was maintained as a Christian realm. The implications of this for the papacy were immense. For Europeans, there was only one Holy Catholic Church and outside it there was no salvation. This church had one head, Christ, who ruled through his vicar, Simon Peter, and his successors on the throne of the church in Rome. The line of succession from Simon Peter to the various Popes was said to be an unbroken line of authority. This power and its potential were the occasion for both excellence and abuse by the medieval Popes.

In the chaos that followed the decline of the Roman Empire, the papacy was often the only secure leadership in Europe, and the Popes of the Christian church exercised much of the same power as did temporal rulers. Indeed, they were the makers of many temporal rulers, as it was the custom of those who would be emperors of the Holy Roman Empire to be crowned by the Popes. Naturally, this power led to abuses. The papacy gathered lands, wealth, and art treasures and went to war in a manner similar to that of any other feudal fiefdom. Frequently, ecclesiastical offices were given to relatives (nepotism) or sold to the highest bidder (simony) because they carried so much potential power and wealth.

The strength of the papacy over European politics was never more clearly illustrated than in the conflict between Gregory VII (1073–1085) and Emperor Henry VI (d. 1106). The issue between them was who was to appoint German bishops, the Pope or the emperor. The emperor wished to appoint his own bishops, for obvious reasons; but when he did so, the Pope excommunicated him. To gain a reversal of this decision, the emperor crossed the Alps in the dead of winter, January 1077, and stood for three days as a barefoot penitent before the palace of the Pope. Finally, Gregory absolved him. Such was the power of the Church over the secular rulers of that time.

In terms of its moral leadership, the papacy reached its weakest point between 1309 and 1377, a period called the Babylonian Captivity of the Church. During this period, the headquarters of the papacy moved from Rome to Avignon. All of the Popes and most of the cardinals of this era were French; at times, the papacy was virtually captive to the king of France, which weakened its power and prestige with nations that were not friendly to France. This was a period of papal wealth, luxury, moral laxity, and abuse. The result was the Great Schism.

In 1378, the Avignon cardinals elected a new Pope, Urban VI, who then refused to return to Avignon with them and instead restored the papacy to Rome. The cardinals declared Urban's election void and elected another Pope, who would rule from Avignon. Thereupon, Urban selected another college of cardinals. The European nations were divided in their support of the two men who claimed to be the successor to Saint (Simon) Peter. The Council of Pisa was called in 1409 to settle the issue but instead selected a third Pope, who also claimed to be Christ's vicar on earth. The Great Schism was finally healed by the Council of Constance, which met from 1414 to 1418, and the papacy was returned to one Pope, with his capital in Rome.

Thomas Aquinas

No discussion of medieval Christianity or Christianity in general would be complete without mention of one of the greatest—if not the greatest—thinker the Church ever produced, Thomas Aquinas (d. 1274).

The tenth through fourteenth centuries in Western Europe were a time of intense intellectual activity. During this period, many of the great universities were founded and their main intellectual pursuit was theology. The writings of Plato, Aristotle, and others had been preserved from destruction by the Arab philosophers; by the late medieval period, there was enough peaceful contact between Muslim and Christian scholars to allow Christians to have access to these writings so that they could translate them into Latin. These translations gave impetus to the intellectual movement.

The issue that most concerned Christian thinkers was the relationship between faith and reason. Were Christian beliefs, which had been communicated through scripture and the Church, consistent with what people perceived to be the truth by means of their ability to reason? The most outstanding Christian scholar to address this issue was Thomas Aquinas, a Dominican monk whose entire life was given over to scholarship. He was a student of Albertus Magnus at the University of Paris. Although Aquinas was a prolific writer of hymns, commentaries, and theological studies, he is best remembered for two works. The first was Summa Contra Gentiles, a series of arguments defending the Christian faith against infidels. The second and best known of his works was Summa Theologiae, a massive systemization of the Christian faith that became the standard theological formulation for the Roman Catholic Church.

Aquinas, more than anyone else, attempted to Christianize Aristotle. To prove part of the Christian scheme, Aquinas used Aristotle's arguments (based on reason) for the existence of God. However, Aquinas believed that reason could take the Christian only so far; beyond this point, there had to be divine revelation to complete the message. Therefore, both reason and revelation were necessary for Christian belief.

The Protestant Reformation

In the sixteenth century, the Western church was torn asunder by a violent revolution from which it has never fully recovered. This revolution has been called the **Reformation**, but it went far beyond reforming Christianity; it upset it, destroyed its unified hold on Europe, challenged its authority, and disrupted it for centuries. The causes of this revolution are many, varied, and intricate. However, the major ones may be listed broadly as the rise of European nationalism, the new learning of the Renaissance, and the decline of the papacy.

Early Reform Movements

The beginning of the Protestant Reformation is usually established in 1517, when Martin Luther posted his Ninety-five Theses on the door of the church in Wittenberg, in what is now Germany; however, there were reformers and reform movements more than a century before Luther.

Religion and Violence

One of the earliest reformers was John Wycliffe of England (1320?–1384). Wycliffe was an Oxford scholar who eventually held most of the ideas that were later representative of the Protestant movement. His greatest contribution was the translation of the official Bible of the Church, the Vulgate, from Latin to English. To facilitate the reading of this Bible by the common people, Wycliffe organized a band of wandering preachers known as Lollards, who went about the country preaching and teaching.

Efforts to reform the Church met with fierce resistance. Wycliffe died peacefully in 1384 but was condemned by the Council of Constance in 1415. His remains were unearthed and burned in 1428 as an expression of this condemnation. Even though the Lollard movement was intermittently persecuted by the kings of England, it survived long after Wycliffe.

Religion and Violence

The early Reformation in Bohemia was led by John Hus (1374–1415). Rector of the University of Prague, Hus was influenced by the writings of Wycliffe. Hus denounced the evils of the current papacy and drew a large following from the citizens of Prague.

To raise money for various reasons, the medieval papacy had approved the sale of **indulgences**. For a price, a Christian could buy an indulgence that, drawing upon the treasury of good that the saints had developed, would pay for a sin committed by the living or by the dead who were in purgatory. Hus was particularly bold in denouncing this practice (that naturally led to all manner of corruption). Hus was condemned by the Council of Constance in 1415 and burned at the stake.

Early Reformation was represented in Italy by the fervent preaching of a Dominican monk, Girolamo Savonarola (1452–1498), urging personal moral reform. Savonarola, who was a preacher to the city of Florence in the 1490s, was convinced that Florence was facing troubled times because of God's judgment on the moral laxity of the city. His preaching was so convincing that the Florentines changed their lives and publicly burned their pornography and objects of amusement. The stern Savonarola soon came into conflict with loose-living Alexander VI, who excommunicated him. Eventually, Savonarola and two of his disciples were hanged and their bodies burned.

Martin Luther

Martin Luther is traditionally regarded as the founder of the Protestant Reformation.
(Lucas Cranach, Martin Luther (1483–1546). Oil on wood. The Granger Collection)

The most outstanding figure of the Reformation was Martin Luther of Saxony, in what is now Germany (1483–1546). Luther was born into the rapidly developing middle class of German society. Although he was reared in a very religious home, he had no intention of pursuing a religious vocation. After completing his Master of Arts degree, he began to study law and planned a career as a lawyer. In July 1505, however, Luther was struck down by a bolt of lightning; in terror, he vowed to become a monk. Against his father's wishes, he entered an Augustinian monastery and began his search for the salvation of his soul. Two years later, he was ordained a priest and celebrated his first mass. Still, he sought salvation through fasting, vigils, confession, and self-mortification.

Luther's skills as a scholar were noted by his superiors, and he was sent as a teacher of theology to the University of Wittenberg. There he taught, preached, and obtained his Doctorate of Theology. While at Wittenberg, he lectured on Paul's Letters to the Romans and Galatians. In both of these books, the phrase "the just shall live by faith" caught his eye and became a source of illumination to him. Luther was convinced that he, and all other humans, were unworthy of salvation, but that in return for unconditional faith God would bestow his saving grace.

Like many others, Luther began to call for moral reform within the Church. He was particularly incensed by the sale of **indulgences** by a monk named Tetzel, who promised people that as soon as their money fell into the coffer, a soul rose from purgatory. On the basis of his opposition to this sale of indulgences, Luther chose his Ninety-five Theses as grounds for debate and nailed them to the door of the castle church in Wittenberg on October 31, 1517. These theses were widely read all across Germany and created an immediate sensation. In the publications and debates that followed, Luther was led into more and more controversy with the papacy. He came to declare that every Christian was a priest who could interpret Scripture and that the Popes and the church hierarchy were not superior to the believer. He also challenged the doctrine of transubstantiation, which taught that at the mass the bread and wine literally became the body and blood of Jesus. Luther's writings on these and many other controversial issues were widely distributed using a new technology: the printing press.

Because of the controversy Luther had caused, the emperor of the Holy Roman Empire, Charles V, convened an imperial diet (court) at the city of Worms in April 1521 to try Luther. When questioned, Luther admitted that the writings under scrutiny were his, but he refused to recant or retract any of their contents. He is reported to have said, "Here I stand. I cannot do otherwise." As a result of his actions before the diet, he was placed under an imperial edict that banned the printing and sale of his books and forbade anyone to provide hospitality or shelter for him or his friends. It had been expected that Luther would suffer the same fate as that of Hus 100 years before, but the emperor was too busy with other matters. Instead, Luther was kidnapped by friends and taken to the Wartburg Castle, where he lived in disguise for almost a year. During this time, he wrote nearly a dozen books and translated the New Testament into German. Later, he translated the Old Testament; his translations of Scripture became classics in the German language.

In 1522, Luther returned to Wittenberg where he took charge of the rapidly developing Reformation. He repudiated the acts of radical reformers who wanted to destroy everything in the Christian church that was not specifically mentioned in Scripture. His own style was to remove only those things he felt were contrary to Scripture. In the following years, Luther was busy in many ways. He was, of course, organizing the Reformed Church in Germany. He was writing hymns, such as the Protestant classic, "A Mighty Fortress Is Our God." He was encouraging former priests and nuns to marry. He himself married a nun, Katherine von Bora, and became a father.

In the last years of his life, Luther grew more conservative. His writings were sometimes bitterly anti-Jewish because Jews were no more anxious to accept Lutheran Christianity than they had been to accept Catholic Christianity. He also turned against the peasants who were currently in rebellion and encouraged the nobility to slaughter them. In a time when many, if not most, reformers died violent deaths, Martin Luther died peacefully in February 1546.

The Reformation sprang up in other nations during Luther's lifetime and immediately thereafter. In Germany, the decision to be reformed or to remain Catholic lay with the prince of any particular region. If the ruler were reformed, the region became reformed; if the ruler chose to remain Catholic, the region remained Catholic. Thus, the religious orientation of Germany became a kind of patchwork. The Scandinavian nations—Sweden, Denmark, and Norway—became Lutheran during the following decades.

Ulrich Zwingli

In Switzerland, the reform movement was led by Ulrich Zwingli (1484–1531). Zwingli was a contemporary of Luther and was much influenced by his writings. At first, the Reformed Church in Switzerland was very close to the Lutheran movement. However,

Zwingli and Luther differed substantially over one central issue. Although Luther denied that the bread and wine of communion actually became the body and blood of Christ, he did believe that Christ was spiritually present in the elements. He believed that the words of Jesus at the Last Supper, "This is my body," were to be taken literally. Zwingli chose to emphasize the other words of Jesus at the Last Supper, "Do this in remembrance of me." Therefore, to the Swiss reformer, the communion meal was a memorial, a remembrance of Jesus' death. This issue prevented a union between the Swiss Protestants and the Lutherans.

John Calvin

Probably the greatest and most influential mind of the Reformation was John Calvin (1509–1564). Calvin was born in France and received a classical education at the University of Paris. By 1534, he had come under the influence of the Protestant movement and made his break with the Roman church. By the time he was twenty-six, he had turned his fine mind to theological matters and had written the massive book that became the classic of Protestant theology, *The Institutes of the Christian Religion.* This book, originally written in Latin and later translated into French, was revised four times in Calvin's lifetime. In it, he set forth his understanding of the nature of the true Christian faith before it was corrupted by Rome. He repeated many of the teachings of Augustine, stressing such ideas as the sovereignty of God, original sin, the total depravity of man, predestination, and election. Among the most important of his teachings was that God determined those who were destined for heaven and those doomed to hell prior to the time of creation.

Eventually, Calvin served as a minister in the Reformed Church of Geneva, Switzerland, and then in Strasbourg, on the French-German border. He was invited back to Geneva a second time and remained there from 1541 until his death in 1564. Although he was never more than a minister in Geneva, Calvin's influence over the life of the entire city was enormous. Despite opposition from theological and political foes, he was virtually the ruler of Geneva. He himself was given to hard work and simple living, and he impressed this upon the city. He discouraged frivolity of any kind. He encouraged commerce and industry as well as lending money at reasonable rates of interest.[32] He encouraged education and founded the University of Geneva. Under Calvin's leadership, Geneva became the home of oppressed Protestants from all over Europe.

The importance of John Calvin to the Reformed Church cannot be stressed enough. His writings set the intellectual base for much of the later Protestant theology. His concern for the rightness of labor and thrift as expressions of religion is felt 500 years later among those who have been reared in Calvinistic religion.

Other Reformation Leaders and Movements

Although the Reformation first centered on the writings and teachings of people like Luther and Calvin, and although it attracted large numbers of dissatisfied Christians throughout Europe, it soon became a fragmented movement. Within 100 years of the death of Luther, there were hundreds of denominations (and later, subdenominations) of the Reformed church. In the centuries that followed, the fragmentation continued. There were at least two major reasons for these divisions. First, Protestantism derived much of its force and early growth from nationalistic trends in sixteenth-century Western Europe. Whereas in medieval Europe one emperor was crowned by the Pope and ruled the entire European society, postmedieval Europe began to demand monarchs over each nation, without outside interference from the emperor or Rome. Therefore, when the opportunity came for leaders of European nations to express their freedom from Rome through a new version of Christianity, many were willing to take it.

Interior view of Knox Church, Otago, New Zealand. The elegance and simplicity of the design reflects the Protestant theological notion that there are no intermediaries between God and humankind.
(Mark R. Woodward)

The best example of this expression of freedom was the establishment of the Church of England. Although England had been the home of Wycliffe and had theological differences with Rome, the major reason for the Reformation in that country was political. The strong king of England, Henry VIII, wanted a wife who would bear him a son. Because his wife Catherine did not bear him one, Henry asked the Pope for an annulment so that he might remarry. When the Pope refused, Henry married Anne Boleyn, established the Church of England, and appointed Thomas Cranmer Archbishop of Canterbury in 1533. Although the ostensible cause of the breach between Rome and England was Henry's marital life, the drive toward political independence was perhaps the stronger force behind the establishment of the Church of England.

A second cause for the many divisions within Protestantism was the controversy about the "priesthood of the believer," which had been such a strong part of Luther's teachings. Many of the reformers thought that many priests, who heard confessions, administered the **sacraments,** and interpreted the Bible for the untrained parishioner—indeed, the institution of the priesthood itself—were corrupt. Therefore, these reformers taught that in the spirit of the New Testament each believer was a priest who was qualified to perform many of these tasks. The reformers were strongly in favor of the translation of the Bible into vernacular languages so that it could be read by every Christian. Obviously, if all Christians could read the Bible and were free to interpret it for themselves, differences of interpretation were bound to occur, and these ultimately caused divisions within Protestantism.

One of the most radical dissident groups was the Anabaptists. Whereas Luther and Calvin had rejected only those elements in the Catholic Church that they felt were expressly forbidden in the Bible, the Anabaptists attempted to discard all of those elements not expressly found in the New Testament. Luther and Calvin advocated infant baptism because it was not condemned by the New Testament, but the Anabaptists rejected it because they could not find such a practice in the New Testament. They therefore baptized adults who had formerly been baptized as infants—thus the nickname *Anabaptists* (those who baptize a second time). Because this movement was inherently divisive, there were many Anabaptist subgroups with a great variety of beliefs. Anabaptists have ranged from pacifists to violent revolutionaries. Many of the Anabaptist sects came to view the technological developments of the modern world as evil. Many of them do not use automobiles or other mechanized forms of transportation. Most wear plain unadorned clothing, often without zippers or buttons.

Religion and Violence

Because they were different and their numbers were small, the Anabaptists were persecuted by both Catholics and other Protestants, to the point that they were almost eliminated from the European continent. They survived in southern Germany, Britain, and America as Mennonites and Amish.

Most Amish live in rural communities and continue to farm with horses. Mennonites are more accepting of the modern world, and many are active in peace and human rights movements.

Religion and Violence

Other Reformation groups existed in nearly every European nation. Many of these were suppressed by their governments and either fled their native lands or were crushed completely. One such group was the French Huguenots. The French were deeply impressed by the teachings of John Calvin, and his Reformation encouraged many converts among the French middle class and even the aristocracy. Hostilities between the Catholic majority and the Protestant minority erupted into a series of wars between 1562 and 1594. After these wars, the Huguenots were guaranteed freedom of worship in certain specified locations by the Edict of Nantes. One hundred years later, in 1685, the Edict was formally revoked by the French crown; hundreds of thousands of Huguenots fled to other parts of Europe and America. Only a tiny minority of Protestants remained in France after the seventeenth century. The Reformation also gave rise to what are known as the "Wars of Religion" which raged across Europe until 1648. They were brought to a close with the "Peace of Westphalia" among the terms of which was that the religion of the monarch would be that of the people.

Italy, the home of both the papacy and Savonarola, never produced a Protestant Reformation of any magnitude, nor did Czechoslovakia (the home of Hus), Russia, or Spain. The Scottish Reformation was led by a Calvinist, John Knox, and became the basis of the modern Presbyterian Church.

Modern Christianity

Christianity, like all of the other major religions, has been forced to deal with the problems and challenges of the modern world. In entering the modern age, however, Christianity was first required to overcome the trauma of the Reformation.

The Catholic Counter-Reformation

Protestants were not the only ones who saw the problems within the sixteenth-century Catholic Church. Others were aware of the same grievances that motivated Luther and Calvin, but they wished to purify the Church without establishing another form of Christianity. They wanted a reformation without the attendant revolution. These individuals remained within the Roman Catholic Church and initiated the Counter-Reformation as a response to the Protestant Reformation.

Eastern European Roman Catholic pilgrims. Saint Peter's Square, Rome. *(Mark R. Woodward)*

When it became apparent that large numbers of Christians were leaving the Catholic Church and following the reformers, the Catholic Church responded, in 1545, by convening the Council of Trent. Some who came to the Council wanted to achieve reforms that would bring reconciliation with the Protestants. Others wished to delineate the Catholic position so clearly that there would be no grounds for reconciliation. Generally, the decisions of Trent favored those who preferred the second path. To counter the Protestant emphasis on Scripture as the sole word of God, the Council declared that Catholic tradition was co-equal with Scripture as a source of truth for Christians. Therefore, when Protestants pointed to a Catholic practice that was contrary to Scripture, the Catholics replied that the Church had written Scripture and therefore its traditions were at least equal if not superior.

As a response to such Protestants as Wycliffe and Luther, who insisted on translating Scripture into the vernacular, the Council of Trent stated that the *Latin Vulgate* was to be the true sacred canon of the Church. This also ran counter to the belief of reformers who had chosen to exclude certain Old Testament books not found in the Jewish Scripture. The council further declared that only the Roman Catholic Church had the right to interpret Scripture. This too flew in the face of the Protestant doctrine of the "priesthood of the believer."

Whereas most reformed churches had rejected all of the sacraments except baptism and communion, the Council of Trent reaffirmed the traditional seven sacraments:

1. *Baptism.* Baptism of infants is necessary to wash away the taint of original sin. Any infant who dies without the benefit of baptism is technically destined for hell. Later, however, it became popular to say that the unbaptized infant was to spend eternity in a land called limbo.
2. *Confirmation.* At some point before maturity, usually at about age thirteen, children must be confirmed as an extension of their baptism.
3. *Penance.* Christians must confess their sins regularly in private to priests and receive absolution. Absolution, or forgiveness, may be conditioned upon acts of penance ordered by the priest, depending on the seriousness of the sin confessed.
4. *Eucharist.* This sacrament is known throughout the Christian world as the Lord's Supper or communion. The Council of Trent not only reaffirmed this sacrament but also gave renewed support to the doctrine of transubstantiation. According to this doctrine, the bread and wine literally become the body and blood of Jesus during the mass. The Council held that because the whole Christ was present in both the bread and the wine, it was not necessary to give the wine to the laity.[33]
5. *Extreme Unction.* As a Catholic nears death, he or she is to be visited by a priest and anointed with healing oil. The priest then hears the last confession. In receiving these last rites, the Catholic is properly prepared to die.[34]
6. *Marriage.* Perhaps as early as the eleventh century, the marriage of Christians had come to be regarded as a sacrament.
7. *Holy Orders.* For Christians who choose a religious vocation instead of marriage, taking the holy orders is considered a sacrament.

The Council of Trent also strongly supported relics, the veneration of saints, and sacred images—all contrary to most Protestant teaching. As a positive response to the challenge of

Luther and others, the sale of indulgences was controlled and other abuses of the medieval church were corrected.

Another result of the Catholic Counter-Reformation was the development of the Society of Jesus (Jesuits). The founder of the Society was Ignatius Loyola (1491–1556), a Spanish nobleman whose first career was the military. Loyola was wounded in battle in 1521. During his convalescence, he read about the life of Christ and the various saints and was so moved by this literature that upon recovery he spent time in a monastery; took the vows of poverty, chastity, and obedience; hung up his armor in the chapel of the Virgin Mary; and dedicated himself to becoming a soldier of Christ. In the following years, Loyola developed the Spiritual Exercises, designed as an agency for examining the conscience and as a guide for meditation. These exercises were usually given under the direction of a spiritual leader and required about four weeks.

A nineteenth century Christian grave in a rural area of the South Island of New Zealand.
(Mark R. Woodward)

Realizing his need for education, Loyola went back to school and eventually studied theology at the University of Paris. He gathered around him other scholars to whom he introduced the Spiritual Exercises. Among these early converts was Francis Xavier (1506–1552), who was to become a Christian missionary to India, Malaysia, and Japan. Loyola and his friends went to Rome; in 1540, the Pope gave them permission to found a new order, the Society of Jesus. This order was characterized by its absolute obedience to the Pope and to the general of the order, its scholarship, and its missionary activities. Scholarship was stressed because Loyola and his early followers were university students. Before Loyola died (in 1556), he saw his order grow from just a few friends to over 1,000 members. Although it evoked fear and suspicion among both Protestants and other Catholics, the Jesuit order continued to grow and attracted some of the ablest young men in Catholic Europe.

Catholic Dogmas since the Counter-Reformation

The heart of the modern Catholic Church was established by the end of the sixteenth century. Between that time and the Second Vatican Council, called in 1959, there were no sweeping changes in Catholic theology. A series of dogmas were established by the Church during this period, but many of them had been widely held for centuries. Their establishment as dogmas merely gave them the official seal of approval. The following dogmas have been accepted as major doctrines since the Council of Trent.

1. *The Immaculate Conception of Mary.* It had long been held among Catholics that Mary, the mother of Jesus, not only had conceived as a virgin but had been born without the taint of original sin. In 1854, Pius IX formally declared the Immaculate Conception to be a dogma that should be believed by all faithful Catholics.
2. *The dogma of papal infallibility.* After the Council of Trent closed in 1563, the Roman Catholic Church called no general council until the Vatican Council of 1869. This council dealt with the sensitive issue of papal infallibility. After much debate and controversy, the Council declared as dogma that the Pope was infallible when he spoke *ex cathedra;* that is, as the pastor of all Christians on the issues of faith and morals. Naturally, this dogma widened the gap between Catholics, on the one hand, and Eastern Orthodox and Protestant groups, on the other hand.
3. *The dogma of the bodily assumption of Mary.* In 1950, Pius XII declared as dogma the bodily assumption of Mary. This meant that Mary did not suffer decay in a tomb but was taken directly into heaven after her death.

A Roman Catholic "folk" shrine nearl Globe, Arizona, United States.
(Mark R. Woodward)

Vatican II

Upon the death of Pius XII in 1958, John XXIII became Pope. John was determined to revitalize the Church and bring it into line with the twentieth century. Therefore, he called the Second Vatican Council, which was to be the most revolutionary council since Trent. Invited to the Council were representatives of Eastern Orthodox and Protestant Christian groups acting as observers to the proceedings. Meeting between 1962 and 1965, the Council effected some of the most sweeping changes ever made in the Roman Catholic Church. Non-Catholics were recognized as true Christians, the vernacular was allowed in many parts of the mass, the Index of Prohibited Books was abolished, more congregational participation in worship was encouraged, and the Church officially declared that Jews were no longer to be held responsible for the death of Jesus. There also was an outreach toward dialogue with non-Christian religions. In general, the Second Vatican Council attempted to bring the Church up to date and took several steps toward reconciliation with Orthodox and Protestant groups.

Modern Movements
Modern Protestant Movements

Because of the reasons already discussed, Protestantism has been, until the recent ecumenical movement, a denominational movement. Two Protestants might believe essentially the same doctrines but might differ on baptism or church government and belong to different denominations.

There are so many Protestant denominations that not even the most exhaustive text on the history of Christianity could hope to cover them all effectively. Basically, however, there are four branches of Protestantism: the Lutherans, who are generally found in the Germanic and Scandinavian nations and among immigrants from those nations; the Reformed and Presbyterian denominations, which sprang from the teachings of John Calvin; the Anabaptists, a third branch that sprang from the radical Reformers (this group includes the Baptists, the Mennonites, and the Amish—although the lines of descent are not clear, Anabaptist influence is also apparent in several other Protestant groups, such as the Religious Society of Friends (Quakers) and the Disciples of Christ; and the Church of England (and its daughter churches, the Anglican Communion) and the Methodists.

We have already considered all of these groups except the Methodists. Methodism began in the eighteenth century as a response to the emotional coolness of the Church of England and the plight of urban dwellers during the early industrial revolution. The founder of Methodism was John Wesley (1703–1791). The fifteenth child in the family of an Anglican clergyman, Wesley attended Oxford and was ordained as an Anglican priest in 1728. While at Oxford, he and his brother Charles organized a small group for the purpose of religious support. The group was first called the Holy Club, but because of its disciplined ways it was nicknamed the Methodists.

Protestant Christian prayer service in Tulsa, Oklahoma, United States.
(Corbis)

In 1735, John and Charles were sent to Georgia as missionaries; on the voyage to America, they encountered another Protestant group called the Moravians, who spoke to them of religious conversion. The Wesley brothers experienced this conversion in 1738 in London. They began to preach about their experience, first in the churches and to religious societies and later in the fields and town squares. They were joined by an eloquent and fiery preacher, George Whitefield. Their emotional sermons appealed mainly to the lower and middle classes, and soon they had a large Methodist following. John organized the Methodists into societies formed into circuits and attended by preachers who traveled from society to society. Charles became the hymn writer and contributed hundreds of songs that are still treasured by many Protestants.

Although John Wesley had no desire to separate himself from the Church of England and form a new denomination, the break between the two groups was obvious by the time he died. At the end of the eighteenth century there were over 70,000 Methodists in England, but the denomination's greatest growth came among the colonists in America. The Methodist meeting and its circuit rider were a familiar part of the American frontier; Methodism became one of the largest Protestant denominations in the United States, second only to the various Baptist groups.

The squalor, poverty, despair, and alcoholism of industrial society produced other Protestant movements. In nineteenth-century England, William Booth founded the Salvation Army in an attempt not only to save the souls of the ragged edges of humanity in the slums of industrialized cities, but also to provide food, clothing, and warmth for their bodies. In 1844, a similar concern for the total person produced the Young Men's Christian Association (YMCA) in London.

A concern for the ignorance of slum children caused Robert Raikes to organize the first Sunday school in Gloucester, England, in 1780. Raikes's first objective was to teach the children to read the Bible. Since then, the Sunday school has become almost universally accepted by Protestant denominations as an agency of religious instruction.

The Missionary Movement

Mother Teresa, founder of the Missionaries of Charity, a Roman Catholic order devoted to aiding the poorest of the poor.
(UN/DPI PHOTO)

Christians have been missionaries since the earliest days. The great theologian of the early church, Paul, was a far-traveling, zealous missionary. There is a strong tradition that Thomas, the doubting disciple of Jesus, spread the Christian Gospel in India. We have already spoken of Catholic missionaries, such as Francis Xavier who preached Christianity in Japan. Catholic missionaries accompanied Spanish explorers in the sixteenth century. The Wesleys served as Anglican missionaries in America. Still, Protestant groups, especially those that had been influenced by John Calvin, were slow to enter the mission fields. They were probably impeded by Calvin's doctrine of predestination, which taught that the sovereign God would save only those persons whom he chose to save and it was therefore folly to send missionaries to the heathens. If God wished to save them, they would be saved without the help of missionaries; if God did not wish to save them, it was a waste of time and money for anyone else to try. By the nineteenth century, however, this attitude had changed except among the sternest Calvinists; most Protestant groups came to support some form of mission work.

Religion and Violence

Occasionally this missionary activity was directed at the Roman Catholic population in such areas as Latin America, but generally it was carried on in non-Christian areas in Africa, Asia, and the Pacific islands. The rising nationalism among many nations in these areas in recent years has sparked resistance to missionary activities in many places. In some instances there have been calls for the execution of both missionaries and converts. Even local missionaries are often and violently harassed. Missionary efforts can lead to political controversy and conflict. Christian missions are illegal in many Islamic countries. Missionaries are often assaulted by Hindu fundamentalists in India and Buddhist nationalists in Burma. There are, however, still many active missionary organizations working in Asia, Africa, and Latin America. The collapse of the Soviet Union created new opportunities for missionaries to work in areas in which Christianity and most other religions were suppressed during the period of communist rule.

The Ecumenical Movement

The most outstanding movement among Christians in the twentieth century was the ecumenical movement. As we have noted, Christianity has long been divided into two main branches, Eastern and Western; since the sixteenth century, the Western church has been divided into Protestant and Catholic. In the twentieth century, Christians began the long, hard journey toward reunion. The Roman Catholic contribution to this journey was the Second Vatican Council. There were also attempts to reconcile theological differences dividing Protestant denominations.

The most visible attempt at reunion was the formation of the World Council of Churches in Amsterdam in 1948. This organization has been supported by many Protestant denominations and some representatives of Eastern Orthodoxy. Although the World Council is organized to promote church unity, little actual unification has been produced. In fact, there are few concrete examples of reunion within Christendom. One has been the uniting of a small number of Protestant denominations that had no great theological differences. Other more dramatic unions stemmed from the pressing needs of the mission fields in nations like India, where factions within Christianity had weakened its case for conversions.

Still, the reunification of Christianity is a long way off. Eastern Orthodoxy maintains aloofness toward the Western church. The post-Vatican II Roman Catholic Church is more open to non-Catholic Christians than ever before, but the Protestant-Catholic dialogue, although progressing, still has many hurdles to clear. Protestants, as always, are vastly divided. Although some are anxious for church union and willing to pay almost any price for it, the majority apparently still prefer to go it alone.

The Christian Calendar and Holy Days

At its beginning, the Christian church was a part of Judaism and followed its calendar of holy days and festivals. As the separation between the two religions grew, Christianity began to develop its own unique calendar. Some of Christianity's holidays, such as Easter and the Pentecost, were celebrated early in the life of the church. Others, such as Christmas, developed several centuries later.

As Christianity divided into Eastern and Western branches, these branches developed different sacred calendars. In the Western church, Christmas is celebrated on December 25, whereas many of the Eastern Orthodox churches keep this holiday in January. The calendars for Easter also vary within Christianity. At various times in history, some branches of Christianity, such as the English Puritans, have refused to celebrate Christmas or other major festivals at all because they considered the practice to be essentially pagan. In general, Christians today celebrate the following major holidays.

Sunday

The earliest Christians apparently continued to worship on Saturday, the Jewish Sabbath. By the late '50s, however, references to offerings on the "first day of the week," Sunday, began to appear in the writings of Paul. It is believed that early Christians chose to worship on this day in memory of the Resurrection of Jesus. With rare exceptions, Christians keep Sunday as a day of rest and worship. Some even refer to it as "Sabbath."

Advent, Christmas, and Epiphany

The Christian year begins with the season of Advent, the four weeks before Christmas. During this period, Christians read from the Old Testament, the Prophets, and seek to prepare themselves for the coming of Christmas.

Christmas, which marks the birth of Jesus, is celebrated in Western Christianity on December 25 and in January by Eastern Orthodox Christians. Although Christmas was one of the last major holidays to be accepted, it has become the best known of all Christian celebrations. Even Japan, with less than 3 percent of its population Christian, celebrates Christmas. The season is kept by giving and receiving gifts and by participating in family gatherings, special worship services, and feasts.

Twelve days after Christmas (on January 6), Western Christians celebrate Epiphany to remember the wise men who came to Bethlehem to find the infant Jesus.

Easter

The oldest and most widely accepted holiday in the Christian calendar is Easter. The date for Easter is established each year according to a lunar calendar and may vary by a number of weeks from year to year. Generally, Easter is connected to the vernal equinox.

Forty days before Easter, Christians observe Ash Wednesday. On this day, it is traditional to begin the season leading to Easter with a somber reminder of the burden of sin. Some Christians receive a mark of ashes on their foreheads at special Ash Wednesday services. For the next forty days, Christians observe the season of Lent. During this period, it has been customary for some to abstain from a certain food or habit or to fast on certain days to be more aware of the need for repentance.

The Lenten season closes with Holy Week. The first day of this week is known as Palm Sunday, when Christians commemorate Jesus' triumphal entry into Jerusalem. On Thursday of this week, Christians observe Maundy Thursday. This is traditionally the day of Jesus' last supper with his disciples. Some Christian communities partake of the communion meal, and some practice the ritual of foot washing on this night. The next day is known as Good Friday. On this day, Christians remember the trial, execution, and burial of Jesus. Special services are held to recount Jesus' last words from the cross.

The Sunday following Good Friday is designated as Easter. On this day, Christians remember the Resurrection of Jesus. It is a time of joyous celebration. The early church used Easter as a time to receive its new members with baptism and new robes. The tradition of new clothing has continued in many modern Christian communities. It also is a time of family gatherings and special meals.

Forty days after Easter is Ascension Day, when Christians remember that Christ ascended into heaven after having spent time with his disciples following the Resurrection.

Pentecost

Another of the most ancient of Christian holy days is the Pentecost. The word *Pentecost* was the Greek name for the Jewish festival of Shavuot. It was established fifty days after Passover and commemorated the giving of the law on Mt. Sinai after the Exodus. According to the Book of Acts, this day came fifty days after Jesus' Resurrection: The Holy Spirit came upon the disciples gathered in Jerusalem and sent them into the streets to preach their new faith. Many modern Christians regard the Pentecost to be the birthday of the church and celebrate it with great joy.

Throughout the year, various Christian communities have other celebrations. Some observe the special days of certain saints. Many Christians recognize the first of November as All Saints' Day, in which all of the recently deceased are remembered and honored.

Christianity Today

Christianity is the world's largest religion and is spread over a wider area than any other. It is estimated that there are nearly 34,000 Christian denominations. Because there are so many denominations it is almost impossible to generalize about the church as a whole. It is possible to speak only in the most general terms and to rely on examples or case studies to illustrate general trends.

Despite the ecumenical movement, Christianity is divided by East and West. Branches of Orthodox Christianity, each associated with a particular national or language group, continue to predominate in parts of Eastern Europe, the Middle East, and Northeast Africa. In parts of Eastern Europe there is serious conflict between Orthodox Churches and Uniate Catholics who use Orthodox style liturgies but accept the authority of Rome. The Western Church is divided into Catholic and Protestant communities. Largely because of Luther's teaching of the priesthood of all believers and the translation of the Bible into many languages, the number of Protestant denominations continues to expand rapidly.

At the beginning of the twenty-first century, the Christian community presents many faces. In Europe, even with its system of state churches, Christianity is in decline as the influence of secularism continues to grow. In some European countries church attendance is as low as 2 percent. In the United States, with its vast number of denominations, attendance remains remarkably high. The Roman Catholic Church remains healthy, but has serious difficulty finding enough priests and nuns to serve the lay community. Some Catholic orders recruit priests and nuns abroad. Others encourage vocations with "pop up" advertisements on the Internet.

One of the most popular and controversial issues in modern Christianity is Liberation Theology, which grew out of the needs of the poor of Latin America and tends to view religion in revolutionary terms. Liberation Theology is based in part on portions of the Gospels and Acts that mention social justice and economic equality as basic teachings of Jesus and the early Christian community.[35] It purports to read the Bible through the eyes of the poor and the oppressed and to apply its message to contemporary problems. Its adherents believe that the proper role for Christianity is political identification with the struggles of the poor. The opponents of Liberation Theology see it as being very close to Marxist doctrine. Liberation Theology has been expressed mainly by Roman Catholic clergy, but it also has Protestant supporters.

Fundamentalism is also a powerful force in contemporary Christianity. Christian fundamentalism began at the end of the nineteenth century as an attempt to defend the teaching of biblical inerrancy against modern scientific and philosophical thought.[36] Fundamentalists believe that the Bible must be read as a historical and scientific text, as well as a moral and religious text. Consequently, they have opposed the teaching of evolution and historical criticism of the Old and New Testaments. In recent years they have turned their attention to combating liberalizing trends in American culture, including legalized abortion, feminism, and the push for legal protection for homosexuals, because they believe that these trends conflict with biblical morality. In the days following the attacks of September 11, 2001, some American fundamentalists became embroiled in controversy when they described terrorist attacks as divine retribution for American immorality.

The most growth in Christianity in the United States in recent years has been among the ranks of **evangelical** Protestant groups and "New Christianities," especially the Church of Jesus Christ of Latter Day Saints, or Mormons, as they are often called.

Evangelicals have mastered the techniques of modern mass communication. Evangelical "mega-churches" have thousands of members and offer a wide array of social services from "job banks" to child care, counseling, and even dating services, in addition to preaching the Gospel. They appeal to urban and suburban Americans who live in an increasingly complex and often alienating environment. Many of the more traditional or "Mainline" Protestant denominations are struggling to maintain their memberships, in part because they have not focused enough on the changing social and religious needs of modern Americans.[37]

The Church of Jesus Christ of Latter Day Saints, also known as the Mormons, was founded by Joseph Smith following a series of visions in which he received spiritual instruction from God the Father; Jesus Christ; John the Baptist; the Apostles Peter, James, and John; and an angel known to Church members as Moroni. The angel informed him of the location of a set of gold tablets and bestowed on him the ability to translate them. This is the Book of Mormon, which recounts the history and teaching of the Nephite prophets. The Church teaches that the Nephites were a branch of the Israelites who migrated to the Americas. Its mission is to restore what is held to be the original Christianity. Smith continued to receive revelations concerning doctrinal and ritual matters. These were recorded in *Doctrines and Covenants*. A third Mormon scripture is *Pearl of Great Price*, an inspired translation of an Egyptian papyri.

Mormons are proud to call themselves Christians and at the same time their beliefs and teachings differ substantially from those of other Christian communities. Among the most important teachings of the Church are:

- Our Father in Heaven and Our Mother in Heaven are physical beings. They have spirit children who are subsequently born on earth in human form.
- Marriage is eternal if "sealed" in a Mormon Temple ceremony.
- The afterlife is a transformative process through which humans can ultimately become divine.
- Between the time of his crucifixion and resurrection Jesus preached in the Americas.
- The Church is led by prophets who continue to receive revelations for God.

Religion and Violence

Because of these teachings and of the practice of polygamy, Mormons were severely persecuted. They were driven from Ohio, Missouri, and Illinois before settling in Utah in 1847.[38]

Despite persecution and the hostility of many other Christian denominations, the Church has experienced phenomenal growth. Mormons are enthusiastic missionaries. Young men are expected to devote two years to mission activities. The result has been enormous growth of Church members. In 1900 there were approximately 240,000 Mormons worldwide; today the number is more than 11,000,000. In the late 1990s conversion was responsible for more than 80 percent of annual growth in Church membership.[39]

Although Christianity may be declining in Europe and remaining stable in the United States, it is one of the most rapidly growing religions in other parts of the world. In Africa, Christians are now more numerous than Muslims. In South Korea, which is traditionally Buddhist and Confucian, Christianity is also growing at the rate of 10 percent per year. Most of this growth does not seem to be attributed to the missions of Western Christians but is rather a grassroots movement. The last decade of the twentieth century may be remembered as being one of the great eras of the growth of Christianity. Particularly in Africa, the growth of Christianity has fostered the development of new denominations that use elements of local culture and symbolism to convey a Christian message. In the past, during the period of Western colonization, Christianity was strongly associated with Western cultures. Missionaries were frequently agents of cultural as well as religious change. The end of colonialism has meant that Africans and others formerly subject to colonial rule have come to control their religious destinies. Among the results are Christian theologies and modes of worship that differ sharply from those of Euro-American denominations.

The same trends can be seen in portions of Asia where churches have come under local control.

Religion and Violence

The Naga of Northeast India and Burma are an important example. They formerly practiced a basic religion in which animal sacrifice, ancestor veneration, and head-hunting—which was understood as a way to steal other people's ancestors—were key elements. Since the mid-1870s almost all of them have become American Baptists. Evangelism is a very important part of Naga Christianity. Many proudly use the expression, "We used to be hunters of heads and now we are gatherers of souls" as a motto. They have announced plans to organize an army of 10,000 missionaries to evangelize all of India. Hindu fundamentalists find this to be a disturbing development and have condemned it as an example of "Christian terrorism." The Naga describe themselves as "Baptist Nationalists."

STUDY QUESTIONS

1. Discuss Christianity as a product of first-century Judaism and the Graeco-Roman world.
2. In what sense did Jesus fulfill the role of Jewish messiah? In what sense did he not fulfill this role?
3. According to the New Testament, what were the two basic rituals of early Christianity?
4. In the production of the New Testament, which section was likely to have been written first? When were the Gospels written?
5. Discuss the importance of Constantine to the survival of Christianity. Why is Asoka called "the Constantine of Buddhism"?
6. What are the major differences between Eastern Orthodox and Western Christianity?
7. List several causes of the Reformation.
8. List the seven sacraments of the Roman Catholic Church as defined by the Council of Trent.
9. Discuss Vatican II and relate its actions to the ecumenical movement.
10. Compare Liberation Theology and fundamentalism as modern Christian movements.

SUGGESTED READING

Brown, Robert McAfee. *The Spirit of Protestantism*. New York: Oxford University Press, 1965.

Carmody, Denise Lardner, and John Tully Carmody. *Roman Catholicism: An Introduction*. New York: Macmillan, 1990.

Eco, Umberto. *In the Name of the Rose*. New York: Every Mans Library, 2006

Filson, Floyd V. *Opening the New Testament*. Philadelphia: Westminster Press, 1952.

Hefner, Robert. *Conversion to Christianity. Historical and Anthropological Perspectives on a Great Transformation*. Berkeley: University of California Press, 1993.

Lawrence, Bruce. *Defenders of God, The Fundamentalist Revolt Against the Modern World*. San Francisco: HarperCollins, 1989.

Linberg, Carter. *The European Reformations*. Oxford: Blackwell, 1999.

Reynolds, Stephen. *The Christian Religious Tradition*. Encino, CA: Dickenson, 1977.

Vermes, Geza. *Jesus the Jew*. London: Fontana, 1976.

Walker, Williston, et al. *A History of the Christian Church*, 4th ed. New York: Charles Scribner's Sons, 1985.

SOURCE MATERIAL

Selections from the New Testament

The following selections from the New Testament illustrate some of the key issues and themes of early Christianity. Matthew 5, 6, and 7 contain Jesus' Sermon on the Mount. In this sermon, one finds many of the distinctive Christian materials, such as the Beatitudes (Matthew 5:3–12) and the Lord's Prayer (Matthew 6:9–13). Romans 3 is selected as one of the bases for the Christian understanding of human sinfulness. I Corinthians 13 is perhaps the most beautiful passage from the New Testament as it describes human and divine love. I Corinthians 15 is one of the best statements of early Christian understanding of the Resurrection. Finally, Revelations 20–22 is the clearest statement of Christian eschatology.[40]

Sermon on the Mount

MATTHEW 5–7

5 Seeing the crowds, he went up on the mountain, and when he sat down his disciples came to him. [2]And he opened his mouth and taught them, saying:

[3]"Blessed are the poor in spirit, for theirs is the kingdom of heaven.

[4]"Blessed are those who mourn, for they shall be comforted.

[5]"Blessed are the meek, for they shall inherit the earth.

[6]"Blessed are those who hunger and thirst for righteousness, for they shall be satisfied.

[7]"Blessed are the merciful, for they shall obtain mercy.

[8]"Blessed are the pure in heart, for they shall see God.

[9]"Blessed are the peacemakers, for they shall be called sons of God.

[10]"Blessed are those who are persecuted for righteousness' sake, for theirs is the kingdom of heaven.

[11]"Blessed are you when men revile you and persecute you and utter all kinds of evil against you falsely on my account.

[12]"Rejoice and be glad, for your reward is great in heaven, for so men persecuted the prophets who were before you.

[13]"You are the salt of the earth; but if salt has lost its taste, how shall its saltiness be restored? It is no longer good for anything except to be thrown out and trodden under foot by men.

[14]"You are the light of the world. A city set on a hill cannot be hid. [15]Nor do men light a lamp and put it under a bushel, but on a stand, and it gives light to all in the house. [16]Let your light so shine before men, that they may see your good works and give glory to your Father who is in heaven.

[17]"Think not that I have come to abolish the law and the prophets; I have come not to abolish them but to fulfill them. [18]For truly, I say to you, till heaven and earth pass away, not an iota, not a dot, will pass from the law until all is accomplished. [19]Whoever then relaxes one of the least of these commandments and teaches men so, shall be called least in the kingdom of heaven; but he who does them and teaches them shall be called great in the kingdom of heaven.

[20]For I tell you, unless your righteousness exceeds that of the scribes and Pharisees, you will never enter the kingdom of heaven.

21"You have heard that it was said to the men of old, 'You shall not kill; and whoever kills shall be liable to judgment.' 22But I say to you that every one who is angry with his brother shall be liable to judgment; whoever insults his brother shall be liable to the council, and whoever says, 'You fool!' shall be liable to the hell of fire. 23So if you are offering your gift at the altar, and there remember that your brother has something against you, 24leave your gift there before the altar and go; first be reconciled to your brother, and then come and offer your gift. 25Make friends quickly with your accuser, while you are going with him to court, lest your accuser hand you over to the judge, and the judge to the guard, and you be put in prison; 26truly I say to you, you will never get out till you have paid the last penny.

27"You have heard that it was said, 'You shall not commit adultery.' 28But I say to you that every one who looks at a woman lustfully has already committed adultery with her in his heart. 29If your right eye causes you to sin, pluck it out and throw it away; it is better that you lost one of your members than that your whole body be thrown into hell. 30And if your right hand causes you to sin, cut it off and throw it away; it is better that you lost one of your members than that your whole body go into hell.

31"It also was said, 'Whoever divorces his wife, let him give her a certificate of divorce.' 32But I say to you that every one who divorces his wife, except on the ground of unchastity, makes her an adulteress; and whoever marries a divorced woman commits adultery.

33"Again you heard that it was said to the men of old, 'You shall not swear falsely, but shall perform to the Lord what you have sworn.' 34But I say to you, Do not swear at all, either by heaven, for it is the throne of God, 35or by the earth, for it is his footstool, or by Jerusalem, for it is the city of the great King. 36And do not swear by your head, for you cannot make one hair white or black. 37

38"You have heard that it was said, 'An eye for an eye and a tooth for a tooth.' 39But I say to you, Do not resist one who is evil. But if any one strikes you on the right cheek, turn to him the other also; 40and if anyone would sue you and take your coat, let him have your cloak as well; 41and if any one forces you to go one mile, go with him two miles. 42Give to him who begs from you, and do not refuse him who would borrow from you.

43"You have heard that it was said, 'You shall love your neighbor and hate your enemy.' 44But I say to you, Love your enemies and pray for those who persecute you, 45so that you may be sons of your Father who is in heaven; for he makes his sun rise on the evil and on the good, and sends rain on the just and on the unjust. 46For if you love those who love you, what reward have you? Do not even the tax collectors do the same? 47And if you salute only your brethren, what more are you doing than others? Do not even the Gentiles do the same? 48You, therefore, must be perfect, as your heavenly Father is perfect."

6 "Beware of practicing your piety before men in order to be seen by them; for then you will have no reward from your Father who is in heaven.

2"Thus, when you give alms, sound no trumpet before you, as the hypocrites do in the synagogues and in the streets, that they may be praised by men. Truly, I say to you, they have their reward.

3But when you give alms, do not let your left hand know what your right hand is doing, 4so that your alms may be in secret; and your Father who sees in secret will reward you.

[5]"And when you pray, you must not be like the hypocrites; for they love to stand and pray in the synagogues and at the street corners, that they may be seen by men. Truly, I say to you, they have their reward. [6]But when you pray, go into your room and shut the door and pray to your Father who is in secret; and your Father who sees in secret will reward you.

[7]"And in praying do not heap up empty phrases as the Gentiles do; for they think that they will be heard for their many words. [8]Do not be like them, for your Father knows what you need before you ask him. [9]Pray then like this:

Our Father who art in heaven,

Hallowed be thy name,

[10]Thy kingdom come,

Thy will be done,

On earth as it is in heaven.

[11]Give us this day our daily bread;

[12]And forgive us our debts,

As we also have forgiven our debtors;

[13]And lead us not into temptation,

But deliver us from evil.

[14]"For if you forgive men their trespasses, your heavenly Father also will forgive you; [15]but if you do not forgive men their trespasses, neither will your Father forgive your trespasses.

[16]"And when you fast, do not look dismal, like the hypocrites, for they disfigure their faces that their fasting may be seen by men. Truly, I say to you, they have their reward. [17]But when you fast, anoint your head and wash your face, [18]that your fasting may not be seen by men but by your Father who is in secret; and your Father who sees in secret will reward you.

[19]"Do not lay up for yourselves treasures on earth where moth and rust consume and where thieves break in and steal, [20]but lay up for yourselves treasures in heaven, where neither moth nor rust consumes and where thieves do not break in and steal. [21]For where your treasure is, there will your heart be also.

[22]"The eye is the lamp of the body. So, if your eye is sound, your whole body will be full of light; [23]but if your eye is not sound, your whole body will be full of darkness. If then the light in you is darkness, how great is the darkness!

[24]No one can serve two masters; for either he will hate the one and love the other, or he will be devoted to the one and despise the other. You cannot serve God and mammon.

[25]"Therefore I tell you, do not be anxious about your life, what you shall eat or what you shall drink, nor about your body, what you shall put on. Is not life more than food, and body more than clothing? [26]Look at the birds of the air; they neither sow nor reap nor gather into barns, and yet your heavenly Father feeds them. Are you not of more value than they? [27]And which of you by being anxious can add one cubit to his span of life? [28]And why are you anxious about clothing? Consider the lilies of the field,

how they grow; they neither toil nor spin; [29]yet I tell you, even Solomon in all his glory was not arrayed like one of these. [30]But if God so clothes the grass of the field, which today is alive and tomorrow is thrown into the oven, will he not much more clothe you, O men of little faith? [31]Therefore do not be anxious, saying, 'What shall we eat?' or 'What shall we drink?' or 'What shall we wear?' [32]For the Gentiles seek all these things; and your heavenly Father knows that you need them all. [33]But seek first his kingdom and his righteousness, and all these things shall be yours as well.

[34]"Therefore do not be anxious about tomorrow, for tomorrow will be anxious for itself. Let the day's own trouble be sufficient for the day."

7 "Judge not, that you be not judged. [2]For with the judgment you pronounce you will be judged, and the measure you give will be the measure you get. [3]Why do you see the speck that is in your brother's eye, but do not notice the log that is in your own eye? [4]Or how can you say to your brother, 'Let me take the speck out of your eye,' when there is the log in your own eye? [5]You hypocrite, first take the log out of your own eye, and then you will see clearly to take the speck out of your brother's eye.

[6]"Do not give dogs what is holy; and do not throw your pearls before swine, lest they trample them under foot and turn to attack you.

[7]"Ask, and it will be given you; seek, and you will find; knock, and it will be opened to you. [8]For every one who asks receives, and he who seeks finds, and to him who knocks it will be opened. [9]Or what man of you, if his son asks him for bread, will give him a stone? [10]Or if he asks for a fish, will give him a serpent? [11]If you then, who are evil, know how to give good gifts to your children, how much more will your Father who is in heaven give good things to those who ask him! [12]So whatever you wish that men would do to you, do so to them; for this is the law and the prophets.

[13]"Enter by the narrow gate; for the gate is wide and the way is easy, that leads to destruction, and those who enter by it are many. [14]For the gate is narrow and the way is hard, that leads to life, and those who find it are few.

[15]"Beware of false prophets, who come to you in sheep's clothing but inwardly are ravenous wolves. [16]You will know them by their fruits. Are grapes gathered from thorns, or figs from thistles? [17]So, every sound tree bears good fruit, but the bad tree bears evil fruit. [18]A sound tree cannot bear evil fruit, nor can a bad tree bear good fruit.[19]Every tree that does not bear good fruit is cut down and thrown into the fire. [20]Thus you will know them by their fruits.

[21]"Not every one who says to me, 'Lord, Lord,' shall enter the kingdom of heaven, but he who does the will of my Father who is in heaven. [22]On that day many will say to me, 'Lord, did we not prophesy in your name, and cast out demons in your name, and do many mighty works in your name?' [23]And then will I declare to them, 'I never knew you; depart from me, you evildoers.'

[24]"Every one then who hears these words of mine and does them will be like a wise man who built his house upon the rock; [25]and the rain fell, and the floods came, and the winds blew and beat upon that house, but it did not fall, because it had been founded on the rock. [26]And every one who hears these words of mine and does not do them will be like a foolish man who built his house upon the sand; [27]and the rain fell, and the floods came, and the winds blew and beat against that house, and it fell; and great was the fall of it."

²⁸And when Jesus finished these sayings, the crowds were astonished at his teaching, ²⁹for he taught them as one who had authority, and not as their scribes.

Romans

3 Then what advantage has the Jew? Or what is the value of circumcision? ²Much in every way. To begin with, the Jews are entrusted with the oracles of God. ³What if some were unfaithful? Does their faithlessness nullify the faithfulness of God? ⁴By no means! Let God be true though every man be false, as it is written,

"That thou mayest be justified in thy words,

and prevail when thou art judged."

⁵But if our wickedness serves to show the justice of God, what shall we say? That God is unjust to inflict wrath on us? (I speak in a human way.) ⁶By no means! For then how could God judge the world? ⁷But if through my falsehood God's truthfulness abounds to his glory, why am I still being condemned as a sinner? ⁸And why not do evil that good may come?—as some people slanderously charge us with saying. Their condemnation is just.

⁹What then? Are we Jews any better off? No, not at all; for I have already charged that all men, both Jews and Greeks, are under the power of sin, ¹⁰as it is written:
"None is righteous, no, not one;
¹¹no one understands, no one seeks for God.
¹²All have turned aside, together they have gone wrong; no one does good, not even one."
¹³"Their throat is an open grave,
they use their tongues to deceive."
"The venom of asps is under their lips."
¹⁴"Their mouth is full of curses and bitterness."
¹⁵"Their feet are swift to shed blood,
¹⁶in their paths are ruin and misery,
¹⁷and the way of peace they do not know."
¹⁸"There is no fear of God before their eyes."
¹⁹Now we know that whatever the law says it speaks to those who are under the law, so that every mouth may be stopped, and the whole world may be held accountable to God. ²⁰For no human being will be justified in his sight by works of the law, since through the law comes knowledge of sin.

²¹But now the righteousness of God has been manifested apart from law, although the law and the prophets bear witness to it, ²²the righteousness of God through faith in Jesus Christ for all who believe. For there is no distinction: ²³since all have sinned and fall short of the glory of God, ²⁴they are justified by his grace as a gift, through the redemption which is in Christ Jesus, ²⁵whom God put forward as an expiation by his blood, to be received by faith. This was to show God's righteousness, because in his divine forbearance he had passed over former sins; ²⁶it was to prove at the present time that he himself is righteous and that he justifies him who has faith in Jesus.

²⁷Then what becomes of our boasting? It is excluded. On what principle? On the principle of works? No, but on the principle of faith. ²⁸For we hold that a man is

justified by faith apart from works of law. [29]Or is God the God of Jews only? Is he not the God of Gentiles also? Yes, of Gentiles also, [30]since God is one; and he will justify the circumcised on the ground of their faith and the uncircumcised through their faith. [31]Do we then overthrow the law by this faith? By no means! On the contrary, we uphold the law.

I Corinthians

13 If I speak in the tongues of men and of angels, but have not love, I am a noisy gong or a clanging cymbal. [2]And if I have prophetic powers, and understand all mysteries and all knowledge, and if I have all faith, so as to remove mountains, but have not love, I am nothing. [3]If I give away all I have, and if I deliver my body to be burned, but have not love, I gain nothing.

[4]Love is patient and kind; love is not jealous or boastful; [5]it is not arrogant or rude. Love does not insist on its own way; it is not irritable or resentful; [6]it does not rejoice at wrong, but rejoices in the right. [7]Love bears all things, believes all things, hopes all things, endures all things.

[8]Love never ends; as for prophecies, they will pass away; as for tongues, they will cease; as for knowledge, it will pass away. [9]For our knowledge is imperfect and our prophecy is imperfect; [10]but when the perfect comes the imperfect will pass away. [11]When I was a child, I spoke like a child, I thought like a child, I reasoned like a child; when I became a man, I gave up childish ways. [12]For now we see in a mirror dimly, but then face to face. Now I know in part; then I shall understand fully, even as I have been fully understood. [13]So faith, hope, love abide, these three; but the greatest of these is love.

15 Now I would remind you, brethren, in what terms I preached to you the gospel, which you received, in which you stand, [2]by which you are saved, if you hold it fast—unless you believed in vain.

[3]For I delivered to you as of first importance what I also received, that Christ died for our sins in accordance with the scriptures, [4]that he was buried, and that he was raised on the third day in accordance with the scriptures, [5]and that he appeared to Cephas, then to the twelve. [6]Then he appeared to more than five hundred brethren at one time, most of whom are still alive, though some have fallen asleep. [7]Then he appeared to James, then to all the apostles. [8]Last of all, as to one untimely born, he appeared also to me. [9]For I am the least of the apostles, unfit to be called an apostle, because I persecuted the church of God. [10]But by the grace of God I am what I am, and his grace toward me was not in vain. On the contrary, I worked harder than any of them, though it was not I, but the grace of God which is with me. [11]Whether then it was I or they, so we preach and so you believed.

[12]Now if Christ is preached as raised from the dead, how can some of you say that there is no resurrection of the dead? [13]But if there is no resurrection of the dead, then Christ has not been raised; [14]if Christ has not been raised, then our preaching is in vain and your faith is in vain. [15]We are even found to be misrepresenting God, because we testified of God that he raised Christ, whom he did not raise if it is true that the dead are not raised. [16]For if the dead are not raised, then Christ has not been raised. [17]If Christ has not been raised, your faith is futile and you are still in your sins. [18]Then those also who have fallen asleep in Christ have perished. [19]If for this life only we have hoped in Christ, we are of all men most to be pitied.

20But in fact Christ has been raised from the dead, the first fruits of those who have fallen asleep. 21For as by a man came death, by a man has come also the resurrection of the dead. 22For as in Adam all die, so also in Christ shall all be made alive. 23But each in his own order: Christ the first fruits, then at his coming those who belong to Christ. 24Then comes the end, when he delivers the kingdom to God the Father after destroying every rule and every authority and power. 25The last enemy to be destroyed is death. 26"For God has put all things in subjection under his feet." 27But when it says, "All things are put in subjection under him," it is plain that he is expected who put all things under him. 28When all things are subjected to him, then the Son himself will also be subjected to him who put all things under him, that God may be everything to every one.

29Otherwise, what do people mean by being baptized on behalf of the dead? If the dead are not raised at all, why are people baptized on their behalf? 30Why am I in peril every hour? 31I protest, brethren, by my pride in you which I have in Christ Jesus our Lord, I die every day! 32What do I gain if, humanly speaking, I fought with beasts at Ephesus? If the dead are not raised, "Let us eat and drink, for tomorrow we die." 33Do not be deceived: "Bad company ruins good morals." 34Come to your right mind, and sin no more. For some have no knowledge of God. I say this to your shame.

35But someone will ask, "How are the dead raised? With what kind of body do they come?" 36You foolish man! What you sow does not come to life unless it dies. 37And what you sow is not the body which is to be, but a bare kernel, perhaps of wheat or of some other grain. 38But God gives it a body as he has chosen, and to each kind of seed its own body. 39For not all flesh is alike, but there is one kind for men, another for animals, another for birds, and another for fish. 40There are celestial bodies and there are terrestrial bodies; but the glory of the celestial is one, and the glory of the terrestrial is another. 41There is one glory of the sun, and another glory of the moon, and another glory of the stars; for star differs from star in glory.

42So is it with the resurrection of the dead. What is sown is perishable, what is raised is imperishable. 43It is sown in dishonor, it is raised in glory. It is sown in weakness, it is raised in power. 44It is sown a physical body, it is raised a spiritual body. If there is a physical body, there is also a spiritual body. 45Thus it is written, "The first man Adam became a living being"; the last Adam became a life-giving spirit. 46But it is not the spiritual which is first but the physical, and then the spiritual. 47The first man was from the earth, a man of dust; the second man is from heaven. 48As was the man of dust, so are those who are of the dust; and as is the man of heaven, so are those who are of heaven. 49Just as we have borne the image of the man of dust, we shall also bear the image of the man of heaven. 50I tell you this, brethren: flesh and blood cannot inherit the kingdom of God, nor does the perishable inherit the imperishable.

51Lo! I tell you a mystery. We shall not all sleep, but we shall all be changed, 52in a moment, in the twinkling of an eye, at the last trumpet. For the trumpet will sound, and the dead will be raised imperishable, and we shall be changed. 53For this perishable nature must put on the imperishable, and this mortal nature must put on immortality. 54When the perishable puts on the imperishable, and the mortal puts on immortality, then shall come to pass the saying that is written:

"Death is swallowed up in victory."

55"O death, where is thy victory?

O death, where is thy sting?"

[56]The sting of death is sin, and the power of sin is the law. [57]But thanks be to God, who gives us the victory through our Lord Jesus Christ.

[58]Therefore, my beloved brethren, be steadfast, immovable, always abounding in the work of the Lord, knowing that in the Lord your labor is not in vain.

Revelations

20 Then I saw an angel coming down from heaven, holding in his hand the key of the bottomless pit and a great chain. [2]And he seized the dragon, that ancient serpent, who is the Devil and Satan, and bound him for a thousand years, [3]and threw him into the pit, and shut it and sealed it over him, that he should deceive the nations no more, till the thousand years were ended. After that he must be loosed for a little while.

[4]Then I saw thrones, and seated on them were those to whom judgement was committed. Also I saw the souls of those who had been beheaded for their testimony to Jesus and for the word of God, and who had not worshiped the beast or its image and had not received its mark on their foreheads or their hands. They came to life, and reigned with Christ a thousand years. [5]The rest of the dead did not come to life until the thousand years were ended. This is the first resurrection! Over such the second death has no power, but they shall be priests of God and of Christ, and they shall reign with him a thousand years.

[7]And when the thousand years are ended, Satan will be loosed from his prison [8]and will come out to deceive the nations which are at the four corners of the earth, that is, Gog and Magog, to gather them for battle; their number is like the sand of the sea. [9]And they marched up over the broad earth and surrounded the camp of the saints and the beloved city; but fire came down from heaven and consumed them, [10]and the devil who had deceived them was thrown into the lake of fire and brimstone where the beast and the false prophet were, and they will be tormented day and night for ever and ever.

[11]Then I saw a great white throne and him who sat upon it; from his presence earth and sky fled away, and no place was found for them. [12]And I saw the dead, great and small, standing before the throne, and books were opened. Also another book was opened, which is the book of life. And the dead were judged by what was written in the books by what they had done. [13]And the sea gave up the dead in it, Death and Hades gave up the dead in them, and all were judged by what they had done. [14]Then Death and Hades were thrown into the lake of fire. This is the second death, the lake of fire; [15]and if any one's name was not found written in the book of life, he was thrown into the lake of fire.

The Martyrdom of Perpetua and Felicitas

For the first 300 years of its existence, Christianity underwent intermittent persecution by the Roman government. At times, and in certain places in the Empire, Christianity was tolerated. At other times, persecution was severe. Christians were a special target because they refused to offer simple sacrifices to the emperors. Therefore, they were accused of being atheists and of being unpatriotic. Many stories of martyrdom come from this era. None is more touching or telling than that of Perpetua and Felicitas.

In the late second century, Perpetua, a young woman of the nobility of Carthage, and her slave Felicitas were arrested for the crime of being Christians. The first part of the story was told by Perpetua. The account of her actual death was told by another Christian.

When Perpetua was arrested and imprisoned she had just given birth to a child. The needs of her family caused her father to beg her to give up her faith.[41]

II 1. "After a few days there prevailed a report that we should be heard. And then my father came to me from the city, worn out with anxiety. He came up to me, that he might cast me down, saying, 'Have pity my daughter, on my gray hairs. Have pity on your father, if I am worthy to be called a father by you. If with these hands I have brought you up to this flower of your age, if I have preferred you to all your brothers, do not deliver me up to the scorn of men. Have regard to your brothers, have regard to your mother and your aunt, have regard to your son, who will not be able to live after you. Lay aside your courage, and do not bring us all to destruction; for none of us will speak in freedom if you should suffer anything.' These things said my father in his affection, kissing my hands, and throwing himself at my feet; and with tears he called me not Daughter, but Lady. And I grieved over the gray hairs of my father, that he alone of all my family would not rejoice over my passion. And I comforted him, saying, 'On that scaffold whatever God wills shall happen. For know that we are not placed in our own power, but in that of God.' And he departed from me in sorrow.

2. "Another day, while we were at dinner, we were suddenly taken away to be heard, and we arrived at the town-hall. At once the rumor spread throughout the neighborhood of the public place, and an immense number of people were gathered together. We mounted the platform. The rest were interrogated, and confessed. Then they came to me, and my father immediately appeared with my boy, and withdrew me from the step, and said in a supplicating tone, 'Have pity on your babe.' And Hilarianus the procurator, who had just received the power of life and death in the place of the proconsul Minucius Timinianus, who was deceased, said, 'Spare the gray hairs of your father, spare the infancy of your boy, offer sacrifice for the well-being of the emperors.' And I replied, 'I will not do so.' Hilarianus said, 'Are you a Christian?' And I replied, 'I am a Christian.' And as my father stood there to cast me down from the faith, he was ordered by Hilarianus to be thrown down, and was beaten with rods. And my father's misfortune grieved me as if I myself had been beaten, I so grieved for his wretched old age. The procurator then delivers judgment on all of us, and condemns us to the wild beasts, and we went down cheerfully to the dungeon."

Perpetua, Felicitas, and the other Christians were to be sacrificed on the emperor's birthday. Felicitas was eight months pregnant at the time. Because it was against the law to execute a pregnant woman, Felicitas feared that she would miss martyrdom. However, she delivered her child in prison before the appointed day of execution.

VI 1. The day of their victory shone forth, and they proceeded from the prison into the amphitheater, as if to an assembly, joyous and of brilliant countenances; if perchance shrinking, it was with joy, and not with fear. Perpetua followed with placid look, and with step and gait as a matron of Christ, beloved of God; casting down the luster of her eyes from the gaze of all. Moreover, Felicitas, rejoicing that she had safely brought forth, so that she might fight with the wild beasts; from the blood and from the midwife to the gladiator, to wash after childbirth with a second baptism. And when they were brought to the gate, and were constrained to put on the clothing—the men, that of the priests of Saturn, and the women, that of those who were consecrated to Ceres—that noble-minded woman resisted even to the end with constancy. For she said, "We have come thus far of our own accord, for this reason, that our liberty might not be restrained. For this reason we have yielded our minds, that we might not do any such thing as this: we have agreed on this with you." Injustice acknowledged the justice; the tribune yielded to their being brought as simple as they were. Perpetua sang psalms, already treading under foot the head of the Egyptian; Revocatus, and Saturninus, and Saturus uttered threatenings against the gazing people about this martyrdom. When they came within sight of Hilarianus, by gesture and nod, they began to say to Hilarianus, "Thou judgest us," say they, "but God will judge thee." At this the people, exasperated, demanded that they should be tormented with scourges as they passed along the rank of the venators. And they indeed rejoiced that they should have incurred any one of their Lord's passions.

3. Moreover, for the young women the devil prepared a very fierce cow, provided especially for that purpose contrary to custom, rivaling their sex also in that of the beasts. And so, stripped and clothed with nets, they were led forth. The populace shuddered as they saw one young woman of delicate frame, and another with breasts still dropping from her recent childbirth. So, being recalled, they are unbound. Perpetua is first led in. She was tossed, and fell on her loins; and when she saw her tunic torn from her side, she drew it over her as a veil for her middle, rather mindful of her modesty than her suffering. Then she was called for again, and bound up her disheveled hair; for it was not becoming for a martyr to suffer with disheveled hair, lest she should appear to be mourning in her glory. So she rose up; and when she saw Felicitas crushed, she approached and gave her her hand, and lifted her up. And both of them stood together; and the brutality of the populace being appeased, they were recalled to the Sanavivarian gate. . . .

4. . . . And when the populace called for them into the midst, that as the sword penetrated into the body they might make their eyes partners in the murder, they rose up of their own accord, and transferred themselves whither the people wished; but first they kissed one another, that they might consummate their martyrdom with the kiss of peace. The rest indeed, immovable and in silence, received the sword-thrust; much more Saturus, who also had first ascended the ladder, and first gave up his spirit, for he also was waiting for Perpetua. But Perpetua, that she might taste some pain, being pierced between the ribs, cried out loudly, and she herself placed the wavering right hand of the youthful gladiator to her throat. Possibly such a woman could not have been slain unless she herself had willed it, because she was feared by the impure spirit.

CHAPTER 13

Islam

CHAPTER OBJECTIVES

In this chapter you will:

- Become familiar with relationships between Judaism, Christianity, and Islam.

- Learn about the life of the Prophet Muhammad.

- Come to understand the differences between Sunni and Shi'ite Islam.

- Study the growth of Islam.

- Learn about the place of Islam in the modern world.

KEY TERMS

Qur'an
Hadith
Sufism

Ramadan
Wahhabi

Ka'ba
Hajj

A Timeline of Islam			
570 C.E.	Birth of the Prophet Muhammad	680	Death of Husayn, grandson of the Prophet Muhammad, leads to split between Sunni and Shi'ite Islam
610	Muhammad receives his initial revelation		
622	*Hijrah* (immigration) of the Muslim community from Mecca to Medina	691	Construction of the Dome of the Rock in Jerusalem
630	Muhammad and the Muslim community return to Medina; rapid growth of Islam among Arabs	700–900	Emergence of Sufism
		711	Conquest of Spain
		750–1258	Abbasid Dynasty; Baghdad becomes the intellectual center of Western civilization
632	Death of the Prophet Muhammad		
633–642	Wars of Conquest; spread of Islam across the Middle East and North Africa; large-scale conversion of non-Arabs	732	Battle of Tours; halt of Muslim advance in Western Europe

(Continued)

A Timeline of Islam   (*Continued*)

922	Execution of Mansur al-Hallaj
1095–1270	The Crusades
1258	Conquest of Baghdad by the Mongols; severe persecution of Muslims
1281–1324	Life of Osman, founder of the Ottoman Empire
13th century	Transmission of Islam to Southeast Asia
1453	Constantinople renamed Istanbul following Ottoman conquest
1492	Reconquest of Spain by Christians; Muslim population expelled
1501	Shi'ite Islam becomes official religion of Persia (Iran)
16th century	Expansion of the Ottoman Empire in Arabia, North Africa, and Europe
1556	Founding of India Mughal Empire
1700	British emerge as major power in India
1744	Founding of Wahhabi Islam in Arabia
19th century	Decline of Ottoman Empire
1857	Indian Mutiny; British Christians, Indian Hindus, Muslims, and Sikhs commit atrocities in the name of religion
1882	British occupy Egypt
1918	End of Ottoman Empire; British and French occupation of much of the Middle East
Early 20th century	Emergence of nationalist movements in the Muslim world
1945–present	Growth of Islam in Europe and North America
1945–60	Muslims in colonial territories regain independence
1947	Partition of British India into India and Pakistan sparks massive outbreaks of violence among Hindus, Muslims, and Sikhs
1979	Iranian Revolution and establishment of the Islamic Republic
1990s	Growth of Islamist extremism. Taliban rule in Afghanistan; severe repression of Shi'ites, liberal Sunnis, and women
1996–2001	Taliban rule in Afghanistan
9/11/2001	Extremists attacks in the United States
2001–present	U.S. and Allied Forces occupy Afghanistan
2003–present	U.S. and Allied Forces occupy Iraq

The youngest of the world's major religions is Islam. It is also one of the largest, with more than one billion adherents. Islam is the dominant religion in many of the nations in the Middle East, Africa, and Asia. These factors make Islam one of the most interesting and important religions.

The most basic belief of Islam is that there is only one God, who is called Allah, the same God worshipped by Jews and Christians. He is the sole and sovereign ruler of the universe. Though Allah has made himself known through other prophets at other times, his final revelation was to the Prophet Muhammad in the seventh century C.E. Islam teaches that a person has just one life to live. How believers live this life determines how they will spend their eternal existence. During this one life, believers must submit to the will of Allah. Thus adherents of this religion are called Muslims (those who submit to God).[1]

Pre-Islamic Arab Religion

Islam began among the Arabian desert people in the seventh century C.E. It did not spring out of a religious vacuum. The people of this area had developed religious forms of their own and had been exposed to various other religions for centuries. Although the influence was not strong, Byzantine Christianity had been a factor in the lives of these people. Judea, the home of Christianity, was not too distant from Arabia. Such cities as Damascus, Caesarea, Antioch, and Alexandria were neighbors to Mecca and Yathrib (Medina). Christian princes ruled from these cities, and many of the early church fathers wrote and taught there.

The people of Arabia were also familiar with Judaism. Several of the desert tribes were Jewish. Although the origins of these tribes are unclear, many historians believe they were the descendants of Jews forced out of Judea when the Romans squelched rebellion in the land in 70 C.E. and again in 135. When Muhammad, the prophet of Islam, entered Medina in 622 C.E., many of the residents of that city were Jewish.

Another religion that may have influenced the formulation of Islam was Zoroastrianism. Although the effects on Islam were not as strong as on Judaism and Christianity, it is possible that Muhammad and some of his disciples were in contact with the Persian Zoroastrians.

Perhaps the major religious force from which Islam grew—and reacted against—was the native religion of the Arab people. We know very little about the basic religion of these people because the only material we have about them comes from Muslim sources, including the **Qur'an,** which naturally are critical of the earlier religion.[2] Apparently, the pre-Islamic people worshipped a variety of gods. They recognized one supreme High God, who was separate and unapproachable by human beings, whom they called Allah (literally, "the God"). The deities that received the most worship and attention were the local and tribal gods. Images of these gods were carved and cherished, and blood sacrifices were made to them. In addition to a great pantheon of the gods of heaven and earth, there were lesser divine creatures. There were angels and fairies, who were kind and helpful spirits, and there were demonic creatures, who often sought to harm humans.

Perhaps the most obvious characteristic of basic pre-Islamic religion is its *animism*. Gods and spirits were found in stones, trees, wells, and animals; these spirits had to be placated and implored for aid. The city of Mecca became a holy place because of animistic associations.[3] Mecca is located on the central western coast of Arabia and in early times lay on the major north-south caravan route. Its fame was rooted in a meteoric stone that had fallen there centuries before. The stone

The courtyard of the great mosque of Surakarta, Indonesia.
(Mark R. Woodward)

became an object of veneration to the animistic population; by the time of Muhammad, pilgrims had built an enclosure around it called the Ka'ba.

The Ka'ba gradually filled with images, relics, and paintings. One report claims that it even contained a painting of Jesus and Mary. Islamic legend says that the black stone fell from heaven during the time of Adam and Eve and that Abraham and his son Ishmael built the Ka'ba. A period of several months each year was set aside as a time of truce between warring tribes so pilgrims could travel safely to Mecca to worship at this shrine. Naturally, the black stone was an object of both pride and profit to Meccans, and there was a constant struggle among the various clans of Mecca over who would control the Ka'ba.

The Life of Muhammad

Because Islam is one of the youngest of the world's religions, the details of the life of its founder are more readily available than are those of other founders. No one seriously questions that Muhammad was a historical figure and lived in the seventh century C.E. He was born about 570 C.E. into the clan of Hashim of the tribe of Quraish, the group that controlled the Ka'ba in Mecca. His father, Abd-Allah, died before Muhammad was born, and his mother died before he was six years old. Thereafter, Muhammad was reared by his uncle, abu-Talib, chief of the Quraish tribe. Life for an orphan in those times was very difficult. There was no chance for any kind of formal education, and Islam makes much of the fact that Muhammad was illiterate. Thus the revelation of the Qur'an to him was even more miraculous.[4]

In the sixth century C.E., the merchants of Mecca controlled the trading caravans that moved between the Indian Ocean and the Mediterranean Sea. This, along with the Ka'ba, brought great wealth to the city of Mecca and allowed the young Muhammad an opportunity to work and travel with the caravans. It is likely that during these travels Muhammad had contact with representatives of the religions and cultures of the Middle East. Covering the Arabian peninsula and traveling to Byzantine cities such as Damascus, he no doubt met Christians, Jews, and perhaps Zoroastrians. Each of these religions had several things in common and must have influenced Muhammad. They all believed in one God; they all had a Scripture believed to be the word of God. Their eschatology taught that the world would one day end and that the righteous would be rewarded, while the evil would be tormented in hell. Muhammad seems to have been especially affected by eschatology, and he became concerned about the future of his people, who worshipped a multitude of gods and idols.

These years as a caravan worker also afforded Muhammad the opportunity to meet the woman who would become his wife: Khadija, the owner of a caravan. Khadija was a wealthy widow who was about forty years old when she married the twenty-five-year-old Muhammad. Although it was permissible to have more than one wife, Muhammad was married only to Khadija as long as she lived. During their marriage of twenty-five years, she bore him two sons and four daughters. The sons died in infancy; only one daughter, Fatima, survived her father. Khadija provided the wealth and love that the orphaned Muhammad had never had as a child. She became his strongest supporter and one of the first converts to Islam. Her wealth gave him the freedom to consider theological questions.

In the years following his marriage to Khadija, Muhammad began to go into the hills surrounding Mecca to ponder the fate of his people. He was especially concerned about their idolatry and the fate they would have on Judgment Day, when the world ended. During these periods of meditation, he received a visit from an angel, whom he later identified as Gabriel (who is mentioned in both the Hebrew and Christian Bibles). Tradition says that during the month of Ramadan, in a cave on Mount Hira, Gabriel brought the following command from God:

From the Source

Recite: In the Name of thy Lord who created, created Man of a blood-clot.
Recite: And thy Lord is the Most Generous,

who taught by the Pen, taught Man what he knew not.[5]

At frequent intervals during the rest of his life, Muhammad received revelations from God in this fashion. Islamic tradition teaches that inspiration came like the painful sounding of a bell and Muhammad's forehead became covered with sweat. At times, visions came to him in his sleep. Muhammad memorized the contents of these divine messages and taught them to his companions; eventually, they were committed to writing, to become the Scripture of Islam, called the Qur'an.

After a series of revelations, Muhammad became convinced that there was only one God, whom his people had called Allah and whom other religions called by other names. He also became convinced that he was the last of a series of God's prophets, who included Abraham, Moses, and Jesus, among others, that these former prophets had had only an incomplete revelation of Allah, but that he had the complete and final revelation. Thus Islam, at its very inception, did not deny the validity of other religions but rather looked upon itself as the completion of what others had begun. It is also noteworthy that Muhammad never considered himself to be anything more than a prophet. He was not divine; he died like any other person. His mission was much like that of the classical Hebrew prophet: to present the word of God to his people.

As the Prophet of Allah, Muhammad began to preach his new understanding of

Muslims at Friday prayer in front of a mosque in Mopti, Mali, in West Africa.
(UN/DPI PHOTO)

religion to the citizens of Mecca. He received little encouragement from his neighbors; indeed, there was much discouragement and open hostility. He was preaching that there was only one God, who was not to be worshipped with idols. This of course worked against the livelihood of many Meccans, who depended on pilgrims' coming to Mecca to worship idols at the Ka'ba.

Muhammad's first convert was his wife Khadija. There is debate in the traditions regarding the first male convert. It was either Ali, a cousin, or Zayd, a slave boy who had been freed by Muhammad. The third convert was a friend, abu-Bakr. In the following years, other converts joined the Muslim movement. They came mainly from the young and the poorer classes in Mecca. As opposition grew from the older, richer, established clan leaders of the city, Muhammad received protection from his uncle abu-Talib and other members of his clan, even those who were not Muslims. As the opposition and persecution became more severe, however, Muhammad finally had to urge some of his followers to leave the country.

In 615 C.E., about fifteen Muslim families fled Mecca and took refuge in the Christian kingdom of Abyssinia (Ethiopia today). The Prophet and the remainder of the Muslims stayed behind in Mecca to continue to preach and face persecution. This persecution took the form of a boycott against Muhammad and his entire clan by the rest of the Meccans, but it proved ineffective.

In 619 C.E. Muhammad suffered the loss of his two greatest benefactors, his uncle abu-Talib and his beloved Khadija. After the death of his wife, the Prophet married the first of a number of wives whom he was to have during the remainder of his life. The death of abu-Talib left him without the protection of his clan, and life became very difficult for Muslims. Muhammad tried to move out of Mecca to a nearby town but was rejected there and had to return.

Religion and Violence

One of the most significant events in the history of Islam occurred in the year 620 C.E., when a group of six men journeyed from the city of Yathrib (later renamed Medina in honor of the Prophet), located 250 miles to the north, to Mecca to confer with Muhammad. They were impressed with his honesty, his sense of justice, and the power of his personality. Yathrib was a city torn by clan warfare and internal strife. It needed an impartial judge to settle its disputes, and the delegation believed Muhammad could be that judge. The following year, twelve delegates came from Yathrib to meet the Prophet. Ten of the twelve were from Jewish tribes, some of whom believed that Muhammad might possibly be the Messiah. An invitation was extended to him to become the ruler of the city.

It was 622 C.E. before Muhammad could leave Mecca because a group of assassins had pledged to kill him, and he had to avoid them with great care. His followers slipped out a few at a time, and finally the Prophet made the journey. On 24 September 622 C.E. Muhammad arrived to be the judge of the city of Yathrib. The journey from Mecca to Yathrib is called *Hijrah* (migration), and it is the time from which Muslims have since dated their calendars. Dates are listed as A.H. (*anno hegirae*).

In Yathrib, the Muslims were established as a clan among other clans, and although Muhammad had been brought to the city as an arbitrator, his religion was by no means widely accepted. An agreement that became known as the "Medina Charter" granted political authority to Muhammad but gave freedom of religious belief and practice to members of other communities. Three of the tribes in Yathrib were Jewish. There also was a Christian community. Up to this point, Muhammad had only had to deal with the polytheists of Mecca; but in Yathrib, he met with resistance from Jewish monotheists. Eventually a division developed between the Prophet and the Jews. At first, Muhammad commanded the Muslims to pray toward Jerusalem, but with the passing of time he commanded his disciples to pray toward Mecca instead. Jerusalem remains, however, the third-holiest city in Islam, following Mecca and Medina.

Religion and Violence

In 623, Muhammad married Aishah, the daughter of his friend abu-Bakr. This also was the year of the first conflict between the Medinans, under the leadership of Muhammad, and the Meccans. The natural rivalry between these two cities was of course intensified by the *Hijrah*. At first, the conflicts were merely scattered raids against the Meccan caravans, but they later developed into full military campaigns.

Arabs did not consider it dishonorable to raid caravans during this era. Such raids gave Muslims a way not only to take vengeance against the Meccans but also to acquire money and goods. The most successful of these early encounters was the battle of Badr in 624, when the Muslims defeated the Meccans, killed up to seventy men, and took many prisoners and much booty. Tradition says that this was accomplished because the Prophet was present during the battle, praying for his troops. A victory like this was a great stimulus for the Muslims; it reinforced their loyalty to the Prophet and his cause and attracted many others to Islam. The following year brought another battle with the Meccans. In this battle, the Muslims lost more men than the Meccans, and Muhammad himself was wounded. Because the forces of Mecca had not altogether wiped out the Muslims, however, it was considered a victory for the Prophet.

Conflict between the Muslims and the Jewish tribes in the area also intensified during this period. The Jews apparently had rejected any notion that Muhammad was the Messiah and often ridiculed him publicly. At times, they supported the Meccans against the Prophet. As a result, the Jewish tribes were offered the choice of conversion or exile from the city. According to Muslim tradition, the final break occurred when Zainab, a matron from the Jewish community, invited the Prophet and his friends to dinner and fed them poisoned lamb. Although Muhammad ate only a small amount of the meat, he suffered the effects the rest of his life.

In 627, a force of 10,000 Meccans attacked Medina but withdrew after failing to take the city. Islamic historians consider this to have been a great victory for Muhammad and a major turning point in the history of the Muslim community. The following year Muhammad attempted to travel to Mecca for a pilgrimage with his followers, but the Meccans barred the way. A peace treaty was arranged, and the Muslims were allowed to make the pilgrimage the following year. By 629, Islam had grown so strong that when the Muslims entered Mecca on their pilgrimage, no one dared stop them. In 630, Muhammad conquered Mecca with a force of 10,000 men. He went to the Ka'ba and, although he respected the black stone and its enclosure, he destroyed the idols and images. With this symbolic act, the Prophet virtually became the sole leader of the Arabian people.

During the next few years, Islam grew stronger still. Qur'an reciters were sent to convert the Bedouin tribes of the Arabian desert. Muhammad sent messages to surrounding nations inviting them to join the community of Islam. His followers returned from Abyssinia to join him. He married new wives, many of whom were the widows of Muslims who had died in battle. Other marriages strengthened political ties.

In 632, Muhammad led the Muslims in another pilgrimage to Mecca. By this time, he was sixty-two years old and in poor health, having never fully recovered from the effects of the poison he had eaten a few years earlier. Upon his return to Medina, he delivered a farewell message to the Muslims and then died in the arms of his wife Aishah. Because he had made no arrangements regarding his successor, there was, for a time, confusion among Muslims regarding leadership. It was finally agreed that abu-Bakr should be the *caliph*, or successor.[6] At Muhammad's funeral, the following words, attributed to abu-Bakr, summed up the Muslim understanding of the Prophet: "O ye people, if anyone worships Muhammad, Muhammad is dead, but if anyone worships God, He is alive and dies not."[7]

The Qur'an

The Scripture of Islam is called the Qur'an. The word Qur'an literally means "reading" or "recitation," thus the title indicates the basic belief that Muslims hold about this book, that it is a recitation of an eternal Scripture, written in heaven and revealed, chapter by chapter, to Muhammad. The title may also reflect the words of the first *surah*, or chapter, to be revealed, "Recite: In the name of thy Lord who created. . . ."[8]

Perhaps no Scripture has ever been as influential to its people as the Qur'an. Surely no Scripture is read as much or committed to memory as often. Although Christians and Jews take their Bibles seriously, human, though inspired, authorship is acknowledged. Such is not the case in Islam; the Qur'an is the word of God: It is eternal, absolute, and irrevocable. The Qur'an is believed to be God's last word to humanity. Islam respects the Scriptures of the Jews and Christians, but the Qur'an is understood to be God's final message. It was literally revealed to Muhammad, who acted only as a stenographer or loudspeaker for Allah, and has been transmitted virtually unchanged since the days of the Prophet. Recitation of the Qur'an is an important ritual act and a source of Allah's blessing because it reproduces his divine speech. While the meaning of the Qur'an can be rendered into other languages, it cannot be translated. Reading or hearing it recited in a language other than Arabic does not convey the divine blessing that the Arabic original does.

The first things Muslims hear when they are born are selections from the Qur'an. Verses from it are inscribed on the walls of Muslim homes for decoration; its words are often the last a person hears before death. Among Muslims, it is considered a supreme act of piety to commit the entire Qur'an to memory. Any person who does this is given the honorific title *hafiz*.

The Qur'an is said to contain the exact words of Allah to the Prophet, from the time of the first revelation to the end of Muhammad's life. Because Muhammad was illiterate, the messages were memorized by him and passed on to Zayd, his secretary, who wrote them on leaves, stones, bones, or parchment. After Muhammad's death, these materials were collected. Tradition says that the third *caliph*, Uthman, worked with Zayd and others to develop an authorized version of the Qur'an that replaced several variations of the text.

The revelations that make up the Qur'an are organized into 114 chapters called *surahs*. The *surahs* contain approximately 6,000 verses called *ayas*. The entire text is somewhat smaller than the Christian New Testament. With the exception of a brief introductory statement, the text is arranged according to the length of the *surahs*, in descending order. Therefore, the non-Muslim reader is sometimes confused because there is no topical or chronological arrangement of the material. The revelations are a great deal like the materials one finds in the prophetic books of the Hebrew Bible, an anthology of prophetic material without regard to arrangement. The longest *surah* contains 287 verses, the shortest only three.

The Nature of God

Because the Qur'an is the word of God, its messages are the authority for all Muslims on God, how God expects people to live, and the eternal destiny of humankind. Allah is revealed as the one sovereign God over the entire universe. The religion of Islam demands strict monotheism and requires its followers to say each day, "There is no God but Allah; Muhammad is " 'the messenger of Allah' " In contrast to the polytheists of Mecca and the Byzantine Christians who were in dispute over what part Jesus played in the Godhead, Muslims state that there is only the one God, complete, eternal, and undivided. Of all the world's other religions, only Judaism insists on such absolute monotheism.

From the Source

Blessed be He
who has sent down the Salvation upon
His servant, that he may be a warner to all beings;
to whom belongs the Kingdom of the heavens
and the earth; and He has not taken

to Him a son, and He has no associate in the Kingdom[9]
Say: He is God, One,
God, the Everlasting Refuge
who has not begotten, and has not been begotten
and equal to Him is not anyone.[10]

Allah's role as an omnipresent, omniscient, and omnipotent creator of the universe is heavily emphasized in the Qur'an.

From the Source

Surely your Lord is God, who created the heavens
and the earth in six days—
then sat Himself upon the Throne,
covering the day with the night
it pursues urgently—

and the sun, and the moon, and the stars
subservient, by His command.
Verily, His are the creation and the command.
Blessed be God,
the Lord of all Being.[11]

According to Muslim tradition, Allah has ninety-nine names, such as the Holy One, the Merciful, the Compassionate, the Guardian, and the Creator. Devout Muslims repeat these names in a manner similar to that of a Roman Catholic Christian reciting the rosary.

Although Allah possesses the characteristics of power, sovereignty, and majesty, he also is characterized by justice and mercy. He will repay the evil with justice and the righteous with mercy.

From the Source

To God belongs whatsoever is in the heavens and whatsoever is in the earth, that He may recompense those who do evil for what they have done, and recompense those who have done good with the reward most fair. Those who avoid the heinous sins and indecencies, save lesser offenses—

surely thy Lord is wide in his forgiveness. Very well He knows you, when He produced you from the earth, and when you were yet unborn in your mother's wombs; therefore hold not yourselves purified; God knows very well who is the godfearing.[12]

The mercy of Allah is often emphasized in Muslim worship and practice. It is traditional for a Muslim who is giving a speech or writing to begin with the words, "In the name of God, the Merciful and Compassionate."

Though Allah is alone as the God figure in Islam, he is surrounded and aided by certain other heavenly figures. His angels act as his messengers, as did Gabriel when he revealed the Qur'an to Muhammad, and his warriors fight at the side of believers against infidels. Another creation halfway between humans and angels is called the *jinn*. The *jinn* are created of fire. Some are beneficial creatures who act as guardian angels for humankind; others are demons. The good *jinn* are believed to be Muslims, the evil ones unbelievers. The leader of the evil *jinn* is a fallen angel called Iblis.[13] Iblis acts very much like Satan in the biblical Book of Job. He is not so much a secondary god of evil as Angra Mainyu in Zoroastrianism, but he acts as a tempter and a prosecuting attorney against humankind. According to Muslim tradition, Iblis was responsible for the fall of Adam.

Predestination

In the Qur'an it is revealed that humans are the creation of Allah and must be obedient to him. Righteous persons who would win the favor of God must submit to his will. Because of this emphasis on God's power and sovereignty, the words *fatalism* and *predestination* have been used to describe Islam. Carried to its ultimate extreme as it is in some Islamic sects, Calvinism, and early Greek philosophy, the belief in an all-powerful force that rules the universe and knows all things leads one to believe that people have no choice in life. Whether one does good or evil or enjoys success or suffers failure is entirely in the hands of the God who rules the world and who has planned each event in advance. When the idea is carried to this extreme, people do not possess freedom of choice, therefore they are not responsible for their acts. God is all, and people are but his puppets.

It is inaccurate to call Islam a fatalistic religion. Perhaps the most common theological position is that humans have the ability to choose from among a set of divinely created acts. Some Muslim theologians, particularly those of the Mutazila school and many modernist thinkers, maintain that God has endowed humans with reason, through which they are able to distinguish good from evil and choose between them. The Mutazila also believe that Allah can be known through the application of reason as well as through revelation. Most Muslims do not accept the Mutazila view, although they do believe people are somehow responsible for the evil they commit and will be judged for it. Allah in his wisdom and mercy allows human beings to make choices in the areas in which they will be judged. A related view is while God ultimately decides our fates that humans have a religious obligation to vigorously exert themselves in the quest for the common good.

Eschatology

The judgment of humanity by Allah at the conclusion of time is one of the basic beliefs of Islam. The Qur'an says that when a person dies, the body returns to the earth and the soul goes into a state of sleep until resurrection day. On this day, the angel of Allah will sound his trumpet, the earth will split, and the bodies will rejoin their souls.[14] The resurrected are then judged by Allah. Those who have been faithful and virtuous will be rewarded; those who have been evil will be punished. All people are judged on the basis of the record of deeds in a book kept for the purpose.

From the Source

And the Book shall be set in place; and thou wilt see the sinners fearful at what is in it, and saying, 'Alas for us! How is it with this Book, that it leaves nothing behind, small or great, but it has numbered it?' And they shall find all they wrought present, and thy Lord shall not wrong anyone.[15]

Muslim beliefs concerning heaven and hell are similar to those of Zoroastrian, Judaic, and Christian eschatological schemes. The only differences are features that would be particularly appealing or distasteful to a desert dweller. Heaven is located in a beautiful garden with flowing water and shade. The righteous are fed wine—normally forbidden to Muslims—that does not disturb the senses and does not leave the drinker with a hangover. Hell is a horrid place filled with scalding winds, black smoke, and brackish water.

Religious Institutions

From the Qur'an and the early years of Islamic life, certain religious institutions developed that are almost universally recognized by Muslims.

The Mosque

Islam is not a temple-oriented religion. Although certain places are venerated by Muslims, it would not have suited the nomadic life of the Arab people to require them to worship in any sort of temple. The nature of their lives demanded that they be free to worship Allah every day, wherever they might be. Generally, Muslim worship is carried on in a variety of places. Muhammad decreed Friday to be a special day of Muslim worship, as Saturday was the Sabbath for Jews and Sunday was for Christians. Unlike the Jewish and Christian Sabbaths, however, Friday is not a day of rest; rather, it is the only day of the week when the Muslim is required to pray at a mosque with fellow Muslims. There believers are led in prayer by an *imam*. The *imam* is not a priest but a community member who has been chosen to lead the prayers because of his reputation as a knowledgeable and pious man. The Friday service also includes a sermon, which may be delivered in Arabic or the language of the congregation. The remainder of the religious duties of a Muslim can be performed away from the mosque and its leadership.

Mosques have also served as schools and libraries. For much of the history of Islam the mosques of Mecca and Medina were among the most important centers of Islamic learning. In time educational institutions known as *madrasha* developed alongside large urban mosques. These schools offer instruction in Qur'an recitation and interpretation, *Hadith* scholarship, theology, law, and in many cases mystical knowledge and practice. In major centers of Islamic learning there are many *madrashas*. Some of these have developed into great Islamic universities that attract students from around the world. Perhaps the most famous of these is al Azhar in Cairo. Al Azhar is one the world's oldest

The Dome of the Rock, the third-most sacred place in Islam, located in Jerusalem.
(Corbis Digital Stock)

universities and has long been considered to be the most important theological school in the Sunni Muslim world. The *madrashas* of the Iranian city of Qom are comparable centers of Shi'ite learning.

The Five Pillars

Those things that one must do to be a good Muslim are usually referred to as "the five pillars of Islam." These five pillars, or obligations, are repetition of the creed, daily prayer, almsgiving, the fast during the month of **Ramadan**, and the pilgrimage to Mecca.

1. *Repetition of the Creed (Shahadah).* The most common religious act of the Muslim is the frequent repetition of the creed of Islam: *La ilaha illa Allah; Muhammad rasul Allah.* (There is no God but Allah; Muhammad is the messenger of Allah.) This statement is known as *Shahadah* (confession of faith). These are the first words a Muslim child hears, and they are likely to be the last words uttered by the dying Muslim. The devout utter this statement as often as possible every day, and the mere utterance of it makes the reciter a Muslim.
2. *Daily Prayer (salaht).* In addition to the recitation of the creed, the Muslim is expected to pray five times daily. The five accepted times for prayer are dawn, midday, midafternoon, sunset, and nightfall. In many Muslim communities strong-voiced men called *muezzins* climb to the tops of graceful towers known as minarets five times a day and cry out that it is time for prayer. In other communities the call to prayer is spoken at the entrance to the mosque. Wherever Muslims are, they pause for a prescribed prayer. Before they pray, however, they must wash themselves and be cleansed of any impurities. Mosques are frequently built with facilities for washing the hands, feet, and face before prayer. If water is not available, Muslims may cleanse themselves with sand. Properly cleansed, the worshippers prostrate themselves, facing Mecca, and offer their prayers. Men and women may not pray together because of the possibility of inappropriate physical contact. Prayer in the mosque is limited to men in many Middle Eastern countries. In much of Asia, mosques are divided into male and female sections.
3. *Almsgiving (zakaht).* Muslims are expected to share their possessions with the poor, widows, and orphans. Alms may also be used to support religious institutions, scholars, and students. Charity is obligatory according to Islamic law and is assessed as a tax amounting to between 2.5 and 10 percent of one's wealth. Because of its emphasis on almsgiving, Islam has never looked on begging as being dishonorable. Receiving as well as giving alms is considered a source of God's blessing.
4. *Fasting (sawm).* Many religions require fasting in one form or another during the year, but usually it is for a very brief period. Jews, for example, fast on the Day of Atonement. Other religions restrict certain foods at special times; for example, Roman Catholic Christians are expected to keep certain fast days and to avoid meat during the season of Lent. Islam, however, requires the longest and most stringent fast of all. Each year during the month of Ramadan, Muslims are expected to abstain from eating, drinking, smoking, and engaging in sexual relations during the daylight hours. The fast is kept in remembrance of the month when the Prophet first received his revelation. Because of the Muslim lunar calendar, the month of

Islamic Cultural Center and Mosque, Tempe, Arizona, United States. The architecture is based on that of the Dome of Rock.
(Mark R. Woodward)

Ramadan varies from year to year. Some years it may fall in the summer months, when abstaining from water during daylight hours is very difficult. By Muslim tradition, all food, drink, and sexual activity must cease when there is enough light in the morning to distinguish a black thread from a white thread. Nourishment may be taken again in the evening when light has passed, so that the threads may not be distinguished. The only Muslims excused from this fast are the sick, travelers, mothers nursing infants, and small children. When the month of Ramadan concludes, Muslims celebrate with a feast that lasts three days. It is believed that Allah will pardon the sins of all of those believers who complete the fast.

5. *Pilgrimage (hajj)*. Pilgrimage to Mecca was part of pre-Islamic Arab religion. It played an important role in the early history of Islam, and it is mentioned in the Qur'an as a ritual duty. The Prophet Muhammad purged the Ka'ba of its idols and, according to Muslim tradition, re-established it as a shrine dedicated to the one God. Every Muslim who can afford the trip should make the pilgrimage to Mecca once in his or her lifetime. The pilgrimage takes place during a special month in the Muslim calendar called the Dhu al-Hijah. During this month, pilgrims from all over the world arrive at Mecca. The poor sometimes use their life's savings to make the trip. Before the advent of air travel, the elderly and the ill began the long journey with little hope of returning home, but no devout Muslim could ask for a more blessed way to die than on the *hajj* to Mecca. Outside of Mecca the pilgrims must leave whatever mode of transportation they used for the journey and walk the rest

of the way. They must be clad in simple pilgrims' garments with no head covering and only the briefest of sandals, so that rich and poor cannot be distinguished by their apparel. During most of the *hajj*, pilgrims must abstain from food and drink during the daylight hours, they must abstain from sexual intercourse, and they must not cut their hair and nails.

During the days of the pilgrimage, visitors to Mecca visit the Zamzam well, which is believed to have been established by Hagar and Ishmael.[16] They make seven trips around the Ka'ba and kiss the sacred black stone. They offer a sacrifice of a sheep or goat on the tenth day of the *hajj* to commemorate Abraham's willingness to sacrifice even his own son to obey God's command. After these duties, they may visit Medina to pay respect to the grave of the Prophet Muhammad and to visit his mosque. When the pilgrims return home, they may have the title *haji* attached to their names so all the world will know they have fulfilled this religious obligation.

Islam and Women

The position of women in pre-Islamic Arabia was very low. Apparently, female infanticide was common as a way to control the female population. A woman was considered property, owned by her father, husband, or elder brother. If she displeased her husband, he could divorce her without any recourse on her part. Women like Khadija (the first wife of the Prophet) who could control their own wealth and destinies were extremely rare. Although Muhammad did not raise the status of women to that of men, he did raise it significantly.

Religion and Violence

The practice of murdering female babies was forbidden by Islam. Whereas Muhammad allowed polygamy to continue and was married to many women himself, he limited the number of wives a Muslim could have to four, provided a man could afford them and treat them equally. In a society whose males were frequently killed in battle and in which marriage was the only acceptable state for a woman, the polygamy rules probably worked to the benefit of women. Many of the wives of the Prophet were the widows of Muslims killed in battle.

If a Muslim wished to divorce his wife, it was an easy process compared to modern Western methods. When the husband said, "I divorce you, I divorce you, I divorce you," the divorce was final. However, the Muslim woman was not left destitute. She had as her possession the dowry that the husband paid the wife when the marriage was initially arranged. If there was a divorce, the property of the dowry remained the wife's.[17] In most contemporary Muslim societies women have a legal right to demand a divorce if their husbands treat them unjustly or cruelly.

Despite these liberalizing themes, it is clear that in Islam, as in many other religions, women are expected to be subordinate to their fathers, brothers, and husbands. The actual status of women in Muslim societies varies considerably, as status is as much the product of culture as it is of religious conviction. In Saudi Arabia, Iran, and also

Muslim girls at a school in Wonosobo, Indonesia that teaches both religious and secular subjects. *(Mark R. Woodward)*

Afghanistan, for example, women are required to conform to very strict regulations concerning dress and public behavior. They generally are not allowed to work or study with men. In Saudi Arabia, women are not permitted to drive. Prior to the fall of the Taliban government, women could be stoned if they did not conform with dress restrictions. More liberal Muslim scholars have denounced these restrictions and have argued that those who impose them are guilty of the sin of prohibiting that which is not prohibited by Allah. In many Asian and African Muslim societies, women have much more visible public roles. While modest dress is expected, in Indonesia and Malaysia head scarves are often very brightly colored and are important "fashion statements." fragment. Even women who choose to wear head coverings as visible signs of Islamic piety participate in almost all aspects of public life. In Indonesia and Pakistan women have held the offices of President and Prime Minister.

Islamic Taboos

The Qur'an and Muslim tradition have established a series of taboos that in many ways are similar to those described in the Hebrew Bible. Many of these taboos concern foods that are allowed (*halal*) and those that are forbidden (*haram*). Like Jews, Muslims are required to slaughter animals by cutting their throats and must invoke the name of Allah over the beasts. Muslims are not allowed to eat pork, which is considered the most unclean of all meats. Dogs also are considered unclean. They cannot be eaten and can be kept only for the purpose of guarding herds and other property. Eating birds and beast of prey, donkeys, and mules is also prohibited. These restrictions became increasingly important as Islam spread to urban areas and as Muslims came into contact with Christians. Muslims also are forbidden to drink alcohol in any form or to gamble.[18]

Religion and Violence

Jihad

One of the most controversial aspects of Islam is *jihad*, all too often translated as "holy war." In fact, *jihad* is somewhat different. Today, the word *jihad* evokes images of terrorists, suicide bombers, and Usama bin Laden. The real meaning of the term *jihad* is struggle in the path of God. It can mean struggle in the physical sense, which can include building mosques or leaving home to work for the spread of Islam or to avoid religious persecution, as well as armed struggle. It can also mean struggle against the human passions and instincts that can prevent people from acting in accordance with the commandments of the faith. Muslim tradition teaches that Allah rewards both types of struggle.[19]

Historically, Muslim nations waged war to spread Muslim rule, as well as for more clearly political and economic reasons. Muslim scholars teach that only defensive wars are truly *jihad*. Muslim leaders have, however, often used the concept of "holy war" to justify their actions, usually with mixed results. Because Muslim resistance to the Christian Crusades was considered a war to defend Islam, it was rightly called *jihad*. In World War I, a leader of Muslims in Turkey called for *jihad* against the Allied forces. His call was not widely heeded by world Islam. In fact, some Muslims joined the Allies against Turkey. In Algeria, Egypt, Indonesia, and other Muslim societies, post-World War II struggles for national independence were often thought of as *jihad*, but only within the borders of those countries. Some Arab Muslims have called the struggle against the modern nation of Israel *jihad*, while others consider it a political struggle for land, water, and Arab self-determination. Saddam Hussein's attempt to justify Iraq's invasion of Kuwait as a "holy war" was almost completely ignored. More recently Usama bin Laden has called for a global *jihad* against both western and Muslim governments. The vast majority of Muslims believe that attacking non-combatants, especially women and children, violates the Islamic law of war. Most Muslim scholars conclude that this use of the Qur'an to justify the attacks of September 11, 2001, is simplistic, inaccurate, and self-serving.

The Spread of Islam

Islam appeared and developed at exactly the right time in history for expansion. It came at a time when the Arab people were ready for a unifying force; when the Byzantine Empire in the Middle East was on the verge of collapse from internal corruption and misrule; and when the Persian Empire also was vulnerable. In the early seventh century C.E., the Persians had invaded Palestine and had taken Jerusalem and Caesarea. The Byzantine rulers fought back and recaptured the territory, but the battles had left both empires exhausted.

Within a century of the death of the Prophet, the religion of Islam had become the unifying force for Arabs. Muslim armies conquered Palestine, Syria, Persia, and Egypt and swept across North Africa into Spain. In the centuries that followed, Islam spread throughout the Middle East and moved into India, China, and Central and Southeast Asia.[20] There were several reasons for this rapid and massive expansion.

1. Islam is a universal religion. Though it arose in the Arab world, it recognizes no national barriers and knows no distinctions among races. All people were created by Allah and all are accepted as Muslims.
2. Islam is a religion with wide appeal. Unlike religions that require learning, meditation, or great sacrifice, Islam at its most basic level is a simple, easily practiced faith. A person who repeats the creed is a Muslim. A person who keeps the five pillars of Islam is a good Muslim.
3. The world that surrounded the early Muslims was confused and corrupt. Byzantine Christian rulers had mistreated and abused Jews and Arab Christians, therefore the Muslim conquerors were frequently received not as an invading army but as deliverers.

Before the death of Muhammad, Islam had begun to conquer and unite the Arabian peninsula. With every conquest and every addition to Islam, others were encouraged to

Rural Qur'an school in Timbuktu, Mali, West Africa.
(Nic Wheeler)

join and share in the benefits. After the death of the Prophet, the movement gathered momentum and moved outside of Arabia. Damascus was taken in 635; Persia fell by 636; Jerusalem became Muslim in 638; Caesarea was conquered, after stubborn resistance, in 640; and Egypt was also taken in 640. In the following decades, Islam consolidated its victories. Most of North Africa became Muslim by the end of the seventh century.

In 711, the Muslims entered Spain, where they were dominant for the next seven centuries. In 732, they were turned back from further conquest in Europe by Charles Martel, at the Battle of Tours. On the eastern side of the Mediterranean, the expansion also began to slow down. Constantinople, the capital of the Byzantine Empire, resisted Muslim attacks until 1453. The island of Sicily fell to the Muslims in the ninth century and for a period was a base for raids against Italy.

In the eleventh century, the *caliphs* of Baghdad extended their conquests into India and China. Today, the South Asian nations of Pakistan and Bangladesh are almost completely Muslim. There also are large Muslim populations in India and China. In the fifteenth century, most of what now constitutes Indonesia and Malaysia was converted to Islam. The Muslim world remained within these boundaries until the end of the nineteenth century, when missionary activity began to make renewed and rapid strides in Africa. Today, Islam is expanding rapidly in Europe and North America.

The Caliphate

Islam is not highly structured like Roman Catholic Christianity. One reason is that Islam can be practiced privately. Most duties of a good Muslim can be done at home, without a priest. Another reason for its lack of structure is that Muhammad never clearly left a successor or a plan for the succession of his leadership. Only one of his children, Fatima, lived longer than the Prophet, and Muhammad never clearly designated her as the leader who was to follow him. The only hint of succession the Prophet made was to appoint his friend abu-Bakr to lead the community in prayers. After the death of Muhammad, there was great confusion among Muslims, but after a time it was agreed that abu-Bakr should be the *caliph* (from *khalifa*, "deputy" or "representative") who would rule the Muslims in temporal matters. It was presumed that spiritual rule would be left to the Qur'an.

The caliphate is the one central unifying office in the history of Islam. At first, the *caliphs* were friends of the Prophet and acted as pious leaders of the faithful. They were chosen by election or common consent. In later years, the caliphate became hereditary and the office was more like that of king. The first four *caliphs* are often called the orthodox *caliphs* because they were selected from the circle of friends of the Prophet and ruled from Arabia. They include abu-Bakr (632–634), Umar (634–644), Uthman (644–656), and Ali (656–661), the husband of the Prophet's daughter Fatima. Life was not easy for these *caliphs*: abu-Bakr had to suppress rebellion and also try to unify the nation the Prophet had built; Uthman was murdered; and Ali had the caliphate wrested from his hands in 661 by those who formed the first dynasty of Islam—the Umayyads.

Between 661 and 750, Islam was ruled by the Umayyad *caliphs*, who made their headquarters in Damascus, Syria. The Umayyads were more interested in ruling as kings, in conquering territory, and in sharing booty than in being leaders of a religious community. They were succeeded by the Abbasid dynasty, which ruled from Baghdad between 750 and 1258. The Abbasids outdid the Umayyads, ruling with great pomp and splendor in the style depicted in the Arabian Nights. It was in this period that Jews, Christians, and Muslims worked together in studying and preserving the texts of the Greek philosophers and scientists. These efforts contributed directly to the resurgence of learning in Europe at the time of the Italian Renaissance.

After the tenth century, however, the golden age of Muslim civilization began to decline and the caliphate began to lose its power. The Abbasids were replaced by the Mamelukan Turks, who ruled the Muslim Empire from Egypt. The Mamelukes were replaced in the sixteenth century by the Ottoman Turks, who made the title *caliph* synonymous with that of "sultan" of Turkey. When the Ottoman Empire was dissolved after World War I, the caliphate ceased to exist. By that time, however, it was only a title and carried with it none of the glory and power it had once held in the days of the Abbasid *caliphs*.

There have been periodic attempts to restore the caliphate. Some Islamist organizations consider it to be the only legitimate form of government in Muslim societies. Hizbul Tahrir, an organization founded in Jerusalem in the 1950s and now centered in London, seeks to restore the caliphate by means of peaceful persuasion. Usama bin Laden shares this goal, but believes that the destruction of the existing system of nation states cannot be obtained peacefully.

Variations within Islam

Like most large religions, Islam is not a monolithic body. Although most Muslims would agree on the basic principles of Islam, there are many variations in beliefs and practice.

The Sunnis

Eighty-five percent of Muslims are Sunnis (traditionalists). Sunni Muslims think of themselves as the guardians of Islamic orthodoxy and tradition. They base their practice of Islam on the Qur'an and on traditions concerning the early Muslim community. In Sunni Islam, the sources of religious and legal authority are the Qur'an and traditions, known as *hadith*, concerning the words and acts of the Prophet Muhammad and his close companions, as well as analogy and the consensus. *Hadith*, of which there are thousands, expand on the basic teachings of the Qur'an. They have been used by Muslim scholars to answer legal questions as well as to clarify the ritual duties of Islam. The study of the Qur'an and *hadith* continues to form the basics of religious education in Sunni Muslim societies. Analogy and consensus are used to arrive at solutions to problems that are not mentioned in the Qur'an and *hadith*. They are particularly important for Muslim scholars striving to find Islamic solutions to the problems of the modern world.

As Islam grew and adopted the character of the many nations into which it spread, schools of interpretation arose that varied in the amount of weight they gave to the Qur'an, the *hadith*, and human reason in interpreting the life of Islam. There are four of these schools of thought, and every Sunni Muslim is a member of one of them. Generally the four schools represent different geographic regions. The first is the Hanifites, who follow the teachings of abu-Hanifah (d. 767 C.E.). The Hanifites are found today in western Asia, India, and lower Egypt. The second is the Malikites, who follow the teachings of Malik ibn-Anas (d. 795 C.E.) and are found in North and West Africa and upper Egypt. The third is the Shafi'ites, who follow the patterns established by al-Shafi'i (d. 820 C.E.) and are found in lower Egypt, East Africa, Syria, India, Malaysia, and Indonesia. The last is the Hanbalites, who follow Ahmad ibn-Hanbal (d. 855 C.E.) and are today found in Saudi Arabia and communities in other countries influenced by them. Generally, the Hanbalites are the most conservative of the four groups. The Shafi'ites are generally the most liberal and the most willing to strike a balance between the demands of Islamic Scripture and local cultures. It is perhaps for this reason that they are the largest of the four legal schools.

The Shi'ites

The Shi'ite element within Islam represents a basic rupture in the body of the religion. It began as a political dispute over the leadership of Islam but later took on theological overtones. Because Muhammad had left no clear message regarding who was to succeed him, he was followed by three of his close associates. However, some Muslims believed that Muhammad had actually named Ali, his cousin and son-in-law, as his successor. Ali was finally named *caliph* in 656 but gradually lost control of the Muslim world. He was murdered in 661, and the Umayyad dynasty took the caliphate. Ali's youngest son, Husayn, challenged the Umayyad *caliphs* in 680 but was defeated at the Battle of Karbala in Iraq. Husayn and most of his family were killed in the battle. They are considered martyrs by the Shi'ites.

Throughout the history of Islam, certain elements have always believed that the descendants of Ali should be the leaders of the faith. In earlier times, these people were called Alids, but they gradually became known as Shia Ali (the party of Ali) and finally as Shi'ites. The Shi'ites differ from Sunni Muslims in the following ways:

1. The Shi'ites believe that while revelation ended with Muhammad and the Qur'an, in later generations there were divinely inspired figures called *imams*. To Sunnis, an *imam* is one who leads community prayers, but the word carries far more importance for Shi'ites. For them, an *imam* speaks with the authority of God.

2. Shi'ites believe that after the disastrous events of 680, the next *imam* was another son of Ali-Zain. Some believe that Zain was followed by a series of six other *imams*. These Shi'ites are called Seveners because they believe that there was a total of seven *imams* in history. Others believe that Zain was followed by eleven other *imams*, who are called Twelvers. Both the Seveners and the Twelvers believe that some of these *imams* did not die but went into hiding and are now waiting to return to earth.

3. Shi'ites have also traditionally believed in the existence of a *Mahdi* (guided one), a messiah figure who will one day appear on earth and lead the world into an era of justice.[21]

4. Because of the importance of the martyrdom of Husayn, Shi'ites tend to prize martyrdom. Each year, on the tenth of the month of Muharran, the passion of Husayn is re-enacted. The site of his martyrdom and other locations that were important in his life are places of special pilgrimages for Shi'ite Muslims.

5. The traditional Sunni reading and interpretation of the Qur'an is mistrusted by Shi'ites. It is reasoned that because the current version of the Qur'an does not mention Ali as Muhammad's successor it must have been tampered with by his enemies. The Qur'an must have hidden meanings that can be known only through allegorical interpretations.

In 1502, Shia Islam became the established religion of Persia and has maintained its hold on present-day Iran. The neighboring country of Iraq is approximately 60 percent Shi'ite. There are Shi'ite minorities in Saudi Arabia, India, Pakistan, Yemen, and some areas in East Africa. Today there are large Shi'ite populations in the United States and Europe because of the exodus of Muslim moderates following the Iranian revolution. It is estimated that between 10 and 15 percent of all Muslims are Shi'ites.

Religion and Violence

Relations between Sunnis and Shi'ites are usually strained. In some Sunni countries there have been efforts to declare them to be legally non-Muslims. The war in Iraq and especially the destruction of major Shi'ite shrines by Sunni insurgents has contributed to deepening the rift between the two communities.

The Mystical Element

Islam, like Judaism, has always been a religion that emphasizes obedience to the will of God in the here and now. Therefore, it has never encouraged the ascetic life so characteristic of Indian religions and some forms of Christianity. Nevertheless, in every religion there is a hunger for the mystical experience. Furthermore, Islam arose in a land dominated by Byzantine Christianity, which highly prized the ascetic life; in later years it developed in India, where there is also a strong concern for communion with God through asceticism.

Over 500,000 Muslims before the **Ka'ba**, the most sacred site in Islam, within the precincts of the Great Mosque at Mecca.
(Amin Mohamed, Nairobi, K./Getty Images Inc.—Hulton Archive Photos)

In Islam, the concern for mystical union with God was expressed by a group called the Sufis. The word *sufi* means "woolen" and refers to the coarse wool garments worn by early Muslim mystics as a symbol of poverty and the rejection of worldly pleasures. Sufis claim they have always been a part of Islam and trace their origins back to the Prophet and the Qur'an. They teach that in Islam's earlier days Muslims were more pious and more concerned with true spiritual matters than they were later. It is probably true that the expansion of Islam into a world empire caused Muslims to become more materialistic than they had been at the time of the Prophet Muhammad. With the development of the Abbasid dynasty and its grandeur in Baghdad, a cry arose among some for a simpler, more austere life. Therefore, the ninth century probably was the era when the Sufi movement began.

Religion and Violence

One of the most famous Sufis of the early period was Mansur al-Hallaj. His quest for mystical oneness with God finally brought him to proclaim, "I am the truth." For this offense and for ignoring the ritual duties of orthodox Islam, he was executed in 922. He went to his death asking forgiveness for his persecutors. The martyrdom of one of their number and similar persecutions in the following years forced the more extreme elements of the Sufi movement to go underground. As the orthodox Muslim teachers increasingly emphasized the formal and legalistic aspects of Islam, however, the Sufis emphasized the emotional and mystical aspects and thus came to appeal to the common people.

Abu-Hamid al-Ghazali, a professor of theology at the Nizamiyah School in Baghdad, attempted to unite the legalistic and mystical schools of Islam. Al-Ghazali was a brilliant theologian and legal scholar. However, as he grew older, he found less and less personal satisfaction in orthodox Muslim doctrine and ritual. He abandoned his position and his family and, like the Christian Saint Francis of Assisi, set out to find God by experiencing poverty and having mystical experiences. He found his satisfaction among the Sufis. His books, *The Revivification of the Religious Sciences*, *The Folly of the Philosophers*, and the *Niche of the Lights,* had a great impact on Islam and served to make orthodox doctrine more mystical. He prescribed **Sufism** as a remedy for spiritual ills, but he taught that even the most advanced mystics were bound by the ritual duties of the orthodox faith.

Also in the twelfth century the Sufis began to organize themselves into spiritual fraternities, which were usually centered on a Sufi saint. When a convert came to join the order, he was known as a *fakir* or a *dervish*.[22] Traditionally, novices stayed in the order and studied with the master until they became masters themselves. Sufi practices vary but generally emphasize discipline, poverty, and abstinence from worldly pleasures. Sometimes the extremes of asceticism and emotionalism, which Westerners have come to associate with the titles of *fakir* and *dervish*, were experienced. There are recorded reports of Sufis walking on coals, swallowing snakes, and so on; of course, there are various Turkish dervishes who seek oneness with God by whirling in one spot for hours at a time. These are only the extremes of the Sufi movement, however, and are not representative of the totality in any sense. The real contribution of the Sufis to Islamic thought is their insistence on the possibility of knowledge of God through mystical experience.

Muslim boys in Jombong, Indonesia, reading the Qur'an at the grave of Hashim Ashari, a late nineteenthcentury Sufi saint.
(Mark R. Woodward)

Islam in the Modern World

In the years following the glories of the caliphate of Baghdad, Islam settled down to a relatively routine existence. There were the battles with the Christian Crusaders over the holy sites in Palestine in the twelfth and thirteenth centuries, which produced one of the most outstanding Muslim leaders of all time, Saladin; there was the eastward spread of Islam into India, China, Central and Southeast Asia; and there was the development of the Ottoman empire in the sixteenth century. But on the whole, Islam never regained the wealth, power, and political unity it had enjoyed during the golden age of the Abbasid caliphs.

When the European countries were moving out of the medieval twilight into the industrial age, many Islamic nations continued to live in preindustrial societies. Several reasons are suggested for this era of quiet in the Islamic world. One of the most obvious is the conservative nature of the religion itself. Most religions are essentially conservative, but Islam is especially so. Muhammad is believed to have been the last of God's prophets and the Qur'an God's last great message to humankind. To obtain salvation, all that is necessary is to know the Qur'an and how to apply it to one's life. This led conservative Muslim scholars to conclude that there is little point in seeking new knowledge or in being suspicious of change, particularly when it originates outside of the Muslim community. Faced with mounting pressures from the industrialized West, some conservative Muslim scholars and communities retreated into self-imposed isolation.

Newly constructed South Asian style Mosque, Singapore.
(Mark R. Woodward)

Another and perhaps more important reason for the lack of change among Muslims may have been their sense of self-satisfaction relative to European countries. The Muslims had decidedly defeated the Christian Crusaders who had invaded their lands. Later, they had taken the supposedly invincible city of Constantinople from its Christian defenders. The Islamic world therefore had a sense of military and cultural superiority toward Christian countries. Advancements in naval and military technology, along with the newfound wealth of the Americas, shifted the world balance of power in favor of Europeans in the sixteenth century. Particularly in the Middle East, Muslims were slow to understand or appreciate the nature of these developments. Some scholars have suggested that it was not until the conquest of Egypt by Napoleon in the early nineteenth century that Islamic nations became aware that Europeans might be superior to them in any way.

A third reason for the slowness with which Muslim nations moved into the modern era was the development of extremely conservative groups within Islam; these groups took an active leadership in the struggle against any change. The most outstanding force against change occurred with the Wahhabi movement, founded in 1744 by Muhammad ibn-Abd al-Wahhab. The Wahhabis were traditionalists who opposed all forms of change. Naturally they opposed internal innovations, such as those proposed by the Sufis. The Wahhabi movement came to be attached to the house of the Sa'ud family, and when the Sa'ud family came to control Arabia, this puritanical religious movement came with them. In the nineteenth century, the Wahhabis suppressed the Sufis and others whom they considered to have departed from they understand as the Islam of the Prophet Muhammad and his close companions. Today, the Wahhabi movement is strongest in Saudi Arabia. The enormous wealth of the Saudis has enabled them to send missionaries throughout the Muslim world. There are few Muslims societies in which there are not Wahhabi inspired puritanical movements.

The isolation of the Muslim world from the modern world came to an end in the early part of the twentieth century. By that time, transportation and communication had advanced to the point that the Muslim world came within easy reach of the Europeans. World War I brought the Ottoman Empire into the struggle on the side of Germany and Austria. At the end of the war, the victorious Allies (Britain, France, and the United States) broke up the Ottoman Empire. European powers took control of most of the Middle East. During the post–World War I years, the Muslim territories that had been part of the Ottoman Empire developed into independent nations. The boundaries of most of the nations of the modern Middle East are based on these post–World War I developments. They reflect the whims of colonial power and are not natural geographic or cultural entities.

The Middle Eastern Arab nations were found to have the world's largest supply of crude oil. As world demand for oil increased and domestic production in the United States and Europe could no longer meet the demand, the wealth and political power of the Arab states increased dramatically. These factors have caused a resurgence of interest in Islam, both internally and externally. The Muslim states of the Middle East can never again be overlooked; they are extremely important to the industrialized world. The same can be said of Indonesia, which has a population of over 200 million and an enormous petroleum reserve and is destined to play a much larger role in the Asian and Islamic worlds in the twenty-first century.

The internal resurgence of interest in Islam has manifested itself in several ways. First is the reform movements from within. Some Muslims have suggested, and practiced, textual criticism of the Qur'an in a manner similar to that practiced by Christians and Jews with their Bibles. Their purpose is to find what the Pakistani scholar Fazlur Rahman (1919–1988) called the "major themes of the Qur'an" and to use them to formulate solutions to the political and economic problems of the modern world.[23] Others have shifted the focus of traditional Islamic scholarship to questions such as the formulation of a philosophy of science based on Islamic ethical concepts and the search for what the Indonesian reformer Nurcholish Madjid called the "Islamic roots of modern pluralism."[24] Islamic feminists have used portions of the Qur'an and *hadith* concerning the just treatment of women as the basis for expanding the religious, social, and economic roles of women in the modern Islamic world. Many now strongly oppose polygamy.[25]

One of the most obvious results of the resurgence of Islam in the twentieth century was its extremely active missionary movement in Africa. The move south of the Sahara by Muslim missionaries began in the late nineteenth century, when the slave trade had ended and conversion of Africans was possible. Yet Islam has existed in portions of Africa since the seventh century. North Africa was among the first lands to be conquered and converted to Islam. Portions of the interior, particularly the cities, have also known Muslim influence for a long time. Muslim merchants and traders worked in many parts of the Continent. However, European colonial forces in the eighteenth and nineteenth centuries made Muslim missionary activity possible in the interior. The colonial powers opened Africa to both Christian and Muslim missions, with maps, modern transportation, and communications.

The abuses of the Africans by the colonial powers also opened doors for Islam. As African nations struggled for and gained their independence, hostility toward white Europeans and their religion could be expressed by conversion to Islam. Because Islam knows no bias of color or ethnic origin, it has often been thought of as an alternative to the Christianity of European colonialists. For many people in Africa, Asia, and the Middle East, Islam has come to be associated with the struggle for social justice and self-determination.[26]

Muslim Calendar and Holy Days

Islam has its own distinctive calendar, made up of twelve lunar months of twenty-nine or thirty days for a total of 354 days each year. To make up some of the difference between the lunar and solar year, one day is added to the last month of the year eleven times each thirty years. Even with this correction, however, 103 Muslim years are the equivalent of 100 solar years. Muslims date their calendars from the *Hijrah*, so the date of the Prophet's death is not known as 632 C.E. but 10 A.H.

Among the five pillars of Islam, Muslims are commanded to pray each day, to fast during the holy month of **Ramadan**, and to try to make the pilgrimage to Mecca at least once in their lives. Thus these holy times are established for Muslims as being basic to their religion. In addition to these holy times, Muslims are required to participate in two annual feasts.

Feast of Fast-Breaking ('Id al-Fitr)

This feast is kept on the first day of Shawwal, the month after Ramadan, and celebrates a return to normal life after the prolonged fast. It is a time of feasting and may last for three days. In many Muslim societies, it is a time for exchanging gifts, visiting friends and relatives, and paying respect to the dead. Today it is common for Muslims to send 'Id al-Fitr cards in much the same way Christians send Christmas cards.

Feast of Sacrifice ('Id al-Adha)

This feast comes on the tenth of dhul-Hijah, the month of the pilgrimage. It is one of the requirements of the *hajj*, but it is also observed throughout the Muslim world. It commemorates the time when Abraham was commanded by God to sacrifice his son Ishmael.[27] When Abraham's faithfulness was revealed, God provided a ram as a substitute sacrifice. On this date in the Muslim year, the head of each household is to kill an animal and provide a feast. Some of the food is given to the needy in the community.

New Year

The month of Muharram is the beginning of the Muslim year. It also is celebrated because it is believed to have been the month of the *Hijrah*. In Sunni communities, the tenth of Muharram is kept as a day of fasting, called Ashura (ten). Among the Shi'ites, the tenth of Muharram commemorates the Battle of Karbala.

Birthday of the Prophet Muhammad (Mawlid an-Nabi)

The traditional celebration for the birth of Muhammad is established on the twelfth day of the third month. The recitation of the Prophet's biography and prayers for him are among the most common elements of this feast. In many places there are also processions, feasts, and special community prayers. The ultraconservative Wahhabis of Arabia do not celebrate the birthday because they consider it a modern invention. Muslim saints, particularly the founders of the Sufi orders, are remembered on their birthdays by many Muslim communities.

Islam Today

In recent decades, Islam has become an increasingly important force in world politics. Many of the newly emerging nations of the Third World are Muslim. Some of these nations are very important to the world's economy because they control vital natural resources such as oil, natural gas, and minerals.

In the present time, Islam again has become a growing religion. Mention has already been made of Muslim missionary activity in Africa. Islam is growing in other parts of the world as well. The Muslim population of Western Europe has been increasing because of the immigration of workers from Muslim nations and fertility rates higher than those of non-Muslim Europeans. Immigration has also been a factor in the growth of the Muslim population in the United States. There also have been many converts to Islam in the United States, particularly among African Americans. Islam is now the second-most popular religion in the United States and Many European countries.

It remains to be seen if Iran or any other Muslim nation can exist for long in the modern world with a political system based on ancient religious customs. The dreams of Islamic fundamentalism are particularly difficult for Muslims living in the non-Muslim world. This has not, however, prevented the emergence of militant groups in the United States and in many European countries. In most of the Islamic nations of the Middle East, Africa, and Asia, the majority of Muslims and their governments are strongly opposed to fundamentalism. In most Muslim societies, religious scholars are engaged in a struggle to define a vision of modernity that is based on Islamic values and yet is compatible with contemporary concepts of human rights and democracy. In 1999, twenty years after the Iranian revolution, Abdurrahman Wahid, one of most articulate proponents of this understanding of Islam, was elected president of Indonesia, the world's most populous Muslim nation. Pakistan, Malaysia, and Indonesia all have strong pro-democracy movements. It seems likely that the struggle between forces of modernization and those of fundamentalism will continue for many decades to come.

Religion and Violence

European Muslims confront problems integrating into largely secular European populations. This is particularly true in France, where young women have not been allowed to cover their hair in public schools and where there have been violent confrontations between young Muslim men and security forces in impoverished communities.

The most dramatic change occurring in Islam today is the emergence of Islamic fundamentalism. In the 1960s and 1970s, Iran and several other Muslim nations became enriched by oil profits. In many cases, factions within these nations turned to Western society for a model. In time, the introduction of Western universities and customs (such as the increased participation of women in public life) was perceived as a threat by some conservative Muslims. Devout Muslims were shocked by what they perceived as the sexual vices and loose morality of Western Christian nations. They believed that the perceived moral decay of these nations had been caused by secularization of their societies.

This sense of threat produced a call for a return to the old ways and to nations controlled by historic Islamic culture. One sees this movement particularly in Iran, but it can be found, to some extent, throughout Islam. Iran represents the "left wing" of Islamic fundamentalism and has produced a revolution. In 1979, the Shi'ite Muslims of Iran deposed the shah and accepted the Ayatollah Ruhollah Khomeini as their leader. The new government called itself an Islamic Republic and is based on a strict interpretation of Shi'ite Islamic law. Since that time, Iran has supported anti-Western fundamentalist movements in many Islamic countries. Saudi Arabia represents the more conservative or "right wing" of Islamic fundamentalism. The Saudi government has attempted to isolate its people from foreign influences and enforces **Wahhabi** social and religious norms at home, while maintaining close economic and diplomatic relationships with the United States and other Western powers. Saudi dissidents, including Usama bin Laden, advocate the abolition of the monarchy and the establishment of an even stricter Islamic order. They provided financial support and manpower for the Taliban in Afghanistan and have declared a global *jihad* against Muslim rulers and their western allies.

STUDY QUESTIONS

1. Contrast the role of Muhammad as the founder of Islam with that of Jesus as the founder of Christianity. How are they similar?
2. Trace the roots of Islam in Jewish, Christian, and traditional Arab religions.
3. What factors made Islam so widely accepted by so many diverse people in the first two centuries of its life?
4. List the five pillars or duties of a good Muslim.
5. Locate the various places in the modern world where one would find an Islamic majority.
6. Distinguish between Sunni and Shi'ite Muslims. Where are Shi'ites a majority?

SUGGESTED READING

Ahmed, Leila. *Women and Gender in Islam: Historical Roots of a Modern Debate*. New Haven, CT: Yale University Press, 1992.

Arberry, A. J., trans. *The Koran Interpreted*. New York: Macmillan, 1973.

Bodansky, Yossef. *Bin Laden: The Man Who Declared War on America*. New York: Random House, 2001.

Denny, F. M. *An Introduction to Islam*. New York: Macmillan, 1985.

Esposito, John L. *Islam the Straight Path*. New York: Oxford University Press, 1991.

Madjid, Nurcholish, "In Search of Islamic Roots for Modern Pluralism: The Indonesian Experiences." In *Toward a New Paradigm. Recent Developments in Indonesian Islamic Thought*, edited by Mark Woodward. Tempe: Arizona State University, 1996.

Martin, Richard. *Islamic Studies. A History of Religions Approach*. Englewood Cliffs, NJ: Prentice Hall, 1995.

Martin, Richard, Woodward, Mark, and Atmaja, Dwi. *Defenders of Reason in Islam. Mu'tazilism from Medieval School to Modern Symbol*. Oxford: One World, 1997.

Mottaheden, Roy. *The Mantle of the Prophet. Religion and Politics in Iran*. New York: Pantheon Books, 1985.

Rahman, Fazlur. *Islam*, 2nd ed. Chicago: University of Chicago Press, 1979.

———. *Major Themes of the Qur'an*. Minneapolis: Bibliotheca Islam, 1989.

Watt, W. Montgomery. *Muhammad, Prophet and Statesmen*. New York: Oxford University Galaxy Press, 1974.

SOURCE MATERIAL

The Muslim Vision of God

In the following selections from the Qur'an, the qualities of Allah as absolute creator and ruler, the only God, are presented.[28]

II 256–59

God
there is no god but He, the
Living, the Everlasting.
Slumber seizes Him not, neither sleep;
to Him belongs
all that is in the heavens and the earth
Who is there that shall intercede with Him
save by His leave?
He knows what lies before them
and what is after them,
and they comprehend not anything of His knowledge
save such as He wills.
His Throne comprises the heavens and earth;
the preserving of them oppresses Him not;
He is the All-high, the All-glorious.
No compulsion is there in religion.
Rectitude has become clear from error.
So whosoever disbelieves in idols
and believes in God, has laid hold of
the most firm handle, unbreaking; God is
All-hearing, All-knowing.
God is the protector of the believers;

He brings them forth from the shadows
into the light.
And the unbelievers—their protectors are idols, that bring them forth from the light
into the shadows;
those are the inhabitants of the Fire,
therein dwelling forever.

VI 102, 103

That then is God your Lord;
there is no god but He,
the Creator of everything.
So serve Him,
for He is Guardian over everything.
The eyes attain Him not, but He attains the eyes;
He is the All-subtle, the All-aware.

XXVII 61–65

He who created the heavens and earth, and sent down for you
out of heaven water;
and We caused to grow therewith gardens full of loveliness
whose trees you could never grow.
Is there a god with God?
Nay, but they are a people who assign to Him equals!
He who made the earth a fixed place
and set amidst it rivers
and appointed it firm mountains
and placed a partition between the two seas.
Is there a god with God?
Nay, but the most of them have no knowledge.
He who answers the constrained, when he calls unto Him,
and removes the evil
and appoints you to be successors in the earth.
Is there a god with God?
Little indeed do you remember.
He who guides you in the shadows of the land and the sea
and looses the winds,
bearing good tidings before His mercy.
Is there a god with God?
Little indeed do you remember.
He who guides you in the shadows of the land and the sea
and looses the winds,
bearing good tidings before His mercy.
Is there a god with God?
High exalted be God, above that which they associate!
Who originates creation, then brings it back again,

and provides you out of heaven and earth,
Is there a god with God?

XXX 47–54

God is He that looses the winds, that stirs up clouds,
and He spreads them in heaven how He will, and shatters them;
then thou seest the rain issuing out of the midst of them,
and when he smites with it whomsoever of His servants
He will, lo, they rejoice,
although before it was sent down on them before that
they had been in despair.
So behold the marks of God's mercy,
how He quickens the earth after it
was dead, and He is powerful
over everything.
But if We loose a wind, and they see it growing yellow,
they remain after the unbelievers.
Thou shalt not make the dead to hear,
neither shalt thou make the deaf to hear the call
when they turn about, retreating.
Thou shalt not guide the blind out of their error
neither shalt thou make any to hear
except for such as believe in Our signs, and so surrender.
God is He that created you of weakness, then He appointed
after weakness strength, then after strength he appointed
weakness and grey hairs; He creates what He will, and
He is the All-knowing, the All-powerful.

XXXV, 36–39

God knows the Unseen in the heavens and the earth;
He knows the thoughts within the breasts.
It is He who appointed you viceroys in the earth.
So whosoever disbelieves, his unbelief shall be
charged against him; their unbelief increases
the disbelievers only in hate in God's sight;
their unbelief increases the disbelievers only in loss.
Say: "Have you considered your associates on whom
you call, apart from God? Show what they have
created in the earth; or have they a partnership
in the heavens?" Or have We given them a Book,
so that they are upon a clear sign from it?
Nay, but the evildoers promise one another
naught but delusion.
God holds the heavens and the earth, lest they remove;

did they remove, none would hold them after Him.
Surely He is All-clement, All-forgiving.

LVII, 1–5

In the Name of God, the Merciful, the Compassionate
All that is in the heavens and the earth magnifies God;
He is the All-mighty, the All-wise.
To Him belongs the Kingdom of the heavens and the earth;
He gives life, and He makes to die, and He is powerful
Over everything.
He is the First and the Last, the Outward and the Inward;
He has knowledge of everything.
It is He that created the heavens and the earth in six days
then seated Himself upon the Throne.
He knows what penetrates into the earth
and what comes forth from it,
what comes down from heaven, and what goes up into it.
He is with you wherever you are; and God sees
the things you do.
To Him belongs the Kingdom of the heavens and the earth;
and unto Him all matters are returned,
He makes the night to enter into the day
and makes the day to enter into the night
He knows the thoughts within the breasts.

LVII, 7, 8

Hast thou not seen that God knows whatsoever is in the heavens, and whatsoever is in the earth? Three men conspire not secretly together, but He is the fourth of them, neither five men, but He is the sixth of them, neither fewer than that, neither more, but He is with them, wherever they may be; then He shall tell them what they have done, on the Day of Resurrection. Surely God has knowledge of everything.

LIX, 23–25

He is God.
There is no God but He.
He is the knower of the unseen and the Visible;
He is the All-merciful, the All-compassionate.
He is God;
There is no God but He.
He is the King, the All-holy, the All-peaceable.
the All-faithful, the All-preserver,
the All-mighty, the All-compeller,
the All-sublime.
Glory be to God, above that they associate!
He is God;

the Creator, the Maker, the Shaper.
To Him belong the Names Most Beautiful.
All that is in the heavens and the earth magnifies Him;
He is the All-mighty, the All-wise.

The Prescriptions of Islam

In the following sections from the Qur'an, many of the duties of a faithful Muslim are detailed.[29]

II, 166–75, 180–82, 186–93

O believers, eat of the good things
wherewith We have provided you, and give thanks
to God, if it be Him that you serve.
These things only has he forbidden you;
carrion, blood, the flesh of swine,
what has been hallowed to other than God.
Yet whoso is constrained, not desiring,
nor transgressing, no sin shall be on him;
God is All-forgiving, All-compassionate.
Those who conceal what of the Book God has sent down
on them, and sell it for a little price—they shall eat
naught but the Fire in their bellies; God shall not
speak to them on the day of Resurrection
neither purify them; there awaits them
a painful chastisement.
Those are they that have bought error at
the price of guidance, and chastisement at
the price of pardon; how patiently they
shall endure the Fire!
That, because God has sent down the Book
with the Truth, and those that are
at variance regarding the Book
are in wide schism.
It is not piety, that you turn your faces
to the East and to the West.
True piety is this:
to believe in God, and the Last Day,
the angels, the Book, and the Prophets,
to give of one's substance, however cherished,
to kinsmen, and orphans,
the needy, the traveler, beggars,
and to ransom the slave,
to perform the prayer, to pay the alms,
And they who fulfill their covenant

when they have engaged in a covenant,
and endure with fortitude
misfortune, hardship and peril,
these are they who are true in their faith,
these are the truly godfearing.
O believers, prescribed for you is
retaliation, touching the slain;
freeman for freeman, slave for slave,
female for female. But if aught is pardoned
a man by his brother, let the pursuing
be honorable, and let the payment be
with kindliness. That is a lightening
granted you by your Lord, and a mercy;
and for him who commits aggression
after that—for him there awaits
a painful chastisement.
In retaliation there is life for you,
men possessed of mind; happily you
will be godfearing.
O believers, prescribed for you is
the Fast, even as it was prescribed for
those that were before you—haply you
will be godfearing—
for days numbered; and if any of you
be sick, or if he be on a journey,
then a number of other days; and for those
who are able to fast, a redemption
by feeding a poor man. Yet better
it is for him who volunteers good,
and that you should fast is better for you,
if you but know;
the month of Ramadan, wherein the Koran
was sent down to be a guidance
to the people, and as clear signs
of the Guidance and the Salvation.
So let those of you, who are present
at the month, fast it; and if any of you
be sick, or if he be on a journey,
then a number of other days; God desires
ease for you, and desires not hardship
for you; and that you fulfill the number, and
magnify God that he has guided you, and haply
you will be thankful.
Permitted to you, upon the night of
the Fast, is to go in to your wives;
they are a vestment for you, and you are

a vestment for them. God knows that you have been
betraying yourselves, and has turned to you
and pardoned you. So now lie with them,
and seek what God has prescribed for you.
And eat and drink, until the white thread
shows clearly to you from the black thread
at the dawn; then complete the Fast
unto the night, and do not lie with them
while you cleave to the mosques. Those are
God's bounds; keep well within them. So God
makes clear His signs to men; happily they
will be godfearing.
And fight in the way of God with those
who fight with you, but aggress not; God loves
not the aggressors.
And slay them wherever you come upon them,
and expel them from where they expelled you;
persecution is more grievous than slaying.
But fight them not by the Holy Mosque
until they should fight you there;
then, if they fight you, slay them—
such is the recompense of unbelievers—
but if they give over, surely God is
All-forgiving, All-compassionate.
Fight them, till there is no persecution
and the religion is God's; then if they
give over, there shall be no enmity
save for evildoers.
The holy month for the holy month;
holy things demand retaliation.
Whoso commits aggression against you,
do you commit aggression against him
like as he has committed against you;
and fear you God, and know that God is
with the godfearing.
And expend in the way of God;
and cast not yourselves by your own hands
into destruction, but be good-doers; God
loves the good-doers.
Fulfill the Pilgrimage and the Visitation
unto God; but if you are prevented,
then such offering as may be feasible.
And shave not your heads, till the offering
reaches its place of sacrifice. If any
of you is sick, or injured in his head,
then redemption by fast, or freewill offering,

or ritual sacrifice. When you are secure,
then whosoever enjoys the Vision
until the Pilgrimage, let his offering
be such as may be feasible; or if he
finds none, then a fast of three days
in the Pilgrimage, and of seven when
you return, that is ten completely;
that is for him whose family are not
present at the Holy Mosque. And fear
God, and know that God is terrible
in retribution.

On the Day of Judgment

The following passages describe the Islamic understanding of God's ultimate justice on the day of judgment.[30]

LVI, 1–56

In the Name of God, the Merciful, the Compassionate
When the terror descends
and none denies its descending
abasing, exalting
when the earth shall be rocked
and the mountains crumbled
and become a dust scattered,
and you shall be three bands—
Companions of the Right
Companions of the Left
and the Outstrippers: the Outstrippers
those are they brought nigh the Throne,
in the Gardens of delight
a throng of the ancients
and how few of the later folk
upon close wrought couches
reclining upon them, set face to face,
immortal youths going round about them
with goblets and ewers and a cup from a spring
no brows throbbing, no intoxication
and such fruits as they shall choose,
and such flesh of fowl as they desire,
and wide eyed houris
as the likeness of hidden pearls,
a recompense for that they laboured.
Therein they shall hear no idle talk, no cause of sin,
only the saying 'Peace, Peace.' . . .

NOTES

Chapter 1

1. See Chapter 2 for a description of Pueblo people of the American Southwest using symbolic magic to call animals to the hunt.
2. It is estimated that more than 200 of the figurines have been found worldwide.
3. In addition to the megaliths of Europe, these monuments are found in such diverse locations as the Pacific Islands, Korea, North America, India, Southeast Asia, and North Africa. Although the erection of megaliths is primarily connected to Neolithic religion, it is not limited to that time period. Megaliths are still erected by the tribal peoples of South and Southeast Asia.
4. Burial or cremation remains are often found near megaliths. Among the Naga of northeast India and the Toraja of eastern Indonesia, megaliths are erected in conjunction with great sacrificial feasts that honor the **ancestors**.
5. See p. 7.
6. See p. 9.
7. A sign in front of a Jain temple in Bombay said, "Do not enter with shoes on. Women in menstrual cycle not allowed." Madeleine L'Engle, *A Stone for a Pillow* (Wheaton, IL: Harold Shaw, 1985), p. 148.
8. Recent archaeological investigation at the ancient city of Carthage reveals that this rather advanced culture burned hundreds of its children as sacrifices throughout the history of the city. The Aztec of central Mexico regularly sacrificed prisoners and even fought wars for the sole purpose of obtaining victims to sacrifice to the gods.
9. Human sacrifice is mentioned in the Hebrew Bible, for example. It is regarded as a supreme sacrifice, which is usually prompted by extremely rare circumstances. See Genesis 22, Judges 11, II Kings 3:27, and Micah 6:7.
10. For examples of these rites, see the chapters on Native American and African religions.
11. Some have suggested that the twenty-first-century secular version of the puberty rite of passage is the acquisition of a driver's license, with its intensive preparation, its ordeal, and the admission into adulthood for those who "pass."

Chapter 2

1. Although this is the most commonly accepted scientific theory, some Native American religious leaders believe that their people are literally "native," that they originated in the Americas and never migrated from any other continent.
2. Some estimate that prior to the arrival of the Europeans, there may have been as many as 2,000 different Native American cultures in North America.
3. A case in point is the debate over Native American eschatology. Did they believe in life after death and heaven and hell? Where evidence supports these features, the charge is made that it is the result of contact with Christianity.
4. Ruth M. Underhill, *Red Man's Religion* (Chicago: University of Chicago Press, 1965), p. 116.
5. T. C. McLuhan, *Touch the Earth* (New York: Outerbridge & Dienstfrey, 1971), p. 15.
6. Human sacrifice and similar practices, including collecting and saving portions of the bodies of slain enemies, were most common among warlike communities including the Aztec of the Valley of Mexico, the Inca of Peru, and some communities in the Southwest of what is now the United States. They were practiced for one of two reasons: Some of the warrior spirits demanded human victims in return for providing aid in battle. In other cases, the bodies of slain enemies were believed to contain spiritual power. Until very recently, similar practices were found in many other parts of the world.
7. Ake Hultkrantz, *Belief and Worship in Native North America* (Syracuse, NY: Syracuse University Press, 1981), p. 171.
8. Underhill, *Red Man's Religion*, pp. 117, 118.
9. For an analysis of the Sun Dance among contemporary Native Americans, see Joseph G. Jorgensen, *The Sun Dance Religion* (Chicago: University of Chicago Press, 1972). Also Arthur Amiotte, "The Lakota Sun Dance: Historical and Contemporary Perspectives," in *Sioux Indian Religion*, ed. Raymond J. DeMallie and Douglas R. Parks (Norman: University of Oklahoma Press, 1987), pp. 75–89.

10. During colonial times, if individuals had a choice between white and native healing, they would have been well advised to go to the native healer. The medicine man might perform rituals and give the patient herbs, some of which, including aspirin, are now known to be of real medicinal value. The spiritual aspects of Native American medicine may or may not have been effective, but they were certainly harmless. The white healer, on the other hand, often resorted to bleeding the patient or prescribing medicines containing mercury and other substances now known to be poisonous. Such practices frequently weakened the sick person and hastened death.

11. Weston La Barre, *The Peyote Cult* (New York: Schocken Books, 1969), p. 7.

12. See Hultkrantz, *Belief and Worship in Native North America*, p. 283.

13. The use of peyote and other hallucinogenic substances in Native American religious ceremonies is not a social problem in the same sense that drug use is in other contemporary American communities. These substances are used only for religious purposes, in part because their use is accompanied by extended periods of nausea and physical discomfort before a vision is achieved. In Native American communities, the most serious problems with chemical dependency are caused by alcohol abuse. These problems are particularly serious in areas with high rates of unemployment and among some groups who appear to have a genetic predisposition for diabetes, which, when coupled with alcohol abuse, often leads to serious health problems and premature death.

14. Similar practices can be found in ancient Chinese religion and in those of many tribal peoples of southern China and Southeast Asia.

15. My grandfather, the Reverend John Arthur Klein, who was an Anglican missionary in North and South Dakota and later in Oklahoma, often observed that it was music, rather than sermons, that his Native American congregations found most moving. My mother and her sister were born on Lakota reservations and were given native names by the elders of the tribe.—M. R. W.

16. Most of the Native American rugs, paintings, and Kachina dolls made for tourists and non-native art collectors are secular in this sense. Objects used in religious ceremonies are carefully guarded and generally speaking are not sold to non-native people.

17. Frances Densmore, *Teton Sioux Music* (Bureau of American Ethnology, Bulletin 61, 1918), pp. 65–66.

18. James R. Walker, *Lakota Myth*, ed. Elaine A. Jahner (Lincoln: University of Nebraska Press, 1983), pp. 183–186.

Chapter 3

1. From the sixteenth to the nineteenth century many Yoruba were brought to the new world as slaves. Yoruba religion continues to flourish in South America, Brazil, and the Carribean. Immigration from these areas has renewed interest in Yoruba religion and culture in the United States.

2. Susan Feldman, ed., *African Myths and Tales* (New York: Dell, 1963), pp. 36–37.

3. Geoffery Parrinder, *African Traditional Religion* (Chicago: Hutchinson House, 1954), p. 48.

4. Diedre Badejo, *Osun Seegesi. The Elegant Diety of Wealth, Power and Femininity* (Trenton, NJ: Africa World Press, 1996), pp. 103–122.

5. Benjamin C. Ray, *African Religions* (Englewood Cliffs, NJ: Prentice Hall, 1976), p. 149.

6. Ibid., p. 80.

7. Feldman, *African Myths and Tales*, pp. 278–280.

8. Parrinder, *African Traditional Religion*, p. 94. In many African cultures, and in others throughout the world, a clear distinction is made between the mother's brothers and sisters and those of the father, who often play very different roles in the life of a child. Often the mother's brothers and sisters are authority figures, while the father's are regarded in a less formal, often familiar way.

9. Female circumcision is also practiced by some Muslim peoples in North Africa even where it is prohibited by the government. Male circumcision is a universal practice in Muslim and Jewish societies and is very widely practiced by Christians and secular people in the United States. It is less common in European and other Christian communities.

10. Ray, *African Religions*, p. 146.

11. Noel Q. King, *Religions of Africa* (New York: Harper & Row, 1970), p. 30.

12. Ray, *African Religions*, pp. 106–108.

13. In 1900, it was estimated that there were 9 million Christians in Africa. In 1995, there were 348,176,000 Christians, 300,317,000 Muslims, and approximately 72,777,000 followers of traditional African religions. *1998 Encyclopedia Britannica Book of the Year* (Chicago: Encyclopedia Britannica, 1998), p. 269.
14. Monica Wilson, *Communal Rituals of the Nyakyusa* (International African Institute, 1959), pp. 40–46.
15. Maria Leach, *The Beginning: Creation Myths Around the World* (New York: Krishna Press, 1956), pp. 145–147.

Chapter 4

1. One of the best sources of information on pre-Aryan India is Mortimer Wheeler, *Early India and Pakistan* (New York: Praeger, 1959).
2. The most common identifications are of the Indian god Varuna with Uranus, of Dyaus Pitar with the Greek Zeus, and the Roman Jupiter because of mythological and linguistic similarities.
3. See the discussion of *animism* in Chapter 1.
4. *Soma* is frequently identified with the *haoma* plant, which was used in the ancient Persian religions, but that too is not easily identified by modern students of religion or botany.
5. Aldous Huxley named the happiness-producing drug of the future *soma* in his book *Brave New World*. Today, soma is the name of a powerful muscle-relaxing prescription drug used to treat athletic and other injuries.
6. The word *Veda* is used in two ways. Generally, it refers to only the ancient collection of hymns to the Aryan gods. In another sense, it refers to an entire collection of sacred literature that includes the hymns and the later additions: the Brahmanas, the Aranyakas, and the Upanishads. In this text, we use the word in the latter sense.
7. Ralph T. H. Griffith, trans., *The Hymns of the Rig-Veda*, Vol. I (Banaras: E. J. Lazarus and Co., 1920), pp. 133, 134.
8. *The Hymns of the Rig-Veda,* p. 294.
9. Ibid., p. 398.
10. Satapatha Brahmana, 1:8.
11. The basic meaning of the word Upanishad seems to be "near sitting," indicating that these are materials developed in the discussions between teachers (*gurus*) and their students as they sat together and spoke of the philosophical implications of the Vedas.
12. The word *Brahman* is neuter. Basically, it means "ever growing."
13. Maitri Upanishad, VI. 17.
14. Svetasv-átara Upanishad, IV. 9–10.
15. Isavasyam Upanishad, 9.
16. Svetasv-átara Upanishad, IV, 6.
17. Katha-Upanishad, I. 14.
18. Chandogya Upanishad, VI. 13.
19. Rig-Veda, X., 90.
20. *The Law of Manu,* 1:31.
21. In Hinduism, the word *dharma* is used in many ways. It comes from the root word *dhri*, which means "to support." It can mean duty or teaching or truth. Here, *dharma* came to refer to rules that support or maintain a proper society.
22. *The Law of Manu,* 1:88–91.
23. Ibid., 12:9.
24. Ibid., 5:147–149.
25. Ibid., 9:26.
26. Ibid., 6:92.
27. Ibid., 9:326.
28. Ibid., 11:59.
29. Ibid., 11:257.
30. Ibid., 1:64–73.
31. The *Mahabharata* contains 110,000 couplets, or 220,000 lines. The English translation of the *Mahabharata* fills thirteen volumes.
32. I:26–32. This citation and those that follow in this text are taken from R. C. Zaehner, trans., *The Bhagavad Gita* (Oxford: Oxford University Press, 1969).
33. Ibid.
34. Ibid., III:4,5.
35. The word *karma* literally means "deed" or "act." In Indian religions, it usually refers to those deeds or actions that affect future lives.
36. *The Bhagavad Gita,* IV:7.
37. Ibid.
38. The god Brahma is to be distinguished from the all-pervading god-force of the Upanishads, Brahman. The word *Brahman* is neuter. The word *Brahma* is masculine and refers to a distinct entity.
39. Geoffrey Moorhouse, *Calcutta* (San Diego: Harcourt Brace Jovanovich, 1971), p. 6.

40. On the goddesses of postclassical Hinduism, see C. Dimmitt and J. A. van Buitenen, *Classical Hindu Mythology. A Reader in the Sanskrit Puranas* (Philadelphia: Temple University Press, 1978), pp. 219–41.

41. The most common posture used in meditation is the so-called lotus position, in which one sits with the right foot upon the left thigh, the left foot upon the right thigh, and the back is erect. In this extremely balanced position, concentration is easier than in most other seated positions.

42. R. C. Zaehner, *Hinduism* (New York: Oxford University Press, 1962), p. 4.

43. It is estimated that in modern India over 90 percent of all marriages are arranged by parents. While exact figures are not available, the custom of arranged marriages is common in the southern Asian populations of Europe and North America. South Asian newspapers and other periodicals published in the United States and Europe frequently include "matrimonial advertisements" in the classified section, which are generally placed by the parents of young people, sometimes without their children's knowledge. Advances in modern education have done little to change this custom, which seems to produce as many happy marriages as most others.

44. The Sanskrit word that Indians have traditionally applied to the caste system is *jati*, or "birth."

45. Adrian C. Mayer, *Caste and Kinship in Central India. A Village and Its Region* (Berkeley: University of California Press, 1960).

46. Ralph T. H. Griffith, trans., *The Hymns of the Rig-Veda*, vol. I (Banaras: E. J. Lazarus, 1920), pp. 448, 449.

47. Ibid., vol. II, pp. 566, 567.

48. S. Radhakrishnan, ed. and trans., *The Principal Upanishads* (London: George Allen & Unwin, 1953), pp. 269, 270, 296.

49. G. Buhler, trans., *Law of Manu, Sacred Books of the East*, vol. XXV (New York: Charles Scribner's Sons, 1882–1902), pp. 204–10.

50. R. C. Zaehner, trans., *Bhagavad Gita* (New York: Oxford University Press, 1969).

51. George Thibaut, trans., *Shankara, Commentary on Vedanta Sutra*, vol. 1, in *Sacred Books of the East*, vol. XXXIV (Oxford: Clarendon Press, 1890), passim.

Chapter 5

1. According to some Jain legends, the parents of Mahavira died of self-imposed starvation. Because Jainism places such high value on asceticism, this form of death becomes the ideal.

2. Herman Jacobi, trans., "Sutrakrtanga," *Gaina Sutras*, in *The Sacred Books of the East*, vol. XL (Oxford: Clarendon Press, 1895), pp. 1–3, 18.

3. *Tattvartha Sutra*, 10, 2.

4. *Ayaranya Sutra*, 1, 1, 6, 6.

5. When rats were a problem in Bombay, Jains established hospices for them. Captured rats were given a home, were separated by sex so they could not reproduce, and were fed and cared for until they died of natural causes.

6. The well-known story of the blind men and the elephant is said to have been of Jain origin and illustrates the relativity of truth. In this tale, several blind men are asked to describe an elephant. Each touches a different part of the elephant's body, and thus each describes the animal in a different way. To one man, the elephant is like a stone wall because he has touched the side; to another, the elephant is like a rope because he has touched the tail; and to another, the elephant is like a fan because he has touched the ear. Each man truthfully described the animal; but because each had contacted it from a different point, the descriptions varied tremendously.

7. In the fourth century B.C.E., when Alexander the Great entered India, he encountered the naked Jain philosophers and was fascinated by them. The Jains only stamped their feet in Alexander's presence. When he inquired about this strange behavior, he was told, "King Alexander, every man can possess only so much of the earth's surface as this we are standing on. You are but human like the rest of us, save that you are always busy and up to no good, travelling so many miles from your home, a nuisance to yourself and to others. Ah well! You will soon be dead, and then you will own just as much of the earth as will suffice to bury you." (Arrian 7:1.4–7:2.1)

8. *1998 Ontario Consultants on Religious Tolerance*

9. A. L. Basham, trans., in *Sources of Indian Tradition*, ed. William T. de Bary (New York: Columbia University Press, 1958), pp. 56–58.

10. Ibid., pp. 62, 63.

Chapter 6

1. Some chronologies place the Buddha's death as late as 368 B.C.E. Nevertheless, the older and probably more reliable Sri Lankan sources place his life in the sixth century B.C.E.

2. Rahula is an unusual name. It means "fetter," thus indicating that at the time of the child's birth, Gautama was at the point of considering that all things, even a beautiful child, could bind one to life like a fetter. The choice of this name indicates that even at the time of the birth of his first child, Gautama had come to see family life as an impediment to the quest for spiritual liberation.

3. The plump, laughing figures found in Chinese restaurants and curio shops are actually not Buddhas at all, but rather kitchen gods.

4. This tradition continues to influence lay Buddhist practice. In many Buddhist societies, women take the leading role in supporting Buddhist monks and supplying them with food and other necessities of life.

5. Because he found enlightenment (*bodhi*) under this tree, it has become known as the *bo* or *bodhi* tree.

6. Although the Buddha spent little time preaching against the abuses of the caste system, he effectively struck at its heart by admitting persons of any caste into his order. Only in Sri Lanka has Buddhism retianed the caste system. There are monastic orders for each of the major caste groups.

7. E. J. Thomas, trans., "Pali Sermons, Morality (1)." in *Samannaphala-sutta*, Digha I, 47 (London: Kegan Paul International, 1935), pp. 54–69.

8. Unlike Jainism, early Buddhism did not require a vegetarian diet. Monks were allowed to eat meat, as long as the animal from which it came was not killed specifically for the purpose of feeding them.

9. "Tathagata" was the Buddha's term for himself. It means "truth gatherer."

10. E. J. Thomas, trans., "Pali Sermons, the First Sermon." in *Samyutta*, V, 420 (London: Kegan Paul International, 1935), pp. 29–33.

11. In most discussions of Buddhism, the terms Hinayana and Theravada are used interchangeably. Technically, Theravada is a subdivision of Hinayana.

12. Whether these missionaries actually visited the Western nations or whether they succeeded in influencing people for Buddhism is not known. There is evidence of cultural interchange between India and the hellenized world. See A. D. Nock, *Conversion* (Lanham, MD: University Press of America, 1985), pp. 44–47.

13. Although this is the ideal of Theravada Buddhism, many of the laity and even some monks may express devotion to some forms of supernatural beings. However, these beings are not gods. While they have great power in the world and can aid or harm people, they are not believed to have the ability to help one along the path to enlightenment.

14. Dhammapada, 90–94, 98.

15. On the Jataka tradition, see Peter Khoroche, *Once the Buddha Was a Monkey. Arya Sura's Jatakamala* (Chicago: University of Chicago Press, 1989).

16. *Wat* is a Thai word. In Burma, similar clusters are called *phongyi-chaung*, which means "buildings for monks."

17. Theravada Buddhists also believe in the existence of many Buddhas, but they maintain that like other humans they are mortal, and that there can be only one at a time. According to Theravada teachings, long periods of time exist during which there is no Buddha in the world.

18. In China, this Buddha is known as O-mi-tuo, and, in Japan, as Amida.

19. The Land of Bliss, or Pure Land.

20. Edward Conze, trans., "The Pure Land, 15, 16." *Sukhavativyuha* (Oxford: Bruno Cassirer, Ltd. 1954) p. 202.

21. The best illustration of the attitude of Intuitive sects toward the externals of religion is found in a Zen cartoon that shows a monk seeking to warm himself on a cold morning. He has chopped up a statue of the Buddha, set fire to it, and is raising his robe to warm his buttocks by the fire.

22. Similar, though lesser-known, texts can be found in other Buddhist and Hindu traditions. A Theravada text from Thailand, *Phra Malai Kham Luang* (The Legend of the Monk Malai) tells the story of a monk who visits the Buddhist heavens and hells and asks their residents what good or evil deeds caused their rebirths. Bonnie Brereton, *Thai Tellings of Phra Malai. Text and Rituals Concerning a Popular Buddhist Saint* (Tempe: Arizona State University, Program for Southeast Asian Studies, 1995). The Balinese text *Bhima Swarga* (Bhima Goes to the Land of

the Gods), Trans. Idanna Pucci, *Bhima Swarga. The Balinese Journey of the Soul* (Boston: Little, Brown and Company, 1992), tells a similar story from a Hindu perspective.

23. The word *dalai* literally means "ocean" and indicates the vastness and depth of the person.

24. See Chapters 8 and 9 for more detailed information about this and other festivals in China and Japan.

25. On Buddhism in the West, see Rick Fields, *How the Swans Came to the Lake. A Narrative History of Buddhism in America* (Boston: Shambala Publications, 1992).

26. *1998 Encyclopedia Britannica Book of the Year* (Chicago: Encyclopedia Britannica, 1998), p. 298.

27. Lord Chalmers, trans., *Further Dialogues of the Buddha*, vol. 1 (New York: Krishna Press, 1926), pp. 53–57.

28. E. J. Thomas, trans., *Early Buddhist Scriptures* (New York: Krishna Press, 1935), pp. 94–96.

29. Edward Conze et al., *Buddhist Texts Through the Ages*, trans. Edward Conze (Oxford: Bruno Cassirer, 1954), pp. 131–32.

30. William T. de Bary, ed. and trans., *Sources of Japanese Tradition* (New York: Columbia University Press, 1958), pp. 253, 254.

Chapter 7

1. *1998 Encyclopedia Britannica Book of the Year* (Chicago: Encyclopedia Britannica, 1998), p. 298.

2. The same story is told about the death of Kabir.

3. Asa Ki War, Slok VI, *The Sacred Writings of the World's Great Religions*, ed. S. E. Frost (New York: McGraw-Hill, 1943), p. 362.

4. See this text, pages 105–106.

5. The source material is taken from S. E. Frost, ed., *The Sacred Writings of the World's Great Religions* (New York: McGraw-Hill, 1943), pp. 357–60.

Chapter 8

1. D. Howard Smith, *Chinese Religions* (New York: Holt, Rinehart and Winston, 1968), p. 15.

2. Ibid.

3. An exception to this may be the collected writings of Chairman Mao.

4. Arthur Waley, *The Way and Its Power* (London: George Allen & Unwin, 1956), p. 86.

5. Ibid., p. 141.

6. Ibid.

7. Ibid., p. 166.

8. Herbert A. Giles, *Religions of Ancient China* (Salem, NH: Books for Libraries Press, 1969), p. 47.

9. Waley, *The Way and Its Power*, p. 177.

10. Smith, *Chinese Religions*, p. 71.

11. James Legge, trans., "How pure and still the *Tao* is. I do not know whose song it is. It might appear to have been before God." In *The Sacred Books of the East*, vol. XXXIX (Oxford: Clarendon Press, 1891), p. 50.

12. Ibid., p. 73.

13. Waley, *The Way and Its Power*, p. 70.

14. Smith, *Chinese Religions*, p. 100.

15. The principal form of divination taught by Confucius was probably the Chinese classic, the *I Ching*. Current versions of the *I Ching* are believed to have been edited by Confucius.

16. Arthur Waley, trans., *The Analects of Confucius* (London: George Allen & Unwin, Ltd., 1938), 6:20.

17. *Li Chi*, XXVII.

18. *Analects* 15:34.

19. Ibid., 12:1.

20. Matthew 7:12. This quotation and those that follow are from the *Revised Standard Version of the Bible* (New York: Thomas Nelson & Sons, 1952).

21. *Analects* 15:23.

22. His real name was Meng and his private name K'o, but his Chinese name has been latinized by Western scholars as Mencius.

23. S. E. Frost, ed., *The Sacred Writings of the World's Great Religions*. (New York: McGraw-Hill, 1943), p. 114.

24. Smith, *Chinese Religions*, p. 54.

25. Hsün tzǔ, Chapter 19.

26. Self-government, self-support, and self-propagation.

27. In 1991, the *Encyclopedia Britannica* estimated that there were 183,646,000 "Chinese Folk Religionists" in the world and 5,917,000 Confucians. *1992 Encyclopedia Britannica Book of the Year* (Chicago: Encyclopedia Britannica, 1992), p. 269.

28. Arthur Waley, trans., *The Way and Its Power: The Tao Tê Ching and Its Place in Chinese Thought* (London: George Allen & Unwin, 1977), pp. 141, 143, 159, 171, 238.

29. Waley, *The Analects of Confucius*, pp. 94–106.
30. Y. P. Mei, trans., in *Sources of Chinese Tradition*, ed. William T. de Bary (New York: Columbia University Press, 1960), pp. 123, 124.

Chapter 9

1. For a discussion of Memorial Day as American Shinto, see W. Lloyd Warner, *American Life, Dream and Reality* (Chicago: University of Chicago Press, 1953), pp. 1–12.
2. Prior to 1945, many Shinto shrines received the financial support of the government. While most aspects of Shinto are not inherently nationalistic, Japanese nationalists have sometimes used Shinto to emphasize the unique character of Japanese culture.
3. Daniel Clarence Holtom, "Shinto," in *Religion in the Twentieth Century*, ed. Vergilius Ferm (New York: The Philosophical Library, 1948), p. 147.
4. William T. de Bary, ed., *Sources of the Japanese Tradition* (New York: Columbia University Press, 1958), p. 23.
5. For a further discussion of these forms, see Chapter 6 of this text.
6. One frequently hears this term corrupted to sound like "harry carry."
7. A. B. Mitford, *Tales of Old Japan*, vol. I (London: Macmillan, 1871), pp. 231–36.
8. Floyd Ross, *Shinto: The Way of Japan* (Boston: Beacon Press, 1965), pp. 138, 139.
9. Most Japanese found this statement to be highly peculiar because they had never thought of the emperor as a god, but rather as a human descendent of the sun goddess.
10. It has been suggested that the closest American parallel to the Japanese *kami-dana* is the dashboard of an automobile or the mantle above a fireplace, where objects that promise good fortune or bring good memories are often displayed.
11. In 1991, the *Encyclopedia Britannica* estimated that there were 3,162,800 Shintoists in the world. *1992 Encyclopedia Britannica Book of the Year* (Chicago: Encyclopedia Britannica, 1992), p. 269.
12. The following source material is found in an abridged translation of selections from the *Kojiki*, by Joseph M. Kitagawa in Wing-Tsit Chan et al., *The Great Asian Religions: An Anthology* (New York: Macmillan, 1969), pp. 231–36.
13. William T. de Bary, ed., *Sources of Japanese Tradition* (New York: Columbia University Press, 1958), pp. 29–31.

Chapter 10

1. The true name of the founder of this religion is probably "Zarathustra." The name has been latinized into the more familiar form "Zoroaster" by Western writers.
2. The Gathas are contained in the Yasna, which is a portion of the *Avesta*, the sacred book of the Zoroastrian faith.
3. It is suggested that the name of the modern nation, Iran, is actually a shortened version of a name that meant "the land of the Aryans."
4. See Mary Boyce, *A History of Zoroastrianism*, vol. I (Leiden: E. J. Brill, 1975, 1982), pp. 157–60.
5. Ibid., p. 190.
6. James Darmesteter, trans., Zend-Avesta, Vendidad Fargard XIX, 45, 46 in *The Sacred Books of the East*, vol. IV (Oxford: Clarendon Press, 1880), p. 218.
7. L. J. Mills, trans., Yasna 44:4, 5 in *The Sacred Books of the East*, vol. XXXI (Oxford: Clarendon Press, 1887), pp. 113, 114.
8. James Darmesteter, trans., Ormazd Yast 7, 8, in *The Sacred Books of the East*, vol. XXIII (Oxford: Clarendon Press, 1883), pp. 24, 25.
9. Yasna 30:3, 4.
10. Some scholars have suggested that Aeshma is the demon Asmodeus, who tormented Sarah (the heroine of the Apocryphal book of *Tobit*) and killed her seven bridegrooms.
11. Yasna 30:2.
12. Yasna 51:12.
13. Galatians 6:7.
14. Yasna 43:5.
15. Yasna 30:11.
16. Joseph Campbell, *The Masks of God: Occidental Mythology* (New York: Viking, 1964), pp. 198, 199.
17. The Hebrew *Bible* pays tribute to the reliability of the Persians when it refers to "the law of the Medes and Persians which altereth not." Esther 1:19.
18. Sir Rustom Masani, *Zoroastrianism: The Religion of the Good Life* (New York: Macmillan, 1968), p. 78.
19. Vendidad Fargard VIII, II, 10.

20. Jack Finegan, *The Archaeology of World Religions* (Princeton, NJ: Princeton University Press, 1952), p. 95.
21. II Chronicles 36:22, 23; Ezra 1:2–4.
22. I Chronicles 21:1, Job, Zechariah 3, and Psalm 109.
23. The so-called intertestamental literature consists of books written between the conclusion of the Hebrew *Bible* (ca. 400 B.C.E.) and the beginning of the Christian New Testament (ca. 50 C.E.). Many of these books were written in the style of scripture and were popular, but for various reasons they were never accepted into either the Hebrew or Christian *Bible*.
24. R. C. Zaehner, *The Teachings of the Magi* (London: George Allen & Unwin, 1956), pp. 133–38.
25. R. C. Zaehner, trans., *Zurvan: A Zoroastrian Dilemma*, (Oxford: Clarendon Press, 1955), pp. 314–16.

Chapter 11

1. A collection of tablets unearthed at Ebla in Syria in the middle 1970s lists some patriarchal names and some biblical sites in a historical context from as early as the middle of the third millennium B.C.E. Not all of the material from Ebla has yet been translated, and archaeologists are far from being in agreement about their true worth and significance. Other tablets from Mesopotamia from the middle of the second millennium B.C.E. also mention patriarchal names and customs.
2. The use of the plural here is a mystery. It is possible that at one point the **patriarchs** may have been polytheists, in the sense that they recognized a number of gods but chose to worship only one. It is clear that nothing in the narrative points to the worship of any but the one God.
3. The events of the Exodus are mentioned only in biblical literature. Known Egyptian records do not speak of the escape of a nation of slaves. Therefore, the actual date of the Exodus is subject to debate. The most widely accepted date is the early thirteenth century B.C.E., during the reign of Ramses II.
4. The vowels of this name have been lost because Jews preferred not to pronounce the divine name lest it be taken in vain. Many scholars vocalize it as Yahweh.
5. The usual reading of this body of water as "Red Sea" is based on an ancient mistranslation.

6. This is one way to divide the material in Exodus 20:1–17. Differing religious traditions in Judaism and Christianity sometimes divide the commandments differently.
7. I Samuel 19:24.
8. The prophet about whom there is the most information in the *Bible*, and who fits this pattern, is Elisha. See II Kings 2:1–13; 13:21.
9. Amos 2:6, 7a.
10. Amos 5:14, 15.
11. Psalm 137:1–4.
12. The visions of Ezekiel 1 emphasize the mobility of God.
13. Chapters 40–66 of the biblical book of Isaiah are usually attributed to a sixth-century B.C.E. author.
14. Isaiah 44:28.
15. Isaiah 49:6b.
16. The Septuagint. At this time Greek was the language of learning and scholarship throughout the Middle East.
17. Hans Kung, *Judaism: Between Yesterday and Tomorrow*, trans. John Bowden (New York: Crossroad, 1992), p. 141.
18. In the first century C.E., the Hebrew Bible was identified as "the law and the prophets."
19. Herbert Danby, trans., *The Mishnah*, (Oxford: Oxford University Press, 1933), p. 115.
20. B. Talmud, Hullin 60a.
21. Romans 15:24, 28.
22. In the twelfth century, Aaron of York was said to be the richest man in England.
23. Louis I. Newman, trans., *The Hasidic Anthology* (New York: Charles Scribner's Sons, 1934), p. 3.
24. *1998 Encyclopedia Britannica Book of the Year* (Chicago: Encyclopedia Britannica, 1998), p. 298.
25. For its religious festivals, Judaism relies on an ancient lunar calendar that is synchronized with the solar calendar by adding an extra month each leap year. This calendar is dated from the supposed date of creation, which would make the year beginning in the fall of 2000 C.E. the Jewish year 5760.
26. The source material that follows is taken from The *Holy Bible: Revised Standard Version* (New York: Thomas Nelson & Sons, 1952).
27. Herbert Danby, trans., *The Mishnah*, (New York: Oxford University Press, 1933), pp. 139, 140.

Chapter 12

1. "Worldwide Adherents of All Religions by Six Continental Areas, Mid–2000," *Encyclopedia Britannica*, http://search.eb.com/eb/article?eu=371575, accessed November 1, 2002.

2. *Koine*, or common, Greek was that version of the Greek language used throughout the Hellenized world. It differs somewhat from classical Greek.

3. The absence of non-Christian accounts of the life of Jesus of Nazareth cannot be understood as evidence that there was never such a man, but rather that the historical Jesus did not attract serious attention from Roman authors during his lifetime. This is not surprising, particularly in light of the fact that there were so many mystery religions during this period of Roman history.

4. If Matthew is correct, Jesus was born between 6 and 4 B.C. This is possible because those who established the Christian calendar, marking time into B.C. (before Christ) and A.D. (Anno Domini, in the year of our Lord), lived several hundred years after the time of Jesus and simply miscalculated the date by a few years. This calendar corresponds with what is called the Common Era (abbreviated C.E.). There is no year 0 in either system.

5. The translation of the Hebrew word *almah* has been a source of contention between Christians and Jews for years. In other contexts, the word nearly always means "young woman." Matthew translates it with the Greek word *parthenos*, which always means "virgin."

6. Isaiah 7:14. This quotation and those that follow are taken from *The Holy Bible: Revised Standard Version* (New York: Thomas Nelson & Sons, 1952).

7. Acts 19:1–7.

8. Many Buddhist, Hindu, and Islamic scholars have great respect for Jesus and his teachings, even if they are not convinced of the Christian belief that he was, literally speaking, the son of God.

9. Matthew 5:3–12.

10. Luke 10:30–35.

11. Matthew 5:38–41.

12. Matthew 15:11.

13. Matthew 5:17–19.

14. Albert Schweitzer, *The Quest of the Historical Jesus*, trans. W. Montgomery (New York: Macmillan, 1964).

15. Mark 8:27–29.

16. Luke 22:17–20.

17. One of the lesser-known disciples was Simon the Zealot. See Luke 6:15.

18. The Second Vatican Council (1962–1964) issued a statement that said that although Jewish authorities had pressed for the death of Jesus, his execution cannot be charged against all Jews.

19. Luke 24:43.

20. Christians refer to this festival by its Greek name, the Pentecost.

21. Some Christians continue to practice baptism by immersion, arguing that this practice preserves that of the earliest Christian communities.

22. This practice is motivated by the belief that salvation can be obtained only by those who have been baptized. Given the very high infant mortality rates in pre-modern societies, this practice can be understood as an act of mercy.

23. The admonitions of Paul to the church at Corinth indicate that the supper eaten by early Christians was not always sober or simple. See I Corinthians 11.

24. Matthew 16:16–19.

25. On several occasions, the New Testament lists women who served as deacons (see Romans 16:1). This may indicate that at least in the earliest days of the Church, congregations were led by either women or men.

26. The books that are most commonly questioned are Ephesians, I and II Timothy, and Titus.

27. This paragraph states the most widely accepted pattern for the reason for the development of the Gospels, their sequence of writing, and their dates. This pattern, however, is not accepted by all Christian scholars.

28. The name is derived from *gnosis*, the Greek word for "knowledge." Gnostics claimed to possess certain secret knowledge that most mortals could not know.

30. This particular aspect of Gnosticism is called Docetism.

31. See James M. Robinson, gen. ed., *The Nag Hammadi Library* (New York: Harper & Row, 1977).

32. Martin E. Marty, *A Short History of Christianity* (New York: World Publishing Company, 1958), p. 75.

33. Indeed, some scholars, including sociologist Max Weber, have suggested that Calvin's teachings of

worldly asceticism contributed to the development of the spirit of modern capitalism.

34. Although this was the traditional practice of the Roman Catholic Church during much of its history, the Vatican II encouraged the use of both bread and wine for the laity at the Eucharist.

35. In the modern Catholic Church, this sacrament is known as "Anointing of the Sick." It is administered only to the seriously ill and dying.

36. According to Acts 4:32–37, the early Christians held property in common and in other ways emphasized social and economic equality.

37. See Bruce Lawrence, *Defenders of God, The Fundamentalist Revolt Against the Modern World* (San Francisco: HarperCollins, 1989) pp. 153–88.

38. The term *Mainline* refers to Philadelphia's Main Line (i.e., wealthy suburbs along a commuter railroad) and therefore tends to represent the wealthy and educated rather than the mainstream.

39. The Church banned polygamy in 1890.

40. *Desert News 1999–2000 Church Almanac*, Salt Lake City; Desert News 1988, p. 111.

41. The source material that follows is taken from the *Holy Bible: Revised Standard Version* (New York: Thomas Nelson & Sons, 1952), Matthew chapters 5, 6, 7; Romans chapter 3; I Corinthians chapters 13 and 15; Revelations chapters 20–22.

42. Alexander Roberts and James Donaldson, eds., *The Ante-Nicene Fathers* vol. III (Buffalo, NY: The Christian Literature Publishing Co., 1885), pp. 699–706.

Chapter 13

1. It is inaccurate and insulting to refer to this religion as "Mohammadanism" and its adherents as "Mohammadans" because they do not worship Muhammad.

2. The word *Qur'an* is often transliterated as "Koran" in English texts.

3. The name Mecca is probably derived from an old Arabic word meaning "sanctuary."

4. Some Muslims compare Muhammad's illiteracy to the Virgin Birth of Jesus. As Christians believe that Jesus was conceived without a human father, Muslims believe that the *Qur'an* is a miracle that could only have come directly from God. It is considered the most perfect and beautiful poetic work in the Arabic language, yet was first spoken by an uneducated, illiterate man.

5. *Qur'an* 96:1–5. This quotation and those that follow are taken from A. J. Arberry, trans., *The Koran Interpreted* (New York: Macmillan, 1955).

6. The Shia do not accept this interpretation of Islamic history. Their view is that Muhammad designated his cousin and son-in-law Ali as his successor.

7. W. Montgomery Watt, *Muhammad: Prophet and Statesman* (New York: Oxford University Galaxy Press, 1961), p. 228.

8. *Qur'an* 96:1. Unlike the Hebrew and Christian Bibles, the *Qur'an* is not ordered chronologically. The order of chapters is, with the exception of the opening verses, determined by their length—from longest to shortest.

9. *Qur'an* 25:2.

10. *Qur'an* 112.

11. *Qur'an* 7:54.

12. *Qur'an* 53:32,33.

13. It is believed that this word is Arabic for the Greek word "devil," *diabolos*.

14. *Qur'an* 82.

15. *Qur'an* 18:46.

16. According to both Jewish and Muslim tradition, Hagar was the second wife of Abraham and Ishmael was their son. Genesis 21 says that Hagar and Ishmael were driven from the home of Abraham by the jealousy of Abraham's first wife Sarah. It also is believed that Ishmael became the forebearer of all of the Arab people.

17. While these regulations may appear restrictive to modern people, the fact that Islam allows divorce at all can also be understood as a liberal teaching that recognizes the imperfection of humans and their choices. In many modern Muslim nations, the state has taken jurisdiction over divorce and the rights of women are protected. The practice of polygamy is forbidden in Turkey and Tunisia and is allowed only with permission of the first wife in Indonesia. It also is estimated that the universities of some Muslim nations contain a higher percentage of women faculty than those of Europe and Asia.

18. Obtaining *halal* food can be a problem for Muslims living in non-Muslim societies. Many Muslims purchase kosher meats when *halal* varieties cannot be

found. Today it is increasingly common to see prepared foods labeled "100% Halal" in American markets.

19. Many modern Muslim theologians think of the struggle for economic justice and development as a type of *jihad*.

20. Today the Southeast Asian nation of Indonesia has the world's largest Muslim population.

21. The constitution of Iran during the reign of the shah contained a clause stating that if the *Mahdi* should come, the ruler would abdicate.

22. The word *faqir* (*fakir*) literally means "a poor man," and the word *darwish* (*dervish*) connotes "one who comes to the door" (i.e., a beggar). Thus, both words indicated the universal ascetic practices of poverty and begging.

23. Rahman Fazlur, *Major Themes of the Qur'an* (Minneapolis: Bibliotheca Islam, 1989).

24. Nurcholish Madjid, "In Search of Islamic Roots for Modern Pluralism: The Indonesian Experiences," in *Toward a New Paradigm. Recent Developments in Indonesian Islamic Thought*, ed. Mark R. Woodward (Tempe: Arizona State University, 1996).

25. Leila Ahmed, *Women and Gender in Islam: Historical Roots of a Modern Debate* (New Haven: Yale University Press, 1992).

26. In many parts of the Muslim world, hostility toward Christians and Christianity has more to do with the behavior of Christian colonialists than it does with the teachings of Christianity itself.

27. In the Old Testament and in Jewish tradition, Abraham was commanded to sacrifice his son Isaac. In Muslim tradition, Ishmael was the son to be sacrificed. Muslim tradition also says that Abraham took Ishmael to the black stone in Mecca for the sacrifice.

28. A. J. Arberry, trans., *The Koran Interpreted* (London: George Allen & Unwin, 1955), vol. I, pp. 65, 66, 161; vol. II, pp. 81, 82, 110, 111, 142, 258, 264, 270.

29. Ibid., vol. I, pp. 50–54.

30. Ibid, pp. 254–55.

Chapter 14

1. Anonymous, *Baha'u'llah: God's Messenger to Humanity* (Wilmette, IL: The National Spiritual Assembly of the Baha'is of the United States, 1994), p. 4.

2. Bahaullah, *Gleanings from the Writings of Bahaullah*, trans. Shaghi Effend (Wilmette, IL: Baha'i Publishing Trust, 1952), p. 217. Copyright 1952 © 1976 National Spiritual Assembly of the Bahá'ís of the United States.

3. J. E. Esslemont, *Baha'llah and the New Era* (Wilmette, IL: Baha'i Books, 1976), p. 6.

4. Ibid., p. 126.

5. Ibid., p. 165

6. Ibid., p. 202.

7. Ibid., p. 154.

8. Ibid., p. 170. Abdul Baha advocated the adoption of Esperanto as the universal language.

9. Bahaullah, *Glad Tidings*.

10. These thirteen principles are taken from information supplied by the Public Information Department, National Baha'i Headquarters, 112 Linden Avenue, Wilmette, IL 60091.

11. Abdul Baha, *Some Answered Questions* (Wilmette, IL: Baha'i Publishing Trust, 1964), p. 250.

12. Esslemont, Baha'llah and the New Era, p. 103.

13. Bahaullah, *Kitab-i-Aqdas*, trans. Shoghi Effendi (Wilmette, IL: Baha'i Publishing Trust, 1931), p. 182.

14. Abdul Baha, cited by J. E. Esslemont, *Baha'llah and the New Era*, p. 189.

15. "Iran's Nuremberg Laws" (editorial). *New York Times*, 27 February 1993, sect. 1, p. 18, col. 1.

16. *1996 Encyclopedia Britannica Book of the Year* (Chicago: Encyclopedia Britannica, 1996), p. 298.

17. Bahaullah, *Gleanings from the Writings of Bahaullah*, pp. 94–96.

18. Ibid., pp. 250, 251.

GLOSSARY

Agamas. The scriptures of Jainism; some believe that the Agamas contain the actual sermons given by Mahavira to his disciples.

Agni. Aryan god of fire.

Agnostic. Literally, "one who does not know"; usually taken by persons who claim not to know for certain the nature or reality of God. This is in contrast to the atheist, who is certain that there is no God.

Ahimsa. Noninjury of living beings. This term, found in many Indian religions, was introduced by the Jains. Adherents of ahimsa make every effort to care for all forms of life and seek to avoid injuring or killing any creature.

Ahura Mazda. The one true God recognized by Zoroastrians. His symbol is the sacred fire.

Ajwaka. African religious functionary whose primary purpose is to heal by driving out evil spirits believed to cause sickness.

Allah. Literally, "the God"; Arabic name for the deity, used by Muslims and Christian Arabs.

Amaterasu. Sun goddess in Japanese mythology.

Amesha-Spenta. Literally, "Holy Immortals"; six modes through which Ahura Mazda revealed himself to humanity in Zoroastrianism.

Anti-Semitism. Prejudice against Jews for religious reasons.

Amitabha. A *dhyani* Buddha who presides over the paradise called "the Pure Land of the West."

Anabaptist. Literally, "rebaptizer"; a radical group of Protestant reformers who insisted that baptism is for adult believers only.

Anatman (anatta). The state of nonsoulness that, according to the Buddha, was the natural state of humanity.

Ancestor veneration. Veneration of deceased members of the family. It frequently involves upkeep and care of graves, memorization of the names from past generations, and prayers and sacrifices in honor of the dead.

Angra Mainyu (Shaitin, Satan). The evil spirit recognized by Zoroastrians.

Animism. The belief that all nature is alive and filled with unseen spirits that may be worshiped or placated. Animists see a soul or a self existing in trees, stones, rivers, and heavenly bodies.

Apostles. The original twelve followers of Jesus.

Apocalypse. Literally, "that which is revealed"; describes certain forms of literature popular in Christianity, Judaism, and Zoroastrianism in the second century B.C.E. to the second century C.E. Apocalyptic books were often written in secret or coded language and spoke about a dramatic end of the world.

Aranyakas. Literally, "forest treatises"; instruction for hermits in Vedic literature.

Arhat (arahat). Individuals, other than Buddhas, who have attainted nirvana.

Arjuna. Major character in the Bhagavad Gita.

Aryan. Sanskrit word that means "the noble ones"; applied to migrants who moved into the Indus valley from Persia in the second millennium B.C.E.

Asceticism. The practice of self-denial through various means, for the attainment of spiritual goals.

Ashkenazim. Jews who lived in Europe, especially Eastern Europe.

Atharva Veda. The fourth book in the Vedic collection, containing rituals and prayers used in the worship of Aryan gods.

Atheist. One who believes that there are no gods.

Avatar. Incarnation of a deity. In Hinduism, the god Vishnu is believed to have taken human or other forms on several occasions.

Avidya. In the Upanishads, this term means "ignorance."

Baalim. Fertility gods worshiped by the ancient Canaanites.

Babis. Religious group, immediate forerunner of the Baha'i religion.

Bab-u-Din. Founder of the Babi movement.

Bahaullah. Founder of the Baha'i faith.

Babylonian Captivity of the Church. Period between 1309 and 1377 C.E., when the papacy of the Roman Catholic Church was at Avignon, France.

Baptism. Christian initiatory ritual.

Bar Mitzvah, Bat Mitzvah. Jewish rituals in which young men and young women, respectively, are officially recognized as adult members of the community.

Bardo Thodol. Tibetan Book of the Dead.

Beatitudes. First ten verses of Jesus' Sermon on the Mount.

Bhagavad Gita. "The Song of the Blessed Lord." Epic poem of Indian culture and religion.

Bhakti. Devotion to the gods of Hinduism.

Bhakti-marga. "The way of devotion." Salvation in postclassical Hinduism through devotion to a specific god.

Black stone. Meteorite stone in Mecca; the stone was an object of veneration in pre-Islamic Arabia.

Bodhidharma. Legendary monk who brought intuitive Buddhism from India to China in the sixth century C.E.

Bodhisattva. A being destined to become a Buddha.

Bon. Pre-Buddhist native religion of Tibet.

Bot. Hall found in a wat and dedicated to teaching, preaching, and meditation.

Brahma. One of the three important gods in Hindu worship, generally regarded as the creator of the world.

Brahman. Impersonal god seen as total reality in the Upanishads.

Brahmana. Ritual instruction in Vedic literature.

Brahmin. Priestly caste of Indian society.

Buddha. One who obtains Nirvana on the basis of his own efforts.

Bushido. Code of the *Samurai*.

Butsu-dan. Japanese Buddhist household altar.

Cabala (kabbalah). General term for mystical elements in Judaism.

Caliph. From *khalifa* (literally, "deputy," "representative"); successors of Muhammad in leading Islam. At first, the caliphate was limited to the companions of the Prophet Muhammad, but as Islam grew, the caliphate took on the role of a dynastic political leadership.

Caste. From Portuguese, *casta*, "race." The multiple classes into which traditional Indian society has been divided.

Chanukah (Hanukkah). Jewish festival that celebrates the rededicating of the Temple by Judas Maccabaeus in 165 B.C.E.

Chinvat Bridge. Bridge that connects the point of judgment with the region of reward or punishment in Zoroastrianism.

Consubstantiation. Presence of the body and blood of Jesus in the bread and wine of communion.

Copt. Member of the traditional Monophysite Christian church originating and centering in Egypt; the Coptic church traces its history to the earliest Christian communities.

Council of Trent. Convened in 1545 by the Roman Catholic Church to reform the church and oppose the actions of Protestants.

Cro-Magnon. Early humans; the Cro-Magnons lived from approximately 25,000 to 7000 B.C.E.

Daeva. One of various pre-Zoroastrian Aryan deities.

Dakhma. Round structure, open to the sky, in which Zoroastrians expose their dead for disposal by birds.

Dalai Lama. Leader of the Yellow Hat group of Tibetan Buddhists and, until 1950, the spiritual and political ruler of Tibet.

Dasehra. Hindu celebration in honor of Durga.

Deacon. Literally, "servant," "attendant," "minister"; a functionary in Christian churches.

Dervish. Literally, "one who comes to the door"; member of a Muslim mystical brotherhood.

Dharma. Duties incumbent on a person in traditional Hindu life, based on caste and station in life. In Buddhism, the teachings of the Buddha.

Dhyani Buddha. Buddhist deity who dwells in heaven and can aid humans in their struggles through life.

Diaspora. Scattering of the Israelites from their homeland, which began with the Assyrian destruction of Israel in 721 B.C.E.

Digambara. Literally, "the sky clad"; the more conservative sect of Jainism, which holds nudity as an ideal for its monks.

Divali. Hindu festival of lights that welcomes the new year; also celebrated by Jains.

Divination. Prediction of the future through various magical means (e.g., Tarot cards, I Ching, reading of tea leaves).

Docetism. Belief held by some Gnostics that Jesus only appeared to be human while he was actually pure spirit.

Durga (Kali). Consort of Shiva.

Ecumenical Movement. Action among modern Christian denominations to attempt to minimize differences among various Christian groups and achieve some form of unity.

Elohim. Literally, "gods"; one of the names applied to God in Hebrew scriptures.

Eschatology. Doctrines concerning the end of the world.

Epistles. Letters written by Paul to the early Christian churches.

Essenes. Monastic Jewish community whose primary headquarters may have been Wadi Qumran near the Dead Sea. They existed mainly during the first century B.C.E.

and the first century C.E. and were extremely interested in eschatology.

Evangelical. Christian churches following in the tradition of Martin Luther.

Eucharist. Literally, "thanksgiving"; Christian memorial meal of bread and wine that celebrates the sacrifice of Jesus.

Exodus. The flight of the Jewish people from bondage in Egypt.

Extreme unction. Roman Catholic last rite given to the dying.

Fakir. Literally, "poor man"; member of a Muslim mystical brotherhood.

Falasha. Form of Judaism found in Ethiopia.

Falun Dafa. New Chinese religion severely persecuted by authorities.

Fetish. Any object used to control nature in a magical fashion (e.g., lucky coin, rabbit's foot, religious charm).

Filial piety. The concept of devotion to elders in East Asian religions.

Gahambars. Zoroastrian seasonal feasts dedicated to the creation of heaven, water, earth, trees, animals, and humans.

Gaon. A president of the early medieval Jewish academies (plural: geonim).

Gatha. A Zoroastrian hymn that takes on the quality of scripture.

Gemara. Commentary on the Mishnah compiled from the rabbinic academies of Palestine and Babylon. Also contains a great body of material that has no connection to the Mishnah. There are two Gemaras: Palestinian and Babylonian.

Ghetto. Section of certain European cities where Jews were forced to live.

Gnostic. Family of early Christian heresies that were purported to contain the secrets of the universe and were thus considered superior to orthodox Christianity.

Gospel. Literally, "good news"; the message concerning Christ, the kingdom of God, and salvation; the first four books of the New Testament (Matthew, Mark, Luke, and John) tell the story of Jesus' ministry and are called the Gospels.

Granth. Scriptures of Sikhism.

Gurdwara. Sikh temple and meeting place.

Guru. In Hinduism, the word connotes "teacher"; in Sikhism, it refers to the leaders of the religion.

Hadith. Collections of traditions concerning the life and words of the Prophet Muhammad.

Haggadah. Literally, "narrative"; history, folklore, and sermons in the Talmud.

Hajj. Pilgrimage each Muslim is supposed to make once in a lifetime to the shrines in and around Mecca.

Halachah (Halakhah). Legal material, discussions, and rabbinic decisions in the Talmud.

Hara-kiri. See *seppuku.*

Hasidim. Movement founded in the seventeenth century in Poland by Israel ben Eliezer, who taught that God was not to be found in scholarly research or in the Talmud but in simple faith.

High God. Certain basic religions maintain that one Supreme God created the world and then withdrew from active participation. Although this god is often recognized and given token worship, the bulk of active worship is given to lesser deities, who participate more fully in the activities of the world.

Hijrah. Literally, "migration"; the migration of Muhammad and his community from Mecca to Medina in 622 B.C.E.

Holi. Hindu festival dedicated to the god Krishna.

Holocaust. The murder of six million Jews by the Nazis during World War II.

Horse sacrifice. Elaborate, year-long ritual in ancient India; this ritual involved the sacrifice of thousands of animals.

I Ching. Ancient Chinese book of divination.

Iblis. Fallen angel who is the Satan figure in Islam.

'Id al-Adha. Muslim feast of sacrifice.

'Id al-Fitr. Muslim feast of fast breaking. Celebrates a return to normal life after the prolonged fast of Ramadan.

Imam. To Sunni Muslims, the imam leads the community in prayers; to Shi'ite Muslims, imams were the legitimate successors of Ali.

Immaculate Conception of Mary. Dogma of the Roman Catholic Church; holds that Mary (the mother of Christ) was born without the taint of original sin.

Indra. Aryan god of thunder, rain, and the ruler of heaven.

Indulgences. The remission of sin in return for money or other contributions.

Institutes of the Christian Religion, The. John Calvin's statement of Christian theology that became a classic for Protestant theology.

Izanagi and Izanami. Mythological male and female who participated in the creation of the Japanese islands.

Jasan. Zoroastrian feast day; one jasan is celebrated each month of the year.

Jen. Confucian principle translated as "love," "goodness," and "humaneness."

Jihad. Arabic term meaning "struggle in the cause of God." Examples range from mission work to armed conflict.

Jinn. Spiritual creatures recognized in pre-Islamic Arabia. Some could be friendly; others were hostile and demonic.

Jiva and ajiva. Soul and matter in Jain philosophy.

Jnana-marga. Literally "way of knowledge"; salvation is achieved by studying the philosophical implications of Indian sacred writings.

Jok. Name for dangerous spirits among the Acholi of Uganda.

Ka'ba. Enclosure surrounding the black stone in Mecca; this stone became an object of veneration by pilgrims in pre-Islamic Arabia.

Kali. Consort of Shiva; also known as Durga.

Kami. Japanese for "spirits"; some scholars see this word as equivalent to mana, but no exact English translation has been achieved.

Kami-dana. Literally, "god shelf"; the center of domestic Shinto in a Japanese home. A shelf where sacred objects are kept and daily prayers are said.

Karaites. Medieval Jewish group that denied the authority of the Talmud and tried to live exclusively by the rules of the Hebrew bible.

Karma. In Indian thought, that which binds one to the endless cycles of life, death, and rebirth.

Koan. Literally, "case study"; a riddle, tale, or short statement used by Zen masters to bring students to sudden insight.

Kojiki. Literally, "chronicles of ancient events"; the source book of Japanese mythology.

Koran. Var. of *Qur'an*.

Kosher. Literally, "fit," "proper"; that which is ritually clean or acceptable in Judaism; usually applied to food or food preparation.

Krishna. Incarnation of the Hindu god Vishnu, who appears as a main character in the Bhagavad Gita.

Kshatriya. Warrior caste of Indian society.

Kuei. Evil spirits recognized in early Chinese religions.

Kusti. Sacred belt worn by all Zoroastrians.

Li. Confucian term translated as "propriety," "rites," "ceremonies," or "courtesy"; probably means "the course of life as it is intended to go."

Lollards. Wandering preachers; the movement was instituted by John Wycliffe in England during the fourteenth century C.E.

Magic. Attempts to influence the action of nature through special practices, dances, rituals, and incantation. Magicians believe that if they perform their rituals properly, they will cause nature to react favorably toward them.

Mahayana. Literally, "the great vehicle"; the larger, more liberal branch of Buddhism.

Mana. Term from the language of the Melanesian islands; used to describe a mysterious, invisible, and impersonal force that causes nature to act as it does.

Mantra. Ritual sound, word, or phrase used to evoke a certain religious effect.

Manu. Mythical survivor of the Indian flood story.

Manu, Code of. Classical Hindu literature that describes life in India between 300 B.C.E. and 300 C.E.

Marcionism. Early Christian heresy named for Marcion of Rome. Marcionism rejected the God of the Old Testament and all theological and literary attachments to the Old Testament.

Marrano. Spanish Jews who openly converted to Christianity but who secretly continued to practice Judaism.

Maya. False knowledge; in the Upanishads, all that is not Brahman all perceptions, all individuality.

Medicine man. Native American religious functionary whose primary task is to heal by religious means.

Megalith. Large stone monuments (e.g., Stonehenge, statues on Easter Island, megalith fields in Brittany) apparently raised in connection with religious practices.

Mishnah. Collection of oral laws gathered by Judah ha Nasi (born c. 135 C.E.); the Mishnah contained the bulk of extrabiblical Jewish law up to the second century C.E.

Mithra (Mithras). Pre-Zoroastrian Aryan deity who appears in Hindu Vedic literature as Mitra, in Zoroastrianism as the judge of the dead, and as the leading figure in a Roman mystery religion.

Mother Earth. The female earth spirit and personification of nature in Native American religions.

Mughal Empire. Muslim rule of portions of India between the sixteenth and eighteenth centuries C.E.

Moksha. Release from the cycle of death and rebirth in Indian religions.

Monotheism. The belief in a single Supreme God.

Mosque. Muslim house of prayer.

Muezzin. One who calls the Muslim community to prayer five times a day.

Muktad. Zoroastrian All Soul's Day honoring departed ancestors.

Muslim. Literally, "submitter" (one who submits to the will of God); one becomes a Muslim by utterance of the Shahadah: "There is no God but God, and Muhammad is the messenger of God."

Myth/Mythology. Religious narratives common to most all traditions.

Native American Church. Religious movement combining elements of Christianity and Native American religions.

Neanderthal. Predecessor of *Homo sapiens*; Neanderthals lived from approximately 125,000 to 30,000 B.C.E.

Neolithic. Late Stone Age; era in human prehistory between approximately 7000 and 3000 B.C.E., when most tools, weapons, and the like were constructed from stone.

Nichiren. Literally, "sun lotus"; sociopolitical sect of Mahayana Buddhism found primarily in Japan.

Niiname-sai. National Japanese festival of the harvest.

Ninety-five Theses. Ninety-five points of controversy submitted by Martin Luther as grounds for debate in 1517.

Nirvana. Literally, "blowing out"; cessation of consciousness.

NōRūz. Zoroastrian festival celebrating the New Year.

Nuer. East African ethnic group with a particularly strong belief in the High God.

Nyaya. Hindu philosophical system that uses logical analysis to arrive at truth about the world.

Om mani padmi hum. Mantra in Tibetan Buddhism that means "Om, the jewel of the lotus, hum."

Orisha. In African mythology, lesser deities who participated in the creation of the world.

Paijusana. Jain festival commencing eight days before the new year; a period of fasting and meditation.

Parable. Short, meaningful story that was one of Jesus' chief teaching devices.

Parsi (or Parsee). Name by which Zoroastrians are known in India.

Passover (Pesach). Jewish holiday celebrated in the spring, commemorating the deliverance of the Israelites from Egyptian slavery.

Penance. Sacrament (of the Roman Catholic, Orthodox, and some Anglican churches) in which the Christian confesses sin and receives absolution; also, an act performed to show sorrow or repentance for sin.

Pentecost. Christian festival that comes fifty days after the Passover and celebrates the coming of the Holy Spirit to the church.

Peyote. Cactus plant that bears small button growths. These buttons contain mescaline, a hallucinogenic sometimes used in the religious rites of the Native American Church.

Polytheism. The belief in more than one deity.

Prophet. One who speaks the words of the gods.

Pure Land Buddhism. Version of Mahayana Buddhism popular in Japan; it teaches that its devotees can be reborn in a paradise, called the "Pure Land of the West," where they can reach enlightenment.

Purim. Jewish holiday that celebrates the deliverance of the Jews from destruction at the hands of the Persians.

Purva Mimamsa. A Hindu philosophical system that taught the avoidance of rebirth by adhering to the laws of the Vedas.

Qur'an. Literally, "reading," "recitation"; Muslim scripture.

Rabbi. Literally, "my master"; teacher associated with the Jewish synagogue.

Raja. Originally, this word was applied to Aryan chieftains but later came to describe Indian rulers in general.

Ramadan. Month during which devout Muslims do not eat or drink between sunrise and sunset. The fast celebrates the month in which the Prophet received the Qu'ran.

Rig-Veda. Basic book of Vedic literature, consisting of over one thousand hymns and other mythological elements dedicated to the gods of the Aryan pantheon.

Rite of passage. Any of various rituals that mark the passage from one phase in a person's life to another phase (e.g., baptism, circumcision, puberty rites, marriage, death rituals).

Rosh Hashanah. The Jewish New Year.

Ryobu. Attempted amalgamation between Shinto and Buddhism.

Sabbath (Shabbat). The seventh day, set aside as a day of rest and worship in Judaism.

Sahajdhari.   Conservative sect in Sikhism.

Sama Veda.   Third book in the Vedic collection consisting of verses from hymns dedicated to the gods of the Aryan pantheon.

Samkhya.   Dualistic system of philosophy in postclassical Hinduism.

Samsara.   In the Upanishads and in Buddhism, the endless cycle of birth, life, death, and rebirth experienced by all humans.

Samurai.   Medieval Japanese knights.

Sangha.   Buddhist monastic order.

Sannyasi.   Wandering beggar; in traditional Indian life, the fourth stage in the ideal life of an upper-caste Hindu male.

Saoshyant.   Prophet or reformer who pre-Zoroastrian Aryans believed came to restore the purity of religion.

Satori.   State of enlightenment that one can achieve in Zen Buddhism.

Sefer Hazohar.   Literally, "The Book of Splendor"; the most outstanding example of cabalistic literature in Judaism.

Sephardim.   Jews who fled from Spain and Portugal and took refuge in the Ottoman Empire.

Seppuku.   Ritual suicide by disembowelment (the term *hara-kiri* means "belly slitting"); dictated for certain dishonors and crimes among the samurai.

Shahadah.   Creedal statement of Islam, "There is no God but God, and Muhammad is the messenger of God."

Shaman.   Term from an indigenous language of Eastern Siberia and referring to one who is possessed by the gods and can therefore predict the future.

Shang Ti.   Supreme God recognized by the Chou dynasty of ancient China.

Shavuot.   "Feast of Weeks"; Jewish holiday in remembrance of the giving of the Ten Commandments.

Shema.   Deuteronomy 6:4, "Hear (*shema*) O Israel: The Lord our God is one Lord; and you shall love the Lord your God with all your heart, and with all your soul, and with all your might."

Shen.   Beneficial spirits recognized in early Chinese religion.

Shi'ite.   Literally, "the party of." This Muslim group, which accounts for approximately 14 percent of all Muslims, began as "the Party of Ali." They believe the legitimate successor to Muhammad was his cousin and son-in-law, Ali.

Shinto (Shen Tao).   Literally, "the way of the gods" (the Japanese language equivalent is *Kamino-michi*); the native religion of Japan.

Shirk.   Muslim word for polytheism.

Shiva.   Most popular god in postclassical Hinduism, regarded as the god of death and destruction but also of rebirth and reproduction.

Shivaite (also Shaivite).   Devotee of the god Shiva.

Shogatsu.   Japanese holiday celebrating the New Year.

Shu.   Confucian law of reciprocity.

Shudra.   Slave or servant caste of Indian society.

Sikh.   Literally, "disciple"; an adherent of Sikhism.

Sikhism.   An Indian religion that blends certain elements of Hinduism and Islam.

Singhs.   In Sikhism, a corps of warriors.

Soma.   Sacred plant whose juice was a libation to the gods of India. The exact identification of the soma plant is lost.

Spenta Mainyu.   The beneficent spirit in Zoroastrianism.

Sufi.   Literally, "woolen"; Muslim mystical brotherhoods that seek a direct experience and knowledge of God.

Sukkot.   Jewish autumn festival of thanksgiving.

Summa Theologiae.   Massive systematic theology by Thomas Aquinas, which became the standard for Catholic theology.

Sunni Muslims.   Most Muslims are Sunnis (traditionalists), who accept orthodox Muslim theology and the traditional line of caliphs.

Sun Dance.   Summer celebration performed by Native Americans of the Great Plains.

Surah.   Chapter division within the Qur'an.

Suttee.   In India, the act or custom of burning a live widow on her husband's funeral pyre or burying her alive in his grave. At the insistence of Christians and Hindus, the British government outlawed the practice in 1829.

Svetambara.   Literally, "the white clad"; the more liberal sect of Jainism.

Sympathetic or imitative magic.   Magic that seeks to operate on the basic notion that look-alikes act alike. The voodoo doll and the various rain dances that incorporate the sprinkling of water or the imitation of thunder are examples.

Synagogue.   Literally, "assembly"; the meeting of Jews of the Diaspora for study and prayer.

Synoptic Gospels.   The New Testament books of Matthew, Mark, and Luke, the three Gospels that share the same basic outline and chronology (the other Gospel is John).

Taboo (tabu). Action that must be avoided lest it release harmful effects on a person or his or her group (e.g., walking under a ladder, breaking a mirror, marrying in violation of cultural rules).

Tahkt. Throne of Sikhism at Amritsar, which is a pilgrimage site.

Talmud. Encyclopedic collection of Mishnah and Gemara, the literary source of postbiblical Judaism. There are two Talmudim: Palestinian and Babylonian.

Tanha. Desire, thirst, or craving; a concept identified by Buddha as that which causes karma.

Tantras. Manuals that teach magical words and spells, primarily found in Tibetan Buddhism but also present in other Buddhist sects and in Hinduism, where tantric religion takes on the element of enlightenment by carrying passion to extremes.

Tao. Literally, "The Way," or "The Way of Nature."

Tao Tê Ching. Literally, "The Classic of the Way and its Power or Virtue"; the book that became the basis for the philosophy of Taoism.

Tenrikyo. Literally, "Teaching of Heavenly Reason"; a sect of Shinto that emphasizes faith healing.

Theravada. Literally, "the tradition of the elders"; the smaller, more conservative version of Buddhism.

Thugs. These devotees of Kali specialized in murdering victims as sacrifices to her.

Tien-t'ai. Rationalist sects of Mahayana Buddhism.

Tirthankaras. Literally, "bridge-builders"; the twenty-four founders of Jainism; they forged the bridge between life and Nirvana. The last of the Tirthankaras was Mahavira.

Torah. Usually translated as "law"; general term in the Hebrew bible referring to divine law and instruction but can also refer to the first five books of the Bible or to revelation in general.

Totemism. From the Ojibwa *ototeman*; it involves the recognition of a relationship between a certain type of animal (the totem) and a group of people. The totem becomes sacred to the group and may not be killed by its members except under certain ritual conditions.

Transubstantiation. The miraculous change by which (according to Roman Catholic and Eastern Orthodox dogma) the eucharistic elements at their consecration become the body and blood of Christ while keeping only the appearances of bread and wine.

Trimurti. The three most important Hindu gods: Shiva, Vishnu, and Brahma.

Udasis. Order of holy men in Sikhism.

Ullambana (The Festival of Souls). A Buddhist festival celebrated in China and Japan; families leave gifts of food for the souls of their departed ancestors thought to be wandering the earth.

Upanishads. Philosophical materials in the Vedic literature.

Vaisheshika. Hindu philosophical system that teaches that the universe is made up of nine distinct and uncreated elements.

Vaishya. Merchant caste of Indian society.

Varna. The four major divisions of the Indian caste system.

Vatican II. Council called by the Roman Catholic Church in 1962; it took broad steps to modernize the Church and mend relationships with Jews, members of the Eastern Orthodox Church, and Protestants.

Veda. Basically, a collection of hymns to the Aryan gods. The term also applies to the entire collection of Indian sacred literature, including the Vedas, the Brahamanas, the Aranyakas, and the Upanishads.

Vedanta. Literally, "the end of the Vedas"; this Hindu philosophical system takes its major materials from the Upanishads and assumes that there is only one true reality in the world Brahman.

Vishnu. One of the three most popular gods of postclassical Hinduism, known as the god of love.

Vision Quest. Exercises undertaken by Native Americans seeking contact with the spirit world.

Vohu Mana. Angelic figure who revealed the nature of Ahura Mazda to Zoroaster.

Voodoo. African American religion combining African and Christian elements.

Vulgate. Latin translation of the Bible by Jerome.

Wahabi. Ultraconservative Muslim movement founded in the eighteenth century and opposed to all forms of change within religion and culture.

Wat. Complex of buildings used in Theravada Buddhism for worship and teaching.

Wu-wei. Taoist principle of nonaggression and pacifism.

Yajur-Veda. Second book in the collection of Vedic literature; it is a collection of materials to be recited during sacrifice to the Aryan gods.

Yang. The positive force in nature recognized in early Chinese religion.

Yarmulke. Skull cap worn by Jewish males at worship.

Yazata. Literally, "adorable ones"; hosts of angels surrounding the throne of Ahura Mazda in Zoroastrianism.

YHWH. The God who revealed himself to Moses and became the God of the Israelites.

Yiddish. The language of Ashkenazi Jews. Essentially, it is Middle High German written in the Hebrew alphabet.

Yin. The negative force in nature recognized in early Chinese religions.

Yoga. Philosophical system in postclassical Hinduism that teaches a dualistic world view.

Yom Kippur. Jewish Day of Atonement.

Yoruba. West African ethnic group whose religion strongly influenced the development of African American religions.

Zen, Ch'an Buddhism. Form of Mahayana Buddhism that teaches that the real truth about life comes from intuitive flashes of insight.

Zionism. Movement founded in the late nineteenth century by Theodore Herzl; Zionism sought to find a national home for the Jews scattered throughout the world.

Student Notes

Student Notes